D0729596

MONTANA & WYOMING

2nd Edition

**Where to Stay and Eat
for All Budgets**

**Must-See Sights
and Local Secrets**

Ratings You Can Trust

Fodor's Travel Publications   New York, Toronto, London, Sydney, Auckland
www.fodors.com

FODOR'S MONTANA & WYOMING

Editors: Constance Jones, Matthew Lombardi

Editorial Production: Linda K. Schmidt

Editorial Contributors: Jean Arthur, Linda Cabasin, Jo Deurbrouck, Dustin D. Floyd, T. D. Griffith, Candy Moulton

Maps: David Lindroth, *cartographer;* Bob Blake and Rebecca Baer, *map editors*

Design: Fabrizio La Rocca, *creative director;* Guido Caroti, *art director;* Melanie Marin, *senior picture editor*

Production/Manufacturing: Robert B. Shields

Cover Photo (Jackson Lake and Grand Tetons, Wyoming): David Jensen

Second Edition

ISBN: 1–4000–1667–3

ISBN-13: 978–1–4000–1667–9

ISSN: 1559–0801

SPECIAL SALES

This book is available at special discounts for bulk purchases for sales promotions or premiums. Special editions, including personalized covers, excerpts of existing books, and corporate imprints, can be created in large quantities for special needs. For more information, write to Special Markets/Premium Sales, 1745 Broadway, MD 6-2, New York, New York 10019, or e-mail specialmarkets@randomhouse.com.

AN IMPORTANT TIP & AN INVITATION

Although all prices, opening times, and other details in this book are based on information supplied to us at press time, changes occur all the time in the travel world, and Fodor's cannot accept responsibility for facts that become outdated or for inadvertent errors or omissions. So **always confirm information when it matters,** especially if you're making a detour to visit a specific place. Your experiences—positive and negative—matter to us. If we have missed or misstated something, **please write to us.** We follow up on all suggestions. Contact the Montana & Wyoming editor at editors@fodors.com or c/o Fodor's at 1745 Broadway, New York, NY 10019.

PRINTED IN THE UNITED STATES OF AMERICA

10 9 8 7 6 5 4 3 2 1

Be a Fodor's Correspondent

Your opinion matters. It matters to us. It matters to your fellow Fodor's travelers too. And we'd like to hear it. In fact, we *need* to hear it.

When you share your experiences and opinions, you become an active member of the Fodor's community. That means we'll not only use your feedback to make our books better, but we'll publish your names and comments whenever possible. Throughout our guides, look for "Word of Mouth," excerpts of your unvarnished feedback.

Here's how you can help improve Fodor's for all of us.

Tell us when we're right. We rely on local writers to give you an insider's perspective. But our writers and staff editors—who are the best in the business—depend on you. Your positive feedback is a vote to renew our recommendations for the next edition.

Tell us when we're wrong. We're proud that we update most of our guides every year. But we're not perfect. Things change. Hotels cut services. Museums change hours. Charming cafés lose charm. If our writer didn't quite capture the essence of a place, tell us how you'd do it differently. If any of our descriptions are inaccurate or inadequate, we'll incorporate your changes in the next edition and will correct factual errors at fodors.com *immediately*.

Tell us what to include. You probably have had fantastic travel experiences that aren't yet in Fodor's. Why not share them with a community of like-minded travelers? Maybe you chanced upon a trail or bistro or B&B that you don't want to keep to yourself. Tell us why we should include it. And share your discoveries and experiences with everyone directly at fodors.com. Your input may lead us to add a new listing or highlight a place we cover with a "Highly Recommended" star or with our highest rating, "Fodor's Choice."

Give us your opinion instantly at our feedback center at www.fodors.com/feedback. You may also e-mail editors@fodors.com with the subject line "Montana & Wyoming Editor." Or send your nominations, comments, and complaints by mail to Montana & Wyoming Editor, Fodor's, 1745 Broadway, New York, NY 10019.

You and travelers like you are the heart of the Fodor's community. Make our community richer by sharing your experiences. Be a Fodor's correspondent.

Happy Trails!

Tim Jarrell, Publisher

CONTENTS

CLOSEUPS

MAPS

ABOUT THIS BOOK

Our Ratings

Sometimes you find terrific travel experiences and sometimes they just find you. But usually the burden is on you to select the right combination of experiences. That's where our ratings come in.

As travelers we've all discovered a place so wonderful that its worthiness is obvious. And sometimes that place is so unique that superlatives don't do it justice: you just have to be there to know. These sights, properties, and experiences get our highest rating, Fodor's Choice ★, indicated by orange stars throughout this book.

Black stars highlight sights and properties we deem Highly Recommended ★, places that our writers, editors, and readers praise again and again for consistency and excellence.

By default, there's another category: any place we include in this book is by definition worth your time, unless we say otherwise. And we will.

Disagree with any of our choices? Care to nominate a place or suggest that we rate one more highly? Visit our feedback center at www.fodors.com/feedback.

Budget Well

Hotel and restaurant price categories from ¢ to $$$$ are defined within each chapter. For attractions, we always give standard adult admission fees; reductions are usually available for children, students, and senior citizens. Want to pay with plastic? **AE, D, DC, MC, V** following restaurant and hotel listings indicate whether American Express, Discover, Diner's Club, MasterCard, and Visa are accepted.

Restaurants

Unless we state otherwise, restaurants are open for lunch and dinner daily. We mention dress only when there's a specific requirement and reservations only when they're essential or not accepted—it's always best to book ahead.

Hotels

Hotels have private bath, phone, TV, and air-conditioning and operate on the European Plan (aka EP, meaning without meals), unless we specify that they use the Continental Plan (CP, with a continental breakfast), Breakfast Plan (BP, with a full breakfast), or Modified American Plan (MAP, with breakfast and dinner) or are all-inclusive (AI, including all meals and most activities). We always

list facilities but not whether you'll be charged an extra fee to use them, so when pricing accommodations, find out what's included.

Many Listings
- ★ Fodor's Choice
- ★ Highly recommended
- ⊠ Physical address
- ✛ Directions
- ⌂ Mailing address
- ☎ Telephone
- 🖷 Fax
- ⊕ On the Web
- ✎ E-mail
- 🎫 Admission fee
- ☉ Open/closed times
- ⊳ Start of walk/itinerary
- Ⓜ Metro stations
- ☰ Credit cards

Hotels & Restaurants
- 🏨 Hotel
- ⇥ Number of rooms
- ⌕ Facilities
- ⦿ Meal plans
- ✕ Restaurant
- ⌕ Reservations
- 🏛 Dress code
- ↘ Smoking
- ⊗ BYOB
- ✕🏨 Hotel with restaurant that warrants a visit

Outdoors
- 🏌 Golf
- ⛺ Camping

Other
- ☺ Family-friendly
- 🛈 Contact information
- ⇨ See also
- ⊠ Branch address
- ☞ Take note

WHAT'S WHERE

YELLOWSTONE NATIONAL PARK

When mountain men like John Colter and Jim Bridger first saw the geyser basins of Yellowstone, in what's now Wyoming's northwest corner, they knew at once that this wondrous place was unique. Nearly 200 years later, the land that became Yellowstone National Park in 1872 remains just as alluring. Millions of people visit the park annually, but in Yellowstone you can still find solitude and listen to the sounds of nature: bubbling mud pots, steaming geysers, and the wind in the pine trees.

No matter where you enter Yellowstone, you'll find yourself driving in circles: the park's road system is laid out in a figure eight known as the Grand Loop. Along the road there are eight primary developed areas: Grant Village, Old Faithful, Madison, Norris, Canyon Village, Mammoth Hot Springs, Roosevelt–Tower Fall, and Lake Village/Fishing Bridge. They all have places to gas up your car at the very least, and some have hotels, restaurants, museums, and information centers.

The park's famous geysers are found throughout the area but are most prevalent in the western sections of the park near Old Faithful, Norris, and Mammoth. Yellowstone Lake attracts boaters and anglers, while the steep Yellowstone Canyon is a rich geological display spanning millions of years. Wildlife abounds everywhere, but particularly in open meadows and along the river valleys. You will see bison, elk, and coyotes in virtually all areas; bears are most visible in the Pelican Valley–Fishing Bridge area, near Dunraven Pass, and near Mammoth; wolves can often be spotted in the Lamar Valley and areas south of Mammoth. Watch for trumpeter swans and other waterfowl along the Yellowstone River and for sandhill cranes near the Firehole River and Madison Valley.

GRAND TETON NATIONAL PARK & JACKSON HOLE

You might think Grand Teton National Park would suffer in comparison to its larger, more historic neighbor just to the north—Yellowstone—but when you see the Tetons rising out of Jackson Hole you realize that the park is its own spectacular destination. Jackson Hole is the valley to the east of the Tetons, and it's home to world-class skiing, with literally thousands of ways to get down the slopes. The town of Jackson, located within the valley, works to maintain its small-town charm while at the same time serving as the area's cultural center. South of Jackson Hole—and off the beaten

WHAT'S
WHERE

path—is the Wind River mountain range. The Oregon-California-Mormon Trail sites in the area near South Pass merit a visit, and you can learn about Native American traditions on the Wind River Reservation.

SOUTHWEST MONTANA

Montana's southwest corner was built on the promise of gold-rush riches. More than 30,000 miners and merchants arrived in the five years after the first news of gold strikes on Grasshopper Creek started circulating in 1862. The gold and silver did not last long, but the unexpected discovery of a massive vein of copper beneath Butte ushered in the greatest era of Montana's colorful mining history. Today the region's real treasures are its untamed national forests, blue-ribbon trout streams, and state parks. The Gold West Country also has an ample supply of museums and art galleries, as well as numerous historic sites—the Big Hole National Battlefield, the Grant-Kohrs Ranch, and the stately restored gold camps of Bannack, Virginia City, and Helena's Last Chance Gulch. Wildlife, water, and wilderness are the hallmarks of the region bordering Yellowstone National Park to the south. Three of Yellowstone's five entrances are here, as are the incredible Beartooth Highway, the Absaroka-Beartooth Wilderness, and the nation's longest free-flowing river. The region's cities and towns, including Bozeman, Livingston, Red Lodge, and West Yellowstone, sponsor year-round special events and are well equipped to welcome visitors.

GLACIER NATIONAL PARK & NORTHWEST MONTANA

Crowned by Glacier National Park, flanked by the Bob Marshall Wilderness Area, and watered by the lakes of the Seeley Valley, northwest Montana is a wild realm encompassing nearly 3 million acres—roughly the size of Connecticut. Add to this the National Bison Range, the Jewel Basin Hiking Area, the Flathead River, and Flathead Lake—the largest body of fresh water in the West—and you can understand why Glacier Country is Montana's top tourist destination. Tucked between the peaks and forests are numerous farms that yield such traditional crops as barley, wheat, seed potatoes, oats, and hay. But the peculiar soil and climate of the Flathead Valley also produce outstanding cherries, peppermint, Christmas trees, and champagne grapes. The largest city in the region, Missoula, is home to the University of Montana and the state's most thriving arts community.

THE MONTANA PLAINS	Nestled up against the eastern edge of the Rocky Mountains are the high plains of Montana, vast expanses of grassy prairie where cattle often outnumber people. Though much of the land has a lonesome, empty look to it, it's rich with the history of America's last frontier in places such as the Little Bighorn Battlefield National Monument, where Lakota and Cheyenne warriors scored a major victory over government troops, and in Ekalaka, where an entire town sprang up around a log saloon in the middle of nowhere. The region is also home to two metropolitan areas that serve as bastions of education, culture, and commerce: Billings, situated along the banks of the Yellowstone River just north of Wyoming, is the state's largest community and one of the largest industrial centers between Minneapolis and Seattle; and Great Falls, nestled at the base of the Rocky Mountains in the north, prides itself on its Western art tradition and beautiful parks.
CODY, SHERIDAN & NORTHERN WYOMING	Northern Wyoming is divided almost exactly in half by the Big Horn Mountains, an easterly Rocky Mountain range with peaks towering more than 13,000 feet above sea level. The wide-open plains of the Powder River Basin lie to the east of these mountains, extending for 150 mi to the Black Hills that straddle the Wyoming–South Dakota border. Although the centrally located and coal-rich town of Gillette is northern Wyoming's most populous city (21,840 residents), the city of Sheridan, with its proud ranching heritage and convenient location near the ski slopes and snowmobile trails of the Big Horns, is more visited by travelers. West of these lofty peaks is the Big Horn Basin, a giant earthen bowl almost as arid as most deserts. The storied settlement of Cody, founded by the great showman Buffalo Bill Cody, sits on its western edge near the border with Yellowstone National Park. Rodeos, museums, guest ranches, hiking trails and winter sports are among the area's biggest draws.
THE SOUTH DAKOTA BLACK HILLS	A few hundred miles east of the Rocky Mountains sit the Black Hills, an ancient mountain range that straddles the Wyoming–South Dakota border. A sacred land that was once the Great Sioux Indian Reservation, it saw America's last great gold rush. Western legends such as Deadwood Dick and the Sundance Kid roamed its creek-carved canyons and windswept prairies. Some, such as Calamity Jane and Wild Bill Hickok, never left. Today you can see their legacy in places

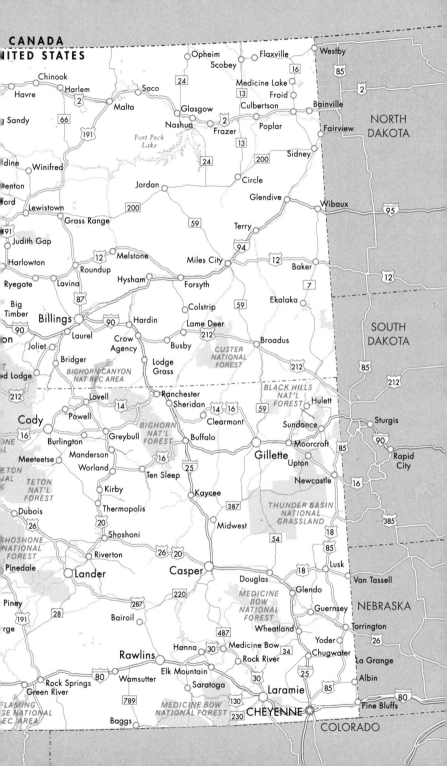

WHAT'S
WHERE

such as Deadwood, the site of one of the country's largest on-going historic preservation projects. You are unlikely to forget a visit to the weathered buttes and otherworldly canyons of Badlands National Park, or to the labyrinthine passages of Jewel Cave National Monument and Wind Cave National Park, two of the longest caves in the world. But the big draw for most visitors (2.8 million in 2005) is Mount Rushmore National Memorial, a mountain sculpted into the unblinking granite faces of George Washington, Thomas Jefferson, Theodore Roosevelt, and Abraham Lincoln.

SOUTHERN WYOMING

Southern Wyoming spans the wheat fields of the southeast, the lush meadows of the Platte River and Bridger valleys, and the wide-open sagebrush lands of the southwest; the region is populated by the world's largest free-ranging pronghorn antelope herds, wild horses, deer, elk, and other wildlife. Cheyenne, Wyoming's state capital, anchors the southeast, and there are major services in Laramie, Rawlins, Rock Springs, Green River, and Evanston, towns that got their start because of the Union Pacific Railroad. Any trip across southern Wyoming involves some miles on I–80, where you'll share the road with lots of 18-wheelers, but the best way to appreciate the region is to take side trips whenever possible. Between Cheyenne and Laramie, use Wyoming Route 210 (Happy Jack Road); follow the old Lincoln Highway—U.S. 30—between Laramie and Walcott Junction; cross the Snowy Range Scenic Byway (open from late May through early October) between Laramie/Centennial and Saratoga to see the rugged beauty of the Snowy Range mountains; and take Wyoming Route 70 (the Battle Highway) between Encampment and Baggs to explore the Medicine Bow National Forest and see the copper mines of the early 1900s. The Red Desert between Rawlins and Green River may seem stark, but in the early morning and late evening shadows lengthen, adding depth and color to the landscape.

WHEN TO GO

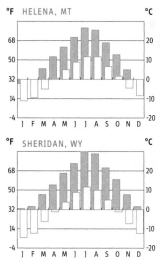

°F HELENA, MT °C

°F SHERIDAN, WY °C

Hotels in tourist destinations book up early, especially in July and August, and hikers spread into the backcountry from June through Labor Day. Ski resorts buzz from December to early April, especially during Christmas and Presidents' Day holiday weeks.

If you don't mind capricious weather, spring and fall are opportune seasons to visit—prices drop and crowds are nonexistent. Spring's pleasures are somewhat limited, since snow usually blocks the high country well into June. But spring is a good time for fishing, rafting on rivers swollen with snowmelt, birding, and wildlife viewing. In fall, aspens splash the mountainsides with gold, and wildlife comes down to lower elevations. The fish are spawning, and the angling is excellent.

Climate

Summer in the area begins in late June or early July. Days are warm, with highs often in the 80s, and nighttime temperatures fall to the 40s and 50s. Afternoon thunderstorms are common over the higher peaks. Fall begins in September, often with a week of unsettled weather around mid-month, followed by four to six gorgeous weeks of Indian summer—frosty nights and warm days. Winter creeps in during November, and deep snows arrive by December. Temperatures usually hover near freezing by day, thanks to the warm mountain sun, dropping considerably overnight, occasionally as low as -60°F. Winter tapers off in March, though snow lingers into April on valley bottoms and into July on mountain passes. The Rockies have a reputation for extreme weather, but no condition ever lasts for long.

⑦ Forecasts Weather Channel Connection ☎ 900/932-8437 95¢ per minute from a Touch-Tone phone ⊕ www.weather.com.

Above are charts of average daily maximum and minimum temperatures for each month within the region.

QUINTESSENTIAL MONTANA & WYOMING

Living with Animals

Whether they're wrangling a herd of cattle, waiting for a trout to bite, or sharing a trail with a mountain goat, people in these parts interact with other members of the animal kingdom to a degree you just don't find in many other places in the United States. Sharing the environment isn't some lofty concept—it's a part of everyday life.

What results is an unromanticized respect for animals and the places they live. It's an attitude worthy of emulation. Spotting the abundant, beautiful wildlife that populate Montana and Wyoming is a thrill, whether you're driving the Grand Loop in Yellowstone or hiking through the backcountry. The locals get a kick out of it, too—but they know to tread softly and keep a safe distance, for the animals' benefit as well as their own.

Rodeos, Rendezvous & Powwows

The Western tradition of working hard and then cutting loose is alive and well—look no further than Cheyenne Frontier Days, the rodeo extravaganza that's known simply as "The Daddy of 'Em All." It's the biggest event on the calendar, but it's hardly alone. In July and August a weekend doesn't go by without some sort of a celebration: there are rodeos, Native American powwows (such as the Plains Indian Powwow in Cody), and rendezvous (events commemorating 19th-century trappers and traders—the Green River Rendezvous in Pinedale, Wyoming, is one of the best).

Winter begins with torchlight ski parades and traditional Christmas celebrations, but as the season wears on, things turn wacky. In Whitefish, Montana, contestants race down the slopes in their favorite furniture, and it's golf on ice at The Wild West Winter Carnival in Riverton, Wyoming.

Montana and Wyoming are states where the buffalo still roam and a cowboy sensibility endures—people tend to look you in the eye, and they consider you a friend until proven otherwise. Below are a few classic elements of the regional culture worth keeping in mind when you make your visit.

Meat & Potatoes

You're in the land of the unrepentant carnivore here: fine dining first and foremost means steaks grilled to perfection. It's also prime hunting and fishing territory. Antelope, elk, venison, and grouse make regular appearances on menus, and you often have a choice of rainbow trout, salmon, and bass pulled from someone's favorite fishing spot. You can find adventurous chefs doing creative things in the kitchen, but anything that smacks of "highfalutin" is a cardinal sin. No matter where you go, your server is likely to greet you with a smile, and blue jeans are always okay.

Microbreweries are another noteworthy phenomenon—a leader in the regional market is Montana's Black Dog, but you'll find smaller local operations all over. And the fruits are exceptional: huckleberries are used in everything from muffins to ice cream, and apples, peaches, and pears from roadside stands are full of tree-ripened goodness.

The Big Sky

"The Big Sky State" is Montana's motto, but you can have the Big Sky experience in Wyoming too. It happens when the vastness of the land (and the sky above it) becomes so great it nearly overwhelms you. The horizon heads off toward infinity in every direction, a few high clouds drift by overhead, and the only sign of civilization is the road beneath your feet.

How you feel about the Big Sky says a lot about the type of person you are. For some people it's exhilarating—they've found a place where they can stretch their legs, take a deep breath, and consider their day-to-day life from a new, broader perspective. On the flip side, if you have a hint of agoraphobia in your blood, you'll feel it here. One way or the other, the Big Sky tends to provoke strong reactions.

IF YOU LIKE . . .

Horseback Riding

Horseback riding in Montana and Wyoming can mean anything from a quick trot around a ring to a weeklong stay at a working dude ranch where guests rise at dawn and herd cattle.

Horse-pack trips are a great way to visit the backcountry, since horses can travel distances and carry supplies that would be impossible for hikers. Northwest Montana's Bob Marshall Wilderness Area is the perfect example: in the state's largest stretch of roadless wilderness, a horse-pack trip is just about the only way to travel the huge expanses. Although horsemanship isn't required for most trips, it's helpful, and even an experienced rider can expect to be a little sore for the first few days. June through August is the peak period for horse-pack trips; before signing up with an outfitter, ask what skills are expected.

Dude ranches fall roughly into two categories: working ranches and guest ranches. Working ranches, where guests participate in such activities as roundups and cattle movements, sometimes require experienced horsemanship. Guest ranches offer a wide range of activities in addition to horseback riding, including fishing, four-wheeling, spa services, and cooking classes. At a typical dude ranch, guests stay in log cabins and are served meals family-style in a lodge or ranch house; some ranches now have upscale restaurants on-site too. For winter, many ranches have added such snow-oriented amenities as sleigh rides, snowshoeing, and cross-country skiing.

The ranches are equipped to handle guests arriving with no gear, although all offer lists of what to bring for travelers who want to use their own gear. Jeans and cowboy boots are still the preferred attire for horseback, although hiking boots and Gore-Tex have long since become fashionable, especially in colder months and at higher altitudes. Long pants are a must either way. Layering is key; plan to have some kind of fleece or heavier outer layer no matter the time of year, since the mountains will be cooler the higher you go.

When choosing a ranch, consider whether the place is family-oriented or adults-only, and check on the length-of-stay requirements. Working ranches plan around the needs of the business, and thus often require full-week stays for a fixed price, while guest ranches operate more like hotels.

- **Encampment, Southern Wyoming.** You feel a little like an old-time cowboy when you ride with the outfitters based here. Trips take you through desert country and up into the Sierra Madres, past old mines and ghost towns.

- **Gunsel Horse Adventures, Yellowstone.** To get a taste of Yellowstone far from the traffic jams, pack up and head into the backcountry on trips ranging from 4 to 10 days.

- **Paradise Guest Ranch, Buffalo, Northern Wyoming.** For a hundred years this ranch has been putting guests on horseback. You can take rodeo training, hit the trail for a multiday pack trip, and get out of the saddle for barbecues and square dances.

- **Seven Lazy P Guest Ranch, Bob Marshall Wilderness Area, Northwest Montana.** From this comfortable all-inclusive ranch you can take rides into "the Bob," where the terrain has changed little since the days of Lewis and Clark.

Skiing & Snowboarding

The champagne powder of the Rocky Mountains can be a revelation for skiers and snowboarders familiar only with the slopes of other regions.

Forget treacherous sheets of rock-hard ice, single-note hills where the bottom can be seen from the top, and mountains that offer only one kind of terrain from every angle. In the Rockies, the snow builds up quickly, leaving a solid base that hangs tough all ski season, only to be layered upon by thick, fluffy powder that holds an edge, ready to be groomed into rippling corduroy or left in giddy stashes along the sides and through the trees. Volkswagen-size moguls and half-pipe–studded terrain parks are the norm, not the special attractions.

Skiing the Rockies means preparing for all kinds of weather, sometimes in the same day, because the high altitudes can start a day off sunny and bright but kick in a blizzard by afternoon. Layers help, as well as plenty of polypropylene to wick away sweat in the sun, and a water-resistant outer layer to keep off the powdery wetness that's sure to accumulate—especially if you're a beginner snowboarder certain to spend time on the ground. Must-haves: plenty of sunscreen, because the sun is closer than you think, and a helmet, because the trees are too.

The added bonus of Rocky Mountain terrain is that so many of the areas have a wide variety of easier (green circle), intermediate (blue square), advanced (black diamond), and expert (double black diamond) slopes—often in the same ski resort. Turn yourself over to the rental shops, which are specialized enough at each resort to offer experts in helping you plan your day and the types of equipment you'll need. Renting is also a great chance for experienced skiers and snowboarders to try out the latest technology before investing in a purchase.

Shop around for lift tickets before you leave home. Look for package deals, multiple day passes, and online discounts. Call the resort and ask if there are any off-site locations (such as local supermarkets) where discount tickets can be purchased. The traditional ski season usually runs from mid-December until early April, with Christmas, New Year's, and the month of March being the busiest times at the resorts.

- **Big Mountain, Whitefish, Northwest Montana.** The highlight here is the long high-speed quad, the Glacier Chaser. The scene isn't as glamorous as Jackson Hole or Aspen, and skiers here think that's just fine.

- **Big Sky, Southwest Montana.** An easygoing atmosphere combined with the second-greatest vertical drop in the U.S. makes for a first-rate ski destination.

- **Jackson Hole, Wyoming.** The steep descents draw America's best skiers, but with thousands of ways to get down the mountain, this is a world-class experience no matter what your skill level.

- **Lone Mountain Ranch, Southwest Montana.** If cross-country skiing is your thing, this is the place to go. The 75 miles of groomed trails are beautiful and wonderfully varied.

IF YOU LIKE . . .

Hiking

Hiking is easily the least expensive and most accessible recreational pursuit. Sure, you could spend a few hundred dollars on high-tech hiking boots, a so-called "personal hydration system," and a collapsible walking staff made of space-age materials, but there's no need for such expenditure. All that's really essential are sturdy athletic shoes, water, and the desire to see the landscape under your own power.

Hiking in the Rockies is a three-season sport that basically lasts as long as you're willing to tromp through snow. (You could look at snowshoeing as winter hiking—the trails are often the same.) One of the greatest aspects of this region is the wide range of hiking terrain, from high-alpine scrambles that require stamina, to flowered meadows that invite a relaxed pace, to confining slot canyons where flash floods are a real danger and can be fatal to the unwary adventurer.

There are few real hazards to hiking, but a little preparedness goes a long way. Know your limits, and make sure the terrain you are about to embark on does not exceed your abilities. It's a good idea to check the elevation change on a trail before you set out—a 1-mi trail might sound easy, until you realize how steep it is—and be careful not to get caught on exposed trails at elevation during afternoon thunderstorms in summer. Dress appropriately by bringing layers to address changing weather conditions, and always carry enough drinking water. Also make sure someone knows where you're going and when to expect your return.

There are literally thousands of miles of hiking trails in Montana and Wyoming. The national parks have particularly well-marked and well-maintained trails, and admission to all trails is free. In fact, hiking is sometimes the only way to get close to certain highlights on protected land. Primarily for safety reasons, overnight hikers are usually expected to register with park or forest rangers. Also keep in mind that run-ins with bears and mountain lions are increasingly common.

- **Clear Creek Trail, Buffalo, Northern Wyoming.** An easy 11-mile path goes through the historic town of Buffalo and out into nature, with good spots to stop for fishing and photography.

- **The Highline Trail, Glacier National Park.** This gorgeous seven-mile hike leads from Logan Pass to Granite Chalet, a rustic National Landmark lodge where you can bed down for the night.

- **Jewel Basil Hiking Area, Flathead Lake, Northwest Montana.** Thirty-five miles of well-maintained trails run past 27 trout-filled alpine lakes.

- **Yellowstone Association Institute, Yellowstone National Park.** This is the group to contact for guided hikes through the park, from day trips to overnight backpacking in the backcountry.

Bicycling

The Rockies are a favorite destination for bikers. Wide-open roads with great gains and losses in elevation test and form road cyclists' stamina, while riders who prefer pedaling fat tires have plenty of mountain and desert trails to test their skills. Unmatched views often make it difficult to keep your eyes on the road.

Thanks to the popularity of the sport here, it's usually easy to find a place that rents bicycles if you'd prefer to leave yours at home. Shops often rent a variety of bikes from entry-level to high-end, though the latter come at a premium, and if you're in the market for a used bike, good deals can often be found when shops unload one season's rentals to make room for next year's models. Bike shops are also a good bet for information on local rides and group tours.

Mountain biking has a huge following—it's more popular in the region than touring on paved roads. The Montana-based Adventure Cycling Association ⊕ www. adventurecycling.org has mapped interconnecting back roads, logging and forest-service roads, and trails stretching from Canada to Mexico. Few people ride the whole route, which covers close to 2,500 mi, but it's easy to pick a segment to suit any rider's stamina. Although the route does follow, very approximately, the Continental Divide, the riding is not all big-mountain climbing and descending. Portions of the trip are negotiable by children as young as 10. The Adventure Cycling Association leads tours and can provide detailed maps (complete with lodging and camping options), information, and advice for self-guided trips.

The rules of the road are the same here as elsewhere, though some areas are less biker-friendly than others. On the road, watch for trucks and stay as close as possible to the side of the road, in single file. On the trail, ride within your limits and keep your eyes peeled for hikers and horses (both have the right of way), as well as dogs. Always wear a helmet and carry plenty of water.

- **Adventure Cycling, Missoula, Southwest Montana.** This organization is the first stop for mountain bikers looking for routes, maps, advice, and guided tours.

- **Mickelson Trail, Deadwood, South Dakota.** Over a hundred miles of former railroad line run the length of the Black Hills.

- **Railroad-Daly Loop, Darby, Northwest Montana.** Sixteen miles of mountainous terrain provide lots of opportunities for spotting moose, deer, and elk.

- **Rimrocks, Billings, Montana Plains.** Trails to suit every level of mountain biker are within easy reach in the terrain surrounding Billings.

IF YOU LIKE . . .

Rafting

Rafting brings on emotions varying from the calm induced by flat waters surrounded with stunning scenery, backcountry scenery, and wildlife, to the thrill and excitement of charging a raging torrent of foam.

For the inexperienced, the young, and the aged, dozens of tour companies offer relatively tame floats ranging from one hour to one day starting at $20, which are ideal for anyone from 4 years old to 90. Others fulfill the needs of adventure tourists content only with chills, potential spills, and the occasional wall of water striking them smack-dab in the chest. Beginners and novices should use guides, but experienced rafters may rent watercraft.

Seasoned outfitters know their routes and their waters as well as you know the road between home and work. Many guides offer multiday trips in which they do everything, including searing your steak in a beach barbecue, setting up your tent, and rolling out your sleeping bag. Select an outfitter based on recommendations from the local chamber, experience, and word of mouth.

The International Scale of River Difficulty is a widely accepted rating system that ranks waters from Class I (the easiest) to Class VI (the most difficult—think Niagara Falls). Ask your guide about the rating on your route before you book. Remember, ratings can vary greatly throughout the season due to run-off and weather events.

Wear a swimsuit or shorts and sandals and bring along sunscreen and sunglasses. Outfitters are required to supply a life jacket for each passenger, although most states don't require that it be worn. Midsummer is the ideal time to raft in the West, although many outfitters will stretch the season, particularly on calmer routes.

Numerous outfitters and guide services offer rafting trips in Wyoming and Montana, and the journey can vary from relaxing family outings to white-knuckled runs through raging waters. In all cases you'll discover scenery, wildlife, and an off-the-road experience that you'll never get looking through a windshield.

- **Alberton Gorge near Missoula, Northwest Montana.** This canyon section of the Clark Fork River is perfect for a hot summer day.

- **North Platte River, near Casper, Northern Wyoming.** Outfitters offer trips ranging from one hour to a full day on this tranquil stretch of water, ideal for the whole family.

- **Snake River Canyon, south of Jackson, Wyoming.** Some of the wildest white water in the Rockies, a winding stretch lined with trees, steep granite walls, alpine meadows and abundant wildlife.

- **Upper middle fork of the Flathead River, Northwest Montana.** A white-water rafting adventure into the 286,700-acre Great Bear Wilderness.

- **Yellowstone River near Gardiner, Southwest Montana.** Raft through Yankee Jim Canyon and experience Boxcar, Big Rock, and Revenge rapids.

Fishing

Trout do not live in ugly places.

And so it is in Montana and Wyoming, where you'll discover unbridled beauty, towering pines, rippling mountain streams, and bottomless pools. It's here that blue-ribbon trout streams remain much as they were when Native American tribes, French fur trappers, and a few thousand faceless miners, muleskinners, and sodbusters first placed a muddy footprint along their banks.

Those early-day settlers had one advantage that you won't—time. To make the best use of that limited resource, consider the following advice.

Hire a guide. You could spend days locating a great fishing spot, learning the water currents and fish behavior, and determining what flies, lures, or bait the fish are following. A good guide will cut through the options, get you into fish, and turn your excursion into an adventure complete with a full creel.

If you're comfortable with your fishing gear, bring it along, though most guides loan or rent equipment. Bring a rod and reel, waders, vest, hat, sunglasses, net, tackle, hemostats, and sunscreen. Always buy a fishing license.

If you're not inclined to fork over the $250-plus that most quality guides charge per day for two anglers and a boat, your best bet is a stop at a reputable fly shop. They'll shorten your learning curve, tell you where the fish are, what they're biting on, and whether you should be "skittering" your dry-fly on top of the water or "dead-drifting" a nymph.

Famed fisherman Lee Wolff wrote that "catching fish is a sport. Eating fish is not a sport." Most anglers practice "catch and release" in an effort to maintain productive fisheries and to protect native species.

Season is always a consideration. Spring run-offs can cloud the waters; summer droughts may reduce stream flows; and fall weather can be unpredictable. But, as many fishing guides will attest, the best time to come and wet a line is whenever you can make it.

- **Black Feet Reservation, near Browning, Northwest Montana.** Twenty-some stocked reservoirs regularly yield lunker lake trout from two to eight pounds.

- **Flaming Gorge Reservoir, Southern Wyoming.** Home to state records for smallmouth bass, Kokanee salmon, brown trout, channel catfish, Utah chub, and lake trout.

- **Gallatin Canyon, south of Bozeman, Southwest Montana.** The clarity and variety of water is outstanding; the scenery incredible.

- **North Fork of Shoshone River, west of Cody, Northern Wyoming** The river drops roughly 3,000 feet in 70 miles from the Silvertip Basin to Buffalo Bill Reservoir.

- **Platte River, near Casper, Northern Wyoming.** With depths ranging from 1 to 15 feet, this blue-ribbon water attracts fishermen from all over the world.

- **Yellowstone National Park.** Simply a tremendous fishing destination.

- **Yellowstone River through Paradise Valley, Southwest Montana.** Fish surrounded by snow-capped peaks, free-roaming wildlife and soaring hawks and eagles.

GREAT ITINERARY

GLACIER LAKES TO THE TETONS

This drive will take you to Glacier, Yellowstone, and Grand Teton national parks—three spectacular crown jewels of the national park system.

Day 1

Start your tour in Glacier National Park, with its 1,500 square mi of exquisite ice-carved terrain. A drive on the cliff-hugging Going-to-the-Sun Road over the Continental Divide is a must. Overnight at Lake McDonald Lodge. Opened in 1914, Lake McDonald is one of the great lodges of the West.

Day 2

Devote your second day in Glacier to river rafting, horseback riding, or hiking.

Day 3

Drive southwest on U.S. 2 to Kalispell, then south on U.S. 93, where you'll hug the western shoreline of Flathead Lake for about 43 mi to the town of Polson. Flathead is the largest natural freshwater lake in the western United States—take time to breathe it all in.

It's only 123 mi from Kalispell to Missoula, but the sheer beauty of the scenery in the Flathead Indian Reservation, looking to the east at the vast Mission Range, makes it a trip worth lingering over.

Stop by the National Bison Range near Ravalli. The range is a 30-square-mi preserve of natural grasslands established in 1908 to protect one of the few surviving herds of American bison.

Overnight in Missoula, at the intersection of five valleys and the junction of three great rivers. This is Montana's hippest town, with excellent galleries, gift shops, and restaurants, as well at the University of Montana and the Missoula Children's Theatre.

Day 4

Day 4 of your trek takes you 119 mi southeast on I–90 to the century-old mining town of Butte, where the lavish Copper King Mansion reveals what you could buy back in the day with an unlimited household budget.

To get to West Yellowstone from Butte, follow I–90 east 28 mi to U.S. 287; then turn south and drive 106 mi. Overnight in one of Yellowstone's old hotels, or if you don't want to drive the whole way, spend the night in Butte or Bozeman.

Day 5

Devote the day to a tour of Yellowstone National Park. The 142-mi Grand Loop Road passes nearly every major attraction in the park, and you'll discover interpretive displays, overlooks, and short trails along the way. Most motorists easily spend a day on the Loop.

You really can't go wrong with a stay at the Old Faithful Inn, where lodgepole-pine walls and ceiling beams, an immense volcanic rock fireplace, and green-tinted, etched windows provide the ideal example of what national park lodgings were originally meant to be.

Day 6

Spend a second day in Yellowstone, this time getting off the Grand Loop to explore the park's hiking trails or to go fishing.

Day 7

On the final day of your tour, get an early start in an easterly direction on the Grand Loop Road, turning south at Grant Village onto U.S. 89–287. Proceed 43 mi south to Grand Teton National Park, whose northern boundary is 7 mi from Yellowstone's south entrance.

The sheer ruggedness of the Tetons makes them seem imposing and unapproachable, but a drive on Teton Park Road, with frequent stops at scenic turnouts, will get you up close and personal with the peaks. Overnight in one of the park lodges.

ON THE CALENDAR

WINTER Dec.	Christmas celebrations blanket most Rockies towns. For the holidays, many ski areas mount torchlight parades, with large groups of torch-bearing ski instructors tracing patterns down mountainsides. Contact specific resorts for details. *Montana:* Bozeman's Christmas Stroll ☎ 406/586–4008 features sleigh rides, carolers, hot-chocolate stands, holiday lights, and late shopping hours. *Wyoming:* Take a candlelight tour of the Historic Governor's Mansion ☎ 307/777–7878 in Cheyenne to get into the holiday spirit. Members of Company I, Third U.S. Volunteer Infantry and the museum at Fort Caspar Historic Site ☎ 307/235–8462 in Casper celebrate Christmas with candlelight tours.
Jan.	*Montana:* Settle in for cowboy music, poetry, and art at the Montana Cowboy Poetry Wintercamp ☎ 406/932–4227 in Big Timber. Introduce your children to snowboarding or skiing during Take Your Children to the Snow Week ☎ 406/862–1948 at Big Mountain Resort in Whitefish. *Wyoming:* The Wild West Winter Carnival ☎ 800/325–2732 or 800/645–6233 at Boysen State Park, near Shoshoni, has dog races, a demolition derby, softball, and golf, all on ice, as well as snowmobile races and a "snowdeo."
Feb.	*Montana:* Mid-February's Race to the Sky ☎ 406/442–4008 or 800/847–4868 begins with activities in Helena, including contests for mutt pulling and stupid pet tricks, a microbrew review, and Cool Dog Ball. The 350-mi, six-day dogsled race itself crisscrosses the Continental Divide at elevations of up to 7,000 feet, beginning and ending in Lincoln. The trail passes through Seeley Lake and Condon. *Wyoming:* On Presidents' Day weekend, horses race down the track pulling two-wheel carts at the Donald E. Erickson Memorial Chariot Races ☎ 307/326–8855, near Saratoga.
SPRING Mar.	*Montana:* Irish folk and other wearers of the green flock to Butte for the St. Patrick's Day Parade ☎ 406/782–0742, one of the West's largest and most rollicking, and for other Irish-accented events. Collectors from around the world attend the C. M. Russell Auction of Original Western Art ☎ 406/761–6453 or 800/803–3351, held in Great Falls. *Wyoming:* The Western Spirit Art Show and Sale ☎ 307/778–1416 at the Old West Museum in Cheyenne includes displays by top regional and national artists. The Wyoming State Winter Fair ☎ 307/

	332–5345 features livestock displays and arts and crafts for sale in Lander.
Apr.	*Montana*: The International Wildlife Film Festival ☎ 406/728–9380 in Missoula is one of two such film festivals in the world. The Rendezvous Cross-country Ski Race ☎ 406/646–7701 attracts 700 skiers and an entourage 1,500 strong to the 50-km (and other) races at West Yellowstone. *Wyoming*: Cowboy Songs and Range Ballads ☎ 307/587–4771 in Cody includes concerts, jam sessions, and a symposium all about cowboy music.
May	*Montana*: At the annual Big Timber Bull-A-Rama ☎ 406/932–6228 or 406/932–6697, the West's top bull riders test their skills and spurs on 1,800-pound bucking-mad bulls. In Miles City, rodeo stock for the upcoming season is auctioned off at the Bucking Horse Sale ☎ 406/232–7700; the horses demonstrate their bucking prowess in rodeo competitions, and the event also features bull riding, a wild-horse race, and street dances. St. Ignatius hosts the Buffalo Feast and Powwow ☎ 406/745–2951 with three days of dancing and games capped by a free feast of pit-roasted buffalo. You can sample fine beers from Montana and the Northwest at the Garden City Micro B. R.I.W. Fest ☎ 406/721–6061 in Missoula. *Wyoming*: The huge Flaming Gorge Fishing Derby ☎ 307/362–3771 in Rock Springs draws 350 teams of anglers. Dubois hosts Pack Horse Races ☎ 307/455–2556 or 307/455–2174, where teams break camp, pack up on horses, and run an obstacle course.
SUMMER June	*Montana*: The Lewis and Clark Festival ☎ 406/761–4434 or 800/735–8535 in Great Falls highlights the expedition across the West two centuries ago. Tours, a kids' day camp, float trips, and courses mark the five-day event. On the third or fourth weekend in June, Great Falls puts on the Montana Traditional Dixieland Jazz Festival ☎ 406/771–1642. The Augusta Rodeo ☎ 406/562–3477 is one of the largest one-day rodeos in Montana and features the old-time Wild Cow Milking and parade. The Battle of the Little Bighorn Reenactment ☎ 406/665–3577 or 888/450–3577 in Hardin enlists more than 200 riders who portray cavalry and Native American participants in that 1876 battle. There is also a historical symposium. *Wyoming*: Bozeman Trail Days ☎ 307/684–7687 or 307/684–7629 has tours and programs about Bozeman Trail travel and Indian wars. On the third full weekend in June, competing lumberjacks

ON THE CALENDAR

	make wood chips fly at the Woodchoppers Jamboree & Rodeo ☎ 307/326–8855 in Encampment.
July	*Montana*: The Grant-Kohrs Ranch National Historic Site in Deer Lodge, Montana, celebrates cowboy lore and skills during Western Heritage Days ☎ 406/846–2070 or 406/846–3388 with roping, branding, chuck-wagon cooking, and traditional cowboy music and poetry. And don't miss the Montana State Fair ☎ 406/727–8900 in Great Falls at the end of the month.
	Wyoming: The old-fashioned Cody Stampede ☎ 307/587–5155 or 800/207–0744 in Buffalo Bill Cody's eponymous hometown is one of the Rockies' larger July 4 celebrations, complete with rodeos. The Green River Rendezvous ☎ 307/367–4101, near Pinedale, stages a reenactment of 1830s mountain life. For the king of out-door rodeos, see the world's largest, Cheyenne Frontier Days ☎ 307/778–7222 or 800/227–6336, in late July. For something in a more arty line, check out the Grand Teton Music Festival ☎ 307/733–1128 in Teton Village. Celebrate cowboy and ranching heritage with music and poetry at the Grand Encampment Cowboy Gathering ☎ 307/327–5308 or 307/326–8855, plus living-history activities at the Grand Encampment Museum.
Aug.	*Montana*: The Crow Fair and Rodeo ☎ 406/638–2601 takes place in Crow Agency—the self-styled teepee capital of the world. The Crow Indian Reservation is off I-90, 45 mi southeast of Billings. At the Montana Cowboy Poetry Gathering ☎ 406/538–8278 in Lewis-ton, U.S. and Canadian performers share verses about a man and a horse following a cow.
	Wyoming: Livestock shows, rodeos, and Western entertainers are part of the Wyoming State Fair ☎ 307/358–2398 in Douglas. Enjoy music and brews at the Steinley Cup Festival ☎ 307/326–8855, held on an island in the North Platte River in Saratoga. Top brewers from the region compete, and there is also a chili cook-off.
FALL Sept.	*Montana*: Libby's four-day Nordicfest ☎ 406/293–6430 celebrates Scandinavian food, costumes, music, dance, and crafts. The Running of the Sheep ☎ 406/326–2288 in Reed Point is a surrealistic ver-sion of Pamplona's running of the bulls, with hundreds of sturdy Montana-bred woollies charging down Main Street. Seventeen species of raptors and magnificent golden eagles soar over the Bridger Mountains' knife-edge ridge during their southern migra-tion. The Bridger Raptor Festival ☎ 406/585–1211 is arranged around the event. Celebrate with the Labor Day Wagon Train ☎ 406/547–

		2209 held at Culbertson. See arts and crafts ranging from photography to beadwork at the **Labor Day Arts Festival** ☎ 406/446–1370 in Red Lodge.
		Wyoming: The **Jackson Hole Fall Arts Festival** ☎ 307/733–3316 marks the season with concerts, art, poetry, dance, and crafts workshops and lectures throughout the valley. Hundreds of buckskinners gather over Labor Day Weekend for the **Fort Bridger Rendezvous** ☎ 307/782–3842. There is a parasol parade and dance contest as part of the **Lander Jazz Festival** ☎ 307/433–0662 held over Labor Day weekend.
	Oct.	*Montana*: The four-day **Glacier Jazz Stampede** ☎ 406/758–2800 belts out ragtime, Dixieland, swing, modern, and big-band jazz in Kalispell.
		Wyoming: **Oktoberfest** ☎ 307/587–2777 in Cody includes German food and drink, and polka dancing.
	Nov.	*Montana:* Look to the heavens in Great Falls at the **Central Montana Astronomy Star Party** ☎ 406/727–8733, which has plenty of large telescopes available for public viewing. See a wide array of local products at Bozeman's **Holiday Festival of the Arts** ☎ 406/586–3333.
		Wyoming: Horse-drawn vehicles are part of the **Buffalo Christmas Parade** ☎ 307/684–5544, and there is free admission to Buffalo's Jim Gatchell Museum open house and Christmas sale. Cheyenne has dozens of lighted entries, music, and other activities as part of its **Christmas Parade** ☎ 307/778–3133.

SMART TRAVEL TIPS

Finding out about your destination before you leave home means you won't squander time organizing everyday minutiae once you've arrived. You'll be more on top of things when you hit the ground as well, better prepared to explore the aspects of Montana and Wyoming that drew you here in the first place. The organizations in this section can provide information to supplement this guide; contact them for up-to-the-minute details, and consult the A to Z sections that end each chapter for facts on the various topics as they relate to the states' different regions. Happy landings!

AIR TRAVEL

Absolutely the best connections to Montana and often the shortest flights to Wyoming are through the Rockies hub cities, Salt Lake City and Denver. Montana also receives transfer flights from Minneapolis, Seattle, and Phoenix.

BIKES IN FLIGHT

Most airlines accommodate bikes as luggage, provided they are dismantled and boxed; check with individual airlines about packing requirements. Some airlines sell bike boxes, which are often free at bike shops, for about $20 (bike bags can be considerably more expensive). International travelers often can substitute a bike for a piece of checked luggage at no charge; otherwise, the cost is about $100. Most U.S. and Canadian airlines charge $40–$80 each way.

BOOKING

When you book, look for nonstop flights and remember that "direct" flights stop at least once. Try to avoid connecting flights, which require a change of plane. Two airlines may operate a connecting flight jointly, so ask whether your airline operates every segment of the trip; you may find that the carrier you prefer flies you only part of the way. To reach Wyoming and most Montana cities, you will have to take a connecting flight. To find more booking tips and to check prices and make online flight reservations, log on to www.fodors.com.

CARRIERS

United and Delta have the most flights to the region. The regional carrier Big Sky connects Montana cities; America West and Northwest (among others) provide connections to Big Sky from outside the state.

Major Airlines Air Canada ☎ 888/247-2262 ⊕ www.aircanada.com. **American Airlines** ☎ 800/433-7300 ⊕ www.aa.com. **British Airways** ☎ 800/247-9297 ⊕ www.ba.com. **Continental** ☎ 800/525-0280 ⊕ www.continental.com. **Delta** ☎ 800/221-1212 ⊕ www.delta.com. **Northwest** ☎ 800/225-2525 ⊕ www.nwa.com. **United Airlines** ☎ 800/241-6522 ⊕ www.united.com. **US Airways** ☎ 800/428-4322 ⊕ www.usair.com.

Smaller Airlines America Trans Air (ATA) ☎ 800/225-2995 ⊕ www.ata.com. **America West** ☎ 800/235-9292 ⊕ www.americawest.com. **Big Sky** ☎ 800/237-7788 ⊕ www.bigskyair.com. **Frontier** ☎ 800/432-1359 ⊕ www.frontierairlines.com. **Horizon Air** ☎ 800/547-9308 ⊕ www.alaskaair.com. **Mesa Airlines** ☎ 800/637-2247 ⊕ www.mesa-air.com. **Midwest Airlines** ☎ 800/452-2022 ⊕ www.midwestairlines.com. **Southwest** ☎ 800/435-9792 ⊕ www.southwest.com.

CHECK-IN & BOARDING

Always **find out your carrier's check-in policy.** Plan to arrive at the airport about two hours before your scheduled departure time for domestic flights and 2½ to 3 hours before international flights. You may need to arrive earlier if you're flying from one of the busier airports or during peak air-traffic times. But at smaller airports, you may only need to be on hand an hour before the flight.

If you're traveling during snow season, **allow extra time for the drive** to the airport, as weather conditions can slow you down. If you'll be checking skis, arrive even earlier.

To avoid delays at airport-security checkpoints, try not to wear any metal. Jewelry, belt and other buckles, steel-toe shoes, barrettes, and underwire bras are among the items that can set off detectors.

Assuming that not everyone with a ticket will show up, airlines routinely overbook planes. When everyone does, airlines ask for volunteers to give up their seats. In return, these volunteers usually get a several-hundred-dollar flight voucher, which can be used toward the purchase of another ticket, and are rebooked on the next available flight out. If there are not enough volunteers, the airline must choose who will be denied boarding. The first to get bumped are passengers who checked in late and those flying on discounted tickets, so get to the gate and check in as early as possible, especially during peak periods.

Always **bring a government-issued photo I.D.** to the airport; even when it's not required, a passport is best.

CUTTING COSTS

The least expensive airfares to the Rockies and plains are often priced for round-trip travel and must usually be purchased in advance. Airlines generally allow you to change your return date for a fee; most low-fare tickets, however, are nonrefundable. It's smart to call a number of airlines and check the Internet; when you are quoted a good price, book it on the spot—the same fare may not be available the next day, or even the next hour. Always check different routings and look into using alternate airports. Also, price off-peak flights and red-eye, which may be significantly less expensive than others. Travel agents, especially low-fare specialists (⇨ Discounts & Deals), are helpful.

Consolidators are another good source. They buy tickets for scheduled flights at reduced rates from the airlines, then sell them at prices that beat the best fare available directly from the airlines. (Many also offer reduced car-rental and hotel rates.) Sometimes you can even get your money back if you need to return the ticket. Carefully read the fine print detailing penalties for changes and cancellations, purchase the ticket with a credit card, and confirm your consolidator reservation with the airline.

Consolidators AirlineConsolidator.com ☎ 888/468-5385 ⊕ www.airlineconsolidator.com; for international tickets. **Best Fares** ☎ 800/880-1234 ⊕ www.bestfares.com; $59.90 annual membership. **Cheap Tickets** ☎ 800/377-1000 or 800/652-4327 ⊕ www.cheaptickets.com. **Expedia** ☎ 800/397-3342 or 404/728-8787 ⊕ www.expedia.com. **Hotwire** ☎ 866/468-9473 or 920/330-9418 ⊕ www.hotwire.com. **Now Voyager Travel** ☎ 212/

459-1616. Onetravel.com ⊕ www.onetravel.com. Orbitz ☎ 888/656-4546 ⊕ www.orbitz.com. Price-line.com ⊕ www.priceline.com. Travelocity ☎ 888/709-5983, 877/282-2925 in Canada, 0870/111-7061 in the U.K. ⊕ www.travelocity.com.

ENJOYING THE FLIGHT

State your seat preference when purchasing your ticket, and then repeat it when you confirm and when you check in. For more legroom, you can request one of the few emergency-aisle seats at check-in, if you're capable of moving obstacles comparable in weight to an airplane exit door (usually between 35 pounds and 60 pounds)—a Federal Aviation Administration requirement of passengers in these seats. Seats behind a bulkhead also offer more legroom, but they don't have under-seat storage. Don't sit in the row in front of the emergency aisle or in front of a bulkhead, where seats may not recline. SeatGuru.com has more information about specific seat configurations, which vary by aircraft.

Ask the airline whether a snack or meal is served on the flight. If you have dietary concerns, request special meals when booking. These can be vegetarian, low-cholesterol, or kosher, for example. It's a good idea to pack some healthful snacks and a small (plastic) bottle of water in your carry-on bag. On long flights, try to maintain a normal routine, to help fight jet lag. At night, get some sleep. By day, eat light meals, drink water (not alcohol), and **move around the cabin** to stretch your legs. For additional jet-lag tips consult *Fodor's FYI: Travel Fit & Healthy* (available at bookstores everywhere).

Smoking policies vary from carrier to carrier. Most airlines prohibit smoking on all of their flights; others allow smoking only on certain routes or certain departures. Ask your carrier about its policy.

FLYING TIMES

Once you have made your way to Denver or Salt Lake City, which are two of the major hubs providing air service to Montana and Wyoming, you will still have one or two hours of flying time to reach your final airport destination. Many of the airports in these states are served by commuter flights that have frequent stops, though generally with very short layovers. There are no direct flights from New York to the area, and most itineraries from New York take between seven and nine hours. Likewise, you cannot fly direct from Los Angeles to Montana or Wyoming; it will take you four or five hours to get here from the West Coast.

HOW TO COMPLAIN

If your baggage goes astray or your flight goes awry, complain right away. Most carriers require that you **file a claim immediately.** The Aviation Consumer Protection Division of the Department of Transportation publishes *Fly-Rights,* which discusses airlines and consumer issues and is available online. You can also find articles and information on mytravelrights.com, the Web site of the nonprofit Consumer Travel Rights Center.

🔲 **Airline Complaints Aviation Consumer Protection Division** ✉ U.S. Department of Transportation, Office of Aviation Enforcement and Proceedings, C-75, Room 4107, 400 7th St. SW, Washington, DC 20590 ☎ 202/366-2220 ⊕ airconsumer.ost.dot.gov. **Federal Aviation Administration Consumer Hotline** ✉ for inquiries: FAA, 800 Independence Ave. SW, Washington, DC 20591 ☎ 800/322-7873 ⊕ www.faa.gov.

RECONFIRMING

Check the status of your flight before you leave for the airport. You can do this on your carrier's Web site, by linking to a flight-status checker (many Web booking services offer these), or by calling your carrier or travel agent.

AIRPORTS

The major gateways include, in Montana, Missoula International Airport and Glacier Park International Airport (in Kalispell); and in Wyoming, Jackson Hole Airport, Cheyenne Regional Airport, Natrona County International Airport (in Casper), and Yellowstone Regional Airport (in Cody).

🔲 **Colorado Airport Information Denver International Airport** ☎ 303/342-2000, 800/247-2336, 800/688-1333 TTY ⊕ www.flydenver.com.

⛟ Montana Airport Information Glacier Park International Airport ☎ 406/257-5994 ⊕ www.glacierairport.com. **Missoula International Airport** ☎ 406/728-4381 ⊕ www.msoairport.org.
⛟ Utah Airport Information Salt Lake City International Airport ☎ 801/575-2400 ⊕ www.slcairport.com.
⛟ Wyoming Airport Information Cheyenne Municipal Airport ☎ 307/634-7071 ⊕ www.cheyenneairport.com. **Jackson Hole Airport** ☎ 307/733-7682 ⊕ www.jacksonholeairport.com. **Natrona County International Airport** ☎ 307/472-6688 ⊠ casperwyoming.org/airport. **Yellowstone Regional Airport** ☎ 307/587-5096 ⊕ www.flyyra.com.

BIKE TRAVEL

Bike travel is popular throughout the Rockies and plains, particularly among folks who like to ride roads that follow the Continental Divide. Generally bike travel is prohibited on interstate highways; there are few bike lanes anywhere, though you'll find some in resort areas in both Montana and Wyoming. As a result bike riders share the road with cars, trucks, RVs, and other traffic. In summer there is almost always construction on roads throughout the region, which can create problems for bike riders. Rentals are available in resort areas particularly, and often in other cities as well. Expect to pay $15 to $30 for a half- or full-day rental of either a mountain bike or a touring bike. Local bike shops are the best places to get bike maps and other information about cycling. For more information, see "Bicycling" under "Sports & the Outdoors" below.
⛟ Resources Adventure Cycling Association ⊕ Box 8308, Missoula, MT 59807 ☎ 406/721-1776 or 800/755-2453 ⊕ www.adventurecycling.org. **National Geographic/Trails Illustrated** ☎ 800/962-1643. **Off-Road Publications** ☎ 888/477-3374.

BUS TRAVEL

Greyhound Lines has regular intercity routes throughout Montana and Wyoming, with connections from Cheyenne, Rawlins, and Rock Springs to Salt Lake City, which also connects with Bozeman and Missoula. Smaller bus companies provide service within state and local areas.

⛟ Bus Information Coach USA/Powder River Transportation ⊠ Wyoming ☎ 800/442-3682 in Wyoming. **Greyhound Lines** ☎ 800/231-2222 ⊕ www.greyhound.com. **Rimrock/Trailways** ⊠ Montana ☎ 800/255-7655.

BUSINESS HOURS

Most retail stores are open from 9 or 9:30 until 6 or 7 daily in downtown locations and until 9 or 10 in suburban shopping malls and in resort towns during high seasons. Downtown stores sometimes stay open later Thursday night. Normal banking hours are weekdays 9–5; some branches are also open on Saturday morning.

CAMERAS & PHOTOGRAPHY

Photographers love the Rockies and the Great Plains—and with good reason. The scenery is arguably America's best, and every season offers a multitude of breathtaking images. When you're at Native American sites, be sure to ask if taking pictures is appropriate. The *Kodak Guide to Shooting Great Travel Pictures* (available at bookstores everywhere) is loaded with tips.
⛟ Photo Help Kodak Information Center ☎ 800/242-2424 ⊕ www.kodak.com.

EQUIPMENT PRECAUTIONS

Wind, dust, and dirt are the biggest problems you'll face with camera equipment throughout the Rockies and plains, though if you are traveling in winter you might experience problems because of extremely cold temperatures (it can get down to 20°F–30°F below zero and stay there for days at a time). The best way to take care of your gear is to keep it in a case or bag whenever possible, and clean it often with canned air and other lens-cleaning gear. In winter keep it out of the cold as much as possible; tuck it inside your jacket when you are not actually shooting. **Don't pack film or equipment in checked luggage,** where it is much more susceptible to damage. X-ray machines used to view checked luggage are extremely powerful and therefore are likely to ruin your film. Try to ask for hand inspection of film, which becomes clouded after repeated exposure to airport X-ray machines, and keep videotapes and computer disks away from metal detectors. Always keep film, tape, and computer disks out of the sun. Carry an extra supply of batteries, and be prepared to turn on your camera, camcorder, or laptop to prove to airport security personnel that the device is real.

CAR RENTAL

Rates in most Montana and Wyoming cities run about $50 a day and $275–$325 a week for an economy car with air-conditioning, automatic transmission, and unlimited mileage. In resort areas such as Jackson or Kalispell, you'll usually find a variety of 4X4s and SUVs for rent, many of them with ski racks. Unless you plan to do a lot of mountain exploring, a four-wheel drive is usually needed only in winter, but if you do plan to venture onto any back roads, an SUV (about $85 a day) is the best bet because it will have higher clearance. Rates do not include tax on car rentals, which is 6% in Wyoming. There is no tax in Montana, but if you rent from an airport location, there is an airport concession fee.

Major Agencies Alamo ☎ 800/327–9633 ⊕ www.alamo.com. **Avis** ☎ 800/331–1212, 800/ 879–2847 or 800/272–5871 in Canada, 0870/606–0100 in the U.K., 02/9353–9000 in Australia, 09/526–2847 in New Zealand ⊕ www.avis.com. **Budget** ☎ 800/527–0700 ⊕ www.budget.com. **Dollar** ☎ 800/800–4000, 0800/085–4578 in the U.K. ⊕ www.dollar.com. **Hertz** ☎ 800/654–3131, 800/ 263–0600 in Canada, 0870/844–8844 in the U.K., 02/9669–2444 in Australia, 09/256–8690 in New Zealand ⊕ www.hertz.com. **National Car Rental** ☎ 800/227–7368 ⊕ www.nationalcar.com.

CUTTING COSTS

Rental rates are similar whether at the airport or at an in-town agency. Many people fly in to Salt Lake City or Denver and drive a rental car from there to cut travel costs. This makes sense if you're traveling to southern Wyoming, but if your goal is Jackson or Cody, that's a 10- to 11-hour drive from Denver. From Salt Lake City, it's about a six-hour drive to Jackson and a nine-hour trip to Cody.

For a good deal, book through a travel agent who will shop around. Also, price

local car-rental companies—whose prices may be lower still, although their service and maintenance may not be as good as those of major rental agencies—and research rates on the Internet. Consolidators that specialize in air travel can offer good rates on cars as well (⇨ Air Travel). Remember to ask about required deposits, cancellation penalties, and drop-off charges if you're planning to pick up the car in one city and leave it in another. If you're traveling during a holiday period, also make sure that a confirmed reservation guarantees you a car.

INSURANCE

When driving a rented car you are generally responsible for any damage to or loss of the vehicle. You also may be liable for any property damage or personal injury that you may cause while driving. Before you rent, see what coverage you already have under the terms of your personal auto-insurance policy and credit cards.

For about $9 to $25 a day, rental companies sell protection, known as a collision- or loss-damage waiver (CDW or LDW), that eliminates your liability for damage to the car; it's always optional and should never be automatically added to your bill. In most states (including Montana and Wyoming), you don't need a CDW if you have personal auto insurance or other liability insurance. However, **make sure you have enough coverage to pay for the car.** If you do not have auto insurance or an umbrella policy that covers damage to third parties, purchasing liability insurance and a CDW or LDW is highly recommended.

REQUIREMENTS & RESTRICTIONS

In the Rockies and plains you must be 21 to rent a car with a valid driver's license; some companies charge an additional fee for drivers ages 21–24, and others will not rent to anyone under age 25; most companies also require a major credit card.

SURCHARGES

Before you pick up a car in one city and leave it in another, ask about drop-off charges or one-way service fees, which can be substantial. Also inquire about early-return policies; some rental agencies charge extra if you return the car before the time specified in your contract while others give you a refund for the days not used. Most agencies note the tank's fuel level on your contract; to avoid a hefty refueling fee, return the car with the same tank level. If the tank was full, refill it just before you turn in the car, but be aware that gas stations near the rental outlet may overcharge. It's almost never a deal to buy a tank of gas with the car when you rent it; the understanding is that you'll return it empty, but some fuel usually remains. Surcharges may apply if you're under 25 or if you take the car outside the area approved by the rental agency. You'll pay extra for child seats, which are compulsory for children under five (under eight in Wyoming) and cost $5 to $10 a day, and usually for additional drivers (up to $25 a day, depending on location).

CAR TRAVEL

You'll seldom be bored driving through the Rockies and plains, which offer some of the most spectacular vistas and challenging driving in the world. Montana's interstate system is driver-friendly, connecting soaring summits, rivers, glacial valleys, forests, lakes, and vast stretches of prairie, all capped by that endless "Big Sky." Wyoming's interstates link classic, open-range cowboy country and mountain-range vistas with state highways headed to the geothermal wonderland of Yellowstone National Park. In Wyoming everything is separated by vast distances, so be sure to leave each major city with a full tank of gas and be prepared to see lots of wildlife and few other people.

Before setting out on any driving trip, it's important to **make sure your vehicle is in top condition.** It's best to have a complete tune-up. At the least, you should check the following: lights, including brake lights, backup lights, and emergency lights; tires, including the spare; oil; engine coolant; windshield-washer fluid; windshield-wiper blades; and brakes. For emergencies, take along flares or reflector triangles, jumper cables, an empty gas can, a fire extinguisher, a flashlight, a plastic tarp, blan-

kets, water, and coins or a calling card for phone calls (cell phones don't always work in high mountain areas).

BORDER CROSSING

Driving a car across the U.S.–Canadian border is simple. Personal vehicles are allowed entry into the neighboring country, provided they are not to be left behind. Drivers must have owner registration and proof of insurance coverage handy. If the car isn't registered in your name, carry a letter from the owner that authorizes your use of the vehicle. Drivers in rental cars that are permitted to cross the border should **bring along a copy of the rental contract,** which should bear an endorsement stating that the vehicle is permitted to cross the border.

GASOLINE

In major cities throughout Montana and Wyoming, gas prices are roughly similar to those in the rest of the continental United States; in rural and resort towns, prices are sometimes considerably higher. Although gas stations are relatively plentiful in many areas, you can drive more than 100 mi on back roads without finding gas.

ROAD CONDITIONS

Roads range from multilane blacktop to barely graveled backcountry trails. Many twisting switchbacks are considerately marked with guardrails, but some primitive roads have a lane so narrow that you must back up to the edge of a steep cliff to make a turn. Scenic routes and lookout points are clearly marked, enabling you to slow down and pull over to take in the views.

One of the more unpleasant sights along the highway is roadkill—animals struck by vehicles. Deer, elk, and even bears may try to get to the other side of a road just as you come along, so **watch out for wildlife on the highways.** Exercise caution, not only to save an animal's life, but also to avoid possible extensive damage to your car.

🚓 Road Condition Information **Montana** ☎ 406/444-6339 or 800/262-6171. **Wyoming** ☎ 307/772-0824 or 800/996-7623.

RULES OF THE ROAD

You'll find highways and the national parks crowded in summer, and almost deserted (and occasionally impassable) in winter. You may turn right at a red light after stopping if there is no sign stating otherwise and no oncoming traffic. When in doubt, wait for the green. Follow the posted speed limit, drive defensively, and **make sure your gas tank is full.** In Montana and Wyoming the law requires that the driver and all passengers **wear seat belts.**

SNOWY DRIVING

Modern highways make mountain and plains driving safe and generally trouble free even in cold weather. Although winter driving can occasionally present some real challenges, road maintenance is good and plowing is prompt. However, in mountain areas, tire chains, studs, or snow tires are essential. If you're planning to drive into high elevations, be sure to **check the weather forecast and call for road conditions** beforehand. Even main highways can close. Winter weather isn't confined to winter months in the high country (it's been known to snow on July 4), so be prepared year-round: **carry an emergency kit** containing warm clothes, a flashlight, some food and water, and blankets. It's also good to carry a cell phone, but be aware that the mountains, and sheer distances from cell towers, can disrupt service. If you do get stalled by deep snow, **do not leave your car.** Wait for help, running the engine only if needed (making sure to keep the exhaust clear and occasionally opening a window for fresh air), and remember that assistance is never far away.

SPEED LIMITS

The speed limit on U.S. interstates is 75 mph in rural areas and 65 mph in urban zones. The speed limit on most two-lane roads is 55 or 65 mph; in Montana there are lower speed limits at night.

CHILDREN IN MONTANA & WYOMING

The Rockies and plains are tailor-made for family vacations, offering dude ranches; historic railroads; mining towns; the extreme natural features of national parks such as Yellowstone, Grand Teton, Glacier, and Badlands; rafting; and many other outdoor activities. Visitor centers and lodgings are often good at recommending places to spend time with children. Attractions sometimes offer reduced family admission tickets.

The Wyoming State Tourism guide has a section geared toward children. Montana has a small flyer for kids as well as more extensive information on children's activities in the state. Good car reading includes the activity guidebooks *Following Lewis & Clark's Trail* ($7.95) and *Reading, Writing & Riding along the Oregon Trail,* both published by the Oregon-California Trails Association.

🖪 Guidebooks for Children **Oregon-California Trails Association** 🖃 Box 1019, Independence, MO 64051-0519 ☎ 816/252-2276 or 888/811-6282.

CAR TRAVEL

If you are renting a car, don't forget to arrange for a car seat when you reserve. For general advice about traveling with children, consult *Fodor's FYI: Travel with Your Baby* (available in bookstores everywhere).

Always **strap children under age five into approved child-safety seats.** In Wyoming children must be in a child restraint seat if they are under age eight and less than 80 pounds. Children in Wyoming also may not ride in the front seat of any vehicle that has more than one row of seats.

FLYING

If your children are two or older, ask about children's airfares. As a general rule, infants under two not occupying a seat fly at greatly reduced fares or even for free. But if you want to guarantee a seat for an infant, you have to pay full fare. Consider flying during off-peak days and times; most airlines will grant an infant a seat without a ticket if there are available seats.

Experts agree that it's a good idea to use safety seats aloft for children weighing less than 40 pounds. Airlines set their own policies: if you use a safety seat, U.S. carriers usually require that the child be ticketed, even if he or she is young enough to ride free, because the seats must be strapped into regular seats. And even if you pay the full adult fare for the seat, it may be worth it, especially on longer trips. Do **check your airline's policy about using safety seats during takeoff and landing.** Safety seats are not allowed everywhere in the plane, so get your seat assignments as early as possible.

When reserving, request children's meals or a freestanding bassinet (not available at all airlines) if you need them. But note that bulkhead seats, where you must sit to use the bassinet, may lack an overhead bin or storage space on the floor.

LODGING

Most hotels in the Rockies and plains allow children under a certain age to stay in their parents' room at no extra charge, but others charge for them as extra adults; be sure to find out the cutoff age for children's discounts. Many lodging properties that have restaurants also allow children to eat free or at reduced prices.

Although most dude ranches are ideal for children of all ages, be sure you know not only the activities a ranch offers but also which are emphasized before booking your vacation. A few ranches may have age restrictions excluding very young children.

SIGHTS & ATTRACTIONS

Places that are especially appealing to children are indicated by a rubber-duckie icon (☺) in the margin. In all four of the region's national parks—Yellowstone, Grand Teton, Glacier, and Badlands—children can participate in Junior Ranger programs that encourage learning about the natural wonders and wildlife of the area. There are interactive exhibits at the Buffalo Bill Historical Center in Cody, a chance to see elk up close at the National Elk Refuge near Jackson, and opportunities to dig for dinosaurs at various sites in Montana and Wyoming.

SPORTS & THE OUTDOORS

Altitude can be even more taxing on small lungs than on adult lungs, so **be conservative** when evaluating what level of activity your child will enjoy.

Some trip organizers arrange backpacking outings for families with small children, especially for family groups of eight or more. Short half-day or full-day bike trips with plenty of flat riding are possible at many Rocky Mountain and northern plains resorts. Ask at local bike shops for recommended rides for children. One of the better resorts for biking and children's ski programs is Jackson Hole Mountain Resort in Wyoming. The Lodging and Learning programs offered in Yellowstone by the Yellowstone Association and Xanterra Parks & Resorts have special activities geared toward families with younger children.

It is not advisable to take children under seven on any extended rafting trip, except those specifically geared toward young children. Before taking an extended trip, you might want to test the waters with a half-day or one-day excursion. For families with younger children, trips aboard larger, motorized rafts are probably safest. Floating the gentle Snake River in Wyoming is one of the area's best options for young children. Outfitters designate some trips as "adults only," with the cutoff usually being 16 years old.

CONSUMER PROTECTION

Whether you're shopping for gifts or purchasing travel services, **pay with a major credit card** whenever possible, so you can cancel payment or get reimbursed if there's a problem (and you can provide documentation). If you're doing business with a particular company for the first time, contact your local Better Business Bureau and the attorney general's offices in your state and (for U.S. businesses) the company's home state as well. Have any complaints been filed? Finally, if you're buying a package or tour, always consider travel insurance that includes default coverage (⇨ Insurance).

🔲 **BBBs Council of Better Business Bureaus** ✉ 4200 Wilson Blvd., Suite 800, Arlington, VA 22203 ☎ 703/276-0100 🖷 703/525-8277 ⊕ www. bbb.org.

CUSTOMS & DUTIES

When shopping abroad, keep receipts for all purchases. Upon reentering the country, **be ready to show customs officials what**

you've bought. Pack purchases together in an easily accessible place. If you think a duty is incorrect, appeal the assessment. If you object to the way your clearance was handled, note the inspector's badge number. In either case, first ask to see a supervisor. If the problem isn't resolved, write to the appropriate authorities, beginning with the port director at your point of entry.

IN AUSTRALIA

Australian residents who are 18 or older may bring home A$900 worth of souvenirs and gifts (including jewelry), 250 cigarettes or 250 grams of cigars or other tobacco products, and 2.25 liters of alcohol (including wine, beer, and spirits). Residents under 18 may bring back A$450 worth of goods. If any of these individual allowances are exceeded, you must pay duty for the entire amount (of the group of products in which the allowance was exceeded). Members of the same family traveling together may pool their allowances. Prohibited items include meat products. Seeds, plants, and fruits need to be declared upon arrival.

⑦ **Australian Customs Service** ⑤ Customs House, 10 Cooks River Dr., Sydney International Airport, Sydney, NSW 2020 ☎ 02/6275–6666 or 1300/363263, 02/8334–7444 or 1800/020–504 quarantine-inquiry line ⑤ 02/8339–6714 ⊕ www.customs.gov.au.

IN CANADA

Canadian residents who have been out of Canada for at least seven days may bring in C$750 worth of goods duty-free. If you've been away fewer than seven days but more than 48 hours, the duty-free allowance drops to C$200. If your trip lasts 24 to 48 hours, the allowance is C$50; if the goods are worth more than C$50, you must pay full duty on all of the goods. You may not pool allowances with family members. Goods claimed under the C$750 exemption may follow you by mail; those claimed under the lesser exemptions must accompany you. Alcohol and tobacco products may be included in the seven-day and 48-hour exemptions but not in the 24-hour exemption. If you meet the age requirements of the province or territory through which you reenter

Canada, you may bring in, duty-free, 1.5 liters of wine *or* 1.14 liters (40 imperial ounces) of liquor *or* 24 12-ounce cans or bottles of beer or ale. Also, if you meet the local age requirement for tobacco products, you may bring in, duty-free, 200 cigarettes, 50 cigars or cigarillos, and 200 grams of tobacco. You may have to pay a minimum duty on tobacco products, regardless of whether or not you exceed your personal exemption. Check ahead of time with the Canada Border Services Agency or the Department of Agriculture for policies regarding meat products, seeds, plants, and fruits.

You may send an unlimited number of gifts (only one gift per recipient, however) worth up to C$60 each duty-free to Canada. Label the package UNSOLICITED GIFT—VALUE UNDER $60. Alcohol and tobacco are excluded.

⑦ **Canada Border Services Agency** ⊠ Customs Information Services, 191 Laurier Ave. W, 15th floor, Ottawa, Ontario K1A 0L5 ☎ 800/461-9999 in Canada, 204/983-3500, 506/636-5064 ⊕ www.cbsa.gc.ca.

IN NEW ZEALAND

All homeward-bound residents may bring back NZ$700 worth of souvenirs and gifts; passengers may not pool their allowances, and children can claim only the concession on goods intended for their own use. For those 17 or older, the duty-free allowance also includes 4.5 liters of wine or beer; one 1,125-ml bottle of spirits; and either 200 cigarettes, 250 grams of tobacco, 50 cigars, *or* a combination of the three up to 250 grams. Meat products, seeds, plants, and fruits must be declared upon arrival to the Agricultural Services Department.

⑦ **New Zealand Customs** ⊠ Head office: The Customhouse, 17–21 Whitmore St., Box 2218, Wellington ☎ 09/300–5399 or 0800/428–786 ⊕ www.customs.govt.nz.

IN THE U.K.

From countries outside the European Union, including the United States, you may bring home, duty-free, 200 cigarettes, 50 cigars, 100 cigarillos, or 250 grams of tobacco; 1 liter of spirits or 2 liters of fortified or sparkling wine or liqueurs; 2 liters of still table wine; 60 ml of perfume; 250 ml of toilet water; plus £145 worth of other goods, including gifts and souvenirs. Prohibited items include meat and dairy products, seeds, plants, and fruits.

HM Customs and Excise ✉ Portcullis House, 21 Cowbridge Rd. E, Cardiff CF11 9SS ☎ 0845/010-9000 or 0208/929-0152 advice service, 0208/929-6731 or 0208/910-3602 complaints ⊕ www.hmce.gov.uk.

EATING & DRINKING

Dining in Montana and Wyoming is generally casual. Menus are becoming more varied with such regional specialties as trout, elk, or buffalo, but you can nearly always order a hamburger or a steak. Authentic ethnic food—other than Mexican—is hard to find outside of cities. Dinner hours are from 6 PM to 9 PM. Outside the large cities and resort towns in the high seasons, many restaurants close by 9 or 10 PM.

The restaurants we list are the cream of the crop in each price category. Properties indicated by a ✕🏠 are lodging establishments whose restaurant warrants a special trip.

In general, when you order a regular coffee, you get coffee with milk and sugar.

MEALTIMES

Unless otherwise noted, the restaurants listed in this guide are open daily for lunch and dinner.

RESERVATIONS & DRESS

Reservations are always a good idea; we mention them only when they're essential or not accepted. Book as far ahead as you can, and reconfirm as soon as you arrive. (Large parties should always call ahead to check the reservations policy.) We mention dress only when men are required to wear a jacket or a jacket and tie—which is almost never.

SPECIALTIES

You can find all types of cuisine in the major cities and resort towns, but don't forget to try native dishes such as trout, elk, and buffalo (the latter two have less fat than beef and are just as tasty); organic fruits and vegetables are also readily available. When in doubt, go for a steak, forever a Rocky Mountain and northern plains mainstay.

Rocky Mountain oysters, simply put, are bull testicles. They're generally served fried, although you can get them lots of different ways. You can find them all over the West, usually at down-home eateries, steak houses, and the like.

WINE, BEER & SPIRITS

Microbreweries throughout the region produce a diverse selection of beers. Snake River Brewing Company in Jackson Hole, Wyoming has won awards for its lager, pale ale, Zonker Stout, and numerous other releases. Missoula, Montana–based Big Sky Brewing Company's best-seller is Moose Drool (a brown ale); the company also markets an award-winning pale ale and several other brews.

DISABILITIES & ACCESSIBILITY

The Rockies and plains offer countless recreational opportunities to travelers with disabilities. Most ski areas offer adaptive ski programs. DREAM—Adaptive Recreation, Inc. serves the ski areas of Big Mountain and Blacktail in Montana.

The majority of United States Forest Service campgrounds have limited wheelchair-accessible sites and there are accesible sites in Yellowstone and Grand Teton National Parks. Access Tours leads nine-day trips for people who use wheelchairs or walk slowly and can customize trips for groups of four or more.

Local Resources **DREAM—Adaptive Recreation, Inc.** ⬡ Box 4085, Whitefish, MT 59937 ☎ 406/862-1817. **Grand Teton National Park** ☎ 307/739-3300 accessibility coordinator Jon Christensen, 307/739-3581 or 307/739-3400 TDD. **Wyoming Tourism** ☎ 307/777-7777. **Yellowstone National Park** ☎ 307/344-7381 accessibility coordinator Doug Madsen, 307/344-2017.

Tour Operator **Access Tours** ⬡ Box 499, Victor, ID 83455 ☎ 800/929-4811 🖷 208/787-2332 ⊕ www.accesstours.org.

LODGING

Despite the Americans with Disabilities Act, the definition of accessibility seems to differ from hotel to hotel. Some properties may be accessible by ADA standards for people with mobility problems but not for people with hearing or vision impairments, for example.

If you have mobility problems, ask for the lowest floor on which accessible services are offered. If you have a hearing impairment, check whether the hotel has devices to alert you visually to the ring of the telephone, a knock at the door, and a fire/emergency alarm. Some hotels provide these devices without charge. Discuss your needs with hotel personnel if this equipment isn't available, so that a staff member can personally alert you in the event of an emergency.

If you're bringing a guide dog, get authorization ahead of time and write down the name of the person with whom you spoke.

RESERVATIONS

When discussing accessibility with an operator or reservations agent, ask hard questions. Are there any stairs, inside *or* out? Are there grab bars next to the toilet *and* in the shower/tub? How wide is the doorway to the room? To the bathroom? For the most extensive facilities meeting the latest legal specifications, opt for newer accommodations. If you reserve through a toll-free number, consider also calling the hotel's local number to confirm the information from the central reservations office. Get confirmation in writing when you can.

SIGHTS & ATTRACTIONS

People with disabilities will generally find Yellowstone National Park a great place to visit. There are many boardwalks with easy grades so you can see wildlife, geysers, and other Yellowstone attractions; lodging and dining properties are generally accessible, and there are even backcountry campsites specially designed for people with disabilities. Grand Teton and Glacier national parks aren't quite so accessible as Yellowstone, but that's due more to terrain than lack of effort on the part of the National Park Service. Larger cities usually have better services for people with disabilities. You'll often find it more difficult to get around in a wheelchair in small

towns, though most places have curb cuts and designated parking areas.

Many resort towns have created opportunities for all types of visitors (on Casper Mountain in Wyoming, for example, there is a short trail with sights marked in Braille for the visually impaired). However, you'll find services for people with hearing and visual impairments to be more limited in smaller communities.

TRANSPORTATION

The U.S. Department of Transportation Aviation Consumer Protection Division's online publication *New Horizons: Information for the Air Traveler with a Disability* offers advice for travellers with a disability, and outlines basic rights. Visit DisabilityInfo.gov for general information.

Most major tour companies have buses that can accommodate people with disabilities; obtaining rental cars with hand controls will be more of a problem unless you get your vehicle in a major hub city such as Denver or Salt Lake City. Handicap parking is allowed with a windshield card from any state.

🚺 Information and Complaints Aviation Consumer Protection Division (⇨ Air Travel) for airline-related problems; ⊕ airconsumer.ost.dot.gov/publications/horizons.htm for airline travel advice and rights. **Departmental Office of Civil Rights** ⊠ for general inquiries, U.S. Department of Transportation, S-30, 400 7th St. SW, Room 10215, Washington, DC 20590 ☎ 202/366-4648, 202/366-8538 TTY 🖬 202/366-9371 ⊕ www.dotcr.ost.dot.gov. **Disability Rights Section** ⊠ NYAV, U.S. Department of Justice, Civil Rights Division, 950 Pennsylvania Ave. NW, Washington, DC 20530 ☎ ADA information line 202/514-0301, 800/514-0301, 202/514-0383 TTY, 800/514-0383 TTY ⊕ www.ada.gov. **U.S. Department of Transportation Hotline** ☎ for disability-related air-travel problems, 800/778-4838 or 800/455-9880 TTY.

TRAVEL AGENCIES

In the United States, the Americans with Disabilities Act requires that travel firms serve the needs of all travelers. Some agencies specialize in working with people with disabilities.

🚺 Travelers with Mobility Problems Access Adventures/B. Roberts Travel ⊠ 1876 East Ave.,

Rochester, NY 14610 ☎ 800/444-6540 ⊕ www. brobertstravel.com, run by a former physical-rehabilitation counselor. **Accessible Vans of America** ✉ 37 Daniel Rd. W, Fairfield, NJ 07004 ☎ 877/282-8267, 888/282-8267, 973/808-9709 reservations 🖶 973/808-9713 ⊕ www.accessiblevans.com. **Flying Wheels Travel** ✉ 143 W. Bridge St., Box 382, Owatonna, MN 55060 ☎ 507/451-5005 🖶 507/451-1685 ⊕ www.flyingwheelstravel.com.

DISCOUNTS & DEALS

Be a smart shopper and compare all your options before making decisions. A plane ticket bought with a promotional coupon from travel clubs, coupon books, and direct-mail offers or purchased on the Internet may not be cheaper than the least expensive fare from a discount ticket agency. And always keep in mind that what you get is just as important as what you save.

DISCOUNT RESERVATIONS

To save money, look into discount reservations services with Web sites and toll-free numbers, which use their buying power to get a better price on hotels, airline tickets (⇨ Air Travel), even car rentals. When booking a room, always **call the hotel's local toll-free number** (if one is available) rather than the central reservations number—you'll often get a better price. Always ask about special packages or corporate rates.

🚩 Hotel Rooms **Accommodations Express** ☎ 800/444-7666 or 800/277-1064. **Hotels.com** ☎ 800/246-8357 ⊕ www.hotels.com. **Quikbook** ☎ 800/789-9887 ⊕ www.quikbook.com. **Turbotrip.com** ☎ 800/473-7829 ⊕ w3.turbotrip.com.

PACKAGE DEALS

Don't confuse packages and guided tours. When you buy a package, you travel on your own, just as though you had planned the trip yourself. Fly/drive packages, which combine airfare and car rental, are often a good deal. In cities, ask the local visitor's bureau about hotel and local transportation packages that include tickets to major museum exhibits or other special events.

ECOTOURISM

Although neither the Bureau of Land Management (BLM) nor the National Park Service has designated any particular parts of the Rockies endangered ecosystems, many areas are open only to hikers; vehicles, mountain bikes, and horses are banned. It is wise to respect these closures, as well as the old adage—**leave only footprints, take only pictures.** Recycling is taken seriously throughout Montana and Wyoming, and you will find yourself very unpopular if you litter or fail to recycle your cans and bottles (locals can be strident about protecting their wilderness).

All archaeological artifacts, including rock etchings and paintings, are protected by federal law and must be left untouched and undisturbed.

🚩 **National Park Service** ☎ 800/436-7275. **U.S. Bureau of Land Management** ☎ 307/775-6256.

GAY & LESBIAN TRAVEL

Resort towns, most of which are gay-friendly, tend to be more tolerant than smaller communities, though some of those are quite welcoming, too. Even more liberal areas experience occasional incidents of homophobic violence. Until you are sure of your surroundings, you are best off being discreet. For details about the gay and lesbian scene, consult *Fodor's Gay Guide to the USA* (available in bookstores everywhere).

🚩 Gay- & Lesbian-Friendly Travel Agencies **Different Roads Travel** ✉ 1017 N. LaCienega Blvd., Suite 308, West Hollywood, CA 90069 ☎ 310/289-6000 or 800/429-8747 (Ext. 14 for both) 🖶 310/855-0323 ✉ lgernert@tzell.com. **Kennedy Travel** ✉ 130 W. 42nd St., Suite 401, New York, NY 10036 ☎ 800/237-7433 or 212/840-8659 🖶 212/730-2269 ⊕ www.kennedytravel.com. **Now, Voyager** ✉ 4406 18th St., San Francisco, CA 94114 ☎ 415/626-1169 or 800/255-6951 🖶 415/626-8626 ⊕ www.nowvoyager.com. **Skylink Travel and Tour/Flying Dutchmen Travel** ✉ 1455 N. Dutton Ave., Suite A, Santa Rosa, CA 95401 ☎ 707/546-9888 or 800/225-5759 🖶 707/636-0951; serving lesbian travelers.

HOLIDAYS

Major national holidays are New Year's Day (Jan. 1); Martin Luther King Day (3rd Mon. in Jan.); Presidents' Day (3rd Mon. in Feb.); Memorial Day (last Mon. in May); Independence Day (July 4); Labor Day (1st Mon. in Sept.); Columbus Day

(2nd Mon. in Oct.); Thanksgiving Day (4th Thurs. in Nov.); Christmas Eve and Christmas Day (Dec. 24 and 25); and New Year's Eve (Dec. 31).

INSURANCE

The most useful travel-insurance plan is a comprehensive policy that includes coverage for trip cancellation and interruption, default, trip delay, and medical expenses (with a waiver for preexisting conditions).

Without insurance you'll lose all or most of your money if you cancel your trip, regardless of the reason. Default insurance covers you if your tour operator, airline, or cruise line goes out of business—the chances of which have been increasing. Trip-delay covers expenses that arise because of bad weather or mechanical delays. Study the fine print when comparing policies.

U.K. residents can buy a travel-insurance policy valid for most vacations taken during the year in which it's purchased (but check preexisting-condition coverage).

Always **buy travel policies directly from the insurance company**; if you buy them from a cruise line, airline, or tour operator that goes out of business you probably won't be covered for the agency or operator's default, a major risk. Before making any purchase, review your existing health and home-owner's policies to find what they cover away from home.

🚆 Travel Insurers In the U.S.: **Access America** ✉ 2805 N. Parham Rd., Richmond, VA 23294 ☎ 800/284-8300 🖶 804/673-1469 or 800/346-9265 ⊕ www.accessamerica.com. **Travel Guard International** ✉ 1145 Clark St., Stevens Point, WI 54481 ☎ 800/826-1300 or 715/345-1041 🖶 800/955-8785 or 715/345-1990 ⊕ www.travelguard.com.

FOR INTERNATIONAL TRAVELERS

For information on customs restrictions, *see* Customs & Duties.

CAR RENTAL

When picking up a rental car, non-U.S. residents need a reservation voucher for any prepaid reservations that were made in the traveler's home country, a passport, a driver's license, and a travel policy that covers each driver. Note that in most cases, cars rented in the region are not allowed to cross into Canada.

CAR TRAVEL

In the Rockies and plains, as across the nation, gasoline costs fluctuate often. Stations are plentiful. Most stay open late (24 hours along large highways and in big cities), except in rural areas, where Sunday hours are limited and where you may drive long stretches without a refueling opportunity. Highways are well paved. Interstate highways—limited-access, multilane highways whose numbers are prefixed by "I–"—are the fastest routes. Interstates with three-digit numbers encircle urban areas, which may have other limited-access expressways, freeways, and parkways as well. Tolls may be levied on limited-access highways. So-called U.S. highways and state highways are not necessarily limited-access but may have several lanes.

Along larger highways, roadside stops with restrooms, fast-food restaurants, and sundries stores are well spaced. State police and tow trucks patrol major highways and lend assistance. If your car breaks down on an interstate, pull onto the shoulder and wait for help, or have your passengers wait while you walk to a roadside emergency phone. If you carry a cell phone, dial 911, noting your location from the small green roadside mileage markers.

Driving in the United States is on the right. Do **obey speed limits** posted along roads and highways. Watch for lower limits in small towns and on back roads. On weekdays between 6 and 10 AM and again between 4 and 7 PM expect heavy traffic. To encourage carpooling, some freeways have special lanes for so-called high-occupancy vehicles (HOV)—cars carrying more than one passenger.

Bookstores, gas stations, convenience stores, and rest stops sell maps (about $3) and multiregion road atlases (about $10).

CURRENCY

The dollar is the basic unit of U.S. currency. It has 100 cents. Coins include the copper penny (1¢); the silvery nickel (5¢), dime (10¢), quarter (25¢), and half-dollar (50¢); and the golden $1 coin, replacing a now-rare silver dollar. Bills are denominated $1, $5, $10, $20, $50, and $100, all green and identical in size; designs vary. The exchange rate at this writing was US$ .75 per Australian dollar, US$1.76 per British pound, US$ .87 per Canadian dollar, US$ .68 per New Zealand dollar, and US$1.22 per euro.

ELECTRICITY
The U.S. standard is AC, 110 volts/60 cycles. Plugs have two flat pins set parallel to each other.

EMERGENCIES
For police, fire, or ambulance, **dial 911** (0 in rural areas).

INSURANCE
Britons and Australians need extra medical coverage when traveling overseas.

🛈 **Insurance Information** In the U.K.: **Association of British Insurers** ✉ 51 Gresham St., London EC2V 7HQ ☎ 020/7600-3333 🖷 020/7696-8999 ⊕ www. abi.org.uk. In Australia: **Insurance Council of Australia** ✉ Level 3, 56 Pitt St. Sydney, NSW 2000 ☎ 02/9253-5100 🖷 02/9253-5111 ⊕ www.ica.com. au. In Canada: **RBC Insurance** ✉ 6880 Financial Dr., Mississauga, Ontario L5N 7Y5 ☎ 800/387-4357 or 905/816-2559 🖷 888/298-6458 ⊕ www. rbcinsurance.com. In New Zealand: **Insurance Council of New Zealand** ✉ Level 7, 111-115 Customhouse Quay, Box 474, Wellington ☎ 04/472-5230 🖷 04/473-3011 ⊕ www.icnz.org.nz.

MAIL & SHIPPING
You can buy stamps and aerograms and send letters and parcels in post offices. Stamp-dispensing machines can occasionally be found in airports, bus and train stations, office buildings, drugstores, grocery stores, and the like. You can also deposit mail in the stout, dark blue, steel bins at strategic locations everywhere and in the mail chutes of large buildings; pickup schedules are posted. You can deposit packages at public collection boxes as long as the parcels are affixed with proper postage and weigh less than one pound. Packages weighing one or more pounds must be taken to a post office or handed to a postal carrier.

For mail sent within the United States, you need a 39¢ stamp for first-class letters

weighing up to 1 ounce (24¢ for each additional ounce) and 24¢ for postcards. You pay 84¢ for 1-ounce airmail letters and 75¢ for airmail postcards to most other countries; to Canada and Mexico, it costs 63¢ for a 1-ounce letter and 55¢ for a postcard. An aerogram—a single sheet of lightweight blue paper that folds into its own envelope, stamped for overseas airmail—costs 75¢.

To receive mail on the road, have it sent c/o General Delivery at your destination's main post office (use the correct five-digit ZIP code). You must pick up mail in person within 30 days and show a driver's license or passport.

PASSPORTS & VISAS
When traveling internationally, carry your passport even if you don't need one (it's always the best form of I.D.) and **make two photocopies of the data page** (one for someone at home and another for you, carried separately from your passport). If you lose your passport, promptly call the nearest embassy or consulate and the local police.

Visitor visas aren't necessary for Canadian or European Union citizens, or for citizens of Australia who are staying fewer than 90 days.

🛈 **Australian Citizens Passports Australia** ☎ 131-232 ⊕ www.passports.gov.au. **United States Consulate General** ✉ MLC Centre, Level 59, 19-29 Martin Pl., Sydney, NSW 2000 ☎ 02/9373-9200, 1902/941-641 fee-based visa-inquiry line ⊕ usembassy-australia.state.gov/sydney.

🛈 **Canadian Citizens Passport Office** ✉ to mail in applications: 70 Cremazie St., Gatineau, Québec J8Y 3P2 ☎ 800/567-6868, 866/255-7655 TTY ⊕ www. ppt.gc.ca.

🛈 **New Zealand Citizens New Zealand Passports Office** ✉ For applications and information, Level 3, Boulcott House, 47 Boulcott St., Wellington ☎ 0800/22-5050 or 04/474-8100 ⊕ www. passports.govt.nz. **Embassy of the United States** ✉ 29 Fitzherbert Terr., Thorndon, Wellington ☎ 04/462-6000 ⊕ usembassy.org.nz. **U.S. Consulate General** ✉ Citibank Bldg., 3rd floor, 23 Customs St. E, Auckland ☎ 09/303-2724 ⊕ usembassy. org.nz.

🛈 **U.K. Citizens U.K. Passport Service** ☎ 0870/ 521-0410 ⊕ www.passport.gov.uk. **American Con-**

sulate General ⊠ Danesfort House, 223 Stranmillis Rd., Belfast, Northern Ireland BT9 5GR ☎ 028/9038-6100 🖷 028/9068-1301 ⊕ www.usembassy. org.uk. **American Embassy** ⊠ for visa and immigration information or to submit a visa application via mail (enclose an SASE), Consular Information Unit, 24 Grosvenor Sq., London W1A 2LQ ☎ 090/5544-4546 or 090/6820-0290 for visa information (per-minute charges), 0207/499-9000 main switchboard ⊕ www.usembassy.org.uk.

TELEPHONES

All U.S. telephone numbers consist of a three-digit area code and a seven-digit local calling number. Within many local calling areas, you dial only the seven-digit number. Within some area codes, you must dial "1" first for calls outside the local area. To call between area-code regions, dial "1" then all 10 digits; the same goes for calls to numbers prefixed by "800," "888," "866," and "877"—all toll free. For calls to numbers preceded by "900" you must pay—usually dearly.

For international calls, dial "011" followed by the country code and the local number. For help, dial "0" and ask for an overseas operator. The country code is 61 for Australia, 64 for New Zealand, 44 for the United Kingdom. Calling Canada is the same as calling within the United States, although you might not be able to get through on some toll-free numbers. Most local phone books list country codes and U.S. area codes. The country code for the United States is 1.

For operator assistance, dial "0." To obtain someone's phone number, call directory assistance at 555–1212 or occasionally 411 (free at many public phones). To have the person you're calling foot the bill, phone collect; dial "0" instead of "1" before the 10-digit number.

At pay phones, instructions often are posted. Usually you insert coins in a slot (usually 25¢–50¢ for local calls) and wait for a steady tone before dialing. When you call long-distance, the operator tells you how much to insert; prepaid phone cards, widely available in various denominations, are easier. Call the number on the back, punch in the card's personal identification number when prompted, then dial your number.

LODGING

Accommodations in the Rockies and plains vary from the very posh resorts in ski areas such as Jackson Hole to basic chain hotels and independent motels. Dude and guest ranches often require a one-week stay, and the cost is all-inclusive. Bed-and-breakfasts can be found throughout the Rockies and plains.

The lodgings we list are the cream of the crop in each price category. We always list the facilities that are available—but we don't specify whether they cost extra. When pricing accommodations, always ask what's included and what costs extra. Properties indicated by a ╳🏠 are lodging establishments whose restaurant warrants a special trip. In almost all cases, parking is free and only in a resort area like Jackson Hole's Teton Village will you have to pay a charge.

Assume that hotels operate on the European Plan (EP, with no meals) unless we specify that they use the Continental Plan (CP, with a Continental breakfast), Breakfast Plan (BP, with a full breakfast), Modified American Plan (MAP, with breakfast and dinner), or the Full American Plan (FAP, with all meals).
🖪 General Information **Travel Montana** ⊠ Department of Commerce, 1424 9th Ave., Helena, MT 59620 ☎ 406/444-2654, 800/548-3390 in Montana, 800/847-4868 nationwide. **Wyoming Division of Tourism** ⊠ I-25 at College Dr., Cheyenne, WY 82002 ☎ 307/777-7777 or 800/225-5996.

BED & BREAKFASTS

Charm is the long suit of these establishments, which generally occupy a restored older building with some historical or architectural significance. They tend to be small, with fewer than 20 rooms. Breakfast is usually included in the rates.
🖪 Reservation Services **Cody Lodging Co.** ⊠ 927 14th St., Cody, WY 82414 ☎ 307/587-6000 or 800/587-6560 🖷 307/587-8048 ⊕ www. codyguesthouses.com. **Jackson Hole Central Reservations** ⊠ 140 E. Broadway, Suite 24, Jackson, WY 83001 ☎ 307/733-4005 or 800/443-6931 ⊕ www. jacksonholewy.com.

CAMPING

Camping is invigorating and inexpensive, and Montana and Wyoming are full of state and national parks and forests. Sites range from rustic (pit toilets and cold running water) to campgrounds with bathhouses with hot showers, paved trailer pads that can accommodate even jumbo RVs, and full hookups. Some national forest campgrounds are free or as low as $5 for tent and RV sites, though there are fewer amenities.

Sometimes site reservations are accepted, and then only for up to seven days (early birds reserve as much as a year in advance); more often, they're not. Campers who prefer a more remote setting may camp in the backcountry; it's free but you might need a permit, available from park visitor centers and ranger stations. If you're visiting in summer, **plan well ahead.**

The facilities and amenities at privately operated campgrounds are usually more extensive (swimming pools are common), reservations are more widely accepted, and nightly fees are higher: $15 and up for tents, $28 and up for RVs.

⚑ _The National Parks: Camping Guide_ ✉ Superintendent of Documents, U.S. Government Printing Office, Washington, DC 20402 ☎ 800/365-2267; $3.50.

CONDO & CABIN RENTALS

If you want a home base that's roomy enough for a family and comes with cooking facilities, consider a furnished rental. These can save you money, especially if you're traveling with a group. Home-exchange directories sometimes list rentals as well as exchanges.

There are rental opportunities throughout Montana and Wyoming, with the best selection in resort areas such Big Sky and Whitefish (Big Mountain), Montana; and Jackson and Cody, Wyoming. You'll find a variety of properties ranging from one-bedroom condos to multibedroom vacation homes. The widest selection is offered by developer-owner consortiums.

⚑ International Agents Hideaways International ✉ 767 Islington St., Portsmouth, NH 03801 ☎ 603/430-4433 or 800/843-4433 📠 603/430-4444 ⊕ www.hideaways.com, annual membership $185.

⚑ Local Montana Agents Glacier Village Property ✉ 3840 Big Mountain Rd., Whitefish, MT 59937 ☎ 406/862-3687 or 800/858-5439 📠 406/862-0658 ⊕ www.stayatbigmountain.com. **Mountain Home-Montana Vacation Rentals** 🗁 Box 1204, Bozeman, MT 59771 ☎ 406/586-4589 or 800/550-4589 ⊕ www.mountain-home.com. **Resortquest Big Sky** ✉ 3080 Pine Dr., Big Sky, MT 59716 ☎ 406/995-4800 or 800/548-4488 📠 406/995-2447 ⊕ www.resortquestbigsky.com.

⚑ Local Wyoming Agents Cody Area Central Reservations ✉ 1115 13th St., Cody, WY 82414 ☎ 307/527-6837 or 888/468-6996 📠 307/754-3493. **Cody Lodging Co.** ✉ 927 14th St., Cody, WY 82414 ☎ 307/587-6000 or 800/587-6560 📠 307/587-8048 ⊕ www.codyguesthouses.com. **Jackson Hole Central Reservations** ✉ 140 E. Broadway, Suite 24, Jackson, WY 83001 ☎ 307/733-4005 or 800/443-6931 ⊕ www.jacksonholewy.com. **Jackson Hole Resort Lodging** ✉ 3200 McCollister Dr., Teton Village, WY 83025 ☎ 307/733-3990 or 800/443-8613 ⊕ www.jhresortlodging.com.

GUEST RANCHES

If the thought of sitting around a campfire after a hard day on the range makes your heart beat faster, consider playing dude on a guest ranch. These range from wilderness-rimmed working ranches that accept guests and encourage them to pitch in with chores and other ranch activities to luxurious resorts on the fringes of small cities, with an upscale clientele, swimming pools, tennis courts, and a lively roster of horse-related activities such as breakfast rides, moonlight rides, and all-day trail rides. Rafting, fishing, tubing, and other activities are usually available; at working ranches you may even be able to participate in a cattle roundup. In winter, cross-country skiing and snowshoeing keep you busy. Lodgings can run the gamut from charmingly rustic cabins to the kind of deluxe quarters you expect at a first-class hotel. Meals may be gourmet or plain but hearty. Many ranches offer packages as well as children's and off-season rates. The various state tourism offices also have information on dude ranches. _See_ Dude Ranches _in_ Sports & the Outdoors.

⚑ Montana Dude Ranchers' Association ✉ 1627 West Main, Suite 434, Bozeman, MT 59715 ☎ 406/284-9933 ⊕ www.montanadra.com. **Wyoming**

Dude Ranchers Association 🖂 Box 618, Dubois, WY 82513 ☎ 307/455-2084 🖷 307/455-2634 ⊕ www.wyomingdra.com.

HOME EXCHANGES

If you would like to exchange your home for someone else's, join a home-exchange organization, which will send you its updated listings of available exchanges for a year and will include your own listing in at least one of them. It's up to you to make specific arrangements.

🔟 **Exchange Clubs HomeLink USA** 🖂 2937 NW 9th Terrace, Wilton Manors, FL 33311 ☎ 954/566-2687 or 800/638-3841 🖷 954/566-2783 ⊕ www. homelink.org; $75 yearly for a listing and online access; $45 additional to receive directories. **Intervac U.S.** 🖂 30 Corte San Fernando, Tiburon, CA 94920 ☎ 800/756-4663 🖷 415/435-7440 ⊕ www. intervacus.com; $128 yearly for a listing, online access, and a catalog; $68 without catalog.

HOSTELS

Montana has hostels in Bozeman, East Glacier, Polebridge, and Whitefish that cater mainly to backpackers. Wyoming has a hostel in Teton Village.

No matter what your age, you can save on lodging costs by staying at hostels. In some 4,500 locations in more than 70 countries around the world, Hostelling International (HI), the umbrella group for a number of national youth-hostel associations, offers single-sex, dorm-style beds and, at many hostels, rooms for couples and family accommodations. Membership in any HI national hostel association, open to travelers of all ages, allows you to stay in HI-affiliated hostels at member rates; one-year membership is about $28 for adults (C$35 for a two-year minimum membership in Canada, £15 in the U.K., A$52 in Australia, and NZ$40 in New Zealand); hostels charge about $10–$30 per night. Members have priority if the hostel is full; they're also eligible for discounts around the world, even on rail and bus travel in some countries.

HI is also an especially helpful organization for road cyclists.

🔟 **Organizations Hostelling International–USA** 🖂 8401 Colesville Rd., Suite 600, Silver Spring, MD 20910 ☎ 301/495-1240 🖷 301/495-6697 ⊕ www.

hiusa.org. **Hostelling International–Canada** 🖂 205 Catherine St., Suite 400, Ottawa, Ontario K2P 1C3 ☎ 613/237-7884 or 800/663-5777 🖷 613/237-7868 ⊕ www.hihostels.ca. **YHA England and Wales** 🖂 Trevelyan House, Dimple Rd., Matlock, Derbyshire DE4 3YH, U.K. ☎ 0870/870-8808, 0870/770-8868, 0162/959-2600 🖷 0870/770-6127 ⊕ www.yha.org.uk. **YHA Australia** 🖂 422 Kent St., Sydney, NSW 2001 ☎ 02/9261-1111 🖷 02/9261-1969 ⊕ www.yha.com.au. **YHA New Zealand** 🖂 Level 1, Moorhouse City, 166 Moorhouse Ave., Box 436, Christchurch ☎ 03/379-9970 or 0800/278-299 🖷 03/365-4476 ⊕ www.yha.org.nz.

HOTELS

In Montana and Wyoming most city hotels cater to business travelers, with such facilities as restaurants, cocktail lounges, swimming pools, exercise equipment, and meeting rooms. Room rates usually reflect the range of amenities offered. Most cities also have less expensive hotels that are clean and comfortable but have fewer facilities. In resort towns, hotels are decidedly more deluxe, with every imaginable amenity in every imaginable price range; rural areas generally offer simple, and sometimes rustic, accommodations.

Many properties offer special weekend rates, sometimes up to 50% off regular prices. However, these deals are usually not extended during peak summer months, when hotels are normally full. The same discounts generally apply for resort-town hotels in the off-seasons.

All hotels listed have private bath unless otherwise noted.

🔟 **Toll-Free Numbers Best Western** ☎ 800/528-1234 ⊕ www.bestwestern.com. **Choice** ☎ 800/424-6423 ⊕ www.choicehotels.com. **Comfort Inn** ☎ 800/424-6423 ⊕ www.choicehotels.com. **Days Inn** ☎ 800/325-2525 ⊕ www.daysinn.com. **Doubletree Hotels** ☎ 800/222-8733 ⊕ www. doubletree.com. **Embassy Suites** ☎ 800/362-2779 ⊕ www.embassysuites.com. **Fairfield Inn** ☎ 800/228-2800 ⊕ www.marriott.com. **Hilton** ☎ 800/445-8667 ⊕ www.hilton.com. **Holiday Inn** ☎ 800/465-4329 ⊕ www.ichotelsgroup.com. **Howard Johnson** ☎ 800/446-4656 ⊕ www.hojo.com. **Hyatt Hotels & Resorts** ☎ 800/233-1234 ⊕ www.hyatt. com. **La Quinta** ☎ 800/531-5900 ⊕ www.lq.com. **Marriott** ☎ 800/228-9290 ⊕ www.marriott.com. **Quality Inn** ☎ 800/424-6423 ⊕ www.choicehotels.

com. **Radisson** ☎ 800/333-3333 ⊕ www.radisson.
com. **Ramada** ☎ 800/228-2828, 800/854-7854 international reservations ⊕ www.ramada.com or
www.ramadahotels.com. **Sheraton** ☎ 800/325-
3535 ⊕ www.starwood.com/sheraton. **Sleep Inn**
☎ 800/424-6423 ⊕ www.choicehotels.com. **Westin
Hotels & Resorts** ☎ 800/228-3000 ⊕ www.
starwood.com/westin.

MOTELS

The once-familiar roadside motel is fast
disappearing from the American landscape. In its place are chain-run motor
inns at highway intersections and in rural
areas off the beaten path. Some of these
establishments offer very basic facilities;
others provide restaurants, swimming
pools, and other amenities.

🔢 **Motel Chains Motel 6** ☎ 800/466-8356. **Quality Inn** ☎ 800/228-5151. **Rodeway Inns** ☎ 800/
228-2000. **Shilo Inn** ☎ 800/222-2244. **Super 8
Motels** ☎ 800/800-8000. **Travelodge** ☎ 800/
578-7878.

RESORTS

Ski towns throughout the Rockies—including Big Sky and Whitefish in Montana
and Jackson Hole in Wyoming—are home
to dozens of resorts in all price ranges; the
activities lacking in any individual property can usually be found in the town itself, in summer as well as winter. In the
national parks there are both wonderfully
rustic and luxurious resorts, such as Jackson Lake Lodge and Jenny Lake Lodge in
Grand Teton National Park, Lake Yellowstone Hotel and the Old Faithful Snow
Lodge in Yellowstone, and Many Glacier
Lodge in Glacier National Park.

MEDIA

NEWSPAPERS & MAGAZINES

The largest daily newspapers in Montana
are the *Billings Gazette,* the *Bozeman
Chronicle,* the *Missoulian,* and the *Great
Falls Tribune.* In Wyoming the biggest
newspapers are the statewide *Casper Star-
Tribune* and Cheyenne's *Wyoming State
Tribune-Eagle.*

RADIO & TELEVISION

You will find National Public Radio across
the region, plus local radio stations, most
targeted to country music listeners. Televi-

sion stations include major network affiliates, and many areas also have cable or
satellite television service. Near mountain
passes or other road hazards, signs often
indicate where on your radio dial you can
hear road information.

MONEY MATTERS

First-class hotel rooms in Missoula and
Cheyenne cost from $85 to $225 a night,
while "value" hotel rooms might go for
$60–$75, and, as elsewhere in the United
States, rooms in national budget chain motels go for around $60 nightly. Weekend
packages, offered by most city hotels, cut
prices up to 50% (but may not be available in peak winter or summer seasons).
As a rule, costs outside cities are lower, except in the deluxe resorts.

In both cities and rural areas, sit-down
restaurants charge between 50¢ and $1
for a cup of coffee (specialty coffeehouses
charge $2–$5) and between $4 and $8 for
a hamburger. A beer at a bar generally
costs between $1.50 and $5, with microbrews and imports at the higher end of
the range. Expect to pay double for food
and drink in resort towns. Prices throughout this guide are given for adults. Sub-
stantially reduced fees are almost always
available for children, students, and senior citizens. For information on taxes,
see Taxes.

ATMS

You will find ATMs at banks and other
locations, including grocery stores, and
occasionally at lodging properties, such as
those in Yellowstone National Park. You
will usually be able to locate an ATM
even in small communities, where they
might be placed at convenience stores or
lodging properties.

CREDIT CARDS

Throughout this guide, the following ab-
breviations are used: **AE,** American Express; **D,** Discover; **DC,** Diners Club; **MC,**
MasterCard; and **V,** Visa.

🔢 **Reporting Lost Cards American Express**
☎ 800/992-3404. **Diners Club** ☎ 800/234-6377.
Discover ☎ 800/347-2683. **MasterCard** ☎ 800/
622-7747. **Visa** ☎ 800/ 847-2911.

NATIONAL PARKS

Look into discount passes to save money on park entrance fees. For $50, the National Parks Pass admits you (and any passengers in your private vehicle) to all national parks, monuments, and recreation areas, as well as other sites run by the National Park Service, for a year. (In parks that charge per person, the pass admits you, your spouse and children, and your parents, when you arrive together.) Camping and parking are extra. The $15 Golden Eagle Pass, a hologram you affix to your National Parks Pass, functions as an upgrade, granting entry to all sites run by the NPS, the U.S. Fish and Wildlife Service, the U.S. Forest Service, and the Bureau of Land Management. The upgrade, which expires with the parks pass, is sold by most national-park, Fish-and-Wildlife, and BLM fee stations. A major percentage of the proceeds from pass sales funds National Parks projects.

Both the Golden Age Passport ($10), for U.S. citizens or permanent residents who are 62 and older, and the Golden Access Passport (free), for persons with disabilities, entitle holders (and any passengers in their private vehicles) to lifetime free entry to all national parks, plus 50% off fees for the use of many park facilities and services. (The discount doesn't always apply to companions.) To obtain them, you must show proof of age and of U.S. citizenship or permanent residency—such as a U.S. passport, driver's license, or birth certificate—and, if requesting Golden Access, proof of disability. The Golden Age and Golden Access passes are available only at NPS-run sites that charge an entrance fee. The National Parks Pass is also available by mail and phone and via the Internet.

National Park Foundation ✉ 11 Dupont Circle NW, Suite 600, Washington, DC 20036 ☎ 202/238-4200 ⊕ www.nationalparks.org. **National Park Service** ✉ National Park Service/Department of Interior, 1849 C St. NW, Washington, DC 20240 ☎ 202/208-6843 ⊕ www.nps.gov. **National Parks Conservation Association** ✉ 1300 19th St. NW, Suite 300, Washington, DC 20036 ☎ 202/223-6722 or 800/628-7275 ⊕ www.npca.org.

Passes by Mail & Online National Park Foundation ⊕ www.nationalparks.org. **National Parks Pass** National Park Foundation ⌖ Box 34108, Washington, DC 20043 ☎ 888/467-2757 ⊕ www.nationalparks.org; include a check or money order payable to the National Park Service, plus $3.95 for shipping and handling (allow 8 to 13 business days from date of receipt for pass delivery), or call for passes.

PACKING

Informality reigns in the mountains and on the plains: jeans, sport shirts, and T-shirts fit in almost everywhere, for both men and women. The few restaurants and performing arts events where dressier outfits are required, usually in resorts and larger cities, are the exception.

If you plan to spend much time outdoors, and certainly if you go in winter, **choose clothing appropriate for cold and wet weather.** Cotton clothing, including denim—although fine on warm, dry days—can be uncomfortable when it gets wet and when the weather's cold. A better choice is clothing made of wool or any of a number of new synthetics that provide warmth without bulk and maintain their insulating properties even when wet.

In summer, you'll want shorts during the day. But because early morning and evenings can be cold, and high mountain passes windy, pack a sweater and a light jacket, and perhaps also a wool cap and gloves. Try layering—a T-shirt under another shirt under a jacket—and peel off layers as you go. For walks and hikes, you'll need sturdy footwear. To take you into the wilds, boots should have thick soles and plenty of ankle support; if your shoes are new and you plan to spend much time on the trail, break them in at home. Bring a day pack for short hikes, along with a canteen or water bottle, and don't forget rain gear, a hat, sunscreen, and insect repellent.

In winter, prepare for subzero temperatures with good boots, warm socks and liners, long johns, a well-insulated jacket, and a warm hat and mittens. Dress in layers so you can add or remove clothes as the temperatures fluctuate.

If you attend dances and other events at Native American reservations, dress conservatively—skirts or long pants for women, long pants for men—or you may be asked to leave. Be aware that you should obtain permission before you take photographs of Native Americans or their programs such as powwow dances. Generally, at a powwow, the dance master will announce when it is appropriate to take photos.

When traveling to mountain areas, **remember that sunglasses and a sun hat are essential at high altitudes**; the thinner atmosphere requires sunscreen with a greater SPF than you might need at lower elevations.

In your carry-on luggage, pack an extra pair of eyeglasses or contact lenses and enough of any medication you take to last a few days longer than the entire trip. You may also ask your doctor to write a spare prescription using the drug's generic name, as brand names may vary from country to country. In luggage to be checked, **never pack prescription drugs, valuables, or undeveloped film.** And don't forget to carry with you the addresses of offices that handle refunds of lost traveler's checks. Check *Fodor's How to Pack* (available at online retailers and bookstores everywhere) for more tips.

To avoid customs and security delays, carry medications in their original packaging. Don't pack any sharp objects in your carry-on luggage, including knives of any size or material, scissors, nail clippers, and corkscrews, or anything else that might arouse suspicion.

To avoid having your checked luggage chosen for hand inspection, don't cram bags full. The U.S. Transportation Security Administration suggests packing shoes on top and placing personal items you don't want touched in clear plastic bags.

CHECKING LUGGAGE

You're allowed to carry aboard one bag and one personal article, such as a purse or a laptop computer. Make sure what you carry on fits under your seat or in the overhead bin. Get to the gate early, so you can board as soon as possible, before the overhead bins fill up.

Baggage allowances vary by carrier, destination, and ticket class. On international flights, you're usually allowed to check two bags weighing up to 70 pounds (32 kilograms) each, although a few airlines allow checked bags of up to 88 pounds (40 kilograms) in first class. Some international carriers don't allow more than 66 pounds (30 kilograms) per bag in business class and 44 pounds (20 kilograms) in economy. If you're flying to or through the United Kingdom, your luggage cannot exceed 70 pounds (32 kilograms) per bag. On domestic flights, the limit is usually 50 to 70 pounds (23 to 32 kilograms) per bag. In general, carry-on bags shouldn't exceed 40 pounds (18 kilograms). Most airlines won't accept bags that weigh more than 100 pounds (45 kilograms) on domestic or international flights. Expect to pay a fee for baggage that exceeds weight limits. Check baggage restrictions with your carrier before you pack.

Airline liability for baggage is limited to $2,500 per person on flights within the United States. On international flights it amounts to $9.07 per pound or $20 per kilogram for checked baggage (roughly $640 per 70-pound bag), with a maximum of $634.90 per piece, and $400 per passenger for unchecked baggage. You can buy additional coverage at check-in for about $10 per $1,000 of coverage, but it often excludes a rather extensive list of items, shown on your airline ticket.

Before departure, itemize your bags' contents and their worth, and label the bags with your name, address, and phone number. (If you use your home address, cover it so potential thieves can't see it readily.) Include a label inside each bag and **pack a copy of your itinerary.** At check-in, make sure each bag is correctly tagged with the destination airport's three-letter code. Because some checked bags will be opened for hand inspection, the U.S. Transportation Security Administration recommends that you leave luggage unlocked or use the plastic locks offered at check-in. TSA screeners place an inspection notice inside searched bags, which are re-sealed with a special lock.

If your bag has been searched and contents are missing or damaged, file a claim with the TSA Consumer Response Center as soon as possible. If your bags arrive damaged or fail to arrive at all, file a written report with the airline before leaving the airport.

F Complaints U.S. Transportation Security Administration Contact Center ☎ 866/289–9673 ⊕ www.tsa.gov.

PASSPORTS & VISAS

When traveling internationally, carry your passport even if you don't need one. Not only is it the best form of I.D., but it's also being required more and more. As of December 31, 2005, for instance, Americans need a passport to re-enter the country from Bermuda, the Caribbean, and Panama. Such requirements also affect re-entry from Canada and Mexico by air and sea (as of December 31, 2006) and land (as of December 31, 2007). **Make two photocopies of the data page** (one for someone at home and another for you, carried separately from your passport). If you lose your passport, promptly call the nearest embassy or consulate and the local police.

Montana borders Canada, and if you plan to enter that country, have the proper papers with you (⇨ Car Travel, as well). Citizens and legal residents of the United States do not need a passport or a visa to enter Canada, but proof of citizenship (a birth certificate or valid passport) and some form of photo identification will be requested. Naturalized U.S. residents should carry their naturalization certificate. Permanent residents who are not citizens should carry their "green card." Citizens of the United Kingdom need only a valid passport to enter Canada for stays of up to six months.

U.S. passport applications for children under age 14 require consent from both parents or legal guardians; both parents must appear together to sign the application. If only one parent appears, he or she must submit a written statement from the other parent authorizing passport issuance for the child. A parent with sole authority must present evidence of it when applying; acceptable documentation includes the

child's certified birth certificate listing only the applying parent, a court order specifically permitting this parent's travel with the child, or a death certificate for the nonapplying parent. Application forms and instructions are available on the Web site of the U.S. State Department's Bureau of Consular Affairs (⊕ travel.state.gov).

SAFETY

Regardless which outdoor activities you pursue or your level of skill, safety must come first. Remember: **know your limits.**

Many trails in the Rockies and northern plains are remote and sparsely traveled. In the high altitudes of the mountains, oxygen is scarce. Hikers, bikers, and riders should **carry emergency supplies** in their backpacks. Proper equipment includes a flashlight, a compass, waterproof matches, a first-aid kit, a knife, a cell phone with an extra battery (although you may have to climb atop a mountain ridge to find a signal), and a light plastic tarp for shelter. Backcountry skiers should add a repair kit, a blanket, an avalanche beacon, and a lightweight shovel to their lists. Always **bring extra food and a canteen of water,** as dehydration is a common occurrence at high altitudes. **Never drink from streams or lakes,** unless you boil the water first or purify it with tablets. Giardia, an intestinal parasite, may be present.

Always **check the condition of roads and trails, and get the latest weather reports** before setting out. In summer, **take precautions against heat stroke or exhaustion** by resting frequently in shaded areas; in winter, **take precautions against hypothermia** by layering clothing. Ultimately, proper planning, common sense, and good physical conditioning are the strongest guards against the elements.

ALTITUDE

You may feel dizzy and weak and find yourself breathing heavily—signs that the thin mountain air isn't giving you your accustomed dose of oxygen. Take it easy and **rest often for a few days until you're acclimatized.** Throughout your stay drink plenty of water and watch your alcohol consumption. If you experience severe headaches and nausea, see a doctor. It is easy to go too high too fast. The remedy for altitude-related discomfort is to go down quickly, into heavier air. Other altitude-related problems include dehydration and overexposure to the sun because of the thin air.

EXPOSURE

The high elevation, severe cold temperatures, and sometimes windy weather in Montana and Wyoming can often combine to create intense and dangerous outdoor conditions. In winter, exposure to wind and cold can quickly bring on hypothermia or frostbite. Protect yourself by dressing in layers, so you don't become overheated and then chilled. Any time of year, the region's clear air and high elevation make sunburn a particular risk. Always wear sunscreen, even when skies are overcast.

FLASH FLOODS

Flash floods can strike at any time and any place with little or no warning. Mountainous terrain can become dangerous when distant rains are channeled into gullies and ravines, turning a quiet streamside campsite or wash into a rampaging torrent in seconds. Similarly, desert terrain floods quickly when the land is unable to absorb heavy rain. Check weather reports before heading into the backcountry and be prepared to head for higher ground if the weather turns severe.

WILD ANIMALS

One of the most wonderful parts of the Rockies and plains is the abundant wildlife. And although a herd of grazing elk or a bighorn sheep high on a hillside is most certainly a Kodak moment, an encounter with a bear or mountain lion is not. To avoid such a dangerous situation while hiking, **make plenty of noise, keep dogs on a leash, and keep small children between adults.** While camping, be sure to store all food, utensils, and clothing with food odors far away from your tent, preferably high in a tree (also far from your tent). If you do come across a bear or big cat, **do not run.** For bears, back away quietly; for lions, make yourself look as

big as possible. In either case, be prepared to fend off the animal with loud noises, rocks, sticks, and so on. And as the saying goes, do not feed the bears—or any wild animals, whether they're dangerous or not. When in the wilderness, **give all animals their space and never attempt to feed any of them.** If you want to take a photograph, use a long lens rather than a long sneak to approach closely. This is particularly important for winter visitors. Approaching an animal can cause it stress and affect its ability to survive the sometimes brutal climate. In all cases remember that the animals have the right-of-way; this is their home, and you are the visitor.

SENIOR-CITIZEN TRAVEL

Senior citizens will often find reduced rates for meals and lodging throughout Montana and Wyoming. Many attractions also have lower fees for senior travelers.

To qualify for age-related discounts, mention your senior-citizen status up front when booking hotel reservations (not when checking out) and before you're seated in restaurants (not when paying the bill). Be sure to have identification on hand. When renting a car, ask about promotional car-rental discounts, which can be cheaper than senior-citizen rates.

🚩 Educational Programs **Elderhostel** ✉ 11 Ave. de Lafayette, Boston, MA 02111 ☎ 877/426–8056, 978/323–4141 international callers, 877/426–2167 TTY 🖨 877/426–2166 ⊕ www.elderhostel.org.

SHOPPING

Although there are plenty of modern shopping malls across the Rockies and plains, independent shops throughout the West stock authentic memorabilia and clothing such as cowboy boots, cowboy hats, bolero ties, and the like. This is also a great place to find Native American crafts. Small artisan colonies often neighbor ritzy resorts. These enclaves of creative souls produce some of the finest handcrafted wares anywhere; look for local galleries and boutiques that showcase their work.

KEY DESTINATIONS

For authentic Native American products visit galleries and shops near Indian reservations in communities such as Fort

Washakie, Wyoming, and Browning, Montana. You'll find extensive shopping opportunities in resort areas such as Jackson, Wyoming, and Kalispell, Montana. Smaller shops often feature local products ranging from huckleberry syrup and candies to jewelry and custom-designed clothing. Western items such as boots, hats, and clothing can be found throughout the region in stores such as Lou Taubert Ranch Outfitters in Billings, Montana, and Casper, Wyoming; in Corral West stores across the area; and at Just Dandy in Cheyenne, Wyoming.

SMART SOUVENIRS

A quintessential Wyoming souvenir is anything involving a "jackalope" (a small fictional animal that is a cross between a jackrabbit and an antelope). For a real taste of Montana take home something made from huckleberries—wine, candy, jelly, syrup. Other popular souvenirs include Native American products such as beaded bags or bracelets; cowboy music and artwork; or an autographed copy of a book written by a local author. Most local bookstores have a stock of signed titles by area writers, including Mary Clearman Blew, W. Michael Gear and Kathleen O'Neal Gear, Richard S. Wheeler, C. J. Box, and Candy Moulton.

SPORTS & THE OUTDOORS

The Rockies and plains are among America's greatest playgrounds, and many area residents make outdoor recreation a high priority. Local jocks can do their thing in the midst of exquisite scenery—not boxed in at a gym watching ceiling-mounted televisions.

Whatever activity you choose to pursue, there is an outfitter who can help you have the best (and safest) possible experience. Many trip organizers specialize in only one type of activity; however, a few companies guide a variety of active vacations. (In some cases, these larger companies also act as clearinghouses or agents for smaller trip outfitters.) Always ascertain from another source that your outfitter is reliable; getting stuck with a shoddy operator can be disappointing, uncomfortable, and even dangerous. Guides for some sports—

white-water rafting and mountaineering, for example—are licensed or certified by industry organizations. Be sure that the guide you're with is properly accredited.

🏃 **Outfitter Referrals America Outdoors** 🖂 Box 10847, Knoxville, TN 37939 ☎ 865/558-3595 ⊕ www.americaoutdoors.org. **Montana Outfitters and Guides Association** 🖂 2 N. Last Chance Gulch, Helena, MT 59624 ☎ 406/449-3578 🖷 406/449-9769 ⊕ www.moga-montana.org. **Wyoming Outfitters and Guides Association** 🖂 Box 2650, Casper, WY 82602 ☎ 307/265-2376 ⊕ www.wyoga.org.

BICYCLING

High, rugged country puts a premium on fitness. Even if you can ride 40 mi at home without breaking a sweat, you might find yourself struggling terribly on steep climbs and in elevations often exceeding 10,000 feet. If you have an extended tour in mind, you might want to come a couple of days early to acclimate yourself to the altitude and terrain. Pretrip conditioning is likely to make your trip more enjoyable.

On tours where the elevation may vary 4,000 feet or more, the climate can change dramatically. Although the valleys may be scorching, high-mountain passes may still be lined with snow in summer. Pack clothing accordingly. (Bicycle racers often stuff newspaper inside their jerseys when descending from high passes to shield themselves from the chill.) Although you shouldn't have much problem renting a bike (trip organizers can usually arrange rentals), it's a good idea to bring your own pair of sturdy, stiff-bottom cycling shoes to make riding easier, and your own helmet. Some experienced riders bring not only their own shoes but their own pedals if they use an interlocking shoe-and-pedal system. If you do decide to bring your own bike, be prepared to spend as much as $150 in special luggage handling on the airlines. Summer and early fall are the best times to plan a trip; at other times, snow and ice may still obstruct high-terrain roads and trails.

Guided bike trips generally range in price between $80 and $150 a day, depending on lodging and meals. The Adventure Cycling Association is perhaps the best general source of information on biking in the

Rockies and plains—including detailed maps and information on trip organizers. They also guide trips stretching along the Continental Divide. Hostelling International (⇨ Lodging) is a good connection for cycling tours as well. Also, when you're in a ski resort town, check whether lifts service mountain bikes. Remember that biking is not permitted in national wilderness areas.

🚩 **Adventure Cycling Association** ⌂ Box 8308, Missoula, MT 59807 ☎ 406/721-1776 or 800/755-2453 ⊕ www.adventurecycling.org.

DUDE RANCHES

Most dude ranches don't require any previous experience with horses, although a few working ranches reserve weeks in spring and fall—when the chore of moving cattle is more intensive than in summer—for experienced riders. No special equipment is necessary on a dude ranch, although if you plan to do much fishing, you're better off bringing your own tackle (some ranches have tackle to lend or rent). Be sure to check with the ranch for a list of items you might be expected to bring. If you plan to do much riding, a couple of pairs of sturdy pants, boots, a wide-brim hat to shield you from the sun, and outerwear as protection from the possibility of rain or chill should be packed. Expect to spend at least $175 per day. Depending on the activities you engage in, as well as accommodations, the price can exceed $300 a day. *See* Guest Ranches *in* Lodging, as well.

FISHING

Field and Stream magazine is a leading source of information on fishing destinations, technique, and equipment. For lists of guides to various rivers and lakes of the Rockies and plains, contact the state tourism departments.

Fishing licenses, available at tackle shops and a variety of local stores, are required in Montana and Wyoming. The fishing season may vary from state to state, and from species to species. A few streams are considered "private" streams, in that they are privately stocked by a local club, and other rivers are fly-fishing or catch-and-release only, so be sure you **know the rules before making your first cast.** Tribal fishing licences are necessary on reservation land.

Rocky Mountain and northern plains water can be cold, especially at higher elevations and especially in spring and fall (and winter, of course). You'd do well to **bring waterproof waders** or buy them when you arrive in the region. Outfitters and some tackle shops rent equipment, but you're better off with your own gear. Lures are another story, though: whether you plan to fish with flies or other lures, local tackle shops can usually give you a pretty good idea of what works best in a particular region, and you can buy accordingly.

In the mid-1990s, whirling disease—a parasitic infection that afflicts trout—began to reduce fish populations in some Rocky Mountain streams dramatically. Efforts to curb the spread of the disease have met with some success, but some waters are still suffering from a smaller fish population.

A guide will cost about $250 per day and can be shared by two anglers if they are fishing from a boat and possibly by three if they are wading. Lunch will probably be included and flies might be, although there may be an extra $15–$20 charge for these. Orvis Fly Fishing Schools runs one of the most respected fishing instructional programs in the country and endorses other instructional programs.

🚩 Fishing Licenses Online www.greatlodge.com. 🚩 Information & Licenses **Montana Department of Fish, Wildlife, and Parks** ✉ 1420 E. 6th St., Helena, MT 59620 ☎ 406/444-2535 ⊕ www.fwp.state. mt.us. **Wyoming Game and Fish Department** ✉ 5400 Bishop Blvd., Cheyenne, WY 82006 ☎ 307/777-4600 ⊕ gf.state.wy.us. 🚩 Instruction **Bud Lilly's Trout Shop** ✉ 39 Madison Ave., Box 530, West Yellowstone, MT 59758 ☎ 406/646-7801 or 800/854-9559 ⊕ www. budlillys.com. **Orvis Fly Fishing Schools** ☎ 800/239-2074 Ext. 784 ⊕ www.orvis.com.

GROUP TRIPS

Group sizes for organized trips vary considerably, depending on the organizer and the activity. If you are planning a trip with a large group, trip organizers or outfitters will sometimes offer discounts of 10% and more, and are willing to customize trips. For example, for people specifically interested in photography or in wildlife, trip organizers have been known to get professional photographers or naturalists to join the group. Recreating as a group gives you leverage with the organizer, and you should use it.

One way to travel with a group is to join an organization before going. Conservation-minded travelers might want to contact the Sierra Club, a nonprofit organization, which offers both vacation and work trips. Individuals or groups that want to test their mettle can learn wilderness skills at "outdoor schools" such as the National Outdoor Leadership School. 🏳 **National Outdoor Leadership School** ⊠ 284 Lincoln St., Lander, WY 82520 ☎ 307/332–5300 or 800/710–6657 ⊕ www.nols.edu. **Sierra Club** ⊠ 85 2nd St., 2nd fl., San Francisco, CA 94105 ☎ 415/977–5500 ⊕ www.sierraclub.org.

HIKING

Hiking is popular throughout the Rockies and plains, and you can get information about trails and guided trips at Forest Service offices or national park visitor centers. The national parks have guided hikes during summer and early fall. *Backpacker* magazine (Rodale Press) is the leading national magazine that focuses on hiking and backpacking, and each region in the Rockies and plains has great local publications on places to hike. Organized-trip costs can be as little as $30 a day. *See* Guidebooks for guidebook sources. 🏳 **American Hiking Society** ⊕ Box 20160, Washington, DC 20041 ☎ 301/565–6704 ⊕ www.americanhiking.org.

KAYAKING

The streams and rivers of the Rockies tend to be better suited to kayaking than canoeing. Steep mountains and narrow canyons usually mean fast-flowing water, in which the maneuverability of kayaks is a great asset. A means of transport for less experienced paddlers is the inflatable kayak (it's easier to navigate and it bounces off the rocks).

To minimize environmental impact as well as ensure a sense of wilderness privacy (riverside campgrounds are often limited to one party per night), a reservation policy is used for many rivers of the West. Often, the reserved times—many of the *prime* times—are prebooked by licensed outfitters, limiting your possibilities if you're planning a self-guided trip. For those rivers with restricted-use policies, it's best to reserve through a guide company several months or more in advance. Also, try to be flexible about when and where to go; you might find that the time you want to go is unavailable, or you may find yourself closed out altogether from your river of choice. If you insist on running a specific river at a specific time, your best bet is to sign on with a guided trip (which will cost at least $100 a day).

Outfitters provide life jackets and, if necessary, paddles and helmets; they often throw in waterproof containers for cameras, clothing, and sleeping bags. Bring bug repellent as well as a good hat, sunblock, and warm clothing for overnight trips. The sun on the river can be intense, but once it disappears behind canyon walls, the temperature can drop 30°F or more. The best footwear is a pair of either water-resistant sandals or old sneakers. 🏳 Instruction & Trips **Montana Surf Kayak School** ⊠ 83 Rowland Rd., Bozeman, MT ☎ 406/581–5178 ⊕ www.montanasurf.com. **Snake River Kayak and Canoe** ⊕ Box 4311, Jackson, WY 83001 ☎ 800/529–2501 or 307/733–9999 ⊕ www.snakeriverkayak.com/.

MAPS

If you plan to do much traveling where trails might not be well marked or maintained, you'll need maps and a compass. Topographical maps are sold in outdoor stores (REI or Eastern Mountain Sports, for example) and maps in several different scales are available from the U.S. Geological Survey. Consult the U.S.G.S. index and catalog, which you can see on their Web site (⊕ http://store.usgs.gov/) or request for free by mail, to order the specific maps you need. Many local camping, fishing, and hunting stores carry U.S.G.S. and other detailed maps of the surrounding region. The U.S. Forest Service and the BLM also publish useful maps, which you can purchase at local offices for those agencies. Another source for maps is Maplink, an online retailer. **Maps Maplink** ⌂ 30 S. La Patera La., Unit #5, Santa Barbara, CA 93117 ☎ 800/962-1394 or 805/692-6777 ⊕ www.maplink.com. **U.S. Bureau of Land Management, Montana State Office** ⌂ 5001 Southgate Dr., Billings, MT 59101 ☎ 406/896-5000 ⊕ www.mt.blm.gov. **U.S. Bureau of Land Management, Wyoming State Office** ⌂ 5353 Yellowstone Rd., Cheyenne, WY 82009 ☎ 307/775-6256 ⊕ www.wy.blm.gov. **U.S. Forest Service Northern Region** ⌂ Box 7669, 200 E. Broadway, Missoula, MT 59807 ☎ 406/329-3511 ⊕ http://www.fs.fed.us/r1. **U.S. Forest Service Rocky Mountain Region** ⌂ Box 25127, Lakewood, CO 80225-01277 ☎ 303/275-5350 ⊕ www.fs.fed.us/r2. **U.S. Geological Survey** ⌂ Distribution Center, Box 25286, Federal Center, Denver, CO 80225 ☎ 303/202-4700 or 888/275-8747 ⊕ www.usgs.gov.

PACK TRIPS & HORSEBACK RIDING

Horsemanship is not a prerequisite for most trips, but it is helpful. Even experienced riders can expect to have some saddle discomfort for the first day or two. If you're unsure of how much of this sort of thing you can put up with, sign up for a shorter trip (one to three days) before taking on an adventure of a week or longer. Another option is to spend a few days at a dude or guest ranch to get used to life in the saddle, then try a shorter, overnight pack trip organized by the ranch.

Clothing requirements are straightforward: a sturdy pair of pants, a wide-brim sun hat with a string to keep it from blowing off, and outerwear to protect against rain are about the only necessities. Ask your outfitter or dude ranch for a list of items you'll need, and for any limits on how much gear (extra clothing) or luxuries (e.g. alcoholic beverages) you can bring along. Trip costs typically range between $200 and $300 per day.

In general, pack trips are organized by local outfitters or ranches rather than national organizations. Local chambers of commerce can usually provide lists of outfitters who work in a particular area.

Outfitters Allen's Diamond 4 Ranch ⌂ Box 243, Lander, WY 82520 ☎ 307/332-2995 ⛁ 307/332-7902 ⊕ www.diamond4ranch.com. **Glacier Wilderness Guides** ⌂ Box 535, West Glacier, MT 59936 ☎ 800/521-7238 ⛁ 406/387-5656 ⊕ www.glacierguides.com. **Rimrock Dude Ranch** ⌂ 2728 North Fork Hwy., Cody, WY 82414 ☎ 307/587-3970 or 800/208-7468 ⛁ 307/527-5014 ⊕ www.rimrockranch.com.

RAFTING

Unless you are a rafting expert, **hire a recognized outfitter** to guide you out on the river. You should be a good swimmer and in solid general health. Different companies are licensed to run different rivers, although there may be several companies working the same river. Some organizers combine river rafting with other activities: pack trips, mountain-bike excursions, extended hikes, or fishing.

Rafting ranges from slow, scenic floats to fast, adrenaline-pumping white-water adventures. Likewise, your raft might be an inflated boat in which passengers do the paddling, an inflated raft or wooden dory in which a licensed professional does the work, or a motorized raft on which some oar work might be required. Be sure you know what kind of raft you'll be riding—or paddling—before booking a trip. When arranging a river trip, choose one that's appropriate for your party: most children up to age six, as well as out-of-shape adults, don't belong on white water. Day trips typically run between $50 and $100 per person. Expect to pay between $120 and $150 per day for multiday trips.

Outfitters Glacier Raft Company ⌂ Box 210C, West Glacier, MT 59936 ☎ 406/888-5454 or 800/235-6781 ⊕ www.glacierraftco.com. **Glacier Wilderness Guides** ⌂ Box 535, West Glacier, MT 59936 ☎ 406/387-5555 or 800/521-7238 ⛁ 406/387-5656 ⊕ www.glacierguides.com.

ROCK CLIMBING & MOUNTAINEERING

Before you sign on with any trip, be sure to clarify to the trip organizer your climbing skills, experience, and physical condition. Climbing tends to be a team sport, and overestimating your capabilities can endanger not only yourself but other team members. A fair self-assessment of your abilities also helps a guide choose an appropriate climbing route; routes (not unlike ski trails) are rated according to their difficulty. The way to a summit may be relatively easy or brutally challenging, depending on the route selected. You may want to get some instruction at a climbing wall before a trip to the Rockies.

Most guide services rent such technical gear as helmets, pitons, ropes, and axes, usually on a per-item, per-day basis. Ask what additional equipment and supplies you'll need to bring along. Some mountaineering stores rent climbing equipment. The best strategy for dealing with weather variations at higher elevations, where temperatures can fluctuate dramatically, is to bring several thin layers of clothing, including a sturdy, waterproof/breathable outer shell.

Organized climbing trip costs can vary considerably, depending on group size, length of climb, instruction rendered, and equipment supplied. Count on spending at least $125 a day. However, the cost of a small-group multiday instructional climb can push $300 a day. The American Alpine Institute leads trips around the world, ranging from training climbs to expeditionary first ascents. It is one of the most respected climbing organizations in the country.

Instructional Programs & Outfitters American Alpine Institute ✉ 1515 12th St., N-4, Bellingham, WA 98225 ☎ 360/671-1505 ⊕ www.aai.cc. **Beartooth Mountain Guides** ✉ Box 1985, Red Lodge, MT 59068 ☎ 406/446-9874 ⊕ www. redlodge.com/climbing. **Exum School of Mountaineering** ✉ Box 56, Moose, WY 83012 ☎ 307/733-2297 ⊕ www.exumguides.com. **Jackson Hole Mountain Guides** ✉ Box 7477, Jackson, WY 83001 ☎ 800/239-7642 ⊕ www.jhmg.com.

TOUR COMPANIES

Off the Beaten Path customizes trips within the Rockies that combine outdoor activities and learning experiences. Many trips cross the Montana–Wyoming border. The Yellowstone Association Institute offers guided tours and trips in Yellowstone National Park, ranging from backcountry expeditions to "Lodging and

Learning" experiences within the comfort of park lodging. Some of these trips are specifically for families. Timberline Adventures leads hiking and biking tours in the bigger national parks, such as Glacier and Yellowstone.

Off the Beaten Path ✉ 27 E. Main St., Bozeman, MT 59715 ☎ 800/445-2995 ⊕ 406/587-4147 ⊕ www.offthebeatenpath.com. **Timberline Adventures** ✉ 7975 E. Harvard, Suite J, Denver, CO 80231 ☎ 303/759-3804 or 800/417-2453 ⊕ www.timbertours.com. **The Yellowstone Association Institute** ✉ Yellowstone National Park ☎ 307/344-2293 ⊕ www.YellowstoneAssociation.org.

STUDENTS IN MONTANA & WYOMING

Students can sometimes get discounts for attractions, but it is not routine.

IDs & Services STA Travel ✉ 10 Downing St., New York, NY 10014 ☎ 212/627-3111, 800/777-0112 24-hr service center ⊕ 212/627-3387 ⊕ www.sta.com. **Travel Cuts** ✉ 187 College St., Toronto, Ontario M5T 1P7, Canada ☎ 800/592-2887 in the U.S., 416/979-2406 or 866/246-9762 in Canada ⊕ 416/979-8167 ⊕ www.travelcuts.com.

TAXES

Sales tax is 4% in Wyoming; Montana has no sales tax. Some areas have additional local sales and lodging taxes, which can be quite significant.

If you are crossing the border into Canada, be aware of Canada's goods and services tax (better known as the GST). This is a value-added tax of 7%, applicable on virtually every purchase except basic groceries and a small number of other items. Visitors to Canada, however, may **claim a full rebate of the GST** on any goods taken out of the country as well as on short-term accommodations. Rebates can be claimed either immediately on departure from Canada at participating duty-free shops or by mail within 60 days of leaving Canada. Rebate forms can be obtained from certain retailers, duty-free shops, and customs officials, or by going to the Canada Revenue Agency Web site and searching for document GST176.

Purchases made during multiple visits to Canada can be grouped together for rebate purposes. Instant cash rebates up to a maximum of $500 are provided by some duty-free shops when leaving Canada, and most provinces do not tax goods that are shipped directly by the vendor to the purchaser's home. Always **save your original receipts** from stores and hotels (not just credit card receipts), and **be sure the name and address of the establishment are shown on the receipt.** Original receipts are not returned. To be eligible for a refund, receipts must total at least $200, and each individual receipt must show a minimum purchase of $50.

Canada Tax Refund Canada Revenue Agency www.cra-arc.gc.ca.

TELEPHONES

Cell phones are generally unreliable in the backcountry, especially in canyons and in remote locations far from cell towers.

AREA & COUNTRY CODES

The telephone area codes are 406 for Montana and 307 for Wyoming.

LOCAL CALLS

Pay telephones cost 35¢ for local calls. Charge phones, also common, may be used to charge a call to a telephone-company calling card or a credit card, or for collect calls.

Many hotels place a surcharge on local calls made from your room and include a service charge on long-distance calls. It may be cheaper for you to make your calls from a pay phone in the hotel lobby rather than from your room.

TIME

Montana and Wyoming are in the Mountain Time Zone. Mountain time is two hours earlier than Eastern time and one hour later than Pacific time. It is 1 hour earlier than Chicago, 7 hours earlier than London, and 17 hours earlier than Sydney.

TIPPING

It is customary to tip 15% at restaurants; 20% in resort towns is increasingly the norm. For coat checks and bellhops, $1 per coat or bag is the minimum. Taxi drivers expect 10% to 15%, depending on where you are. In resort towns, ski technicians, sandwich makers, coffee baristas, and the like also appreciate tips.

TOURS & PACKAGES

Because everything is prearranged on a prepackaged tour or independent vacation, you spend less time planning—and often get it all at a good price.

BOOKING WITH AN AGENT

Travel agents are excellent resources. But it's a good idea to collect brochures from several agencies, as some agents' suggestions may be influenced by relationships with tour and package firms that reward them for volume sales. If you have a special interest, find an agent with expertise in that area. The American Society of Travel Agents (ASTA) has a database of specialists worldwide; you can log on to the group's Web site to find one near you.

Make sure your travel agent knows the accommodations and other services of the place being recommended. Ask about the hotel's location, room size, beds, and whether it has a pool, room service, or programs for children, if you care about these. Has your agent been there in person or sent others whom you can contact?

Do some homework on your own, too: local tourism boards can provide information about lesser-known and small-niche operators, some of which may sell only direct.

BUYER BEWARE

Each year consumers are stranded or lose their money when tour operators—even large ones with excellent reputations—go out of business. So check out the operator. Ask several travel agents about its reputation, and try to **book with a company that has a consumer-protection program.** (Look for information in the company's brochure.) In the United States, members of the United States Tour Operators Association are required to set aside funds (up to $1 million) to help eligible customers cover payments and travel arrangements in the event that the company defaults. It's also a good idea to choose a company that participates in the American Society of Travel Agents' Tour Operator Program; ASTA will act as mediator in any disputes between you and your tour operator.

Remember that the more your package or tour includes, the better you can predict the ultimate cost of your vacation. Make sure you know exactly what is covered, and beware of hidden costs. Are taxes, tips, and transfers included? Entertainment and excursions? These can add up.

⚑ Tour-Operator Recommendations American Society of Travel Agents (⇨ Travel Agencies). **CrossSphere–The Global Association for Packaged Travel** ✉ 546 E. Main St., Lexington, KY 40508 ☎ 859/226-4444 or 800/682-8886 🖶 859/226-4414 ⊕ www.CrossSphere.com. **United States Tour Operators Association** (USTOA) ✉ 275 Madison Ave., Suite 2014, New York, NY 10016 ☎ 212/599-6599 🖶 212/599-6744 ⊕ www.ustoa.com.

TRAIN TRAVEL

Amtrak connects the Rockies and plains to both coasts and all major American cities. Trains run through northern Montana, with stops in Essex and Whitefish, near Glacier National Park. Connecting bus services to Yellowstone National Park are provided in the summer from Amtrak's stop in Pocatello, Idaho.

Canada's passenger service, VIA Rail Canada, stops at Jasper, near the Canadian entrance to Waterton/Glacier International Peace Park.

⚑ Amtrak ☎ 800/872-7245 ⊕ www.amtrak.com. **VIA Rail Canada** ☎ 800/561-3949.

SCENIC TRAIN TRIPS

In Montana you can ride refurbished turn-of-the-20th-century touring cars along old rail routes. These trips give you the chance to scout out places beyond the reach of any four-lane freeway.

⚑ Travel Montana ✉ Department of Commerce, 1424 9th Ave., Helena, MT 59620 ☎ 406/444-2654, 800/548-3390 in Montana, 800/847-4868 nationwide.

TRANSPORTATION IN MONTANA & WYOMING

Without a doubt, the best way to travel the Rocky Mountains and northern plains region is by automobile because bus service is limited, there is little possibility of other public transportation, and trains provide access only to limited areas. Of course, once you are in an area, touring specific attractions by hiking, biking, or horseback riding is de rigueur and also is the way to access areas that can't be reached by vehicle.

If you have limited time, choose one area or one state to visit. To visit national parks in both Wyoming and Montana, fly into a gateway community and then rent a car. It takes only about five hours to drive between Yellowstone and Glacier, and there is plenty to see along the way.

TRAVEL AGENCIES

A good travel agent puts your needs first. Look for an agency that has been in business at least five years, emphasizes customer service, and has someone on staff who specializes in your destination. In addition, **make sure the agency belongs to a professional trade organization.** The American Society of Travel Agents (ASTA) has more than 10,000 members in some 140 countries, enforces a strict code of ethics, and will step in to mediate agent-client disputes involving ASTA members. ASTA also maintains a directory of agents on its Web site; ASTA's TravelSense.org, a trip planning and travel advice site, can also help to locate a travel agent who caters to your needs. (If a travel agency is also acting as your tour operator, *see* Buyer Beware *in* Tours & Packages.)

⚑ Local Agent Referrals American Society of Travel Agents (ASTA) ✉ 1101 King St., Suite 200, Alexandria, VA 22314 ☎ 703/739-2782 or 800/965-2782 24-hr hotline 🖶 703/684-8319 ⊕ www.astanet.com and www.travelsense.org. **Association of British Travel Agents** ✉ 68–71 Newman St., London W1T 3AH ☎ 020/7637-2444 🖶 020/7637-0713 ⊕ www.abta.com. **Association of Canadian Travel Agencies** ✉ 130 Albert St., Suite 1705, Ottawa, Ontario K1P 5G4 ☎ 613/237-3657 🖶 613/237-7052 ⊕ www.acta.ca. **Australian Federation of Travel Agents** ✉ Level 3, 309 Pitt St., Sydney, NSW 2000 ☎ 02/9264-3299 or 1300/363-416 🖶 02/9264-1085 ⊕ www.afta.com.au. **Travel Agents' Association of New Zealand** ✉ Level 5, Tourism and Travel House, 79 Boulcott St., Box 1888, Wellington 6001 ☎ 04/499-0104 🖶 04/499-0786 ⊕ www.taanz.org.nz.

VISITOR INFORMATION

Learn more about foreign destinations by checking government-issued travel advisories and country information. For a broader picture, consider information from more than one country.

At each visitor center and highway welcome center, you can obtain maps and information; most facilities have staff on hand to answer questions. You'll also find conveniences such as phones and restrooms.

🚩 Tourist Information **Travel Montana** ✉ Department of Commerce, 1424 9th Ave., Helena, MT 59620 ☎ 406/444-2654 or 800/847-4868 📠 406/444-1800 ⊕ www.visitmt.com. **Wyoming Department of Tourism** ✉ I-25 at College Dr., Cheyenne, WY 82002 ☎ 307/777-7777 or 800/225-5996 📠 307/777-6904 ⊕ www.wyomingtourism.org.

🚩 Government Advisories **Consular Affairs Bureau of Canada** ☎ 800/267-6788 or 613/944-6788 ⊕ www.voyage.gc.ca. **U.K. Foreign and Commonwealth Office** ✉ Travel Advice Unit, Consular Directorate, Old Admiralty Building, London SW1A 2PA ☎ 0870/606-0290 or 020/7008-1500 ⊕ www.fco.gov.uk/travel. **Australian Department of Foreign Affairs and Trade** ☎ 300/139-281 travel advisories, 02/6261-1299 Consular Travel Advice ⊕ www.

smartraveller.gov.au or www.dfat.gov.au. **New Zealand Ministry of Foreign Affairs and Trade** ☎ 04/439-8000 ⊕ www.mft.govt.nz.

WEB SITES

Do check out the World Wide Web when planning your trip. You'll find everything from weather forecasts to virtual tours of famous cities. Be sure to visit Fodors.com (⊕ www.fodors.com), a complete travel-planning site. You can research prices and book plane tickets, hotel rooms, rental cars, vacation packages, and more. In addition, you can post your pressing questions in the Travel Talk section. Other planning tools include a currency converter and weather reports, and there are loads of links to travel resources.

Also keep in mind that many towns, parks, and attractions have their own Web site, often jam-packed with pertinent information. Park sites are particularly helpful to read for safety precautions, as many Rocky Mountain and northern plains area parks are true wilderness.

Yellowstone National Park

WORD OF MOUTH

"Grand Geyser is spectacular by the light of a full moon. It is the one geyser in the park that draws rounds of applause from the viewers."

—bob_brown

"We stayed in the cabins at Canyon—we were willing to make the drives to the other locations. Some of the best wildlife sightings were on the dusk drives back to the cabins."

—keysmom

"I tend to prefer end of September/beginning of October for Yellowstone. You not only get the fall colors, but the moose and elk are in rut. There's a reason why nature photographers descend on Yellowstone in the fall."

—lifelist

By Candy
Moulton

WHERE ELSE BUT YELLOWSTONE can you pull off the empty highway at dawn to see two bison bulls shaking the earth as they collide in battle before the herd, and an hour later be caught in an RV traffic jam? For more than 125 years the granddaddy of national parks has been full of such contradictions, stemming from its twin goals: to remain America's preeminent wildlife preserve as well as its most accessible one. Anyone traveling to Wyoming or Montana should make a point of fitting Yellowstone into the itinerary.

Few places in the world can match Yellowstone's collection of accessible wonders. The Continental Divide slices through the park from southeast to northwest, amid a diverse terrain that includes rugged mountains, lush meadows, pine forests, free-flowing rivers, and the largest natural high-elevation lake in the United States. Yellowstone is exceptional for its abundance of geothermal features, such as rainbow-color hot springs and thundering geysers. As you visit the park's hydrothermal areas, you'll be walking on top of the Yellowstone Caldera—a 28- by 47-mi collapsed volcanic cone that last erupted about 600,000 years ago. The park's geyser basins, hot mud pots, fumaroles (steam vents), and hot springs are kept bubbling by an underground pressure cooker filled with magma. One geophysicist describes Yellowstone as "a window on the Earth's interior."

If you're not here for the geysers, chances are that you've come to spot some of the teeming wildlife, from grazing bison to cruising trumpeter swans. Yellowstone has 51 species of mammals and 209 species of birds, including predators such as grizzly and black bears, coyotes, foxes, hawks, and eagles, as well as less fearsome creatures such as elk, deer, moose, songbirds, and rodents. Controversy swirls around the park's wolves, which were reintroduced in 1995, and its bison, which sometimes roam outside the park in winter. Both draw headlines because neighboring cattle ranchers, particularly in Montana, see both creatures as a threat to their herds.

Yellowstone's attractions are as spectacular today as they were in the days of John Colter, the area's first white explorer. More than 3 million people visit annually to witness the geological wonders, the beautiful scenery, and the diverse array of wildlife. To see a spectacularly different Yellowstone than that experienced by most visitors, come in winter. Then the frosty silence is intruded upon by very few people—even if some of them are riding in snow coaches. Stop along a trail or a road and simply listen; if you're patient, you'll hear the gentle voice of nature. Even in the depths of winter the park is never totally still: mud pots bubble, geysers shoot skyward, and wind soughs through the pine trees. Above these sounds, the cry of a hawk, the yip of a coyote, or—if you're lucky—the howl of a wolf may pierce the air.

EXPLORING YELLOWSTONE

There are two major seasons in Yellowstone: summer (May–September), when by far the majority of visitors come, and winter (mid-December–February), when fewer people venture into the region. Except for

If, like most people who visit Yellowstone, you plan to spend just one full day in the park before heading to the surrounding attractions and cities, you will have to strategize wisely to get a good glimpse of the park's wonders. Your best approach would be to concentrate on one or two of the park's major areas. Many visitors with limited time head for the two biggest attractions: the famous Old Faithful geyser, and the hiking trails in the Upper Geyser Basin and along both rims of Grand Canyon of the Yellowstone. En route between these attractions, you will be able to see some wildlife and some geothermal activity.

1

With more time you can really sink your teeth into Yellowstone. In each of the major park villages—Mammoth, Lake Yellowstone, Fishing Bridge, Roosevelt-Tower, and Grant—you have a choices of activities and experiences. If you want to study a geyser terrace and see elk, go to Mammoth. Head to Roosevelt for hiking in open meadows, a horseback or stagecoach ride, and a cookout, as well as the chance to see or hear wolves and examine the remnants of a petrified forest. In the Lake Yellowstone and Fishing Bridge area, you can fish, watch buffalo and often see grizzly bears, especially in the Pelican Valley. Grant has its own small geyser basin that abuts Lake Yellowstone.

Wherever you go in Yellowstone, spend as much time as possible out of the car to immerse yourself in this natural place. Take a hike on some of the park's dozens of trails, which range from extremely easy and suitable for people with impaired mobility to rigorous enough to challenge the hard-core backpacker. In the easy category, good walks in the outdoors include the Old Faithful, Upper Geyser Basin, and Norris Geyser Basin boardwalks. For a moderate hike, take the trail to Mystic Falls, with its trailhead at Biscuit Basin between Old Faithful and Mammoth, or the South Rim Trail at Canyon. More difficult and longer treks include hikes to Specimen Ridge, in the northeast part of the park, and the trail to the top of Elephant Back, near Lake Yellowstone.

Another good way to learn about the park is to participate in a ranger-led tour or discussion. Take a sunset cruise on Lake Yellowstone or a ride to LeHardy Rapids in a classic 1937 touring bus. In winter there are guided snowmobile or snow-coach trips with options for cross-country skiing or snowshoeing through geyser basins and along the canyon. Sign up for the Yellowstone Association's Lodging and Learning program or one of its field seminars to delve more deeply into specific areas of interest, such as wildlife, geology, flora, or history. If you seek greater solitude, explore Yellowstone's backcountry either on your own or on a guided backpacking or horse-packing trip. For days on end, you might not see a visitor center and you might not sleep in a bed with four walls around you, but you will gain an appreciation for the park's unspoiled wilderness—without running into hordes of other people. Some backcountry campsites are accessible for people with disabilities, so everyone can witness Yellowstone's wild wonders.

services at park headquarters at Mammoth Hot Springs, the park closes from October to mid-December and again from March to late April or early May.

You'll spot Yellowstone's wildlife most often in early morning and late evening, when animals move out of the forest in search of food and water. Bison, elk, and coyotes populate virtually all areas; elk and bison particularly like river valleys and the geyser basins. Moose like marshy areas along Yellowstone Lake and in the northeast corner of the park. Wolves roam throughout the region but are most common in the Lamar Valley and areas south of Mammoth, while bears are most visible in the Pelican Valley–Fishing Bridge area, near Dunraven Pass, and near Mammoth. Watch for trumpeter swans and other waterfowl along the Yellowstone River and for sandhill cranes near the Firehole River and in Madison Valley.

Yellowstone has five primary entrances. The majority of visitors arrive through the South Entrance, north of Grand Teton National Park and Jackson, Wyoming. Other entrances are the East Entrance, with a main point of origin in Cody, Wyoming; the West Entrance at West Yellowstone, Montana (most used during winter); the North Entrance at Gardiner, Montana; and the Northeast Entrance at Cooke City, Montana, which can be reached from either Cody, Wyoming, via the Chief Joseph Scenic Highway, or from Red Lodge, Montana, over the Beartooth Pass. Each entrance has its own attractions: the South has the Lewis River canyon; the East, Sylvan Pass; the West, the Madison River valley; the North, the beautiful Paradise Valley; and the Northeast, the spectacular Beartooth Pass.

No matter where you enter Yellowstone National Park, you'll find yourself driving in circles: the park's road system is laid out in a figure eight known as the Grand Loop, with The Upper Loop to the north and the Lower Loop to the south. The entrance roads feed into the Grand Loop; all told, the park has 370 mi of public roads. All roads except the one linking Mammoth to Cooke City, Montana, close to automobiles in mid-October and remain closed until mid-April. Some roads may close earlier or open later due to snowfall. During winter the park roads are groomed for use by over-snow vehicles.

The park's efforts to upgrade its roads, most of which are now wide and smooth, is ongoing in a few areas: work continues on a segment of the East Entrance Road over Sylvan Pass through 2007, with half-hour delays most days and complete nighttime closures. On holiday weekends all road construction halts so there are no construction delays for travelers. Check with park rangers to determine where you'll encounter construction delays or closures; then give yourself plenty of time and enjoy the scenery and wildlife. Remember that snow is possible any time of year in almost all areas of the park.

Along the Grand Loop are eight primary "communities" or developed areas. Grant Village, near West Thumb, is the farthest south; Old Faithful and Madison are on the western side of the Lower Loop; Norris and Canyon Village are in the central part of the park, where the two loops intersect; Mammoth Hot Springs and Roosevelt–Tower Fall lie at the northern corners of the Upper Loop; and Lake Village/Fishing Bridge is along the eastern segment of the Lower Loop. Each community has parking areas, most have rangers on-site, and some have services such as gas stations, hotels, restaurants, and information centers.

Before you begin your visit, assess your desires and endurance level. If time is limited, don't try to cover the whole park. Instead, read through this chapter and pick an area to concentrate on, such as the Grand Canyon of the Yellowstone or Old Faithful, or plan to drive either the Lower or Upper Loop. There are summer-staffed visitor centers throughout the park, and there's a busy schedule of guided hikes, evening talks, and campfire programs, which are detailed in the park newspaper, *Discover Yellowstone.* In winter some centers and warming huts are open and distribute information about trails and activities. Pamphlets describing hot-spring basins are available for 50¢ at each site or visitor center.

In addition to enjoying frontcountry activities, you can head into Yellowstone's backcountry on your own or with a guide to hike, camp, ski, snowshoe, or horse pack. All overnight backcountry camping requires a backcountry use permit, which must be obtained in person no more than 48 hours before the planned trip. For information, call the backcountry office (☎ 307/344–2160).

As you explore the park keep this thought in mind: Yellowstone is not an amusement park. It is a wild place. The animals may seem docile or tame, but they are wild, and every year careless visitors are injured, sometimes even killed, when they venture too close. Particularly dangerous are female animals with their young, and bison, which can turn and charge in an instant. (Watch their tails: when they are standing up or crooked like a question mark, the bison is agitated.) ✑ *Box 168, Yellowstone National Park, WY 82190* ☎ *307/344–7381, 307/344–2386 TTD* ✒ *307/344–2005* ⊕ *www.nps.gov/yell* ✉ *7-day pass good for both Yellowstone and Grand Teton national parks $25 per motor vehicle, $10 on foot or bicycle, $15 on motorcycle* ☉ *Year-round to Mammoth; early May–Sept. in other areas; winter season mid-Dec.–Feb. to over-snow vehicles and transportation methods (skis/snowshoes) only.*

Numbers in the text correspond to numbers in the margin and on the Yellowstone National Park, Western Yellowstone, and Eastern Yellowstone maps.

Grant Village

Grant Village is the first community you'll encounter if you arrive in the park through the South Entrance. This area along the western edge of Lake Yellowstone has basic lodging and dining facilities and gives you easy access to the West Thumb Geyser Basin. It takes about two hours to hike to Lake Overlook and explore West Thumb Geyser Basin.

What to See

 Lake Overlook. From this hilltop northwest of West Thumb and Grant Village you get an expansive view of the southwest portion of Yellowstone. You reach the promontory by taking a 1½-mi hiking trail through

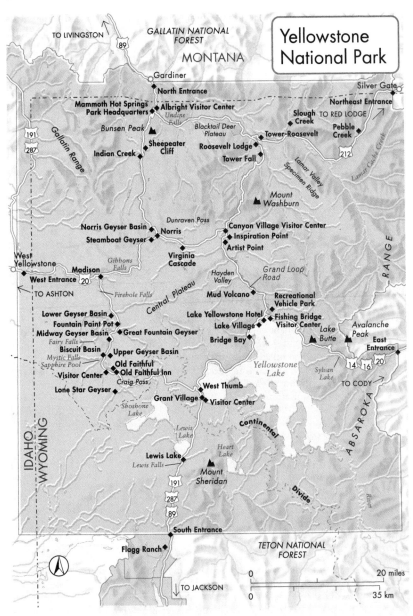

Yellowstone National Park

TO LIVINGSTON

89

GALLATIN NATIONAL FOREST

MONTANA

Gardiner

North Entrance

Silver Gate

Northeast Entrance

Mammoth Hot Springs
Park Headquarters
Albright Visitor Center
Undine Falls

Slough
Creek
TO RED LODGE

191

287

Bunsen Peak

Blacktail Deer Plateau

Tower-Roosevelt

Pebble
Creek

Gallatin Range

Indian Creek
Sheepeater
Cliff

Roosevelt Lodge

Tower Fall

212

Lamar Valley

Specimen Ridge

Lamar Cache Creek

Mount
Washburn

Dunraven Pass

Norris Geyser Basin
Norris

Canyon Village Visitor Center

Inspiration Point

RANGE

Steamboat Geyser

Artist Point

Gibbons Falls

Virginia
Cascade

West
Yellowstone

Madison

Hayden Valley

Grand Loop Road

West Entrance
20

TO ASHTON

Firehole Falls

Central Plateau

Mud Volcano

Recreational
Vehicle Park

Avalanche
Peak

Lower Geyser Basin
Fountain Paint Pot
Midway Geyser Basin
Great Fountain Geyser

Lake Yellowstone Hotel
Lake Village

Fishing Bridge
Visitor Center

*Lake
Butte*

East
Entrance

Bridge Bay

14

16

20

Fairy Falls

Biscuit Basin

Upper Geyser Basin

*Yellowstone
Lake*

Mystic Falls

Sapphire Pool

Old Faithful
Old Faithful Inn

*Sylvan
Lake*

TO CODY

Visitor Center

Craig Pass

Lone Star Geyser

West Thumb

*Shoshone
Lake*

Grant Village
Visitor Center

ABSAROKA

Continental

*Lewis
Lake*

*Heart
Lake*

Lewis Lake
Lewis Falls

Mount
Sheridan

Divide

River

191

287

89

South Entrance

TETON NATIONAL
FOREST

Flagg Ranch

0
20 miles

TO JACKSON

0
35 km

IDAHO
WYOMING

forest still recovering from the massive fires of 1988; the clearing caused by the fire makes this a prime area for sighting elk. ⊠ *1½ mi northwest of Grant Village.*

❶ West Thumb Geyser Basin. The unusual name of this small geyser basin comes from its location along a digitlike projection of Yellowstone Lake. This area, full of geysers and hot springs, is reached by a short boardwalk loop. It is particularly popular for winter visitors who take advantage of the nearby warming hut and a stroll around the geyser basin before continuing their trip via snow coach or snowmobile. ⊠ *Grand Loop Rd., West Thumb, 22 mi north of South Entrance.*

The **West Thumb Information Station** (☉ June–Aug., daily 9–5; Sept., daily 9–6; Dec.–Feb., daily 8–5) is a little log cabin that houses a bookstore run by the nonprofit Yellowstone Association. There are restrooms in the parking area, and during winter the cabin doubles as a warming hut.

Sports & the Outdoors

HIKING   The very difficult 24-mi, 13-hour round-trip on the **Heart Lake–Mt. Sheridan Trail** provides one of the park's top overnight backcountry experiences. After traversing 5½ mi of partly burned lodgepole-pine forest, the trail descends into Heart Lake Geyser Basin, reaching Heart Lake at the 8-mi mark. This is one of Yellowstone's most active thermal areas—the biggest geyser here is Rustic Geyser, which erupts 25–30 feet about every 15 minutes. Circle around the northern tip of Heart Lake and camp at one of five designated backcountry sites on the western shore (remember to get your permit beforehand). Leave all but the essentials here as you take on the 3-mi, 2,700-foot climb to the top of 10,308-foot Mt. Sheridan. To the south, if you look carefully, you can see the Tetons. ⊠ *1 mi north of Lewis Lake on the east side of South Entrance Rd.*

Old Faithful

The world's most famous geyser, Old Faithful, is the centerpiece of this region of the park, which has extensive boardwalks through the Upper Geyser Basin and equally extensive visitor services, including several choices in lodging and dining. It is the one area of Yellowstone that almost all visitors include in their itinerary. You can get views of Old Faithful as it erupts from benches just yards away from the geyser, from a public balcony or some of the guest rooms at the spectacular Old Faithful Inn, and from the dining room at the lodge cafeteria, and even limited views from the Old Faithful Snow Lodge. During winter you can dine and stay in this area and cross-country ski or snowshoe through the Geyser Basin.

a good tour   Begin your tour at **Old Faithful Visitor Center ❸ ▶**, where you can look out at Old Faithful geyser, get maps of the region, watch a movie about geysers, and talk to park rangers about geyser activity. When you depart the visitor center walk to the century-old **Old Faithful Inn ❹** to check out its massive log construction; late afternoon is a good time to relax with a cool drink in the lobby, on the second-floor balcony area, or on the Old Faithful observation deck.

At Old Faithful Village you're in the heart of the **Upper Geyser Basin ❺**, a mile-square area with about 140 geysers. The biggest attraction in the geyser basin is where you should begin your tour: **Old Faithful ❻**, which spouts from 130 to 180 feet every 94 minutes or so. Once you've watched Old Faithful erupt, begin to explore the larger basin with a hike around **Geyser Hill Loop ❼**, where you'll see a variety of wildlife as well as thermal features. Heading the list of attractions is the **Morning Glory Pool ❽**, with its unique flower shape. After you have explored Geyser Hill and Morning Glory Pool, walk or drive to **Black Sand Basin ❾**, which has a dozen or so hot springs and geysers.

From Black Sand Basin, return to your car and drive north 3 mi to **Biscuit Basin ❿**, where you'll find the trailhead for the Mystic Falls Trail. There's a boardwalk through the Biscuit Basin geyser area, and you can get views of the basin and the Upper Geyser Basin from atop the hill on the Mystic Falls Trail. Return to your car and head farther north along **Firehole Lake Drive ⓫** through an area that's sometimes populated by bison and has access to additional thermal areas. Continue north to the **Lower Geyser Basin ⓬**, where you'll see the Great Fountain Geyser and White Dome Geyser as well as the colorful **Fountain Paint Pots ⓭**.

TIMING   It takes at least a day to do justice to the various sights in the Old Faithful area and the geyser basins to its north.

What to See

❾ Black Sand Basin. There are a dozen hot springs and geysers in this basin near the cloverleaf entrance from Grand Loop Road to Old Faithful. ⊠ *North of Old Faithful on Grand Loop Rd.*

❿ Biscuit Basin. Located north of Old Faithful, this basin is also the trailhead for the Mystic Falls Trail. It's an active geyser basin—sometimes there are even steam vents popping through the asphalt in the parking lot. The 2½-mi Biscuit Basin Trail, a boardwalk loop, takes you across the Firehole River to colorful Sapphire Pool. ⊠ *3 mi north of Old Faithful on Grand Loop Rd.*

⓫ Firehole Lake Drive. About 8 mi north of Old Faithful, this one-way, 3-mi road takes you north past Great Fountain Geyser, which shoots out jets of water that occasionally reach as high as 200 feet. If you're touring the park in winter, watch for bison. ⊠ *8 mi north of Old Faithful off Grand Loop Rd.*

⓭ Fountain Paint Pots. Take the easy ½-mi loop boardwalk of Fountain Paint Pot Nature Trail to see fumaroles (steam vents), blue pools, pink mud pots, and minigeysers in this geyser area. It's popular in both summer and winter because it's right next to Grand Loop Road. ⊠ *Between Old Faithful and Madison on Grand Loop Rd.*

Ⓖ **❼ Geyser Hill Loop.** Along the 1⅓-mi Geyser Hill Loop boardwalk you can see active thermal features such as violent Giantess Geyser. Normally erupting only a few times each year, Giantess spouts 100–250 feet high for five to eight minutes once or twice hourly for 12 to 43 hours. Nearby Doublet Pool consists of two adjacent springs whose complex ledges and deep blue waters are highly photogenic. Anemone Geyser

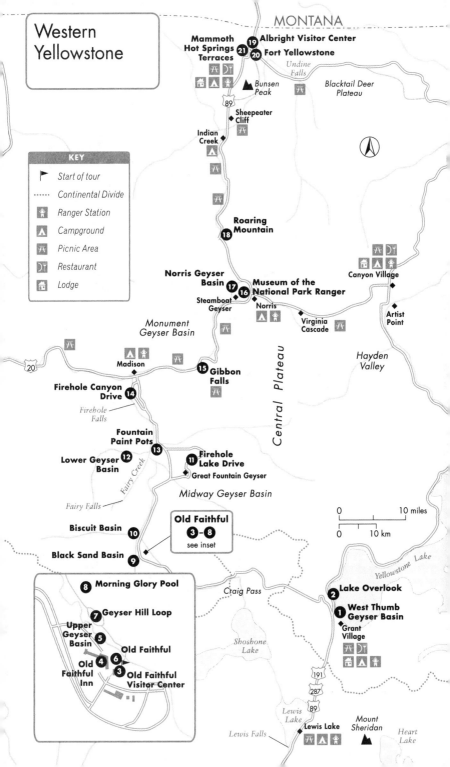

A WORLD OF GEOLOGICAL WONDERS

SPOUTING GEYSERS, bubbling mud pots, and hissing steam vents have earned fame for Yellowstone, which has the greatest concentration of thermal features in the country—nearly 10,000 of them all told.

Cataclysmic volcanoes erupted here 2 million years ago, 1.3 million years ago, and again 600,000 years ago, helping to create the steaming, vaporous landscape of today. The heat from the magma (molten rock) under the Yellowstone Caldera continues to fuel the park's most famous geyser basins—West Thumb, Upper, Lower, Midway, and Norris—which contain most of Yellowstone's 200 to 250 active geysers.

Other traces of the geological past include the basaltic columns near Tower and the steam that hisses from Roaring Mountain. The molten lava beneath the Yellowstone Caldera, one of the world's most active volcanoes, has created two resurgent

domes: Sour Creek, forming the eastern edge of Hayden Valley, and Mallard Lake, which overlooks Old Faithful from the Upper Geyser Basin, at Observation Point. In Firehole Canyon, the Firehole River runs between two lava flows; at West Thumb, a minor eruption created the Lake Yellowstone bay lined with hydrothermal features; in the park's forests, volcanic soils nurture lodgepole pine.

The superheated underground means Yellowstone is a constantly changing landscape. A geyser that is active one month may go dormant while a nearby thermal feature suddenly becomes quite intense. This potential for constant change makes Yellowstone a place where you can see something new and different each time you visit.

starts as a gentle pool, overflows, bubbles, and finally erupts 10 feet or more, repeating the cycle every three to eight minutes. The loop board-walk brings you close to the action, making it especially appealing to children intrigued with the sights and sounds of the geyser basin. Also keep a lookout for elk and buffalo in this area. To reach Geyser Hill, head counterclockwise around the Old Faithful boardwalk ⅓ mi from the visitor center, crossing the Firehole River and entering Upper Geyser Basin. ⊠ *Old Faithful.*

Grand Prismatic Spring. This is Yellowstone's largest hot spring, 370 feet in diameter. It's in the Midway Geyser Basin, and you can reach it by following the boardwalk. The spring is deep blue in color, with yellow and orange rings formed by bacteria that give it the effect of a prism. ⊠ *Midway Geyser Basin off Grand Loop Rd.*

Great Fountain Geyser. This geyser erupts twice a day; rangers predict when it will shoot some 200 feet into the air, but their prediction has a window of opportunity a couple of hours long. Should you see Great Fountain spew, however, you'll be rewarded with a view of waves of water cascading down the terraces that form the edges of the geyser. ⊠ *Firehole Lake Dr., north of Old Faithful.*

⑫ **Lower Geyser Basin.** Shooting more than 150 feet, the Great Fountain Geyser is the most spectacular sight in this basin, midway between Old Faithful and Madison. Less impressive but more regular is White Dome Geyser, which shoots from a 20-foot-tall cone. You'll also find pink mud pots and blue pools at the Fountain Paint Pots, which are a part of this basin. ⊠ *Between Old Faithful and Madison.*

Midway Geyser Basin. A series of boardwalks wind their way through Midway Geyser Basin, a favorite stop of most visitors in Yellowstone, particularly in winter. Among the attractions is Grand Prismatic Spring. ⊠ *Between Old Faithful and Madison on Grand Loop Rd.*

❽ **Morning Glory Pool.** Shaped somewhat like a morning glory flower, this pool once was a deep blue, but tourists dropping coins and other debris into it clogged the plumbing vent. As a result, the color is no longer as striking. To reach the pool, follow the boardwalk past Geyser Hill Loop and stately Castle Geyser, which has the biggest cone in Yellowstone. It erupts every 10 to 12 hours, to heights of 90 feet, for as much as an hour at a time. From Morning Glory Pool it's about 2 mi back to the visitor center. ⊠ *At the north end of Upper Geyser Basin at Old Faithful.*

☾ ❻ **Old Faithful.** Yellowstone's most predictable big geyser—although not
Fodor'sChoice its largest or most regular—sometimes reaches 180 feet, but it averages
★ 130 feet. Sometimes it doesn't shoot as high, but in those cases the eruptions usually last longer. The mysterious plumbing of Yellowstone has lengthened Old Faithful's cycle somewhat in recent years, to every 94 minutes or so. To find out when Old Faithful is likely to erupt, check at the visitor center, or at any of the lodging properties in the area. The ¾-mi Old Faithful geyser Loop boardwalk circles the benches around Old Faithful, filled nearly all day long in summer with tourists. In winter, cross-country and snowshoe trails converge at Old Faithful. ⊠ *Southwest segment, Grand Loop Rd.*

❹ **Old Faithful Inn.** It's hard to imagine that any work could be accomplished when snow and ice blanket the region, but this historic hotel was constructed in winter 1903. It has served as a lodging property for Yellowstone visitors since opening in 1904, and because of the massive log construction it's become an attraction in its own right. Even if you don't plan to spend a night at the Old Faithful Inn, take a walk through or 45-minute guided tour of the building to admire its massive open-beam lobby and rock fireplace (where the tour begins). There are writing desks on the second-floor balcony, and during evening hours a pianist plays there as well. From the outdoor deck, reached from the second floor, you can watch Old Faithful geyser as it erupts. The tour schedule is subject to change, so call ahead to confirm times. ⊠ *Old Faithful* ☎ *307/344–7901* ☾ *Early May–late Oct.; tours daily 9:30, 11, 2, and 3:30* ☞ *Free.*

need a break?	Late afternoon is a good time to relax with a cool drink in the lobby or on the second-floor balcony of the **Old Faithful Inn.** You'll hear piano music floating around the massive log walls and stone fireplace, and witness the hustle and bustle of visitors from around the world.

AMERICA'S FIRST NATIONAL PARK

YELLOWSTONE WAS ESTABLISHED *in 1872 as America's first national park. It's popularly believed that early-19th-century French trappers called the region Yellowstone when they heard a Sioux description of the yellow rock varieties in the deep canyon along the Yellowstone River. Only one small Shoshone band, the Sheepeaters, lived on the land now occupied by the park, but for thousands of years the Blackfeet, Crow, Bannock, Flathead, Nez Perce, and Northern Shoshone have known about the area's plentiful wildlife.*

Mountain man John Colter became the first white American to explore Yellowstone, in 1807–08. His descriptions of geysers and boiling rivers prompted some mapmakers to dub the uncharted region Colter's Hell. Reports coming out of the region in the 1820s through the 1860s eventually prompted exploration by the federal government and designation of

the area as America's first national park. At the time it was administered by the army; the National Park Service didn't come into existence until 1916.

Yellowstone's history is preserved in the park, at Norris's Museum of the National Park Ranger and in the displays and archives at the Albright Visitor Center in Mammoth. During Heritage Days, held twice each summer (generally in June and August), authors and researchers share their knowledge of Yellowstone history in presentations on topics ranging from Chief Joseph and the Nez Perce Indians to the fashions worn by park visitors over the decades.

➤ ❸ **Old Faithful Visitor Center.** Located 600 feet from Old Faithful, this A-frame building has one of the best views in the park of the famous geyser. A 100-seat theater shows a movie about geysers. You can get information from park rangers about all types of services and opportunities within the park and purchase a book that will help you better understand and explore it. ⊠ *Old Faithful* ☎ *307/545–2750* ☉ *June–Aug., daily 8–7; Sept., daily 8–6; Oct., daily 9–5.*

❺ **Upper Geyser Basin.** With Old Faithful as its central attraction, this mile-square basin contains about 140 different geysers—one-fifth of the known geysers in the world. It's an excellent place to spend a day or more exploring. You will find a complex system of boardwalks and trails—some of them used as bicycle trails—that take you to the basin's various attractions. ⊠ *Old Faithful.*

Sports & the Outdoors

BICYCLING A paved 2-mi trail, **Old Faithful to Morning Glory Pool,** starts at the Hamilton Store at Old Faithful Village, loops near Old Faithful geyser, and ends at Morning Glory Pool. The entire route is through a geyser basin, so stay on the trail. Watch for elk and buffalo.

HIKING From the Biscuit Basin boardwalk's west end, **Mystic Falls Trail** gently climbs 1 mi (3½ mi round-trip from Biscuit Basin parking area) through heavily burned forest to the lava-rock base of 70-foot Mystic Falls. It then switchbacks up Madison Plateau to a lookout with the park's least-crowded view of Old Faithful and Upper Geyser Basin. ⊠ *3 mi north of Old Faithful Village off Grand Loop Rd.*

Old Faithful and its environs in the Upper Geyser Basin are rich in short-walk options, starting with three connected loops that depart from Old Faithful Visitor Center. **Observation Point Loop,** a 2-mi round-trip from the visitor center, leaves Geyser Hill Loop boardwalk and becomes a trail shortly after the boardwalk crosses the Firehole River; it circles a picturesque overview of Geyser Hill with Old Faithful Inn as a backdrop. ⊠ *Old Faithful Village.*

Shoshone Lake–Shoshone Geyser Basin Trail is a 22-mi, 11-hour, moderately difficult overnight trip combining several shorter trails. The trail starts at DeLacy Creek Trail, gently descending 3 mi to the north shore of Shoshone Lake. On the way, look for sandhill cranes and browsing moose. At the lake turn right and follow the North Shore Trail 8 mi, first along the beach and then through lodgepole-pine forest. Make sure you've reserved one of the several good backcountry campsites—reservations can be made at any ranger station in the park. Take time to explore the Shoshone Geyser Basin, reached by turning left at the fork at the end of the trail and walking about ¼ mi. The next morning turn right at the fork, follow Shoshone Creek for 2 mi, and make the gradual climb over Grant's Pass. At the 17-mi mark the trail crosses the Firehole River and divides; take a right onto Lone Star Geyser Trail and continue past this fine coned geyser through Upper Geyser Basin backcountry to Lone Star Geyser Trailhead. ⊠ *8 mi east of Old Faithful Village on north side of Grand Loop Rd.*

Madison

The area around the junction of the West Entrance Road and the Lower Loop is a good place to take a break as you travel through the park, because you will almost always see bison grazing along the Madison River, and often elk are in the area as well. You'll find limited visitor services here, though there is an amphitheater for programs as well as a Yellowstone Association bookstore and a picnic area. There are no dining facilities, and the only lodging is a campground.

What to See

🄬 **Firehole Canyon Drive.** This one-way, 2-mi detour off Grand Loop Road runs in a southerly direction just south of Madison Junction. The road twists through the 700- to 800-foot-deep canyon and passes the 40-foot Firehole Falls. ⊠ *1 mi south of Madison on Grand Loop Rd.*

🄭 **Gibbon Falls.** Water rushes over the caldera rim in this 84-foot waterfall on the Gibbon River. ⊠ *4 mi east of Madison on Grand Loop Rd.*

Sports & the Outdoors

BICYCLING Fountain Flats Drive departs the Grand Loop Road south of the Nez Perce picnic area and follows the Firehole River to a trailhead 1½ mi

GETTING ACTIVE IN YELLOWSTONE

YELLOWSTONE IS FILLED with opportunities to enjoy the outdoors and take part in sports—first and foremost hiking, but also bicycling, fishing, and horseback riding. There are more miles of trails than roads, reflecting the importance of hiking in the park.

You'll find here general information and park-wide resources that can help you get active. Details about specific activity locations (such as hiking trails and bike routes) are listed under "Sports & the Outdoors" in community sections within this chapter.

Hiking

There are 1,210 mi of trails and 85 trailheads in Yellowstone. Many of the trails are easy nature walks, often along boardwalks, past popular thermal features; others are more serious hikes. Trails are occasionally closed because of bad weather conditions or bear activity. Guided hikes are led by park rangers and concessionaires.

To help visitors learn about the flora, fauna, and geology of the park, the **Yellowstone Association Institute** offers daylong hiking excursions; multiday "Lodging and Learning" trips geared around hikes, some of them designed for families (there are age restrictions on some trips); and full-blown backcountry backpacking trips. The Lodging and Learning trips include nightly accommodations at park facilities, but for the hikes you bring your own personal gear; they provide group gear and instruction plus permits as needed and some meals. The association also offers courses on topics ranging from nature writing to wolf biology. Taught by college professors or other experts, most courses are for people age 18 and older. ⬠ Box 117, Yellowstone National Park, WY 82190 ☎ 307/344–2293 ⊠ 307/344–2486 ⊕ www.yellowstoneassociation.org

🚃 $150–$320, guided trips; $299–$929, Lodging and Learning trips.

Bicycling

More and more visitors tour Yellowstone by bicycle every year, despite the heavy traffic, large vehicles, and sometimes narrow, shoulderless roads that can make the going hazardous. To be on the safe side, ride single file and wear a helmet and reflective clothing. Remember that some routes, such as those over Craig Pass, Sylvan Pass, and Dunraven Pass, are especially challenging because of their steep climbs. Bikes are prohibited on most hiking trails and in the backcountry.

There are no bike rentals within Yellowstone, but **Free Heel and Wheel,** just outside the West Entrance, rents bikes and dispenses advice, and sells hiking and cross-country skiing gear. ⊠ 40 Yellowstone Ave., West Yellowstone, MT ☎ 406/646–7744 ⊕ www. freeheelandwheel.com.

Boating

Yellowstone Lake attracts the most attention, but the park is filled with pristine waters waiting to be explored. Most of its 175 lakes, except for Sylvan Lake, Eleanor Lake, and Twin Lakes, are open for boating. You must purchase a $5 permit for boats and floatables or a $10 permit for motorized boats at Bridge Bay Marina, Grant Village visitor center, Lewis Lake Campground, or Mammoth Hot Springs visitor center.

Fishing

Anglers flock to Yellowstone on Memorial Day weekend, when fishing season begins. By the time the season ends in November, thousands have found a favorite spot along the park's rivers and streams. Many varieties of trout—cutthroat, brook, lake, and rainbow—along with grayling and mountain whitefish inhabit Yellowstone's waters.

Popular sportfishing opportunities include the Gardner and Yellowstone rivers as well as Soda Butte Creek, but the top fishing area in the region is Madison River, known to fly fishermen throughout the country. Catch and release is the general policy. You can get a copy of the fishing regulations at any visitor center. Fishing supplies are available at general stores found throughout the park; the biggest selection is at Bridge Bay.

Fishing permits are required for people over age 16; they cost $20 for a 7-day permit or $35 for a season permit. Anglers ages 12 to 15 must have a nonfee permit; those younger than 12 don't need a permit but must be with an adult who knows the regulations. Permits are available at all ranger stations, visitor centers, and general stores.

Horseback Riding

About 50 area outfitters lead horse-packing trips and trail rides into Yellowstone. Expect to pay about $1,400 for a four-night backcountry trip, including meals, accommodations, and guides. A guide must accompany all horseback-riding trips.

One- and two-hour horseback trail rides run by **Xanterra Parks & Resorts** leave from three sites in the park: Mammoth Hot Springs, Roosevelt Lodge, and Canyon Village. Children must be at least 8 years old and 48 inches tall; kids 8–11 must be accompanied by someone age 16 or older. ✆ Box 165, Mammoth Hot Springs, Yellowstone, WY 82190 ☎ 307/344-7901 ⊕ www.travelyellowstone.com ✉ $31–$50.

Since 1968, **Gunsel Horse Adventures** has provided 4-, 7-, or 10-day pack trips into the Yellowstone backcountry. The trips are a great way to see moose, bear, deer, elk, and wolves in Yellowstone's forests. Bring only your sleeping bag and personal effects. They also offer day trips several

times a week from May through October. ✆ Box 1575, Rapid City, SD 57709 ☎ 605/343-7608 ⊕ www.gunselhorseadventures.com ✉ $210–$250 per day; $1,400–$1,500 multiday backcountry trips.

Outfitter Gary Fales has been leading multiday pack trips into Yellowstone for decades, operating out of **Rimrock Dude Ranch** west of Cody. His favorite trip heads into the southeast corner of Yellowstone, leaving from near the East Entrance and riding up Eagle Creek into Thorofare country before following the South Fork of the Shoshone River out of the park area. Regular trips include treks between the Cody area and Jackson. Trips last a week and include backcountry camping, fishing, hiking, and horseback activities. All food and camping items are provided. ✉ 2728 Northfork Rte., Cody, WY 82414 ☎ 307/587-3970 or 800/208-7468 🖷 307/527-5014 ⊕ www.rimrockranch.com ✉ $300 per day; $2,000 for trips linking Cody and Jackson.

Outfitters **Tory and Meredith Taylor** offer backcountry horse-packing trips in Yellowstone. All meals are included as well as group equipment; you will need your own sleeping bag and personal gear. ✆ 6360 Hwy. 26, Dubois, WY 82513 ☎ 307/455-2161 🖷 307/455-3169 ✉ $895–$1,495.

With **Wilderness Pack Trips,** you can take a guided day trip, have them pack in your gear and leave it at a drop camp, or take a full multiday guided pack trip in the northeast region of the park, primarily the Lamar Valley. ✆ Box 1146, Livingston, MT 59047 ☎ 406/222-5128 ⊕ www.wildernesspacktrips.com ✉ $350 per day up to $2,400 for multiday trips.

away. From there, the **Fountain Freight Road** continues along the old roadbed, giving bikers access to the Sentinel Meadows Trail and the Fairy Falls Trail. The total length of the route is 5½ mi. Mountain bikes are recommended; you'll share Fountain Flats Drive with one-way automobile traffic and the Freight Road with hikers.

Norris

Norris, at the western junction of the Upper and Lower Loops, has the most active geyser basin in the park. The underground plumbing occasionally reaches such high temperatures—the ground itself has heated up in areas to nearly 200°F—that a portion of the basin is periodically closed for safety reasons. There are limited visitor services: you'll find two museums, a bookstore, and a picnic area.

Allow at least half a day to explore Norris Geyser Basin. It's a good idea to consult with rangers at the Norris Geyser Basin Museum about when different geysers are expected to erupt and to plan your walk accordingly. Rangers also will know whether any areas of the geyser basin are closed.

What to See

🔟 **Museum of the National Park Ranger.** The former Norris Soldier Station, a historic log building that from 1886 to 1916 housed soldiers who guarded the park, is now a museum where you can see a movie telling the history of the National Park Service and exhibits related to army service in Yellowstone and early park rangers. ⊠ *Grand Loop Rd. at Norris* ☉ *June–Sept., daily 10–5.*

Ⓒ 🗗 **Norris Geyser Basin.** The oldest geyser basin in Yellowstone, Norris is
Fodor'sChoice also the most volatile of all the geyser areas of the park. It's constantly
★ changing: some geysers might suddenly stop flowing, while new ones blow and hiss to life. Here you'll discover colorfully named features such as Whirligig Geyser, Whale's Mountain, Emerald Spring, and Arch Steam Vent. The area is accessible via an extensive system of boardwalks, some of them suitable for people with disabilities.

Stop in at the **Norris Geyser Basin Museum** (☉ late May–early Oct., daily 10–5) and have a look at the exhibits on geothermal geology, life in thermal areas, and the features of the basin. The museum building, erected 1929–30, is a National Historic Landmark.

There are several geysers of note in Norris's **Back Basin** area, accessible via the 1½-mi loop of Back Basin Trail. The most famous geyser here, Steamboat, performs rarely—sometimes going for years without an eruption—but when it does, it shoots a stream of water nearly 400 feet, making it the world's tallest geyser. Cistern Spring drains when Steamboat erupts. More dependable Echinus Geyser erupts 50–100 feet every 35–75 minutes.

The **Porcelain Basin** in the eastern portion of the Norris area is reached by a ¾-mi, partially boardwalked loop from the north end of Norris Geyser Basin Museum. In this geothermal field of whitish geyserite stone, the earth bulges and belches from the underground pressure. You'll find bubbling pools, some milky white and others ringed in orange because of the minerals in the water, and small geysers such as extremely active Whirligig.

⓲ Roaring Mountain. There is little vegetation on this bare mountain north of Norris, but the area is a good location for spotting bears, and it's known for steam vents that can be seen all across the acidic hillside. ⊠ *4 mi north of Norris on Grand Loop Rd.*

Mammoth Hot Springs

This part of Yellowstone is known for its massive natural terraces, where mineral water flows continuously, building an ever-changing display. You will almost always see elk grazing in the area. Mammoth Hot Springs is also headquarters for Yellowstone National Park. In the early days of the park, it was the site of Fort Yellowstone, and the brick buildings constructed during that era are still used for various park activities. The Albright Visitor Center has information and displays about the park history, including some of the original Thomas Moran paintings, created on an 1871 government expedition to the area, that made the broader public aware of Yellowstone's beauty and helped lead to its establishment as a national park. There is a complete range of visitor services here as well. Schedule about half a day for exploration. There are lots of steps on the lower terrace boardwalks, so plan to take your time there.

What to See

⓳ Albright Visitor Center. This red-roof building, which served as bachelor quarters for cavalry officers from 1886 to 1918, now holds a museum with exhibits on the early inhabitants of the region and a theater showing films about the history of the park. There are original Thomas Moran paintings of park sites on display here as well. ⊠ *Mammoth Hot Springs* ☎ *307/344–2263* ◷ *June–Aug., daily 8–7; Sept., daily 9–6; Oct.–May, daily 9–5.*

⓴ Fort Yellowstone. The oldest buildings at Mammoth Hot Springs served as Fort Yellowstone from 1886 to 1918, the period when the U.S. Army managed the park. The redbrick buildings cluster around an open area reminiscent of a frontier-era fort parade ground. You can pick up a self-guided tour map of the area to make your way around the historic fort structures. ⊠ *Mammoth Hot Springs.*

㉑ Mammoth Hot Springs Terraces. Multicolored travertine terraces formed by slowly escaping hot mineral water mark this unusual geological formation. It constantly changes as a result of shifts in water flow. You can explore the terraces via an elaborate network of boardwalks. The Lower Terrace Interpretive Trail leads past the most outstanding features: Start at Liberty Cap, at the area's north end, named for its resemblance to Revolutionary War–era tricornered hats. Head uphill on the boardwalks past bright and ornately terraced Minerva Spring. Alternatively, drive up to the Lower Terrace Overlook on Upper Terrace Drive and take the boardwalks down past New Blue Springs (which, inexplicably, is no longer blue) to the Lower Terrace. This route works especially well if you can park a second vehicle at the foot of Lower Terrace. Either route should take about an hour. ⊠ *Northwest corner of Grand Loop Rd.*

Sports & the Outdoors

BICYCLING   Automobiles and bicycles share the gravel **Old Gardiner Road** running parallel to U.S. 89 between Mammoth Hot Springs and the nearby town of Gardiner; cars can travel only north, but bikes are allowed in both directions. The 5-mi route has views of the Gardner River. Mountain bikes are recommended.

HIKING   **Beaver Ponds Loop Trail** is a 2½-hour, 5-mi round-trip starting at Liberty Cap. It climbs 400 feet through ½ mi of spruce and fir, passes through open meadows and past beaver ponds (look for their dams), and has spectacular views of Mammoth Terraces on the way down. Moose, antelope, and occasional bears may be sighted. ⊠ *Grand Loop Rd. at Old Gardiner Rd.*

Past the entrance to Bunsen Peak Road, the moderately difficult **Bunsen Peak Trail** is a 4-mi, three-hour round-trip climbing 1,300 feet to Bunsen Peak for a panoramic view of Blacktail Plateau, Swan Lake Flats, the Gallatin Mountains, and the Yellowstone River valley. (Use a topographical map to find these landmarks.) ⊠ *Grand Loop Rd., 1½ mi south of Mammoth Hot Springs.*

The 4-mi **Osprey Falls Trail,** a two-hour round-trip, starts near the entrance of Bunsen Peak Road. A series of switchbacks drops 800 feet to the bottom of Sheepeater Canyon and the base of the Gardner River's 151-foot Osprey Falls. As at Tower Fall, the canyon walls are basalt columns formed by ancient lava flow. ⊠ *Bunsen Peak Rd., 3 mi south of Mammoth Hot Springs.*

In the park's northwest corner, the extremely difficult 16½-mi, 10-hour **Skyline Trail** is a combination trail that climbs up and over numerous peaks whose ridgelines mark the park's northwest boundary before looping sharply back down via Black Butte Creek. For much of its length the trail follows the ridgetops, with steep drop-offs on either side. ⊠ *U.S. 191, 25 mi north of West Yellowstone.*

Starting at Specimen Creek Trailhead, follow the **Specimen Creek Trail** 2½ mi and turn left at the junction, passing petrified trees to your left. At the 6½-mi mark, turn left again at the fork and start climbing 1,400 feet for 2 mi up to Shelf Lake, one of the park's highest bodies of water, at 9,200 feet altitude. Stay at one of the pair of designated backcountry campsites, which you can reserve at any ranger station in the park. Just past the lake is the trailhead for Skyline Trail. Watch for bighorn sheep as you approach Bighorn Peak's summit. The trail's most treacherous section is just past the summit, where it drops 2,300 feet in the first 2½ mi of descent; make sure you take a left where the trail forks at the big meadow just past the summit to reach Black Butte Creek Trail. Moose and elk can be seen along this last 2½-mi stretch. ⊠ *U.S. 191, 27 mi north of West Yellowstone.*

Tower-Roosevelt

The northeast region of Yellowstone is the least-visited part of the park, making it a great place to explore without running into lots of other people. You can hike or ride horseback to sights in the area, such as a petri-

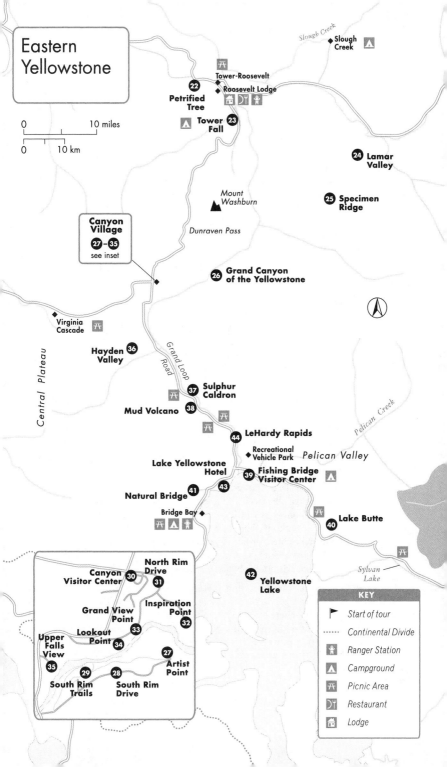

Eastern Yellowstone

0 ——— 10 miles

0 ——— 10 km

Slough Creek

◆ Slough Creek

Tower-Roosevelt

22 ◆ Roosevelt Lodge

Petrified Tree

△ **23** **Tower Fall**

24 **Lamar Valley**

25 **Specimen Ridge**

Mount Washburn

Canyon Village

27–**35** see inset

Dunraven Pass

26 **Grand Canyon of the Yellowstone**

◆ *Virginia Cascade*

Central Plateau

36 **Hayden Valley**

Grand Loop Road

37 **Sulphur Caldron**

Mud Volcano **38**

44 **LeHardy Rapids**

Pelican Creek

◆ Recreational Vehicle Park

Pelican Valley

Lake Yellowstone Hotel

39 **Fishing Bridge Visitor Center** △

Natural Bridge **41** **43**

Bridge Bay ◆

40 **Lake Butte**

42 **Yellowstone Lake**

Sylvan Lake

Canyon Village Inset

Canyon Visitor Center **30** **North Rim Drive** **31**

Grand View Point **Inspiration Point** **32**

33

Upper Falls View **35** **Lookout Point** **34**

27 **Artist Point**

29 **28**

South Rim Trails **South Rim Drive**

KEY

⚑ *Start of tour*

····· *Continental Divide*

🚹 *Ranger Station*

△ *Campground*

🌲 *Picnic Area*

🍴 *Restaurant*

🏠 *Lodge*

fied tree and a ridge filled with fossil specimens. This is where wolves were first reintroduced to the park; packs are often seen in the Lamar Valley. The area gets its appellation from the junction of the Northeast Entrance Road and the Upper Loop—named for Theodore Roosevelt—and Tower Fall, located south of the junction. It will take you a couple of hours to drive through this area and a full day if you decide to explore on foot.

What to See

㉔ Lamar Valley. The Northeast Entrance Road between Cooke City and Roosevelt slices through the broad Lamar Valley, where you are likely to see an abundance of wildlife, ranging from elk and moose to bison and wolves (which were transplanted in this area in 1995). The main wolf-watching activities in the park occur here during early-morning and late-evening hours year-round. ⊠ *Northeast Entrance Rd. between Cooke City and Roosevelt.*

㉒ Petrified Tree. A short hike takes you to this ancient petrified redwood tree, one of the most accessible specimens of its kind in the park. ⊠ *Grand Loop Rd., 1 mi west of Tower-Roosevelt.*

㉕ Specimen Ridge. The world's largest concentration of standing petrified trees can be found on this ridge in the park's northeast region, to the southwest of the Lamar Valley. There are also plenty of unusual fossils, such as impressions of leaves left behind on rocks. Access is via a difficult but rewarding 3.2-mi (one way) hike. ⊠ *About 2 mi east of Tower-Roosevelt on Northeast Entrance Rd.*

㉓ Tower Fall. View volcanic pinnacles in the area of the 132-foot Tower Fall, one of the major waterfalls on the Yellowstone River. From the lookout point at Tower Fall, the ½-mi (round-trip) Tower Fall Trail switchbacks down through pine trees matted with luminous green wolf lichen to the base of the waterfall. There you'll find yourself at the northern end of the Grand Canyon of the Yellowstone. ⊠ *2 mi south of Roosevelt on Grand Loop Rd.*

Sports & the Outdoors

BICYCLING Running parallel to Grand Loop Road, **Blacktail Plateau Drive** is a gravel road with one-way traffic for cars traveling east, but bicycles are allowed in both directions. The road meanders through forest where you might see deer, coyotes, or elk. The western entrance to the road is 9 mi east of Mammoth Hot Springs, and the eastern entrance is 2 mi west of Tower-Roosevelt. Mountain bikes are recommended.

HIKING **Slough Creek Trail,** starting at Slough Creek Campground, climbs steeply for the first 1½ mi before reaching expansive meadows and prime fishing spots, where moose are common and grizzlies occasionally wander. From this point the trail, now mostly level, meanders another 9½ mi to the park's northern boundary. ⊠ *7 mi east of Tower-Roosevelt off Northeast Entrance Rd.*

Canyon

With its waterfalls and the steep canyon walls surrounding the Yellowstone River, the Canyon area is one of the most spectacular places in Yellowstone. Here in the central part of the park, near the eastern meeting point of the Upper and Lower Loops, you will find all types of visitors' services and lots of hiking opportunities—as well as lots of other visitors.

a good tour

Most Canyon visitors catch their first view of the **Grand Canyon of the Yellowstone** ▶ from **Artist Point** ㉗, where there are two viewing levels, the lower one accessible by wheelchair. After you have peered into the canyon, take at least a short hike along the rim; then return to your vehicle and backtrack along **South Rim Drive** ㉘ to the Uncle Tom's parking area. If your schedule allows, park there and hike along the **South Rim Trail** ㉙, with impressive views of the yellow walls above the river.

After your explorations from the South Canyon rim, return to the Grand Loop Road and proceed to the Canyon Village, where you should begin explorations at the **Canyon Visitor Center** ㉚; there park rangers can give you specific details about hiking opportunities, and you can learn more about bison. From the village, travel south on the one-way **North Rim Drive** ㉛, which gives you access to **Inspiration Point** ㉜, **Grand View Point** ㉝, and **Lookout Point** ㉞. Farther south you'll find a spur road that takes you to the **Upper Falls View** ㉟.

For a great early-morning or late-evening side trip with opportunities to see a variety of wildlife, travel south of Canyon and into the open meadows of the **Hayden Valley** ㊱, which is home to hundreds of bison, waterbirds, and other wildlife.

TIMING   Depending on how much hiking you want to do, it can take you anywhere from half a day to a couple of days to explore the Grand Canyon of the Yellowstone.

What to See

★ ㉗ **Artist Point.** The most spectacular view of the Lower Falls of the Yellowstone is seen from this point, which has two different viewing levels, one of which is accessible for people with disabilities. The South Rim Trail goes right past this point, and there is a nearby parking area open in both summer and winter. ⊠ *East end of South Rim Rd., Canyon.*

㉚ **Canyon Visitor Center.** An exhibit on bison, dealing with the history of the animals and their current status in the park, is one attraction at Canyon Visitor Center, where you can also obtain park information and specific details about hiking options in the Canyon area. A new visitor center is slated to open in spring 2006. ⊠ *Canyon Village* ☎ *307/242–2552* ☉ *June–Sept., daily 8–7.*

▶ ㉖ **Grand Canyon of the Yellowstone.** If you have time in Yellowstone to visit

Fodor'sChoice   only two locations, this should be one of them (the other being Old Faith-

★   ful). The cascading waterfall and rushing river carved this 24-mi-long canyon. The red-and-ochre canyon walls are topped with an emerald-green forest. The best view of the falls is from Artist Point. There are hiking trails on both the north and south rims of the canyon. ⊠ *Canyon.*

㉝ **Grand View Point.** You have a view of the Lower Falls of the Yellowstone from this spot on the north canyon rim. ⊠ *Off North Rim Dr., Canyon.*

36 Hayden Valley. You will almost always see bison grazing in this area—summer and winter—and as a result you will also often see coyotes and other predators. This broad valley was once a lake, and the rolling hills and sagebrush flats are popular grazing areas for bison, deer, and elk. A wide array of waterfowl also spends time here, lured by the placid waters of the Yellowstone River, which has not yet reached the canyon country, where it becomes a raging torrent. ⊠ *Between Canyon and Fishing Bridge on Grand Loop Rd.*

32 Inspiration Point. A spur road off North Rim Road at Canyon and a short loop walk take you to Inspiration Point, from which you can see the Grand Canyon of the Yellowstone. This is also a starting or ending point on the North Rim Trail. ⊠ *Off Spur Rd. and North Rim Dr., Canyon.*

34 Lookout Point. Located midway on the North Rim Trail, or accessible via the one-way North Rim Drive, Lookout Point gives you a view of the Grand Canyon of the Yellowstone from above the falls. From there you can descend a steep trail to stand above the lower falls. The best time to hike the trail is early morning, when sunlight reflects off the mist from the falls to create a rainbow. ⊠ *Off North Rim Dr., Canyon.*

31 North Rim Drive. This one-way, southbound road passes through Canyon Village and past Canyon Lodge to give you access to Inspiration Point, Grand View, and Lookout Point as well as to the 1¾-mi North Rim Trail, a paved, mostly flat walkway. ⊠ *Canyon.*

28 South Rim Drive. Trailheads to Uncle Tom's Trail and the South Rim Trail can be reached from South Rim Drive, as can Artist Point, the site where most visitors capture a classic view of the Yellowstone Falls on film. ⊠ *1 mi south of Canyon, off Grand Loop Rd.*

29 South Rim Trail. Partly paved and fairly flat, this 4½-mi loop along the south rim of the Grand Canyon of the Yellowstone affords impressive views and photo opportunities of the canyon and falls of the Yellowstone River. It starts at Chittenden Bridge. Along the way you can take a break for a snack or a picnic but you'll need to sit on the ground, as there are no picnic tables. Beyond Artist Point, the trail crosses a high plateau and meanders through high mountain meadows, where you're likely to see bison grazing. ⊠ *Off South Rim Dr., Canyon.*

35 Upper Falls View. A spur road off Grand Loop Road south of Canyon gives you access to the west end of the North Rim Trail and takes you down a fairly steep trail for a view of Upper Falls from almost directly above. ⊠ *¾ mi south of Canyon, off Grand Loop Rd.*

Sports & the Outdoors

HIKING Take in some great views from the several **Grand Canyon of the Yellowstone trails.** You can wander along small sections of the trails or combine them into a three-hour trek through one of the park's most breathtaking areas. To hear and feel the Yellowstone River's power, follow the steep side trails into the canyon. ⊠ *1 mi south of Canyon Village.*

★ Especially scenic, the **Brink of the Lower Falls Trail** branches off of the North Rim Trail at the Brink of the Upper Falls Parking Area. The steep

EVER-CHANGING YELLOWSTONE

YELLOWSTONE IS DEFINITELY NOT *a sleepy world of natural wonders. The park truly feels alive when you see mud pots, steam vents, fumaroles, and paint pots—all different aspects of the park's geyser basins, and all intriguing. Beyond the geyser activity, seasonal changes in wildlife and vegetation make Yellowstone fascinating to visit over and over again.*

Though Old Faithful continues to spew routinely, even it has changed in recent years because of various factors. The geyser now erupts about every 94 minutes (up from 78 minutes in 1990), and it may look different each time. Monitoring shows that Old Faithful almost always spews forth the same amount of water at each eruption, but how it does so varies. Sometimes it shoots higher and faster, whereas other times it lasts longer but doesn't reach so high in the sky.

Other geyser basin features aren't so reliable. The force and nature of the various geysers depend on several factors, including the complex underground geology at Yellowstone. Rangers say the greatest threats to the geyser basin activity are earthquakes (which occur regularly in the region, though they are usually very small tremors) and the impact caused by people. In past years, for example, people threw hundreds of coins into the bright blue Morning Glory Pool. The coins eventually clogged the pool's water vents, causing it to change color to a sickly green. Though it has been cleaned and people are warned not to throw anything into it, the Morning Glory Pool has never regained its pristine color.

Besides its unique geology, Yellowstone has many other faces. There are petrified forests and fossil remains of both plants and animals. The ongoing ecological development of the region draws widespread interest. The reintroduction of

wolves to the ecosystem and efforts to control the movement of bison—to keep them from wandering out of the park during the winter months in search of food—are just two examples of issues that divide opinions on the management of Yellowstone.

Bison leave the park in winter—mainly through the North and West entrances—in part because of overpopulation and the need to find adequate feed. Their movements are sometimes made easier by the winter grooming of Yellowstone roads for use by over-snow vehicles.

Wolves were brought back to Yellowstone in 1995. They acclimated so well that they quickly formed several packs, some of which have ventured outside the park's boundaries. (Wolves from Yellowstone's packs have been spotted as far south as northern Utah and Colorado.) Their presence has had a lasting effect on wildlife populations. The wolves feed on both elk and buffalo, and researchers have noted a significant decline in elk calf survival throughout the region as a result of wolf predation. Park rangers have also reported a significant decline in Yellowstone's coyote population. Since the wolves are bigger and stronger than coyotes, they kill coyotes or force them to find a new range.

When massive wildfires tore through Yellowstone in 1988, some believed it would take generations for the park to recover. Already, the park has begun to renew itself. Certainly, when you visit Yellowstone now you will see reminders of fires from 1988 and more recent fires in 2001 and 2002, but you will also see the new growth. Lodgepole-pine forests need fire to release their seeds, and once seeds get a start, trees grow quickly. The new growth provides excellent cover for animals, making it harder for visitors to see wildlife such as elk, deer, and bears.

½-mi one-way trail switchbacks 600 feet down to within a few yards of the top of the Yellowstone River's Lower Falls.

The spectacular and very strenuous 700-step **Uncle Tom's Trail** (⊠ Artist Point Dr., about ½ mi east of Chittenden Bridge) descends 500 feet from the parking area to the roaring base of the Lower Falls of the Yellowstone. Much of this walk is on steel sheeting, which can have a film of ice on early summer mornings or anytime in spring and fall.

Fishing Bridge

In this part of the park you might see grizzly bears; they like to hunt for fish spawning or swimming near Yellowstone Lake's outlet to the Yellowstone River. It is also a popular fishing area and a trailhead for routes headed into the Pelican Valley. At this important park junction, where the East Entrance Road meets the Lower Loop, there are some visitor services, including limited dining, but no lodging other than the Fishing Bridge RV Park, where only hard-sided vehicles are allowed because of the presence of grizzly bears.

What to See

㊴ Fishing Bridge Visitor Center. With a distinctive stone-and-log design, this building, dating from 1931, has been designated a National Historic Landmark. It has exhibits on birds and other wildlife found in Yellowstone. Take note, particularly, of the overhead light made from the skulls and horns of Rocky Mountain bighorn sheep. ⊠ *East Entrance Rd.* ☎ *307/242–2450* ☺ *Memorial Day–Sept., daily 8–7.*

㊵ Lake Butte. Reached by a spur road off the East Entrance Road, this wooded promontory rising 615 feet above Yellowstone Lake is a prime spot for watching the sun set over the lake. ⊠ *2 mi east of Fishing Bridge on East Entrance Rd.*

㊳ Mud Volcano. The ¾-mi round-trip Mud Volcano Interpretive Trail loops gently around seething, sulfuric mud pots with names such as Black Dragon's Cauldron and Sizzling Basin and makes its way around Mud Volcano itself, a boiling pot of brown goo. ⊠ *10 mi south of Canyon; 4 mi north of Fishing Bridge on Grand Loop Rd.*

㊶ Natural Bridge. You can take an easy 1-mi hike or bicycle ride from Bridge Bay Campground to Natural Bridge, which was formed by erosion of a rhyolite outcrop by Bridge Creek. The top of the bridge is about 50 feet above the creek, and there is a trail to its top, though travel over the bridge itself is restricted. ⊠ *1 mi west of Bridge Bay Campground.*

㊲ Sulphur Caldron. You can smell the sulphur before you even leave your vehicle to walk to the overlook of Sulphur Caldron, where hissing steam escapes from a moonscape-like surface as superheated bubbling mud. ⊠ *9½ mi south of Canyon; 4½ mi north of Fishing Bridge on Grand Loop Rd.*

off the
beaten
path

PELICAN VALLEY – The long valley following Pelican Creek is some of the best wildlife habitat in the lower 48 states. A hike up it is likely to include sightings of bison, elk, moose, osprey, eagles, sandhill cranes, and possibly grizzly bears. There is a variety of trails in the valley, ranging from the 3.4-mi trail to Pelican Creek Bridge, to the 16-mi trail that takes you clear across the broad meadow and forest ecosystem. Because this area is so widely used by grizzly bears, there are certain restrictions, including no trail hiking during evening and night hours. For backcountry users, campsites are established outside the valley itself. The trailhead for Pelican Valley is east of Fishing Bridge; inquire at the visitor center there for trail conditions and restrictions. ⊠ *3 mi east of Fishing Bridge.*

Yellowstone Lake

The tranquillity of massive Yellowstone Lake, located in the southeastern segment of the park, permeates Lake Village, where you will find lodging and dining geared to a slower pace, as well as opportunities to take part in water sports, including boating and fishing.

What to See

43 **Lake Yellowstone Hotel.** Completed in 1891 and spiffed up for its centennial in 1991, this historic structure feels fresh and new as you lounge in white wicker chairs and watch the waters of Yellowstone Lake through massive windows. It got its columned entrance in 1903, when the original bland facade was reworked by the architect of the Old Faithful Inn. Now it is on the National Register of Historic Places. ⊠ *Lake Village Rd.* ☎ *307/344–7901* ☉ *Mid-May–late Sept.*

Fodor'sChoice
★

44 **LeHardy Rapids.** This is the point where Yellowstone Lake feeds into the Yellowstone River. It's a good place for an evening drive to watch for waterfowl. ⊠ *2 mi north of Fishing Bridge on Grand Loop Rd.*

If you feel like letting someone else do the driving, you can opt for the **LeHardy Rapids-Lake Butte Bus Tour.** The sunset tour originates at the Lake Yellowstone Hotel, where you board a 1937 touring bus to travel to the rapids and then on to the Lake Butte Overlook in time to watch the sun go down over the western mountains. The driver delivers a narrative of historical and natural information as you travel along the shores of Yellowstone Lake. You're likely to spot a variety of wildlife, ranging from bison and elk to waterbirds or coyotes. The tour takes a couple of hours. ⊠ *Lake Yellowstone Hotel* ☑ *$25* ☉ *Daily, sunset.*

42 **Yellowstone Lake.** Yellowstone Lake is one of the largest alpine lakes in the world, encompassing 136 square mi and located in a caldera—crater formed by a volcano—that filled with the melt from glaciers. The lake has 110 mi of shoreline, much of it followed by the East Entrance Road and Grand Loop Road, along which you will often see moose, elk, waterfowl, and other wildlife. During winter you will often see coyotes and otters along the lakeshore. Streams flowing into the lake mean it has an abundant supply of fish. ⊠ *East Entrance Rd. and southeast segment, Grand Loop Rd.*

Sports & the Outdoors

BICYCLING Leading off Grand Loop Road at Bridge Bay along the western shore of Yellowstone Lake, **Natural Bridge Road** is an easy 1-mi bike loop leading to Natural Bridge, a 50-foot cliff cut through by Bridge Creek.

CloseUp

PLAYING IN THE SNOW

EVEN IF YOU'VE VISITED *Yellowstone many times in summer, you might not recognize it after the first snowfall. Rocky outcroppings are smoothed over. Waterfalls are transformed into jagged sheets of ice. The most satisfying—and often the only—way to explore this world by snowshoe, ski, or snowmobile.*

Nordic Skiing & Snowshoeing

The **Yellowstone Association Institute** *offers everything from daylong cross-country skiing excursions to multiday "Lodging and Learning" trips geared around skiing and snowshoeing treks. You bring your own personal gear; they provide group gear and instruction plus permits as needed and some meals. Ski instruction is available.* ✇ Box 117, Yellowstone National Park, WY 82190 ☎ 307/344–2293 🖷 307/344–2486 ⊕ www.yellowstoneassociation.org ✉ $150–$255, excursions; $673–$823, Lodging and Learning trips.

At Mammoth Hot Springs Hotel and Old Faithful Snow Lodge, **Xanterra Parks & Resorts** *rents skis and snowshoes. Skier shuttles run from Mammoth Hotel to Mammoth Terraces and to Tower and from Old Faithful Snow Lodge to Fairy Falls.* ☎ 307/344–7901 ⊕ www. travelyellowstone.com ✉ $11–$28.

Lone Star Geyser Trail *is an easy 2.3 mi to the Lone Star Geyser, starting south of Keppler Cascades. You can ski back to the Old Faithful area.* ✉ Shuttle at Old Faithful Snow Lodge; trailhead 3½ mi west of Old Faithful Village.

Five ski trails begin at the **Madison River Bridge** *trailhead. The shortest is 4 mi and the longest is 14 mi.* ✉ West Entrance Rd., 6 mi west of Madison.

When you need a break from the cold, you can stop at a strategically located hut. Warming huts at Canyon Village, West Thumb, and Madison are intermittently

staffed; huts at Indian Creek, Fishing Bridge, and Old Faithful Village are unstaffed. All are open 24 hours.

Free Heel and Wheel, *outside the West Yellowstone entrance gate, is a source for cross-country ski gear and advice.* ✉ 40 Yellowstone Ave., West Yellowstone, MT ☎ 406/646–7744 ⊕ www. freeheelandwheel.com.

Snowmobiling

Snowmobiling is an exhilarating way to experience Yellowstone. It's also controversial: there's heated debate about the pollution and disruption to animal habitats. The number of riders per day is limited, and you must have a reservation, a guide, and a four-stroke engine (which is less polluting than the two-stroke variety). Regulations are subject to change.

Xanterra Parks & Resorts *rents snowmobiles from Mammoth Hotel and Old Faithful Snow Lodge and leads tours through the park from Mammoth Hot Springs.* ☎ 307/344–7311 ⊕ www. travelyellowstone.com ✉ Rentals $115–$150 per day.

Jackson-based **National Park Adventures** *conducts one- and multiday snowmobile trips into Yellowstone, centering on Canyon and Old Faithful. Lodging is is sometimes within the park, sometimes just outside.* ✉ 155 W. Broadway, Jackson, WY ☎ 307/733–1572 or 800/255–1572 ✉ $225 per day includes breakfast and lunch; multiday tours from $300 per day, including lodging.

Yellowstone Tour & Travel *rents snowmobiles and leads trips into the park. Longer-term packages include lodging in West Yellowstone.* ✉ 211 Yellowstone Ave., West Yellowstone, MT ☎ 406/646–9310 or 800/221–1151 ⊕ www. yellowstone-travel.com ✉ Rentals $140–$184 per day.

BOATING Watercraft from rowboats to powerboats are available at **Bridge Bay Marina** by the hour or by the day for trips on Yellowstone Lake. You can even rent 22- and 34-foot cabin cruisers. ⊠ *Grand Loop Rd., 2 mi south of Lake Village* ☎ *307/344–7311* ⌨ *$8–$37 per hour* ◔ *Mid-June–mid-Sept., daily 8 AM–9:30 PM.*

Yellowstone Lake Scenic Cruises, run by Xanterra Parks & Resorts, operates the *Lake Queen II* from out of Bridge Bay Marina on Yellowstone Lake. The one-hour cruises make their way to Stevenson Island and then return to Bridge Bay. Boats depart throughout the day. ⊠ *Bridge Bay Marina* ☎ *307/344–7311* ⌨ *$10.50* ◔ *June–mid-Sept., daily.*

FISHING The park concessionaire **Xanterra Parks & Resorts** offers guided Yellowstone Lake fishing charters on boats large enough for as many as six guests. The cost of a charter includes your guide plus fishing gear. Charters are on 22- and 34-foot cabin cruisers that accommodate as many as three people fishing at one time. ⊠ *Grand Loop Rd., 2 mi south of Lake Village* ☎ *307/344–7311* ⌨ *$66–$85 per hour* ◔ *Mid-June–early Sept.*

HIKING Starting across from a parking area, the difficult 4-mi, four-hour round-trip on **Avalanche Peak Trail** climbs 2,150 feet to the peak's 10,566-foot summit, from which you'll see the rugged Absaroka Mountains running north and south. Some of these peaks have patches of snow year-round. Look around the talus and tundra near the top of Avalanche Peak for alpine wildflowers and butterflies. Don't try this trail before late June or after early September—it may be covered in snow. At any time of year, carry a jacket: the winds at the top are strong. ⊠ *19 mi east of Lake Junction on the north side of East Entrance Rd.*

★ Well marked and mostly flat, **Storm Point Trail,** a 1½-mi loop, leaves the south side of the road for a perfect beginner's hike out to Yellowstone Lake. The trail rounds the western edge of Indian Pond, then passes moose habitat on its way to Yellowstone Lake's Storm Point, named for its frequent afternoon windstorms and crashing waves. Heading west along the shore, you're likely to hear the shrill chirping of yellow-bellied marmots, rodents that grow as long as 2 feet. Also look for ducks, pelicans, and trumpeter swans. ⊠ *3 mi east of Lake Junction on East Entrance Rd.*

WHERE TO EAT

When traveling in Yellowstone it's always a good idea to bring along a cooler—that way you can carry some snacks and lunch items for a picnic or break and not have to worry about making it to one of the more developed areas of the park, where there are restaurants and cafeterias. Generally you'll find burgers and sandwiches at cafeterias and full meals at restaurants. The prices in Yellowstone are comparable to what you'd pay outside the park. You will not find any chain restaurants or fast-food establishments in the park, but you will find a good selection of entrées such as free-range beef and chicken; game meats such as elk, venison, and trout; plus organic vegetables. At the several delis and general stores in the park you can purchase picnic items, snacks, and sandwiches.

	WHAT IT COSTS				
	$$$$	**$$$**	**$$**	**$**	**¢**
AT DINNER	over $23	$16–$22	$10–$16	$7–$11	under $7

Restaurant prices are for a main course at dinner, excluding sales tax of 5%–6%.

In Yellowstone

Grant Village

$$–$$$$ ✕ **Grant Village Restaurant.** The floor-to-ceiling windows of this lakeshore restaurant provide views of Yellowstone Lake through the thick stand of pines. The most contemporary of the park's restaurants, it makes you feel at home with pine-beam ceilings and cedar-shake walls. You'll find dishes ranging from pork and duck to prime rib; in late season you'll find a sandwich buffet on Sundays. ⊠ *Grant Village* ☎ *307/344–7311* ⌒ *Reservations essential* ⊟ *AE, D, DC, MC, V* ⊘ *Closed late Sept.–late May.*

Old Faithful

$$–$$$$ ✕ **Old Faithful Inn Dining Room.** Lodgepole-pine walls and ceiling beams, a giant volcanic rock fireplace graced with a painting of Old Faithful, and green-tinted windows etched with scenes from the 1920s set the mood here. Soaked in history, the restaurant has always been a friendly place where servers find time amid the bustle to chat with diners. Don't pass up the prime rib or elk medallions, although you can also get a burger or seafood. ⊠ *Old Faithful Village* ☎ *307/344–7311* ⌒ *Reservations essential* ⊟ *AE, D, DC, MC, V* ⊘ *Closed late Oct.–early May.*

$$–$$$$ ✕ **Old Faithful Snow Lodge.** From the wood-and-leather chairs etched with **Fodor$Choice** figures of park animals to the intricate lighting fixtures that resemble ★ snowcapped trees, there's lots of atmosphere at Old Faithful Snow Lodge. The huge windows give you a view of the Old Faithful area, and you can sometimes see the famous geyser as it erupts. Aside from Mammoth Hot Springs Dining Room, this is the only place in the park where you can enjoy a full lunch or dinner in winter. The French onion soup will warm you up on a chilly afternoon; among the main courses, look for elk, beef, or salmon. ⊠ *Old Faithful Village, far end of Old Faithful Bypass Rd.* ☎ *307/344–7311* ⊟ *AE, D, DC, MC, V* ⊘ *Closed mid-Oct.–mid-Dec. and mid-Mar.–mid-May.*

☾ ¢–$$ ✕ **Old Faithful Lodge Cafeteria.** Serving kid-friendly fare such as pizza, this noisy, family-oriented eatery has some of the best views of Old Faithful. ⊠ *South end of Old Faithful Bypass Rd.* ☎ *307/344–7311* ⊟ *AE, D, DC, MC, V* ⊘ *Closed mid-Sept.–mid-May.*

☾ ¢–$ ✕ **Geyser Grill.** When the kids are hungry, stop by this spot in the Old Faithful Snow Lodge for burgers, sandwiches, and french fries. ⊠ *Old Faithful Village* ☎ *307/344–7311* ⊟ *AE, D, DC, MC, V* ⊘ *Closed early Oct.–late May.*

Mammoth Hot Springs

$–$$$ ✕ **Mammoth Hot Springs Dining Room.** A wall of windows overlooks an expanse of green that was once a military parade and drill field at Mammoth Hot Springs. The art deco–style restaurant, decorated in shades of gray, green, and burgundy, has an airy feel with its bentwood chairs.

PICNICKING IN YELLOWSTONE

THERE ARE 49 PICNIC AREAS in the park, ranging from secluded spots with a couple of tables to more popular stops with a dozen or more tables and more amenities. Only nine areas—Snake River, Grant Village, Spring Creek, Nez Perce, Old Faithful East, Bridge Bay, Cascade Lake Trail, Norris Meadows, and Yellowstone River—have fire grates. Only gas stoves may be used in the other areas. None have running water; all but a few have pit toilets.

You can stock up your cooler at any of the general stores in the park; there is one in each major developed area. It is also possible to purchase box lunches that include drinks, snacks, sandwiches, and fruit, or vegetarian or cheese-and-crackers selections from restaurants within Yellowstone.

When you choose a picnic area, keep an eye out for wildlife; you never know when a herd of bison might decide to march through. In that case, it's best to leave your food and move a safe distance away from the big animals.

At the **Firehole River** (⊠ Grand Loop Rd., 3 mi south of Madison) you might see elk grazing along the banks. This picnic area has 12 tables and one pit toilet.

There are 11 tables in the vicinity of the busy **Fishing Bridge** (⊠ East Entrance Rd., 1 mi from Grand Loop Rd.). The picnic area is within walking distance of the amphitheater, store, and visitor center.

You are likely to see elk or buffalo along the **Gibbon Meadows** (⊠ Grand Loop Rd., 3 mi south of Norris) from one of nine tables at its area, which has a wheelchair-accessible pit toilet.

Beef, pork, and chicken are on the menu as well as a selection of pasta and vegetarian dishes. ⊠ *Mammoth Hot Springs* ☎ *307/344–7311* ⚐ *Reservations essential* ⊟ *AE, D, DC, MC, V* ☉ *Closed mid-Oct.–mid-Dec. and mid-Mar.–mid-May.*

¢–$ ✕ **Terrace Grill.** Although the exterior looks rather elegant, this restaurant in Mammoth Hot Springs serves only fast food, ranging from biscuits and gravy for breakfast to hamburgers and veggie burgers for lunch and dinner. ⊠ *Mammoth Hot Springs* ☎ *307/344–7311* ⊟ *AE, D, DC, MC, V* ☉ *Closed late Sept.–mid-May.*

Tower-Roosevelt

$$–$$$ ✕ **Roosevelt Lodge Dining Room.** At this rustic log cabin set in a pine forest, the menu ranges from barbecued ribs and Roosevelt beans to hamburgers and french fries. For a real Western adventure, call ahead to join a chuck-wagon cookout ($$$$) that includes an hour-long trail ride or a stagecoach ride. ⊠ *Tower-Roosevelt* ☎ *307/344–7311* ⊟ *AE, D, DC, MC, V* ☉ *Closed early Sept.–early June.*

Canyon

¢–$$ ✕ **Canyon Lodge Cafeteria.** The park's busiest lunch spot serves such traditional American fare as country-fried steak and hot turkey sandwiches. For early risers, it also has a full breakfast menu. ⊠ *Canyon Village* ☎ *307/344–7311* ▭ *AE, D, DC, MC, V* ⊗ *Closed mid-Sept.–early June.*

Yellowstone Lake

$$–$$$$
Fodor'sChoice
★
× **Lake Yellowstone Hotel Dining Room.** This double-colonnaded dining room off the hotel lobby will have you gazing through the big square windows overlooking the lake. Because this is one of the park's most elegant restaurants, it tends to attract an older clientele. The menu includes steak, pasta, seafood, and buffalo prime rib. Reservations are required for dinner. ⊠ *Lake Village Rd.* ☎ *307/344–7311* ▭ *AE, D, DC, MC, V* ⊗ *Closed early Oct.–mid-May.*

¢–$$
× **Lake Lodge Cafeteria.** This casual eatery, popular with families, serves hearty lunches and dinners such as spaghetti, pot roast, and fried chicken. It also has a full breakfast menu. ⊠ *Lake Village Rd.* ☎ *307/344–7311* ▭ *AE, D, DC, MC, V* ⊗ *Closed mid-Sept.–early June.*

Near the Park

Consult Chapter 2 for dining options in Jackson, Wyoming, and Grand Teton National Park, and Chapter 6 for dining options in Cody, Wyoming.

$$–$$$
× **Trapper's Inn.** This popular restaurant recalls the days of the mountain men with massive breakfasts featuring sourdough pancakes, biscuits, and rolls. Trout with eggs will fortify you for a day exploring Yellowstone. Lunch standouts include buffalo burgers on sourdough bread, and hearty steaks are a favorite for dinner. ⊠ *315 Madison Ave., West Yellowstone, MT* ☎ *406/646–9375* ▭ *AE, D, MC, V.*

$–$$$
× **Yellowstone Mine.** Decorated with mining equipment such as picks and shovels, this is a place for casual family-style dining. Town residents come in for the steaks and seafood. ⊠ *U.S. 89, Gardiner, MT* ☎ *406/848–7336* ▭ *AE, D, MC, V* ⊗ *No lunch.*

WHERE TO STAY

Park lodgings range from two of the national park system's magnificent old hotels to simple cabins to bland modern motels. They are operated by **Xanterra Parks & Resorts** (⌂ Yellowstone National Park, Box 165, Mammoth Hot Springs 82190 ☎ 307/344–7311, 307/344–7901 to contact a guest 🖷 307/344–7456 ⊕ www.travelyellowstone.com), and all accept major credit cards. Make reservations at least two months in advance for July and August for all park lodgings. Old Faithful Snow Lodge and Mammoth Hot Springs Hotel are the only accommodations open in winter; rates are the same as in summer.

Ask about the size of beds, bathrooms, thickness of walls, and room location when you book, especially in the older hotels, where accommodations vary and upgrades are ongoing. Telephones have been put in some rooms, but there are no TVs. All park lodging is no-smoking. There are no roll-away beds available.

Prices

Prices in Yellowstone are generally comparable to costs outside the park, though some of the budget options, such as simple cabins, are often less expensive in the park. In general, accommodations in the park will have fewer amenities. For example, park lodgings have no televisions, some have no telephones, and there is no air-conditioning (though it's not needed at these elevations).

WHAT IT COSTS					
	$$$$	$$$	$$	$	¢
FOR 2 PEOPLE	over $220	$159–$220	$111–$160	$70–$110	under $70

Hotel prices are for two people in a standard double room in high season, excluding service charges and 6%–9% tax.

In Yellowstone

Grant Village

$$ 🏨 **Grant Village Lodge.** The six humble lodge buildings that make up this facility have rough pine exteriors painted gray and rust. Reminiscent of a big-city motel, the complex offers basic rooms with few features beyond a bed and nightstand. ⊠ *Grant Village* ☎ *307/344–7901* 🖷 *307/344–7456* ⊕ *www.travelyellowstone.com* 📞 *300 rooms* ♻ *2 restaurants, hiking, bar, shops; no a/c, no room TVs, no smoking* ☰ *AE, D, DC, MC, V* ⊘ *Closed mid-Sept.–late May.*

Old Faithful

★ **$$$** 🏨 **Old Faithful Snow Lodge.** Built in 1998, this massive structure brings back the grand tradition of park lodges by making good use of heavy timber beams and wrought-iron accents in a distinctive facade. Inside you'll find soaring ceilings, natural lighting, and a spacious lobby with a stone fireplace. Nearby is a long sitting room where writing desks and overstuffed chairs invite you to linger. Rooms combine traditional style with modern amenities. This is one of only two lodging facilities open in winter, when the only way to get here is on over-snow vehicles. Snow Lodge also has older cabins with basic amenities. ⊠ *Far end of Old Faithful Bypass Rd.* ☎ *307/344–7901* 🖷 *307/344–7456* ⊕ *www.travelyellowstone.com* 📞 *95 rooms, 33 cabins* ♻ *Restaurant, snack bar, hiking, cross-country skiing, ski shop, snowmobiling, bar, shops; no a/c, no room TVs, no smoking* ☰ *AE, D, DC, MC, V* ⊘ *Closed mid-Oct.–mid-Dec. and mid-Mar.–May.*

$–$$$ 🏨 **Old Faithful Inn.** When you push open the massive, iron-latched front
FodorsChoice door, you enter the log-pillared lobby of one of the most distinctive na-
★ tional park lodgings. From the main building, where many gables dot the wood-shingled roof, you can watch Old Faithful erupt. Rooms in the 1904 "Old House" have brass beds, and some have deep claw-foot tubs. Rooms in the 1927 west wing contain antique cherrywood furniture, and those in the 1913 east wing have Stickley furniture and tremendous four-poster beds. First-floor rooms in the Old House are the hotel's noisiest, so ask for a rear-facing room if you are seeking some quiet. Some

of the rooms in the older sections share hallway bathrooms, though they do have sinks. Renovations to the inn are underway; a lobby renovation and roof repairs were completed in 2005 and other work will continue until 2007. The inn remains open, but its historic ambience is compromised by the construction. ⊠ *Old Faithful Village* ☎ *307/344–7901* 🖷 *307/344–7456* ⊕ *www.travelyellowstone.com* ⮌ *327 rooms, 6 suites* ⟂ *Restaurant, snack bar, hiking, bar, lobby lounge, piano bar, shops; no a/c, no phones in some rooms, no room TVs, no smoking* ▭ *AE, D, DC, MC, V* ☉ *Closed late Oct.–early May.*

¢–$ 🏨 **Old Faithful Lodge Cabins.** These older cabins located behind the Old Faithful Lodge are a good budget option. They're small and plainly decorated and have no views of Old Faithful geyser. Many do not have bathrooms. ⊠ *South end of Old Faithful Bypass Rd.* ☎ *307/344–7901* 🖷 *307/344–7456* ⊕ *www.travelyellowstone.com* ⮌ *97 cabins* ⟂ *Restaurant, snack bar, hiking, shops; no a/c, no room TVs, no smoking* ▭ *AE, D, DC, MC, V* ☉ *Closed mid-Sept.–mid-May.*

Mammoth Hot Springs

$ 🏨 **Mammoth Hot Springs Hotel and Cabins.** Built in 1937, this hotel has a spacious art deco lobby, where you'll find an espresso cart after 4 PM. The rooms are smaller and less elegant than those at the park's other two historic hotels, but the Mammoth Hot Springs Hotel is less expensive and usually less crowded. In summer the rooms can get hot, but you can open the window and there are fans. Some rooms do not have bathrooms, so you must use a bathroom down the hall. The cabins, set amid lush lawns, are the nicest inside the park. This is one of only two lodging facilities open in winter. Some cabins have hot tubs, a nice amenity after a day of cross-country skiing or snowshoeing. ⊠ *Mammoth Hot Springs* ☎ *307/344–7901* 🖷 *307/344–7456* ⊕ *www.travelyellowstone.com* ⮌ *97 rooms, 67 with bath; 2 suites; 115 cabins, 76 with bath* ⟂ *Restaurant, snack bar, hiking, horseback riding, cross-country skiing, ice-skating, ski shop, snowmobiling, bar, shops; no a/c, no room TVs, no smoking* ▭ *AE, D, DC, MC, V* ☉ *Closed mid-Sept.–mid-Dec. and mid-Mar.–late May.*

Tower-Roosevelt

¢–$ 🏨 **Roosevelt Lodge.** Near the beautiful Lamar Valley in the park's northeast corner, this simple lodge dating from the 1920s surpasses some of the more expensive options. The rustic accommodations, in nearby cabins set around a pine forest, require that you bring your own bedding. Some cabins have bathrooms, but most do not. There is a bathhouse nearby. Some rooms also have woodstoves. You can make arrangements here for horseback and stagecoach rides. ⊠ *Tower-Roosevelt Junction on Grand Loop Rd.* ☎ *307/344–7901* 🖷 *307/344–7456* ⊕ *www.travelyellowstone.com* ⮌ *80 cabins, 12 with bath* ⟂ *Restaurant, hiking, horseback riding, shops; no a/c, no room TVs, no smoking* ▭ *AE, D, DC, MC, V* ☉ *Closed early Sept.–early June.*

Canyon

$$ 🏨 **Cascade Lodge.** Pine wainscoting and brown carpets set the tone in this newer motel-style facility in the trees above the Grand Canyon of the Yellowstone. The lodge is at the farthest edge of the Canyon Vil-

lage, which means it's quite a hike to the nearest dining facilities, but it's quiet because it's away from the major traffic at Canyon. ⊠ *North Rim Dr. at Grand Loop Rd.* ☎ *307/344–7901* 🖨 *307/344–7456* ⊕ *www.travelyellowstone.com* ⤬ *40 rooms* ⚘ *Picnic area, hiking, horseback riding, bar, shops; no a/c, no room TVs, no smoking* ⊟ *AE, D, DC, MC, V* ⊘ *Closed early Sept.–early June.*

$$ ⊡ **Dunraven Lodge.** This motel-style lodge with pine wainscoting and brown carpets is in the pine trees at the edge of the Grand Canyon of the Yellowstone, adjacent to the essentially identical Cascade Lodge. It's at the farthest edge of the Canyon Village, so it's a distance to the nearest dining facilities. ⊠ *North Rim Dr. at Grand Loop Rd.* ☎ *307/344– 7901* 🖨 *307/344–7456* ⊕ *www.travelyellowstone.com* ⤬ *41 rooms* ⚘ *Picnic area, hiking, horseback riding, bar, shops; no a/c, no room TVs, no smoking* ⊟ *AE, D, DC, MC, V* ⊘ *Closed early Sept.–early June.*

¢–$$ ⊡ **Canyon Cabins.** With clusters of plain pine-frame cabins that are all duplex or fourplex units surrounding a main lodge building, this is one of Yellowstone's most bare-bones places to stay. Cabins have beds but no other amenities to speak of. Most have no running water; instead you use a bathhouse at the main lodge. ⊠ *North Rim Dr. at Grand Loop Rd.* ☎ *307/344–7901* 🖨 *307/344–7456* ⊕ *www.travelyellowstone. com* ⤬ *532 cabins* ⚘ *2 restaurants, cafeteria, picnic area, hiking, horseback riding, bar, shops; no a/c, no room TVs, no smoking* ⊟ *AE, D, DC, MC, V* ⊘ *Closed Sept.–May.*

Yellowstone Lake

★ $$$ ⊡ **Lake Yellowstone Hotel.** This distinguished hotel, dating from 1891, is popular with older visitors, who gather in the sunroom each afternoon to gaze at the lake while a pianist plays. Others browse behind the etched green windows of the expensive Crystal Palace gift shop or warm themselves on chilly days before the tile-mantel fireplace in the colonnaded lobby. Rooms have white wicker furnishings, giving them a light, airy feeling; some have lake views. There is one two-room suite with lake views that has been used as accommodations for more than one U.S. president. ⊠ *Lake Village Rd.* ☎ *307/344–7901* 🖨 *307/344– 7456* ⊕ *www.travelyellowstone.com* ⤬ *158 rooms* ⚘ *Restaurant, snack bar, boating, fishing, hiking, bar, lobby lounge, piano bar, shops; no a/c, no room TVs, no smoking* ⊟ *AE, D, DC, MC, V* ⊘ *Closed late Sept.–mid-May.*

¢–$$ ⊡ **Lake Lodge.** Among the pines not far from Lake Yellowstone Hotel, this lodge was built in 1920 but has been modernized so that the accommodations resemble those of a fairly standard motel. There are views of the lake from the lodge but not from the rooms. ⊠ *Lake Village Rd.* ☎ *307/ 344–7901* 🖨 *307/344–7456* ⊕ *www.travelyellowstone.com* ⤬ *186 rooms* ⚘ *Restaurant, snack bar, hiking, bar, shops; no a/c, no room TVs, no smoking* ⊟ *AE, D, DC, MC, V* ⊘ *Closed mid-Sept.–mid-June.*

¢–$$ ⊡ **Lake Lodge Cabins.** Located near Yellowstone Lake, these older cabins, brightened up with yellow paint, provide basic, no-frills accommodations. ⊠ *Lake Village Rd.* ☎ *307/344–7901* 🖨 *307/344–7456* ⊕ *www.travelyellowstone.com* ⤬ *186 cabins* ⚘ *Cafeteria, boating, fishing, hiking, shops; no a/c, no room TVs, no smoking* ⊟ *AE, D, DC, MC, V* ⊘ *Closed mid-Sept.–mid-June.*

$ 🏨 **Lake Yellowstone Hotel Cabins.** Set unobtrusively in the trees behind the Lake Yellowstone Hotel, these pine-paneled cabins with yellow exteriors provide basic accommodations. ⊠ *Lake Village Rd.* ☎ *307/ 344–7901* 🖷 *307/344–7456* ⊕ *www.travelyellowstone.com* ⮑ *102 cabins ♻ Restaurant, snack bar, boating, fishing, hiking, bar, shops; no a/c, no room TVs, no smoking* ☰ *AE, D, DC, MC, V* ☉ *Closed mid-Sept.–mid-June.*

Near the Park

Consult Chapter 2 for lodging options in Jackson, Wyoming, and Grand Teton National Park, and Chapter 6 for additional lodging options in Cody, Wyoming.

$–$$ ✕🏨 **Three Bear Lodge.** Earth-tone walls, carpets, and draperies and pine furnishings help set a casual and woodsy mood at this lodge. You can eat a hearty breakfast, arrange an all-day snowmobile tour, then return to this log lodge for a dinner ($–$$$) of prime rib, steak, or buffalo burgers. They don't serve lunch, but will pack a boxed meal for your day in the park. ⊠ *217 Yellowstone Ave., West Yellowstone, MT 59758* ☎ *406/ 646–7353 or 800/646–7353* 🖷 *406/646–4767* ⊕ *www.threebearlodge. com* ⮑ *73 rooms ♻ Restaurant, cable TV, Wi-Fi, outdoor pool, exercise equipment, hot tubs, snowmobiling, bar, no-smoking rooms* ☰ *AE, D, MC, V* ☉ *No lunch.*

$–$$ 🏨 **Pahaska Teepee Resort.** Just 2 mi from Yellowstone's East Entrance, these cabins in a pine forest are a good base for summer and winter recreation, both inside and outside the park. This was Buffalo Bill's original getaway in the high country—one lodge building remains from his time. The cabins, some of which stand alone and some of which are grouped together, have two, four, or six bedrooms. With seven bedrooms and a kitchen, the Reunion Lodge is ideal for big groups. A trailhead for an extensive cross-country-ski-trail network is at Pahaska, as are a gas station and trail rides. ⊠ *183 Yellowstone Hwy., Cody, WY 82414* ☎ *307/ 527–7701 or 800/628–7791* 🖷 *307/527–4019* ⊕ *www.pahaska.com* ⮑ *48 cabins, 1 lodge ♻ Restaurant, hiking, horseback riding, cross-country skiing, shop, bar, travel services, no-smoking rooms; no a/c, no room TVs* ☰ *D, MC, V.*

Camping & RV Facilities

Yellowstone has a dozen campgrounds scattered around the park. Most campgrounds have flush toilets, and some have coin-operated showers and laundry facilities. Most are operated by the National Parks Service and are available on a first-come, first-served basis. Those campgrounds run by Xanterra Parks & Resorts—Bridge Bay, Canyon, Fishing Bridge, Grant Village, and Madison—accept bookings in advance. To reserve, call 307/344–7311. Larger groups can reserve space in Bridge Bay, Grant, and Madison from late May through September.

Camping outside designated areas is prohibited, with exceptions during the winter season (October 15–May 15). There are about 300 backcountry sites available all over the park. Permits are free, and sites can be reserved for $20, regardless of the length of time spent in the park or the number of people in the group. You can make reservations by visiting any ranger station or by mail at Backcountry Office, Box 168, Yellowstone National Park, WY 82190.

All overnight backcountry camping requires a backcountry use permit, which must be obtained in person no more than 48 hours before the planned trip. For information, call the backcountry office (307/344–2160). In summer you can usually get these free permits seven days a week, from 8 to 4:30, at Mammoth Ranger Station/Visitor Center, Canyon Ranger Station/Visitor Center, Grant Village Visitor Center, South Entrance Ranger Station, Bechler Rangers Station, and Old Faithful Ranger Station. Hours vary off-season. All backcountry campsites have restrictions on group size and length of stay. Boating is prohibited throughout the backcountry, and pit fires are prohibited at certain campsites.

In Yellowstone

🏕 **Bridge Bay.** The park's largest campground, Bridge Bay rests in a wooded grove. You can rent boats at the nearby marina, take guided walks, or listen to rangers lecture about the history of the park. Don't expect solitude, as there are more than 400 campsites. Generators are allowed from 8 AM to 8 PM. Hot showers and laundry are 4 mi north at Fishing Bridge. ♻ *Flush toilets, dump station, drinking water, showers, bear boxes, fire pits, picnic tables, public telephone, ranger station* ⤳ *431 sites* ⊠ *3 mi southwest of Lake Village on Grand Loop Rd.* ☎ *307/344–7311* 🖷 *307/344–7456* ⊕ *www.travelyellowstone.com* ☎ *$17* 🖃 *AE, D, DC, MC, V* ☺ *Late May–mid-Sept.*

☺ 🏕 **Canyon.** The campground is accessible to Canyon's many short trails, which makes it a hit with families. The location is near laundry facilities and the visitor center. Generators are allowed from 8 AM to 8 PM. ♻ *Flush toilets, drinking water, guest laundry, showers, bear boxes, fire pits, picnic tables, public telephone, ranger station* ⤳ *272 sites* ⊠ *North Rim Dr., ¼ mi east of Grand Loop Rd.* ☎ *307/344–7311* 🖷 *307/344–7456* ⊕ *www.travelyellowstone.com* ☎ *$17* 🖃 *AE, D, DC, MC, V* ☺ *Early June–early Sept.*

🏕 **Fishing Bridge RV Park.** Although Fishing Bridge is on Yellowstone Lake, there's no boat access here. Near Bridge Bay Marina, this is the only facility in the park that caters exclusively to recreational vehicles. Because of bear activity in the area, only hard-sided campers are allowed. Liquid propane is available. Generators are allowed from 8 AM to 8 PM. ♻ *Flush toilets, full hookups, dump station, drinking water, guest laundry, showers, bear boxes, picnic tables, public telephone, ranger station* ⤳ *346 sites* ⊠ *East Entrance Rd. at Grand Loop Rd.* ☎ *307/344–7311* 🖷 *307/344–7456* ⊕ *www.travelyellowstone.com* ☎ *$33* 🖃 *AE, D, DC, MC, V* ☺ *Mid-May–late Sept.*

🏕 **Grant Village.** The park's second-largest campground, Grant Village has some sites with great views of Yellowstone Lake. Some of the sites are wheelchair accessible. The campground has a boat launch but no dock. Generators are allowed from 8 AM to 8 PM. ♻ *Flush toilets, dump station, drinking water, guest laundry, showers, bear boxes, picnic tables, public telephone, ranger station* ⤳ *425 sites* ⊠ *South Entrance Rd., 2 mi south of West Thumb* ☎ *307/344–7311* 🖷 *307/344–7456*

⊕ *www.travelyellowstone.com* ✉ *$17* ▭ *AE, D, DC, MC, V* ☉ *Late June–late Sept.*

⚠ **Indian Creek.** In a picturesque setting next to a creek, this campground is in the middle of a prime wildlife-viewing area. There are some combination sites that can accommodate trailers of up to 45 feet. ♿ *Pit toilets, bear boxes, fire pits, picnic tables* ⤵ *75 sites* ✉ *8 mi south of Mammoth Hot Springs on Grand Loop Rd.* ☎ *307/344–2017* ✉ *$12* ▭ *No credit cards* ☉ *Early June–mid-Sept.*

⚠ **Lewis Lake.** It's a bit off the beaten track, which means this campground south of Grant Village is quieter than most. Also, it's a good choice for boaters who don't want to fight the crowds, because it's the only campground besides Bridge Bay and Grant Village that has a boat launch. ♿ *Pit toilets, drinking water, bear boxes, fire pits, picnic tables* ⤵ *85 sites* ✉ *6 mi south of Grant Village on South Entrance Rd.* ☎ *307/344–2017* ✉ *$12* ▭ *No credit cards* ☉ *Late June–early Nov.*

⚠ **Madison.** This campground is beside the Madison River, with plenty of hiking trails nearby. It can accommodate trailers up to 45 feet. ♿ *Flush toilets, dump station, drinking water, bear boxes, fire pits, picnic tables, public telephone, ranger station* ⤵ *277 sites* ✉ *Grand Loop Rd. at Madison* ☎ *307/344–7311* 🖶 *307/344–7456* ⊕ *www.travelyellowstone.com* ✉ *$17* ▭ *AE, D, DC, MC, V* ☉ *Early May–mid-Oct.*

⚠ **Mammoth Hot Springs.** The sagebrush-covered hillside where Mammoth Hot Springs is located often attracts elk and mule deer. There are plenty of things to do at the nearby visitor center, including evening talks by park rangers. The campground is more exposed than most, so it gets hot on summer days. There are wheelchair-accessible sites at this campground. ♿ *Flush toilets, drinking water, bear boxes, fire pits, picnic tables, public telephone, ranger station* ⤵ *85 sites* ✉ *North Entrance Rd. at Mammoth Hot Springs* ☎ *307/344–2017* ✉ *$14* ▭ *AE, D, DC, MC, V.*

⚠ **Norris.** Because it adjoins the Gibbon River, this campground is a favorite among anglers. Brook trout and grayling are the prizes caught here. The campground can accommodate trailers up to 45 feet. Generators are allowed from 8 AM to 8 PM. ♿ *Flush toilets, drinking water, bear boxes, fire pits, picnic tables, ranger station* ⤵ *116 sites* ✉ *Grand Loop Rd. at Norris* ☎ *307/344–2177* ✉ *$14* ▭ *No credit cards* ☉ *Mid-May–late Sept.*

⚠ **Pebble Creek.** Near a 10,554-foot peak called the Thunderer, this campground offers some unforgettable views. It's also smaller than most, which means it tends to be a little quieter. It allows trailers up to 45 feet. ♿ *Pit toilets, bear boxes, fire pits, picnic tables* ⤵ *36 sites* ✉ *Northeast Entrance Rd., 22 mi east of Tower-Roosevelt Junction* ☎ *307/344–2017* ✉ *$12* ▭ *No credit cards* ☉ *June–late Sept.*

⚠ **Slough Creek.** Reached by a little-used spur road, this creekside campground is about as far from the beaten path as you can get without actually camping in the backcountry. It's popular among fishing aficionados, who come here for the trout. ♿ *Pit toilets, bear boxes, fire pits, picnic tables* ⤵ *29 sites* ✉ *Northeast Entrance Rd., 10 mi east of Tower-Roosevelt Junction* ☎ *307/344–2017* ✉ *$12* ▭ *No credit cards* ☉ *Late May–late Oct.*

⚠ **Tower Fall.** It's within hiking distance of the roaring waterfall, so this campground gets a lot of foot traffic. It can accommodate shorter trailers. Hot water and flush toilets are at Tower Store restrooms nearby. ⌂ *Pit toilets, bear boxes, fire pits, picnic tables* ⌁ *32 sites* ⊠ *3 mi southeast of Tower-Roosevelt on Grand Loop Rd.* ☎ *307/344–2017* ⌦ *$12* 🖃 *No credit cards* ☉ *Mid-May–late Sept.*

Near the Park

Consult Chapter 2 for camping options in Jackson, Wyoming, and Grand Teton National Park, and Chapter 6 for campgrounds in Cody, Wyoming.

⚠ **Wagon Wheel Campground and Cabins.** Located within West Yellowstone a few blocks west of the park, this campground has tent and RV sites along with cozy one-, two-, and three-bedroom cabins with porches, barbecue grills, and cable TV. No pets are allowed, and there's no smoking in the cabins. Two cabins are open year-round. ⌂ *Flush toilets, full hookups, drinking water, guest laundry, showers, public telephone* ⌁ *40 RV sites, 8 tent sites; 9 cabins* ⊠ *408 Gibbon Ave., West Yellowstone, MT 59758* ☎ *406/646–7872* ⊕ *www.wagonwheelrv.com* ⌦ *$26–$36 tent and RV sites, $55–$85 camping cabins, 3-day minimum rental* 🖃 *No credit cards* ☉ *Memorial Day–Sept. 15.*

NIGHTLIFE & THE ARTS

Nightlife

The terrace room of **Lake Yellowstone Hotel** (⊠ Lake Village Rd. ☎ 307/344–7901) has nightly piano music; the hotel also has a bar. You can listen to piano music during most summer evenings or hear a ranger talk in the large sitting room at **Mammoth Hot Springs Hotel** (⊠ Mammoth Hot Springs ☎ 307/344–7901). Piano music resounds from the second-floor balcony of the **Old Faithful Inn** (⊠ Old Faithful ☎ 307/344–7901) on summer evenings, and the inn has a cocktail bar.

Family campfire programs are held some evenings at the amphitheater of **Bridge Bay Campground** (⊠ 3 mi southwest of Lake Village on Grand Loop Rd. ☎ 307/344–7311), with information geared particularly to families with young children. These programs begin in early evening; later on most evenings there is another campfire talk geared more to adults and families with older children. Campfire programs occur at the **Canyon Campground** (⊠ North Rim Dr., ¼ mi east of Grand Loop Rd. ☎ 307/344–7311) amphitheater, including talks on Yellowstone's natural and cultural history. Rangers present some evening slide-show programs at the **Grizzly and Wolf Discovery Center** (⊠ 201 South Canyon St., West Yellowstone, MT ☎ 406/646–7001 ⊕ www.grizzlydiscoveryctr. com). The slide program is free, though there is a charge if you want to tour the center itself.

Take in the stars over Yellowstone at the amphitheater of **Madison Campground** (⊠ Grand Loop Rd. at Madison ☎ 307/344–7311). There are Friday and Saturday evening programs at 9, plus general night-sky observing some Friday and Saturday evenings beginning at 10:30. These talks help you find constellations and give you an opportunity to view celestial objects through telescopes. Meet west of the amphitheater; dress warmly and take a flashlight. Park rangers also present slide shows most summer evenings at the amphitheater. Details about programs are available in the park newspaper and from visitor centers.

Talks about natural or cultural history in Yellowstone take place nightly during summer at **Mammoth Hot Springs Campground** (⊠ North Entrance Rd. at Mammoth Hot Springs ☎ 307/344–2017) amphitheater. Information about specific programs is available in the park newspaper and from visitor centers. Family campfire programs take place nightly during the summer at the campfire circle of **Norris Campground** (⊠ Grand Loop Rd. at Norris ☎ 307/344–2177). Times and topics for programs are included in the park newspaper. Park rangers present slide shows most summer evenings in the auditorium of **Old Faithful Visitor Center** (⊠ Old Faithful ☎ 307/545–2750), with details about park history and culture. For specific times and topics, check the park newspaper or inquire at visitor centers.

The Arts

You can learn more about photography techniques and participate in early-morning photography walks at **Canyon Visitor Center** (⊠ Canyon Village ☎ 307/242–2552). Kids and adults can participate in separate photography walks and demonstrations at **Fishing Bridge Visitor Center** (⊠ East Entrance Rd. ☎ 307/242–2450). To find out about the specific times and locations for programs, check the park newspaper or a visitor center. In the map room of **Mammoth Hot Springs Hotel** (⊠ Mammoth Hot Springs ☎ 307/344–7901) a Kodak ambassador presents a program titled "Portrait of Yellowstone" one evening each week, with details on how to take better photos of Yellowstone attractions.

A one-hour or longer stroll through Geyser Hill from **Old Faithful Visitor Center** (⊠ Old Faithful ☎ 307/545–2750) is held at least once a week with the focus on photography and how to capture images of the geysers with your camera. Rangers conduct morning and evening photo walks from the parking lot at **West Thumb Geyser Basin** (⊠ Grand Loop Rd., West Thumb), giving you ample opportunity to walk through the geyser basin and learn about taking photos of the various Yellowstone features in either morning or evening light.

SHOPPING

Some of Yellowstone's stores are interesting destinations themselves. The Old Faithful Basin Lower Store, for example, has a knotty-pine porch with benches that beckon tired hikers, as well as an inexpensive and very busy lunch counter. All stores sell souvenirs ranging from the tacky (cowboy kitsch and rubber tom-toms) to the authentic ($60 buffalo-hide moccasins and $200 cowboy coats). From May to September, most stores are open 7:45 AM to 9:45 PM; Mammoth Hot Springs is open year-round. All the stores accept credit cards.

Light meals, snacks, photography supplies, and gifts are all available at the **Canyon Lodge Gift Shop** (✉ Canyon Village ☎ 307/242–7377).

Souvenirs, T-shirts and other clothing, and fishing gear are among the items you can purchase at **Fishing Bridge General Store** (✉ Fishing Bridge ☎ 307/242–7200). There's also one-hour film processing here.

Fast food, snacks, light meals, and general supplies are available at the **Grant Village General Store** (✉ Grant Village ☎ 307/242–7390).

For general supplies, including light meals, snacks, and beverages, head to the **Lake General Store** (✉ Yellowstone Lake Village ☎ 307/242–7563).

FodorsChoice ★ You will find a good selection of stoneware with fishing motifs and other fishy kinds of goods at the **Lake Yellowstone Hotel Gift Shop** (✉ Lake Village Rd. ☎ 307/344–7901).

Outdoor gear and clothing are sold at the **Mammoth Hot Springs Hotel Gift Shop** (✉ Mammoth Hot Springs ☎ 307/344–7901).

★ Top-quality Native American artwork and goods, ranging from cradle boards to jewelry, are sold at the **Old Faithful Inn Gift Shop** (✉ Old Faithful ☎ 307/344–7901).

Stock up on outdoor clothing for kids and adults plus guidebooks at the **Old Faithful Lodge Gift Shop** (✉ South end of Old Faithful Bypass Rd. ☎ No phone).

★ ☺ You can purchase outdoor clothing for winter and summer, pick up goods with a bear-related theme (stuffed animals, clothing with bear designs, carved bears), and browse the "Yellowstone Kids" section at the **Old Faithful Snow Lodge Bear Den Gift Shop** (✉ Far end of Old Faithful Bypass Rd. ☎ 307/344–7901).

For goods ranging from groceries to hiking gear to camera accessories, check out the **Yellowstone General Store** (✉ Mammoth ☎ 307/344–7702).

You can get fuel, tires, and automobile accessories, as well as towing and repair services (in an emergency, dial 911), at **Yellowstone Park Service Stations,** located at Canyon Village, Old Faithful, Grant Village, Fishing Bridge, Mammoth Hot Springs, and Tower-Roosevelt Junction.

YELLOWSTONE NATIONAL PARK A TO Z

To research prices, get advice from other travelers, and book travel arrangements, visit www.fodors.com.

AIR TRAVEL

CARRIERS There is no commercial air service to Yellowstone itself. The airlines listed here have service to neighboring regional airports.

▐ Airlines & Contacts Delta/Sky West ☎ 800/221-1212 ⊕ www.delta.com. Frontier Airlines ☎ 800/432-1359 ⊕ www.frontierairlines.com. Great Lakes Aviation ☎ 800/544-5111 ⊕ www.greatlakesav.com. Northwest Airlines ☎ 800/225-2525 ⊕ www.nwa.com. United Express ☎ 800/241-6522 ⊕ www.united.com.

AIRPORTS

Yellowstone National Park is served by airports in nearby communities, including Cody, Wyoming, one hour east; Jackson, Wyoming, one hour south; Bozeman, Montana, 90 minutes north; and West Yellowstone, Montana, just outside the park's west gate, which has only summer service.

🛈 Airport Information **Gallatin Field** ✉ 850 Gallatin Field Rd., Belgrade MT ☎ 406/388-6632 ⊕ www.gallatinfield.com. **Jackson Hole Airport** ✉ 1250 E. Airport Rd., 5 mi north of Jackson off U.S. 189/191, Jackson ☎ 307/733-7682 or 307/733-4005 ⊕ www.jacksonholeairport.com. **Yellowstone Airport** ✉ West Yellowstone, MT ☎ 406/646-7631. **Yellowstone Regional Airport** ✉ 3001 Duggleby Dr., Cody ☎ 307/587-5096 ⊕ www.flyyra.com.

BUS TRAVEL

There is no commercial bus service to Yellowstone, though several companies offer tours of the park.

🛈 Bus Information **Gray Line of Jackson Hole** ☎ 307/733-4325.

CAR RENTAL

The best places to rent cars in the region are at airports in Cody, Jackson, Bozeman, and West Yellowstone. The following companies all rent cars in the region.

🛈 **All Trans Company** ☎ 307/733-3135. **Aspen Rent-A-Car** ✉ 345 W. Broadway, Jackson Hole ☎ 307/733-9224 or 877/222-7736. **Avis** ☎ 800/331-1212. **Budget** ☎ 800/527-0700. **Eagle Rent-A-Car** ✉ 375 N. Cache Dr., Jackson Hole ☎ 307/739-9999 or 800/582-2128. **Hertz** ☎ 800/654-3131. **National** ☎ 800/328-4567.

CAR TRAVEL

Yellowstone National Park is well away from the interstates, so drivers make their way here on two-lane highways that are long on miles and scenery. From I–80, take U.S. 191 north from Rock Springs; it's about 177 mi to Jackson, then another 60 mi north to Yellowstone National Park. From I–90, head south at Livingston, Montana, 80 mi to Gardiner and the park's North Entrance. From Bozeman travel south 90 mi to West Yellowstone.

ROAD INFORMATION & EMERGENCY SERVICES Contact the Wyoming Department of Transportation for road and travel reports October–April. For emergency situations dial 911 or contact the Wyoming Highway Patrol. Most cell phones work in the developed areas of the park, and there are emergency phones located along some park roads.

🛈 **Montana Highway Patrol** ☎ 406/388-3190 or 800/525-5555 ⊕ www.mdt.mt.gov. **Wyoming Department of Transportation** ☎ 307/777-4484, 307/772-0824 from outside Wyoming for road conditions, 888/996-7623 from within Wyoming for road conditions ⊕ www.wyoroad.info. **Wyoming Highway Patrol** ☎ 307/777-4301, 800/442-9090 for emergencies, #4357 (#HELP) from a cell phone for emergencies.

EMERGENCIES

There are hospitals with 24-hour emergency rooms in Jackson, Cody, and Bozeman. Within Yellowstone there are clinics at Lake, Mammoth, and Old Faithful. In all cases you can call 911 if you have any type of emergency.

▓ Ambulance or Police Emergencies ☎ 911.
▓ Bozeman Deaconess Hospital ✉ 915 Highland Blvd., Bozeman Mont. ☎ 406/585–5000. **Grand Teton Medical Clinic** ✉ Next to Jackson Lake Lodge ☎ 307/543–2514. **Lake Clinic** ✉ Lake Yellowstone ☎ 307/242–7241 ☉ Mid-May–Sept., daily 8:30–8:30. **Mammoth Clinic** ✉ Mammoth Hot Springs ☎ 307/344–7965 ☉ June–Sept., daily 8–1 and 3–5; Oct.–May, Mon., Tues., Thurs., Fri. 8:30–noon and 1–5, Wed. 8:30–noon. **Old Faithful Clinic** ✉ Old Faithful ☎ 307/545–7325 ☉ Mid-May–mid-Sept., daily 7–7; mid-Sept.–mid-Oct., daily 8:30–5. **St. John's Hospital** ✉ 625 E. Broadway Ave., Jackson, Wyo. ☎ 307/733–3636. **West Park Hospital** ✉ 707 Sheridan Ave., Cody, Wyo. ☎ 307/527–7501.

LODGING

The best way to find accommodations in Yellowstone is to contact Xanterra Parks & Resorts, which manages all of the in-park lodging.
▓ Xanterra Parks & Resorts ✉ Box 165, Yellowstone National Park, 82190 ☎ 307/344–7901 general information, 307/344–7311 reservations ⊕ www.travelyellowstone.com.

CAMPING There are a variety of campgrounds both inside Yellowstone National Park and in the surrounding national forests and gateway communities.
▓ Xanterra Parks & Resorts ☎ 307/344–7311 ⊕ www.travelyellowstone.com.

MEDIA

NEWSPAPERS & There are no newspapers published in Yellowstone except the official
MAGAZINES park publication, *Yellowstone Today*, that you receive free when you enter the park. In the park you can generally purchase regional papers such as the *Casper Star-Tribune* and *Billings Gazette* that cover major park stories.

TELEVISION & There are no radio or television stations within the park, and no broad-
RADIO cast reception from outside.

TOURS

A quieter way than snowmobiling to sight buffalo herds, trophy-size bull elk, moose, and other winter wildlife is within a comfortable van of the **Yellowstone Alpen Guides Co.** (✉ 555 Yellowstone Ave. ☎ 406/646–9591 or 800/858–3502 ⊕ www.yellowstoneguides.com). The naturalist guides also lead cross-country ski trips and summer trips in and around the park.
▓ Tour Operators Xanterra Parks & Resorts ✉ Box 165, Yellowstone National Park, 82190 ☎ 307/344–7901 general information, 307/344–7311 reservations ⊕ www.travelyellowstone.com. **The Yellowstone Association Institute** ✉ Box 117, Yellowstone National Park, 82190 ☎ 307/344–2293 ⊕ www.yellowstoneassociation.org.

VISITOR INFORMATION

▓ Tourist Information Bozeman Chamber of Commerce ✉ 2000 Commerce Way, Bozeman, MT 59715 ☎ 406/586–5421 or 800/228–4224 ⊕ www.bozemanchamber.com. **Cody Chamber of Commerce** ✉ 836 Sheridan Ave., Box 2777, Cody, WY 82414 ☎ 307/587–2297 🖷 307/527–6228 ⊕ www.codychamber.org. **Gardiner Chamber of Commerce** ✉ 221 Park St., Gardiner, MT 59030 ☎ 406/848–7971 🖷 406/848–2446 ⊕ www.gardinerchamber.com. **Jackson Hole Chamber of Commerce** ✉ 990 W. Broadway, Box E, Jackson, WY 83001 ☎ 307/733–3316 🖷 307/733–5585 ⊕ www.jacksonholeinfo.com. **Travel Montana** ✉ 301 South Park, Helena, MT 59620-0133 ☎ 406/841–2870 or 800/

847-4868 ⊕ www.visitmt.com. **West Yellowstone Chamber of Commerce** ✉ 30 Yellowstone Ave., West Yellowstone, MT 59758 ☎ 406/646-7701 📠 406/646-9691 ⊕ www. westyellowstonechamber.com. **Wyoming Division of Tourism** ✉ I-25 at College Dr., Cheyenne, WY 82001 ☎ 307/777-7777 or 800/225-5996 📠 307/777-2877 ⊕ www. wyomingtourism.org.

WINTER TRANSPORTATION

You can't enter Yellowstone by car in the winter months. At present you can ride a snowmobile, so long as you have a guide and a four-stroke machine, but the controversy over snowmobile use in the park has continued for several years and further restrictions could be implemented. Snow coaches are the only certain means of motorized winter transportation into the park. They range from old-style, bright yellow Bombardier coaches to modern vans with their wheels converted to tracks so they can travel over the snow. Snow coaches carry from six to a dozen passengers, make frequent stops, have guides to interpret the park's attractions, and serve as both tour vehicles and shuttles within the park. 🚩 **Xanterra Parks & Resorts** ✉ Box 165, Yellowstone National Park, 82190 ☎ 307/344-7901 ⊕ www.travelyellowstone.com.

Grand Teton
National Park &
Jackson Hole

WITH THE WIND RIVER RANGE

2

By Candy
Moulton

NORTHWEST WYOMING IS MOUNTAIN COUNTRY, where high peaks—some of which remain snowcapped year-round—tower above deep, glacier-carved valleys. Indeed, the mountains of the Bridger-Teton and Shoshone national forests define the region, as do the state's two national parks, both along the Continental Divide. Yellowstone National Park, with its wildlife and geothermal wonders, is the state's most popular destination. Just to the south lies Grand Teton National Park, which encompasses the spectacular Teton Range jutting into the sky above the Snake River. This part of Wyoming has the tallest, most spectacular peaks in the state and a diverse wildlife population that includes wolves, grizzly bears, Rocky Mountain bighorn sheep, and antelope. Here you can hike through mountain meadows, challenge white water, explore Native American culture, and trace the history of westbound 19th century emigrants.

You might think Grand Teton National Park would suffer in comparison to larger, more historic Yellowstone, but when you see the Tetons rising out of Jackson Hole, you realize that nothing overshadows soaring peaks like these. Jackson Hole, the valley to the east of the Tetons, is a world-class ski destination, with literally thousands of ways to get down the slopes. In the valley, the town of Jackson works to maintain its small-town charm while at the same time serving as the area's cultural center. In the Wind River Mountains, the Oregon-California-Mormon trail sites near South Pass merit a visit, and you can learn about Native American traditions on the Wind River Reservation.

Wildlife-watching in northwest Wyoming ranks among the best in the state: look for Rocky Mountain bighorn sheep at Whiskey Mountain near Dubois; buffalo, elk, and even wolves in Jackson Hole; and moose near Pinedale or north of Dubois. One of the best ways to admire the landscape—mountain flowers, alpine lakes, and wildlife ranging from fat little pikas to grizzly bears—is to pursue an outdoor activity.

Name an outdoor activity and you can probably do it here, whether it be hiking, mountain biking, climbing, fishing, picnicking, and camping in summer, or downhill skiing, cross-country skiing, dogsledding, and snowmobiling in winter. You can hike or ride a horse along one of the backcountry trails near Grand Teton National Park, Dubois, or Lander; scale mountain peaks in the Wind River or Grand Teton ranges; or fish or float the Snake River near Jackson. Come winter, take a sleigh ride through the National Elk Refuge, snowmobile on hundreds of miles of trails, cross-country ski throughout the region, or hit the slopes at Snow King Mountain, Grand Targhee, or Jackson Hole Mountain Resort, one of the great skiing destinations in the country.

There's more to northwest Wyoming than the great outdoors. A handful of museums, well worth a few hours of your trip, offer a window on the history of the American West. The Jackson Hole Museum concentrates on the early settlement of Jackson Hole, while the Museum of the Mountain Man in Pinedale takes an informative look at

2

Any tour of northwest Wyoming should include a day or two, at minimum, in Jackson Hole, where you can explore Grand Teton National Park. The massive mountain range, with its lakes, rivers, and miles of trails, is an ideal venue for outdoor activities ranging from horseback riding to hiking and from river floating to bicycling. Also in Jackson Hole is the small but bustling town of Jackson, with its one-of-a-kind town square entered through elk antler arches and a stagecoach that gives rides throughout the day during summer. In winter, action is concentrated at nearby Teton Village, where you'll find unparalleled winter sports offerings at the Jackson Hole Mountain Resort. You're likely to share the slopes with Olympic champion skiers and snowboarders.

If you can extend your stay, travel over Togwotee Mountain Pass to little Dubois, where you can stay at a guest ranch, ride horses in the Bridger-Teton National Forest, learn about local history at the Wind River Historical Center, and glimpse the region's wildlife at the National Bighorn Sheep Interpretive Center. After Dubois and environs, head south onto the Wind River Indian Reservation to find exceptional shops filled with arts and crafts locally made by Northern Arapaho and Eastern Shoshone tribal members.

Spend some time in Lander and explore the Wind River Mountains before heading south and then west to South Pass City State Historic Site, near Atlantic City. From here, follow the emigrant trail corridor west and then northwest to Pinedale and its excellent Museum of the Mountain Man.

---

the trapper heritage. The Indian Arts Museum, within the Colter Bay Visitor Center at Grand Teton National Park, houses Plains Indians artifacts, including toys, clothing, and instruments; it occasionally hosts crafts demonstrations by tribal members and ranger programs on Native American culture. At Fort Washakie, the Gallery of the Wind and Museum celebrates the heritage of northwest Wyoming's earliest residents.

Exploring Northwest Wyoming

You will need a car to tour northwest Wyoming; to reach the really spectacular backcountry a four-wheel-drive vehicle is best. Major routes through the area include U.S. 191, which runs north–south through Jackson, on the western edge of the state, and U.S. 26/287, which runs east of Grand Teton National Park (also on the western edge of the state, within the Jackson Hole valley) toward Dubois. Much of the driving you do here will take you through the mountains—including the Absaroka and Wind River ranges that dominate the region.

The best bases for an exploration of Grand Teton National Park are the adjacent gateway towns of Jackson, Pinedale, and Dubois to the south. You can also stay at one of the lodges within the park itself.

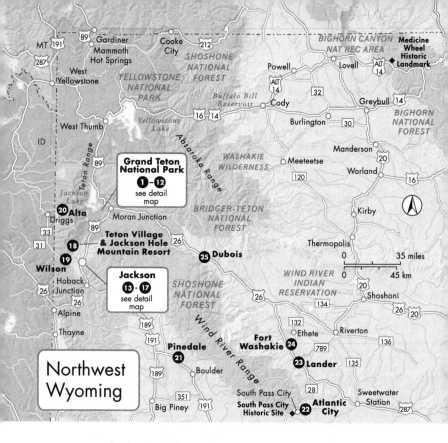

About the Restaurants

Northwest Wyoming has a lot of restaurants. Anyplace you go you'll find basic Western fare such as steaks, chicken, and burgers; in Jackson there's a wider selection, with menus listing everything from Chinese and Thai dishes to trout, buffalo, and elk. There are also a few fine-dining establishments in the region, such as Jenny Lake Lodge. Arguably the best steaks in all of Wyoming are prepared at Svilars, a steak house in the tiny community of Hudson, east of Lander.

About the Hotels

No other part of Wyoming has such a variety of lodging properties that appeal to all budgets. Lodging options in the area include elegant and expensive properties such as the Amangani resort in Jackson Hole, guest ranches in the Dubois and Jackson areas, historic inns, simple cabins, and dozens of chain motels.

It's a good idea to reserve well ahead for lodging near Grand Teton National Park, including the town of Jackson, in July and August. You should also reserve lodgings at Teton Village well in advance for skiing at Jackson Hole Mountain Resort.

WHAT IT COSTS					
	$$$$	**$$$**	**$$**	**$**	**¢**
RESTAURANTS	over $22	$17–$22	$12–$16	$7–$11	under $7
HOTELS	over $220	$161–$220	$111–$160	$70–$110	under $70

Restaurant prices are for a main course at dinner, excluding sales tax of 4%–7%. Hotel prices are for two people in a standard double room in high season, excluding service charges and 5%–10% tax.

Timing

Most people visit northwest Wyoming in summer, although winter draws skiing enthusiasts (the ski season generally lasts December through March). The months between Memorial Day and Labor Day are the busiest, with all attractions operating at peak capacity. If you don't mind a few limitations on what you can do and where you can stay and eat, the best times to visit the region are in late spring (May) and early fall (September and October). Not only will you find fewer people on the roads and at the sights, but you also will have some of the best weather (although springtime can be wet, and it can and does snow here every month of the year). In general, spring is the best time to see wildlife, particularly young animals. Fall brings a rich blaze of colors, painting the aspen and cottonwood trees with a palette of red, gold, and orange. The days are warm, reaching into the 60s and 70s, and the nights are cool in fall. There are also fewer thunderstorms than in midsummer, plus fewer biting insects (such as mosquitoes) to bother you.

GRAND TETON NATIONAL PARK

Your jaw may well drop the first time you see the Teton Range jutting up from the Jackson Hole valley floor. With no foothills to get in the way, you'll have a close-up view of magnificent, jagged peaks capped with snow. This massif is long on natural beauty. Before your eyes, mountain glaciers creep imperceptibly down 12,605-foot Mount Moran. Lakes are strung along the range's base, multicolored wildflowers cover the valley floor, and Wyoming's abundance of wildlife scampers about the meadows and mountains.

In Grand Teton National Park, short trails lead through willow flats near Jackson Lake, connecting with longer trails that lead into the canyons of the Teton Range. Boats skim the waters of Jackson and Jenny lakes, depositing people on the wild western shore of Jenny, and guided float trips meander down a calm stretch of the tortuous Snake River. A trip to the backcountry—which has more than 200 mi of trails, from the novice-accessible Cascade Canyon to the expert-level Teton Crest—reveals the majesty of what the Shoshone tribes called *Teewinot* (Many Pinnacles).

Numbers in the text correspond to numbers in the margin and on the Grand Teton National Park map.

Exploring Grand Teton National Park

Most people explore the park either from the south—usually out of Jackson—or from the north at Yellowstone National Park. By starting from

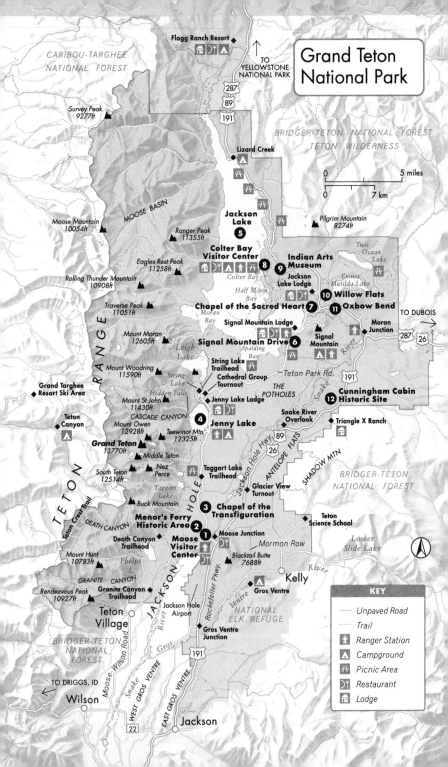

Grand Teton National Park

Flagg Ranch Resort

TO YELLOWSTONE NATIONAL PARK

CARIBOU-TARGHEE NATIONAL FOREST

287
89
191

BRIDGER-TETON NATIONAL FOREST
TETON WILDERNESS

Survey Peak 9277ft

Lizard Creek

0 — 5 miles
0 — 7 km

Two Ocean Lake

Moose Mountain 10054ft

MOOSE BASIN

Ranger Peak 11355ft

Jackson Lake
5

Pilgrim Mountain 8274ft

Colter Bay Visitor Center
8 **9**

Indian Arts Museum

Eagles Rest Peak 11258ft

Colter Bay

Jackson Lake Lodge

Emma Matilda Lake

Rolling Thunder Mountain 10908ft

Half Moon Bay

10 Willow Flats

Traverse Peak 11051ft

Chapel of the Sacred Heart **7**

11 Oxbow Bend

TO DUBOIS

Moran Bay

Moran Junction

287 26

Mount Moran 12605ft

Signal Mountain Lodge

Signal Mountain Drive **6**

Signal Mountain

RANGE

Leigh Lake

Spalding Bay

Snake River

Teton Park Rd.

191

Mount Woodring 11590ft

String Lake

THE POTHOLES

String Lake Trailhead

Grand Targhee Resort Ski Area

Hidden Falls

Cathedral Group Tournout

Cunningham Cabin Historic Site **12**

Teton Canyon

Mount St John 11430ft

Jenny Lake Lodge

CASCADE CANYON

Snake River Overlook

Triangle X Ranch

Mount Owen 12928ft

4

Jenny Lake

Grand Teton 13770ft

Teewinot Mtn 12325ft

Middle Teton

89
26

ANTELOPE FLATS

South Teton 12514ft

Nez Perce

Taggart Lake Trailhead

SHADOW MTN

BRIDGER-TETON NATIONAL FOREST

TETON

Buck Mountain

Taggart Lake

Glacier View Turnout

Teton Crest Trail

DEATH CANYON

JACKSON

Jackson Hole Hwy.

3 **Chapel of the Transfiguration**

Teton Science School

Mount Hunt 10783ft

Menor's Ferry Historic Area

2

Moose Junction

Death Canyon Trailhead

Phelps L.

HOLE

Mormon Row

Lower Slide Lake

GRANITE CANYON

1 **Moose Visitor Center**

Blacktail Butte 7688ft

Rendezvous Peak 10927ft

Granite Canyon Trailhead

River

NATIONAL ELK REFUGE

Kelly

Jackson Hole Airport

Gros Ventre

Teton Village

Rockefeller Pkwy.

Gros Ventre Junction

Gros Ventre River

BRIDGER-TETON NATIONAL FOREST

191

TO DRIGGS, ID

Wilson

Moose-Wilson Road

Snake River

WEST GROS VENTRE

EAST GROS VENTRE

22

Jackson

the south, as is suggested by the tour below, you can make your first stop at Moose, which is park headquarters. The visitor center here can give you a good, quick overview of the park.

There are two main routes through the park. U.S. 26/89/191/287 runs north–south along the eastern edge of the park; it remains open year-round. Teton Park Road diverges from this highway at Moose, running north through the center of the park and hooking up with the highway again near Jackson Lake. This second route—which is open seasonally, generally from May until October—more closely hugs the Teton Range.

A seven-day pass that can also be used at Yellowstone National Park costs $25 per car, $15 per motorcycle, and $10 per hiker or biker.

a good tour

Start your tour at **Moose Visitor Center ❶**, which has exhibits on the geology and wildlife of the area, plus information on the park. Follow Teton Park Road north for about ½ mi and then head east on the path to **Menor's Ferry Historic Area ❷**, which illustrates how people crossed the Snake River before bridges were built. Also here is the tiny **Chapel of the Transfiguration ❸**. Drive north for 10 mi on Teton Park Road to scenic **Jenny Lake ❹**. If you want to hike, you can spend the rest of the day exploring trails in the Jenny Lake area. However, if you prefer a driving tour, return to the Teton Park Road and travel north.

Jackson Lake ❺, popular with boaters and anglers, starts several miles north of Jenny Lake, off Teton Park Road. Teton Park Road intersects with U.S. 89/191/287 west of Moran Junction; follow U.S. 89/191/287 north for about 5 mi as it skirts the lake to Jackson Lake Lodge, which is a good place for lunch. After eating, continue north to **Colter Bay Visitor Center ❽**, which hosts daily programs on wildlife and Native American culture. Within the visitor center, the **Indian Arts Museum ❾** houses numerous Plains Indians artifacts and it's well worth the miles to see the collection. From the Colter Bay Visitor Center, retrace your route south on U.S. 89/191/287 to the **Willow Flats ❿**, where you have a good chance of seeing moose grazing. Continue east on U.S. 89/191/287 to the scenic **Oxbow Bend ⓫**, home to several species of birds. Drive southeast to Moran Junction and then head south for 6 mi on U.S. 191 to the late-19th-century cabin at **Cunningham Cabin Historic Site ⓬** before returning to Jackson.

TIMING Plan to spend at least a full day on this tour, and budget even more time if you want to hike or pursue other outdoor activities in the park. This tour is meant to be done between late spring and early fall, as much of the park shuts down in winter to all but skiing and snowmobiling (Teton Park Road and many of the restaurants and lodgings in the area are closed between October and April).

The Main Attractions

★ ❸ **Chapel of the Transfiguration.** Still a functioning Episcopal church, this tiny chapel was built in 1925. Couples come here to exchange vows with the Tetons as a backdrop, and tourists come to take photos of the small church with its awesome view. The church is generally open, but unattended, year-round. ✉ *½ mi off Teton Park Rd., 2 mi north of Moose Junction* ☎ *No phone* ☉ *Late May–late Sept., Sun. services at 8 AM and 10 AM.*

❽ Colter Bay Visitor Center. The auditorium here hosts several free daily programs about Native American culture and natural history. Ranger programs are presented hourly on topics ranging from grizzly bears and bison to nature activities in the park. The center is named for explorer John Colter, who may or may not have passed through the Grand Teton region in 1807 when he became the first white person to explore the Yellowstone area (no one is sure of his exact route). ✉ *2 mi off U.S. 89/191/287, 5 mi north of Jackson Lake Junction* ☎ *307/739–3594* ☉ *Mid-Sept.–early June, daily 8–5; early June–mid-Sept., daily 8–8.*

❾ Indian Arts Museum. You could easily spend an hour or two looking at examples of Plains Indian clothing, weapons, and other artifacts at this museum within the Colter Bay Visitor Center. Among the displays are Crow blanket strips with elegant beadwork, sashes from both the Shawnee and Hopi tribes, and various weapons, games and toys, flutes and drums, and a large collection of moccasins from many tribes. June through September, you can watch crafts demonstrations by tribal members, take ranger-led tours of the museum, and listen to a daily 45-minute ranger program on Native American culture (call for times). ✉ *2 mi off U.S. 89/191/287, 5 mi north of Jackson Lake Junction* ☎ *307/739–3594* ✆ *Free* ☉ *Mid-Sept.–early June, daily 8–5; early June–mid-Sept., daily 8–7.*

FodorśChoice ★

❹ Jenny Lake. This alpine lake south of Jackson Lake draws boaters to its pristine waters and hikers to its tree-shaded trails. The lake is named for the Native American wife of mountain man Beaver Dick Leigh, who guided surveyors through this region in 1872. ✉ *Jenny Lake Rd., 2 mi off Teton Park Rd., 12 mi north of Moose Junction.*

Geology exhibits, including a relief model of the Teton Range, are on display at the **Jenny Lake Visitor Center.** ✉ *S. Jenny Lake Junction, ½ mi off Teton Park Rd., 7 mi north of Moose Junction* ☎ *No phone* ☉ *Early June–early Sept., daily 8–7; early Sept.–late Sept., daily 8–5.*

★ **❷ Menor's Ferry Historic Area.** The ferry on display is not the original, but it's an accurate re-creation of the craft built by Bill Menor in the 1890s, and it demonstrates how people crossed the Snake River before bridges were built. The original buildings used by Menor house historical displays, including a photo collection; one building has been turned into a small general store. You can pick up a pamphlet for a self-guided tour, and guided tours are available here in summer. ✉ *½ mi off Teton Park Rd., 2 mi north of Moose Junction* ☎ *No phone* ✆ *Free* ☉ *Year-round, daily 24 hrs; tours late May–late Sept., daily 8–4:30.*

▶ **❶ Moose Visitor Center.** With information on activities and a knowledgeable staff, this center at the south entrance is a good place to begin a visit to Grand Teton National Park. Also here are exhibits of rare and endangered species and the geology and natural history of the Greater Yellowstone area. In the auditorium you can watch a video called *The Nature of Grand Teton* and other videos on topics that range from geology to wolves. The center sells maps and books related to the history and natural history of the area. ✉ *Teton Park Rd., ½ mi north of Moose Junction* ☎ *307/739–3399* ☉ *Sept.–1st week June, daily 8–5; 2nd week June–Aug., daily 8–7.*

Also Worth Seeing

⑦ Chapel of the Sacred Heart. This small log chapel sits in the pine forest and affords a nice view of Jackson Lake. The chapel is open only for services, but you can appreciate the view from here at any time. ⊠ *Off Teton Park Rd., ¼ mi east of Signal Mountain Lodge, 4 mi south of Jackson Lake Junction* ☎ *No phone* ☉ *Services June–Aug., Sat. at 5:30 PM and Sun. at 8 AM.*

⑫ Cunningham Cabin Historic Site. At the end of a gravel spur road, an easy ¾-mi trail runs through sagebrush around Pierce Cunningham's 1890 log-cabin homestead. Cunningham, an early Jackson Hole homesteader and civic leader, built his cabin in Appalachian dogtrot style, joining two halves with a roofed veranda. The cabin is closed to the public, but you can peek in through the windows. Watch for badgers, coyotes, and Uinta ground squirrels in the area. The site is open year-round, and a pamphlet is available at the trailhead. ⊠ *½ mi off Jackson Hole Hwy., 6 mi south of Moran Junction.*

★ ⑤ Jackson Lake. The biggest of Grand Teton's glacier-scooped lakes at 39 square mi, this body of water in the northern reaches of the park was enlarged by construction of the Jackson Lake Dam in 1906. You can fish, sail, and windsurf on the lake, or hike trails near the shoreline. Three marinas (Colter Bay, Leeks, and Signal Mountain) provide access for boaters, and several picnic areas, campgrounds, and lodges overlook the lake. ⊠ *Along U.S. 89/191/287 between Lizard Creek and Jackson Lake Junction, along Teton Park Rd. between Signal Mountain Lodge and Jackson Lake Junction.*

★ ⑪ Oxbow Bend. This spot overlooks a quiet backwater left by the Snake River when it cut a new southern channel. White pelicans stop here on their spring migration (many stay on through summer), trumpeter swans visit frequently, and great blue herons nest amid the cottonwoods along the river. Binoculars can help you locate bald eagles, ospreys, moose, beaver, and otter. In early morning in particular, look for the reflection of Mount Moran in the Oxbow's calm waters. ⊠ *U.S. 26/89/191/287, 2 mi east of Jackson Lake Junction.*

⑥ Signal Mountain Drive. Climbing 800 feet up Signal Mountain, this drive leads to an overlook with spectacular panoramic views of the surrounding mountains and Jackson Hole. Note that this narrow road is unsuitable for RVs. *Off Teton Park Rd.*

⑩ Willow Flats. You will almost always see moose grazing in the marshy area of Willow Flats, in part because it has a good growth of willow trees, which moose both eat and hide in. You can also often spot birds here, including bald eagles, ospreys, white pelicans, and sandhill cranes. ⊠ *U.S. 89/191/287, 1 mi north of Jackson Lake Junction.*

Sports & the Outdoors

Bicycling

Jackson Hole's long, flat profile and mountain scenery attract road and mountain bikers of all skill levels. Teton Park Road and Jackson Hole Highway are generally flat with long, gradual inclines, and have well-marked shoulders. Grand Teton has few designated bike paths, so cyclists should be very careful when sharing the road with vehicles, especially RVs and trailers. A bike lane allows for northbound bike traffic along the one-way Jenny Lake Loop Road, a one-hour ride. The River Road, 4 mi north of Moose, is an easy four-hour mountain-bike ride along a ridge above the Snake River. Bicycles are not allowed on trails or in the backcountry.

May through October, **Adventure Sports** (⊠ U.S. 191, Moose ☎ 307/733–3307), at Dornan's Chuckwagon in Moose, rents Diamondback, Cannondale, Giant, and Marin mountain bikes and can provide information on good places to bike in the area. May through September, **Teton Mountain Bike Tours** (⊠ Jackson ☎ 800/733–0788 ⊕ www.tetonmtbike.com) runs guided half-, full-, and multiday mountain-bike tours into both Grand Teton and Yellowstone national parks, as well as to the Bridger-Teton and Targhee national forests. Tours are available for all skill levels and include some specially designed for families. The Grand Teton tours are all half- or full-day outings. Prices start at $45 for half-day trips, $75 for full-day trips.

Bird-Watching

More than 300 species of birds inhabit Grand Teton National Park, and you can pick up a free bird guide at the park's visitor centers. Teton-country birds include bald eagles and ospreys, which nest near Oxbow Bend throughout summer. White pelicans also stop at the Oxbow on their northerly migration in spring. Nearby Willow Flats attracts similar birdlife plus sandhill cranes. You can see trumpeter swans at Oxbow Bend and Two Ocean Lake (in the northeast section of the park). Look for songbirds, such as pine and evening grosbeaks and Cassin's finches, in surrounding open pine and aspen forests. Similar songbirds inhabit Grandview Point, in the northeast section of the park, as do blue and ruffed grouse. It's a good idea to keep binoculars handy while traveling along Antelope Flats Road: you may spot red-tailed hawks and prairie falcons. Woodpeckers, bluebirds, and hummingbirds gather around Taggart Lake, which is several miles south of Jenny Lake.

Phelps Lake (⊠ Moose-Wilson Rd., about 3 mi off Teton Park Rd., 1 mi north of Moose Junction) is a great spot for bird-watching. The moderate 1⅕-mi round-trip Phelps Lake Overlook Trail takes you up conifer- and aspen-lined glacial moraine to a view that's accessible only by trail. Expect abundant birdlife: Western tanagers, northern flickers, and ruby-crowned kinglets thrive in the bordering woods, and hummingbirds feed on scarlet gilia beneath the overlook.

Boating

Motorboats are allowed on Jenny, Jackson, and Phelps lakes. On Jenny Lake, there's an engine limit of 7½ horsepower. On Jackson Lake you can launch your boat at Colter Bay, Leek's Marina, Signal Mountain, or Spalding Bay.

At **Colter Bay Marina** (⊠ 2 mi off U.S. 89/191/287, 5 mi north of Jackson Lake Junction ☎ 307/543–2811), all types of services are available to boaters early June through mid-August, including free parking for boat trailers and vehicles, free mooring, boat rentals, guided fishing trips, and fuel. The marina, on Jackson Lake, is operated by the Grand Teton Lodge Company. Due to current low lake levels the marina may have limited service. You can rent motorboats, rowboats, and canoes from **Grand Teton Lodge Company** (☎ 307/543–3100, 307/543–2811, or 800/ 628–9988 ⊕ www.gtlc.com) at Colter Bay Marina. Motorboats start at $23 per hour, rowboats at $10 per hour, and canoes at $11 per hour. Boats are available for rent mid-May through mid-October, and reservations are not accepted. The company also offers cruises on Jackson Lake, including scenic cruises starting at $18, breakfast cruises starting at $30, and evening steak-fry cruises starting at $50. Snake River cruises are $44 for a scenic float, $52 for a lunch float, and $57 for an evening supper float.

Both day and short-term parking for boat trailers and vehicles is available for up to three nights maximum mid-May through mid-September at **Leek's Marina** (⊠ U.S. 89/191/287, 6 mi north of Jackson Lake Junction ☎ 307/543–2516). There are no boat rentals, but you can get fuel, and there's free short-term docking plus a pizza restaurant. Park concessionaire Signal Mountain Lodge operates this marina. Mid-May through mid-September, **Signal Mountain Lodge Marina** (⊠ Teton Park Rd., 3 mi south of Jackson Lake Junction ☎ 307/543–2831 ⊕ www.signalmtnlodge. com) rents pontoon boats ($62 per hour), deck cruisers ($70 per hour), motorboats ($25 per hour), and canoes ($12 per hour) by the hour or for full- or half-day cruising. Also available are fuel, oil, overnight mooring ($20 per night), and guided sailboat tours ($75 per hour or $225 for a half day). You can launch your boat at **Spalding Bay** (⊠ 2 mi off Teton Park Rd., 7 mi south of Jackson Lake Junction) and park your trailer and vehicle for the day. There's no docking or mooring available.

Cross-Country Skiing

Grand Teton National Park has some of North America's finest and most varied cross-country skiing. Ski the gentle 5-km (3-mi) Swan Lake–Heron Pond Loop near Colter Bay Visitor Center, the mostly level 9-mi Jenny Lake Trail, or the moderate 6.5-km (4-mi) Taggart Lake–Beaver Creek Loop and 8-km (5-mi) Phelps Lake Overlook trail, which have some steep descents. Advanced skiers should head for the Teton Crest Trail. In winter all overnight backcountry travelers must register at park headquarters in Moose to obtain a free permit.

Fishing

Rainbow, brook, lake, and native cutthroat trout inhabit the park's waters. The Snake's 75 mi of river and tributary are world renowned for their fishing. To fish in Grand Teton National Park you need a Wyoming fishing license. A day permit for nonresidents costs $10, and an annual permit costs $65 plus a $10 conservation stamp; for state residents a license costs $15 per season plus $10 for a conservation stamp. You can buy a fishing license at Colter Bay Marina, Dornan's General Store in Moose, Signal Mountain Lodge, and at area sporting-goods stores. Or you can get one directly from the **Wyoming Game and Fish Department** (⊠ 360 N. Cache St., Box 67, Jackson 83001 ☎ 307/733–2321 ⊕ gf. state.wy.us/).

June through September, **Grand Teton Lodge Company** (⊠ Colter Bay Marina or Jackson Lake Lodge ☎ 307/543–3100 or 800/628–9988 ⊕ www.gtlc.com), the park's major concessionaire, operates guided Jackson Lake fishing trips that include boat, guide, and tackle. The company also offers guided fly-fishing trips on the Snake River. Fishing trips start at $63 per hour and cost $375 per day for two people. Make reservations at the activities desks at Colter Bay Village or Jackson Lake Lodge, where trips originate. Guided half- and full-day fishing trips on Jackson Lake depart from the marina at **Signal Mountain Lodge** (⊠ Teton Park Rd., 3 mi south of Jackson Lake Junction ☎ 307/543–2831 ⊕ www.signalmtnlodge.com). Trips run mid-May through September and cost $200 per half day, $386 per full day.

Golf

Jackson Hole Golf and Tennis Club (⊠ 5000 Spring Gulch Rd. ☎ 307/733–3111 ⊕ www.gtlc.com) is a championship 18-hole course near the Jackson Hole Airport, with tennis, fly-fishing, horseback riding, and swimming facilities.

Hiking

Much of the spectacular mountain scenery of Grand Teton is best seen by hiking. You can get trail maps and information about hiking conditions from rangers at the park visitor centers at Moose, Jenny Lake, or Colter Bay. Rangers lead a variety of hikes for people of varying skill levels. Popular trails are those around Jenny Lake, the Leigh and String lakes area, and Taggart Lake Trail, with views of Avalanche Canyon. Other trails let you experience the Grand Teton backcountry on longer hikes lasting from a few hours to several days. You can also do some off-trail hiking in the park. You can register for backcountry hiking and pick up backcountry trail information from any ranger station or visitor center. Wherever you go hiking in the park you may see moose and bears; keep your distance. Pets are not permitted on trails or in the backcountry, but you can take them on paved front-country trails so long as they are on a leash no more than 6 feet in length.

A 10-minute boat ride from the Jenny Lake dock ($7) takes you to the start of **Cascade Canyon Trail** (⊠ Jenny Lake Rd., 2 mi off Teton Park Rd., 12 mi south of Jackson Lake Junction), a moderate, ½-mi climb to 200-foot Hidden Falls, the park's most popular and crowded trail destination. Listen here for the distinctive bleating of the rabbitlike pikas among the glacial boulders and pines. The trail continues ½ mi to Inspiration Point over a rocky path that is moderately steep. There are two points on the climb that afford good views of Jenny Lake and the surrounding area, but keep climbing; after passing a rock wall you'll finally reach the true Inspiration Point, with the best views. To avoid crowds, try to make your way to Inspiration Point in early morning or late afternoon.

Colter Bay Nature Trail Loop (⊠ 2 mi off U.S. 89/191/287, 5 mi north of Jackson Lake Junction), a very easy, 1¾-mi round-trip excursion, treats you to views of Jackson Lake and the Tetons. As you follow the level trail from Colter Bay Visitor Center and along the forest's edge, you may see moose and bald eagles. Allow yourself two hours to complete the walk.

THE BEAR ESSENTIALS

THE NORTHERN ROCKIES are bear country—grizzlies and black bears are a presence throughout the region. Seeing one across a valley, through a pair of binoculars, is fun, but meeting one at closer range isn't. There have been few fatal encounters, but almost every summer there are incidents involving bears.

Wherever you venture in Wyoming and Montana, keep in mind these tips for travel in bear country:

Practical Precautions
Avoid sudden encounters. Whenever possible, travel in open country, during daylight hours, and in groups. Make noise—talking or singing is preferable to carrying "bear bells"—and leave your dog at home. Most attacks occur when a bear is surprised at close quarters or feels threatened.

Stay alert. Look for signs of bears, such as fresh tracks, scat, matted vegetation, or partially consumed salmon.

Choose your tent site carefully. Pitch the tent away from trails, streams with spawning salmon, and berry patches. Avoid areas that have a rotten smell or where scavengers have gathered; these may indicate the presence of a nearby bear cache, and bears aggressively defend their food supplies.

Keep food away from campsites. Cook meals at least 100 feet from tents, and store food and other items that give off odors (including personal products such as soap, shampoo, lotions, and even toothpaste) away from campsites. Hang food between trees where possible, or store your food in bear-resistant food containers. Avoid strong-smelling foods, and clean up after cooking and eating. Store garbage in airtight containers or burn it and pack up the remains.

If You Encounter a Bear
Identify yourself. Talk to the bear, to identify yourself as a human. Don't yell. And don't run. Running will trigger a bear's predatory instincts, and a bear can easily outrun you. Back away slowly, and give the bear an escape route. Don't ever get between a mother and her cubs.

Bigger is better. Bears are less likely to attack a larger target. Therefore, increase your apparent size. Raise your arms above your head to appear larger and wave them slowly, to better identify yourself as a human. With two or more people, it helps to stand side by side. In a forested area it may be appropriate to climb a tree, but remember that black bears and young grizzlies are agile tree climbers.

As a last resort, play dead. If a bear charges and makes contact with you, fall to the ground, lie flat on your stomach or curl into a ball, hands behind your neck, and remain passive. If you are wearing a pack, leave it on. Once a bear no longer feels threatened, it will usually end its attack. Wait for the bear to leave before you move. The exception to this rule is when a bear displays predatory behavior. Instead of simply charging, a bear hunting for prey will show intense interest while approaching at a walk or run and it may circle, as if stalking you. But remember that such circumstances are exceedingly rare and most often involve black bears, which are much smaller and less aggressive than grizzlies (and can be driven off more easily).

Death Canyon Trail (⊠ Off Moose-Wilson Rd., 4 mi south of Moose Junction), a strenuous 7⅗-mi hike, with lots of hills to traverse, ends with a climb up into Death Canyon. The view from the top includes huge boulders and rock formations and scattered pine trees and aspens.

★ You can walk to Hidden Falls from the Jenny Lake ranger station by following the mostly level **Jenny Lake Trail** (⊠ S. Jenny Lake Junction, ½ mi off Teton Park Rd., 8 mi north of Moose Junction) around the south shore of the lake to Cascade Canyon Trail. Jenny Lake Trail continues around the lake for 6½ mi. It's an easy trail that will take you two to three hours, depending on how fast you walk.

The flat **Leigh Lake Trail** (⊠ String Lake Trailhead, ½ mi west of Jenny Lake Rd., 14 mi north of Moose Junction) follows String Lake's northeastern shore to Leigh Lake's south shore, covering 2 mi in a round-trip of about an hour. You can extend your hike into an easy 7½-mi, four-hour round-trip by following the forested east shore of Leigh Lake to Bearpaw Lake. Along the way you'll have views of Mount Moran across the lake, and you may be lucky enough to spot a moose.

Lunchtree Hill Trail (⊠ U.S. 89/191/287, ½ mi north of Jackson Lake Junction), one of the park's easiest trails, begins at Jackson Lake Lodge and leads ½ mi to the top of a hill above Willow Flats. The area's willow thickets, beaver ponds, and wet, grassy meadows make it prime bird-watching territory. Look for sandhill cranes, hummingbirds, and many types of songbirds. You might also see moose. The round-trip walk takes no more than a half hour.

In the shadows of 11,144-foot Rockchuck Peak and 11,430-foot Mount Saint John, the easy 3½-mi, three-hour **String Lake Trail** (⊠ ½ mi west of Jenny Lake Rd., 14 mi north of Moose) loops around String Lake.

An easy-to-moderate path, **Taggart Lake Trail** (⊠ ½ mi south of Jenny Lake on Teton Park Rd.) runs for more than 1½ mi from the trailhead to the lake. You can continue around the lake to complete the 4-mi loop, but note that the terrain becomes steeper near Beaver Creek. The loop affords views of Avalanche Canyon, and you may see moose.

Horseback Riding

June through August, Grand Teton Lodge Company arranges one-, two-, and three-hour rides from **Colter Bay Village Corral** (⊠ 2 mi off U.S. 89/191/287, 5 mi north of Jackson Lake Junction ☎ 307/543–3100 or 800/628–9988 ⊕ www.gtlc.com) to several destinations. Half-day trips, for advanced riders only, go to Hermitage Point. Some rides include breakfast or dinner eaten along the trail. Prices vary, from $30 for short rides to $52 for dinner rides.

Several trail rides depart daily from the **Jackson Lake Lodge Corral** (⊠ U.S. 89/191/287, ½ mi north of Jackson Lake Junction ☎ 307/543–3100 or 800/628–9988 ⊕ www.gtlc.com), operated by Grand Teton Lodge Company June through August. One-hour rides give an overview of the Jackson Lake Lodge area; two- and three-hour rides go to Emma Matilda Lake, Oxbow Bend, and Christian Pond. Experienced riders can take a half-day ride to Two Ocean Lake. Some rides include breakfast or dinner eaten along the trail. Prices vary, from $25 for short rides to $47 for dinner rides.

Mountain Climbing

The Teton Range offers the nation's most diverse general mountaineering. Excellent rock, snow, and ice routes abound for climbers of all experience levels.

Started by climbing pioneers Paul Petzoldt and Glen Exum, **Exum Mountain Guides** (✉ Lupine Meadows, near Jenny Lake ☎ 307/733–2297) offers a variety of climbing experiences and instruction, ranging from one-day mountain climbs to ice climbing and backcountry adventures on skis and snowboards. Though most of their climbing is on the Teton Range, they also lead trips to other sites in Wyoming and the region, and they have an international climbing program as well. One-day climbs range from $200 to $325; climbing classes cost from $95 to $170.

Mountain climbers get a leg up in the Tetons from **Jackson Hole Mountain Guides** (✉ 165 N. Glenwood St., Jackson ☎ 307/733–4979). There are classes on rock and ice climbing for beginners and more-experienced climbers. Guided trips concentrate on the Tetons and other Wyoming locations. One-day guided climbs cost between $180 and $225; climbing classes range from $90 to $125.

River Expeditions

If you want to float the Snake River on your own, you are required to purchase a permit that costs $10 per raft and is valid for the entire season. Permits are available year-round at Moose Visitor Center and at Colter Bay, Signal Mountain, and Buffalo (near Moran entrance) ranger stations in summer. Before you set out, check with park rangers for current conditions.

You may prefer to take one of the many guided float trips through calm-water sections of the Snake; outfitters pick you up at the float-trip parking area near Moose Visitor Center for a 10- to 20-minute drive to upriver launch sites. All concessionaires provide ponchos and life preservers. Early morning and evening floats are your best bets for wildlife viewing, but be sure to carry a jacket or sweater. Float season runs mid-May to mid-September.

Barker-Ewing River Trips (✉ 45 W. Broadway, Jackson ☎ 800/448–4204 or 307/733–1000 ⊕ www.barker-ewing.com) runs white-water trips down the Snake River late May through late September. A four-hour trip costs $44–$50. Breakfast trips are $76–$82; overnight trips are $140; and scenic trips (no white water) are $14–$20. If you'd like to sit back and be a passenger, travel the peaceful parts of the Snake looking for wildlife with **Barker-Ewing Scenic Float Trips** (✉ Moose ☎ 307/733–1800 or 800/365–1800 ⊕ www.barkerewingscenic.com), which operates exclusively on the scenic Snake in Grand Teton National Park. Trips run June through August and cost $40.

Grand Teton Lodge Company Snake River Float Trips (☎ 307/543–3100 or 800/628–9988 ⊕ www.gtlc.com) operates exclusively within Grand Teton National Park. Choose from a simple scenic float trip ($44), one that also includes lunch ($51), or an evening trip that includes a steak-fry dinner ($57). Make reservations at the activities desk at Colter Bay Village or Jackson Lake Lodge.

To experience some wet and wild stretches of river, get in touch with the folks at **Lewis and Clark River Expeditions** (⌧ 145 W. Gill St., Jackson ☎ 307/733–4022 or 800/824–5375 ⊕ www.lewisandclarkexpeds.com), who put you in big rubber rafts for an exhilarating ride. You can also take a more leisurely scenic float or have a steak fry along with your river trip. Some trips are in Grand Teton National Park waters and others are outside the park. Trips run mid-May through mid-September and cost between $30 and $64.

Mad River Boat Trips (⌧ 1255 S. U.S. 89, Jackson ☎ 307/733–6203 or 800/458–7238 ⊕ www.mad-river.com), which worked on the movie *A River Runs Through It,* leads several white-water and scenic float trips, some combined with breakfast, lunch, or dinner. Start or end your trip with a visit to the company's river museum, which has photos and information. There are even old boats from expeditions on Wyoming waters, dating back to explorer John Wesley Powell's expedition on the Green River in the 1870s. Some trips are in park waters and others are outside Grand Teton. Trips run mid-May through August and cost between $25 and $60.

Triangle X Float Trips (⌧ 2 Triangle X Ranch Rd., Moose ☎ 307/733–2183, 307/733–6445, or 888/860–0005 ⊕ www.trianglex.com) are subdued river trips in Grand Teton National Park, including short 10-mi floats and a sunset dinner float. Trips are available June through August and cost $38 to $48.

Snowmobiling

Designated unplowed sections of Teton Park Road are open to snowmobiles, and you can also snowmobile on Jackson Lake. You must first purchase an annual $15 permit at a park entrance station. The speed limit within the park is 45 mph.

You can rent a snowmobile at **Togwotee Mountain Lodge** (⌧ U.S. 26/287, Moran ☎ 307/543–2847 or 800/543–2847 ⊕ www.togwoteelodge.com), on the eastern edge of Grand Teton National Park, and then ride it on an extensive trail network along the Continental Divide. Rentals cost $139–$179.

Where to Stay & Eat

$$–$$$ ✕ **Dornan's Chuckwagon.** An Old West theme, mountain views, and good food make this a popular local hangout. Choose from mountain red trout or salmon, barbecue chicken or baby-back ribs, and steak; on weekends you can also get prime rib. There are also Mexican platters, and in summer Dornan's cooks up an outdoor Dutch-oven buffet (roast beef, ribs, and cowboy beans). Meals are eaten outside at picnic tables or inside tepees. On the same premises as a pizzeria and a good wine store, the chuckwagon serves no alcohol. ⌧ *U.S. 191, 12 mi north of Jackson, Moose* ☎ *307/733–2415* ▭ *MC, V* ⛾ *BYOB* ⊗ *Closed Oct.–Apr.*

$–$$ ✕ **Dornan's Pizza & Pasta Co.** Noisy, packed with families and a younger crowd, this joint offers a good selection of pizza, pasta, homemade soups, salads, and sandwiches. They have a kid's menu and do not serve alcohol, but you can pick up something nice at the wine shop next door. ⊠ *U.S. 191, 12 mi north of Jackson, Moose* ☎ *307/733–2415* ▤ *MC, V* ⏚ *BYOB* ⊗ *Closed Oct.–Apr.*

★ **$$$$** ✕▥ **Jenny Lake Lodge.** In the most exclusive of the park's resorts, elegant yet rustic cabins are bedecked with handmade quilts, down comforters, and even walking sticks. You can request a phone in your room, but you may prefer to sit undisturbed in a rocker on the cabin porch and watch for moose and fox. Activities, such as riding a horse or 1950s-style bicycle along park trails, are included in the price along with breakfast and dinner. The dining room ($$$$) serves a set dinner menu with a choice of entrées emphasizing Rocky Mountain cuisine, including roast prime rib of buffalo and breast of pheasant. Jackets are requested for evening dining, and you should reserve ahead. ⊠ *Jenny Lake Rd.* ⏚ *Grand Teton Lodge Co., Box 250, Moran 83013* ☎ *307/733–3100 or 800/628–9988* 🖷 *307/543–3143* ⊕ *www.gtlc.com* ➥ *30 cabins, 6 suites* ⏚ *Restaurant, boating, bicycles, horseback riding, bar, no-smoking rooms; room phones, no room TVs, no a/c* ▤ *AE, DC, MC, V* ⊗ *Closed mid-Oct.–May* ⏁ *MAP.*

$$$–$$$$ ✕▥ **Jackson Lake Lodge.** Two large fireplaces adorn the lounge, Native American designs decorate the walls, and huge picture windows look out on Willow Flats. There are 30 rooms in the main lodge; the others, in one-story motor-lodge-style buildings, are larger and preferable. Some rooms have Teton views and a higher price tag as a result. The park's only pool is here, and you can arrange for horseback riding, float trips, and boating excursions that depart from the lodge. The Mural Room ($$$–$$$$) serves buffalo, cedar-plank king salmon, and rack of lamb. You can eat by the pool at the Western barbecue (reservations required, ☎ *307/543–2811 Ext. 1911*) or at the snack bar. ⊠ *U.S. 89 north of Jackson Lake Junction* ⏚ *Grand Teton Lodge Co., Box 250, Moran 83013* ☎ *307/733–3100 or 800/628–9988* 🖷 *307/543–3143* ⊕ *www. gtlc.com* ➥ *385 rooms* ⏚ *2 restaurants, pool, boating, hiking, horseback riding, bar, recreation room, business services, meeting rooms, airport shuttle, no-smoking rooms; no a/c, no room TVs* ▤ *AE, DC, MC, V* ⊗ *Closed late Oct.–mid-May.*

$–$$$ ✕▥ **Signal Mountain Lodge.** Volcanic stone and pine shingles were used in the construction of this lodge on the eastern shore of Jackson Lake. Guest rooms are clustered in cabinlike units, and many of them have lake views; some have kitchenettes. The lobby has a fireplace, a piano, and Adirondack furniture. You can rent boats, take scenic float trips, or fish. The Peaks restaurant ($$–$$$$) offers buffalo steak, trout, and free-range chicken along with views of the lake and the Tetons. The Trapper Grill, which has a children's menu, serves sandwiches and burgers that can be eaten indoors or out on the deck. ⊠ *Teton Park Rd.* ⏚ *Box 50, Moran 83013* ☎ *307/543–2831* ⊕ *www.signalmtnlodge.com* ➥ *79 rooms* ⏚ *2 restaurants, some kitchenettes, refrigerators, microwaves, laundry, boating, fishing, bar, shops, some pets allowed (fee); no room TVs, no a/c, no smoking* ▤ *AE, DC, MC, V* ⊗ *Closed mid-Oct.–early May.*

¢–$$ ✕▦ **Colter Bay Village.** Less expensive than its posher cousins, Colter Bay Village, near Jackson Lake, may not be fancy, but it has splendid views and an excellent marina and beach for the windsurfing crowd. (You'll need a wet suit.) A Western theme decorates the cabins. With their concrete floors, hanging bunks, canvas exteriors, and shared bathrooms, the tent cabins are by no means luxurious, but they do keep the wind and rain off. There's also an RV park with showers, a service station, and a marina. The family-oriented Chuckwagon restaurant ($–$$$$) serves lasagna, trout, and barbecue spareribs. This is a full-service lodging, with a grocery store, canoe and kayak rentals, and a service station. ⊠ *Off U.S. 89* ⬠ *Grand Teton Lodge Co., Box 250, Moran 83013* ☎ *307/733–3100 or 800/628–9988* 🖷 *307/543–3143* ⊕ *www. gtlc.com* 🗨 *166 cabins, 66 tent cabins with shared bath* ⌂ *2 restaurants, grocery, lake, boating, hiking, horseback riding, bar, shops, laundry facilities, no-smoking rooms; no a/c, no room phones, no room TVs* ▤ *AE, DC, MC, V* ⊗ *Closed late Sept.–late May (tent cabins have slightly shorter season).*

$$–$$$$ ▦ **Spur Ranch Log Cabins.** These log cabins, at the popular and busy Dornan's in Moose and adjacent to the Snake River, have views of the Teton Range. They range from small one-bedroom cabins to large two-bedroom units. Lodgepole-pine furniture fills the cabins' bedrooms and living areas. There is a canoe and kayak school here as well. ⊠ *U.S. 191, 12 mi north of Jackson* ⬠ *Box 39, Moose 83012* ☎ *307/733–2522* 🖷 *307/739–9098* ⊕ *www.dornans.com* 🗨 *12 cabins* ⌂ *2 restaurants, grocery, kitchens, boating, fishing, mountain bikes, hiking, cross-country skiing, bar, wine shop, shops; no a/c, no room phones, no room TVs, no smoking* ▤ *D, MC, V.*

$–$$$ ▦ **Moulton Ranch Cabins.** With a view of the Tetons and just a short walk away from two of the most photographed barns in Wyoming, this is one of Jackson Hole's most historic lodgings. Some of the cabins originally served the T. A. Moulton Ranch as a granary and bunkhouse, but they have been completely modernized. The friendly hosts are descendants of the homesteaders who first claimed this land in 1907 and they can regale you with stories about the early settlers. A portion of one barn has been turned into a dance hall/function space. There's a three-night minimum stay and no Sunday check-in. ⊠ *Off Antelope Flats Rd., U.S. 26/89/191, 2 mi north of Moose Junction, Grand Teton National Park, 83012* ☎ *307/733–3749 or 208/529–2354* ⊕ *www.moultonranchcabins. com* 🗨 *6 cabins* ⌂ *Some kitchenettes, picnic area, hiking; no smoking, no room phones, no room TVs, no a/c* ▤ *MC, V* ⊗ *Closed Oct.–Memorial Day.*

¢–$$$ ▦ **Flagg Ranch Resort.** Located north of Grand Teton National Park and just 2 mi south of Yellowstone, this sprawling resort has cabins, a big campground, and a main lodge with a convenience store, gas station, bar, and restaurant, plus acres of parking. You can arrange a tour to Yellowstone or Grand Teton, a fly-fishing trip on the Snake River, or a river float. ⊠ *Moran, 83013* ☎ *800/443–2311* 🖷 *307/543–2356* ⊕ *www.flaggranch.com* 🗨 *92 cabins, 97 full hookups, 74 tent sites* ⌂ *Restaurant, laundry facilities, hiking, horseback riding* ▤ *AE, D, DC, MC, V.*

Camping

🏕 **Colter Bay Campground.** Busy, noisy, and filled by noon, this campground has sites for tents, trailers, or RVs and one great advantage: its central location, about ¼ mi from Jackson Lake. Try to get a site as far from the nearby cabin road as possible. This is the only national-parks-operated campground in the park that has hot showers. The maximum stay is 14 days. ⚐ *Flush toilets, dump station, drinking water, guest laundry, showers, bear boxes, fire grates, picnic tables* ⚑ *350 sites* ✉ *2 mi off U.S. 89/191/287, 5 mi north of Jackson Lake Junction* ☎ *307/543–3100* ⊕ *www.gtlc.com* ✍ *$26–$39* ⚐ *Reservations not accepted* ▤ *AE, D, MC, V* ☉ *Mid-May–late Sept.*

🏕 **Colter Bay RV Park.** This campground, part of Colter Bay Village and next to Colter Bay Campground, is the only RV park in Grand Teton where you can get full hookups. There's also a marina here. ⚐ *Flush toilets, full hookups, dump station, drinking water, guest laundry, showers, bear boxes, fire grates, picnic tables* ⚑ *112 full hookups* ✉ *2 mi off U.S. 89/191/287, 5 mi north of Jackson Lake Junction* ☎ *307/543–2811* ✍ *$26–$39* ▤ *AE, D, MC, V* ☉ *Late May–late Sept.*

🏕 **Gros Ventre.** The park's biggest campground is set on an open, grassy area on the bank of the Gros Ventre River, away from the mountains and in the southeast corner of the park. Try to get a site close to the river. The campground usually doesn't fill until nightfall, if at all. There's a maximum stay of 14 days. ⚐ *Flush toilets, dump station, drinking water, bear boxes, fire grates, picnic tables* ⚑ *372 tent or RV sites* ✉ *4 mi off U.S. 26/89/191, 1½ mi southwest of Kelly on Gros Ventre River Rd., 6 mi south of Moose Junction* ☎ *No phone* ✍ *$12* ⚐ *Reservations not accepted* ▤ *AE, D, MC, V* ☉ *May–mid-Oct.*

★ 🏕 **Jenny Lake.** Wooded sites and Teton views make this the most desirable campground in the park, and it fills early. The small, quiet facility allows tents only and limits stays to a maximum of seven days. ⚐ *Flush toilets, drinking water, bear boxes, fire grates, picnic tables* ⚑ *51 sites* ✉ *Jenny Lake Rd., ½ mi off Teton Park Rd., 8 mi north of Moose Junction* ☎ *No phone* ✍ *$12* ⚐ *Reservations not accepted* ▤ *No credit cards* ☉ *Mid-May–late Sept.*

🏕 **Lizard Creek.** Views of Jackson Lake, wooded sites, and the relative isolation of this campground make it a relaxing choice. There's a maximum stay of 14 days, and no vehicles more than 30 feet long are allowed. ⚐ *Flush toilets, drinking water, bear boxes, fire grates* ⚑ *60 tent or trailer sites* ✉ *U.S. 89/191/287, 12 mi north of Jackson Lake Junction* ☎ *No phone* ✍ *$15* ⚐ *Reservations not accepted* ▤ *AE, D, MC, V* ☉ *Early June–early Sept.*

🏕 **Signal Mountain.** In a hilly setting on Jackson Lake, this campground has boat access. No vehicles or trailers more than 30 feet long are allowed. There's a maximum stay of 14 days. ⚐ *Flush toilets, dump station, drinking water, fire grates, picnic tables* ⚑ *86 tent or trailer sites* ✉ *Teton Park Rd., 3 mi south of Jackson Lake Junction* ☎ *No phone* ✍ *$12* ⚐ *Reservations not accepted* ▤ *AE, D, MC, V* ☉ *Early May–mid-Oct.*

Nightlife & the Arts

Ranger programs on topics ranging from wildlife to the geology of the park are presented during summer evenings at **Colter Bay Visitor Center** (⌗ 2 mi off U.S. 89/191/287, 5 mi north of Jackson Lake Junction ☏ 307/739–3594).

Shopping

Colter Bay General Store (⌗ Colter Bay Village, off U.S. 89 ☏ No phone) sells groceries, gifts, sporting goods, fishing tackle, and books, including hiking guides. Many of the items bear pictures of moose. You can buy gifts, wine, marshmallows, and other food items at **Dornan's General Store** (⌗ Teton Park Rd. near Moose Visitor Center ☏ 307/733–2415 Ext. 301). This is also a good place to stock up on mountaineering and camping equipment. **Jackson Lake Lodge** (⌗ U.S. 89 north of Jackson Lake Junction ☏ No phone) has four shops, including a newsstand that sells postcards, film, and other useful items; the Apparel and Teton shops, where you will find clothing and reference books; and the Gift Shop, which sells Indian crafts, sculptures, hiking supplies, and snacks, as well as a good selection of beer, wine and liquor.

★ Original watercolors by Joanne Hennes, custom jewelry, leather coats, antler knives, and hand-pressed-flower photo albums are among the unique items sold at **Jenny Lake Lodge Gift Shop** (⌗ Jenny Lake Lodge, Jenny Lake Rd. ☏ 307/733–4647). **Jenny Lake Store** (⌗ South end of Jenny Lake ☏ No phone) sells backpacks, waist packs, water bottles, and camping and hiking gear (socks, compasses, and even sandwiches). For a good selection of bird feeders and jewelry, head to **Needles Gift Shop** (⌗ Signal Mountain Lodge, Teton Park Rd. ☏ 307/543–2831). You can purchase hiking guides, hats, and T-shirts at **Timbers Gift Shop** (⌗ Signal Mountain Lodge, Teton Park Rd. ☏ 307/543–2831).

JACKSON

Most visitors to northwest Wyoming come to Jackson, which remains a small Western town, "howdy" in the daytime and hopping in the evening. For active types, it's a good place to stock up on supplies before heading for outdoor adventures in Grand Teton National Park and the surrounding Jackson Hole area. For those looking to rest their feet awhile, it's a good stop for its wealth of galleries, Western-wear shops, varied cuisines, and active nightlife centering on bars and music.

Jackson's charm and popularity put it at risk. On busy summer days, traffic can slow to a crawl where the highway doglegs through downtown. Proposals for new motels and condominiums sprout like the purple asters in the spring, as developers vie for a share of the vacation market. Old-timers suggest that the town—in fact, the entire Jackson Hole—has already lost the dusty charm it had when horses stood at hitching rails around Town Square. However, with national parks and forests and state lands occupying some of the most beautiful real estate in the country, there's only so much ground on which to build. These

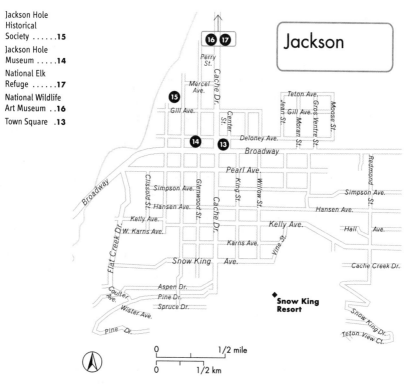

limitations, along with the cautious approach of locals, may keep Jackson on a human scale.

Exploring Jackson

The best way to explore Jackson's downtown, which is centered on vibrant Town Square, is on foot, since parking can be a challenge during the busy summer months. To go beyond downtown—the National Wildlife Art Museum or National Elk Refuge, for example—you'll need to hop into your car.

Start your visit at the corner of Cache and Broadway at **Town Square** ⓭ ▶, easily identifiable by its elk-antler arches and bustle of activity. Stroll around the square and visit the various shops here. Walk one block west to Glenwood Street and the **Jackson Hole Museum** ⓮ for a lesson on local history. Once you have done the town, hop into your car and drive 3 mi north on Cache Drive to the **National Wildlife Art Museum** ⓰, with its wonderful collection devoted to depictions of animals. From a deck at the museum you can see the real thing—thousands of elk in winter, plus waterfowl, coyotes, and more at various times of the year—at the **National Elk Refuge** ⓱. If you want to see the animals up close, you can take a sleigh ride to the refuge in winter.

TIMING   If you don't plan to shop on Town Square, you can easily do this tour in a few hours. If you want to hit the stores, budget a full day for this tour. Note that the Jackson Hole Museum is open only in summer.

The Main Attractions

⑭ Jackson Hole Museum. For some local history, visit this museum, where you can get acquainted with the early settlers and find out how Dead Man's Bar got its name. You'll also learn how Jackson had the first all-female town government. Among the exhibits are Native American, ranching, and cowboy artifacts. ✉ *Corner of Glenwood and Deloney Ave.* ☎ *307/733-2414* ⊕ *www.jacksonholehistory.org* ☎ *$3* ☉ *Memorial Day–Sept., Mon.–Sat. 9:30–6, Sun. 10–5.*

⚙ **⑰ National Elk Refuge.** Wildlife abounds on this 25,000-acre refuge year-
Fodor's Choice   round, but from approximately late November through March, the
★   real highlight is the more than 7,500 elk, many with enormous antler racks, that winter here, three miles north of Jackson. You can see them from various pullouts along U.S. 191, or up close by taking a horse-drawn sleigh ride through the refuge. The elk stand or eat calmly as sleighs loaded with families and supplied with alfalfa pellets move in their midst. Among the other animals that make their home here are coyotes, trumpeter swans, and other waterfowl. Arrange for sleigh rides through the Jackson Hole & Greater Yellowstone Visitor Center (*see* Sleigh Rides, *below*) in Jackson; wear warm clothing including hats, gloves, boots, and coats. ✉ *532 N. Cache St.* ☎ *307/733-5771* ⊕ *nationalelkrefuge. fws.gov* ☎ *Free, sleigh ride $15* ☉ *Year-round; sleigh rides, generally mid-Dec.–Mar., daily 10–4.*

★ **⑯ National Wildlife Art Museum.** Among the paintings and sculptures of bighorn sheep, elk, and other animals of the West at this museum devoted to representations of wildlife are works by such artists as George Catlin and Charles M. Russell. The collection includes works in various mediums and styles, and the earliest pieces date to 2000 BC. A deck here affords views across the National Elk Refuge, where, particularly in winter, you can see wildlife in a natural habitat. ✉ *2820 Rungius Rd., 3 mi north of Jackson* ☎ *307/733-5771* ⊕ *www.wildlifeart.org* ☎ *$6* ☉ *Daily 9–5.*

▶ **⑬ Town Square.** You can spend an entire day wandering around Jackson's always-bustling Town Square, a parklike area crisscrossed with walking paths and bedecked with arches woven from hundreds of elk antlers. Various shops and restaurants surround the square, and there's often entertainment going on in the square itself, including a melodramatic "shoot-out" summer evenings at approximately 6:30. At the southwest corner of the square you can board a stagecoach for a ride around the area; it should cost about $6 per adult.

Also Worth Seeing

⑮ Jackson Hole Historical Society. Displays at this log cabin illuminate local history. In addition to historic artifacts and photographs, the society houses manuscripts, maps, and an oral-history collection. ✉ *105 Mercill Ave.* ☎ *307/733-9605* ⊕ *www.jacksonholehistory.org* ☎ *Free* ☉ *Weekdays 8–5.*

off the beaten path

GRANITE HOT SPRINGS – South of Jackson Hole, concerted local and national efforts have preserved both the wildlands and the ranches that dot the Teton Valley floor. The Snake River turns west and the contours steepen; by Hoback Junction there's white-water excitement. The drive south along U.S. 191 provides good views of the river's twists and turns and the life-jacketed rafters and kayakers who float the canyon. About 13 mi south of Jackson at Hoback Junction, head east on U.S. 189/191 and follow the Hoback River south up its beautiful canyon. A tributary canyon 10 mi south of the junction is followed by a well-maintained and marked gravel road to Granite Hot Springs, in the Bridger-Teton National Forest, 10 mi east of U.S. 189/191 on Granite Creek Road. People come for the shady, creek-side campground, the pool fed by hot springs, and moderate hikes up Granite Canyon to passes with panoramic views. In winter, there's a popular snowmobile and dogsled trail from the highway.

Sports & the Outdoors

Bicycling

The trip up to **Lower Slide Lake,** north of town, is a favorite of cyclists. Turn east off U.S. 26/89/191 to Kelly, and then follow Slide Lake Road. Cyclists ride the **Spring Gulch Road,** part pavement, part dirt, off Route 22, along the base of Gros Ventre Butte, rejoining U.S. 26/89/191 near the Gros Ventre River.

Bike rentals for all skill levels and age groups are available at **Edge Sports** (✉ 409 W. Broadway ☎ 307/734–3916); the company also leads guided bike tours. You can rent a mountain bike to explore on your own or take a tour at **Hoback Sports** (✉ 40 S. Millward St. ☎ 307/733–5335). General tours are geared to intermediate and advanced riders, but Hoback can also custom-design a tour to suit your abilities and interests. **Teton Cyclers** (✉ 175 N. Glenwood St. ☎ 307/733–4386) rents bikes and leads tours, including family-style outings to the National Elk Refuge and intermediate or advanced tours from the top of Snow King Mountain. **Teton Mountain Bike Tours** (✉ Box 7027 ☎ 307/733–0712 or 800/733–0788 ⊕ www.wybike.com) leads tours throughout Jackson Hole.

Canoeing, Kayaking & Rafting

South of Jackson, where the Hoback joins the Snake River and the canyon walls become steep, there are lively white-water sections. But the Snake, whose rating is Class I and Class II, is a river for those who value scenery over white-water thrills. For the most part, floating rather than taking on rapids is the theme of running the Snake (with trips usually incorporating Jackson Lake, at the foot of the Tetons); as such, it's a good choice for families with children. What makes the trip special is the Teton Range, looming as high as 8,000 feet above the river. This float trip can also be combined with two or more days of kayaking on Jackson Lake. Raft trips take place between June and September. Experienced paddlers run the Hoback, too.

The Snake River has earned a strange footnote in history as the river that Evel Knievel tried (and failed miserably) to jump over on a rocket-powered motorcycle in the mid-1970s.

At **Snake River Kayak and Canoe** (⊠ 365 N. Cache St. ☎ 307/733–9999 or 800/529–2501 ⊕ www.snakeriverkayak.com) you'll receive instruction in the fine art of paddling, after which you can test yourself on the river. Canoe and kayak rentals are also available. **Teton Aquatics** (⊠ 155 W. Gill Ave. ☎ 307/733–3127) offers boating lessons plus canoe and kayak rentals.

Dogsledding

Dogsledding excursions are available through **Iditarod Sled Dog Tours** (⊠ 11 Granite Creek Rd. ☎ 307/733–7388 or 800/554–7388 ⊕ www.jhsleddog. com). Frank Teasley, a veteran Iditarod racer, leads half-day introductory trips and full-day trips to Granite Hot Springs.

Hiking

Bridger-Teton National Forest (⊠ 340 N. Cache St., Box 1888, 83001 ☎ 307/739–5500 ⊕ www.fs.fed.us/btnf) covers hundreds of thousands of acres of western Wyoming and shelters abundant wildlife. Permits for backcountry use of the forest are necessary only for groups and commercial operators such as outfitters. Contact the forest office for more information.

You can take part in wilderness camping, climbing, and exploration of alpine areas with experienced guides on day trips, overnight excursions, or as part of regular classes offered by **Jackson Hole Mountain Guides** (⊠ 165 N. Glenwood St. ☎ 307/733–4979 ⊕ www.jhmg.com). The guides at **The Hole Hiking Experience** (⊠ Box 7779 83002 ☎ 866/733–4453 or 307/690–4453 ⊕ www.holehike.com) will take you to mountain meadows or to the tops of the peaks on half- or full-day tours. Some outings are suitable for the very experienced, others for any well-conditioned adult, and still others for families.

Skiing

Jack Dennis Sports (⊠ 50 E. Broadway ☎ 307/733–3270, 307/733–4505, or 307/733–5838 ⊕ www.jackdennis.com) sells and rents skis and snowboards, plus outdoor gear for any season. Ski rental costs $25 to $40; snowboard and boot rental costs $25.

☺ **Snow King Resort** (⊠ 400 E. Snow King Ave. ☎ 307/733–5200 or 800/522–5464 ⊕ www.snowking.com), at the western edge of Jackson, has 400 acres of ski runs for daytime use and 110 acres suitable for night skiing, plus an extensive snowmaking system on Snow King Mountain. Also here are a half pipe, snowboard park, and snow-tubing park. In summer there's a waterslide.

Lessons and groomed cross-country trails are available for a fee at **Spring Creek Ranch** (⊠ 1800 Spirit Dance Rd. ☎ 307/733–8833 or 800/443–6139).

Sleigh Rides

☺ Sleigh rides into the National Elk Refuge last about 45 minutes and depart from in front of the **Jackson Hole & Greater Yellowstone Visitor Cen-**

ter (⊠ 532 N. Cache St. ☎ 307/733–5771) daily in winter, 10 to 4, about every 20 minutes. Dinner sleigh rides are available through **Spring Creek Ranch** (⊠ 1800 Spirit Dance Rd. ☎ 307/733–8833 or 800/443–6139), with dinner at its Granary restaurant.

Snowmobiling

Numerous companies in the Jackson area rent snowmobiles. Contact the **Jackson Hole Chamber of Commerce** (⊠ 990 W. Broadway, Box E, 83001 ☎ 307/733–3316 ⊕ www.jacksonholeinfo.com) for information on snowmobile rentals and guides.

Rocky Mountain Snowmobile Tours (⊠ 1050 S. Hwy. 89 ☎ 307/733–2237 or 800/647–2561 ⊕ www.rockymountainsnow.com or www.snowmobiletours.net) guides one- to five-day trips beginning at $190 per day, to such areas as Granite Hot Springs, Togwotee Pass, Gros Ventre Mountains, Grey's River near Alpine, and Yellowstone National Park.

Where to Stay & Eat

There are three reservations services for Jackson Hole. You can make reservations for most lodgings in Jackson through **Central Reservations** (☎ 800/443–6931). Properties managed by **Jackson Hole Resort Lodging** (☎ 800/443–8613 🖷 307/733–1286 ⊕ www.jacksonholewy.com) include rooms, condominiums, and vacation homes at Teton Village, Teton Pines, and the Jackson Hole Racquet Club. **Mountain Property Management** (⊠ 250 Veronica La., Box 2228, Jackson 83001 ☎ 800/992–9948 🖷 307/739–1686 ⊕ www.mpmjh.com) offers condominium, cabin, and luxury-home rentals throughout Jackson Hole.

$$$–$$$$ ✕ **The Snake River Grill.** Choose from fresh fish, free-range meats, and organic produce at this restaurant overlooking Town Square. Buffalo short ribs, vegetarian pasta with mushrooms and artichokes, and grilled elk chops round out the menu, and there's an extensive wine list. ⊠ *84 E. Broadway* ☎ *307/733–0557* ✅ *AE, D, MC, V* ⊗ *No lunch.*

$$$–$$$$ ⧉✕ **Sweetwater Restaurant.** Imaginative takes on salmon, pork tenderloin, and buffalo pot roast are on the dinner menu in this log building with antique oak furnishings. For lunch, you can have a wrap, salad, or sandwich in the outdoor dining area. ⊠ *85 S. King St.* ☎ *307/733–3553* ✅ *AE, D, MC, V.*

$$–$$$$ ✕ **The Blue Lion.** Consistently excellent, distinctive fare is the rule at this white-and-blue clapboard house two blocks from Town Square. Dishes range from Dijon-mustard-rubbed rack of lamb to grilled elk with a brandy-peppercorn sauce to fresh fish, perhaps herb-crusted rainbow trout. There's patio dining in summer. ⊠ *160 N. Millward St.* ☎ *307/733–3912* ✅ *AE, D, MC, V* ⊘ *No smoking* ⊗ *No lunch.*

$$–$$$$ ✕ **Nani's Genuine Pasta House.** The ever-changing menu (each month the menu represents a different region) at this cozy, almost cramped restaurant may contain braised veal shanks with saffron risotto or other regional Italian cooking. Almost hidden behind a motel, Nani's is designed to attract gourmets, not tourists. Vegan dishes are also served, and you can dine in or take out. ⊠ *242 N. Glenwood St.* ☎ *307/733–3888* ✅ *MC, V.*

$$–$$$$ ✕ **Off Broadway Grill.** In addition to seafood and pasta dishes such as Cajun shrimp with black linguine, this spot with a snazzy neon look serves roast pork and grilled venison. There's indoor and outdoor seating. ⊠ *30 King St.* ☎ *307/733–9777* ⊟ *AE, MC, V* ☸ *No lunch.*

$–$$$ ✕ **Billy's Giant Hamburgers.** True to its name, Billy's serves big—really big—burgers that are really, really good, along with several sandwiches. The portions in general are huge. The dining room is casual and noisy at this restaurant sharing an entrance with the Cadillac Grille. Seating options consist of a few booths, tall tables with stools, or the bar. ⊠ *55 N. Cache Dr.* ☎ *307/733–3279* ⊟ *AE, MC, V.*

★ **$–$$$** ✕ **The Bunnery.** Lunch is served year-round and dinner is served in summer at the Bunnery, but it's the breakfasts of omelets and home-baked pastries that are irresistible. All of the breads are made on the premises, mostly of a combined grain known as OSM (oats, sunflower, millet). It's elbow to elbow inside and you may have to wait to be seated on busy mornings, but any inconvenience is well worth it. There's also a decent vegetarian selection here. Try a sticky bun or a piece of Very Berry Pie made from raspberries, strawberries, and blueberries. ⊠ *130 N. Cache St., Hole-in-the-Wall Mall* ☎ *307/733–5474* ⊴ *Reservations not accepted* ⊟ *MC, V* ☸ *No dinner Oct.–Apr.*

$–$$ ✕ **Bubba's Barbecue Restaurant.** Succulent baby-back ribs and mouthwatering spareribs are the specialties at this busy barbecue joint, which evokes the Old West with its large wooden porch, wooden booths, Western paintings, and antique signs. Sandwiches and a huge salad bar with plenty of nonmeat choices are also available. The desserts include homemade pies of the chocolate-buttermilk and fudge-pecan variety. The locals who started this restaurant have since gone on to open other branches in Wyoming. ⊠ *515 W. Broadway* ☎ *307/733–2288* ⊟ *AE, D, MC, V.*

$–$$ ✕ **Jedediah's House of Sourdough.** Friendly, noisy, and elbow knocking, this restaurant a block east of Town Square makes breakfast and lunch for those with big appetites. There are plenty of "sourjacks" (sourdough flapjacks) and biscuits and gravy. Burgers are mountain-man size, and dinners include trout, barbecue chicken, and steak. ⊠ *135 E. Broadway* ☎ *307/733–5671* ⊴ *Reservations not accepted* ⊟ *AE, D, MC, V* ☸ *No dinner Labor Day–Memorial Day.*

$$$$ ✕⊡ **Rusty Parrot.** An imposing river-rock fireplace in the cathedral lounge lends warmth to this timber inn near the center of Jackson. You can walk the four blocks to shops, galleries, and restaurants on Town Square. Handcrafted wooden furnishings fill the rooms, some of which have fireplaces and oversize whirlpool tubs. With body wraps, massages, and facials, the spa is a nice extra. Have dinner at the Wild Sage Restaurant ($$$$), which serves quail, duck, pork, and halibut. This property is not recommended for children under age 12. ⊠ *175 N. Jackson St., 83001* ☎ *307/733–2000 or 800/458–2004* ⊟ *307/733–5566* ⊕ *www.rustyparrot.com* ↘ *31 rooms* ⊘ *Room service, some in-room hot tubs, cable TV, hot tub, spa, library, business services; no smoking* ⊟ *AE, D, DC, MC, V* ⫩⊙⫫ *CP.*

$$$$ ✕⊡ **Spring Creek Ranch.** Outside Jackson on Gros Ventre Butte, this luxury resort has beautiful views of the Tetons. Among the numerous amenities are horseback riding, tennis, and cross-country skiing and sleigh rides in winter. Aside from hotel rooms, there's a mix of studios and condos; many of the accommodations have wood-burning fireplaces and lodgepole-pine furniture. The lobby has Wi-Fi. Among the fine food served at the Granary ($$$–$$$$) are Alaskan halibut, fillet of beef, elk tenderloin, and New Zealand lamb. You can also eat in the Rising Sage Cafe. ⊠ *1800 Spirit Dance Rd., Box 4780, 83001* ☎ *307/733–8833 or 800/443–6139* 🖷 *307/733–1524* ⊕ *www.springcreekranch.com* ➤ *36 rooms, 76 studios and condos* ♿ *2 restaurants, room service, kitchenettes, cable TV, in-room broadband, 2 tennis courts, pool, spa, horseback riding, cross-country skiing, sleigh rides, bar, no-smoking rooms* ▭ *AE, D, DC, MC, V* ⟨○⟩ *BP.*

$$$$
Fodor'sChoice
★
✕▥ **Wort Hotel.** This brick Victorian hotel near Town Square seems to have been around as long as the Tetons, but it feels fresh inside (there's even Wi-Fi in the lobby). A fireplace warms the lobby, and a sitting area is just up the stairs. Locally made Western-style furnishings, including lodgepole-pine beds and pine dressers, decorate the rooms, along with carpets, drapes, and bedcoverings in warm, muted blues and mauves. You can sip a drink in the Silver Dollar Bar ($–$$$$)—aptly named for the 2,032 silver dollars embedded on top of the bar—or sit down for a fine meal there or in the Plug Nickel Cafe. Try the mixed grill of buffalo and elk medallions or the nightly veal special. ⊠ *50 N. Glenwood St., 83001* ☎ *307/733–6964, 307/733–2190, or 800/322–2727* 🖷 *307/733–2067* ⊕ *www.worthotel.com* ➤ *57 rooms, 3 suites* ♿ *2 restaurants, cable TV, in-room broadband, gym, hot tub, bar, business services, meeting rooms, no-smoking rooms* ▭ *AE, D, MC, V.*

★ $$$$
▥ **Amangani.** This exclusive resort built of sandstone and redwood melds into the landscape of Gros Ventre Butte, affording beautiful views of Spring Creek Valley from its cliff. The warm hospitality is Western, but the setting is that of Eastern (as in Asian) simplicity, with tall ceilings, clean lines, and rooms with platform beds, large soaking tubs, and plenty of space. The amenities here are the best in Jackson Hole, and include horseback riding, tennis, and nearby cross-country skiing and sleigh rides in winter. ⊠ *1535 N.E. Butte Rd., Box 15030, 83002* ☎ *307/734–7333 or 877/734–7333* 🖷 *307/734–7332* ⊕ *www.amangani. com* ➤ *40 suites* ♿ *Restaurant, room service, in-room safes, minibars, refrigerators, cable TV, in-room VCRs, in-room data ports, 2 tennis courts, pool, health club, spa, horseback riding, cross-country skiing, sleigh rides, lobby lounge, library, dry cleaning, concierge, meeting room, airport shuttle, no-smoking rooms* ▭ *AE, D, DC, MC, V.*

★ $$$–$$$$
▥ **Parkway Inn.** Each room has a distinctive look, with oak or wicker furniture, and all are filled with antiques, from 19th-century pieces onward. The overall effect is homey and delightful, especially appealing if you plan to stay several days or longer. Breakfast is served in an antiques-filled lounge. This quiet property is just three blocks from the Town Square. ⊠ *125 N. Jackson St., 83001* ☎ *307/733–3143 or 800/247–8390* 🖷 *307/733–0955* ⊕ *www.parkwayinn.com* ➤ *37 rooms, 12 suites* ♿ *Indoor pool, gym, hot tub, sauna, no-smoking rooms; no room TVs, no a/c* ▭ *AE, D, DC, MC, V* ⟨○⟩ *BP.*

$$–$$$
▥ **Trapper Inn.** This motel is within walking distance of Town Square and has some of the best-appointed rooms for people with disabilities in Jackson. ⊠ *235 N. Cache St., 83001* ☎ *307/733–2648* 🖷 *307/739–*

9351 ⊕ *www.trapperinn.com* ⊅ *54 rooms* ⌂ *Cable TV, refrigerators, microwaves, outdoor hot tub, laundry facilities, no-smoking rooms* ▤ *AE, D, DC, MC, V.*

$–$$$ ▨ **Cowboy Village Resort.** Stay in your own small log cabin with covered decks and barbecue grills. There is a ski-waxing room, and both the START Bus and Targhee Express buses that serve the ski areas stop here. Continental breakfast is served in winter. ⊠ *120 S. Flat Creek, 83001* ☎ *307/733–3121 or 800/962–4988* ⊞ *307/739–1955* ⊕ *www.townsquareinns. com* ⊅ *82 cabins* ⌂ *Some kitchenettes, cable TV, hot tub, laundry facilities, business services, no-smoking rooms* ▤ *AE, D, MC, V.*

$$ ▨ **Days Inn.** Like other chain properties, this motel is familiar, but the lodgepole-pine swing out front, the lobby's elk-antler chandelier, and the rooms' Teton, Wind River Range, or Snake River views remind you where you are. There are ski-boot and glove dryers in the lobby, plus in-room ski racks and safes. ⊠ *350 S. Hwy. 89, 83001* ☎ *307/739–9010* ⊞ *307/733–0044* ⊅ *91 rooms* ⌂ *In-room safes, some microwaves, some refrigerators, hot tub, sauna, ski storage, cable TV, no-smoking rooms* ▤ *AE, D, DC, MC, V* ⦿⟊ *CP.*

$–$$ ▨ **Antler Inn.** As real estate agents say, location, location, location, and perhaps no motel in Jackson has a better location than the Antler, one block south of Town Square. Some rooms have fireplaces, but they are otherwise standard motel rooms (indeed, the neon sign calls this place the Antler Motel). In winter there's a complimentary ski shuttle. ⊠ *43 W. Pearl St., 83001* ☎ *307/733–2535 or 800/483–8667* ⊞ *307/733–2002* ⊕ *www.townsquareinns.com* ⊅ *110 rooms* ⌂ *Restaurant, cable TV, in-room data ports, exercise equipment, hot tub, sauna, laundry facilities, meeting room, some pets allowed, no-smoking rooms* ▤ *AE, D, MC, V.*

Camping

⚠ **Curtis Canyon.** Numerous trees surround this simple campground northeast of Jackson Hole. Part of Bridger-Teton National Forest, the campground is near a popular mountain-biking area and sits at an elevation of 6,600 feet. ⌂ *Pit toilets, drinking water, fire pits, picnic tables* ⊅ *11 sites* ⊠ *Off Broadway, 7 mi northeast of Jackson* ☎ *307/739–5400 or 307/543–2386* ⊕ *www.fs.fed.us/btnf/* ⊡ *$12* ⌂ *Reservations not accepted* ▤ *No credit cards* ⊙ *Late May–Sept.*

⚠ **Granite Creek.** Part of Bridger-Teton National Forest, this wooded campground is a big, noisy place convenient to hiking and mountain-biking trails. An added bonus are the small pools of Granite Hot Springs. The elevation is 7,100 feet and there are wheelchair-accessible sites. ⌂ *Flush toilets, pit toilets, drinking water, fire pits, picnic tables* ⊅ *52 sites* ⊠ *Granite Creek Rd. off U.S. 189/191, 35 mi southeast of Jackson* ☎ *307/739–5400 or 307/543–2386* ⊕ *www.fs.fed.us/btnf* ⊡ *$15* ⌂ *Reservations not accepted* ▤ *No credit cards* ⊙ *Late May–Sept.*

Nightlife & the Arts

Nightlife

There's never a shortage of live music in Jackson, where local performers play country, rock, and folk. Some of the most popular bars are on Town Square. At the **Million Dollar Cowboy Bar** (⊠ 25 N. Cache St. ☎ 307/733–2207), everyone dresses up in cowboy garb and tries to two-step into the Old West. There's live country music most nights at the **Rancher Bar** (⊠ 20 E. Broadway ☎ 307/733–3886). Various musical performers and dancing are nightly events at the **Shady Lady Saloon** (⊠ 400 E. Snow King Ave. ☎ 307/733–5200) at the Snow King Resort. Folks head to the **Virginian Saloon** (⊠ 750 W. Broadway ☎ 307/733–2792) to shoot a game of pool, listen to live music, and sip a drink by the fireplace.

The Arts

Artists who work in a variety of mediums show and sell their work at the **Jackson Hole Fall Arts Festival** (☎ 307/733–3316), with special events highlighting art, poetry, and dance. Festival events take place throughout town in September, and many art galleries in Jackson have special programs and exhibits. At the **Jackson Hole Playhouse** (⊠ 145 W. Deloney Ave. ☎ 307/733–6994) you can attend live theater from late May to September; some of the performances are dinner shows.

Shopping

Jackson's peaceful Town Square is surrounded by storefronts with a mixture of specialty and outlet shops—most of them small scale—with moderate to expensive prices. North of Jackson's center, on Cache Street, is a small cluster of fine shops on Gaslight Alley.

Books

One of Gaslight Alley's best shops is **Valley Bookstore** (⊠ 125 N. Cache St. ☎ 307/733–4533). It ranks among the top bookstores in the region, with a big selection of regional history, guidebooks on flora and fauna, and fiction by Wyoming and regional authors.

Clothing

Hide Out Leather (⊠ 40 N. Center St. ☎ 307/733–2422) carries many local designs and has a diverse selection of men's and women's coats, vests, and accessories such as pillows and throws. Try **Jackson Hole Clothiers** (⊠ 45 E. Deloney Ave. ☎ 307/733–7211) for women's Western wear, belts, purses, and leather jackets.

Craft & Art Galleries

Jackson's art galleries serve a range of tastes. **Di Tommaso Galleries** (⊠ 172 Center St. ☎ 307/734–9677) has a collection of 19th- and 20th-century art by Michael Coleman, Harry Jackson, Francois Koch, and Tony Eubanks, and also sells fine furniture and African art. The fine nature photography of Tom Mangelson is displayed at his **Images of Nature Gallery** (⊠ 170 N. Cache St. ☎ 307/733–9752). **Trailside Galleries** (⊠ 105 N. Center St. ☎ 307/733–3186) sells traditional Western art

Fodor'sChoice and jewelry. The photography of Abi Garaman is highlighted at **Under**
★ **the Willow Photo Gallery** (⊠ 50 S. Cache St. ☎ 307/733–6633). He has been photographing in Jackson Hole for decades and has produced a wide selection of images of wildlife, mountains, barns, and both summer and winter scenes. **Wilcox Gallery** (⊠ 1975 N. Hwy. 89 ☎ 307/733–6450) showcases wildlife and landscape paintings, sculpture, pottery,

and other works by contemporary artists. **Wild By Nature Gallery** (⊠ 95 W. Deloney Ave. ☎ 307/733–8877) displays wildlife and landscape photography by Henry W. Holdsworth, plus books and notecards. **Wild Exposures Gallery** (⊠ 60 E. Broadway ☎ 307/739–1777) represents photographers Jeff Hogan, Scott McKinley, and Andrew Weller, all of whose work has appeared on National Geographic and BBC programs.

Sporting Goods

Jackson's premier sports shop, **Jack Dennis Sports** (⊠ 50 E. Broadway ☎ 307/733–3270) is well stocked with the best in outdoor equipment for winter and summer activities. It also has a store at Teton Village. **Skinny Skis** (⊠ 65 W. Deloney Ave. ☎ 307/733–6094) offers everything a cross-country skier might need. **Teton Mountaineering** (⊠ 170 N. Cache St. ☎ 307/733–3595) specializes in Nordic-skiing, climbing, and hiking equipment and clothing. **Westbank Anglers** (⊠ 3670 N. Moose-Wilson Rd. ☎ 307/733–6483) can provide all the equipment necessary for fly-fishing.

AROUND JACKSON HOLE

In this part of Wyoming you need to keep one thing straight: there is Jackson, and then there is Jackson Hole, both named for fur trapper David Jackson, who spent a great deal of time in the area in the late 1820s and early 1830s. The first is the small town; the second is the larger geographic area surrounding the town (and called a hole because it is encircled by mountains). In addition to Jackson, Jackson Hole includes Grand Teton National Park and the small towns of Kelly, Moose, Moran, and Wilson. Also here is Teton Village, the center for the Jackson Hole Mountain Resort, best known for skiing in winter but popular for summer activities as well.

Although you might headquarter in Jackson, most of the outdoor activities in the region occur in Jackson Hole. The valley has a world-class ski mountain and hiking and biking trails, and the Snake River, ideal for fishing or floating, runs right through the middle of it.

Teton Village & Jackson Hole Mountain Resort

⑱ *11 mi northwest of Jackson via Hwy. 22 and Teton Village Rd.*

Teton Village resounds with the clomping of ski boots in winter and with the sounds of violins, horns, and other instruments at the Grand Teton Music Festival in summer. The village mostly consists of the restaurants, lodging properties, and shops built to serve the skiers who flock to Jackson Hole Mountain Resort. This is possibly the best ski resort area in the United States, and the expanse and variety of terrain are incredible. In summer, folks come here to hike, ride the tram, and attend high-caliber concerts.

As it travels to the summit of Rendezvous Peak, the **Aerial Tramway** affords spectacular panoramas of Jackson Hole. There are several hiking trails at the top of the mountain. Trams depart every 15 to 30 minutes. The tram will be will be closed and dismantled in September 2006, after the summer season, and replaced by chairlifts or a new tram. ⊠ *Teton Village* ☎ *307/733–2292 or 800/333–7766* ☜*$17* ☼ *Memorial Day–late Sept., daily 9–5 or 6.*

Sports & the Outdoors

GOLF The 18-hole **Teton Pines Golf Club** (⊠ 3450 N. Clubhouse St. ☎ 307/733–1733 ⊕ www.tetonpines.com) lies south of the Jackson Hole Mountain Resort.

HIKING The plus here is that much of the uphill legwork can be dispensed with by the **Aerial Tramway** (⊠ Teton Village ☎ 307/733–2292 or 800/333–7766), the same one that carries Jackson Hole skiers upward in winter (note that the tramway will close permanently in September 2006, to be replaced by either a new tram or chairlifts). From the top of Rendezvous Peak you can walk through high-mountain basins filled with wildflowers in summer or along cliff-line ridges, all against the stunning backdrop of the Tetons. The weather and wildflowers are best between July and August.

A loop of about 30 mi can be made by picking up the Teton Crest Trail, then branching off on the Death Canyon Trail. Don't necessarily expect solitude; most of the time, you're in Grand Teton National Park, an exceedingly popular tourist destination. However, this route keeps you well away from the visitor crush at the park's main gate, so you aren't likely to encounter hiker traffic jams, either.

Downhill Skiing & Snowboarding

Fodor'sChoice A place to appreciate both as a skier and as a voyeur, **Jackson Hole Moun-**
★ **tain Resort** is truly one of the great skiing experiences in America. There are literally thousands of ways of getting from top to bottom, and not all of them are hellishly steep, despite Jackson's reputation. First-rate racers such as Olympic champion skier Tommy Moe and snowboarders Julie Zell, A. J. Cargill, and Rob Kingwill regularly train here. As Kingwill has put it, "nothing really compares to Jackson Hole . . . This place has the most consistently steep terrain. You can spend years and years here and never cross your trail."

On the resort map, about 111 squiggly lines designate named trails, but this doesn't even begin to suggest the thousands of different skiable routes. The resort claims 2,500 skiable acres, a figure that seems unduly conservative. And although Jackson is best known for its advanced to extreme skiing, it is also a place where imaginative intermediates can go exploring and have the time of their lives. It is not, however, a good place for novice skiers.

A word of caution. High snowfall some winters can lead to extreme avalanche danger in spite of efforts by the Ski Patrol to make the area as safe as possible. Before venturing from known trails and routes, check with the Ski Patrol for conditions. Ski with a friend, and always carry an emergency locator device. ⌂ *Box 290, Teton Village 83025* ☎ *307/733–2292 or 800/333–7766* ⊕ *www.jacksonhole.com.*

FACILITIES 4,139-foot vertical drop; 2,500 skiable acres; 10% beginner, 40% intermediate, 50% expert; 1 gondola, 6 quad chairs, 2 triple chairs, 1 double chair, 1 surface lift.

LESSONS & PROGRAMS
Half-day group lessons at the **Jackson Hole Ski & Snowboard School** (☎ 307/733–2292 or 800/450–0477) start at $85. There are extensive children's programs, including lessons for kids 6 to 13 years old and day care for children from 6 months to 2 years old. Nordic-skiing lessons start at $45. For expert skiers, the **Jackson Hole Ski Camps** (☎ 307/739–2791 or 800/450–0477), headed by such skiers as Tommy Moe, the 1994 Olympic gold medalist, and top snowboarders like Julie Zell, A. J. Cargill, and Jessica Baker, run for five days, teaching everything from big-mountain free-skiing to racing techniques. The cost is $820 per person.

LIFT TICKETS
Lift tickets cost $70. You can save about 10%–30% on five- to seven-day tickets.

RENTALS
Equipment can be rented at ski shops in Jackson and Teton Village. **Jackson Hole Sports** (☎ 307/733–4005 or 800/443–6931), at the Bridger Center at the ski area, offers ski and snowboard rental packages starting at $20 a day. You can buy or rent skis or snowboards at **Pepi Stegler Sports Shop** (☎ 307/733–3270 ⊕ www.jackdennis.com), a branch of the Jackson-based Jack Dennis Sports. Ski rentals cost between $25 and $40; snowboard rentals are $25. The store is at the base of Rendezvous Peak.

HELI-SKIING
In general, heli-skiing is best done when there has been relatively little recent snowfall. For two or three days after a storm, good powder skiing can usually be found within the ski area. Daily trips can be arranged through **High Mountain Helicopter Skiing** (✉ Jackson Hole Mountain Resort base area ☎ 307/733–3274 ⊕ www.heliskijackson.com).

Nordic Skiing

BACKCOUNTRY SKIING
Few areas in North America can compete with Jackson Hole when it comes to the breadth, beauty, and variety of backcountry opportunities. For touring skiers, one of the easier areas (because of flatter routes) is along the base of the Tetons toward Jenny and Jackson lakes. Telemark skiers (or even skiers on alpine gear) can find numerous downhill routes by skiing in from Teton Pass, snow stability permitting. A guide isn't required for tours to the national park lakes but might be helpful for those unfamiliar with the lay of the land; trails and trail markers set in summer can become obscured by winter snows. When you are touring elsewhere, a guide familiar with the area and avalanche danger is a virtual necessity. The Tetons are big country, and the risks are commensurately large as well.

Alpine Guides (☎ 307/739–2663) leads half-day and full-day backcountry tours into the national parks and other areas near the resort, for more downhill-minded skiers. Arrangements can also be made through the Jackson Hole Ski School. **Jackson Hole Mountain Guides** (✉ 165 N. Glenwood St., Jackson ☎ 307/733–4979 ⊕ www.jhmg.com) leads strenuous backcountry tours. The **Jackson Hole Nordic Center** (☎ 307/733–2292 or 800/450–0477) at Teton Village has cross-country, telemark, and snowshoe rentals and track and telemark lessons. The center also leads naturalist tours into the backcountry. Rental packages begin at $25 and lessons start at $75, including rental equipment and a $10 trail pass. Forest Service rangers lead free snowshoe tours; the Nordic Center also runs snowshoe tours, starting from $60. Sled dog tours start at $120.

TRACK SKIING   The **Jackson Hole Nordic Center** (☎ 307/739–2292 or 800/450–0477 ⊕ www.jacksonhole.com) is at the ski-resort base. The scenic 17 km (10½) mi of groomed track is relatively flat. Because the Nordic Center and the downhill ski area are under the same management, downhill skiers with multiday passes can switch over to Nordic skiing in the afternoon for no extra charge. Otherwise, the cost is $10 for a day pass. Rentals and lessons are available; alpine lift tickets are also good at the Nordic Center.

Where to Stay & Eat

In the winter ski season, it can be cheaper to stay in Jackson, about 20 minutes away; in summer it's generally cheaper to stay at Teton Village.

$$$$ ✕ **Solitude Cabin Dinner Sleigh Rides.** Climb aboard a horse-drawn sleigh and ride through the trees to a log cabin for a dinner of prime rib, broiled salmon, or a vegetarian entrée. Live entertainment is provided. ⊠ *Jackson Hole Mountain Resort* ☎ *307/739–2603* ⚛ *Reservations required* ▭ *AE, D, DC, MC, V* ⊗ *Closed Apr.–early Dec.*

$$–$$$$ ✕ **Mangy Moose.** Folks pour in off the ski slopes for a lot of food and talk at this two-level restaurant with a bar and an outdoor deck. There's a high noise level but decent food consisting of prime rib, steak, ribs, buffalo meat loaf, and even crab legs. The place is adorned with antiques, including a full-size stuffed caribou and sleigh suspended from the ceiling. ⊠ *3295 W. McCollister St.* ☎ *307/733–4913* ▭ *AE, MC, V.*

$$$$ ▥ **R Lazy S Ranch.** Jackson Hole, with the spectacle of the Tetons in the background, is true dude-ranch country, and the R Lazy S is one of the largest dude ranches in the area. Horseback riding and instruction are the main attraction, with a secondary emphasis on fishing, either in private waters on the ranch or at other rivers and streams. One of the regular activities is a scenic float on the Snake River. You stay in log-cabin guest cottages and gather for meals in the large main lodge. There's a one-week minimum stay. ⊠ *1 mi north of Teton Village, Box 308, 83025* ☎ *307/733–2655* 🖷 *307/734–1120* ⊕ *www.rlazys.com* ⇆ *14 cabins* ⚛ *Dining room, fishing, horseback riding, no-smoking rooms; no kids under 7, no room TVs, no a/c* ▭ *No credit cards* ⊗ *Closed Oct.–mid-June* ⦿ *FAP.*

$$$–$$$$ ▥ **Alpenhof Lodge.** This small Austrian-style hotel is in the heart of Jackson Hole Mountain Resort, next to the tram. Hand-carved Bavarian furniture fills the rooms. All the deluxe rooms have balconies, and some have fireplaces and Jacuzzis. Standard rooms are smaller and don't have balconies. Entrées such as wild game loaf, Wiener schnitzel, and fondue are served in the dining room, and Dietrich's Bar and Bistro is a relatively quiet nightclub that also offers casual dining. The lobby and some rooms have Wi-Fi. ⊠ *3255 W. McCollister Dr., 83025* ☎ *307/ 733–3242 or 800/732–3244* 🖷 *307/739–1516* ⊕ *www.alpenhoflodge. com* ⇆ *42 rooms* ⚛ *Dining room, cable TV, in-room broadband, pool, spa, ski storage, bar, nightclub; no smoking, no a/c* ▭ *AE, D, DC, MC, V* ⊗ *Closed Oct., Nov., and mid-Apr.–May* ⦿ *CP.*

¢ ▥ **The Hostelx.** Although the classic hostel accommodations at this lodge-style inn are basic, you can't get any closer to Jackson Hole Mountain Resort for a better price. It's popular with young, budget-conscious people. Rooms, some of which have bunk beds, sleep two to four people. Downstairs common areas include a lounge with a fireplace, a movie room, and a ski-waxing room. ⊠ *3315 McCollister Dr., Box 546, 83025* ☎ *307/733–3415* 🖷 *307/739–1142* ⊕ *www.hostelx.com* ⟿ *55 rooms* ♿ *Lounge, library, recreation room, laundry facilities, Internet room, no-smoking rooms; no room phones, no room TVs, no a/c* ⊟ *MC, V* ⎰⎱ *BP.*

The Arts

In summer the symphony orchestra performances of the **Grand Teton Music Festival** (⊡ Box 490, Teton Village, 83025 ☎ 307/733–1128 or 800/959–4863 ⊕ www.gtmf.org) are held outside at Teton Village. A winter series takes place in Walk Festival Hall. Tickets cost between $16 and $75.

Shopping

At the **Mountainside Mall** (⊠ Teton Village ☎ No phone), not to be mistaken for a big suburban mall (to its credit), you can find goggles, snowboards, skis, and clothing ranging from parkas to swimsuits.

Wilson

⑲ *6 mi south of Teton Village on Teton Village Rd., 4 mi west of Jackson on Hwy. 22.*

If you want to avoid the hustle and bustle of Jackson, Wilson makes a good alternative base for exploring Grand Teton National Park or skiing at Jackson Hole Mountain Resort. This small town takes its name from Nick Wilson, one of the first homesteaders in the area, a man who spent part of his childhood living with the Shoshone Indians.

Where to Stay & Eat

$$–$$$$ ✕ **Nora's Fish Creek Inn.** Among the dishes served at this casual log inn are honey-hickory baby-back ribs, prime rib, and nut-crusted trout, plus nightly specials. There's also a kids' menu. You can dine in one of two large rooms or sit at the counter for quick service. Breakfast, but not lunch, is served on weekends. ⊠ *Hwy. 22* ☎ *307/733–8288* ⊟ *AE, D, MC, V* ⊗ *No lunch weekends.*

$$$ ✕ **Bar J Chuckwagon.** At the best bargain in the Jackson Hole area,
Fodor'sChoice you'll get a true ranch-style meal along with some of the best Western
★ entertainment in the region. The food, served on a tin plate, includes barbecued roast beef, chicken, or rib-eye steak, plus potatoes, beans, biscuits, applesauce, spice cake, and ranch coffee or lemonade. The multitalented Bar J Wranglers sing, play instruments, share cowboy stories and poetry, and even yodel. "Lap-size" children eat free. The doors open at 5:30, so you can explore the Bar J's Western village—including a saloon and several shops—before the dinner bell rings at 7:30. The dining area is covered, so no need to worry if the sun isn't shining. ⊠ *4200 Bar J Chuckwagon Rd.* ☎ *307/733–3370* ⊟ *D, MC, V.*

$–$$ ⨯ **Vista Grande.** You'll get a generous portion of Mexican fare here, but if you like a lot of heat and spice, you may find this food a bit bland. Favorites include blackened-chicken tostada salad, fresh veggie burritos, and crab chimichangas. Service can be on the slow side, but gazing at the Tetons from the window or from the deck is a great way to pass the time. This is a popular place, so it can get crowded and noisy. ⊠ *2550 Teton Village Rd., near Wilson turnoff* ☎ *307/733–6964* ⚠ *Reservations not accepted* ▤ *MC, V.*

$$$–$$$$ 🏠 **The Painted Porch Bed and Breakfast.** Cozy, clean, and comfortable, this traditional red-and-white farmhouse built in 1901 is nestled on 3½ acres of pine and aspen about midway between Jackson and Teton Village. The rooms, both with private entrances, blend Western-style furnishings, antiques, and designer linens. There is a two-night minimum stay. ⊠ *3755 N. Moose-Wilson Rd., 83002* ☎ *307/733–1981* 🖶 *307/733–1564* ⊕ *www.jacksonholebedandbreakfast.com* 🛏 *2 rooms, 1 cabin* ♨ *In-room hot tubs, library; no room TVs, no a/c, no smoking* ▤ *AE, D, MC, V* ⏃ *BP.*

$$–$$$ 🏠 **Teton Tree House.** On a steep hillside and surrounded by trees, this is a real retreat. Ninety-five steps lead to this cozy lodgepole-pine bed-and-breakfast tucked away in the forest. Decks abound, rooms are full of wood furniture and warm Southwestern colors, and an inviting common area has a two-story old-fashioned adobe fireplace. ⊠ *6175 Heck of a Hill Rd., Box 550, 83014* ☎ *307/733–3233* 🖶 *307/733–3233* 🛏 *6 rooms* ♨ *Dining room, hot tub; no room TVs, no a/c, no smoking, no kids under 6* ▤ *D, MC, V* ⏃ *BP.*

Nightlife

The **Stagecoach Bar** (⊠ Hwy. 22 ☎ 307/733–4407) fills to bursting when local bands play, and is a good place to enjoy a drink and conversation at other times.

Shopping

Clothing, groceries, and camping supplies are available at **Hungry Jack's General Store** (⊠ 5855 W. Hwy. 22 ☎ 307/733–3561), next to the post office in Wilson.

en route   The drive between Wilson and Alta over the **Teton Pass** on Highway 22 affords outstanding views of Idaho's Teton Valley, known as Pierre's Hole to the mountain men of the 1800s, on the west and Jackson Hole on the east. The steep and winding road closes sometimes in winter due to avalanche danger, but in summer it is a wildflower paradise.

Alta

20   *27 mi northwest of Wilson via Hwy. 22 to Hwy. 33 (in Idaho) to Alta cutoff (back to Wyoming).*

Alta is the site of the Grand Targhee Ski and Summer Resort, famed for its deep powder and family atmosphere. The slopes never feel crowded, but to experience complete solitude, try a day of Sno-Cat skiing in untracked powder.

Sports & the Outdoors

An average of 500 inches of powder attracts skiers to **Grand Targhee Ski & Summer Resort** (⊠ Ski Hill Rd. ☎ 307/353–2300 or 800/827–4433 ⊕ www.grandtarghee.com), with 2,000 acres, 1,000 of which are dedicated to powder Sno-Cat skiing. There are four lifts and one rope tow, and the vertical drop is 2,400 feet. Lift tickets are $55 per day; Nordic trail permits are $10. Classes are available.

Where to Stay & Eat

$$–$$$$　✕▥ **Grand Targhee Ski and Summer Resort.** This modern facility perched on the west side of the Tetons has a handsome, natural-wood look and the atmosphere of an alpine village. Clustered around common areas with fireplaces, the motel-style rooms are simply furnished with Western furniture; the condominium rooms are brighter and more spacious. Targhee Steakhouse ($$–$$$$) is the resort's foremost restaurant. The Trap Bar and Grille and Wild Bill's Grille serve quicker, less expensive food, while Snorkel's has bakery items, espresso, and deli sandwiches. ⊠ *Ski Hill Rd., Box SKI, 83422* ☎ *307/353–2300 or 800/827–4433* ⊕ *www.grandtarghee.com* ↝ *65 rooms, 32 condos* ⚋ *4 restaurants, some kitchenettes, cable TV, pool, hot tubs (indoor and outdoor), spa, cross-country skiing, downhill skiing, sleigh rides, shops, airport shuttle, free parking, no-smoking rooms* ▭ *AE, D, MC, V.*

THE WIND RIVER RANGE

Rising to the east and southeast of Jackson Hole is the Wind River Range, which remains snowcapped year-round and still holds small glaciers. Much of this range is rugged wilderness, ideal for backcountry hiking and horseback riding. Several towns here make good bases for exploring the area, including Pinedale on the west side of the range; Atlantic City, within the range itself; and Lander, Fort Washakie, and Dubois on the east side of the range.

Pinedale

㉑ *77 mi southeast of Jackson on Hwy. 191.*

A southern gateway to Jackson Hole, Pinedale has much to offer on its own, for the spirit of the mountain man lives on here. Fur trappers found the icy streams of the Green River watershed to be among the best places to capture beaver. In the mid-1800s they gathered on the river near what is now Pinedale for seven annual rendezvous. Now, the Museum of the Mountain Man preserves their heritage, and modern-day buckskinners continue to meet in the area each summer.

To the east are millions of acres of Bridger-Teton National Forest, much of it off-limits to all but foot and horse traffic. The peaks reach higher than 13,000 feet, and the area is liberally sprinkled with more than a thousand high-mountain lakes where fishing is generally excellent. Contact the **Bridger-Teton National Forest, Pinedale Ranger District** (⊠ 29 E. Fremont Lake Rd., Box 220, 82941 ☎ 307/367–4326 ⊕ www.fs.fed.us/btnf) for more information. Although outdoor activities still beckon in the forest, an oil and gas development boom in the area keeps motel rooms full year-round, and restaurants can be busy.

Buckskinners and reenactors gather in Pinedale annually during the second weekend of July for the **Green River Rendezvous** (☎ 307/367–4101 ⊕ www.pinedaleonline.com), which commemorates the get-togethers the fur trappers and traders staged between 1825 and 1843 (seven of which were in what is now Pinedale). Highlights include a parade, crafts, booths, and a historical pageant.

★ ♨ The **Museum of the Mountain Man** depicts the trapper heritage of the area with displays of 19th-century guns, traps, clothing, and beaver pelts. There's also an exhibit devoted to the pioneer and ranch history of Sublette County. In summer the museum hosts living-history demonstrations, children's events, and lectures. ✉ 700 E. Hennick Rd. ☎ 307/367–4101 ⊕ www.museumofthemountainman.com ☜ $5 ☉ May–Sept., daily 10–5; call for winter hrs.

Sports & the Outdoors

Encompassing parts of the Wind River range, the **Bridger-Teton National Forest, Pinedale Ranger District** (✉ Forest office, 29 E. Fremont Lake Rd. ☎ 307/367–4326 ⊕ www.fs.fed.us/btnf) holds hundreds of thousands of acres to explore. The fishing is generally excellent in the numerous mountain lakes, and you can also hike, snowmobile, camp, and picnic here.

Where to Stay & Eat

$$–$$$$ ✕ **Stockmen's Restaurant.** The salad bar is shaped like a tepee, and there's a 1903 map of the area at this restaurant, a local hangout since 1933. On the menu are burgers, salads, prime rib, steaks, and seafood. Smoking is allowed, so it can get hazy at times. ✉ 117 W. Pine St. ☎ 307/367–4562 or 307/367–4563 ▤ MC, V.

$–$$$ ✕ **McGregors Pub.** Built in 1905, this converted hotel has a classic Western interior with a restaurant on the ground floor. Local folks like the steaks and seafood; the menu also has Italian dishes, and there's a kids' menu. You can eat inside or outside on the patio. ✉ 21 N. Franklin St. ☎ 307/367–4443 ▤ AE, D, DC, MC, V.

$–$$$ ✕ **Moose Creek Trading Company.** As the name suggests, this downtown restaurant employs a moose motif, reflected, for example, in the wrought-iron bar tables with carvings of the animal. The menu includes various sandwiches, plus homemade pies and desserts. Try the chunky chicken salad for a light summer meal. ✉ 44 W. Pine St. ☎ 307/367–4616 ▤ AE, D, DC, MC, V ☉ No dinner.

★ $$ ▥ **Chambers House B&B.** Huge pine trees surround this 1933 log home filled with the owner's family antiques. Downstairs there's a sitting room where you can relax with a book or chat with other guests. The master bedroom, with a fireplace, private bathroom, and private entrance, is also on the ground floor. Three of the upstairs bedrooms share bathroom facilities; a fourth has a private bathroom and a fireplace. ✉ 111 W. Magnolia St., 82941 ☎ 307/367–2168 or 800/367–2168 ⊕ www. chambershouse.com ➾ 5 rooms, 2 with bath ⚹ Dining room, some pets allowed (fee); no phones in some rooms, no TV in some rooms, no smoking, no a/c ▤ AE, D, DC, MC, V ⊚ BP.

CloseUp

TOUGH MEN, STRONG WOMEN

HISTORY IS EVERYWHERE you look in northwest Wyoming. Seeking their fortunes and a better life out West, hundreds of thousands of pioneers made their way through the South Pass section of the Wind River Range between 1843 and 1870. A representative from South Pass City, south of Lander, introduced the legislation that made Wyoming the first territory in the nation to grant women the right to vote. Countless others in this ruggedly beautiful region wrote their own chapters in the story of the American West.

Native Americans

Northwest Wyoming was originally populated by the Eastern Shoshones and Northern Arapahos, and the Gros Ventres, Bannocks, and Crows also spent time here. You can see evidence of their ancient presence throughout the area, at sites such as the Medicine Wheel outside Lovell. Numerous powwows manifest the enduring Native American presence; members of the Northern Arapaho and Shoshone tribes still live on the Wind River Indian Reservation at Fort Washakie.

Mountain Men

John Colter was the first white man known to visit this part of Wyoming. He spent the winter of 1807 here and "discovered" the area that became Yellowstone National Park.

Other mountain men followed, seeking beaver began filtering into the region. In 1825, Andrew Henry met and traded with beaver trappers on the Black Fork of the Green River, in what came to be known as the first mountain-man rendezvous. For the next 18 years, trappers and traders, along with Native Americans and even a few missionaries, gathered annually. The trappers sold or exchanged the beaver pelts (called "plews") they'd harvested during the previous winter for goods brought by the traders, such as weapons,

ammunition, food, clothing, and other supplies they would need for another year of trapping.

Although the first rendezvous was a quiet affair, simply an opportunity to exchange furs for supplies, subsequent gatherings were often raucous events soaked with whiskey. A rendezvous could last anywhere from a few days to several weeks. At least seven rendezvous took place on the Upper Green River near present-day Pinedale, where you can learn more at the Museum of the Mountain Man. Two other rendezvous took place on the Wind River near present-day Riverton.

Women's Rights

Such a rough-and-tumble beginning might not seem to portend a bright future for women in the region, but it became a pioneer in women's rights. In 1869, the territory enacted a law granting women the right to vote, to serve on juries, and to hold office, making it the first territory to grant women such broad political rights. The following year, 70-year-old Louisa "Grandma" Swain cast the first woman's ballot in Laramie.

Wyoming was not the first place in the United States where women voted—Utah Territory holds that honor—but it was here that the first all-female jury heard a case, in Laramie. The northwest part of the territory played a prominent role in the history of women's rights: America's first female justice of the peace (Esther Hobart Morris) was appointed at South Pass City in February 1870, and in 1920 an all-female town council, believed to be the first of its kind in the country, served in Jackson. To learn more about women's rights in Wyoming, visit the home of Esther Hobart Morris in South Pass City and the Jackson Hole Museum.

$-$$ 🏨 **The Lodge at Pinedale.** This three-story motel is across a parking lot from the town's movie theater and bowling alley. Green carpeting and bed coverings decorate the rooms. ⊠ *1054 W. Pine St., 82941* ☎ *307/367–8800 or 866/995–6343* 🖷 *307/367–8812* ⊕ *www.pinedalelodge. com* ➘ *41 rooms, 2 suites* ⚹ *Microwaves, refrigerators, cable TV, in-room data ports, indoor pool, hot tub, some pets allowed (fee), business services; no smoking* ⊟ *AE, D, DC, MC, V* ⧖ *CP.*

$ 🏨 **Best Western Pinedale Inn.** On the north side of town, this hotel is within three blocks of downtown shopping and restaurants. The rooms aren't large, but they have contemporary furniture. ⊠ *850 W. Pine St., 82941* ☎ *307/367–6869* 🖷 *307/367–6897* ⊕ *www.bestwestern.com* ➘ *58 rooms* ⚹ *Some refrigerators, cable TV, indoor pool, exercise equipment, hot tub, some pets allowed, no-smoking rooms* ⊟ *AE, D, DC, MC, V* ⧖ *CP.*

The Arts

The annual **Blues Festival** (⊠ Rendezvous Rodeo Grounds ☎ 307/367–2448 ⊕ www.pinedableblues.com), highlighting blues and bluegrass, takes place the third weekend in June.

Photographs by Dan Abernathy, plus watercolors and sculpture, are on display and for sale at **Rock Rabbit Gallery** (⊠ 36 W. Pine St. ☎ 307/367–2448).

Shopping

The Cowboy Shop (⊠ 129 W. Pine St. ☎ 877/567–6336) stocks Western and cowpoke clothing for all ages, including hats and boots, and also sells leather goods and regional books.

en route | As you drive south of Pinedale along U.S. 191, the mountains of the Wind River Range seem to fade down to a low point. This is **South Pass,** the area through which some 500,000 emigrants traveled over the Oregon, Mormon, and California trails between 1843 and 1870.

Atlantic City

🄴 *36 mi south of Pinedale via U.S. 191 to Farson, then 25 mi east on Hwy. 28.*

Now a near ghost town, this onetime boomtown has a few residents, a couple of tourist-oriented businesses, dirt streets, late-19th-century buildings, and a whole lot of atmosphere. The town formed in 1868 when gold rushers flocked to the area seeking their fortune. Known for its red-light district, Atlantic City was where Wyoming Territory's first brewery opened in the late 1860s. Once the gold boom had petered out less than a decade later, however, residents deserted the town. Atlantic City had a few more smaller rushes over the years, but it never boomed again.

South Pass City, 2 mi west of Atlantic City, was established with the discovery of gold in the region in 1867, and in its heyday it had around 1,000 residents. The town went bust in the 1870s, and the ghost town that remained is now the **South Pass City State Historic Site.** You can tour many of the original buildings that survive and have been restored, and

Fodor'sChoice
★

you can even try your hand at gold panning. With artifacts and photographs of the town at its peak, the small museum here gives an overview of the South Pass gold district.

South Pass City has another claim to fame. Julia Bright and Esther Hobart Morris are two of the women from the community who firmly believed that women should have the right to vote. It is suspected that they encouraged Bright's husband, Representative William Bright, to introduce a bill for women's suffrage in the Wyoming Territorial Legislature. He did so, the bill was ratified, and South Pass went down in history as the birthplace of women's suffrage in Wyoming. In 1870 Morris became the first female justice of the peace in the nation, serving South Pass City. ⊠ *South Pass City Rd., off Hwy. 28, South Pass* ☎ *307/332–3684* ⊕ *wyoparks.state.wy.us/SPCslide.htm* 🎫 *$2* ☉ *Mid-May–early Sept., daily 9–5:30.*

Where to Stay & Eat

★ **$–$$$** ✕ **Atlantic City Mercantile.** The town's oldest saloon, known as the Merc, serves refreshment in a room that has seen its share of gold miners, perhaps an outlaw or two, and certainly some ruffians. When you step through the doors of this 1893 building with tin ceilings, a massive back bar, and an assortment of mismatched oak tables and chairs, you may feel as though you've walked directly into an episode of *Gunsmoke.* At times a honky-tonk piano player is on hand. The menu includes steak, chicken, and seafood, plus sandwiches and big burgers. If you're here on the fourth Wednesday of the month, from November through May, try the seven-course Basque dinner. ⊠ *100 E. Main St.* ☎ *307/332–5143* ▭ *D, MC, V.*

¢–$ 🏨 **Miner's Delight B & B.** Rooms in the lodge, which was built in 1895 as the town's hotel, are larger and have private bathrooms, but if you want to do things the way the gold miners did in the boom of the late 1860s, stay in the simple, authentic, rustic cabins. Each one has a small washstand with a bowl and a pitcher of water, and there are patchwork curtains and bedcoverings. It's a short walk to the bathroom in the main lodge. ⊠ *290 Atlantic City Rd., 82520* ☎ *307/332–0248 or 888/292–0248* ⊕ *www.wyomingbnb-ranchrec.com/MinersDelight. htm* 🛏 *3 lodge rooms; 5 cabins without bath* ♨ *Dining room, picnic area, no-smoking rooms; no a/c, no room phones, no room TVs* ▭ *AE, MC, V* ❂ *BP.*

Shopping

South Pass Trading Company (⊠ 50 South Pass Main ☎ 307/332–6810) sells Wyoming-made products ranging from vintage clothing to books by local and regional authors.

Lander

㉓ *28 mi northeast of Atlantic City via Hwy. 28.*

At the southwestern edge of the Wind River Indian Reservation and in the heart of country held dear by Chief Washakie (circa 1804–1900), one of the greatest chiefs of the Shoshone tribe, and his people, Lander has always had a strong tie to the Native American community. East of the Wind River Range, Lander makes a good base for pursuing mountain sports and activities ranging from backcountry hiking to horse-packing trips.

At **Sinks Canyon State Park,** a rushing river—the Popo Agie (pronounced pa-*po*-sha)—flows into a limestone cavern, known as the Sinks, only to resurface ¼ mi downstream. In the Rise, where the water reemerges, huge fish swim in the still pool. Rocky Mountain bighorn sheep and other wildlife wander the grounds of this park 8 mi south of Lander. The park is ideal for hiking, camping, and picnicking. ⊠ *8 mi south of Lander on Hwy. 131* ☎ *307/332–6333* ⊕ *wyoparks.state.wy.us/SCslide.htm* 🖆 *Park free, camping $4* ☉ *Park daily 24 hrs; visitor center Memorial Day–Labor Day, daily 9–7.*

Sports & the Outdoors

You can learn all aspects of mountaineering, from low-impact camping and hiking to horseback riding on pack trips, by taking a course from the **National Outdoor Leadership School** (⊠ 284 Lincoln St. ☎ 307/332–6973 ⊕ www.nols.edu).

FISHING There's great fishing on the Wind River Indian Reservation, but you must first obtain a tribal license; contact **Shoshone and Arapaho Tribes** (⊠ Fish and Game Dept., 1 Washakie, Fort Washakie 82520 ☎ 307/332–7207) for more information.

Kayak, Fishing & Scenic Tours (⊠ 466 Cascade St. ☎ 307/332–0305) leads guided fishing trips to area waters.

HORSEBACK **Allen's Diamond Four Ranch** (⊠ Off U.S. 287, 35 mi northwest of Lan-
RIDING der ☎ 307/332–2995) arranges mountain horse-packing trips and other horseback excursions. Some trips originate at the ranch, where you stay in cabins and take day rides; others are overnight backcountry adventures. Children must be seven or eight years old to go on extended pack trips. Also available are drop-camp services. Ride the Oregon Trail, take pack trips into the high country, or participate in an "outlaw ride" with **Rocky Mountain Horseback Adventures** (☎ 307/332–8535 or 800/408–9149).

Where to Stay & Eat

$$$–$$$$ ✕ **Svilars.** Inside this small, dark, family-owned restaurant, you'll find
Fodor's Choice what many locals say is the best food in all of Wyoming. It's rivaled only
★ by the Club El Toro steak house across the street. A meal here usually begins with *sarma* (cabbage rolls) and other appetizers. Your server will then place before you one of the biggest, if not *the* biggest, and best steaks you've likely ever seen. ⊠ *175 S. Main St., Hudson, 10 mi east of Lander* ☎ *307/332–4516* ▭ *No credit cards* ☉ *Closed Sun. and alternate Mon. No lunch.*

¢–$$ ✕ **Gannett Grill.** This crowded, noisy place serves large sandwiches and hand-tossed New York–style pizzas. ⊠ *148 Main St.* ☎ *307/332–8228* ▭ *D, MC, V.*

$ 🏠 **The Inn at Lander.** This two-story Best Western motel sits on a hill overlooking Lander and is beautifully landscaped with grassy areas and trees. It's within walking distance of restaurants and discount-store shopping. The small outdoor area has picnic tables. ⊠ *260 Grandview Dr., 82520* ☎ *307/332–2847* 🖷 *307/332–2760* ⊕ *www.bestwestern.com* ⇨ *100 rooms* ⚬ *In-room safes, some refrigerators, cable TV, pool, hot tub, exercise room, meeting room, business services, in-room data ports, no-smoking rooms* ⊟ *AE, D, MC, V* ⏐◉⏐ *CP.*

$ ▣ **Blue Spruce Inn.** Highlights of this 1920 home named for five enormous spruce trees on the property include a front porch with a swing, interior design from the Arts and Crafts period, hardwood floors, and beautiful gardens. The sun porch is a nice spot to curl up with a book and a cup of tea. The guest rooms are on the second floor, accessible only by a staircase. ⊠ *677 S. 3rd St., 82520* ☎ *307/332–8253 or 888/ 503–3311* 🖷 *307/332–1386* ⊕ *www.bluespruceinn.com* ⇨ *4 rooms* ⚬ *Dining room, library, Wi-Fi; no a/c, no TV in some rooms, no smoking* ⊟ *AE, D, MC, V* ⏐◉⏐ *BP.*

CAMPING ⚴ **Sleeping Bear Ranch.** There's a re-created Old West town at this RV park and campground that sits beside the Little Popo Agie River. There are lots of amenities here, including a restaurant, shops, and horseshoes, and you can take a hayride or swim in the river. ⚬ *Grills, flush toilets, full hookups, drinking water, guest laundry, showers, picnic tables, general store, play area, swimming (river)* ⇨ *65 full hookups, 20 tent sites* ⊠ *U.S. 287, 9 mi southeast of Lander, 1 mi south of junction with Hwy. 28* ☎ *307/332–3836 or 800/914–9226* ▦ *$18 tent sites, $22 full hookups* ⊟ *D, MC, V.*

⚴ **Sleeping Bear RV Park.** Next to a golf course, this campground and RV park has lots of grass and shade trees. You can join in various activities here, including basketball, horseshoes, and volleyball, and there's often evening entertainment in the form of campfires and storytelling. ⚬ *Grills, flush toilets, full hookups, partial hookups (electric and water), drinking water, showers, fire grates, picnic tables, public telephone, general store, play area* ⇨ *21 full hookups, 20 partial hookups, 6 tent sites* ⊠ *715 E. Main St.* ☎ *307/332–5159 or 888/757–2327* ⊕ *www. sleeping-rv-park.com* ▦ *$16 tent sites, $23 partial hookups, $26 full hookups* ⊟ *D, MC, V.*

Nightlife & the Arts

NIGHTLIFE   On weekends the **Lander Bar** (⊠ 146 Main St. ☎ 307/332–8228) gets crowded with people who come to dance and listen to live country bands.

THE ARTS   Dixieland bands converge on Lander for the **Lander Jazz Festival** (⊠ Lander Community Center ☎ 800/433–0662), with performances taking place over Labor Day weekend. June through August the **Native American Cultural Program** (☎ 307/856–7566 or 800/433–0662) has storytelling and Native American dancing at Jaycee Park each Monday evening. Native American traditional dancing is part of the **Yellow Calf Memorial Powwow** (☎ 307/856–7566 or 800/433–0662), held in late May (often over Memorial Day weekend) in Ethete, about 15 mi north of Lander.

Shopping

The shelves at **The Booke Shoppe** (⊠ 160 N. 2nd St. ☎ 307/332–6221 or 800/706–4476) are lined with regional-history books and works by Wyoming authors. You can also buy cards and journals here. Antiques and one-of-a-kind treasures are sold at **Charlotte's Web** (⊠ 228 Main St. ☎ 307/332–5989).

Distinctive, flamboyant women's clothing and unique jewelry are available at **Whippy Bird** (⊠ 306 Main St. ☎ 307/332–3444), in an old mercantile store. Everything is for the birds at **Wild Bird Marketplace** (⊠ 645 Main St. ☎ 307/332–7600), including bird feeders, birdbaths, gift items (with birds on them), and field guides.

Fort Washakie

㉔ *15 mi north of Lander via U.S. 287.*

This town named for Chief Washakie is the headquarters for the Eastern Shoshone tribe on the Wind River Indian Reservation. Fort Washakie was established in 1871, and some of the buildings here date from the town's early days.

A parade, rodeo, and buffalo barbecue are part of **Shoshone Indian Days** (☎ 307/856–7566 or 800/433–0662), held in mid-June.

The **Shoshone Tribal Cultural Center** examines Shoshone history, important treaties, and the development of the Wind River Indian Reservation. Tours of Fort Washakie are available; they last from one to four hours (the longer tours include visits to the Washakie and Sacajawea cemeteries). Some tours include a traditional Native American meal with such highlights as stew and fry bread, Indian tacos, and traditional berry pudding. ⊠ *90 Ethete Rd.* ☎ *307/332–9106 or 307/332–3177* 🎫 *Center free, tours $30–$150* ⊙ *Weekdays 8–4:45; call ahead for tour times and reservations.*

★ The small, private **Gallery of the Wind and Museum** displays 19th-century Native American tools, weapons, drums and musical instruments, and clothing, including headdresses and moccasins. Most of the items were gathered from the Wind River Indian Reservation. You can also purchase Native American crafts here. ⊠ *U.S. 287, ½ mi south of Fort Washakie* ☎ *307/332–3267 or 307/332–4231* 🎫 *Free* ⊙ *May–Sept., daily 8–7; Oct–Apr., daily 9–6.*

Shopping

★ Don't let the metal exterior of **Ancient Ways Indian Arts and Tanning** (⊠ U.S. 287, 1 mi south of Fort Washakie ☎ 307/332–6001) fool you. This store sells the highest-quality products made by Native Americans, including flutes, moccasins, cradle boards (used by mothers to carry babies on their backs while they worked), jewelry, and tanned hides. From squash-blossom necklaces made by Southwestern tribes to Pendleton blankets and beaded moccasins made by the Shoshone and Arapaho, you can choose any variety of Native American–crafted items at **Gallery of the Wind and Museum** (⊠ U.S. 287, ½ mi south of Fort Washakie ☎ 307/332–3267 or 307/332–4231).

Dubois

 56 mi northwest of Fort Washakie via U.S. 287 and U.S. 26; 86 mi east of Jackson via U.S. 26 and U.S. 287.

The mountains around Dubois attracted explorers as early as 1811, when members of the Wilson Price Hunt party crossed through the region en route to Fort Astoria in Oregon. These high peaks still attract folks who like to hike, climb, ride horses, camp, and experience wilderness. The largest concentration of free-ranging bighorn sheep in the country—more than 1,400 animals—lives here, roaming the high country in summer and wintering just above town on Whiskey Mountain.

South and east of Grand Teton and Yellowstone, Dubois is the least well known of the gateway communities to the parks, but this town of 1,000 provides all the services a visitor in Jackson or Cody might need. You can still get a room during the peak summer season without making a reservation months in advance, although it's a good idea to call a week or so before you arrive.

Displays at the **Wind River Historical Center** focus on Wind River tie hacks (workers who cut ties for railroads), local geology, and the archaeology of the Mountain Shoshone. Outbuildings include the town's first schoolhouse, a saddle shop, a homestead house, and a bunkhouse. The center also offers Elderhostel programs for senior citizens. With advance notice you can examine the historical-photograph collection, oral-history tapes, and library. ⊠ *909 W. Ramshorn Ave.* 🕾 *307/455–2284* ⊕ *www.windriverhistory.org* 🖭 *$1* ⊙ *June–Sept., daily 9–5.*

★ ☾ You can learn about bighorn sheep, including Rocky Mountain bighorn, at the **National Bighorn Sheep Interpretive Center** on the north side of Dubois. Among the mounted specimens here are the "super slam," with one of each type of wild sheep in the world, and two bighorn rams fighting during the rut. Hands-on exhibits illustrate a bighorn's body language, characteristics, and habitat. Winter tours (reserve ahead) to Whiskey Mountain provide an opportunity to see the wild sheep in its natural habitat; reservations are required. ⊠ *907 Ramshorn Ave.* 🕾 *307/455–3429 or 888/209–2795* ⊕ *www.bighorn.org* 🖭 *$5, Whiskey Mountain tours $25* ⊙ *Memorial Day–Labor Day, daily 9–8; Labor Day–Memorial Day, daily 9–5; wildlife-viewing tours mid-Nov.–Mar., daily at 9.*

⎛ off the ⎞
⎜ beaten ⎟
⎝ path ⎠
BROOKS LAKE RECREATION AREA – About 20 mi west of Dubois, easy to moderate hiking trails lead around Brooks Lake, across alpine meadows, and through pine forest to high mountain points with expansive views of Brooks Lake Mountain and the Pinnacles. You can picnic here, and boat, fish, or swim on the lake. Brooks Lake Lodge, a private dude ranch, stands on the lakeshore. ⊠ *20 mi west of Dubois on U.S. 26/287, then 7 mi northeast on gravel road to Brooks Lake Recreation Area* 🕾 *USDA Forest Service Shoshone National Forest: 307/578–1200* ⊕ *www.fs.fed.us/r2/shoshone.*

Sports & the Outdoors

CROSS-COUNTRY
SKIING
Among the best places for cross-country skiing is **Togwotee Pass,** east of Jackson and north of Dubois on U.S. 26/287, in Bridger-Teton and Shoshone national forests.

MOUNTAIN CLIMBING Much of the appeal of the Wind River Range, which you can access from the west near Pinedale, or the east near Lander and Dubois, is the (relatively difficult) access to major peaks, the most significant of which is Gannett Peak, at 13,804 feet the highest mountain in Wyoming. The trip to the base of Gannett Peak can take two days, with considerable ups and downs and stream crossings that can be dangerous in late spring and early summer. The reward for such effort, however, is seclusion: climbing Gannett Peak might not be as dramatic as climbing the Grand Teton to the west, but you won't have to face the national-park crowds at the beginning or end of the climb. Wind River is a world of granite and glaciers, the latter (though small) being among the last active glaciers in the U.S. Rockies. Other worthy climbs in the Wind River Range are Gannett's neighbors Mount Sacajawea and Fremont Peak. **Jackson Hole Mountain Guides** (⊠ 165 N. Glenwood St., Jackson ☎ 307/733–4979 ⊕ www.jhmg.com) leads trips in the area.

Where to Stay & Eat

$$–$$$ ✕ **Rustic Pine Steakhouse.** The bar here is one of Wyoming's more memorable spots, where locals and visitors congregate to share news about hunting or hiking. The adjoining steak house serves mouthwatering steak and seafood in quiet surroundings with white tablecloths and candles. Get your greens at the salad bar. ⊠ *123 Ramshorn Ave.* ☎ *307/455–2772* ⊟ *MC, V* ⊘ *No lunch.*

$–$$$ ✕ **Cowboy Cafe.** Among the homemade dishes served at this small restaurant in downtown Dubois are sandwiches, steaks, buffalo burgers, chicken, pork, and fish. ⊠ *115 Ramshorn Ave.* ☎ *307/455–2595* ⊟ *AE, D, MC, V.*

$$$$ 🏨 **Brooks Lake Lodge.** This mountain lodge on Brooks Lake combines

FodorsChoice great scenery with service and amenities. Built in 1922, the lodge has

★ massive open-beam ceilings, spacious rooms, subtle lighting, and log, leather, and wicker furnishings. Each of the lodge bedrooms and cabins has handcrafted lodgepole-pine furniture. Some cabins have woodburning stoves; the lodge suite has a full kitchen, living room, two-person Jacuzzi tub, and king bed. All cabins have panoramic views of the Wind River Range; some have views of Brooks Lake. Take a guided hike, go horseback riding, or fly-fish or canoe on the lake in summer. In the winter you can take dogsled or snowmobile rides with outfitters. Dinner is served in the lodge dining room, or you can enjoy a drink in the small bar or tea in the adjoining den. Many evenings include music and other entertainment before or during dinner. ⊠ *458 Brooks Lake Rd., 20 mi west of Dubois, 82513* ☎ *307/455–2121* 🖶 *307/455–2121* ⊕ *www.brookslake.com* 🛏 *6 rooms, 6 cabins* ⚹ *Restaurant, lake, outdoor hot tub, spa, gym, fishing, hiking, horseback riding, cross-country skiing, snowmobiling, tobogganing, bar; no room TVs, no a/c, no smoking* ⊟ *AE, MC, V* ⚹ *FAP.*

$$$ 🏨 **Absaroka Ranch.** Surrounded by mountains, this ranch offers traditional activities such as horseback riding, hiking, fishing, and relaxing. Five Mile Creek runs right through the property, which is 16 mi west of Dubois. There are special programs for children, and you can take an overnight pack trip deep into mountain country. The ranch takes weeklong bookings only. ✉ *306 Dunoir, off U.S. 26/287, Box 929, 82513* ☎ *307/455–2275* 🖷 *307/455–2275* ⊕ *www.absarokaranch.com* ⇆ *4 cabins* ⚭ *Dining room, fishing, hiking, horseback riding, recreation room, children's programs (ages 8–12); no smoking, no room TVs, no a/c* ⊟ *No credit cards* ⊘ *Closed mid-Sept.–mid-June* ⏍⦙ *FAP.*

$$$ ▥ **T Cross Ranch.** At this traditional guest ranch in an isolated valley 15 mi north of Dubois, the cozy cabins have porches with rocking chairs, fireplaces or woodstoves, and handmade log furniture. You can snuggle under a down quilt by night and spend your days riding horses. Hosts Ken and Garey Neal have been in the guest-ranch business for decades, and they know how to match people to horses. Only weeklong stays are available. ✉ *15 mi north of Dubois off Horse Creek Rd., Box 638 KRW, 82513* ☎ *307/455–2206 or 877/827–6770* 🖷 *307/455–2720* ⊕ *www.tcross.com* ⇆ *8 cabins* ⚭ *Dining room, hot tub, fishing, hiking, horseback riding, library, recreation room, children's programs (ages 6 and up), laundry facilities, playground, no-smoking rooms; no room TVs, no a/c, no room phones* ⊟ *No credit cards* ⊘ *Closed mid-Sept.–mid-June* ⏍⦙ *FAP.*

$ ▥ **Stagecoach Motor Inn.** This locally owned downtown motel has a large backyard with a picnic area and playground equipment, and there's even a reproduction stagecoach for kids to climb on. But the play area is bordered by Pretty Horse Creek, so young children need some supervision. Some rooms have full kitchens, others have refrigerators. ✉ *103 E. Ramshorn Ave., 82513* ☎ *307/455–2303 or 800/455–5090* 🖷 *307/455–3903* ⊕ *www.stagecoachmotel-dubois.com* ⇆ *47 rooms, 6 suites* ⚭ *Picnic area, some kitchens, some refrigerators, cable TV, pool, hot tub, fishing, basketball, horseshoes, playground, laundry facilities, airport shuttle, some pets allowed, no-smoking rooms; no a/c* ⊟ *AE, D, MC, V.*

¢–$ ▥ **Black Bear Country Inn.** The Wind River runs behind this redwood cabin-style motel, which has basic rooms with outdoor patios and tables. There's also a large seven-person apartment with a full kitchen. ✉ *505 W. Ramshorn Ave., 82513* ☎ *307/455–2344 or 800/873–2327* 🖷 *307/455–2626* ⇆ *16 rooms, 1 apartment* ⚭ *Kitchenettes, cable TV, no-smoking rooms; no a/c.*

¢–$ ▥ **Riverside Inn & Campground.** Located 3 mi east of Dubois with a view of the painted badlands, this family-owned lodging has cabins and a small camping area/RV park located in a cottonwood grove. ✉ *5810 U.S. 26, 82513* ☎ *307/455–2337 or 877/489–2337* ⊕ *www.riversideinnandcampground.com* ⇆ *14 cabins, 10 RV sites, 10 tent sites* ⚭ *Some kitchenettes, horseback riding, laundry facilities, some pets allowed, no-smoking rooms; no room phones, no room TVs, no a/c* ⊟ *D, MC, V.*

Shopping

From leather couches to handmade lamps and wall hangings, you can furnish your home with the Western-style items sold at **Absaroka Western Designs** (✉ 1416 Warm Springs Dr. ☎ 307/455–2440). The sounds of Native American music set the tone at **Stewart's Trapline Gallery & Indian Trading Post** (✉ 120 E. Ramshorn Ave. ☎ 307/455–2800). You'll find original oil paintings, old-pawn silver Indian jewelry, Navajo rugs, katsina dolls, Zuni fetishes, and quality Plains Indian artwork.

Fodor'sChoice
★

NORTHWEST WYOMING A TO Z

To research prices, get advice from other travelers, and book travel arrangements, visit www.fodors.com.

AIR TRAVEL

CARRIERS American, Delta Connection, and United Airlines/United Express provide multiple flights to Jackson daily, with connections in Chicago, Denver, and Salt Lake City. Scheduled jet service increases during the ski season. United flies between Denver and Riverton.

🔏 Airlines & Contacts **American Airlines** ☎ 800/433-7300 ⊕ www.aa.com. **Great Lakes Aviation** ☎ 307/587-7683 or 800/554-5111 ⊕ www.greatlakesav.com. **Delta** ☎ 800/221-1212 ⊕ www.delta-air.com. **United Airlines/United Express** ☎ 800/241-6522 ⊕ www.ual.com.

AIRPORTS

The major airports in the region are Jackson Hole Airport, north of Jackson in Grand Teton National Park and about 40 mi south of Yellowstone National Park; and Riverton Airport in Riverton, 25 mi northeast of Lander and 78 mi east of Dubois.

Many lodgings have free shuttle-bus service to and from Jackson Hole Airport. All Star Transportation, Alltrans, and Jackson Hole Transportation are shuttle services that serve the Jackson Hole Airport. If you're coming into the area from the Salt Lake City or Idaho Falls airport, you can travel to Jackson and back on a Jackson Hole Express shuttle.

🔏 Airport Information **Jackson Hole Airport** ✉ 1250 E. Airport Rd., Jackson Hole ☎ 307/733-7682 or 307/733-4005. **Riverton Regional Airport** ✉ 4800 Airport Rd., Riverton ☎ 307/856-1307 ⊕ www.flyriverton.com.

🔏 Transfer Information **All Star Transportation** ☎ 307/733-2888. **Alltrans** ☎ 307/733-3135 or 800/443-6133. **Jackson Hole Express** ☎ 307/733-1719 or 800/652-9510. **Jackson Hole Transportation** ☎ 307/733-3135.

BUS TRAVEL

During the ski season, START buses shuttle people between Jackson and the Jackson Hole Mountain Resort. The fare is $3 one way, and the buses operate from 6 AM to 11 PM. In summer START buses are free, operating from 6 AM to 10:30 PM. They stop at more than 40 locations in Jackson. People with disabilities must make reservations 48 hours in advance for START buses.

The Targhee Express runs between Jackson and the Grand Targhee Ski and Summer Resort, with pickups at various lodging properties in Jackson and Teton Village. The cost is $20 per day, or you can buy a combination shuttle/Grand Targhee lift ticket for $56. Advance reservations are required. All Star Transportation runs a nightly shuttle bus between Jackson and Teton Village; the cost is $22 for up to three people.

🔏 Bus Information **All Star Transportation** ☎ 307/733-2888. **START** ☎ 307/733-4521. **Targhee Express** ☎ 307/734-9754 or 307/733-3101.

CAR RENTAL

If you didn't drive to Wyoming, rent a car once you arrive. The airports have major car-rental agencies, which offer four-wheel-drive vehicles and ski racks. Aspen Rent-A-Car, a local agency in Jackson, rents cars, full-size vans, and sport utility vehicles; another local agency in Jackson, Eagle Rent-A-Car, provides cars and package deals with sport utility vehicles and snowmobiles. Rent-A-Wreck, in Lander, rents used cars.

🚗 **Aspen Rent-A-Car** ⊠ 345 W. Broadway, Jackson ☎ 307/733-9224 or 877/222-7736. **Avis** ⊠ Jackson Hole Airport ☎ 307/733-3422. **Budget** ⊠ Yellowstone Regional Airport ☎ 307/587-6066. **Eagle Rent-A-Car** ⊠ 375 N. Cache Dr., Jackson ☎ 307/739-9999 or 800/582-2128. **Hertz** ⊠ Jackson Hole Airport ☎ 800/654-3131 ⊠ Riverton Regional Airport ☎ 307/856-2344. **Rent-A-Wreck** ⊠ 715 E. Main St., Lander ☎ 307/332-5159. **Thrifty** ⊠ Jackson Hole Airport ☎ 307/734-9306.

CAR TRAVEL

Northwest Wyoming is well away from the interstates, so drivers make their way here on two-lane highways that are long on miles and scenery. To get to Jackson from I–80, take U.S. 191 north from Rock Springs for about 177 mi. From I–90, drive west from Sheridan on U.S. 14 or Alternate U.S. 14 to Cody. U.S. 14 continues west to Yellowstone National Park, and you can also hook up with U.S. 191, which leads south to Jackson.

Be extremely cautious when driving in winter; whiteouts and ice on the roads are not uncommon. Contact the Wyoming Department of Transportation for road and travel reports. For emergency situations dial 911 or contact the Wyoming Highway Patrol.

🚗 **Grand Teton Park Road Conditions** ☎ 307/739-3300. **Wyoming Department of Transportation** ☎ 307/777-4484, 307/772-0824 from outside Wyoming for road conditions, 888/996-7623 from within Wyoming for road conditions ⊕ www.wyoroad. info. **Wyoming Highway Patrol** ☎ 307/777-4301, 800/442-9090 for emergencies, #4357 (#HELP) from a cell phone for emergencies.

EMERGENCIES

There are hospitals in Jackson and Riverton and clinics in most other towns throughout the region.

🚨 **Ambulance or Police Emergencies** ☎ 911.

🏥 **Hospitals & Clinics Grand Teton Medical Clinic** ⊠ next to Jackson Lake Lodge ☎ 307/543-2514. **Riverton Memorial Hospital** ⊠ 2100 West Sunset Dr., Riverton ☎ 307/856-4161 ⊕ www.riverton-hospital.com. **St. John's Medical Center** ⊠ 625 E. Broadway, Jackson ☎ 307/733-3636 ⊕ www.tetonhospital.org.

LODGING

APARTMENT & CABIN RENTALS There are three reservations services for Jackson Hole.

🏠 **Central Reservations** ☎ 800/443-6931. **Jackson Hole Resort Lodging** ⊠ Jackson 83002 ☎ 800/443-6931 🖷 307/733-1286 ⊕ www.jacksonholewy.com. **Mountain Property Management** ⊠ 250 Veronica La., Box 2228, Jackson 83001 ☎ 800/992-9948 🖷 307/739-1686 ⊕ www.mpmjh.com.

CAMPING There are numerous campgrounds within Grand Teton National Park and Bridger-Teton, Shoshone, and Targhee national forests (Targhee National Forest borders Grand Teton National Park on the west; most of the forest lies within Idaho). Few of these campgrounds accept reservations. Campgrounds in the national forests tend to fill up more slowly than those in Grand Teton.

Reservations can be made for a small number of national-forest campgrounds near Jackson through U.S. Forest Reservations.

🚩 **Bridger-Teton National Forest** ☎ 307/739-5500. **Grand Teton** ☎ 307/739-3300. **Targhee National Forest** ☎ 208/624-3151. **U.S. Forest Reservations** ☎ 800/280-2267.

MEDIA

NEWSPAPERS & MAGAZINES   The weekly *Jackson Hole News & Guide* prints local news as well as information on ski conditions and events in the region; they also publish the free *Jackson Hole Daily*. Other major publications in the region, all published weekly, are the *Pinedale Roundup, Dubois Frontier, Riverton Ranger,* and *Wyoming State Journal,* in Lander.

TELEVISION & RADIO   NBC/KCWY Channel 13, broadcast out of Casper, serves much of the area. KGWL Channel 5 is a local station based in Lander. You can pick up ABC, CBS, and NBC from Salt Lake City or Idaho Falls, depending where you are in the region.

In Jackson, KSGT 1340 AM plays talk radio, KMTN 100.3 FM plays current and classic rock, and KZJH 95.7 FM plays classic rock. In Lander, KOVE 1330 AM plays country, KDLY 97.5 FM plays classic rock, and KTRZ 95.3 FM plays Top 40 music. KTHE 1240 AM in Thermopolis is a country-music station.

SAFETY

You can encounter a grizzly bear, mountain lion, wolf, or other wild animal anywhere in the Yellowstone ecosystem, which encompasses the mountains and valleys around Pinedale, Dubois, Jackson, and both Grand Teton and Yellowstone national parks. If you plan on hiking on backcountry trails, be sure to carry bear repellent, make noise, and travel with a companion. Check with forest or park rangers for other tips to protect yourself. (There are different tactics, depending on the animal species.) Always let someone know where you are going and when you plan to return.

Take particular care with female animals, particularly moose, with young by their side. These animal mothers are fiercely protective of their offspring. Buffalo can and do charge visitors every year. The best safety rule with all animals is to give them plenty of space.

SPORTS & THE OUTDOORS

Northwest Wyoming has the best the state has to offer in the way of outdoor activities, including camping, climbing, fishing, mountain biking, horseback riding, hiking, cross-country and downhill skiing, snowmobiling, and even dogsledding. Grand Teton National Park and Jackson Hole Mountain Resort in particular are popular playgrounds. Throughout the region there are countless outfitters and tour guides who can help you pursue any of these activities.

FISHING   To fish in Wyoming you must obtain a fishing license, usually available at sporting-goods stores; you can also request a license through the Wyoming Game and Fish Department.

The Wind River Indian Reservation has some of the best fishing in the Rockies. A separate license is required here. Contact Shoshone and Arapaho Tribes.

🔳 **Shoshone and Arapaho Tribes** ⊠ Fish and Game Dept., 1 Washakie, Fort Washakie 82520 ☎ 307/332-7207. **Wyoming Game and Fish Department** ⊠ 360 N. Cache St., Box 67, Jackson 83001 ☎ 307/733-2321 ⊕ gf.state.wy.us/.

SKIING For up-to-date information on ski conditions and snowfall at the Jackson Hole Mountain Resort, contact the number below or visit the Web site.

🔳 **Snow report** ☎ 307/733-4005 ⊕ www.jacksonhole.com/snowreport.asp.

TOURS

For leisurely appreciation of the area, try a multiday covered wagon and horseback trip with Teton Wagon Train and Horse Adventure. Wild West Jeep Tours has naturalist guides who will show you the backcountry.

🔳 **Teton Wagon Train and Horse Adventure** ⟟ Box 10307, Jackson 83002 ☎ 888/734-6101 ⊕ www.tetonwagontrain.com. **Wild West Jeep Tours** ⟟ Box 7506, Jackson 83002 ☎ 307/733-9036 ⊕ www.wildwestjeeptours.com.

VISITOR INFORMATION

🔳 **Dubois Chamber of Commerce** ⟟ Box 632, Dubois 82513 ☎ 307/455-2556 🖳 307/455-3168 ⊕ www.duboiswyoming.org. **Grand Teton National Park** ⟟ Drawer 170, Moose 83012 ☎ 307/739-3300 ⊕ www.nps.gov/grte. **Jackson Hole Chamber of Commerce** ⊠ 990 W. Broadway, Box E, Jackson 83001 ☎ 307/733-3316 🖳 307/733-5585 ⊕ www.jacksonholechamber.com. **Jackson Hole Mountain Resort** ⟟ Box 290, Teton Village 83025 ☎ 307/733-2292 or 800/443-6931 🖳 307/733-2660 ⊕ www.jacksonhole.com. **Lander Chamber of Commerce** ⊠ 160 N. 1st St., Lander 82520 ☎ 307/332-3892 or 800/443-0662 🖳 307/332-3893 ⊕ www.landerchamber.org. **Pinedale Chamber of Commerce** ⊠ 32 E. Pine St., Pinedale 82941 ☎ 307/367-2242 🖳 307/367-6830 ⊕ www.pinedalechamber.com.

Southwest Montana

3

WORD OF MOUTH

"The beauty of the Bozeman area is that you can so easily access such a great variety of activities *and* the Gallatin Canyon area is gorgeous!"
—NoCal_Jo

"Big Sky is incredible—we vacation there in summer and winter. Been to most mountain-state resort areas—Big Sky is our favorite for atmosphere—not stuffy—and astounding natural beauty. Bozeman is like being in the city—Big Sky is heaven in the mountains."

—MellyZ

Updated by
T. D. Griffith &
Dustin D. Floyd

GLISTENING, GLACIATED, AND GRAND, the Absarokas, Crazies, Gallatins, and other mountains send cooling summer winds to roil among the grasslands and forests of southwest Montana. This is a wild place inhabited by hundreds of animal species. Abundant wildlife is a daily sight, from the pronghorn sprinting across grasslands to the 17,000-strong northern elk herd in and north of Yellowstone National Park. Bald eagles and ospreys perch in tall snags along the rivers, watching for fish. Mules and white-tailed deer spring over fences (and across roads, so watch out when driving). Golden eagles hunt above hay fields. Riparian areas come alive in spring with ducks, geese, pelicans, and great blue herons. The south-central area known as Yellowstone Country shares the topography, wildlife, rivers, and recreational opportunities of its namesake national park.

Critters outnumber people in southwest Montana, which should come as no surprise when you consider that some counties have fewer than one person per square mile. The region's ranches are measured in the thousands of acres, though they are bordered by ranchettes of fewer than 20 acres around the towns of Bozeman, Big Timber, Red Lodge, and Dillon. But even the most densely populated area, Yellowstone County, has only about 34 people per square mile. That leaves thousands of square miles in the region wide open for exploration. Hiking, fishing, mountain biking and rock climbing are popular outdoor activities in summer, while in winter the thick pillows of snow make skiing and snowmobiling conditions near perfect.

Southwest Montana's human history reaches back only about 12,000 years, and the non–Native American presence dates back only 200 years. Yet this place is full of exciting tales and trails, from the path followed by the Lewis and Clark Expedition to the Bozeman and Nez Perce trails. To the west, in Montana's southwesternmost corner, is Gold West Country, which includes the gold-rush towns of Helena, Virginia City, and Bannack. Roadside historic signs along various routes in the region indicate the sites of battles, travels, and travails.

Exploring Southwest Montana

A private vehicle is far and away the best means of exploring southwest Montana, and it allows you to appreciate the grandeur of the area. Wide-open terrain affords startling vistas of mountains and prairies, where you're likely to see abundant wildlife. I–90 is the major east–west artery through the region; I–15 is the major north–south route. Most of the other routes here are paved and in good shape, but be prepared for gravel and dirt roads the farther off the beaten path you go. Driving through the mountains in winter can be challenging; a four-wheel-drive vehicle, available from most car-rental agencies, is best.

About the Restaurants

This is ranch country, so expect numerous Angus-steer steak houses. Many restaurants also serve bison meat and various vegetarian meals but few ethnic dishes. Restaurants here are decidedly casual: blue jeans, crisp shirts, and cowboy boots are dressy for the region.

Southwest Montana encompasses a multitude of landscapes, from rolling plains and creek-carved coulees to massive mountain ranges and raging rivers fed by snowfields atop towering peaks. The region's beauty, arguably unmatched elsewhere in the United States, is best experienced at a leisurely pace—one that allows you to do some wildlife viewing, to spend an afternoon on the banks of a stunning stream, and to watch the slow descent of the sun as it drops behind ragged mountains. In this land of the Big Sky, slow down and take a big breath.

3

Growing numbers of city-dwellers are immigrating to southwest Montana in search of their own slice of paradise. Fortunately, state and federal management of massive land holdings and the enduring strength of the ranch economy and lifestyle have kept development in check. Millions of acres of the region remain much as they have been for time immemorial.

For the best tour of southwest Montana, drive the unforgetable roadways that seem to reach the top of the world, make frequent stops in historic towns and parks, and take at least a short outdoor adventure. Drive up the Beartooth Pass from Red Lodge and, between late May and early October, go on some day hikes along myriad trails right from the highway. (Don't forget your camera, a light lunch, and plenty of drinking water.) Stop in Big Timber to browse some great galleries, ride a white-water raft on the Stillwater River, or fly-fish the Yellowstone River with a knowledgable outfitter. From Livingston, one of Montana's prettiest towns, drive south into ever more beautiful countryside, through the Paradise Valley toward Yellowstone National Park. A float trip on this section of the Yellowstone, combined with a stay at Chico Hot Springs, is the stuff of which great memories are made.

During summer in Virginia City, Ennis, or Three Forks, return to gold-rush days along the historic streets or live for today with a fly rod in hand and a kreel waiting to be filled beside you. Trail rides, float trips, steam trains—not to mention long walks in the long-gone footsteps of Lewis and Clark, Sacajawea, and a few thousand forgotten trappers, traders, cavalry soldiers, and Native Americans—all await you around these towns.

Bozeman, Big Sky, and the Gallatin Canyon are premier destinations in any season, with more than enough museums, galleries, historical sites, and scenic stops to fill your itinerary. Southwest Montana offers ample opportunities for outdoor recreation even when the snow flies. In places like Big Sky, Bridger Bowl, and the Gallatin National Forest you can experience some of the best skiing and snowmobiling in America, and after a day on the slopes or the trails plunge into the hot springs in Bozeman, Butte, or Boulder.

In making the most of your time, take time to breathe in the air filtered through a few million pines, to listen to the sounds of nature all around, to feel the chill of a mountain stream or the welcome warmth of a thermal spring. Small moments like these stick with you and become the kind of memories that will beckon you back to this high, wide and handsome land.

About the Hotels

Lodging varies from national chain hotels to mom-and-pop motor inns. More and more elegant guest ranches are inviting lodgers, historic hotels are being restored, and new bed-and-breakfasts are opening their doors. If you plan to visit in summer and during the ski season (December–mid-March), it's best to reserve rooms far in advance.

WHAT IT COSTS				
$$$$	**$$$**	**$$**	**$**	**¢**
RESTAURANTS over $22	$16–$22	$11–$16	$7–$11	under $7
HOTELS over $220	$160–$220	$110–$160	$70–$110	under $70

Restaurant prices are for a main course at dinner. Hotel prices are for two people in a standard double room in high season, excluding service charges and a 7% bed tax.

Timing

December through March is the best time to visit for skiers, snowboarders, snowshoers, and people who love winter. Summer draws even more visitors. That's not to say that southwest Montana gets crowded, but you may find more peace and quiet in spring and fall, when warm days and cool nights offer pleasant vacationing under the Big Sky.

Temperatures will drop below freezing in winter (and in fall and spring in the mountains) and jump into the 80s in summer. The weather can change quickly, particularly in the mountains and in the front range area north of Helena, and temperatures have been known to vary by as much as 70°F within a few hours, bringing winds, thunderstorms, and the like.

Numbers in the text correspond to numbers in the margin and on the Southwest Montana, Bozeman, and Helena maps.

NORTH OF YELLOWSTONE

This mountainous stretch of land from the town of Red Lodge west to the resort region at Big Sky is mostly roadless, glaciated, and filled with craggy heights. Winter often refuses to give up its grasp on this high alpine region until late spring. Snowpack assures that streams feeding the mighty Yellowstone River will flow throughout the hot summer, satiating the wildlife, native plants, and numerous farms downstream.

Red Lodge

❶ *60 mi southwest of Billings via U.S. 212.*

Nestled against the foot of the pine-draped Absaroka-Beartooth Wilderness and edged by the Limestone Palisades, this little burg is listed on the National Register of Historic Places and has become a full-blown resort town, complete with a ski area, trout fishing, access to backcountry hiking, horseback riding, and a golf course. Red Lodge was named for a band of Cheyenne who marked their tepee lodges with paintings of red earth. It became a town in the late 1880s, when the Northern Pacific Railroad laid tracks here to take coal back to Billings. One of Red Lodge's most colorful characters from this time was former sheriff "Liver Eatin' " Jeremiah Johnson, the subject of much Western lore and an eponymous movie starring Robert Redford. Red Lodge is a favored stop-over for motorcyclists heading to Yellowstone National Park.

Each August, Red Lodge holds an eight-day **Festival of Nations** (☎ 406/446–1718 ⊕ www.festivalofnations.us) to celebrate the numerous ethnic heritages of early settlers, many of whom worked in coal mines nearby. The festival includes music and dance.

🕙 When the snow flies in late February, the annual **Winter Carnival** (✉ 601 N. Broadway ☎ 888/281–0625 ⊕ www.redlodge.com) draws skiers, snowboarders, and other fans of the cold to three days of events such as the zany Firehose Race, in which teams of skiing firefighters compete while carrying a 50-foot hose. Other events include an obstacle ski course, the Snow Ball, a children's treasure hunt, and a snow-sculpture contest.

In addition to artifacts that once belonged to the famous Ridin' Greenoughs, a rodeo family, the **Peaks to Plains Museum** houses a historic gun collection, a reproduction of a coal mine, and Liver Eatin' Johnson exhibits. ✉ *224 N. Broadway* ☎ *406/446–3667* 🎟 *$3* ☉ *Mid–May–Sept., weekdays 10–5, weekends 1–5; Oct.–mid-May, Tues.–Fri. 10–5, Sat. 1–5.*

Sports & the Outdoors

DOWNHILL SKIING In winter there are 69 ski trails on 1,600 acres at **Red Lodge Mountain Resort** (✉ 305 Ski Run Rd. ☎ 406/446–2610 or 800/444–8977 ⊕ www. redlodgemountain.com). The family-friendly resort has a 2,400-foot vertical drop, a large beginner area, plenty of groomed intermediate terrain, and the Cole Creek area for powder-loving advanced and expert skiers. The best snow conditions are from February through April.

FISHING **Montana Trout Scout** (✉ 213 W. 9th St. ☎ 406/855–3058) conducts fly-fishing float trips and wade fishing on local streams and rivers such as the Yellowstone, Clark's Fork, Stillwater, and Rock Creek.

GOLF The surrounding mountains form a backdrop for the 18-hole **Red Lodge Mountain Golf Course** (✉ 828 Upper Continental St. ☎ 406/446–3344 or 800/444–8977 ⊕ www.redlodgemountain.com/golf).

HORSEBACK RIDING Ride the Beartooth high country among 12,000-foot peaks with **Silver Run Outfitting & Guide Service** (✉ 303 W. Rosebud Rd., Fishtail ☎ 406/328–4412 ⊕ www.silverrunoutfitting.com) on a horse or mule. You may see elk, bighorn sheep, birds of prey, and some of the 25 glacier-flanked peaks of the Absaroka-Beartooth Wilderness along the West Rosebud River. You can also join in a cattle drive in summer.

WHITE-WATER RAFTING The Stillwater River's foaming white water flows from the Absaroka-Beartooth Wilderness, providing exhilarating rafting with **Adventure Whitewater** (✉ 1 mi north of Absarokee on Hwy. 78 ☎ 406/446–3061 or 800/897–3061 ⊕ www.adventurewhitewater.com), which also has a combined rafting and horseback-riding trip.

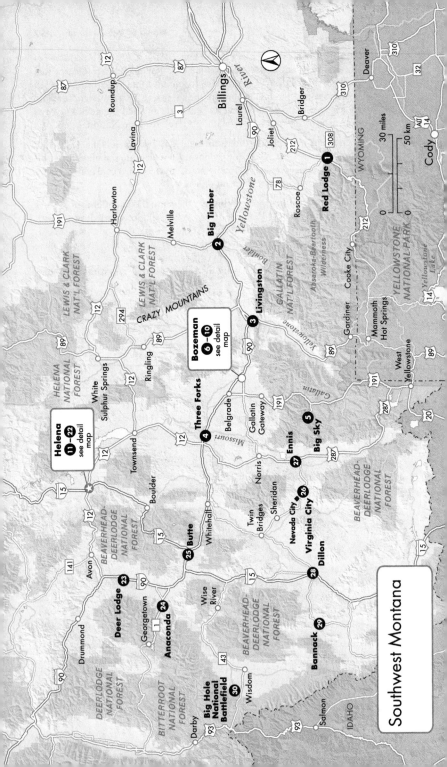

Southwest Montana

Where to Stay & Eat

The friendly folks at **Red Lodge Reservations** (✉ 1119 S. Broadway, 59068 ☎ 406/446–3942 or 877/733–5634 📠 406/446–4701 ⊕ www. redlodgereservations.com) can help you make lodging reservations in and around town—from snug cottages and cabins to historic B&Bs and hotels.

$$–$$$$ ✕ **Bridge Creek Backcountry Kitchen & Wine Bar.** This casual restaurant, often decorated with local artwork by schoolkids or professional artists, prepares fine dinners using naturally raised Montana beef. For lunch, try one of the three soups du jour, such as smoked turkey bisque, country Dijon vegetable chowder, or clam chowder. ✉ *116 S. Broadway* ☎ *406/446–9900* ⊕ *www.eatfooddrinkwine.com* 🖃 *MC, V.*

$–$$$ ✕ **Carbon County Steakhouse.** Saddles, saddle blankets, bridles, and other cowboy and ranch paraphernalia prepare you for the certified Angus beef from the grill, perhaps in the form of a hearty rib eye or even an appetizer of Rocky Mountain oysters (calf testicles). Vegetarian pasta dishes and seafood pasta are local favorites. ✉ *121 S. Broadway* ☎ *406/ 446–4025* 🖃 *AE, DC, MC, V* ☉ *Closed Mon. and Tues.*

★ $$–$$$$ ✕🖿 **Pollard Hotel.** This 1893 landmark in the heart of Red Lodge's historic district has been restored to the charms of an earlier era, when the likes of Calamity Jane and Liver Eatin' Johnson frequented the hotel. Reproduction Victorian furniture throughout vivifies a fin de siècle feeling, and handsome oak paneling and green, brown, and gold flocked wallpapers decorate the public rooms. Arthur's restaurant specializes in steaks, chops, and exotic game such as ostrich. The sautéed steelhead trout is served with crayfish crème fraîche sauce and saffron-spinach rice. ✉ *2 N. Broadway, 59068* ☎ *406/446–0001 or 800/765–5273* 📠 *406/446– 0002* ⊕ *www.pollardhotel.com* 🛏 *39 rooms* 🖔 *Restaurant, cable TV, gym, hot tub, sauna, racquetball, bar; no smoking* 🖃*AE, D, MC, V* ⭗❙*BP.*

$–$$$$ ✕🖿 **Rock Creek Resort.** After negotiating the cliff-hanging Beartooth Pass Highway between Red Lodge and Yellowstone National Park, this resort is a welcome respite. A Southwestern motif decorates the wood, log, and stone lodge, cabin, and condos, which perch along a babbling, boulder-strewn creek. Some of the rooms have hot tubs. A historic old cabin holds the wonderful Old Piney Dell restaurant ($$–$$$$), where locals go for intimate celebrations. The menu lists simple American, Mexican, and regional food. ✉ *6382 U.S. 212 S., on the Beartooth Hwy., Box 3500, 59068, 4½ mi south of Red Lodge* ☎ *406/446–1111 or 800/ 667–1119* 📠 *406/237–9851* ⊕ *www.rockcreekresort.com* 🛏 *38 rooms, 48 condos, 1 cabin* 🖔 *2 restaurants, some in-room hot tubs, some kitchenettes, some microwaves, cable TV, in-room data ports, 4 tennis courts, indoor pool, sauna, fishing, basketball, soccer, volleyball, cross-country skiing, 2 bars, shop, playground, laundry facilities, convention center, meeting rooms, airport shuttle, free parking; no smoking* 🖃 *AE, D, DC, MC, V* ⭗❙ *CP.*

$$–$$$$ 🖿 **The Torgrimson Place.** A 1904 fully restored log home sits amid the 5,000 acres of the working Bench Ranch, a place of bald eagles, deer, elk, sheep, cattle, and peace. Part of the trout-rich West Rosebud River runs through the property. The house has five bedrooms (note

CloseUp

MONTANA'S MOUNTAIN BOOM

THE DISCOVERY OF GOLD *accelerated white settlement in Montana—especially in its southwestern corner. Though a few fur trappers and missionaries arrived in the wake of the Lewis and Clark Expedition of 1804-1806, it wasn't until the gold strikes of the early 1860s that permanent settlements were established here. Bannack, Virginia City, and Nevada City were among the first communities to spring up, followed shortly by Butte, Helena, and Bozeman.*

Although Native Americans did not necessarily live in the mountains themselves, the mass migrations triggered by the gold rush led to conflicts between whites and the regional tribes. U.S. government troops engaged Chief Joseph's Nez Perce warriors in several famous skirmishes in southwest Montana. The most notable is commemorated at Big Hole National Battlefield, where a clash in 1877 led to severe losses on both sides.

Mining continues to play an important role in southwest Montana's economy, but the growth of tourism has changed the state forever. When Yellowstone National Park was established in 1872, the tiny hamlet of Gardiner served as its first year-round entrance. It wasn't until after World War II, however, that good roads, reliable automobiles, and a strong national economy made family vacations to Montana commonplace. World-class ski resorts were soon developed. By the 1970s, tourism had supplanted mining as the region's top industry, providing a much more stable economic base. As a result, southwest Montana is the state's fastest-growing area, and some of the world's most luxurious mountain lodges, alpine inns, and valley retreats are right here.

that you must rent the entire house). The master bedroom, with its king-size lodgepole-pine bed and plump comforter, looks out upon glacier-sculpted peaks. The bunkhouse next door, available for rent separately, is ideal for kids. Other cabins are nestled in an aspen grove. The ranch can cater barbecues and also arranges summer horse-pack trips and other guided tours. ⊠ *303 W. Rosebud Rd., Fishtail 59028, 37 mi west of Red Lodge* ☎ *406/328–6923* 🖷 *406/328–6971* ⊕ *www. benchranch.com* 🛏 *1 house, 1 bunkhouse, 2 cabins* ⚒ *Kitchens, fishing, mountain bikes, horseback riding, cross-country skiing, babysitting, laundry facilities; no TV in some rooms, no smoking, no a/c* ⊟ *No credit cards.*

CAMPING   ⚠ **Greenough Campground and Lake.** Pine trees, a small trout-stocked lake, and gentle hiking trails provide summer respite in Greenough, one of a dozen U.S. Forest Service campgrounds in the Red Lodge vicinity. ⚒ *Pit toilets, drinking water, fire grates, picnic tables, swimming (lake)* 🛏 *18 sites* ⊠ *10½ mi south of Red Lodge on U.S. 212, then 1 mi west on Hwy. 421* ☎ *406/446–2103* ⊕ *www.fs.fed.us/r1/custer* 🗒 *$10* 🖳 *Reservations essential* ⊟ *AE, D, MC, V* ☉ *May–Sept.*

⚠ **Red Lodge KOA.** With its heated pool, playground, and trout-filled brook for fishing, this tidy campground is ideal for families. Sites are along the banks of small creeks and among shady willows and pine trees. The group site, popular for reunions, hosts up to 50 guests. ♿ *Pool, laundry facilities, flush toilets, full hookups, partial hookups (water), drinking water, showers, fire grates, picnic tables, food service, electricity, public telephone, play area* ⤴ *13 full hookups, 35 partial hookups, 20 tent sites; 6 cabins* ✉ *7464 U.S. 212, 4 mi north of Red Lodge* ☎ *406/446–2364 or 800/562–7540* 🖷 *406/446–2364* ⊕ *www.koa.com* 💲 *$24 partial hookups and tent sites, $32 full hookups, $52–$56 cabins* ♿ *Reservations essential* ▭ *D, MC, V* ☺ *Mid-May–mid-Sept.*

Nightlife & the Arts

NIGHTLIFE You can sit back with a beer and watch the Bearcreek Downs' Pig Races at the **Bear Creek Saloon** (✉ 108 W. Main St., Bearcreek, 7 mi east of Red Lodge on Hwy. 308 ☎ 406/446–3481), a bar and steak house. Piglets streak through the miniature race courses while patrons bet on favorite oinkers; the proceeds from the betting fund local scholarships. The races take place summer evenings at 7, from Thursday through Sunday, and off-season races feature piglets mid-December through March at 7 Friday and Saturday evenings.

THE ARTS Internationally recognized painter Kevin Red Star, a Crow Indian, displays his oils, acrylics, lithographs, and etchings at **Kevin Red Star Studio & Gallery** (✉ 103 S. Main St., Roberts, 13 mi north of Red Lodge on U.S. 212 ☎ 406/445–2211 or 800/858–2584). His works are in the permanent collections of the Smithsonian Institution, the Institute of American Indian Art, and the Pierre Cardin Collection in Paris.

The historic **Round Barn Restaurant and Theater** (✉ 7193 U.S. 212 N, 2 mi north of Red Lodge ☎ 406/446–1197) hosts year-round plays, concerts, and comedy acts, mostly on weekends.

Shopping

☺ **Magpie Toymakers** (✉ 115 N. Broadway ☎ 406/446–3044) sells a dizzying array of toys, some crafted locally. From hiking accessories to cross-country-skiing gear, **Sylvan Peak Mountain Shoppe** (✉ 9 S. Broadway ☎ 406/446–1770 or 800/249–2563) carries a large selection of top-quality mountain-country dry goods, locally made fleece jackets, hats, and kids' togs. Distinctive clothing, handmade jewelry, handcrafted furniture, and gifts are just some of the offerings at **Twin Elk** (✉ 6382 U.S. 212 ☎ 406/446–3121 or 877/894–6355), at the Rock Creek Resort.

en route Driving south from Red Lodge on U.S. 212 will take you over the precipitous **Beartooth Pass,** which winds its way through lush alpine country to the "back door" of Yellowstone National Park in Wyoming. The highway is usually open from May to September, but wintery weather can close it at any time of the year. It's a good idea to fill the gas tank and cooler before you leave Red Lodge, because it's 64 mi to the next gas station. Several hiking trails lead off the highway; for hiking maps and more information, contact the **Beartooth Ranger District** (☎ 406/446–2103) in Red Lodge.

HITTING THE TRAIL

HUNDREDS OF HIKING TRAILS *crisscross the region's mountains, forests, and grasslands. Many are marked; you can buy trail maps at sporting-goods shops and Forest Service and state lands offices. Others are unmarked and only partially maintained. They often lead into the quietest, most remote areas of Montana.*

Serious backpackers might consider the Gallatin National Forest south of Bozeman, with alpine trails at elevations over 10,000 feet. The 27-mile Devil's Backbone, on the west side of Paradise Valley, is another challenging hike.

You're almost guaranteed wildlife sightings. Elk, deer, antelope, bighorn sheep, mountain goats, eagles, hawks, and herons are likely to appear along your trail. You might also come across petrified wood and fossils, as well as pictographs, arrowheads, or other signs of earlier human existence.

Absaroka-Beartooth Wilderness

12 mi south of Red Lodge via Beartooth Hwy.; 10 mi west of Red Lodge via Rock Creek Rd.

Although millions of summer visitors swarm into Yellowstone National Park to the south, the Absaroka-Beartooth Wilderness is blissfully unpeopled year-round, except for the relatively few hikers and dedicated backcountry travelers who come precisely for its emptiness. Unlike in Yellowstone, no paved roads lead into the wilderness area, although a four-wheel-drive vehicle is not essential for access. The wilderness encompasses Montana's highest mountains, including 12,799-foot Granite Peak; because of that, the prime hiking season (August) is relatively short. Many of the 640 high-mountain lakes may remain partially frozen even into August, especially in the high plateau region. Hikes are moderate to strenuous. Perhaps the most popular trails are those in the East Fork–Rosebud Creek area (35 mi one way), where numerous lakes rest in alpine basins above 9,000 feet. Keep in mind that this is grizzly bear country. You can get information and permits from Custer National Forest in Billings, or Gallatin National Forest in Bozeman.

For information on the western half of the wilderness, contact **Gallatin National Forest** (⊠ Federal Bldg., 3017 Fallon St., Suite C, Bozeman 59718 ☎ 406/522–2520 ⊕ www.fs.fed.us/r1/gallatin). For information on the eastern half of the wilderness, contact **Custer National Forest** (⊠ 1310 Main St., Billings 59105 ☎ 406/657–6200 ⊕ www.fs.fed.us/r1/custer).

Sports & the Outdoors

Because the Beartooths are rugged and remote, it's best to get outfitted in Billings or another city before heading here. Climbing guides and horse-pack trail guides—recommended unless you are familiar with the backcountry—can lead trips to remarkable and scenic places, safely. Most important, know backcountry rules regarding travel in grizzly bear country.

HORSEBACK Ride the high alpine wilderness trails on one- to five-day pack trips with
RIDING **Beartooth Plateau Outfitters** (⊠ 819 Clear Creek Rd., Roberts, 14 mi north of Red Lodge on U.S. 212 ☎ 800/253–8545 ⊕ www.beartoothoutfitters. com), which also runs fly-fishing expeditions.

MOUNTAIN Experienced climbers from **Beartooth Mountain Guides** (☎ 406/446–
CLIMBING 9874) lead outings to the top of Montana's tallest mountain, the challenging 12,799-foot Granite Peak. They also offer daylong and multiday trips of rock climbing, alpine and ski mountaineering, and ice climbing for beginners and experts.

Camping

⚠ **Beartooth Lake Campground.** More than a dozen U.S. Forest Service campgrounds on the edge of the wilderness are open for summer car camping. Beartooth Lake, at a 9,000-foot elevation, allows for outstanding views, water sports, and alpine scenery. ⚐ *Pit toilets, drinking water, swimming (creek)* ⬤ *20 sites* ⊠ *U.S. 212, 31 mi south of Red Lodge* ☎ *307/527–6921 or 877/444–6777* 🖶 *406/446–3918* ⊕ *www.fs.fed. us/r1/custer* ⬜ *$9* ▤ *D, MC, V* ☉ *July–early Sept.*

Big Timber & the Boulder River

❷ *88 mi northwest of Red Lodge via Hwy. 78 north and I–90 west; 81 mi west of Billings via I–90.*

People come to Big Timber to shop at its galleries and antiques shops, fly-fish the blue-ribbon trout streams, float the Yellowstone River, or unwind in front of the Crazy Mountains (so called because a homesteader supposedly went crazy from living in such a remote setting). South of town you can follow the Boulder River in its mad dash out of the Absaroka-Beartooth Wilderness. This journey along Highway 298 will take you into wild country, with craggy peaks rising on either side of a lush, ranch-filled valley.

The **Sweet Grass Chamber of Commerce** (⊠ I–90, Exit 367 ☎ 406/932–5131 ⊕ www.bigtimber.com) can provide information about sightseeing in the region; of particular interest in the area are a prairie-dog park and a natural bridge.

Explore the Boulder Valley and drop by the **Yellowstone River Trout Hatchery** to gaze at cutthroat trout. The best time to visit the hatchery is in spring, when you can see the fingerlings. ⊠ *Fairgrounds Rd.* ☎ *406/ 932–4434* ⬜ *Free* ☉ *Daily, 24 hrs.*

A striking lodge-style building constructed with native stone and logs houses the **Crazy Mountain Museum,** with exhibits on Big Timber's history and people, as well as the Crazy Mountains. Highlights include the famous Cramer Rodeo, sheep and wool exhibits, and a room dedicated to pioneers that includes artifacts dating from the late 1890s. Also here are a detailed miniature model of Big Timber in 1907, the restored Sour Dough School House, and a reconstruction of a *stabbur* (a Norwegian-style grain storehouse). ⊠ *Frontage Rd., Exit 367 off I–90* ☎ *406/932–*

5126 ⊕ www.bigtimber.com ✉ Donations accepted ☉ Late May–early Sept., Tues.–Sun. 1–4:30 or by appointment.

The comical critters at **Greycliff Prairie Dog Town State Park** pop out of their underground homes, sound their chirping alarms, and dash across the grassland to another hole. Explorers Meriwether Lewis and William Clark referred to these "barking squirrels" in their journals. At this large protected habitat, you can wander the trails for easy viewing. Watch out for rattlesnakes. ✉ I–90, Exit 377, Greycliff ☎ 406/247–2940 ⊕ www. fwp.state.mt.us ✉ $2 ☉ Apr.–Oct., daily dawn–dusk.

At **Natural Bridge State Monument,** the Boulder River disappears underground, creating a natural bridge, then reappears as roaring falls in the Boulder River canyon. Hiking trails and interpretive signs explain how this geologic wonder occurred. ✉ Hwy. 298, 27 mi south of Big Timber ☎ 406/247–2940 ⊕ www.fs.fed.us/r1/gallatin/ ✉ Free ☉ Daily.

The annual one-day **"Running of the Sheep" Sheep Drive** (✉ I–90, Exit 392, Reed Point, 25 mi west of Big Timber ☎ 406/326–2325) in September celebrates the hundreds of sturdy Montana-bred sheep and the state's agriculture history with humor. In addition to the sheep run (the sheep are let loose down the main street, sort of like the bulls in Pamplona, Spain, only a lot tamer), you can see a precision draft-horse event (in which the handlers and horses maneuver together) and a contest for the ugliest sheep and the prettiest ewe.

off the beaten path

INDIAN CAVES PICTOGRAPHS – Native Americans lived in the area for more than 10,000 years, leaving evidence of their presence on cave walls here, including a depiction of a bison hunt. To get to the cave you'll have to hike 1½ mi along the Grouse Creek Trail, near the main Boulder Ranger Station on U.S. 298. The cave is always open and accessible, but in poor weather the trail can be difficult to hike. A flashlight is useful for visiting the cave, particularly on overcast days. ✉ U.S. 298, 26 mi south of Big Timber on the Main Boulder River ☎ 406/932–5155.

Sports & the Outdoors

FISHING You're likely to see white pelicans, bald eagles, white-tailed deer, and cutthroat trout on float and fishing trips on the Yellowstone River with **Big Timber Guides and Rollin' Boulder Outfitters** (✉ 529 E. Boulder Rd., McLeod ☎ 406/932–4080 or 406/932–5836). The company also offers horseback riding and pack trips.

You can fish in private lakes or streams at the 2,300-acre **Burns Ranch** (✉ 333 Swamp Creek Rd. ☎ 406/932–4518, 406/932–4150, 406/220–6690, or 406/932–4891). The 40-acre Burns Lake, with rainbow, cutthroat, brown, and brook trout, is limited to a few anglers a day. The cost is $80 per rod, and reservations are required. The ranch is 4 mi north of Big Timber on U.S. 191 and then another 4 mi west on Swamp Creek Road.

HORSEBACK RIDING Ride the 11,000-acre range with cowboys on the **Range Riders Ranch** (✉ 238A Bridger Creek Rd., Reed Point ☎ 406/932–6538), a working cattle ranch. Trail rides take you to scenic spots with view of the Crazy and Beartooth mountains. You can also arrange for overnight campouts or a weeklong cattle drive.

Where to Stay & Eat

$–$$ ✕ **Prospector Pizza Plus.** You can dine in or take out at this popular downtown pizza joint. Aside from basic pizzas, Prospector prepares deli sandwiches, burgers, ribs, and steaks. ⊠ *121 McLeod St.* ☎ *406/932–4846* 🚬 *D, MC, V* ☺ *Closed Sun.*

¢–$ ✕ **Cole Drug.** Behind the historic brick-front facade of this pharmacy is an old-fashioned soda fountain, where friendly folks whip up Italian sodas, milk shakes, and the giant Big Timber, with nine scoops of ice cream and various toppings. ⊠ *136 McLeod St.* ☎ *406/932–5316 or 888/836–4146* 🚬 *AE, D, MC, V* ☺ *Closed Sun. No dinner.*

★ **¢–$$** ✕🏠 **Grand Hotel.** Fine dining and an 1890s saloon are two of the attractions of this classic Western hotel in the middle of downtown Big Timber. The romantic restaurant ($$$–$$$$) serves steaks, seafood, and lamb for lunch and dinner, plus decadent desserts. The antiques-furnished rooms are small, clean, and comfortable—the kind of accommodations you might find over the Longbranch Saloon in *Gunsmoke*. A full breakfast is included in the room rate. ⊠ *139 McLeod St., 59011* ☎ *406/932–4459* 🖶 *406/932–4248* ⊕ *www.thegrand-hotel.com* ⇖ *11 rooms, 4 with bath* ⌂ *Restaurant, bar, meeting room; no TV in some rooms, no smoking* 🚬 *D, MC, V* ❏ *BP.*

$$ 🏠 **Carriage House Ranch.** This B&B ranch retreat, named for an 1886 Dutch carriage barn on the premises, has trail rides, fishing, carriage rides, and a café. Events such as team steer roping and training for carriage driving are held in the ranch equestrian center, which also houses rare Holstein horses from Holland. There are even bed and barn facilities for the equines of the family. The rooms have an eclectic Western style, with period furnishings and wallpaper. ⊠ *771 U.S. 191 N, 59011* ☎ *406/932–5339 or 877/932–5339* 🖶 *406/932–5863* ⇖ *4 rooms* ⌂ *Café, some kitchens, fishing, mountain bikes, horseback riding, shop, laundry facilities, meeting rooms, helipad, some pets allowed; no TV in some rooms, no smoking, no a/c* 🚬 *AE, MC, V* ❏ *BP.*

CAMPING ⛺ **Halfmoon Campground.** At the end of a dusty road leading into the remote and lovely Crazy Mountains, this respite with tent sites is ideal for scenic picnicking, hiking, and fishing. ⌂ *Pit toilets, drinking water, some fire grates, picnic tables, swimming (creek)* ⇖ *8 sites* ⊠ *11 mi north of Big Timber on U.S. 191, then 12 mi west on Big Timber Canyon Rd.* ☎ *406/932–5155* ⊕ *www.fs.fed.us/r1/gallatin* ▨ *$5* ⌂ *Reservations not accepted* 🚬 *No credit cards.*

⛺ **Hicks Park Campground.** On the Main Boulder River, this remote jewel is en route to one of the entrances to the Absaroka-Beartooth Wilderness and has good fishing access. ⌂ *Pit toilets, drinking water, fire pits, picnic tables* ⇖ *16 sites* ⊠ *Rd. 212 ; head 25 mi south of Big Timber on U.S. 298, then 15½ mi south on Rd. 212* ☎ *406/932–5155* ⊕ *www.fs.fed.us/r1/gallatin* ▨ *$5* ⌂ *Reservations not accepted* 🚬 *No credit cards.*

🏕 **West Boulder Campground and Cabin.** Shady and cool, this remote setting is known for good fishing, access to the Absaroka-Beartooth Wilderness, and quiet camping. The cabin has electricity, a woodstove, a refrigerator, and water in summer. Reservations are essential for the cabin. ⛺ *Pit toilets, drinking water, fire pits, picnic tables* ⊠ *West Boulder Rd.; head 16 mi south of Big Timber on U.S. 298 to McLeod, 6½ mi southwest on Rd. 30, and 8 mi southwest on West Boulder Rd.* ☎ *406/932–5155* ⊕ *www.fs.fed.us/r1/gallatin* ⤴ *10 tent sites, 1 cabin* ⊟ *$5 tent sites, $35 cabin* ⊟ *No credit cards.*

Nightlife & the Arts

NIGHTLIFE The name may evoke unsavory images, but that doesn't stop fly-fishing anglers, ranchers, and curious tourists from filling the **Road Kill Cafe and Bar** (⊠ 1557 Boulder Rd., U.S. 298, McLeod, 15 mi south of Big Timber ☎ 406/932–6174). Beer, burgers, and Road Kill T-shirts are big sellers.

THE ARTS Cowboy music, poetry, and good humor spur the annual **Cowboy Poetry Wintercamp** (⊠ 110 E. 3rd Ave. ☎ 406/932–4227), which takes place at the American Legion Hall in mid-January. Day shows are free; evening shows cost $12.

Livingston & the Yellowstone River

❸ *35 mi west of Big Timber via I–90; 116 mi west of Billings via I–90.*

The stunning mountain backdrop to the town of Livingston was once Crow territory, and a chief called Arapooish said about it: "The Crow country is good country. The Great Spirit has put it in exactly the right place. When you are in it, you fare well; when you go out of it, you fare worse."

Livingston, along the banks of the beautiful Yellowstone River, was built to serve the railroad and the white settlers it brought. The railroad still runs through the town of 12,000, but now tourism and outdoor sports dominate the scene, and there are some 14 art galleries. Robert Redford chose the town, with its turn-of-the-20th-century flavor, to film parts of the movie *A River Runs Through It*.

Antique creels, fly rods, flies, and aquarium exhibits are among the displays at the Federation of Fly Fishers' **International Fly Fishing Center,** housed in a former school. The museum–education center hosts year-round classes, such as the free summer casting lesson every Tuesday and Thursday evening from 5 to 7. ⊠ *215 E. Lewis St.* ☎ *406/222–9369* ⊕ *www. fedflyfishers.org* ⊟ *$3* ⊙ *June–Sept., Mon.–Sat. 10–6, Sun. noon–5; Oct.–May, weekdays 10–4.*

The old **Livingston Depot Center in the Northern Pacific Depot** is now a museum with displays on Western and railroad history and works by artists from the region and across the country. The 1902 depot, an Italian villa–style structure, has mosaic trim, a terrazzo floor, and wrought-iron ticket windows. ⊠ *200 W. Park St., Exit 333 off I–90 and turn right onto Park St.* ☎ *406/222–2300* ⊟ *$3* ⊙ *Mid-May–Oct., Mon.–Sat. 9–5, Sun. 1–5.*

The **Yellowstone Gateway Museum,** on the north side of town in a turn-of-the-20th-century schoolhouse, holds an eclectic collection, including finds from a 10,000-year-old Native American dig site and a flag fragment associated with the Battle of the Little Bighorn. Outdoor displays include an old caboose, a sheep wagon, a stagecoach, and other pioneer memorabilia. ⊠ *118 W. Chinook St.* ☎ *406/222–4184* ⌦ *$3* ☉ *Late May–early Sept., daily 10–5; rest of Sept., daily noon–4; Oct.–late May, by appointment.*

Just south of Livingston and north of Yellowstone National Park, the **Yellowstone River** comes roaring down the Yellowstone Plateau and flows through Paradise Valley. Primitive public campsites (available on a first-come, first-served basis; for information contact Montana Fish, Wildlife and Parks Department at ☎ 406/247–2940) and fishing access sites can be found at various places along the river, which is especially popular for trout fishing, rafting, and canoeing. With snowcapped peaks, soaring eagles and an abundance of wildlife, a float on this section of the Yellowstone is a lifetime experience. U.S. 89 follows the west bank of the river, and East River Road runs along the east side.

Since the 1920s, cowboys and cowgirls have ridden and roped at the annual **Livingston Roundup Rodeo,** held on Independence Day weekend at the Park County Fairgrounds. A 3 PM parade, queen-selecting contest, and hoedown kick off the celebration. ⊠ *46 View Vista Dr.* ☎ *406/222–0850 or 406/222–3199* ⊕ *www.yellowstone-chamber.com* ⌦ *$12* ☉ *Independence Day weekend, 8 PM nightly.*

Since the 1950s the **Wilsall Rodeo** (⊠ U.S. 89 N, east on Clark St. past grain elevator to rodeo grounds, Wilsall ☎406/578–2290) has been showcasing cowboy and cowgirl events in late June at this ranching community at the base of the Crazy Mountains.

---

off the beaten path

PARADISE VALLEY LOOP – A drive on this loop takes you along the spectacular Yellowstone River for a short way and then past historic churches, schoolhouses, hot springs, and expansive ranches, all backed by the peaks of the Absaroka-Beartooth Wilderness. From Livingston head 3 mi south on U.S. 89, turn east onto East River Road, and follow it over the Yellowstone River and for 32 mi through the tiny towns of Pine Creek, Pray, Chico, and Emigrant. You'll eventually hit U.S. 89 again, where roadside historic markers detail early inhabitants' lives; follow it north to Livingston. ☎ *406/222–0850* ⊕ *www.yellowstone-chamber.com.*

Sports & the Outdoors

From the spring hatch of "Mother's Day" caddis flies through late-fall streamer fishing, the Yellowstone River and its tributary streams draw fly fishers from around the globe to the blue-ribbon streams for Yellowstone cutthroat, brown, and rainbow trout. Hiking trails lead into remote accesses of surrounding peaks, often snowcapped through June.

BOATING   In late July, the annual three-day **Yellowstone Boat Float** (☎406/222–4414), a boating get-together with canoes, kayaks, and fishing and drift boats, begins at Livingston, with overnight stops in Big Timber and Reed

CloseUp
WELCOME TO FLY-FISHING HEAVEN

MONTANA HAS THE BEST *rainbow, brown, and brook trout fishing in the country. This is the land of A River Runs Through It, the acclaimed Norman Maclean novel that most people know as a movie. Although the book was set in Missoula, the movie was filmed in the trout-fishing mecca of southwest Montana and the Gallatin River played the role of Maclean's beloved Big Blackfoot. Several rivers run through the region, notably the Madison, Gallatin, and Yellowstone (more or less parallel to one another flowing north of Yellowstone National Park), as well as the Big Hole River to the west. These are among the rivers that get the most recognition in the region, though it's hard to go wrong in these parts. All are easily accessible from major roads, which means that in summer you might have to drive a ways to find a fishing hole to call your own.*

If you're only a casual fisherman, all you'll really need is a basic rod and reel, some simple tackle (hooks, sinkers, floaters, and extra line) and a few worms, which can all be bought at most outfitting and sporting goods stores for less than $40. Many non-fly fishers use open-face reels with lightweight line and spinners, which makes for a nice fight when they connect with trout. If you would like to try your hand at the more elegant stylings of fly-fishing, hire a local guide. Not only will he show you the good fishing holes; a knowledgable outfitter can teach city slickers how not to work otherwise tranquil waters into a froth. Many guide services will provide you with fly-fishing equipment for the day.

Stream fishing in southwest Montana is a year-round enterprise. Even if you never catch a fish, your time on the water will be well spent: the mountain ranges that separate the rivers are among the most beautiful in the Rockies.

Point, and ends at Laurel. Some people camp overnight; others stay in hotels or go home.

Boaters eager to explore the Yellowstone River will find a one-stop shop at **Rubber Ducky River Rentals** (⊠ 15 Mt. Baldy Dr. ☎ 406/222–3746 ⊕ www.riverservices.com). Aside from guide and drop-off services, the store rents and sells boats and equipment, including its own line of rafts and kayaks. Guided rafting and kayaking trips down the Yellowstone, Gallatin, and Madison rivers are available from the **Yellowstone Raft Company** (⊠ 406 Hwy. 89, Gardiner ☎ 800/858–7781 or 800/348–4376 ⊕ www.yellowstoneraft.com). Be sure you make reservations for your trip in advance.

FISHING **George Anderson's Yellowstone Angler** (⊠ 5256 U.S. 89 S ☎ 406/222–7130 ⊕ www.yellowstoneangler.com) specializes in catch-and-release fly-fishing trips floating on the Yellowstone River, wade trips on spring creeks, access to private lakes and streams, and fly-casting instruction.

The fishing experts at **Dan Bailey's** (⊠ 209 W. Park St. ☎ 406/222–1673 ⊕ www.dan-bailey.com) can help you find the right fly, tackle, and outdoor clothing. Rental equipment, fly-fishing clinics, and float and wade trips are also available at this world-renowned shop.

HORSEBACK **Bear Paw Outfitters** (⊠ 136 Deep Creek Rd. ☎ 406/222–6642 or 406/
RIDING 222–5800) runs day rides and pack trips in Paradise Valley, the Absaroka-
Beartooth Wilderness, and Yellowstone National Park; prices start at
$25 per hour aboard horses or mules.

SCENIC FLIGHTS **Paradise Valley Flying Service** (⊠ 3693 U.S. 89 S, 17 mi south of Livingston
☎ 406/333–4788) takes you soaring over the mountains and vales of
Paradise Valley.

Where to Stay & Eat

★ $$-$$$$ ✕ **Chathams Livingston Bar and Grill.** The enlightened Continental cui-
sine and owner Russell Chatham's elegant drawings and lithographs of
landscapes create a comfortable dining experience. The seasonal menu
may include fresh blue-crab salad topped with avocado, or a tomato
salad with Spanish anchovies. Fresh seafood is flown in daily and served
with imported Italian pastas. The most popular dish is the filet mignon,
topped with a port sauce or a bourbon-honey glaze. Chatham's work
is also displayed down the block at Legends Fine Art. ⊠ *130 N. Main
St.* ☎ *406/222–7909* ▤ *DC, MC, V.*

$-$$$ ✕ **Montana's Rib & Chop House.** Here, in the middle of cattle country,
you can expect the juiciest, tenderest steaks—such as the flavorful hand-
cut rib eye—all made from certified Angus beef. Jambalaya, baby back
ribs, and catfish are also on the menu. ⊠ *305 E. Park St.* ☎ *406/222–
9200* ▤ *AE, D, MC, V.*

¢-$ ✕ **Paradise Valley Pop Stand & Grill.** You can dine in or order takeout
from this 1950s-style burger and ice-cream joint. The ice cream is made
locally. ⊠ *5006 U.S. 89, 2 mi south of Livingston* ☎ *406/222–2006*
▤ *No credit cards* ⊘ *Closed Mon.*

★ $$$$ ▦ **B Bar Ranch.** In winter, this 20,000-acre working cattle ranch invites
guests for spectacular winter adventures in cross-country skiing and
wildlife tracking. The ranch shares a 6-mi boundary with Yellowstone
National Park, in Tom Miner Basin, 36 mi south of Livingston. Some
of the 24 mi of impeccably groomed trails are created by rare Suffolk
Punch draft horses from the country's largest herd, which lives here on
the B Bar. Sleigh rides and naturalist-led trips into Yellowstone are some
of the activities. Rates include meals and activities, and there's a two-
night minimum stay. ⊠ *818 Tom Miner Creek Rd., Emigrant 59027*
☎ *406/848–7729* 🖷 *406/847–7793* ⊕ *www.bbar.com* ➽ *6 cabins, 3
lodge rooms* ⚹ *Dining room, outdoor hot tub, cross-country skiing, ice-
skating, piano, shop, meeting rooms; no room phones, no room TVs,
no smoking, no a/c* ▤ *No credit cards* ⊘ *Closed Mar.–mid-Dec.* ⫢ *FAP.*

$$$$ ▦ **Mountain Sky Guest Ranch.** This full-service guest-ranch resort in the
middle of scenic Paradise Valley and 30 mi north of Yellowstone National Park is a family favorite. The log cabins feel luxurious after a day
in the saddle. The children's programs offer age-appropriate activities
such as hiking, swimming, crafts, hayrides, campfires, and a talent
show. Dinners range from Western barbecue to gourmet treats such as
grilled lamb loin topped with fig-and-port-wine glaze. Everyone learns
to dance the two-step to a local band. There's a seven-night minimum
stay in summer only. ⊠ *Big Creek Rd., Emigrant, U.S. 89 29 mi south
of I–90, then west 4½ mi on Big Creek Rd.* ✆ *Box 1219, Bozeman 59715*

☎ *406/333–4911 or 800/548–3392* ᕀ *406/587–3977 or 406/333–4911* ⊕ *www.mtnsky.com* ⬅ *30 cabins* ⚸ *Dining room, refrigerators, tennis court, pool, outdoor hot tub, sauna, fishing, mountain bikes, hiking, horseback riding, horseshoes, volleyball, bar, dance club, recreation room, shop, babysitting, children's programs (ages 1–18), playground, laundry facilities, laundry service, Internet, meeting rooms, airport shuttle; no room phones, no room TVs, no a/c* ▭ *MC, V* ⍥ *FAP.*

★ ¢–$$$$ ▦ **Chico Hot Springs Resort.** During the gold rush of the 1860s, a miner noted that he "washed [his] dirty duds" in the hot-springs water near the Yellowstone River. Soon, a series of bathhouses sprang up, attracting people to the medicinal waters. The Chico Warm Springs Hotel opened in 1900, drawing famous folks such as painter Charlie Russell (1864–1926) to the 104°F–107°F pools. The hotel is surrounded by large outdoor soak pools, a convention center, and upscale cottages that open to views of 10,920-foot Emigrant Peak and the Absaroka-Beartooth Wilderness beyond. The Easter buffet is exceptional. ⊠ *1 Old Chico Rd., Pray 59065* ☎ *406/333–4933 or 800/468–9232* ᕀ *406/333–4694* ⊕ *www.chicohotsprings.com* ⬅ *82 rooms, 4 suites, 16 cottages* ⚸ *Restaurant, pizzeria, snack bar, room service, some in-room hot tubs, some kitchens, some refrigerators, in-room data ports, spa, fishing, hiking, horseback riding, cross-country skiing, 2 bars, piano, shop, business services, convention center, airstrip, free parking, some pets allowed, no-smoking rooms; no room TVs, no a/c in some rooms* ▭ *AE, D, MC, V.*

$$$ ▦ **63 Ranch.** Owned by the same family since 1929, this 2,000-acre working cattle ranch is one of Montana's oldest. Only weeklong packages are available, and they include a full range of activities, from horseback riding to fishing to pack trips. The rustic cabins are commodious yet comfortable, with log furniture and private baths. ⊠ *Off Bruffey La., 12 mi southeast of Livingston;* ⍰ *Box MA979, 59047* ☎ *406/222–0570* ᕀ *406/222–9446 or 406/222–6363* ⊕ *www.sixtythree.com* ⬅ *12 cabins* ⚸ *Dining room, pond, fishing, horseback riding, laundry facilities; no a/c, no room TVs, no room phones* ▭ *No credit cards* ⊗ *Closed mid-Sept.–mid-June* ⍥ *FAP.*

¢–$$ ▦ **The Murray Hotel.** Even cowboys love soft pillows, which is why they come to this 1904 town centerpiece, whose floors have seen silver-tipped cowboy boots, fly-fishing waders, and the sparkling heels of Hollywood celebrities. Antiques reflect a different theme in each guest room. Historic photos and stuffed game animals decorate the comfortable lobby and surround the antique elevator, which is still in use. ⊠ *201 W. Park St., 59047* ☎ *406/222–1350* ᕀ *406/222–2752* ⊕ *www. murrayhotel.com* ⬅ *30 rooms* ⚸ *Cable TV, in-room data ports, outdoor hot tub, bar, no-smoking floors* ▭ *AE, D, MC, V.*

CAMPING ⚠ **Paradise Valley/Livingston KOA.** Set among willows, cottonwoods, and small evergreens, this full-service campground is well situated along the banks of the Yellowstone River, 50 mi north of Yellowstone National Park. It's popular with families, who enjoy the heated pool. It's a good idea to reserve ahead. ⚸ *Swimming (indoor pool), laundry facilities, flush toilets, full hookups, dump station, drinking water, showers, fire grates, picnic tables, electricity, public telephone, general store* ⬅ *82 RV sites,*

27 tent sites, 22 cabins, 1 cottage ⊠ 163 Pine Creek Rd.; 10 mi south of Livingston on U.S. 89, then ½ mi east on Pine Creek Rd. ☎ 406/222–0992 or 800/562–2805 ⊕ www.koa.com ➷ $20 tent sites, $30 full hookups, $45–$55 cabins, $130 cottage ☰ AE, D, MC, V ⊗ May–Oct.

⚠ **Pine Creek Campground.** A thick growth of pine trees surrounds this relatively flat campground at the base of the mountains. It's near the trailhead for challenging hikes to Pine Creek Waterfalls and the Absaroka-Beartooth Wilderness. ♿ *Pit toilets, drinking water, fire pits, picnic tables* ♺ *24 sites ⊠ End of Pine Creek Rd.; 9 mi south of Livingston on U.S. 89, then 6 mi east on Pine Creek Rd. ☎ 406/222–1892 or 877/444–6777 ⊕ www.fs.fed.us/r1/gallatin ➷ $9 ☰ AE, MC, V ⊗ Late May–early Sept.*

Nightlife & the Arts

NIGHTLIFE With dancing and country music, microbrews, video poker, and keno, the **Buffalo Jump Steakhouse & Saloon** (⊠ 5237 U.S. 89 S ☎ 406/222–2987) has livened up many a Saturday night in Livingston. Friday and Saturday evenings June through August, the **Pine Creek Cafe** (⊠ 2496 East River Rd. ☎ 406/222–3628) serves up live bluegrass music, barbecue burgers, and beer under the stars. The fun starts at 7.

THE ARTS Livingston's beauty has inspired artists, as evidenced by the many fine art galleries in town. The **Danforth Gallery** (⊠ 106 N. Main St. ☎ 406/222–6510) is a community art center that displays and sells works by local and regional artists. Subtle, moody images by Russell Chatham and ★ other artists line the walls of **Legends Fine Art** (⊠ 120 N. Main St. ☎ 406/222–0317 ⊕ www.legendsfineart.com), and bronzes, oils, and lithographs fill the studio. **Visions West Gallery** (⊠ 108 S. Main St. ☎ 406/222–0337 ⊕ www.visionswestgallery.com) specializes in Western and wildlife art, including numerous works on the fly-fishing theme, from paintings and bronzes to hand-carved flies.

The historic district's **Blue Slipper Theatre** (⊠ 113 E. Callender St. ☎ 406/222–7720) presents various full-length productions, including one-act plays, popular melodramas, and an annual Christmas variety show. The **Firehouse 5 Playhouse** (⊠ Sleeping Giant Trade Center, 5237 U.S. 89 S ☎ 406/222–1420) stages comedies, dramas, and musicals year-round.

Shopping

The floorboards creak as you walk through **Sax and Fryer's** (⊠ 109 W. Callender St. ☎ 406/222–1421), an old-time bookstore specializing in Western literature and especially books by Montana authors. It's the oldest store in Livingston and also sells newspapers, cards, and gifts.

In addition to selling outdoor clothing, boots, and bicycles, **Timber Trails** (⊠ 309 W. Park St. ☎ 406/222–9550) helps mountain bikers, hikers, and cross-country skiers with trail maps, directions, and friendly advice.

Three Forks

❹ *51 mi west of Livingston via I–90; 29 mi west of Bozeman via I–90.*

While the scenery in Three Forks is striking, it's the historical sites that make this place worth a visit. Sacajawea (circa 1786–1812), famed for helping Lewis and Clark, traveled in the area with her Shoshone family before she was kidnapped as a child by a rival tribe, the Hidatsas. Five years later she returned here as part of the Lewis and Clark expedition. In 1805 they arrived at the forks (of the Madison, Jefferson, and Gallatin rivers), now in Missouri Headwaters State Park, looking for the river that would lead them to the Continental Divide. A plaque in the city park commemorates her contribution to the expedition's success.

★ The Madison, Jefferson, and Gallatin rivers come together to form the mighty Missouri River within **Missouri Headwaters State Park**, a National Historic Landmark. At 2,315 mi, the Missouri is the country's second-longest river, after the Mississippi. Lewis and Clark named the three forks after Secretary of the Treasury Albert Gallatin, Secretary of State James Madison, and President Thomas Jefferson. The park has historical exhibits, interpretive signs, picnic sites, hiking trails, and camping. ⊠ *Trident Rd., 3 mi northeast of Three Forks on I–90, exit at the Three Forks off-ramp, then go east on 205, and 3 mi north on 286* ☎ *406/994–4042* ⊕ *www.fwp.state.mt.us* ⊠ *$5 per vehicle (includes admission to Madison Buffalo Jump)* ⊙ *Daily dawn–dusk.*

Within the **Madison Buffalo Jump** historic site is a cliff where Plains Indians stampeded bison to their deaths for more than 2,000 years, until European guns arrived in the West. An interpretive center explains how the technique enabled Native Americans to gather food and hides. Picnic areas provide a restful break from touring. Be on the lookout for rattlesnakes here, and avoid wandering off the paths; do not turn over any rocks or logs, where the rattlers often hide. ⊠ *Buffalo Jump Rd., 5 mi east of Three Forks on I–90, exiting at Logan, then 7 mi south on Buffalo Jump Rd.* ☎ *406/994–4042* ⊕ *www.fwp.state.mt.us* ⊠ *$5 per vehicle (includes admission to Missouri Headwaters State Park)* ⊙ *Daily dawn–dusk.*

☾ The **Lewis and Clark Caverns,** Montana's oldest state park, hold some of the most beautiful underground landscape in the nation. Two-hour tours lead through narrow passages and vaulted chambers past colorful, intriguingly varied limestone formations. The temperature stays in the 50s year-round; jackets and rubber-soled shoes are recommended. Note that the hike to the cavern entrance is mildly strenuous and that the cave trip involves lots of bending and stooping. Each cave area is lighted during the tour, but it's still a good idea to bring a flashlight. A campground sits at the lower end of the park. ⊠ *Hwy. 2, 19 mi west of Three Forks* ☎ *406/287–3541* ⊠ *$8* ⊙ *June–early Sept., daily 9–6:30; May and early Sept.–late Sept., daily 9–4:30.*

Thousands of local historical artifacts are on display in the **Headwaters Heritage Museum**, including a small anvil, all that is left of a trading post, Fort Three Forks, established in 1810. There's also an exhibit of a one-room schoolhouse. ⊠ *Main and Cedar Sts.* ☎ *406/285–4778* ⊠ *Donations accepted* ⊙ *June–Sept., Mon.–Sat. 9–5, Sun. 1–5; Oct.–May by appointment.*

Sports & the Outdoors

BOATING   In addition to arranging fly-fishing float trips, **Canoeing House and Guide Service** (⊠ 11227 U.S. 287 ☎ 406/285–3488) rents canoes for trips down the Madison, Gallatin, and Jefferson rivers.

SCENIC FLIGHTS "Flightseeing" trips with **Bridger Aviation** (✉ 1680 Airport Rd. ☎ 406/285–4264) take you a thousand feet above the confluence of the Madison, Gallatin, and Jefferson rivers. The knowledgeable pilots can show you several otherwise inaccessible historic sites from the air, including tepee rings, bison herds, and buffalo jumps.

Where to Stay & Eat

★ $–$$$ ✕ **Historic Headwaters Restaurant.** This 1908 brick restaurant once served railroad passengers on their way to see Yellowstone National Park. The smoke-free dining area now includes a summertime dining patio surrounded by native plants, flowers, and a stream. Today diners eat better than Lewis and Clark: the Culinary Institute of America–trained chef-owner prepares such dishes as buffalo-chorizo enchiladas with black-bean sauce and smoked-corn salsa, and melt-in-your-mouth barbecue beef. ✉ 105 S. Main St. ☎ 406/285–4511 ▤ MC, V ✹ Closed Mon. and Tues.

¢–$ ✕ **Wheat Montana.** A local ranching family grows and grinds its wheat, then bakes it into sandwich bread and bakery items for one of the best lunch meals in the state. Try the gigantic cinnamon rolls. Also for sale is grind-your-own flour from several kinds of wheat, including Prairie Gold Whole Wheat and Bronze Chief Hard Red Spring Wheat. Note that the shop closes at 7 PM. ✉ 10778 Hwy 287, I–90 at Exit 274 ☎ 406/285–3614 or 800/535–2798 ▤ MC, V.

$ ▦ **Sacajawea Hotel.** The original portion of this hotel, built in 1910 by the Old Milwaukee Railroad, was rolled on logs from a site about a mile away to its current location, where it became a railroad hotel for travelers heading to Yellowstone National Park. The lofty lobby and cozy rooms retain their period style, and the front porch has rockers where you can relax with a book or watch the sunset. The restaurant prepares basic steak and fish, and the bar serves lighter fare. ✉ 5 N. Main St., 59752 ☎ 406/285–6515 or 888/722–2529 ▤ 406/285–4210 ∰ www.sacajaweahotel.com ⇩ 30 rooms, 1 suite ⟁ Restaurant, cable TV, in-room data ports, fishing, bar, piano, meeting rooms, some pets allowed (fee); no smoking ▤ AE, D, DC, MC, V ⍾ CP.

CAMPING ⚠ **Missouri Headwaters State Park.** Tent sites are strewn among the cottonwood trees of the campground at this park. An interpretive kiosk details the Lewis and Clark adventure through the area. Be prepared for mosquitoes and rattlesnakes along the 4 mi of hiking trails. Reservations are taken only for groups. ⟁ Flush toilets, pit toilets, drinking water, fire grates, picnic tables ⇩ 23 sites ✉ Hwy. 286; 4 mi northeast of Three Forks on Hwy. 205, then north on Hwy. 286 ☎ 406/994–6934 ∰ www.fwp.state.mt.us ▤ $12–$15 ▤ No credit cards ⍾ May–Sept.

Big Sky & Gallatin Canyon

❺ 75 mi southeast of Three Forks via I–90 and then U.S. 191; 43 mi south of Bozeman via U.S. 191 and west on Big Sky Rd.

The name of Lone Peak, the mountain that looms over the isolated community beneath Big Sky, is a good way to describe **Big Sky Ski and Sum-**

mer Resort, one of the most remote major ski resorts in the country. Here you can ski a true wilderness. Yellowstone National Park is visible from the upper mountain ski runs, as are 11 mountain ranges in three states. The park's western entrance at West Yellowstone is about 50 mi away, along a route frequented by elk, moose, and bison (use caution when driving U.S. 191).

Conceived in the 1970s by national TV newscaster Chet Huntley, the resort area is the solitary node of civilization in otherwise undeveloped country, between Bozeman and West Yellowstone. Getting here invariably means at least one plane change en route to Bozeman and about an hour's drive to the resort through Gallatin Canyon, a narrow gorge of rock walls, the frothing Gallatin River, and the occasional snow-glazed grass benchland. Big Sky's 1,220 locals are used to driving through the canyon for such simple pleasures as a fresh head of lettuce.

This is not to suggest that Big Sky is primitive. Indeed, being just a few decades old and still growing, the resort is quite modern in its design and amenities. You won't find crowds amongst all this rugged nature, but you don't have to give up the creature comforts of a warm bed and a good meal. It's not as if you can't get a daily newspaper, cable TV, or a well-prepared cocktail. All are readily available in Big Sky's three villages. One is in the Gallatin Canyon area along the Gallatin River and U.S. 191. Another, Meadow Village, radiates from the 18-hole Big Sky Golf Course. The third enclave, 9 mi west of U.S. 191, is the full-service ski resort itself, overlooking rugged wilderness areas and Yellowstone National Park.

Major real-estate developments around Big Sky have started to impinge upon the resort-in-the-wild atmosphere. Still, outdoor pleasures abound. In addition to skiing, golfing, hiking, horseback riding, and other activities, Big Sky hosts many festivals, musical events, races, and tournaments. ⊠ *1 Lone Mountain Trail, Box 160001, Big Sky 59716* ☎ *406/995–5000 or 800/548–4486* ⊕ *www.bigskyresort.com.*

A restored early-20th-century homestead and cattle ranch, **Historic Crail Ranch** makes a pleasant picnic spot in the midst of Big Sky's Meadow Village area. To get here drive west on Big Sky Spur Road, make a right on Little Coyote, go past the chapel, and make a left onto Spotted Elk Road in Meadow Village. ⊠ *Spotted Elk Rd.* ☎ *406/995–3000* ⊕ *www. bigskychamber.com* ⊠ *Free* ☉ *Memorial Day–Labor Day, daily sunrise–sunset.*

FISHING Rivers such as the **Gallatin,** which runs along U.S. 191, the Madison (one
Fodor'sChoice valley west), and the Yellowstone (one valley east) have made southwest
★ Montana famous among fly fishers, most of whom visit during the nonwinter months. However, that's not to say the trout stop biting in winter; on almost any day of the winter, no matter how bitter or nasty the weather, usually a dozen or more die-hard anglers lay out lines in the Gallatin River.

East Slope Anglers (⊠ 47855 Gallatin Rd. ☎ 406/995–4369 or 888/359–3974 ⊕ www.eastslopeanglers.com) arranges guides for winter and summer fly-fishing. You can also rent or buy flies, rods and reels, clothing, and gifts here. Flies, rods and reels, clothing, and equipment rentals are available at **Gallatin Riverguides** (✉ U.S. 191 ☎ 406/995–2290 or 888/707–1505 ⊕ www.montanaflyfishing.com), ½ mi south of the Big Sky entrance. Rental equipment and guide service is offered through **Lone Mountain Ranch** (✉ 4 mi west of U.S. 191, 6 mi from Big Sky resort, and ½ mi down gravel ranch Rd. ☎ 406/995–4644 or 800/514–4644).

GOLF   The 18-hole Arnold Palmer–designed **Big Sky Golf Course** (✉ Black Otter Rd., Meadow Village ☎406/995–5780 or 800/548–4486) has challenging holes along the fork of the Gallatin River, cooling breezes from snowy Lone Peak, and the occasional moose, elk, or deer on the green.

HORSEBACK   **Jake's Horses & Outfitting** (✉ U.S. 191 and Beaver Creek Rd., 3 mi south
RIDING   of Big Sky ☎ 406/995–4630 or 800/352–5956) will take you riding
☾   through mountainous trails on Forest Service lands for one- and two-hour rides year-round. Weeklong pack trips inside Yellowstone National Park are also available.

KIDS' ACTIVITIES   The kids-only Outdoor Youth Adventures program at **Lone Mountain Ranch**
☾   (✉ 4 mi west of U.S. 191 on Westfork Meadows and ½ mi down gravel ranch Rd. ☎ 406/995–4644) includes building snow caves, tubing, snowshoeing, playing snow kick ball, and cross-country skiing over snowy trails and through obstacle courses.

RAFTING   **Geyser Whitewater Expeditions** (✉ 46651 Gallatin Rd. ☎406/995–4989 or 800/914–9031) has guided raft trips on the Gallatin River. Since 1978,
★   **Yellowstone Raft Company** (✉ 55265 Gallatin Rd. ☎ 406/995–4613 or 800/348–4376) has been arranging guided raft trips and kayak lessons on the Gallatin and Yellowstone rivers.

SNOWMOBILING   Far and away the most popular nonskiing activity in the region is snowmobiling into and around Yellowstone National Park. West Yellowstone, about 50 mi south of Big Sky on U.S. 191, prides itself on being the "Snowmobile Capital of the World," and in winter there are more snowmobiles in town than cars. The most popular excursion is the 60-mi round-trip between West Yellowstone and Old Faithful. Recent attempts to ban snowmobiling in the park have ended up in court but, to date, the sleds are still allowed.

SNOWSHOEING   You can rent snowshoes through **Big Sky Rentals** (✉ Snowcrest Lodge, Plaza Area ☎ 406/995–5841) for use on the resort's 2-mi Moose Tracks trail, which wends through aspen groves. Quiet and picturesque snowshoe trails lead through the woods and meadows of **Lone Mountain Ranch** (✉ 4 mi west of U.S. 191 on Westfork Meadows and ½ mi down gravel ranch Rd. ☎ 406/995–4644 or 800/514–4644), where you can get a trail map and rent snowshoes and poles. **Montana Backcountry Adventures** (✉ Big Sky Spur Rd.; 1 mi outside Mountain Village ☎ 406/995–3880 or 866/766–9622 ⊕ www.skimba.com) offers guided half-day snowshoe tours through the Lee Metcalf Wilderness, where naturalists discuss fire ecology and native flora and fauna.

Downhill Skiing & Snowboarding

For many years, the attitude of more advanced skiers toward Big Sky was "big deal." There wasn't nearly enough challenging skiing to keep

CloseUp

HITTING THE SLOPES

IT'S CALLED "COLD SMOKE"—*the exceedingly light, dry snow that falls on the mountains of southwest Montana—and it doesn't go to waste. All told, the region has six downhill ski areas and more than 390 km (245 mi) of cross-country trails. The season generally begins in late November or early December and runs through early to mid-April.*

Downhill ski areas like Bridger Bowl, Discovery, Moonlight Basin, and Maverick are family friendly, inexpensive, and

relatively uncrowded. For steep skiers, Big Sky, one of the country's largest resorts, has more than 500 turns on a single slope; it's also a fine mountain for beginner and intermediate skiers.

The cross-country tracks of Lone Mountain Ranch stand out among the 40 or 50 trails in southwest Montana. They're groomed daily or weekly and are track-set for both classic and skate skiing. Backcountry skiing has no limits, with hundreds of thousands of skiable acres on public land.

expert skiers interested for long, and certainly not for an entire ski week. As a remedy, the Big Sky people strung up the Challenger chairlift, one of the steepest in the country, and then installed a tram to the summit of Lone Peak, providing access to an array of steep chutes, open bowls, and at least one scary-steep couloir. The tram also gave Big Sky the right to claim the second-greatest vertical drop—4,350 feet—of any resort in the country. Those changes now provide big action for experts.

None of that, however, has diminished Big Sky's otherwise easy-skiing reputation. There is, indeed, a good deal of intermediate and lower-intermediate terrain, a combination of wide-open bowl skiing higher up and trail skiing lower down. And as on the Challenger terrain, the skiing on these slopes is fairly unpopulated. Additionally, there are 75 km (47 mi) of groomed cross-country skiing trails nearby at Lone Mountain Ranch.

The other plus about skiing Big Sky is its wide variety of exposures. Many of the ski areas here are built on north-facing slopes, where snow usually stays fresher longer, protected from the sun. In addition to these, Big Sky also has plenty of runs facing south and east, and the differing snow textures that result make for more interesting skiing.

FACILITIES 4,350-foot vertical drop; 3,600 skiable acres; 150 runs; 17% beginner, 25% intermediate, 37% advanced, 21% expert; 1 aerial tram, one 4-passenger gondola, 4 high-speed quads, 1 quad chair, 3 triple chairs, 5 double chairs, 3 surface lifts.

LESSONS & PROGRAMS Half-day group-lesson rates at the **ski school** (☎ 406/995–5743 or 800/548–4486) are $49; a learn-to-ski package (half-day lesson, equipment rentals, and restricted lift ticket) is $71. Racing, powder, mogul, and snowboarding clinics are also available. There's also a ski school just for kids—whether they're first-timers or speedsters—with enthusiastic instructors and a day camp.

LIFT TICKETS Lift tickets cost $65. Multiday tickets (up to 10 days) are available, with savings of up to $12 per day. Kids 10 and under ski free.

RENTALS The resort's **Big Sky Ski Rentals** (☎ 406/995–5841) at the base of the mountain offers rental packages for $28, and performance ski packages for $43. Moderate rental packages (starting at $16 per day) are available from **Mad Wolf Ski & Sport** (✉ U.S. 191, 8 mi from ski area ☎ 406/995–4369).

OUTSIDE OF BIG SKY The Big Sky resort still dominates downhill skiing in the area, but the 2003–2004 ski season saw the debut of a new resort at **Moonlight Basin** (✉ 2 mi east of Big Sky resort on Big Sky Spur Rd. ☎ 406/993–6000 ⊕ www.moonlightbasin.com), with north-facing slopes overlooking the Lee Metcalf Wilderness Area. The runs here may not be as lengthy as they are next door at Big Sky, but the terrain offers some unique knolls, chutes, and glades. Best of all, tickets are competitively priced at $40 a day for the four chairlifts. Lifts access 1,900 acres of skiing, with 1,850 feet of lift-served descent and an additional 1,200 feet of hike-to terrain.

Nordic Skiing

BACKCOUNTRY SKIING **Lone Mountain Ranch** (☎ 406/995–4644 or 800/514–4644 ⊕ www.lmranch.com) offers guided cross-country ski and snowshoe tours in the nearby backcountry as well as in Yellowstone National Park. Ski tours near Big Sky are best for experienced skiers; they tend to cover steeper terrain, with opportunities for telemarking, backcountry skiing, and snowboarding. Tours in Yellowstone generally cover flat or gently rolling terrain, for which little or no cross-country skiing experience is necessary. In some cases, snow "coaches" (essentially, over-the-snow buses and vans) take skiers from West Yellowstone to scenic parts of the park for skiing.

Cat-ski adventures from Big Sky in the nearby yet remote Moonlight Basin are run daily in winter by **Montana Backcountry Adventures** (✉ 1020 Big Sky Spur Rd. [Hwy. 64], 1 mi west of resort at Moonlight Basin Ranch ☎ 406/995–3880 or 866/766–9622 ⊕ www.skimba.com); you'll have access to 1,800 acres of untracked powder ski terrain with views into the Lee Metcalf Wilderness Area.

Using snowmobile or helicopter services, **Montana Powder Guides** (✉ 15792 Bridger Canyon Rd. ☎ 406/587–3096) leads backcountry expeditions into several mountain ranges for untracked powder skiing and snowboarding. The best conditions are late February through late April.

TRACK SKIING ★ **Lone Mountain Ranch** (☎ 406/995–4644 or 800/514–4644 ⊕ www.lmranch.com) is a rare bird in cross-country circles. Not only are there 75 km (47 mi) of groomed trails, but the network is superb, with everything from a flat, open, golf-course layout to tree-lined trails with as much as 1,600 feet of elevation gain (and loss). Much of the trail network provides a genuine sense of woodsy mountain seclusion. If there is a drawback, it's that moose sometimes wander onto the trails, causing pockmarked tracks and occasional moose-skier confrontations.

Mountain Meadows Guest Ranch (☎ 406/849–5459 or 888/644–6647 ⊕ www.lakemaryronan.com) has 24 km (15 mi) of groomed cross-country and snowshoe trails for lodging guests in a beautiful log facility on a mountaintop above Big Sky.

Where to Stay & Eat

$$$$ ✕ **Moonlight Dinners by Montana Backcountry Adventures.** For a unique dining experience, ride a Sno-Cat into the pristine Moonlight Basin for a meal under the stars. While the chef prepares French onion soup, filet mignon, and garlic mashed potatoes on a woodstove, you can sled on hills under the light of the moon and tiki lamps. Yurt dining is accompanied by acoustic music and candlelight. ⊠ *1020 Big Sky Spur Rd. (Hwy. 64); 1 mi outside Mountain Village* ☎ *406/995–3880* ⚎ *Reservations essential* ⊟ *AE, MC, V* ⊗ *Closed mid-Apr.–late Nov.*

$$$–$$$$ ✕ **Buck's T-4 Lodge and Restaurant.** Within a historic log lodge and bar, this restaurant is known for its dinners of wild game (try the antelope satay) and steaks. There's live jitterbug music after dark. ⊠ *U.S. 191, 1½ mi south of Big Sky entrance* ☎ *406/995–4111* ⊟ *MC, V* ⊗ *Closed mid-Apr.–May.*

$$$–$$$$ ✕ **Cafe Edelweiss.** Stepping into this cozy post-and-beam lodge is a bit like wandering into the Tirol. Among the traditional Austrian and German dishes on the menu are schnitzel, bratwurst, and *schweinebraten* (pork roast with homemade sauerkraut). ⊠ *Meadow Village, Big Sky Spur Rd.* ☎ *406/995–4665* ⊟ *AE, D, MC, V* ⊗ *Closed late Apr.–mid-June.*

$–$$$$ ✕ **The Corral.** Trucker-size portions of everything from steak and eggs to burgers and local brews feed cowboys and skiers at this local hangout. Stuffed elk, moose, and deer heads watch over diners from walls lined with posters and humorous photos. ⊠ *42895 Gallatin Rd., 5 mi south of Big Sky entrance* ☎ *406/995–4249* ⊕ *www.corralbar.com* ⊟ *AE, D, MC, V* ⊗ *Closed 2 wks in late Nov. and late Apr.–mid-May.*

$$–$$$ ✕ **By Word of Mouth.** By day this café is filled by sunlight, and by night, by noise, particularly Friday nights, when the after-ski crowd gathers for an all-you-can-eat fish fry. The menu includes Thai chicken strips served with soba, and *opa* (a Hawaiian sunfish) sautéed in teriyaki sauce and served with organic vegetables and rice. The wine list is lengthy, and there are several local beers on tap. ⊠ *2815 Aspen Dr., in West Fork Meadow* ☎ *406/995–2992* ⊕ *www.bigskycatering.com* ⊟ *AE, D, MC, V.*

$–$$$ ✕ **Big Horn Cafe.** This spacious café, possibly the best value in the area, serves contemporary fare, with starters such as hummus with roasted garlic, olives, peppers, and pita chips. The real treat is the wonton lasagna: layers of wontons, spinach, peppers, and portobello mushrooms. ⊠ *Big Horn Center, U.S. 191, 1 block north of Big Sky entrance* ☎ *406/995–3880* ⊟ *MC, V* ⊗ *Closed Mon.*

$$$$ ✕⌂ **Lone Mountain Ranch.** Four-night to one-week packages include seasonal activities such as naturalist-guided trips to Yellowstone, cross-country ski lessons, downhill skiing, and kids' camps. The ranch maintains 75 km (47 mi) of groomed trails for classic and skate cross-country skiing. An additional four trails totaling 10 km (6 mi) are for snowshoers only. Some activities cost extra, such as fly-fishing with world-renowned, Orvis-endorsed guides. Lodging ranges from rustic, historic cabins to elegant log homes. Nonguests fill the log-lodge dining room (try the bison steak) or partake of a night of backcountry sleigh rides, dinner, and entertainment. 🏠 *Box 160069, 59716* ✉ *4 mi west of U.S. 191, 6 mi from Big Sky resort, and ½ mi down gravel ranch Rd.* 🕿 *406/995–4644 or 800/514–4644* 🖷 *406/995–4670* ⊕ *www.lmranch.com* ⇨ *23 cabins, 7 rooms* ⌂ *Restaurant, hot tub, fishing, hiking, horseback riding, cross-country skiing, sleigh rides, bar, recreation room, shop, children's programs (all ages), airport shuttle, travel services; no smoking, no room TVs, no room phones, no a/c* ⊟ *D, MC, V* ⊗ *Closed Oct., Nov., Apr., and May* ⍩ *FAP.*

$$$–$$$$
Fodor'sChoice
★
✕⌂ **Rainbow Ranch.** Lovely log-accented cabins and a fully updated 1919 log lodge perch alongside the Gallatin River. A fishing motif decorates the spacious rooms in the cabins, which have fireplaces, lodgepole-pine beds, and down comforters. The exceptional restaurant, decorated with Western paintings, has the state's largest collection of wines, 6,500 bottles, displayed in the Bacchus Room, where groups of up to 14 can dine. Fresh fish is flown in daily. Among the game dishes are pistachio-crusted antelope and bison rib eye prepared with *chimichurri* herbs. ✉ *42950 Gallatin Rd., 5 mi south of Big Sky entrance, 59716* 🕿 *406/995–4132 or 800/937–4132* 🖷 *406/995–2861* ⊕ *www.rainbowranch.com* ⇨ *16 rooms* ⌂ *Restaurant, cable TV, in-room VCRs, in-room data ports, outdoor hot tub, fishing, cross-country skiing, bar, shop, meeting rooms; no smoking* ⊟ *AE, D, MC, V* ⍩ *FAP.*

$$$$
Fodor'sChoice
★
⌂ **The Big EZ.** Atop a mountain at a 7,500-foot elevation, the Big EZ lodge overlooks other mountains and the Gallatin River drainage. Each luxury suite is appointed with Western-style furnishings, an eclectic collection of fine art, and state-of-the-art technology, including laptops and Internet access. The property includes an 18-hole, par-72 championship putting course and one of the state's largest outdoor hot tubs. Dinners are unusual, elegant, and savory: try pan-roasted caribou loin or African pheasant, and save room for Tasmanian-honey crème brûlée. ✉ *7000 Beaver Creek Rd., 59716* 🕿 *406/995–7003 or 877/244–3299* 🖷 *406/ 995–7007* ⊕ *www.bigezlodge.com* ⇨ *12 suites* ⌂ *Restaurant, cable TV, in-room VCRs, in-room data ports, putting green, exercise equipment, outdoor hot tub, fishing, bar, shop, laundry service, concierge, Internet, business services, meeting rooms, airport shuttle; no smoking* ⊟ *AE, MC, V* ⍩ *FAP.*

$$$$
⌂ **Big Sky Resort Condominiums.** These comfortable on-mountain units—with one, two, or three bedrooms—have large kitchens, dining rooms, fireplaces, and underground parking. Stone and wood accents give the otherwise utilitarian decor some mountain character. Many of the units are ski-in, ski-out properties. ✉ *1 Lone Mountain Trail, 59716* 🕿 *406/ 995–5000 or 800/548–4486* 🖷 *406/995–8095* ⊕ *www.bigskyresort.com* ⇨ *600 condos* ⌂ *6 restaurants, kitchens, minibars, microwaves, refrigerators, cable TV, golf privileges, 3 indoor-outdoor pools, gym, spa, mountain bikes, horseback riding, cross-country skiing, downhill skiing, ski shop, ski storage, 5 bars, shops, babysitting, children's programs (ages 2–12), laundry facilities, business services, convention center, meeting rooms, airport shuttle, no-smoking rooms* ⊟ *AE, D, MC, V* ⊗ *Closed late Apr.–early June and late Oct.–mid-Nov.* ⍩ *FAP.*

★ **$$$$** ⊞ **Summit at Big Sky.** The rooms of this slope-side, full-service hotel take in the full view of Lone Mountain and several ski runs. A Euro-Western flavor decorates the spacious rooms and suites, which are ideal for discriminating business travelers and families looking to be at the center of the mountain action. The best things about the Summit just may be the underground, heated parking garage, unusual in Montana, and the outdoor, year-round soaking pool. ⊠ *1 Lone Mountain Trail, 59716* ☎ *406/995–5000 or 800/548–4486* 🖷 *406/995–8095* ⊕ *www. bigskyresort.com* ↜ *213 rooms, 8 suites* ⌂ *2 restaurants, room service, kitchenettes, minibars, refrigerators, cable TV, in-room data ports, golf privileges, indoor-outdoor pool, gym, spa, mountain bikes, downhill skiing, ski shop, ski storage, bar, shops, babysitting, children's programs (ages 2–12), concierge, business services, meeting rooms, airport shuttle, no-smoking rooms* ⊟ *AE, D, MC, V* ❮◯❯ *FAP.*

¢–**$$** ⊞ **Comfort Inn of Big Sky.** This is a family-friendly, affordable lodging option, sitting right along the Gallatin River, less than 1 mi south of the Big Sky entrance. A Southwestern theme permeates the simple, comfortable, clean rooms, which have pine accents and queen-size beds. Kids love the 90-foot waterslide that spills into the pool. ⊠ *47214 Gallatin Rd., 59716* ☎ *406/995–2333 or 800/228–5150* 🖷 *406/995–2277* ⊕ *www. comfortinnbigsky.com* ↜ *62 rooms* ⌂ *Some kitchens, some microwaves, cable TV, indoor pool, gym, hot tub, ski storage, laundry facilities, some pets allowed (fee), no-smoking floors* ⊟ *AE, D, MC, V* ❮◯❯ *CP.*

CAMPING ⚠ **Greek Creek.** Squeezed into the narrow Gallatin Canyon, this Forest Service campground with tent sites snuggles up to the Gallatin River under a canopy of tall evergreens. ⌂ *Pit toilets, drinking water, fire grates, picnic tables, swimming (river)* ↜ *14 sites* ⊠ *U.S. 191, 13 mi south of Bozeman* ☎ *406/522–2520 or 877/444–6777* ⊕ *www.fs.fed.us/r1/ gallatin* 🖃 *$10* ⊟ *AE, D, MC, V* ☉ *Mid-May–mid-Sept.*

Nightlife & the Arts

NIGHTLIFE Some weekends the **Corral** (⊠ 42895 Gallatin Rd., 5 mi south of Big Sky entrance ☎ 406/995–4249) rocks to the house band. Other entertainment comes from quirky bartenders, pool-table bets, and legions of skiers, snowmobilers, and locals in for the Montana brews. There's live rock music at **Dante's Inferno** (⊠ Mountain Mall, 1 Lone Mountain Trail ☎ 406/995–3999), where the dancing often spills out onto the deck for a boogie in ski boots.

THE ARTS Every July and August, the **Music in the Mountains** (⊠ Meadow Village
★ Pavilion ☎406/995–2742 or 877/995–2742) summer concert series showcases such headliners as Taj Mahal, Willie Nelson, and the Bozeman Symphony Orchestra in outdoor venues.

Gallatin River Gallery (⊠ 50 Meadow Village Dr., No. 102, in the Ringston Bldg., Meadow Village ☎ 406/995–2909), the only contemporary gallery in Big Sky, showcases one-of-a-kind jewelry, paintings, sculptures, and more from international, national, and local artists.

Shopping

Top-of-the-line ski and snowboard equipment and outerwear are sold at **Big Sky Sports** (⊠ Mountain Mall, 1 Lone Mountain Trail ☎ 406/

995–5840). **Lone Mountain Ranch Outdoor Shop** (✉ 4 mi west of U.S. 191, 6 mi from Big Sky resort, and ½ mi down gravel ranch Rd. ☎ 406/ 995–4644) sells beautiful Nordic sweaters, cross-country-skiing and snowshoeing accessories, summer outdoor wear, fly-fishing gear, and unique gifts.

BOZEMAN

This recreation capital offers everything from trout fishing to white-water river rafting to backcountry mountain biking. The arts have also flowered in Bozeman, the home of Montana State University; the mix of cowboys, professors, students, skiers, and celebrities make it one of the more diverse communities in the northern Rockies.

Bozeman has a strong Western heritage, readily evident at local museums, downtown galleries, and even the airport. In 1864 a trader named John Bozeman led his wagon train through this valley en route to the booming goldfields of Virginia City and southwest Montana. For several years this was the site of Fort Ellis, established to protect settlers making their way west along the Bozeman Trail, which extended into Montana Territory.

Exploring Bozeman

You can easily maneuver downtown Bozeman's mix of Old West bars, saddle shops, upscale stores and restaurants, and espresso cafés on foot or by bicycle. A vehicle is necessary—in winter, a four-wheel-drive vehicle is best—to explore the parks, trails, and recreation areas in the mountain ranges surrounding Bozeman.

Free, guided walking tours from the Pioneer Museum, on Main Street, take you through three areas of town: Main Street, historic neighborhoods, and Sunset Hills Cemetery and parks.

a good tour

Main Street, the original Bozeman Trail, running east–west through town, runs past some 700 homes and buildings listed on the National Register of Historic Places. Many have signs detailing their history. Begin a walking tour at the former Gallatin County Jail, now the **Pioneer Museum** ⑥, at Main Street and 4th Avenue. Head east on Main Street, noting the former **Gallatin County High School** ⑦ complex, comprising two distinct buildings, across the street. Turn left onto Grand Avenue and walk north one block to the elegant Victorian **Ketterer Building** ⑧. Walk south on Grand Avenue for two blocks (you'll cross Main Street) to the Gothic Revival **Emerson Cultural Center** ⑨, a former school and now a center for the arts. Return to Main Street, turn right, and continue east for a leisurely stroll past several notable historic buildings that now house shops, offices, and apartments. Once your feet wear down, return to the Pioneer Museum and hop in the car; drive to the south side of town to the **Museum of the Rockies** ⑩.

TIMING This tour should take about three hours, including time for visiting the museums. Note that some of the downtown businesses close on Sun-

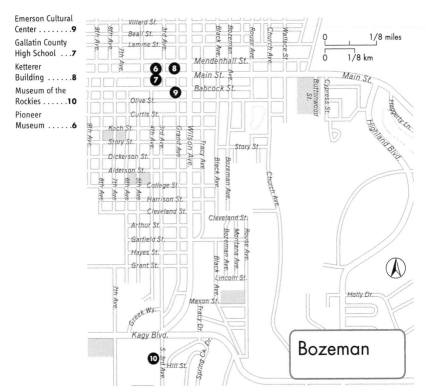

days. It's a good idea to carry a jacket around, even on warm days, in case of sudden changes in the weather.

The Main Attractions

9 Emerson Cultural Center. A school until 1990, this 1918 Gothic Revival brick building now houses 37 galleries, studios, and classrooms, plus a performing-arts hall. You can watch craftspeople at work, purchase artwork, take a class, or catch a performance here. ⌧ *111 S. Grand Ave.* ☎ *406/587-9797* ⊕ *www.theemerson.org* ⌧ *Free* ☉ *Daily 10–5 and for scheduled evening performances.*

7 Gallatin County High School. In the 1920s, actor Gary Cooper was a student at this high school. The original structure, constructed in 1901–02, includes neoclassical and Romanesque elements. An Art Deco addition was built in the 1930s. This is the only school building still standing in town that was built before the Great Depression. Today it houses offices. ⌧ *404 W. Main St.* ☎ *406/586-5421* ⊕ *www.bozemanchamber.com.*

8 Ketterer Building. This 1901 building, which now houses law offices, was built in the Queen Anne style, with some colonial touches. It was the home of Emil Ketterer, a German immigrant, blacksmith, and carriage maker. ⌧ *35 N. Grand Ave.* ☎ *406/586-5421* ⊕ *www. bozemanchamber.com.*

⊕ ⑩ **Museum of the Rockies.** Here you'll find a celebration of the history of the Rockies region, with eclectic exhibits on everything from prehistory to pioneers, plus a planetarium with laser shows. You can watch workers clean dinosaur fossils and see displays of dinosaur bones and eggs excavated around Montana. Children love the hands-on science activities in the Martin Discovery Room and the outdoors Tensley Homestead, with home-crafts demonstrations, including butter churning, weaving, and blacksmithing. May through mid-September, sheep, donkeys, and horses graze among the tall pasture grasses of the homestead. ⊠ *600 W. Kagy Blvd., south end of university campus* ☎ *406/994–3466 or 406/994–2251* ⊕ *www.museumoftherockies.org* ⊡ *$8 museum, $5 planetarium laser shows* ⊙ *Mon.–Sat. 9–5, Sun. 12:30–5.*

❻ **Pioneer Museum.** West of downtown, this redbrick former jail, built in 1911 in the Gothic Revival style, serves as a reminder of the rough-and-tumble days of the past. Inside, the Gallatin County Historical Society displays Native American artifacts, Fort Ellis items, an 1870s authentic log cabin, a library, photo archives, and a bookstore. Free guided tours of the museum are available by arrangement, and outside you can often pick up a historic walking tour of the town (for a small fee). ⊠ *317 W. Main St.* ☎ *406/522–8122* ⊕ *www.pioneermuseum.org* ⊡ *$3* ⊙ *June–Sept., Mon.–Sat. 10–5; Oct.–May, Tues.–Fri. 11–4.*

Also Worth Seeing

Bozeman Hot Springs. You can soak for an hour or a day at Bozeman Hot Springs, with nine indoor pools, one outdoor pool, a sauna, spa, gym, and juice bar. Individual pools of varying temperatures allow soakers to slowly adapt to hotter pools. ⊠ *81123 Gallatin Rd., 5 mi west of Bozeman at Four Corners Junction of Huffine La. (Main St.) and U.S. 191* ☎ *406/586–6492* ⊡ *$6.50* ⊙ *Mon.–Thurs. 7 AM–10 PM, Fri. 7 AM–7:15 PM, Sat. 8:15 PM–midnight, Sun. 8 AM–10 PM.*

Sports & the Outdoors

Bicycling
Austin Lehman Adventures (⊠ 2111 Fourth Ave. N. ☎ 406/655–4591 or 800/575–1540 ⊕ www.austinlehman.com) offers bike and multisport tours in the Gallatin Valley and all over the state.

Fishing
The **Bozeman Angler** (⊠ 23 E. Main St. ☎ 406/587–9111) sells fly rods and gear and arranges guided trips on several lakes, streams, and rivers, including the Gallatin and Yellowstone rivers.

Rafting
★ **Yellowstone Raft Company** (⊠ 55265 Gallatin Rd. ☎ 406/995–4613 or 800/348–4376) provides guided scenic and white-water raft trips and kayak instruction on the Gallatin and Yellowstone rivers.

Skiing
Bridger Bowl (⊠ 15795 Bridger Canyon Rd. ☎ 406/587–2111 or 800/ 223–9609 ⊕ www.bridgerbowl.com) is known for skiing in "cold smoke," light, dry powder. The terrain, from steep, rocky chutes to gentle slopes and meadows, is the headline act at this city-owned moun-

tain, where lift tickets are half the price of those at upscale resorts. In late September the ski area hosts the Bridger Raptor Festival to celebrate the golden-eagle flyway along the mountain-range crest. Some days, more than 200 goldens are spotted gliding the thermals.

Using Sno-Cat or helicopter services, **Montana Powder Guides** (✉ 15792 Bridger Canyon Rd. ☎ 406/587–3096) leads expeditions into the snowy backcountry for untracked powder skiing and snowboarding.

Where to Stay & Eat

$$–$$$$ ✕ **Cafe International.** This classic white-tablecloth restaurant inside the Emerson Cultural Center attracts the business crowd for lunch with a large selection of hot and cold salads and sandwiches. The elegant presentation of specials such as the portobello-mushroom lobster chowder draws oohs and ahs. ✉ *207 W. Olive St.* ☎ *406/586–4242* ▭ *AE, D, MC, V.*

$$–$$$$ ✕ **Montana Ale Works.** A cavernous brick building, the former Northern Pacific Railroad depot houses a brewery and restaurant with outdoor dining in summer. In addition to the 42 beers on tap, the Ale Works serves bison burgers, wild game, baked pasta dishes, and nightly specials such as fresh grilled yellowfin tuna. ✉ *611 E. Main St.* ☎ *406/ 587–7700* ▭ *AE, D, MC, V* ⊘ *No lunch.*

$$–$$$$ ✕ **Sophia's Restaurant and Looie's Downunder.** Two eateries are packed under one roof in the historic downtown area. Upstairs, Sophia's serves Italian specialties such as the penne Looie, with mushrooms, chicken, and Gorgonzola cream sauce. Downstairs, Looie's is popular for both the atmosphere (casual and intimate) and the food; try the nightly specials such as curried halibut with sushi and seaweed salad, coupled with a selection from the extensive wine list. ✉ *101 E. Main St.* ☎ *406/ 582–0393 or 406/522–8814* ▭ *AE, D, MC, V.*

$$–$$$$ ✕ **John Bozeman's Bistro.** Located in Bozeman's historic downtown district, this contemporary café changes its menu regularly. Expect dishes such as Jamaican jerk chicken, coconut fried shrimp, Sonoran pork roulade, and fettuccine carbonara. ✉ *125 W. Main St.* ☎ *406/587–4100* ⊕ *www.johnbozemansbistro.com* ⌦ *Reservations essential* ▭ *AE, D, MC, V* ⊘ *Closed Sun.*

¢–$$ ✕ **La Parrilla.** At this cottage turned café, you choose the ingredients and watch the crew build your burrito wrap. The Bombay wrap includes beans, rice, chicken, ginger, and chutney. Dining is indoors or outside on the flower-draped deck. ✉ *1533 W. Babcock St.* ☎ *406/582–9511* ▭ *No credit cards.*

$–$$$ ✕▣ **Gallatin Gateway Inn.** The Milwaukee Railroad built this sumptuous inn 10 mi from town on U.S. 191 as a stopping-off point for visitors to Yellowstone National Park. After a stint as a seedy bar, the inn has recaptured its reputation. A modern, Western style decorates the uniquely furnished rooms painted in soothing pastels. The bathrooms, with original tile work and brass fixtures, exude simple elegance. Crisp white linens and candlelight set the formal tone in the wonderful restaurant, which serves regional cuisine. The Baggage Room Pub's casual fare complements a day of recreation. ✉ *U.S. 191, Box 376, Gallatin Gateway 59730* ☎ *406/763–4672 or 800/676–3522* 🖷 *406/763–4777*

⊕ *www.gallatingatewayinn.com* ↝ *33 rooms* ♨ *Restaurant, cable TV, tennis court, pool, pub, Wi-Fi; no smoking* ⊟ *AE, MC, V* ⭍ *CP.*

$$$$ ⊡ **Gallatin River Lodge.** On the property of a 350-acre ranch, this full-service, year-round fly-fishing lodge perches on the banks of the famed fly-fishing river for which it is named. Packages include guided fishing. The elegant country inn has six suites, with rustic furnishings and views of the river. ⊠ *9105 Thorpe Rd., 59718* ☎ *406/388–0148 or 888/387–0148* 🖷 *406/388–6766* ⊕ *www.grlodge.com* ↝ *6 suites* ♨ *Dining room, cable TV, Wi-Fi, fishing, bar, library, business services, meeting rooms, airport shuttle, free parking; no a/c, no smoking* ⊟ *MC, V* ⭍ *BP.*

★ **$–$$** ⊡ **Voss Inn.** This B&B occupies an elegant 1883 Victorian house and is lavishly furnished with antiques and knickknacks. Stop by the parlor to enjoy afternoon tea or to catch up on the news with other guests who drop in to watch TV or to chat. Huge breakfasts are served in rooms or in the parlor. The lovely English garden makes a great spot for a quiet conversation. ⊠ *319 S. Willson Ave., 59715* ☎ *406/587–0982* 🖷 *406/585–2964* ⊕ *www.bozeman-vossinn.com* ↝ *6 rooms* ⊟ *AE, D, MC, V* ⭍ *BP.*

Nightlife & the Arts

Nightlife

On weekends, young professionals, university professors, and tourists head to the **Robin** (⊠ 105 W. Main St. ☎ 406/522–0362), a smoke-free bar at the Baxtor Hotel, for live jazz, drink specials, and casual socializing. A smoke-free downtown saloon, the **Rocking R Bar** (⊠ 211 E. Main St. ☎ 406/587–9355) draws a young crowd with its classic-rock bands and original local acts, suds, and dancing. Pool tables, a jukebox, a poker room, and foosball fill one side of the **Zebra Cocktail Lounge** (⊠ 321 E. Main St. ☎ 406/585–8851), a downtown basement hangout. The other side has a dance floor, couches, and live music on weekends, all in swanky surroundings.

The Arts

The **Bozeman Symphony Society** (⊠ 104 W. Main St., #102 ☎ 406/585–9774) runs a year-round concert series, often featuring talented university students and traveling artists. Performances take place at the Willson Auditorium, and there's one outdoor summer concert each year in Big Sky.

Shopping

Antiques, collectibles, and more fill the 12,000-square-foot **Antique Barn** (⊠ 5 Wheeler Mountain Way, ½ mi north of Gallatin Gateway Inn ☎ 406/763–4676). Among the more unusual items are antler light fixtures and animal hides. Outdoor wear, cross-country-skiing equipment, and boating gear are sold at **Northern Lights Trading Co.** (⊠ 1716 W. Babcock St. ☎ 406/586–2225). Don't be surprised to see any of the helpful staff members out on the trails, tracks, or rivers beside you.

HELENA

Montana's state capital is a city of 28,000, with 25 city parks, several museums, a thriving arts community, and its own minor-league baseball team. The southern part of the city, near the State Capitol Building and neighboring museums, mansions, and parks, is hilly and thick with lush greenery in summer. This quiet town, where the prairie meets the mountains, started as a rowdy mining camp in 1864 and became a banking and commerce center in the Montana Territory. At the turn of the 20th century, Helena had more millionaires per capita than any other town in the country. Some of that wealth came from ground now occupied by main street: called Last Chance Gulch, it was the first of several gulches that yielded more than $15 million in gold during the late 1800s. With statehood came a fight between the towns of Anaconda and Helena over which would be the capital. In a notoriously corrupt campaign in which both sides bought votes, Helena won. The iron ball of urban renewal has since robbed the town of much of its history, but Helena still has ornate brick and granite historic buildings along Last Chance Gulch.

Exploring Helena

The downtown historic area has a pedestrian-only mall on Last Chance Gulch with shops, coffeehouses, and restaurants. There are several historic sights here that you can see on foot, but other sights are spread out in the city and best accessed by automobile.

The **Downtown Helena Office** (⊠ 121 N. Last Chance Gulch ☎ 406/442–9869 ⊕ www.downtownhelena.com) in the center of Helena's historic downtown can provide a brochure for a self-guided walking tour.

TIMING   If you wish to hit all of the major sights in town, set aside an entire day for a walk. Plan on spending at least two hours strolling around the historic district and another two hours visiting the capitol, Montana Historical Society Museum, and the Governor's Mansion.

The Main Attractions

㉑ Cathedral of St. Helena. Modeled after the cathedral in Cologne, Germany, this Gothic Revival building has stained-glass windows from Bavaria and 230-foot-tall twin spires that are visible from most places in the city. Construction began in 1908 and was completed 16 years later. Note the white marble altars, statues of Carrara marble, and gold leaf decorating the sanctuary. Guided tours are available with one day's advance notice. ⊠ 530 N. Ewing St. ☎ 406/442–5825 ☜ Donations accepted ☉ Daily 7–6.

㉒ Great Northern Carousel. Hand-carved ponies gallop through the center of town on this carousel, open 365 days a year. You can buy homemade Painted Pony ice cream and fudge here. ⊠ 924 Bicentennial Plaza, at 14th Ave. W ☎ 406/457–5353 ⊕ www.gncarousel.com ☜ $1 ☉ Sun.–Thurs. 11:30–8, Fri. 11:30–9, and Sat. 10–9.

⑬ Last Chance Gulch. Four down-and-out prospectors designated this spot their "last chance" after they'd followed played-out gold strikes across

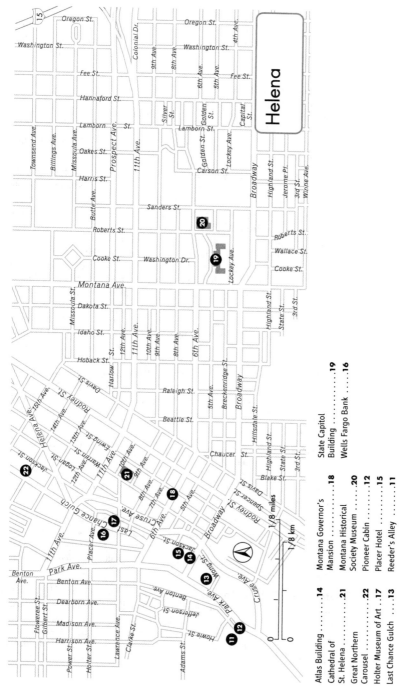

Helena

Atlas Building **14**
Cathedral of
St. Helena **21**
Great Northern
Carousel **22**
Holter Museum of Art ...**17**
Last Chance Gulch **13**

Montana Governor's
Mansion **18**
Montana Historical
Society Museum **20**
Pioneer Cabin **12**
Placer Hotel **15**
Reeder's Alley **11**

State Capitol
Building **19**
Wells Fargo Bank **16**

the West. Their perseverance paid off when they discovered the first of several gold deposits here, which propelled Helena to the ranks of Montana's leading gold producers. Many of the mansions and businesses that resulted from the discovery of gold still stand on this historic route, also known as Main Street.

18 **Montana Governor's Mansion.** Governors lived in this Victorian mansion between 1913 and 1959. You can take a scheduled guided tour, but call ahead, because some tours are unexpectedly canceled. ⊠ *304 N. Ewing St.* ☎ *406/444–4789* ⊕ *www.montanahistoricalsociety.org* ☞ *$4* ⊙ *Tours May–Sept., Tue. and Sat. at noon, 1, 2, 3, and 4; Oct.–Apr. Sat., noon–4.*

20 **Montana Historical Society Museum.** Highlights here include the MacKay Gallery, which displays one of the most important collections of Western artist Charlie Russell's work, and the Haynes Gallery where early black-and-white photos of Yellowstone National Park taken by F. Jay Haynes are on display. The expansive Montana Homeland exhibit, which contains nearly 2,000 historical artifacts, documents, and photographs, takes a thorough look at Montana from the time of the first native settlers to the present. The venue also hosts special events and family days in summer, including programs on folk music, Native American culture, and cowboys. Call ahead for information on upcoming events. Out in front of the Historical Society Museum, catch the **Last Chance Train Tour** (☎ 406/442–1023 or 888/423–1023 ⊕ www.lctours. com) for an hour-long tour through historic neighborhoods of miners' mansions on the west side to the site where four miners made their first gold discovery on the gulch. Train tours cost $6 and take place daily on the hour, 10–6 in July and August, and 10–3 in May, June, and September. ⊠ *225 N. Roberts St., across from the State Capitol* ☎ *406/444–2694 or 800/243–9900* ⊕ *www.montanahistoricalsociety.org* ☞ *$5* ⊙ *Memorial Day–Labor Day, daily 9–5; Labor Day–Memorial Day, Tue.–Sat., 9–5.*

12 **Pioneer Cabin.** This 1864 hand-hewn log structure now houses a museum of the gold-rush days of the 1860s. This is Helena's oldest extant home. ⊠ *212 S. Park Ave.* ☎ *406/443–7641* ☞ *$1* ⊙ *Memorial Day–Labor Day, daily 9–5; Labor Day–Memorial Day by appointment only.*

11 **Reeder's Alley.** Miners' houses and distinctive shops built between 1872 and 1884 line this carefully restored area of old Helena. Also here are some restaurants and a visitor center. Note the stone pillars and wooden stringers of the Morelli Bridge, spanning a dry gulch. ⊠ *Near south end of Last Chance Gulch.*

19 **State Capitol Building.** The Greek Renaissance capitol is topped by a dome of Montana copper and holds Charlie Russell's largest painting, a 12-by 25-foot depiction of Lewis and Clark. Self-guided-tour booklets are available. This building was thought so beautiful, South Dakota modeled its capitol in Pierre on the same design. ⊠ *6th Ave. and Montana Ave.* ☎ *406/444–4789 or 800/243–9900* ☞ *Free* ⊙ *May–Sept., Mon.–Sat. 9–3, Sun. noon–4; Oct.–Apr., Sat. 10–2.*

Also Worth Seeing

⑭ Atlas Building. A statue of Atlas himself and two lizards and a salamander crown this building, symbols of insurance protection offered by the company housed in this 1887 neo-Romanesque structure. ⊠ *7 Last Chance Gulch* ☑ *Free* ☉ *Mon.–Sat. 9–5, Sun. noon–5.*

⑰ Holter Museum of Art. Displays at this museum not far from Last Chance Gulch include folk art, crafts, photography, painting, and sculpture, with an emphasis on homegrown Montana artists. ⊠ *12 E. Lawrence Ave.* ☎ *406/442–6400* ⊕ *www.holtermuseum.org* ☑ *Donations accepted* ☉ *Memorial Day–Labor Day, Mon.–Sat. 10–5, Sun. noon–5; Labor Day–Memorial Day, Tues.–Fri. 10–5, weekends noon–5.*

⑮ Placer Hotel. Now housing apartments, this 1913 building is one of only two historic hotels that remain in downtown Helena. Early on in its history, the hotel was a favorite after-hours gathering place for prominent state politicians; it was the site of closed-door lobbying by powerful companies. Note the statue of the bullwhacker (a man using a stick to urge cattle along the trails), symbol of the making of Montana, at one corner of the building. ⊠ *15-27 N. Last Chance Gulch.*

⑯ Wells Fargo Bank. The lobby of this bank on the corner of Last Chance Gulch and Lawrence Street displays a collection of gold nuggets, including one nugget worth $600,000, taken from area diggings. ⊠ *350 N. Last Chance Gulch* ☎ *406/447–1530* ☑ *Free* ☉ *Weekdays 9–4.*

Sports & the Outdoors

To stretch your legs, consider taking an hour-long hike to the top of Mt. Helena, which towers over the Last Chance Gulch pedestrian mall on the west edge of town. From the summit, you'll have panoramic views of the city, the Helena Valley, and the Rocky Mountains to the west.

Bicycling

Old logging roads such as the MacDonald Pass area, 20 mi west of town on the Continental Divide, offer challenging mountain biking. Other trails closer to town, such as the Mount Helena Ridge Trail, the Birdseye Loop, and the Helena Valley Loop, lead to mining towns and thick forests.

To find out more about bike routes, check the Web site of the **Helena Bicycle Club** (⊕ www.helenabicycleclub.org). The **Helena National Forest** (☎ 406/449–5201) can provide bike route information by phone.

Boating

The more than 75 mi of shoreline of the **Canyon Ferry Recreation Area** (⊠ Hwy. 284, Townsend, near Helena ☎ 406/475–3310) are a great place to fish, boat, sail, camp, and watch wildlife. Herds of pronghorns often blanket the surrounding plains. The Missouri River once flowed freely here, though now a dam has created a lake. You can rent canoes, Jet Skis, and pontoon, fishing, and pedal boats from **Kim's Marina, RV Park and Store** (⊠ 8015 Canyon Ferry Rd., 2 mi east of dam on Hwy. 284 ☎ 406/475–3723).

CloseUp

ON THE TRAIL OF LEWIS & CLARK

AMERICA'S GREATEST ADVENTURE *began with the stroke of a pen, when in 1803 President Thomas Jefferson purchased the vast Louisiana Territory from cash-strapped France, effectively doubling the size of the United States. The land, stretching from the Gulf of Mexico to Canada and from the Mississippi River to the Rockies, was unmapped and virtually unknown to outsiders.*

To understand what his $16 million had bought, Jefferson appointed a secret "Corps of Discovery" to venture west, make contact with native peoples, chart the landscape, and observe the growing British presence in the Pacific Northwest. The group would be headed by Jefferson's personal secretary, Meriwether Lewis, and another intrepid explorer, William Clark.

Time in Montana

On May 14, 1804, Lewis and Clark set out from St. Louis on their expedition with a party of 45 seasoned soldiers, scouts, interpreters, and others, poling up the Missouri River in well-stocked flatboats and keelboats. After wintering with the Mandans in North Dakota, the corps continued upriver in canoes and keelboats as soon as ice jams had cleared the waterway.

They entered what is now Montana on April 27, 1805, and followed the Missouri to its Montana headwaters—the confluence of the Jefferson, Madison, and Gallatin rivers. After they reached the Continental Divide, Shoshone Indians helped them cross the Rockies. The party then followed the Snake, Clearwater, and Columbia rivers, reaching the Pacific Ocean that fall.

On the return trip, the expedition split into two groups in Montana and explored several rivers, including the Yellowstone. The explorers arrived back in St. Louis on September 23, 1806, having traveled

more than 8,000 mi. They had spent more than a quarter of their time in Montana, where much of the land they observed remains unchanged today.

Following in Their Footsteps

If you want to trace Lewis and Clark's path, the best place to start is the Lewis and Clark National Historic Trail Interpretive Center in Great Falls, where the 200-year-old adventure unfolds before you. Nearby Giant Springs State Park marks the place where Clark discovered a large "fountain or spring" during an 18-mi portage around a series of waterfalls.

Missouri Headwaters State Park near Three Forks preserves the spot where the explorers traced the river to its origin. The Lolo Pass Visitor Center, on U.S. 12 at the Montana-Idaho border, also interprets the expedition.

Another way to connect with Lewis and Clark history is a boat tour on the "Mighty Mo." Several operators offer tours at Gates of the Mountains, north of Helena off I-15, and also at the White Cliffs area of the Upper Missouri National Wild and Scenic River below Fort Benton. A canoe rental and shuttle service on the Missouri near Loma gives you a self-guided option. And look for Lewis and Clark Trail signs along state, U.S., and interstate highways that follow the expedition's route.

★ In their travels on the Missouri River, Lewis and Clark made note of towering limestone cliffs. **Gates of the Mountains** (⊠ Off I–15, 20 mi north of Helena ☎ 406/458–5241 ⊕ www.gatesofthemountains.com) boat tours take you past these same great stone walls, which rise 1,200 feet above the river.

Fishing

Western Rivers Outfitters (⊠ Box 772, East Helena 59635 ☎ 406/227–5153), with more than 25 years and 16,000 miles of river experience, offers day trips, overnight camping and base-camp fishing excursions, and float trips on the Bitterroot, Blackfoot, Clark Fork, Missouri, Madison, Gallatin, and Jefferson rivers.

Where to Stay & Eat

★ **$$$$** ✕ **Last Chance Ranch.** After a wagon ride, which is included in the price, there's dinner, usually prime rib, salads, potatoes, and huckleberry cheesecake. Dinner is served family style at 7 PM in Montana's largest tepee, with seating for 50, and is accompanied by singing and storytelling. ⊠ *2884 Grizzly Gulch, 8 mi southwest of Helena* ☎ *406/442–2884 or 800/505–2884* ⊕ *http://lastchanceranch.biz* ▤ *MC, V* ☺ *Closed Oct.–May.*

$$–$$$$ ✕ **On Broadway.** Wooden booths, discreet lighting, and brick walls contribute to the comfortable ambience at this Italian restaurant. Popular dishes include New York strip steak and pasta puttanesca (sautéed Greek olives, artichoke hearts, red bell peppers, red onions, capers, and pine nuts). When the state legislature is in session, representatives make this a boisterous place. ⊠ *106 Broadway* ☎ *406/443–1929* ⌔ *Reservations not accepted* ▤ *AE, D, DC, MC, V* ☺ *No lunch. Closed Sun.*

★ **$$–$$$** ✕ **Windbag Saloon & Grill.** This historic restaurant in the heart of downtown was called Big Dorothy's until 1973, when a crusading county attorney forced Dorothy to shut down her house of ill repute. Now it's a family restaurant, named for the political debates you're likely to hear while dining on burgers, quiche, salads, and sandwiches. It also has a large selection of imported beer, on tap and in bottles. Old photos of Helena characters and a bounty of cherrywood give the place a warm, comfortable feel. ⊠ *19 S. Last Chance Gulch* ☎ *406/443–9669* ▤ *AE, D, MC, V* ☺ *Closed Sun.*

¢–$ ✕ **The Staggering Ox.** The unique deli sandwiches here have even more unique, often political, names and humorous descriptions. Try the Capitol Complex (loaded with different deli meats and cheese) or the Clinton Shuffle (with chicken, ham, Swiss cheese, and guacamole). The sandwiches are served on specialty breads shaped like a can of beans. Zany decor ranges from old records dangling from the ceiling to wildlife oil paintings. ⊠ *Lundy Center, 400 Euclid St.* ☎ *406/443–1729* ▤ *MC, V.*

★ **$–$$$** ▥ **Canyon Ferry Mansion.** Saved from inundation in 1954 when the Canyon Ferry Reservoir was created, this former cattle baron's home was relocated to a premier perch above the lake. Antiques, many of which are for sale, accent the frilly modern furnishings and lovingly restored woodwork throughout the B&B. In addition to several private rooms, there's a dorm-style bunkhouse that sleeps seven. Outdoorsy types come here for summer water sports and winter ice boating. In summer there are lots of weddings and outdoor events. ⊠ *7408 U.S. 287, Townsend 59644, 20 mi southeast of Helena at mi marker 74* ☎ *406/266–3599 or 877/933–7721* 🖷 *406/266–4003* ⊕ *www.canyonferrymansion.com* 🛏 *7 rooms, 3 with bath; 1 bunkhouse* ⚒ *Dining room, in-room data ports, cable TV, lake, outdoor hot tub, spa, beach, boating, fishing, mountain bikes, concierge, meeting rooms, free parking, no-smoking rooms; no a/c* ⊟ *AE, D, MC, V* ⧐ *BP.*

★ $ 🏨 **Sanders–Helena Bed and Breakfast.** Colonel Wilbur Sanders, one of the first senators of Montana, built this three-story Victorian mansion in 1875. The colonel's rock collection is still in the front hall, and the B&B has retained his furnishings. Most of the rooms overlook mountain-ringed downtown Helena. Breakfasts are a work of art: Grand Marnier French toast, orange soufflé, or gingerbread waffles. ⊠ *328 N. Ewing St., 59601* ☎ *406/442–3309* 🖷 *406/443–2361* ⊕ *www.sandersbb.com* 🛏 *7 rooms, 6 with bath* ⊟ *AE, MC, V* ⧐ *BP.*

Camping

△ **Cromwell-Dixon Campground.** High above Helena on MacDonald Pass at 6,320 feet, this forested spot is frequented by migrating birds in spring and fall. ⚒ *Grills, pit toilets, drinking water, fire grates, picnic tables* 🛏 *14 sites* ⊠ *MacDonald Pass, U.S. 12* ☎ *406/449–5490* ⊕ *www.fs.fed.us/ r1/helena* 🍴 *$8* ⊟ *AE, D, MC, V* ☉ *Early June–early Oct.*

Nightlife & the Arts

Late May through mid-September, live music plays in downtown parks and plazas Wednesday evenings from 5 to 9 as part of the **Alive at Five** (☎ 406/447–1535 ⊕ www.downtownhelena.com) series. The type of music and the venues vary, but it's always free and fun for the whole family.

In a remodeled historic stone jail, the **Myrna Loy Center for the Performing Arts** (⊠ 15 N. Ewing St. ☎ 406/443–0287 ⊕ www.myrnaloycenter. com)—named after the Montana-born actress—hosts live performances by nationally and internationally recognized musicians and dance troupes. Two theaters show foreign and independent films, usually two films per night.

Shopping

★ Since 1951, many of the nation's best ceramic artists have come to work in residency at the **Archie Bray Foundation** (⊠ 2915 Country Club Ave. ☎ 406/443–3502 ⊕ www.archiebray.org). Wander near the five antiquated, 8-foot-high, dome-shape brick kilns on a self-guided walking tour, and visit the gift shop, which sells work produced by foundation artists. It's open Monday–Saturday 9–5 and Sunday 1–5.

The **Made in Montana Store and Gallery** (⊠ 21 N. Last Chance Gulch ☎ 406/442–3136 or 800/700–3136 ⊕ www.madeinmontanastore.com) stocks the largest selection of Montana-made foods and gifts, including huckleberry and chokecherry treats, T-shirts, and books. There's also an Old West photo studio. A refreshing stop in the historic center of town, the independent **Montana Book and Toy Company** (⊠ 331 N. Last Chance Gulch ☎ 406/443–0260 ⊕ www.mtbookco.com) lines its shelves with regional and hard-to-find books, unique toys, games, and gifts.

⊘ For an old-fashioned sweet treat, pull up a stool at the **Parrot Confectionery** (⊠ 42 N. Main St. ☎ 406/442–1470), a soda fountain and candy store built in the 1920s that sells everything from chocolate malts with homemade ice cream to hand-dipped chocolates and a regional favorite, a cherry phosphate. The building's ornate facade resembles a wedding cake.

en route At the turn of the 20th century, radon health mines were considered cure-alls. Several of these underground mines still operate outside of Helena, including the **Merry Widow Health Mine,** where you sit in lighted chambers and breathe radon gas. ⊠ *93 Basin Rd., at Basin exit off I–15, Basin, 40 mi south of Helena* ☎ *406/225–3220* ⊕ *www.merrywidowmine.com* 🖃 *$3.50 per hour* ⊙ *Mar.–mid-Nov., daily 8–7.*

THE SOUTHWEST CORNER

In Montana Territory days, the mineral wealth of this remote area drew hard-drinking miners, women of easy virtue, thieves, and the people who became rich on it all. Abundant winter snowfall coats the mountains and feeds the lush valleys, where ranching and forestry are the main industries and where remnants of the mining era abound.

Deer Lodge

㉓ *60 mi southwest of Helena via U.S. 12 and I–90.*

Deer Lodge, a quiet community of 3,400 residents, maintains a complex of history museums in and near its old penitentiary. Many locals make their living by ranching, which came to the 55-mi-long Deer Lodge Valley in 1862, when John Grant built the area's first cabin and began a cattle operation, selling beef to miners. Ranching remained the primary industry as the town of Deer Lodge developed. Its name derives from a 40-foot-high geothermal mound that used to emit steam from its top; Native Americans though it resembled a large medicine lodge. The minerals and water attracted deer, and so the Native Americans named the place Deer Lodge. The mound is hidden behind trees and buildings at the Warm Springs State Hospital.

A single admission charge ($9) grants you access to the Old Montana Prison Museum, the Montana Automobile Museum, the Frontier Montana Museum, and Yesterday's Playthings.

Built in 1871, the old Montana Territorial Prison did not shut down until 1979. It's now the **Old Montana Prison Museum,** where you can enter cells and learn about early Montana law. Also on display is the gallows tree taken from town to town in territorial days to hang convicted prisoners. ⊠ *1106 Main St.* ☎ *406/846–3111* 🖃 *$9 (includes admission* *to other three complex museums)* ☾ *June–Aug., daily 8–8; Sept.–May, daily 8:30–5.*

The **Montana Automobile Museum** is a car buff's delight. Displays include more than 100 vintage Fords and Lincolns dating from 1903 to the 1970s, including such rarities as a Fordson tractor and a Model A snowmobile. Admission here also grants you entrance to the Old Montana Prison Museum, the Frontier Montana Museum, and Yesterday's Playthings doll and toy museum. ⊠ *1106 Main St.* ☎ *406/846–3111* 💲 *$9 (includes admission to other three complex museums)* ☾ *Late May–early Sept., daily 8–8; early Sept.–Oct. and Apr.–late May, daily 8:30–5:30. Call for hrs rest of yr.*

The **Frontier Montana Museum** displays hats, saddles, spurs, chaps, and all things cowboy. Also here are Civil War items, Native American artifacts, and Desert John's Saloon, complete with whiskey memorabilia. Admission here also grants you entrance to the Old Montana Prison Museum, the Montana Automobile Museum, and Yesterday's Playthings doll and toy museum. ⊠ *1106 Main St.* ☎ *406/846–0026* 💲 *$9 (includes admission to other three complex museums)* ☾ *Mid-May–Sept., daily 10:30–5:30.*

Whimsical old toys and dolls and a large, excellent clown collection inhabit **Yesterday's Playthings** in an 1880s print shop on the National Register of Historic Places. Admission here grants you access to the Montana Automobile Museum, Frontier Montana Museum, and the Old Montana Prison Museum. ⊠ *1017 Main St.* ☎ *406/846–1480* 💲 *$9 (includes admission to other three complex museums)* ☾ *Mid-May–Sept., daily 9–5.*

The **Powell County Museum** focuses on local history; it includes an antique gun collection, photographs, and a 1926 Model T Ford. ⊠ *1193 Main St.* ☎ *406/846–3111* 💲 *Free* ☾ *June–Sept., daily 8:30–5:15; Oct.–May, daily noon–5.*

☾ Daily tours of the 1,600-acre **Grant-Kohrs Ranch National Historic Site**, a working cattle ranch run by the National Park Service, give insight into ranching life in the 1850s. You can learn about roping steers, watch blacksmith demonstrations, and bounce along on a hayride. The annual Western Heritage Days Celebration, with demonstrations and kids' programs, takes place in mid-July. ⊠ *Grant Circle, ½ mi off I–90* ☎ *406/846–2070* ⊕ *www.nps.gov/grko* 💲 *Free* ☾ *June–Aug., daily 8–5:30; Sept.–May, daily 9–4:30.*

Where to Stay & Eat

¢–$$ ✕ **The Coffee House.** Remember to save room for one of the 40 different milk shakes and malts at this Western-front eatery, which serves a bit of everything: pizza, calzones, cold and grilled sandwiches, salads, and baked potatoes. ⊠ *200 Main St.* ☎ *406/846–1750* ⌣ *Reservations not accepted* ▤ *AE, MC, V* ☾ *Closed Sun.*

$ ▦ **Deer Lodge Super 8.** This cookie-cutter motel is clean and convenient to the interstate, historic sights, and restaurants. ⊠ *1150 N. Main St., 59722* ☎ *406/846–2370 or 800/800–8000* 📠 *406/846–2373* ⊕ *www.super8.com* ⇆ *57 rooms* ⌣ *Restaurant, cable TV, some pets allowed, no-smoking rooms* ▤ *AE, D, DC, MC, V.*

CAMPING   ⚠ **Indian Creek Campground.** Set among brush and flats, this campground along tiny Indian Creek has large campsites, plus cable TV hookups. For a small fee you can use the Internet at the office. It's a good idea to make reservations. ⚐ *Flush toilets, full hookups, drinking water, guest laundry, showers, picnic tables, electricity, public telephone, general store* ⚑ *65 full hookups, 20 tent sites* ✉ *745 Maverick La.* ☎ *406/846–3848 or 800/294–0726* ⊕ *www.indiancreekcampground.com* ⚑ *$15 tent sites, $22 full hookups* ▤ *MC, V* ☾ *Mid-Apr.–Oct.*

Nightlife & the Arts

Bluegrass bands perform outdoors (weather permitting) at the three-day **Prison Breakout Bluegrass Festival** (☎ 406/846–1843) in late June. Barbecues, vendors, and concessions are set up at this annual event 10 mi west of town at Garrison Junction's Riverfront RV Park.

Anaconda

㉔ *22 mi south of Deer Lodge via I–90.*

Nicknamed the Smelter City, Anaconda is a window on the age of the copper barons, who ran this town in the 1880s through the 1950s. A number of sites preserve traces of Anaconda's rough-and-tumble history, including the dormant 585-foot smokestack, visible for miles, of the copper-smelting works around which the town was built. Copper is no longer the chief industry here, but even the Jack Nicklaus–designed golf course uses smelter-tailings slag for sand traps. Anaconda is also an ideal spot for fishing and hiking, and it sits at the base of the rugged Pintlar Mountains, popular for cross-country skiing, downhill skiing, and backcountry adventures.

The **Anaconda Visitor Center,** in the old railroad depot, displays memorabilia of the town's railroad and copper history. It also hosts tours, performances, and exhibits. You can even buy a pen with ink made from slag. At the visitor center, board a 1931 **Vintage Bus** for a tour of historic Anaconda. ✉ *306 E. Park Ave.* ☎ *406/563–2400* ⊕ *www. anacondamt.org* ⚑ *Visitor center free, bus $5* ☾ *Visitor center June–Sept., daily 9–5; Oct.–May, weekdays 9–5. Bus mid-May–mid-Sept., Mon.–Sat. at 10 and 2.*

The **Copper Village Museum and Arts Center** houses displays on the area's history along with video presentations and local artwork. The center also hosts musical performances and special events. ✉*401 E. Commercial St.* ☎ *406/563–2422* ⚑ *Free* ☾ *Daily 10–4.*

The classic Art Deco **Washoe Theatre** (✉ 305 Main St. ☎406/563–6161), built in 1931, was ranked by the Smithsonian as the fifth-most-beautiful theater in the nation. Murals and ornamentation in silver, copper, and gold leaf are some of the highlights of this theater, which is open nightly for movies and other events.

At 585 feet tall, "the Stack" at **Anaconda Smoke Stack State Park** is a solid reminder of the important role the Anaconda Copper Company played in the area's development. Built in 1919, the stack, one of the tallest freestanding brick structures in the world, is listed on the National Register of Historic Places. Smelting operations ceased in 1980. There's a viewing and interpretive area with displays and historical information, but you cannot access the smokestack itself. ⊠ *Hwy. 1* ☎ *406/542–5500* ⊕ *http://fwp.mt.gov* 🖃 *Free* ⊙ *Daily, sunrise–sunset.*

off the beaten path

ANACONDA-PINTLAR WILDERNESS – Overlapping three ranger districts of the Beaverhead-Deerlodge National Forest, the 159,000-acre Anaconda-Pintlar wilderness area extends more than 30 mi along the Continental Divide to the southwest of Anaconda. Elevations range from 5,400 feet near the Bitterroot River to 10,793 feet at the summit of West Goat Peak. Glaciation formed many spectacular cirques, U-shape valleys, and glacial moraines in the foothills. The habitat supports mountain lions, deer, elk, moose, bears, and many smaller animals and birds. About 280 mi of Forest Service trails cross the area. If you hike or ride horseback along the Continental Divide, at times you can view the Mission Mountains to the northwest and the mountains marking the Idaho-Montana border to the southwest. If you want to explore the wilderness, you must obtain a detailed map and register your plans with a Forest Service office. Stock forage is scarce, so if you're riding a horse, bring concentrated feed pellets. Note that no motorized travel is permitted in the wilderness area. There are more than 20 access points to the area, including popular ones at Moose Lake, Georgetown Lake, and the East Fork of the Bitterroot River. ⊠ *Access to East Fork of Bitterroot River via U.S. 93* ☎ *406/821–3201* 🖃 *Free* ⊙ *Daily, 24 hrs.*

PINTLAR SCENIC HIGHWAY – The 63 mi of mountain road on this highway pass a ghost town, historic burgs, and Georgetown Lake. The road begins in Anaconda and ends on I–90 at Drummond, backdropped by the 159,000-acre Anaconda-Pintlar Wilderness. ☎ *406/563–2400 for information on highway.*

Sports & the Outdoors

BICYCLING Need a mountain bike or just some suggested bike routes? Check with **Sven's Bicycles of Anaconda** (⊠ 220 Hickory St. ☎ 406/563–7988) for local advice, including the best mountain-biking routes, from back roads to challenging mile-high trails. In winter, Sven's rents ice skates and cross-country-skiing equipment and can provide ski-trail maps and telemarking suggestions.

CROSS-COUNTRY SKIING Beautifully groomed skate and classic-ski trails climb nearly to the Continental Divide at the **Mt. Haggin Cross-Country Ski Trails** area, the state's largest wildlife management area, with more than 54,000 acres. There's a warming hut but no services. Ski rentals and information are available at Sven's Bicycles on Hickory Street. To get to the area from Anaconda, head southwest on Highway 1, cross the railroad tracks, and look for the sign to Wisdom; from here, make a left onto Highway 274 and follow it for 11 mi to the parking area.

DOWNHILL SKIING Powder skiing at **Discovery Ski Area** (⊠ Hwy. 1, 23 mi northwest of Anaconda at Georgetown Lake ☎ 406/563–2184 ⊕ www.skidiscovery.

com), an inexpensive family resort, offers thrills on the extreme steeps and extensive beginner and intermediate runs.

GOLF At the public, 18-hole, Jack Nicklaus–designed **Old Works Golf Course** (⌂ 1205 Pizzini Way ☎ 406/563–5989), on the site of Anaconda's historic Old Works copper smelter, hazards are filled with smelter-tailings slag instead of sand.

Where to Stay & Eat

$$–$$$ ✕ **Barclay II.** This supper club and lounge is known for its steak, and folks come especially for the huge set meal of tenderloin served with salad, a relish tray, spaghetti, salami and cheese, and ice cream. Dim lighting, white tablecloths, mirrors, and historic photos of Anaconda decorate the restaurant. ⌂ 1300 E. Commercial St. ☎ 406/563–5541 ⊟ AE, D, MC, V ⊘ Closed Mon.

¢ ✕▥ **Seven Gables Resort.** At Georgetown Lake, this simple, clean lodge has views of the Pintlar Mountains and is 4 mi from skiing and across the road from fishing. The restaurant ($–$$) serves simple fare such as pressure-fried chicken and burgers; there's also a salad bar. ⌂ 20 Southern Cross Rd., 59711 ☎▤ 406/563–5052 ⊕ www.sevengablesmontana. com ⇱ 9 rooms ⌂ Restaurant, cable TV, lake, beach, dock, boating, fishing, cross-country skiing, downhill skiing, bar, casino, no-smoking rooms; no a/c ⊟ AE, D, MC, V.

$$–$$$$ ▥ **Fairmont Hot Springs Resort.** This resort between Anaconda and Butte is a great option if you have children. Although not much to look at, the Fairmont has naturally heated indoor and outdoor swimming pools, a 350-foot waterslide, a playground, and a wildlife zoo in a beautiful setting. There's also an 18-hole golf course on the grounds. ⌂ 1500 Fairmont Rd., Fairmont 59711 ☎ 406/797–3241 or 800/332–3272 ▤ 406/ 797–3337 ⊕ www.fairmontmontana.com ⇱ 129 rooms, 23 suites ⌂ Restaurant, coffee shop, 18-hole golf course, 2 tennis courts, 2 pools (1 indoor), massage, volleyball, bar, playground, cable TV, in-room data ports; no smoking ⊟ AE, D, DC, MC, V.

CAMPING ⛺ **Lost Creek State Park.** A short trail at this scenic recreation area leads to the Lost Creek Falls. Views of limestone cliffs rising 1,200 feet above the canyon floor, and frequent sightings of bighorn sheep and mountain goats are some of the attractions of this park. The campground has hiking trails and creek fishing. ⌂ Pit toilets, drinking water, fire grates, picnic tables, swimming (creek) ⇱ 25 sites ⌂ 1½ mi east of Anaconda on Hwy. 1, then 2 mi north on Hwy. 273, then 6 mi west ☎ 406/542– 5500 ⊕ www.state.mt.us ▤ Free ⌂ Reservations not accepted ⊟ No credit cards ⊘ May–Oct.

The Arts

Washoe Park, with its flower gardens, tennis courts, picnic areas, an outdoor swimming pool, and the Montana State Fish Hatchery, hosts **Art in Washoe Park** (☎ 406/723–6656 ⌂ Park St.). The three-day celebration in July includes juried art and crafts booths, ethnic foods, and professional entertainment.

The Art Deco **Washoe Theatre** (✉ 305 Main St. ☎ 406/563–6161) presents movies, concerts, and other kinds of performances.

Butte

㉕ *30 mi east of Anaconda via Hwy. 1 and I–90; 79 mi northwest of Virginia City via Hwy. 287 and Hwy. 55.*

Dubbed the "Richest Hill on Earth," Butte was once a wealthy and rollicking copper-, gold-, and silver-mining town. During its heyday 100,000 people from around the world lived here; by 1880 Butte had generated about $22 billion in mineral wealth. The revived historic district, Uptown Butte, is now a National Historic Landmark area. Numerous ornate buildings recall the Old West days, and several museums preserve the town's past. Today about 34,000 people live in the Butte–Silver Bow County area. The city maintains a strong Irish flavor, and its St. Patrick's Day Parade celebration is one of the nation's most notorious.

Butte's uptown district, with several historic buildings and museums, is easily walkable, but you'll want a car to drive to some of the outlying attractions. You can catch narrated tours on a red trolley at the **Butte-Silver Bow Chamber of Commerce Visitor and Transportation Center** (✉ 1000 George St. ☎ 800/735–6814 or 406/723–1377 ⊕ www.butteinfo.org), just off I–90 at exit 126. You also can pick up free information about the area and take a stroll down the scenic Blacktail Creek Walking Path.

TIMING   Like most places in Montana, many attractions in Butte are either closed or have limited hours in winter. Summer or autumn are the ideal seasons for visiting the city, as the warm weather allows for walks through the old mining town's historic uptown district. It takes at least half a day to visit the house-museums and explore the shops and eateries. Another half day can be spent visiting worthwhile locations outside the city, including Our Lady of the Rockies.

The Main Attractions

Keeping watch over Butte is **Our Lady of the Rockies,** on the Continental Divide. The 90-foot-tall, 80-ton statue of the Virgin Mary is lighted at night. For a 2½-hour bus tour, stop by the visitor center, a nonprofit, nondenominational organization. ✉ *3100 Harrison Ave., at the Butte Plaza Mall* ☎ *406/782–1221 or 800/800–5239* ⊕ *www.ourladyoftherockies. org* 🚌 *Bus tour $12* ⊙ *June–Sept., Mon.–Sat. at 10 and 2, Sun. at 11 and 2, weather permitting.*

Thanks to old mining waste, Butte has dubious distinction as the location of the largest toxic-waste site in the country. The underground copper mines were dug up in the 1950s, creating the **Berkeley Open Pit Mine,** which stretches 1½ by 1 mi, reaches 1,800 feet deep, and is filled with toxic water some 800 feet deep. A viewing platform allows you to look into the now-abandoned, mammoth pit where more than 20 billion pounds of copper, 704 million ounces of silver, and 3 million ounces of gold were extracted from the Butte mining district. ✉ *Continental Dr.*

at Park St. ☎ *406/723–3177 or 800/735–6814* ✉ *Free* ☉ *Daily 8–dusk, weather permitting.*

William Clark, one of Butte's richest copper barons, built the **Copper King Mansion** between 1884 and 1888. Tours of the house take in the hand-carved oak paneling, nine original fireplaces, antiques, a lavish ballroom, and frescoes. ⊠ *219 W. Granite St.* ☎ *406/782–7580* ⊕ *www. thecopperkingmansion.com* ✉ *$7* ☉ *May–Sept., daily 9–4; Oct. and Apr., weekends 9–4; Nov.–Mar., by appointment.*

Also Worth Seeing

Built in 1890 as a sporting house, the **Dumas Brothel Museum** was America's longest-running house of ill repute: it was shut down in 1982 and reopened as a museum. Tours are available of the building and of Butte's red-light district, Venus Alley. ⊠ *45 E. Mercury St.* ☎ *406/494–6908* ⊕ *www.thedumasbrothel.com* ✉ *$5* ☉ *May–Aug., daily 10–5.*

More than 1,300 mineral specimens are displayed at Montana Tech University's **Mineral Museum**, including a 27½-troy-ounce gold nugget and a 400-pound smoky quartz crystal. ⊠ *1300 W. Park St.* ☎ *406/ 496–4414* ⊕ *www.mbmg.mtech.edu* ✉ *Free* ☉ *Late May–early Sept., daily 9–6; early May–late May and mid-Sept.–Oct., weekdays 9–4, weekends 1–5.*

The **Mai Wah Museum** contains exhibits on the history of the Chinese and other Asian settlers of Butte. The two restored historic buildings it occupies were constructed to house Chinese-owned businesses: the Wah Chong Tai Company and the Mai Wah Noodle Parlor. ⊠ *17 W. Mercury St.* ☎ *406/723–6731* ⊕ *www.maiwah.org* ✉ *Donations accepted* ☉ *Tues.–Sun. 11–5.*

★ The **Arts Chateau Museum**, an elegant 1898 four-story Victorian mansion, now serves as a gallery space and an interactive youth center. The collection includes 18th- and 19th-century furniture, textiles, and collectibles as well as artwork. ⊠ *321 W. Broadway* ☎ *406/723–7600* ✉ *$5* ☉ *Tues.–Sat. 10–4.*

off the beaten path

SHEEPSHEAD MOUNTAIN RECREATION AREA – At this designated Wildlife Viewing Area you might glimpse elk, deer, moose, and birds of prey. There's a picnic area and drinking water. ⊠ *13 mi north of Butte on I-15 to Exit 138 (Elk Park), west on Forest Service Rd. 442, follow signs for 6 mi* ☎ *406/494–2147* ⊕ *www.fs.fed.us/r1/bdnf* ✉ *Free* ☉ *Memorial Day–Labor Day, daily.*

Sports & the Outdoors

FISHING **Tom's Fishing and Bird Hunting Guide Service** (⊠ 3460 St. Ann St. ☎ 406/ 723–4753 or 800/487–0296) arranges float and wade trips for blue-ribbon trout fishing.

HORSEBACK RIDING **Cargill Outfitters** (⊠ 40 Cedar Hills Rd., Whitehall ☎ 406/494–2960 ⊕ www.ironwheel.com), which is just over the Continental Divide, 20 minutes east of Butte, offers two-hour to full-day horseback riding into the Highland Mountain range.

ICE-SKATING You can speed skate on ice at the **U.S. High Altitude Sports Center** (✉ 5155 Continental Dr. ☎ 406/494–7570) with international speed-skaters or beginners. The ice track is open for general ice-skating as well; call for times. Skate rentals are available.

Where to Stay & Eat

$$–$$$$ ✕ **Acoma.** Renovations haven't altered the authentic Art Deco decor of this restaurant on the National Register of Historic Places. Dine on game hen chasseur, prepared hunter-style with tomatoes, mushrooms, and duchess potatoes, or veal Acoma sautéed with artichoke hearts and mushrooms and finished with white-wine cream sauce. ✉ 60 E. Broadway ☎ 406/728–7001 ⊟ AE, D, MC, V.

$$–$$$$ ✕ **Uptown Café.** Fresh seafood, steaks (try the Cajun prime rib), poultry, and pasta are served in this informal, smoke-free café. Try the artichoke ravioli or the chicken zingara, a boneless breast sautéed with Italian ham, olives, and onions. A rotating exhibit of paintings by local artists lines the walls. ✉ 47 E. Broadway ☎ 406/723–4735 ⊟ AE, D, MC, V.

$–$$$ ✕ **Spaghettini's.** In the historic district, this Italian trattoria squeezes a bit of the Mediterranean into a narrow brick building. Surrounded by thick ferns and murals of Old Italy, tuck into seafood and pasta wonders such as shrimp spaghettini, with shrimp, asparagus, prosciutto, and artichoke bottoms sautéed in pesto sauce. ✉ 26 N. Main St. ☎ 406/ 782–8855 ⊟ No credit cards.

¢–$$ ✕ **Broadway Café.** This turn-of-the-20th-century building is the place for pizzas and salads. Try the ginger tahini salad or the "madhouse" pizza, with red onions, sun-dried tomatoes, olives, artichokes, feta, and mozzarella cheese. Thursday and Friday nights there's live music, usually contemporary jazz. It's right near the Berkeley Open Pit Mine. ✉ 302 E. Broadway ☎ 406/723–8711 ⌕ Reservations essential ⊟ AE, D, MC, V ⊘ Closed Sun.

¢ ✕ **Town Talk Bakery.** No visit to Butte is complete without trying a pasty, the traditional miner's dinner of meat, potatoes, and onion baked inside a pastry shell. This bakery is one of the best of several eateries that serve these pocket-size meals, generally to go. There are two tables for dining here, but most people order takeout. ✉ 611 E. Front St. ☎ 406/ 782–4985 ⊟ No credit cards ⊘ Closed Mon.

$–$$$ ▦ **Toad Hall Manor Bed and Breakfast.** Built as a private home in the early
Fodor'sChoice 1990s, this mansion has a historic feel thanks to hardwood accents, mar-
★ ble tile, and a classic redbrick exterior. Each of the four guest rooms is named after a character from Kenneth Grahame's The Wind in the Willows. The ground-floor Papa Otter's Place, with its Victorian-style furnishings, marble-accented Jacuzzi, and French doors opening to a private garden, probably offers the best value. Sir Badger's Suite, which takes up the entire fifth floor with two bedrooms, a two-person Jacuzzi, walk-in closet, and loft-style windows, ranks as the most luxurious option. ✉ 1 Green La., 59701 ☎ 406/494–2625 or 866/443–8623 ⊟ 406/494–8025 ⊕ www.toadhallmanor.com ⟿ 4 rooms ⌂ Microwaves, cable TV with movies, Internet, meeting rooms; no smoking ⊟ AE, D, MC, V ⍩ BP.

$–$$ ▦ **Best Western Butte Plaza Inn.** Butte's largest lodging is convenient to shopping, sports events, and the interstates. The rooms are clean and comfortable, if somewhat bland. ☒ *2900 Harrison Ave., 59701* ☎ *406/494–3500 or 800/543–5814* 🖷 *406/494–7611* ⊕ *www.bestwestern.com* ⇨ *134 rooms* ⚘ *Restaurant, cable TV, in-room data ports, indoor pool, sauna, steam room, bar, laundry facilities, meeting rooms, airport shuttle, free parking, some pets allowed, no-smoking rooms* ☴ *AE, D, MC, V* ¶◯¶ *CP.*

CAMPING ⚠ **Butte KOA.** This large and grassy campsite with cottonwood trees has a playground and allows fishing and swimming in the on-site Silver Bow Creek. It's next to a tourism office and is easily accessed from the interstate. It's a good idea to reserve ahead. ⚘ *Laundry facilities, flush toilets, full hookups, partial hookups (water), dump station, drinking water, showers, picnic tables, food service, electricity, public telephone, general store, swimming (creek, pool)* ⇨ *100 RV sites (full or partial hookups), 20 tent sites, 4 cabins* ☒ *1601 Kaw Ave., off I–90 at Exit 126* ☎ *406/782–8080 or 800/562–8089* ⊕ *www.koa.com* 🖃 *$25 tent sites, $27 partial hookups, $32 full hookups, $45 cabins* ☴ *D, MC, V* ☼ *Mid-Apr.–Oct.*

Nightlife & the Arts
Every August, the Montana Gaelic Cultural Society hosts the **An Ri Ra, Montana Irish Festival** (☒ Park St. between Main and Montana Sts. ☎ 800/735–6814), with an art show, a film festival, children's activities, and the Pipers' Parade in Uptown Butte. On March 17, the annual **St. Patrick's Day Parade** (☒ Uptown Butte ☎ 406/782–0742 ⊕ www.butteamerica.com) celebrates Butte's Irish heritage, but the real festivities occur in the local bars, a few of which reportedly have never locked their doors.

Community and children's theater productions at the **Mother Lode** (☒ 316 W. Park St. ☎ 406/723–3602) include Broadway shows and concerts. This 1922 grand theater is the last of several that once embellished Uptown.

Shopping
Find everything from Butte collectibles to fine porcelain and antique furniture at **D&G Antiques** (☒ 16 N. Montana St. ☎ 406/723–4552), one of eight antiques shops in the historic district. Montana's largest bookstore, **Second Edition Books** (☒ 112 S. Montana St. ☎ 406/723–5108 or 800/298–5108), buys, sells, and trades books on many different subjects but specializes in hard-to-find regional tomes. While visiting the historic district, stop at the **Uptown Butte Farmers' Market** (☒ Main St. between Park St. and Broadway ☎ 406/723–3177 or 800/735–6814) for fresh garden produce, fruit, flowers, baked goods, and local crafts. It's open Saturday in summer from 9 to 1.

Virginia City

➋➏ *72 mi southeast of Butte via Hwys. 2, 41, and 287.*

Remnants of Montana's frontier days, Virginia City and its smaller neighbor, Nevada City, are two of the the state's standout attractions. Boardwalks pass in front of partially restored historic buildings, and 19th-century goods stock the stores. Virginia City prospered when miners stampeded into Montana Territory after the 1863 discovery of gold. The diggings were rich in Alder Gulch, and Virginia City eventually became the territorial capital. Enticed by the city's wealth, criminals came to prey on the miners. In turn, vigilance committees—eager to maintain order—held lightning-fast trials and strung up the bad guys. The outlaws were buried atop Boot Hill, overlooking town.

Begin a visit at the **Virginia City Depot Visitor Center,** where you can get information on theater, historic accommodations, and gold panning. There's also a gift shop. ⊠ *Lower Wallace St.* ☎ *406/843–5247* ⊕ *www. virginiacitymt.com* ⊡ *Free* ⊗ *May–Oct., daily 9–5.*

The eclectic assortment of items dating from 1860 to 1900 at the **Thompson-Hickman Memorial Museum** includes a petrified wedding cake, the eponymous limb of "Club Foot" George Lane, rifles, and numerous photographs. The collection is made up of the heirlooms of three local families. The local library is upstairs. ⊠ *Wallace St.* ☎ *406/843–5238* ⊡ *Donations accepted* ⊗ *May–Sept., daily 10–5.*

An old-time narrow-gauge steam train, the **Baldwin Locomotive No. 12,** Montana's only operating steam locomotive run by volunteer crews, travels between Virginia City and Nevada City on weekends. On weekdays, a smaller locomotive, the **Alder Gulch Shortline Railroad,** makes the same journey. ☎ *406/843–5812* ⊡ *$10 round-trip* ⊗ *Memorial Day–Labor Day, 5 trips daily (on either Baldwin or Alder Gulch); select weekends rest of yr.*

The annual **Heritage Days** festival celebrates the Victorian West, with historical reenactments, activities along the boardwalk, and the evening **Victorian Ball,** with authentic music, dancing, and costumes. The event lasts for two days in mid-August. ⊠ *Victorian Ball: Virginia City Gymnasium, Van Buren and Idaho Sts.* ☎ *406/843–5583 or 800/829–2969* ⊕ *www.virginiacitychamber.com* ⊡ *Festival free; $30 for ball and dinner, $5 to observe ball from balcony.*

★ The living-history **Nevada City Open Air Museum,** next door to Virginia City, preserves the town as it was at the turn of the 20th century, with restored buildings, thousands of artifacts from the gold-rush era, and demonstrations. New to the collection is the **Frontier House Museum,** from the PBS television series of the same name. ⊠ *U.S. 287, 1½ mi west of Virginia City* ☎ *406/843–5247* ⊕ *www.virginiacitychamber.com* ⊡ *$9* ⊗ *Mid-May–mid-Sept., daily sunrise–sunset.*

After they were hanged by vigilantes, the outlaws who preyed on miners ended up in graves at **Boot Hill** cemetery. Come to have a look at the old markers and to take in the hill's view of the town and surrounding mountains. ⊠ *From Wallace St. turn north on Spencer St. and follow signs for ROAD AGENTS' GRAVES* ☎ *406/843–5555 or 800/829–2969* ⊕ *www.virginiacitychamber.com.*

Sports & the Outdoors
Spend a day moving cattle from high in the saddle with **Upper Canyon Outfitters/Tate Ranch** (⊠ 2149 Upper Ruby Rd., 35 mi southwest of Vir-

ginia City ☎ 800/735–3973). You can also sleep under the stars on the six-day cattle drive on the ranch and into the Gravelly Range.

Where to Stay & Eat

¢ ✕ **City Bakery.** Fresh pastries and gingerbread keep people coming back for more at this bakery. Wash your order down with a huckleberry iced tea. There's no seating in the bakery, but there are benches on the sidewalk outside. ⊠ *325 W. Wallace St.* ☎ *406/843–5227* ♨ *Reservations not accepted* ▤ *MC, V* ☉ *Closed Oct., Nov., and Jan.–May.*

$ ▥ **Stonehouse Inn Bed & Breakfast.** Period charm pervades this 1884 Gothic Revival home with antiques, brass beds, 12-foot ceilings, and a teddy-bear collection. The full breakfast might include strawberry French toast with cream cheese and fresh fruit. ⊠ *306 E. Idaho St., 59755* ☎ *406/843–5504* ⊕ *www.stonehouseinnbb.com* ⇖ *5 rooms* ♨ *Dining room, fishing, piano, babysitting, laundry facilities, meeting room; no room phones, no room TVs, no a/c, no smoking* ▤ *MC, V* ❠ *BP.*

¢–$ ▥ **Fairweather Inn and the Nevada City Hotel and Cabins.** Virginia City's Fairweather Inn is a classic Western-Victorian hotel with balconies in the heart of the area's gold-mining country. The two-story 1864 Nevada City Hotel is 1½ mi away in Nevada City; there are Victorian-style hotel rooms, plus rustic miners' cabins. ⊠ *305 W. Wallace St., 59755* ☎ *406/ 843–5377 or 800/829–2969* ♨ *406/843–5235* ⇖ *Fairweather Inn: 14 rooms, 5 with bath. Nevada City Hotel: 11 rooms, 2 suites, 17 cabins* ♨ *No room phones, no room TVs, no smoking* ▤ *D, MC, V* ☉ *Closed Oct.–mid-May.*

CAMPING ⚠ **Virginia City Campground & RV Park.** The large grassy campsites here are close to miniature golf, horseshoes, volleyball, and a recreation field. It's a good idea to reserve ahead. ♨ *Flush toilets, full hookups, partial hookups (some electric, some electric and water), dump station, drinking water, showers, fire pits, picnic tables, electricity, public telephone* ⇖ *10 full hookups, 8 partial hookups, 24 tent sites* ⊠ *Hwy. 287, ¼ mi east of Virginia City* ☎ *406/843–5493 or 888/833–5493* ⊕ *www. virginiacitycampground.com* ▧ *$22 tent sites, $25 partial hookups, $28 full hookups, $55 cabin* ▤ *MC, V* ☉ *Mid-May–mid-Sept.*

Nightlife & the Arts

NIGHTLIFE Weekend evenings in summer there's often live rock music at **Banditos** (⊠ 320 Wallace St. ☎ 406/843–5556), in the historic Wells Fargo building. The **Brewery Follies** (⊠ H. S. Gilbert Brewery building, Cover St. ☎ 406/843–5218 or 800/829–2969) are contemporary comedies (ages 12 and up); shows take place Wednesday through Monday evenings from late May through August.

THE ARTS The historic **Opera House** (⊠ 338 W. Wallace St. ☎ 406/843–5314 or
★ 800/829–2969) is the oldest continuously operating summer theater in the West, in operation since 1949. Early June through early September, the theater hosts an amusing vaudeville show by the Virginia City Players. The cost is $15.

Shopping

Opened in 1864, **Rank's Mercantile** (⊠ 211 Wallace St. ☎ 406/843–5454 or 800/494–5442) is Montana's oldest continuously operating store. Period clothing, books, toys, gifts, and groceries are for sale here.

Ennis

27 *14 mi east of Virginia City via Hwy. 287.*

In addition to being a hub of ranching in the area, this tiny town sits among some of the best trout streams in the West. People come from around the world for the area's blue-ribbon fishing, particularly in the area of Beartrap Canyon. Welcoming you to town is a sign that reads 600 PEOPLE, 11,000,000 TROUT.

Consistently rated among the most exciting and challenging rodeos in Montana, the Independence Day **Ennis Rodeo** (☎ 406/682–4700) attracts top cowpokes to the evening shows.

Each year at the **Ennis National Fish Hatchery,** six strains of rainbow trout produce 23 million eggs used to stock streams throughout the United States. Blaine Springs provides fresh, clean spring water at a constant temperature of 54°F ideal for nurturing trout. Note that the 10-mi access road leading here is bumpy. ⊠ *180 Fish Hatchery Rd.* ☎ *406/682–4847 or 800/344–9453* ⊕ *ennis.fws.gov* ☜ *Free* ⊙ *Daily 8–5.*

For a bit of relaxation, nothing beats soaking in the natural hot water of the **Norris Hot Springs** pool. Note that no kids are allowed in the pool after 7:30 PM. ⊠ *Hwy. 84, 16 mi north of Ennis on U.S. 287, then west through town, Norris* ☎ *406/685–3303* ☜ *$5* ⊙ *Daily noon–9.*

off the beaten path

BEARTRAP CANYON – In this part of the Lee Metcalf Wilderness northeast of Ennis, you can hike, fish, and go white-water rafting on the Madison River. A picnic area and access to Trail Creek are at the head of the canyon below Ennis Lake. To get here, drive north out of Ennis on U.S. 287 to the town of McAllister and turn right down a bumpy dirt road (no number), which takes you around to the north side of the lake across the dam. Turn left after the dam onto an unmarked road and drive across the river to the Trail Creek access point. ☎ *406/683–2337* ☜ *Free* ⊙ *Daily.*

Sports & the Outdoors

FISHING The fly-fishing specialists of **Eaton Outfitters** (⊠ 307 Jeffers Rd. ☎ 800/755–3474) lead trips on the Madison, Beaverhead, Big Hole, and Ruby rivers. The **Tackle Shop** (⊠ 127 E. Main St. ☎ 406/682–4263 or 800/808–2832) offers guided float and wade fishing on the Madison, Big Hole, and other rivers. The full-service Orvis fly shop also sells luggage, clothing, and fishing accessories.

HORSEBACK RIDING Ride the dusty trails with **Bar 88 Horses** (☎ 406/682–4827) on half- and full-day adventures in the Beaverhead National Forest.

Where to Stay & Eat

$$$–$$$$ ✕ **Continental Divide.** This bistro-style restaurant is a pleasant surprise in an area with numerous steak houses. Among the specials are local free-range chicken roasted with tomatoes and vegetables, and lobster ravioli. In summer there's live jazz during Sunday brunch. ⊠ *315 E. Main St.* ☎ *406/682–7600* ☰ *AE, D, MC, V* ⊘ *Closed Nov.–Apr.*

$$$ ✕🏠 **Diamond J Guest Ranch.** Fishing, horseback riding, supervised kids' activities, weekly square dances, and steak cookouts are all part of the fun at this family-run 1930s ranch bordering the Lee Metcalf Wilderness. The lodgepole-pine cabins have stone fireplaces, hardwood floors, hickory furniture, and private baths. There's a seven-day minimum stay. ⊠ *800 Jack Creek Rd., 59747* ☎ *406/682–4867 or 877/929–4867* 🖷 *406/682–4106* ⊕ *www.ranchweb.com/diamondj* ➟ *8 cabins* ⏦ *Dining room, tennis court, pool, hot tub, fishing, hiking, horseback riding, horseshoes, Ping-Pong, volleyball, lobby lounge, library, shop, babysitting, airport shuttle; no room phones, no room TVs, no a/c, no smoking* ☰ *AE, MC, V* ⊘ *Closed mid-Sept.–mid-June* ⏧ *FAP.*

★ $$$$ 🏠 **Potosi Hot Springs.** Western and fishing accents decorate the private cabins at this hot-springs resort. Soak pools vary in size and temperature; the 20- by 50-foot Big Pool is at the base of a mossy granite cliff. You can join in numerous outdoor activities on the resort's 75 acres or in the Tabacco Root Mountains. Dinner, perhaps oven-roasted pheasant or grilled elk tenderloin, is served in your cabin in front of the fireplace. ⊠ *S. Willow Creek Rd., Pony 59747, 35 mi northwest of Ennis,* ☎ *406/685–3330 or 888/685–1695* 🖷 *406/685–3390* ⊕ *www.potosiresort.com* ➟ *4 cabins* ⏦ *Restaurant, room service, kitchens, refrigerators, sauna, fishing, mountain bikes, horseback riding, cross-country skiing, lobby lounge, piano, shop, meeting room, some pets allowed; no room phones, no room TVs, no a/c, no kids under 13, no smoking* ☰ *AE, MC, V* ⏧ *BP, FAP.*

¢ 🏠 **Fan Mountain Inn.** This simple but clean family motel has wonderful views of the Madison Range and is within walking distance of downtown shops and galleries. ⊠ *204 N. Main St., 59729* ☎ *406/682–5200 or 877/682–5200* 🖷 *406/682–5266* ⊕ *www.fanmountaininn.com* ➟ *27 rooms* ⏦ *Some microwaves, some refrigerators, cable TV, shop, meeting rooms, some pets allowed (fee), no-smoking rooms* ☰ *AE, D, MC, V.*

CAMPING 🏕 **Ennis RV Village.** Hiking trails wend past a small stream at this 8-acre park with views of the Madison, Gravelly, and Tabacco Root ranges. Reservations are recommended. ⏦ *Grills, laundry facilities, flush toilets, full hookups, partial hookups, dump station, drinking water, showers, fire pits, picnic tables, electricity, public telephone, general store* ➟ *41 full hookups, 10 partial hookups, 4 tent sites* ⊠ *5034 N. U.S. 287, 1 mi north of Ennis* ☎ *406/682–5272, 866/682–5272, or 888/519–5879* 🖷 *406/682–5245* ⊕ *www.ennisrv.com* ☒ *$15 tent sites, $20 partial hookups, $26 full hookups* ☰ *AE, MC, V* ⊘ *May–Oct.*

Nightlife & the Arts

NIGHTLIFE Live music Friday and Saturday night at the **Claim Jumper Saloon** (⊠ *305 Main St.* ☎ *406/682–5558*) ranges from blues to classic rock. The patio has outdoor seating and horseshoes.

The **River Stone Gallery** (✉ 219 E. Main St. ☎ 406/682–5768) displays original paintings, sculptures, pottery, and contemporary jewelry by Western artists. Local stones are often used in the jewelry. One-of-a-kind abstract sculptures are made of copper and brass at the **Trudi Gilliam Metal Sculpture Studio and Gallery** (✉ 100 W. Main St. ☎ 406/682–7772).

Dillon

28 *65 mi south of Butte via I–90 west and I–15 south.*

From Dillon you can hike and mountain bike into the nearby Ruby and Tendoy mountains. Blue-ribbon trout fishing on the Beaverhead River attracts thousands of fly fishermen and anglers year-round. A capital of southwest Montana's ranch country, Dillon began as a cattle and wool shipping point between Utah and the goldfields of Montana. From the mid-1860s until the early 1900s cattle and sheep remained the primary cargo shipped out of here on the Union Pacific Railroad.

The **Beaverhead County Museum** exhibits Native American artifacts, ranching and mining memorabilia, a homesteader's cabin, mining equipment and agricultural artifacts, and a boardwalk imprinted with the area's ranch brands. ✉ *15 S. Montana St.* ☎ *406/683–5027* 💲 *Donations accepted* ☉ *Memorial Day–Labor Day, weekdays 8:30–8, Sat. noon–4; Labor Day–Memorial Day, weekdays 8:30–5.*

The annual weeklong **Lewis and Clark Festival** (☎ 406/683–5511 ⊕ www. beaverheadchamber.org) in August highlights the explorers' travels through the area. Historic reenactments, presentations, and a buffalo and beef barbecue are all part of the fun. Events take place at various sites around town.

Everyone is a cowboy for the annual **Dillon Jaycee Labor Day Rodeo and Parade** (✉ Fairgrounds, Railroad St. ☎ 406/683–5511), which has been staged here since 1914. Among the activities that take place at this festival running late August through early September are a fair, rodeo, and concert.

Beaverhead Rock State Park takes its name from a rock shaped like the head of a beaver; Native Americans used the landmark when traveling from western valleys to hunt bison on Montana's plains. As the Lewis and Clark expedition traveled along the Beaverhead River in 1805, Sacajawea pointed out the rock, knowing it marked the route across the mountains. Most people view the massive rock from an overlook because the primitive park lacks signs and is populated by rattlesnakes. ✉ *15 mi north of Dillon on Hwy. 41* ☎ *406/834–3413* ⊕ *www.fwp. state.mt.us* 💲 *Free* ☉ *Daily dawn–dusk.*

off the beaten path

RED ROCK LAKES NATIONAL WILDLIFE REFUGE – In the undeveloped and remote Centennial Valley, this 43,500-acre refuge shelters moose, deer, and antelope but is primarily a sanctuary for 230 species of birds, including trumpeter swans. Once threatened with extinction, these elegant birds have survived thanks to refuge protection; today, they build their nests and winter here among the 14,000 acres of lakes and marshes. ✉ *27820 Southside Centennial*

Rd.; 60 mi south of Dillion on I–15 to Monida; follow signs east 28 mi on gravel and dirt road, Lima ☎ *406/276–3536* ⊕ *redrocks.fws. gov* ⊠ *Free* ☉ *Daily 7:30–4.*

Sports & the Outdoors

FISHING Whether they're discussing nymphs, caddis flies, or crane flies, the guides of **Backcountry Angler** (⊠ 426 S. Atlantic St. ☎ 406/683–3462 ⊕ www.backcountryangler.com) know the art of fly-fishing. They lead overnight fishing-lodging trips, plus wade- and float-fishing day adventures. **Watershed Fly Fishing Adventures** (⊠ 11 Pierce Dr. ☎ 406/ 683–6660 or 800/753–6660) arranges float- and wade-fishing trips on private creeks and ponds and the Beaverhead, Big Hole, Jefferson, and Ruby rivers.

HORSEBACK Horse and mule day rides and pack trips traverse the Continental Di-
RIDING vide and the Lima Peaks with **Centennial Outfitters** (⊠ 121 Steel Bridge La., 45 mi south of Dillon via I–15, Lima ☎ 406/276–3463). **Diamond Hitch Outfitters** (⊠ 3405 Ten Mile Rd., 4 mi west of Dillon ☎ 406/683–5494 or 800/368–5494) takes you by horse or mule to high rocky summits, past endless flowery meadows, and along trout fisheries on hourly rides, cookout rides, and overnight pack trips.

SKIING A fun family attraction, **Maverick Mountain Ski Area** (⊠ Hwy. 278 [Mav-
☺ erick Mountain Rd.], 40 mi west of Dillon ☎ 406/834–3454) has a top elevation of 8,620 feet, a vertical drop of 1,927 feet, and 24 runs. Lessons and ski and snowboard rentals and sales are available for kids and adults.

Where to Stay & Eat

★ $$–$$$$ ✕ **Cross Ranch Cookhouse.** Dine in a cookhouse with working ranch hands. In addition to salads, bread, and dessert, there's "pitchfork fondue"—Angus beef sirloin, skewered and then deep-fried in a cauldron via pitchfork. A local fiddle, banjo, and guitar band plays country music. To get here from Dillon, head south on I–15 to Exit 44, drive 12 mi west on Highway 324 to the Bannack turnoff, and then turn right and follow the dirt road for 2 mi. ⊠ *12775 Bannack Rd.; south on I–15, Exit 44, on Hwy. 324 12 mi to Bannack turnoff, right 2 mi ahead on right* ☎ *406/ 681–3133* ⌂ *Reservations essential* ⊟ *No credit cards* ☉ *Closed Sun.*

¢–$ ✕▦ **The Grasshopper Inn.** In the spectacular Pioneer Mountains, this wilderness lodge is ideally situated for snowmobiling, hiking, and fishing. The tidy, colorful rooms have log beds and views of the mountains. The restaurant's back bar dates from the 1800s. The simple yet filling meals (¢–$$$) include burgers, steak, and fish. You can rent snowmobiles here in winter and four-wheel drives in summer. ⊠ *460505 Polaris Rd., 45 mi west of Dillon, Polaris 59746* ☎ *406/834–3456 or 866/ 468–6386* 🖷 *406/834–3507* 🖃 *10 rooms* ⌂ *Restaurant, cable TV, cross-country skiing, snowmobiling, bar, shop, meeting rooms, some pets allowed, no-smoking rooms; no room phones* ⊟ *MC, V* ☉ *Closed weekdays Apr. and May.*

$$ ▦ **Goose Down Ranch.** Darling cabins, one log and one clapboard, have front-porch views of the Blacktail Mountains and are near the famed

Poindexter Slough blue-ribbon fly-fishing spot on the Beaverhead River. The cabins both have two bedrooms, fireplaces, and cozy couches. ⊠ *710 S. Pacific St., 59725* ☎ *406/683–6704 or 406/683–3590* 🖷 *406/683–8390* ⊕ *www.goosedownranch.com* ⤵ *2 cabins* ⚬ *Kitchens, microwaves, in-room VCRs, fishing, laundry facilities; no room phones, no smoking* ⊟ *MC, V.*

$ ⊞ **Guest House Inn & Suites.** This hotel is affordable, clean, and quiet and has an outdoor sundeck off the indoor pool. The staff can direct you to interesting local sights, scenic viewpoints, and perhaps even a good local fishing hole. ⊠ *580 Sinclair St., 59725* ☎ *406/683–3636 or 800/214–8378* 🖷 *406/683–3637* ⊕ *www.guesthouseintl.com* ⤵ *58 rooms* ⚬ *Some kitchens, microwaves, refrigerators, cable TV, in-room VCRs, in-room data ports, pool, hot tub, some pets allowed, no-smoking rooms* ⊟ *AE, D, MC, V* ⦿ *CP.*

CAMPING ⚠ **Dillon KOA.** Pine, aspen, and birch trees shade this campground on the banks of the Beaverhead River. The campground, which is on the edge of Dillon, has views of the Pioneer Mountains and other peaks. ⚬ *Swimming (pool), laundry facilities, flush toilets, full hookups, dump station, drinking water, showers, picnic tables, electricity, public telephone, general store, play area* ⤵ *68 full hookups, 30 tent sites, 4 cabins* ⊠ *735 W. Park St.* ☎ *406/683–2749 or 800/562–2751* ⊕ *www.koa.com* 🖾 *$24 tent sites, $31 full hookups, $39 cabins* ⊟ *D, MC, V.*

Shopping

Watercolor originals of flowers, dragonflies, and other scenes from nature are for sale as posters and cards at the **Cathy Weber–Artmaker** (⊠ 26 N. Idaho St. ☎ 406/683–5493) studio. Antiques and collectibles are for sale in **P & L Antiques** (⊠ 236 N. Idaho St. ☎ 406/683–9863).

Bannack

㉙ *24 mi west of Dillon via I–15 and U.S. 278.*

Bannack was Montana's first territorial capital and the site of the state's first major gold strike, on May 26, 1863, at Grasshopper Creek. Now **Bannack State Historic Park,** this frontier boomtown has historic structures lining the main street, and picnic and camping spots. It was here that the notorious renegade Sheriff Henry Plummer and several of his gang members were caught and executed by vigilantes for murder and robbery. The gallows on which Plummer was hanged still stands. Rumors persist that Plummer's stash of stolen gold was hidden somewhere in the mountains near here and never found. To get to Bannack from Dillon, follow Highway 278 west for 24 mi and watch for a sign just before Badger Pass; take the well-maintained gravel road for 3 mi. ☎ *406/834–3413* 🖾 *$4 per vehicle* ⦿ *Park daily dawn–dusk. Visitor center late May–early Sept., daily 10–6; early Sept.–late May, daily 8–5.*

Lectures, an old-fashioned school day, demonstrations of historical log-cabin construction, and guided tours are all part of **Dale Tash Montana History Day** (☎ 406/834–3413 ⊕ www.bannack.org) at Bannack State Historic Park. It takes place in mid-July.

For two days in mid-July, **Bannack Days** (☏ 406/834–3413 ⊕ www.bannack.org) celebrates life in Montana's first territorial capital with stagecoach rides, a main-street gunfight, old-time music and dancing, and pioneer-crafts demonstrations.

> **off the beaten path**
>
> **PIONEER MOUNTAIN SCENIC BYWAY** – Mountains, meadows, lodgepole-pine forests, and willow-edged streams line this road, which runs north–south between U.S. 278 (west of Bannack) and Highway 43. Headed north, the byway skirts the Maverick Mountain Ski Area and Elkhorn Hot Springs and ends at the town of Wise River on the Big Hole River. ☏ *406/683–5511.*

Camping

⚠ **Bannack Campgrounds.** Grasshopper Creek, where gold was discovered in 1863, flows not far from this rustic campground, which has few amenities but is close to Bannack. Grocery stores and restaurants are in nearby Dillon. It's a good idea to reserve ahead for the single tepee. ⚴ *Pit toilets, drinking water, fire pits, picnic tables* ⟿ *28 tent sites, 1 tepee* ⊠ *4200 Bannack St.* ☏ *406/834–3413* ⊕ *www.fwp.state.mt.us* ▧ *$15 tent sites, $25 tepee* ⊟ *No credit cards.*

Big Hole National Battlefield

30 *60 mi northwest of Bannock via Hwy. 278 northwest and Hwy. 43 west; 87 mi southwest of Butte via I–90 west, I–15 south, and Hwy. 43 west.*

At Big Hole, a visitor center now overlooks meadows where one of the West's greatest and most tragic stories played out. In 1877, Nez Perce warriors in central Idaho killed some white settlers as retribution for earlier killings by whites. Knowing the U.S. Army would make no distinction between the guilty and innocent, several hundred Nez Perce fled, beginning a 1,500-mi, five-month odyssey that has come to be known as the Nez Perce Trail. The fugitives engaged 10 separate U.S. commands in 13 battles and skirmishes. One of the fiercest of these was at Big Hole, where both sides suffered serious losses. From here, the Nez Perce headed toward Yellowstone. The Big Hole battlefield remains as it was when the battle unfolded; tepee poles erected by the park service mark the site of a Nez Perce village and serve as haunting reminders of what transpired here. Ranger-led programs for groups or individuals can be arranged with advance request. The park stays open for winter snowshoeing and cross-country skiing on a groomed trail through the battlefield's sites. Big Hole National Battlefield is one of 38 sites in four states that make up the **Nez Perce National Historic Park** (☏ 406/689–3155 ⊕ www.nps.gov/nepe), which follows the historic Nez Perce Trail. ⊠ *Hwy. 43, 10 mi west of Wisdom* ☏ *406/689–3155* ⊕ *www.nps.gov/ biho* ▧ *$5 per vehicle Memorial Day–Labor Day; free rest of yr* ☉ *May–Labor Day, daily 8:30–6; Labor Day–Apr., daily 9–5.*

The annual **Commemoration of the Battle of Big Hole** (☏ 406/689–3155 ⊕ www.nps.gov/nepe), in early August, includes traditional Nez Perce music, ceremonies, and demonstrations, along with cavalry exhibitions.

Sports & the Outdoors

You can cross-country ski (with your own equipment) or snowshoe through the historic trails of **Big Hole Battlefield** (⊠ Hwy. 43, 10 mi west of Wisdom ☎406/689–3155 ⊕www.nps.gov/biho). A few pairs of snowshoes are available for use for free at the visitor center.

Where to Stay & Eat

¢–$ ✕🏨 **Jackson Hot Springs Lodge.** Lewis and Clark cooked their dinner in the hot springs near the site of this spacious log lodge decorated with elk antlers, a stuffed mountain lion, and other critters. Accommodations are in cabins, many with fireplaces, and there's also tent and RV camping. The Olympic-size outdoor pool is filled with artesian hot water that averages 103°F year-round. The dining room ($$–$$$$) specializes in wild game dishes such as pheasant, bison, and elk steaks. ⊠ *Main St., Box 808, Jackson 59736, 30 mi northwest of Big Hole* ☎ *406/834–3151 or 888/438–6938* 🖷 *406/834–3157* ⊕ *www.jacksonhotsprings.com* 🛏 *20 cabins* ⚘ *Restaurant, pool, fishing, bar, piano, meeting rooms, some pets allowed (fee); no room phones, no room TVs, no a/c, no smoking* ▤ *MC, V.*

CAMPING 🏕 **Miner Lake Campground.** Campsites have a view of the Bitterroot Mountains at this quiet, out-of-the-way lakeside spot. You can fish in 30-acre Miner Lake, which is also popular for nonmotorized boats. ⚘ *Pit toilets, drinking water, fire grates, picnic tables, swimming (lake)* 🛏 *18 tent sites* ⊠ *Forest Rd. 182, Jackson* ☎*406/689–3243* 🖷*406/689–3245* ⊕ *www.fs.fed.us/r1/* 🖼 *$6* ▤ *No credit cards* ☉ *June–mid-Sept.*

SOUTHWEST MONTANA A TO Z

To research prices, get advice from other travelers, and book travel arrangements, visit www.fodors.com.

AIR TRAVEL

CARRIERS Several daily flights link Bozeman's Gallatin Field Airport to Butte, Denver, Minneapolis, Salt Lake City, and Seattle. Butte Airport has service from Bozeman, Salt Lake City, and Seattle. Helena Airport has service from Billings, Great Falls, Minneapolis, and Salt Lake City. Note that major air carriers tend to use smaller planes to serve the area.

🎫 **Airlines & Contacts Delta** ☎ 800/221–1212 ⊕ www.delta-air.com. **Horizon** ☎ 800/547–9308 ⊕ www.horizonair.com. **Northwest** ☎ 800/225–2525 ⊕ www.nwa.com. **Skywest** ☎ 800/453–9417 ⊕ www.skywest.com. **United/United Express** ☎ 800/241–6522 ⊕ www.unitedairlines.com.

AIRPORTS

Butte Airport is 7 mi south of downtown. Gallatin Field Airport is 16 mi west of Bozeman. Helena Airport is 3 mi from downtown.

🎫 **Butte Airport** ⊠ 101 Airport Rd., Butte ☎ 406/494–3771 ⊕ www.butteairport.com. **Gallatin Field Airport** ⊠ 850 Gallatin Field Rd., Belgrade ☎ 406/388–6632 ⊕ www.gallatinfield.com. **Helena Airport** ⊠ 2850 Skyway Dr., Helena ☎406/442–2821 ⊕ www.helenaairport.com.

BUS TRAVEL

Greyhound Lines serves several communities along I–90, including Billings, Livingston, Bozeman, and Butte. Karst Stage/4X4 Stage has regional service in the Bozeman area, plus service from Bozeman to Big Sky. Rimrock Trailways, which is based in Billings, serves major communities in the state.

Greyhound Lines ☎ 800/231-2222 ⊕ www.greyhound.com. **Karst Stage/4x4 Stage** ☎ 800/287-4759 ⊕ www.karststage.com. **Rimrock Trailways** ☎ 800/255-7655 ⊕ www.rimrocktrailways.com.

CAR RENTAL

You can rent anything from an economy car on up at the Bozeman and Butte airports; a four-wheel-drive vehicle may be necessary for some winter travel.

Avis ☎ 406/388-6414 or 800/831-2847 ⊕ www.avis.com. **Budget** ☎ 406/388-4091 or 800/952-8343 ⊕ www.budget.com. **Hertz** ☎ 406/388-6939 or 800/654-3131 ⊕ www.hertz.com. **National** ☎ 406/388-9994 or 800/227-7368 ⊕ www.nationalcar.com. **Thrifty** ☎ 406/388-3484 or 800/344-1705 ⊕ www.thrifty.com.

CAR TRAVEL

Major routes are paved and well maintained, but there are many gravel and dirt roads off the beaten track. When heading into remote regions, be sure to fill up the gas tank, and check road reports for construction delays or passes that may close in severe winter weather. Always carry a flashlight, drinking water and some food, a first-aid kit, and emergency overnight gear (a sleeping bag and extra, warm clothing). Most important, make sure someone is aware of your travel plans. While driving, be prepared for animals crossing roads, livestock on open ranges along the highway, and other hazards such as high winds and dust- or snowstorms.

When driving in the mountains in winter, make sure you have tire chains, studs, or snow tires.

Montana Highway Patrol ☎ 406/388-3190 or 800/525-5555 ⊕ www.doj.state.mt.us/enforcement/highwaypatrol.asp. **Statewide Road Report** ☎ 800/226-7623 ⊕ www.mdt.mt.gov/travinfo/.

EMERGENCIES

Ambulance or Police Emergencies ☎ 911.

24-Hour Medical Care Barrett Hospital ✉ 1260 S. Atlantic St., Dillon ☎ 406/683-3000. **Beartooth Hospital** ✉ 600 W. 21st St., Red Lodge ☎ 406/446-2345. **Bozeman Deaconess Hospital** ✉ 915 Highland Blvd., Bozeman ☎ 406/585-5000. **Livingston Memorial Hospital** ✉ 504 S. 13th St., Livingston ☎ 406/222-3541. **St. James Healthcare** ✉ 400 S. Clark St., Butte ☎ 406/723-2500.

LODGING

Montana Bed & Breakfast Association ☎ 800/453-8870 ⊕ www.mtbba.com. **Montana Dude Ranch Association** ☎ 406/284-9933 ⊕ www.montanadra.com. **Mountain Home–Montana Vacation Rentals** ☎ 406/586-4589 or 800/550-4589 ⊕ www.mountain-home.com. **Montana Innkeepers Association** ☎ 406/449-8408 ⊕ www.montanainnkeepers.com.

CAMPING There are numerous campsites throughout the region, and they vary from rustic (with pit toilets) to relatively plush (with cabins and heated swimming pools). When camping, ask about bears in the area and whether or not food must be stored inside a hard-side vehicle (not a tent). Avoid bringing pets to campgrounds—it can lead to confrontations with the wildlife, and it's against the rules at most campgrounds.

Contact Montana Fish, Wildlife & Parks for information on camping in state parks and the U.S. Forest Service for information on camping at national parks in the area.

🚩 **Montana Fish, Wildlife & Parks** ☎ 406/444-2535 ⊕ www.fwp.state.mt.us/parks. **U.S. Forest Service** ☎ 406/329-3511 ⊕ www.fs.fed.us/r1.

MEDIA

NEWSPAPERS & The largest daily newspapers in the region are the *Billings Gazette,* the
MAGAZINES *Bozeman Chronicle,* the *Missoulian,* and the *Great Falls Tribune.*

TELEVISION & Two National Public Radio affiliates broadcast over most of the state:
RADIO Yellowstone Public Radio, KEMC 91.7 FM, Billings, and Montana Public Radio, KUMF 89.1 FM, Missoula. When driving near mountain passes or other road hazards, look for a sign along your route indicating which radio station to check for road information.

Billings and Bozeman have national televison network affiliate stations: Fox/KHMT Channel 4 and CBS/KBZK Channel 7, respectively. KUSM Channel 9 is the public television station based in Bozeman.

SPORTS & THE OUTDOORS

When you are heading into the backcountry, it's best to hire a guide or outfitter who knows the local trails, weather patterns, and unique features of the region.

BICYCLING Adventure Cycling can create route maps and provide other resources for cycling in the region.

🚩 **Adventure Cycling** ✉ 150 E. Pine St., Missoula 59807 ☎ 406/721-1776 ⊕ www. adventurecycling.org.

FISHING Fishing Outfitters Association of Montana and Montana Outfitters and Guides Association can help you find outfitters who lead fishing excursions throughout the state.

🚩 **Fishing Outfitters Association of Montana** ⓓ Box 67, Gallatin Gateway 59730 ☎406/ 763-5436 ⊕ www.foam-montana.org. **Montana Outfitters and Guides Association** ⓓ Box 1248, Helena 59624 ☎ 406/449-3578 ⊕ www.moga-montana.org.

SKIING The best information for downhill and cross-country skiing is available through the state tourism bureau, Travel Montana. There's detailed information on the Web site, and you can order a free winter guide.

🚩 **Travel Montana** ✉ 301 S. Park Ave., Helena 59620 ☎ 406/841-2870 or 800/847-4868 ⊕ www.visitmt.com.

TOURS

Adventure Cycling specializes in bicycling tours of Montana and other regions of the United States and Canada. Accomplished guides lead Off the Beaten Path outdoor journeys in Montana and the Rockies. Swan

River Tours conducts tours that focus on the Lewis and Clark expedition, Glacier and Yellowstone national parks, fall foliage, and more.

⚏ Tour Operators Adventure Cycling ✉ 150 E. Pine St., Missoula 59807 ☎ 406/721-1776 ⊕ www.adventurecycling.org. **Off the Beaten Path** ✉ 7 E. Beall St., Bozeman 59715 ☎ 800/445-2995 ⊕ www.offthebeatenpath.com. **Swan River Tours** ⌂ Box 1010, Condon 59826 ☎ 877/696-1666 ⊕ www.swanrivertours.com.

VISITOR INFORMATION

Travel Montana is the state's tourism bureau.

⚏ Tourist Information Beaverhead Chamber of Commerce ✉ 125 S. Montana, Box 425, Dillon 59725 ☎ 406/683-5511 ⊕ www.beaverheadchamber.org. **Big Sky Chamber of Commerce** ⌂ Box 160100, Big Sky 59716 ☎ 406/995-3000 or 800/943-4111 ⊕ www.bigskychamber.com. **Bozeman Chamber of Commerce** ✉ 2000 Commerce Way, Bozeman 59715 ☎ 406/586-5421 or 800/228-4224 ⊕ www.bozemanchamber.com. **Gold West Country** ✉ 1155 Main St., Deer Lodge 59722 ☎ 406/846-1943 or 800/879-1159 ⊕ www.goldwest.visitmt.com. **Helena Chamber of Commerce** ✉ 225 Cruse Ave., Helena 59601 ☎ 406/447-1530 or 800/743-5362 ⊕ www.helenachamber.com. **Red Lodge Chamber of Commerce** ✉ 601 N. Broadway, Red Lodge 59068 ☎ 888/281-0625 ⊕ www.redlodge.com. **Travel Montana** ✉ 301 S. Park Ave. Helena 59620 ☎ 406/841-2870 or 800/847-4868 ⊕ www.visitmt.com. **Yellowstone Country** ✉ 1822 W. Lincoln, Bozeman 59715 ☎ 800/736-5276 ⊕ www.yellowstone.visitmt.com.

Glacier National Park & Northwest Montana

WORD OF MOUTH

"Glacier National Park is one of the most spectacular places I've ever been. Every turn on any of the roads gives you a new picture to look at. Going to the Sun highway is spectacular, especially as you wind down the western side."
—lee

"Glacier is a hikers' park. If you aren't hiking you only need a day or two to tour Going to the Sun Road and other areas of the park. There are easy hikes but very few little circuit nature-trail types."
—justme22

"Missoula is a lot of fun due to the influence of the university as well as great local history."
—Gardyloo

By Jean Arthur **NORTHWEST MONTANA'S SEEMINGLY ENDLESS** mountain ranges shimmer under the Big Sky, reflecting the state's motto, *Oro y Plata* (gold and silver). When the Lewis and Clark expedition traveled through the region, they found lush forests surrounding glaciated valleys teeming with wildlife. Not much has changed today, as you can see in 1.2-million-acre Glacier National Park. At the top of any northwest Montana must-see list, Glacier remains open year-round. You'll have the most company in summer, when people come to drive the jaw-dropping Going-to-the-Sun Road, but winter has undeniable charms. The park's cross-country skiing and snowshoeing trails lead to turquoise waterfalls and cedar forests where, if you're lucky, you just might hear the howling of wolves.

Beyond Glacier stretch 2.7 million acres of northern Rockies wilderness, most of it roadless but some of it visible along impossibly scenic drives. Accessible lands offer stellar bird-watching, fishing, golfing, bicycling, and skiing (both downhill and cross-country). Hiking trails lace mountains and meadows, cross streams, and skirt lakes all over northwest Montana.

In the 200 years since Lewis and Clark passed through, Montana's population has grown to 902,000, and much of it has concentrated in the Bitterroot, Missoula, Mission, and Flathead valleys of the northwest. The largest city in the area, with a population of approximately 57,000, Missoula is a business and shopping center and home to the University of Montana, as well as to many arts and cultural attractions. In and between friendly towns such as Hamilton, Stevensville, Kalispell, Polson, and Whitefish are well-preserved historical sites and small yet resourceful museums; entertainment includes everything from local theater to Native American festivals. Civilization, however, perches on the edge of seemingly endless wilderness: visit this part of the world for its wildlife, its water, and its pristine lands.

Exploring Northwest Montana

Rivers, streams, lakes, and mountains dominate landscapes here and attract boaters, fly fishers, and outdoor adventurers. Once here, they discover playhouses, art galleries, and summer festivals and rodeos. In winter, visitors seek out northwest Montana's seven ski areas and scores of miles of cross-country ski trails. Spring and fall, the quiet seasons, are blessed with temperate weather, open tee times, and frequent wildlife sightings.

About the Restaurants

Although Montana generally isn't known for elegant dining, several sophisticated restaurants are tucked away among the tamaracks and cedars, where professionally trained chefs bring herbed nuances and wide-ranging cultural influences to their menus. More typical of the region are steak houses featuring certified Angus beef; in recent years, particularly in resort communities, these institutions have diversified their menus to include bison meat, fresh fish, and savory vegetarian options. Small cafés offer hearty, inexpensive meals, and you can pick up on local history through photographs and artwork on walls and conversation with the local denizens. Attire everywhere is decidedly casual: blue jeans, a clean shirt, and cowboy boots or flip-flops are dress-up for most Montana restaurants.

About the Hotels

From massive log lodges to historic bed-and-breakfasts to chain hotels, you'll find the range of lodging options here that you'd expect from a region that makes a business of catering to tourists. Many historic lodges and cabins do not offer air-conditioning, but in general you won't miss it, since summers here are never humid and temperatures rarely reach 90°. During ski season and the summer vacation months, reservations are necessary. Some hotels are open only in summer and early fall.

WHAT IT COSTS					
	$$$$	**$$$**	**$$**	**$**	**¢**
RESTAURANTS	over $22	$16–$22	$11–$16	$7–$11	under $7
HOTELS	over $220	$160–$220	$110–$160	$70–$110	under $70

Restaurant prices are for a main course at dinner, excluding sales tax of 2%–4% in some resort communities. Hotel prices are for two people in a standard double room in high season, excluding service charges and 7% bed tax.

Timing

Most visitors to northwest Montana come in July and August, enticed by lakes, rivers, golf courses, trails, and fresh mountain air. Arts festivals, rodeos, powwows, and farmers' markets fill the summer calendar. Even during this busiest season, though, you're unlikely to feel cramped among Montana's wide-open spaces. Winter is the second peak season; deep snows attract snowboarders and skiers to the region's seven alpine ski areas. It's also an excellent time to explore cross-country ski and snowshoe trails through the light, fluffy snow.

Spring and fall are the quiet seasons, but they're becoming increasingly popular. In spring, wildlife sightings include newborn elk calves, fawns, and an occasional bear cub. Mountain air cools the nights, and the occasional late-spring storm can cloak the region in snow, if only for a day. Fall's dry, warm days and blessedly cool nights offer the best of weather; there are few other tourists, and most attractions are still open. Lodgings offer off-season rates and there are no crowds, unless it's at a local high-school event, where nearly the entire town shows up. No matter the time of year, keep in mind that weather in this part of the world can change rapidly. Be prepared with extra clothing.

Numbers in the text correspond to numbers in the margin and on the Northwest Montana, Glacier National Park, and Missoula maps.

GLACIER NATIONAL PARK

The massive peaks of the Continental Divide are the backbone of Glacier National Park and its sister across the border, Canada's Waterton Lakes National Park. These parks embody the essence of the Rocky Mountains. Coniferous forests, thickly vegetated creek bottoms, and green-carpeted meadows and basins provide homes for all kinds of wildlife. Melting snow and alpine glaciers yield streaming ribbons of clear, frigid water, the headwaters of rivers that flow west to the Pacific Ocean, north to

Since Northwest Montana is famous for its mountains and waterways, a good place to start your trip here is Glacier National Park. Topping the list of its many don't-miss sites is Logan Pass on the Going-to-the-Sun Road, where you may encounter shaggy, white-coated mountain goats as they lunge across cliff faces or tiptoe through the parking lot. From the visitor center at Logan Pass, several hikes lead to backcountry splendor; the most popular and spectacular is the short trail that climbs to Hidden Lake Overlook. Even for non-hikers, Logan Pass offers magnificent fresh air and great views: both sides of the Continental Divide, numerous lakes, streams, and waterfalls, and wildflowers (especially in July and August).

4

Among the best in the state, northwest Montana's seven alpine ski areas are led by Big Mountain Ski Resort in the Flathead Valley. If you come in summer, be sure to take a chairlift ride to the top: from there you can see the Canadian Rockies, the peaks of Glacier, and the valley. Nearby, railroad fans and history buffs will appreciate Whitefish's Stumptown Historical Museum and Kalispell's Central School Museum, both crammed full of local history, plus a few humorous exhibits. Water lovers find ample room for all kinds of sports on Flathead Lake, the West's largest natural freshwater lake. Artsy types should stop in Bigfork, on the lake's northeast shore, where galleries dominate the main street, and eateries are often galleries, too. Finish off your time in the Flathead Valley with a visit the Flathead Indian Reservation, whose People's Center offers a glimpse of local Native American art, historic photographs, and artifacts.

If your travels include Missoula, you can figure out the lay of the land via a short hike to the M on the mountainside above the University of Montana's Washington-Grizzly Football Stadium. From here you'll see the Clark Fork River, downtown's Missoula Art Museum, and, way off to the west, the Rocky Mountain Elk Foundation Wildlife Visitor Center.

In the forested Bitterroot Valley, where many travelers follow Lewis and Clark's trail, stop at Traveler's Rest State Park for perspective on the expedition. Plan on floating and fishing the Bitterroot and other local rivers, and in early July watch the Senior Pro Rodeo if you're in Hamilton. At one of the valley's guest ranches, be sure to sign up for a trail ride into the Bitterroot or Selway wilderness areas and along surrounding U.S. Forest Service trails. Wherever you go, don't forget your cowboy hat and your "howdy."

---

the Arctic, and southeast to the Atlantic via the Gulf of Mexico. In the backcountry you can see some of the Rockies' oldest geological formations and numerous rare species of mammals, plants, and birds. The Going-to-the-Sun Road, which snakes through the precipitous center of Glacier, is one of the most dizzying rides on the continent.

In the rocky northwest corner of America's fourth-largest state, Glacier encompasses more than 1 million acres (1,563 square mi) of untram-

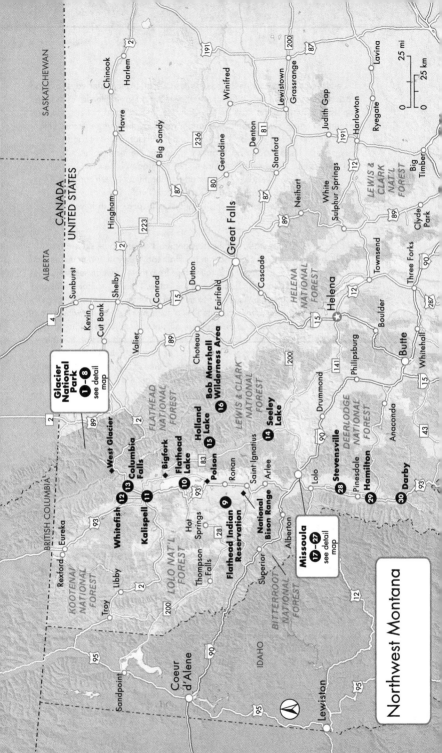

Northwest Montana

meled wilds. It came into being under the aegis of President William Howard Taft in 1910. Great Northern Railway baron Louis Hill's "See America First" campaign drew wealthy Easterners to the new park, where he'd built lodges, chalets, roads, and trails, many of which are still in use today. Along the 720 mi of trails are 37 named glaciers, 200 lakes, and 1,000 mi of streams. Neighboring Waterton Lakes National Park, across the border in Alberta, Canada, covers another 130,000 acres. In 1932, the parks were symbolically unified to form the Waterton-Glacier International Peace Park in recognition of the two nations' friendship and dedication to peace. Both parks continue to be maintained by their respective park services.

Exploring Glacier

Motorized access to the park is limited, but the few roads can take you through a range of settings—from densely forested lowlands to craggy heights. Going-to-the-Sun Road is the main thoroughfare, snaking through the precipitous center of the park. Beginning in 2007, the Federal Highway Administration and the park are embarking upon a multiyear alpine road rehabilitation. The narrow, curving highway, built from 1922 to 1932, will undergo structural repair. While work is underway, a shuttle system will allow access for visitors. Until then and undoubtedly after construction is complete, vehicles more than 21 feet long and 8 feet wide (including mirrors) are not allowed to drive over Logan Pass—a restriction that is enforced at checkpoints at the east and west entrances. Touring cars can take you over the Going-to-the-Sun Road while a driver interprets. Shuttle services will drop off and pick up hikers—useful, since parking at many trailheads is limited. Note that extreme weather conditions occasionally prompt short-term closures of the alpine section of Going-to-the-Sun Road. You can check online or by calling the park service for the most up-to-date road report. Most development and services are concentrated around St. Mary Lake, on the east side of the park, and Lake McDonald, on the west side. Other islands of development occur in Many Glacier, in the northeastern part of the park; Logan Pass Visitor Center; Apgar Village; and West Glacier. Remember that weather in the mountains can change quickly; snow can fall even in August. Be prepared with extra layers, a hat, and rain gear. If you intend to travel to Canada, be sure that everyone in your vehicle has proper identification. A U.S. driver's license will do for adults; kids traveling with one parent need a notarized letter from the other parent giving permission to enter Canada. If you are traveling with pets, you need proof of immunizations to cross the border into Canada. ⊠ *Glacier National Park Headquarters, West Glacier 59936* ☎ *406/888–7800* ⊕ *www.nps.gov/glac* ✉ *$10 for a single person on foot or bicycle; $20 per vehicle for a 7-day permit* ☉ *Year-round. Going-to-the-Sun Road's center section closed over Logan Pass Oct.–June. Limited services in winter. Park headquarters weekdays year-round.*

A Good Tour

Begin in West Glacier at the entrance station, where you'll receive a free park map, newspaper, and wildlife safety information. Drive along the lake's shore and spend some time on one of may the rocky beaches on

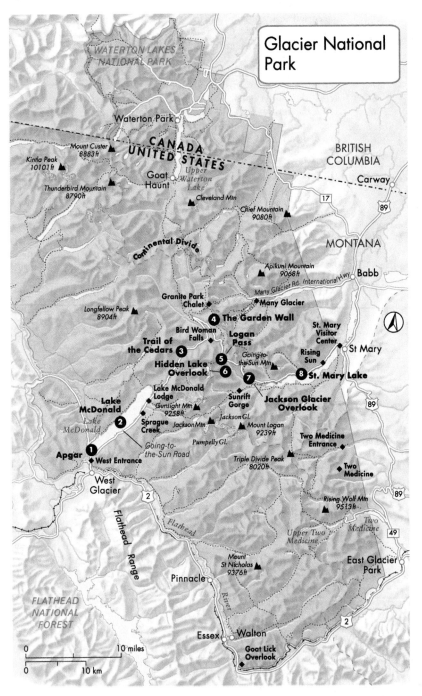

Glacier National Park

WATERTON LAKES NATIONAL PARK

Waterton Park

CANADA
UNITED STATES

BRITISH COLUMBIA

Carway

Mount Custer
8883ft

Kintla Peak
10101ft

Thunderbird Mountain
8790ft

Goat
Haunt

Upper
Waterton
Lake

Cleveland Mtn

Chief Mountain
9080ft

17

89

MONTANA

Continental Divide

Apikuni Mountain
9068ft

Babb

Many Glacier Rd. International Hwy

Longfellow Peak
8904ft

Granite Park
Chalet

Many Glacier

The Garden Wall 4

Bird Woman
Falls

Logan
Pass

St. Mary
Visitor
Center

St Mary

**Trail of
the Cedars** 3

5

Going-to-
the-Sun Mtn

Rising
Sun

**Hidden Lake
Overlook** 6

7

8 **St. Mary Lake**

Lake McDonald
Lodge

Sunrift
Gorge

**Jackson Glacier
Overlook**

**Lake
McDonald**

2

Gunsight Mtn
9258ft

Jackson Mtn

Jackson Gl.

89

Lake
McDonald

Sprague
Creek

Mount Logan
9239ft

Pumpelly Gl.

**Two Medicine
Entrance**

Apgar 1

West Entrance

Going-to-
the-Sun Road

Triple Divide Peak
8020ft

**Two
Medicine**

West
Glacier

2

Rising Wolf Mtn
9513ft

89

Flathead Range

Flathead

Upper Two
Medicine

Two
Medicine

49

FLATHEAD
NATIONAL
FOREST

Mount
St Nicholas
9376ft

East Glacier
Park

Pinnacle

River

2

Essex

Walton

Goat Lick
Overlook

0   10 miles
0   10 km

Lake McDonald ❷. Continue along Going-to-the-Sun Road, making sure to stop at Lake McDonald Lodge for lunch or just a hot coffee and a glimpse at the historic collection of mounted wildlife, then keep driving north to Avalanche Creek, which is the trailhead for the **Trail of the Cedars ❸**. As you drive farther, **The Garden Wall ❹** looms ahead as an impassible rock fortress. The road climbs below its crest to the summit at **Logan Pass ❺**, where you'll want to take photos of the wildflowers, peaks, and mountain goats that graze here. If you have time, climb to the **Hidden Lake Overlook ❻**. Continuing your drive east, you'll find several pull-outs, including the **Jackson Glacier Overlook ❼**. As you drive alongside **St. Mary Lake ❽**, you'll see the lake campgrounds, visitor center, and the end of the Going-to-the-Sun Road where it meets U.S. 89. Either return by retracing your route or turn south on U.S. 89 for the trip back to West Glacier.

If you don't want to drive the Going-to-the-Sun Road, consider making the ride in a Jammer, an antique red bus operated by **Glacier Park, Inc.** (☎ 406/892–2525 ⊕ www.glacierparkinc.com). The drivers double as guides, and they can roll back the tops of the vehicles to give you improved views and the sensation of wind on your face. Reservations are required.

TIMING   A drive along Going-to-the-Sun Road is a satisfying day trip, though you can easily devote days and even weeks to visiting the park; the more time you have to explore in depth, the more rewarding your experience will be. Watch for weather alerts, as snow can fall in any season. The Going-to-the-Sun Road is generally closed from mid-October through late May.

What to See

❶ **Apgar.** Entering Glacier National Park at the west entrance, you come to a stop sign about a mile inside the park. If you turn left, you will reach Apgar, on the southwest end of Lake McDonald. Apgar is a tiny hamlet with a few stores, an ice-cream shop, motels, ranger buildings, a campground, a historic schoolhouse, and lake access for swimming, fishing, and boating. In summer, Apgar is the hub of activity for the west side of the park. From November to mid-May, no services remain open, except the weekend-only visitor center. ⊠ *2 mi north of the west entrance.*

⟳ The small **Apgar Visitor Center** is a great first stop if you're entering the park from the west. You can get all kinds of park information, maps, permits, and books here, plus the Junior Ranger Newspaper (available at all visitor centers) with activities that earn youngsters their Junior Ranger Badge. The large relief map in the center is a model of the park; you can plan your route and get a glimpse of where you're going. In winter, the rangers offer free snowshoe walks—they provide the snowshoes, too. ☎ *406/888–7800 or 406/888–7939 ⊕ www.nps.gov/glac ⊙ Mid-May–Sept., daily 8–8; Oct., daily 8–4:30; Nov.–mid-May, weekends 9–4.*

⟳ The **Apgar Education Cabin**, across the street from the visitor center, is filled with animal posters, kids' activities, and maps. ☎ *406/888–7939 ⊙ Mid-June–Labor Day, daily 2:30–4.*

Baring Falls. For an easy family hike, try the 1³⁄₁₀-mi path from the Sun Point parking area. It leads to a spruce and Douglas fir wood; cross a log bridge over Baring Creek and you arrive at the base of gushing Baring Falls. ⊠ *11 mi east of Logan Pass on Going-to-the-Sun Rd.*

Belly River Country. Trailing through both parks, this valley has lovely low meadows and large alpine lakes. Waters from Belly River eventually drain into Hudson Bay. Backcountry camp spots see few human footprints and lots of bear tracks. One trailhead is south of the Chief Mountain Customs Station on Route 17. Another trailhead lies 2 mi north of the station on Canada Route 6, at the Belly River campground. The trails from the campground provide the only access to Cracker (12 mi round-trip), Cosley (15 mi), Glenns (18 mi), Helen (25 mi), and Elizabeth (16 mi) backcountry lakes. ⊠ *Hwy. 17 to Canada Hwy. 6* ☎ *406/ 888–7800.*

4 The Garden Wall. An abrupt and jagged wall of rock juts above Going-to-the-Sun Road and is visible from the road as it follows Logan Creek from just past Avalanche Creek Campground for about 10 mi to Logan Pass. The knife-edge wall, called an arête, was created by massive glaciers moving down the valleys on either side of it. ⊠ *Going-to-the-Sun Rd.*

Goat Haunt. Reached only by foot trail or tour boat from Waterton Townsite, this spot on the U.S. end of Waterton Lake is the stomping ground for mountain goats, moose, grizzlies, and black bears. The ranger posted at this remote station gives thrice-daily dock talks, free 10-minute overviews of natural and human history in Waterton Valley. You can see exhibits in the ranger station, camp, and picnic. ⊠ *South end of Waterton Lake* ☎ *406/888–7800 or 403/859–2362* ⛴ *Tour boat $22* ⊙ *Mid-May–Oct.*

Goat Lick Overlook. From this highway pull-out, you may see more than a dozen mountain goats at a natural salt lick on a cliff above the Middle Fork of the Flathead River. Take a short, paved trail from the parking lot to the observation point. ⊠ *2½ mi east of Walton Ranger Station on U.S. 2.*

Grinnell and Salamander Glaciers. Formed only about 4,000 years ago, these glaciers were one ice mass until 1926, and they continue to shrink. Icebergs often float in Grinnell Lake across from the glaciers. The best viewpoint is reached by the 5½-mi Grinnell Glacier Trail from Many Glacier. ⊠ *5½ mi from Swiftcurrent campground on Grinnell Glacier Trail.*

6 Hidden Lake Overlook. Take a walk from Logan Pass up to see the crystalline Hidden Lake, which often still has ice clinging to it in early July. It's a 1½-mi hike on an uphill grade, partially on a boardwalk that protects the abundant wildflowers. You'll meet lots of others along the way. ⊠ *Logan Pass, Going-to-the-Sun Rd.*

7 Jackson Glacier Overlook. As you descend Going-to-the-Sun Road on the east side of the Continental Divide, you come into view of Jackson Glacier looming in a rocky pass across the upper St. Mary River valley. If it isn't covered with snow, you'll see sharp peaks of ice. The glacier is shrinking and may disappear in another 100 years. ⊠ *Going-to-the-Sun Rd., 5 mi east of Logan Pass.*

❷ Lake McDonald. From one end to the other, beautiful Lake McDonald is 10 mi long and accessible year-round on Going-to-the-Sun Road. Take a boat ride to the middle for a unique view of the surrounding glacier-clad mountains. You can go fishing and horseback riding at either end of the lake. Three drive-in campgrounds are along the shore at Apgar, Fish Creek, and Sprague Creek. In winter, snowshoe, cross-country ski, or walk along the lakeshore or on the closed, snowed-in portion of Going-to-the-Sun Road. ⊠ *2 mi from the west entrance at Apgar.*

★ ❺ Logan Pass. At 6,660 feet, Logan Pass, the highest point in the park accessible by motor vehicle, presents unparalleled views of both sides of the Continental Divide. It's the apex of Going-to-the-Sun Road, and a must-see. The pass is frequented by mountain goats, bighorn sheep, and grizzly bears—trailheads spread out from the visitor center to wildlife-viewing points. There are no phones or food services here, so be sure to bring along enough water and provisions for the round-trip. The road and the pass are both extremely crowded in July and August. ⊠ *34 mi from West Glacier, 18 mi from St. Mary.*

Built of stone, the **Logan Pass Visitor Center** stands sturdy against the severe weather that forces it to close in winter. Snow often dapples the high alpine terrain around the visitor center late into spring, providing moisture for the summer wildflowers. Park information, books, and maps are stocked inside. Rangers staff the center and give 10-minute talks on the alpine environment. ☎ *406/888–7800* ☽ *Mid-June–Oct., daily 8–4:30.*

★ Many Glacier. On the shore of Swiftcurrent Lake, the historic, Swiss-style Many Glacier Lodge has a restaurant, a bar, a gift shop, and a lovely foyer. You can enjoy the quiet deck overlooking Swiftcurrent Lake. The view of jagged peaks over the lake is worth packing a camera. You can book boat rentals and cruises. Also in the area are a campground, camp store, ranger station, horseback riding outfitter, and several trailheads. ⊠ *12 mi west of Babb on Many Glacier Rd.* ☎ *406/888–7800 or 406/732–7741* ☽ *June–late Sept., daily.*

Running Eagle Falls. This falls, sometimes called Trick Falls, cascades near Two Medicine and is actually two different waterfalls from two different sources. In spring, when the water level is high, the upper falls join the lower falls for a 40-foot drop into Two Medicine River; in summer, the upper falls dry up, revealing the lower, 20-foot falls that start midway down the precipice. ⊠ *2 mi east of the Two Medicine entrance.*

❽ St. Mary Lake. When the breezes calm, the lake acts as a reflecting pool mirroring the snowcapped granite peaks that line the St. Mary Valley. The Sun Point Nature Trail follows the lake's shore 1 mi each way. You can buy an interpretive brochure for 50¢ at the trailhead on the north side of the lake, about halfway between the Logan Pass and the St. Mary Visitor Center. Use it and drop it at the box at the other end of the trail so that it may be recycled. ⊠ *1 mi from St. Mary on Going-to-the-Sun Rd.*

The park's largest visitor complex, the **St. Mary Visitor Center** has a huge relief map of the park's peaks and valleys. Rangers can answer your questions, and they host a 45-minute slide show program each evening at 8. Traditional Blackfeet dancing and drumming performances are held weekly. The center has books and maps for sale, and there are large viewing windows facing 10-mi-long St. Mary Lake. ⊠ *Going-to-the-Sun Rd. off U.S. 89* ☏ *406/732–7750* ☽ *Mid-May–mid-Oct., daily 8* AM*–4:30* PM *and 8* PM*–9* PM.

★ **Sun Tours.** Ride with Blackfeet interpreters to get a historical perspective on the park and region as seen by the Native American community. Tours depart daily from East Glacier and St. Mary in 24-passenger, air-conditioned coaches. ⊠ *29 Glacier Ave., East Glacier* ☏ *406/226–9220 or 800/786–9220* ⊕ *www.glacierinfo.com* ☽ *Mid-May–Sept., daily.*

◑ ➌ **Trail of the Cedars.** This ½-mi-long handicap-accessible boardwalk meanders through the westernmost western red-cedar rain forest. The ancient trees are home to numerous small animals, such as chipmunks. Interpretive signs detail the cedars' resistance to fires and other information about the habitat. ⊠ *15 mi north of Apgar on Going-to-the-Sun Rd.*

Two Medicine Valley. Rugged, often windy, and always beautiful, the valley is a remote 9-mi drive from Route 49 and is surrounded by some of the park's most stark, rocky peaks. On and around the valley's lake you can rent a canoe, take a narrated boat tour, camp, and hike. Be aware that bears frequent the area; sometimes rangers allow only hard-sided camping (not tents) until bears are gone. You'll find a camp store, a gift shop, and a picnic area here, but no formal lodging. The road is closed from late October through late May. ⊠ *Two Medicine entrance, 9 mi east of Hwy. 49* ☏ *406/888–7800, 406/257–2426 boat tours.*

Waterton Information Centre. If you make your way up to Canada, stop here on the eastern edge of Waterton Townsite to orient yourself in Canada's Waterton Lakes National Park. You can pick up brochures and buy maps and books. Rangers are on hand to answer questions and give directions. ⊠ *Waterton Rd.* ☏ *403/859–5133 or 403/859–2224* ⊜ *403/859–2650* ⊕ *www.parkscanada.pch.gc.ca/waterton* ☐ *$6 per person; $15 per family* ☽ *Mid-May–mid-June, daily 8–6; mid-June–early Sept., daily 8–8; early Sept.–Oct. 8, daily 9–6.*

Sports & the Outdoors

◑ The **Glacier Institute** (✉ Box 7457, Kalispell 59901 ☏ 406/755–1211 or 406/888–5215 May–Sept. ⊕ www.glacierinstitute.org), based inside the park near West Glacier at the Field Camp and on the remote western boundary at the Big Creek Outdoor Education Center, offers more than 75 different field courses for kids and adults. Year-round, experts in wildlife biology, native plants, and river ecology lead educational treks into Glacier's backcountry on daylong and multiday programs.

◑ A nearly all-purpose outfitter for the park is **Glacier Wilderness Guides and Montana Raft Company** (⊠ 11970 U.S. 2 E, 1 mi south of West Glacier ☏ 406/387–5555 or 800/521–7238 ⊕ www.glacierguides.com), which operates daylong to weeklong trips that can combine hiking, rafting, and fishing.

Boating

★ See the park's larger lakes with **Glacier Park Boat Tours** (☎ 406/257–2426 ⊕ www.montanaweb.com/gpboats), which offers cruises on Lake Mc-Donald, Lake Josephine, Two Medicine Lake, and St. Mary Lake. Tours last 45 minutes to 1½ hours. You can also rent sea kayaks, canoes, rowboats, and small motorboats.

Tour by boat with **Waterton Inter-Nation Shoreline Cruise Co.** (⊠ Waterton Townsite Marina ☎ 403/859–2362 ⊕ www.watertoninfo.ab.ca/m/cruise) on a two-hour round-trip from Waterton Townsite in Canada, along Upper Waterton Lake to Goat Haunt, Montana. The narrated tour passes scenic bays, sheer cliffs, and snow-clad peaks. Combine a lake cruise and the Crypt Trail hike for a spectacular afternoon.

Fishing

Within Glacier National Park there's an almost unlimited range of fishing possibilities, with a catch-and-release policy encouraged. The sportfishing species include burbot (ling); northern pike; whitefish; kokanee salmon; grayling; and cutthroat, rainbow, lake (mackinaw), and brook trout. You can fish in most waters of the park, but the best fishing is generally in the least accessible spots. A fishing license is required, and you must stop by a park office to pick up a copy of the regulations. It is expected that you familiarize yourself with all park fishing regulations before you use any facilities. If you want a guide for fly-fishing or hiking, contact **Glacier Wilderness Guides and Montana Raft Company** (⊠ 11970 U.S. 2 E, 1 mi south of West Glacier ☎ 406/387–5555 or 800/521–7238 ⊕ www.glacierguides.com).

Golf

Glacier Park Lodge (☎ 406/226–9311), in East Glacier, has a 9-hole, par-36 course, as well as a 9-hole pitch-and-putt course. Take your camera and watch out for moose. **Glacier View Golf Course** (☎ 406/888–5471), in West Glacier, is an 18-hole course. On the Canadian side of the park, you can play 18 holes at the **Waterton Golf Course** (☎ 403/859–2114), just outside Waterton Townsite. Don't be surprised if you see moose, elk, deer, bighorn sheep, and other wildlife on the course.

Hiking & Backpacking

The Hiker's Guide to Glacier National Park, by the Glacier Natural History Association, lists 25 hikes with tips for hiking in the park. Maps for hiking are available at the **Apgar Visitor Center** (☎ 406/888–5441) near the western entrance of Glacier. If you want to backpack, you must pick up a backcountry permit there. Trail closures—often due to bear activity—and a daily backcountry bulletin are posted here and on the park's Web site. Cross-country skiers and snowshoers can pick up maps here, too.

Hiking trails of various lengths and levels are well marked within the park. Novices and those who want the help of an experienced guide can sign up with **Glacier Wilderness Guides and Montana Raft Company** (⊠ 11970 U.S. 2 E, 1 mi south of West Glacier ☎ 406/387–5555 or 800/521–7238 ⊕ www.glacierguides.com). The most spectacular hiking-and-lodging adventure in the state is the gentle 7-mi **Highline Trail** from Logan Pass to Granite Park Chalet, a National Historic Landmark,

Fodor'sChoice
★

which is open for rustic lodging from late July to mid-September. Built in 1914 by the Great Northern Railway, the chalet was one of nine backcountry lodges of which only two remain, the other being Sperry Chalet.

Horseback Riding

Mule Shoe Outfitters (☎ 406/888–5121, 406/732–4203, 928/684–2328 in winter ⊕ www.mule-shoe.com) runs the horseback riding concession in Glacier from early June to September 15, as the weather allows. Rides begin at Apgar, Lake McDonald and Many Glacier. Trips for beginning to advanced riders cover both flat and mountainous territory; all are led by guides who provide information on the park. Rates run from $28 for an hour to $120 for a full day.

Rafting

Glacier Raft Company (✉ 11957 U.S. 2 E, West Glacier ☎ 406/888–5454 or 800/235–6781 ⊕ www.glacierraftco.com) is a river outfitter that also rents bikes, snowshoes, and cabins and has a full-service fly-fishing shop. **Glacier Wilderness Guides and Montana Raft Company** (✉ 11970 U.S. 2 E, 1 mi south of West Glacier ☎ 406/387–5555 or 800/521–7238 ⊕ www.glacierguides.com) will take you on raft trips through the stomach-churning white water of the Middle Fork of the Flathead and combine it with a hike or a barbecue. **Great Northern Whitewater** (✉ 12127 U.S. 2 E, 1 mi south of West Glacier ☎ 406/387–5340 or 800/735–7897 ⊕ www.gnwhitewater.com) offers daily white-water, kayaking, and fishing trips and rents Swiss-style chalets with views of Glacier's peaks. **Wild River Rafting** (✉ 12900 U.S. 2 E, 1 mi south of West Glacier ☎ 406/387–9453 or 800/700–7056 ⊕ www.RiverWild.com) offers rafting, trail rides, and scenic fishing trips on rivers around Glacier Park.

Skiing

Cross-country ski excursions reveal mountain views, frozen lakes and streams, and wildlife such as moose, deer, and bald eagles. Glacier National Park distributes a free pamphlet titled "Ski Trails of Glacier National Park," which describes 16 ski trails. On scenic trails such as Autumn Creek near the Continental Divide, **Glacier Park Ski Tours** (☎ 406/862–2790) guides custom day trips, full-moon ski tours, and winter camping in snow huts or tents.

The 20 mi of groomed track at **Izaak Walton Inn** (✉ U.S. 2, Essex ☎ 406/888–5700 ⊕ www.izaakwaltoninn.com), at the edge of Glacier National Park, nicely combine the pleasures of groomed-trail skiing with the spirit of backcountry skiing with views into the park and the Great Bear Wilderness. Because it's alongside the railroad tracks, it is also accessible from Whitefish by Amtrak train. Track, touring, and telemark rentals, ski lessons, guide service, and multiday packages including skiing, lodging, and meals are available. Be careful when crossing the highway between trails.

Where to Stay & Eat

$$–$$$$ ✕ **Lake McDonald Lodge Restaurants.** The lodge staffs its restaurants with energetic college students. In the Russell's Fireside Dining Room, take in a great view while choosing between standards such as pasta, steak, and salmon. Don't miss the apple bread pudding with caramel-cinnamon sauce for dessert. If you're in a hurry, grab a quick sandwich or appetizer in the Stockade Lounge, or walk across the parking lot to the cheaper alternative, Jammer Joe's Grill & Pizzeria, which serves burgers and pasta for lunch and dinner. ⊠ *10 mi north of Apgar on Going-to-the-Sun Rd.* ☎ *406/888–5431 or 406/892–2525* ☰ *AE, D, MC, V* ☾ *Closed early Oct.–early June.*

$$–$$$$ ✕ **Prince of Wales Lodge Restaurants.** Enjoy upmarket cuisine before a dazzling view of Waterton Lake in the dining room of this century-old chalet high on a hill. Choose from a fine selection of wines to accompany your meal. Every afternoon the lodge's main culinary event unfolds: a British high tea served in Valerie's Tea Room (with the same great view); true to form, tea includes finger sandwiches, scones and other pastries, and chocolate-dipped fruits. Try the Windsor Lounge for snacks, brews, and more views. ⊠ *Waterton Townsite* ☎ *403/859–2231* ☰ *D, MC, V* ☾ *Closed Oct.–May.*

$$–$$$$ **Ptarmigan Dining Room.** Sophisticated cuisine is served in the dining room of early-20th-century chalet-like Many Glacier Hotel. As the sun sets over Swiftcurrent Lake just outside the massive windows, Italian-inflected food is served amid Swiss-style decor. Each night there's a chef's special such as smoked salmon and pasta with a pink marinara sauce, or pork prime rib with a huckleberry demi-glace. For a true Montana creation, have a huckleberry daiquiri. ⊠ *Many Glacier Rd.* ☎ *406/732–4411 or 406/892–2525* ☰ *AE, D, MC, V* ☾ *Closed late Sept.–early June.*

$–$$$ ✕ **Curly Bear Cafe & Pizza Co.** Dine outside on the deck, where you can see Glacier's peaks. Buffalo burgers, rotisserie chicken, and pizza fill the menu. Save room for baked goodies or head to the ice-cream parlor next door. ⊠ *U.S. 89 and Going-to-the-Sun Rd., St. Mary* ☎ *406/732–4431* ⌲ *Reservations not accepted* ☰ *AE, D, MC, V* ☾ *Closed early Oct.–mid-May.*

$$$$ ▥ **Sperry Chalet.** This elegant backcountry lodge, built in 1913 by the Great Northern Railway, is accessible only by a steep, 6.7-mi trail with a 3,300-foot vertical rise. Either hike in or arrive on horseback (hire horses from Mule Shoe Outfitters, *above*). Guest rooms have no electricity, heat, or running water, but who cares when the view includes Glacier's Gunsite peak, Mt. Edwards, Lake McDonald, and mountain goats in wildflowers. Informal meals, such as turkey with the trimmings, are simple yet filling. Note that the reservations office is closed September through October. ⌂ *Box 188, Going-to-the-Sun Rd., West Glacier 59936* ☎ *406/387–5654 or 888/345–2649* ⊕ *www.sperrychalet.com* ⤶ *17 rooms* ⌁ *Dining room, hiking, horseback riding, shop; no a/c, no room phones, no room TVs, no smoking* ☰ *AE, MC, V* ☾ *Closed mid-Sept.–early July* ⁞◎⁞ *FAP.*

$$$–$$$$ ▥ **Glacier Park Lodge.** On the east side of the park, across from the Amtrak station, you'll find this beautiful hotel built in 1913. The full-service lodge is supported by 500- to 800-year-old fir and 3-foot-thick cedar logs. Rooms are sparsely decorated, but there are historic posters on the walls in the halls. Cottages and a house are also available on the grounds next to the golf course. If you golf on the spectacular course, watch out

for moose. Entertainers delight guests with storytelling and singing in the great hall. ⊠ *Off U.S. 2, East Glacier* ⌖ *Box 2025, Columbia Falls 59912* ☎ *406/892–2525 or 406/226–9311* 🖷 *406/226–9152* ⊕ *www. glacierparkinc.com* ⥿ *154 rooms* ⌂ *Restaurant, snack bar, 9-hole golf course, pool, bar, playground; no a/c, no room TVs, no smoking* ☰ *AE, D, MC, V.*

$$–$$$$ 🏨 **Belton Chalet.** This carefully restored 1910 railroad hotel, the original winter headquarters for the park, has a great location just outside the West Glacier entrance. Rooms are cozy and bright, with original woodwork around the windows and period furnishings. Cottages, which remain open in winter, are snug up against the evergreen forest behind the lodge. ⊠ *12575 U.S. 2 E, West Glacier 59936* ☎ *406/888–5000 or 888/235–8665* 🖷 *406/888–5005* ⊕ *www.beltonchalet.com* ⥿ *25 rooms, 2 cottages* ⌂ *Dining room, spa, bicycles, cross-country skiing, bar; no a/c, no room phones, no room TVs, no smoking* ☰ *MC, V* ⦿ *BP.*

$$–$$$$ 🏨 **Great Bear Lodge and Resort at Glacier.** Just outside the park boundary, this full-service resort is a good base for a few days of fishing, hiking, and boating. Of all the lodges in and around the park, this is the most up-to-date and comfy. All rooms have decks, wet bars, sitting areas, and spectacular views of Glacier's peaks. Sparse decor doesn't detract from the view outside. Nearby, the Pinnacle Cottages have river-rock fireplaces, private decks, and barbecue grills. ⊠ *U.S. 89 and Going-to-the-Sun Rd.* ⌖ *Resort at Glacier, St. Mary 59417* ☎ *406/732–4431 or 800/368–3689* ⊕ *www.glcpark.com* ⥿ *48 rooms* ⌂ *Restaurant, café, coffee shop, pizzeria, some kitchens, cable TV, in-room data ports, lake, fishing, mountain bikes, bar, shops, laundry facilities, business services, meeting rooms, no-smoking rooms* ☰ *AE, D, MC, V* ⊗ *Closed mid-Oct.–Apr.*

$$–$$$$ 🏨 **Izaak Walton Inn.** This historic lodge sits on the southern edge of Glacier and under the shadow of the Great Bear Wilderness. You can ride Amtrak to the back door and stay either in quaint lodge rooms or in unique train cabooses, refurbished for guests. Lodge rooms have knotty-pine paneling, lacy curtains, and simple furnishings. Caboose Cottages (three-night minimum for $723) sleep up to four people and have kitchenettes. In winter you can ski or snowshoe from the door or head into Glacier with a guide from the inn. ⊠ *290 Izaak Walton Inn Rd. (off U.S. 2), Essex 59916* ☎ *406/888–5700* 🖷 *406/888–5200* ⊕ *www. izaakwaltoninn.com* ⥿ *33 rooms, 4 caboose cottages* ⌂ *Restaurant, mountain bikes, cross-country skiing, bar, shop, meeting rooms; no a/c, no room phones, no room TVs, no smoking* ☰ *MC, V.*

$$–$$$$ 🏨 **Many Glacier Hotel.** The most isolated of the grand hotels—it's on Swiftcurrent Lake on the northeast side of the park—this is also one of the most scenic, especially if you nab one of the balcony rooms. There are several hiking trails nearby, and a large fireplace in the lobby where guests gather on chilly mornings. Rooms are small and sparsely decorated, but who needs trinkets with views like these? ⊠ *Many Glacier Rd., 12 mi west of Babb* ⌖ *Box 2025, Columbia Falls 59912* ☎ *406/ 892–2525 or 406/732–4411* 🖷 *406/732–5522* ⊕ *www.glacierparkinc. com* ⥿ *211 rooms* ⌂ *Restaurant, ice-cream parlor, hiking, bar; no a/c, no room TVs, no smoking* ☰ *AE, D, MC, V.*

$–$$$ ☷ **Village Inn.** On Lake McDonald at Apgar Village, this motel could use some updating, but it is very popular and offers a view of the lake and surrounding peaks. All of the plain but serviceable rooms, some with kitchenettes, face the lake. It's near the lake outlet and good fishing. A restaurant, bar, and coffee shop are nearby. ⊠ *Apgar Village* ⌂ *Box 2025, Columbia Falls 59912* ☎ *406/756–2444* ⊟ *406/892–1375* ⊕ *www.glacierparkinc.com or www.villageinnatapgar.com* ⟿ *36 rooms* ⌂ *Boating, fishing, hiking; no a/c* ☰ *AE, D, MC, V.*

$$ ☷ **Granite Park Chalet.** This 1914 stone hut perched on a knoll below the Continental Divide and Garden Wall is reachable only by hiking trail or horseback ride. The 7.4-mi trek is fully worth the effort, because from the balcony you see Heaven's Peak and Logan Pass and may even watch grizzly bears digging for glacier-lily bulbs in a meadow nearby. You pack in your own food and bedding (there's optional linen service for a fee). The innkeeper will help you organize in the kitchen, find a good hiking trail, and watch for wildlife. Guided hut hikes can be arranged through Glacier Wilderness Guides. ⊠ *Going-to-the-Sun Rd.* ⌂ *Box 330, West Glacier 59936* ☎ *406/387–5654 or 888/345–2649* ⊕ *www.sperrychalet. com* ⟿ *12 rooms* ⌂ *Dining room, kitchens, horseback riding, library, shop; no a/c, no room phones, no room TVs, no smoking* ⊗ *Closed mid-Sept.–late June* ☰ *AE, MC, V.*

$–$$ ☷ **Lake McDonald Complex.** One of the great historic lodges of the West anchors this complex on the shore of lovely Lake McDonald. Take a room in the lodge itself, where public spaces are filled with massive timbers, stone fireplaces, and animal trophies. Cabins sleep up to four and don't have kitchens; there are also motel-style rooms separate from the lodge. ⊠ *Going-to-the-Sun Rd.* ⌂ *Box 2025, Columbia Falls 59912* ☎ *406/892–2525 or 406/888–5431* ⊕ *www.glacierparkinc.com* ⟿ *30 rooms, 13 cabins* ⌂ *Restaurant, coffee shop, boating, fishing, hiking, bar, no-smoking rooms; no room TVs, no a/c* ☰ *AE, D, MC, V.*

Camping

Most campgrounds within Glacier offer **Ranger-Led Evening Programs** (⊠ Apgar Rd. ☎ 406/888–7800) nightly or several evenings a week at campground amphitheaters. Check the free *Nature with a Naturalist* newspaper, available at the Apgar Ranger Station.

⚠ **Apgar Campground.** On the southern shore of Lake McDonald, this popular and large campground has many activities and services. From here you can hike; boat, fish, or swim in the lake; and sign up for trail rides. Stores and the visitor center are a short walk from the campground. ⌂ *Flush toilets, pit toilets, dump station, drinking water, bear boxes, fire grates, picnic tables, food service, public telephone, general store, ranger station, swimming (lake)* ⟿ *194 sites* ⊠ *Apgar Rd.* ☎ *406/ 888–7800 or 800/365–2267* ⊕ *www.nps.gov/glac* ▨ *$15* ☰ *AE, D, MC, V* ⊗ *Early May–mid-Oct.*

⚠ **Avalanche Creek Campground.** Sheltered by huge red cedars and bordered by Avalanche Creek, this campground sits at trailheads and along the Going-to-the-Sun Road. ⌂ *Flush toilets, drinking water, fire grates, picnic tables, public phone* ⟿ *87 sites* ⊠ *Going-to-the-Sun Rd.* ☎ *406/ 888–7800 or 800/365–2267* ⊟ *406/888–7808* ⊕ *www.nps.gov/glac* ▨ *$15* ☰ *AE, D, MC, V* ⊗ *Early June–early Sept.*

🏕 **Bowman Lake Campground.** In the remote northwestern corner of the park, this quiet camping spot is a fishermen's favorite for the lake and stream fishing. Mosquitoes can be bothersome here, as can the potholes and ruts in the one-lane drive in from Polebridge. ⚬ *Pit toilets, drinking water, bear boxes, fire grates, picnic tables, ranger station, swimming (lake)* ⟿ *48 sites* ✉ *Bowman Lake Rd.* ☎ *406/888–7800 or 800/365–2267* 🖷 *406/888–7808* ⊕ *www.nps.gov/glac* ▧ *$12* ▤ *AE, D, MC, V* ☯ *Mid-May–mid-Sept.*

★ 🏕 **Many Glacier Campground.** One of the most beautiful spots in the park is also a favorite for bears. Several hiking trails take off from here, and often ranger-led hikes climb to Grinnell Glacier. Scenic boat tours and a lovely lodge are nearby. Always check posted notices for areas or trails closed because of bears. ⚬ *Flush toilets, pit toilets, drinking water, showers, bear boxes, fire grates, picnic tables, food service, public telephone, ranger station, swimming (lake)* ⟿ *110 sites* ✉ *Many Glacier Rd.* ☎ *406/888–7800 or 800/365–2267* 🖷 *406/888–7808* ⊕ *www. nps.gov/glac* ▧ *$14* ▤ *AE, D, MC, V* ☯ *May–Sept.*

🏕 **Rising Sun Campground.** As the name says, you can watch the sun rise from your camp, across the peaks and grassy knolls here. The campground is near St. Mary Lake and many hiking trails. ⚬ *Flush toilets, pit toilets, drinking water, showers, bear boxes, fire grates, picnic tables, food service, public telephone, swimming (lake)* ⟿ *83 sites* ✉ *Going-to-the-Sun Rd.* ☎ *406/888–7800 or 800/365–2267* 🖷 *406/ 888–7808* ⊕ *www.nps.gov/glac* ▧ *$14* ▤ *AE, D, MC, V* ☯ *May–Sept.*

🏕 **St. Mary Campground.** This large, grassy spot alongside the lake and stream has mountain views and cool breezes. It's within walking distance of the St. Mary Visitor Center, and it always seems to be the campground that fills first. ⚬ *Flush toilets, pit toilets, drinking water, showers, bear boxes, fire grates, picnic tables, food service, public telephone, swimming (lake)* ⟿ *173 sites* ✉ *Going-to-the-Sun Rd.* ☎ *406/888–7800 or 800/365–2267* 🖷 *406/888–7808* ⊕ *www.nps.gov/glac* ▧ *$14* ▤ *AE, D, MC, V* ☯ *May–Sept.*

☻ 🏕 **St. Mary Glacier Park KOA.** Just outside the park boundary, this tidy, full-service campground 1 mi west of St. Mary offers everything from hot tubs to canoe rentals, and there's lots for kids to do. From here you can watch glaciers melting into the pristine mountain stream that flows right past the camp into lower St. Mary Lake. At the nightly barbecue dinners (mid-June–Aug.), relax while the sun sets over the lake. ⚬ *Flush toilets, full hookups, dump station, drinking water, guest laundry, showers, picnic tables, food service, electricity, public telephone, general store, swimming (pool)* ⟿ *50 full hookups, 51 partial hookups; 27 cabins* ✉ *106 W. Shore Rd.* ☎ *406/732–4122 or 800/562–1504* 🖷 *406/ 732–4327* ⊕ *www.goglacier.com or www.koa.com* ▧ *$22 tent, $23–$29 partial hookups, $33–$43 full hookups, $49–$159 cabins* ▤ *AE, D, MC, V* ☯ *Mid-May–Sept.*

🏕 **Two Medicine Campground.** Situated next to Two Medicine Lake in the remote southeastern side of the park, this is often the last campground to fill during the height of summer. It's not near a town, but a general store, snack bar, and boat rentals are available. The wind can howl across the lake, so plan to boat early in the day. ⚬ *Flush toilets, pit toilets, drink-*

ing water, showers, bear boxes, fire grates, picnic tables, food service, public telephone, general store, swimming (lake) ⤳ *99 sites* ⊠ *Two Medicine Rd.* ☎ *406/888–7800 or 800/365–2267* 🖷 *406/888–7808* ⊕ *www.nps.gov/glac* 🖃 *$15* ⊟ *AE, D, MC, V* ☉ *May–Sept.*

Shopping

Paintings, photographs, and sculptures by regional artists are available at the **Cedar Tree** (⊠ Apgar Rd. ☎ 406/888–5232).

The **Glacier Natural History Association Bookstore** (⊠ U.S. 2, West Glacier ☎ 406/888–5756 ⊕ www.glacierassociation.org) sells guidebooks, maps, and historical publications at its shop inside the Historic Belton Depot, within the visitor centers of the park, and on its Web site.

Gift shops in the park lodges such as the **Lake McDonald Lodge** (⊠ Going-to-the-Sun Rd. ☎ 406/888–5431) sell keepsakes, postcards, books, T-shirts, and sweatshirts.

Montana House of Gifts (⊠ Apgar Rd. ☎ 406/888–5393) displays weavings and other works of art by local and regional artisans. This is the only gift shop open in winter.

Schoolhouse Gifts (⊠ Apgar Rd. ☎ 406/888–5235) sells clothing and high-quality artists' work.

A Side Trip to Browning

35 mi east of Glacier National Park via U.S. 89.

Browning, to the east of Glacier, is the center of the Blackfeet Nation, whose name is thought to have been derived from the color of their painted or dyed black moccasins. Until the late 19th century, the Blackfeet hunted the great northern buffalo, moving with them across the vast northern plains. At one time, the Blackfeet homeland stretched all the way from the Missouri River north to the Bow and Red Deer rivers in Canada, and from the Rocky Mountains 300 mi east. Rugged terrain and remoteness left Blackfeet territory some of the last Native American country in the contiguous United States to be opened to whites. The 1.5-million-acre reservation was established in 1851 and currently has about 13,000 enrolled tribal members. There's outstanding fly-fishing on the reservation.

★ The **Museum of the Plains Indian**, on the north end of town, houses a stunning collection of ancient artifacts from the Blackfeet, who have lived in the region for 7,000 years, and other Plains peoples. Among the exhibits are clothing, saddlebags, and artwork. ⊠ U.S. 2 at U.S. 89 ☎ 406/338–2230 🖃 $4 ☉ *June–Sept., daily 9–4:45; Oct.–May, weekdays 10–4:30.*

During the second weekend of July, the Blackfeet host the free **North American Indian Days** (⊠ Agency Sq. ☎ 406/338–7276). This gathering of tribes is a pageant of drumming, chanting, traditional games, and teepees as far as the eye can see.

Sports & the Outdoors

The Blackfeet reservation has excellent fly-fishing. A tribal fishing permit is required and is available from tribal officials, outfitters in the area, and Browning's **Tribal Headquarters** (⊠ Public Sq. ☎ 406/338–7521).

Where to Stay

¢–$ 🏨 **Western Motel.** A central location and low rates are this small, modest hotel's highlights. There are few amenities, but the rooms do have microwaves and refrigerators, which make it easy to pack lunches for trips into Glacier National Park. The staff is knowledgeable and willing to answer questions about the reservation and the park. The hotel also accepts Canadian currency. ⊠ *121 Central Ave. E, 59417* ☎ *406/338–7572* 📮 *15 rooms* ⚹ *Microwaves, refrigerators; no room TVs, no smoking* ▤ *AE, D, MC, V.*

CAMPING 🏕 **Aspenwood Campground and RV Park.** A nightly bonfire and teepee rentals are some of the fun, numerous extras at this campground 10 mi west of Browning and 2 mi from Glacier National Park. ⚹ *Flush toilets, partial hookups (electric and water), dump station, drinking water, showers, fire pits, picnic tables, food service, electricity, public telephone, general store, play area* 📮 *10 partial hookups, 9 tent sites; 3 teepees* ⊠ *U.S. 89* ☎ *406/338–3009 or 858/945–1801* ⊕ *www.aspenwoodcamp.com* 📧 *$15 tent sites, $20 partial hookups, $35–$45 tepees* ▤ *MC, V* ☺ *Open June–Sept.*

FLATHEAD & MISSION VALLEYS

Between the Canadian border and Missoula, tree-lined lakes and snowy peaks punctuate glaciated valleys scoured out by ice sheets some 12,000 years ago. A growing destination for golf, boating, skiing, and other outdoor recreation, the fertile Flathead and Mission valleys support ranching and farming, and are becoming known for some of the state's best restaurants.

Flathead Indian Reservation

⑨ *20 mi north of Missoula via U.S. 93.*

Home to the Salish and Kootenai tribes, this 1.2-million-acre reservation is a fascinating historical site. Archaeological evidence indicates that Native Americans were here some 14,000 years ago, but it wasn't until the 1700s that the Kootenai, Salish, and Pend d'Oreille shared common hunting grounds in this area. The people hunted bison, descendants of which you can see at the National Bison Range. When Catholic "Black Robes" arrived to convert the Indians, they built the St. Ignatius Mission. For nature-lovers, the main attractions of the **Flathead Indian Reservation** are fishing and water recreation on numerous lakes and streams and bird-watching in Ninepipe National Wildlife Refuge. Of the approximately 6,950 enrolled tribal members of the **Confederated Salish and Kootenai Tribes** (🏠 Box 278, Pablo 59855 ☎ 406/675–2700, 406/657–0160, or 888/835–8766 ⊕ www.cskt.org), about 4,500 live on the reservation, which is interspersed with non-Indian ranches and other property. Both tribes celebrate their heritage during the annual July Powwow.

BIG COUNTRY, BRIEF HISTORY

SCRAPED BY RECEDING GLACIERS and chiseled by weather, the landscape of northwest Montana has a long history, but the region's human history is relatively recent. The earliest Native Americans probably settled here between 10,000 and 12,000 years ago, or traveled through in search of bison herds east of the Rockies. Today, the Confederated Salish and Kootenai tribes live on the Flathead Indian Reservation spread out across the Mission and Flathead valleys; their People's Center is one of the state's best displays of native culture and history.

Explorers such as Lewis and Clark looked at but mostly didn't touch the riches—timber, wild game, and emerald lakes—of northwest Montana, and more permanent white settlers didn't arrive until they had depleted goldfields in other areas of the West. Many of the frontier communities are only now celebrating centennial anniversaries. Even so, the area claims some of Montana's oldest structures, such as St. Mary's Mission, the first Catholic mission in the Northwest, and Fort Connah, a Hudson's Bay Company fur-trading post. During the race across the continent, three railroads laid track through Glacier Country, leaving in their wake elegant train stations and a heritage of rail travel.

Historic sites throughout northwest Montana offer a glimpse back at the rough-and-tumble old days, but the wild lands and wildlife are what you'll write home about. On the National Bison Range, you'll see descendants of the last few free-roaming American bison. Watch for birds of prey wherever you go. From the Lee Metcalf National Wildlife Refuge to the Bob Marshall Wilderness to Glacier National Park, elk, bighorn sheep, mountain goats, and bears thrive. All of these critters are living reminders of centuries of Montana history.

☎ 406/675–0160 ⊕ *indiannations.visitmt.com/flathead.shtm* ⊠ *Free* ⊙ *Weekdays 9–5.*

★ The **Sqelix'u/Aqfsmakni-k Cultural Center (The People's Center)** exhibits artifacts, photographs, and recordings concerning the Salish, Kootenai, and Pend d'Oreille people. The People's Center oversees educational programs, guided interpretive tours, outdoor traditional lodges, and annual festivals. A gift shop sells both traditional and nontraditional work by local artists and craftspeople. ⊠ *53253 U.S. 93 W, Pablo, 6 mi south of Polson* ☎ *406/883–5344 or 800/883–5344* ⊕ *www.peoplescenter. org* ⊠ *$3* ⊙ *Apr.–Sept., weekdays 9–6, Sat. 10–6; Oct.–Mar., weekdays 9–5.*

Fodor'sChoice
★ The Red Sleep Mountain Drive, a 19-mi loop road at the **National Bison Range,** allows close-up views of bison, elk, pronghorn, deer, and mountain sheep. The gravel road rises 2,000 feet and takes about two hours to complete; you're required to begin the drive no later than 6 PM and to finish before the gate closes at dark. The 19,000-acre refuge at the foot of the Mission Mountains was established in 1908 by Theodore Roosevelt. Today the U.S. Fish and Wildlife Service ranches a herd of 400 bison. A visitor center explains the history, habits, and habitat of

the bison. To reach the bison range, follow the signs west, then north from the junction of U.S. 93 and Route 200 in Ravalli. ⊠ *132 Bison Range Rd., Moiese* ☎ *406/644–2211* ⊕ *bisonrange.fws.gov* 💰 *$4 per vehicle* ☉ *Mid-May–Sept., daily 7 AM–9 PM; Oct.–mid-May, weekdays 8–4:30.*

Established in 1846 as a Hudson's Bay Company trading post, **Fort Connah** was used by fur traders until 1871. Of the original three buildings, one remains today; it's believed to be the oldest building still standing in Montana. You can't go inside, but a historical marker details events and inhabitants. ⊠ *U.S. 93 at Post Creek, between St. Ignatius and Charlo* ☎ *406/676–0256 or 406/549–4431* ⊕ *www.montanaweb.com/ftconnah/* 💰 *Donations accepted* ☉ *Dawn–dusk.*

The **St. Ignatius Mission**—a church, cabin, and collection of other buildings—was built in the 1890s with bricks made of local clay by missionaries and Native Americans. The 58 murals on the walls and ceilings of the church were used to teach Bible stories to the natives. In the St. Ignatius Mission Museum (an old log cabin) there's an exhibit of early artifacts and arts and crafts. The mission is still a functioning church; mass is held several mornings a week. To reach the mission from St. Ignatius, take Main Street south to Mission Drive. ⊠ *1 Catholic Mission Dr.* ☎ *406/ 745–2768* 💰 *Donations accepted* ☉ *Mid-Mar.–mid-Oct., daily 9–9; mid-Oct.–mid-Mar., daily 9–5.*

Sprawling **Ninepipe National Wildlife Refuge** is *the* place for bird-watchers. This 2,000-acre wetland complex in the shadow of the Mission Mountains is home to everything from marsh hawks to kestrels to red-winged blackbirds. Flanking both sides of U.S .93 are rookeries for double-crested cormorants and great blue herons; bald eagles fish here in the winter. Roads (including U.S. 93) through the center of the refuge are closed March through mid-July during nesting season, but you can drive along the periphery throughout the year. Maps are available from the nearby National Bison Range, which manages Ninepipe. ⊠ *132 Bison Range Rd.* ☎ *406/644–2211* ⊕ *www.fws.gov/bisonrange/ninepipe/.*

off the beaten path

SYMES HOT SPRINGS HOTEL AND MINERAL BATHS – Truly a unique find on the western edge of the Flathead Indian Reservation, this rustic 1928 hotel has hot mineral pools from continuously flowing springs, spa treatments, massage, live music on weekends, and organic food in its restaurant. The hotel itself isn't a standout, though the rates ($45–$110 for a room) are reasonable. Several historic hot springs in the area attracted Native Americans for centuries. ⊠ *209 Wall St., Hot Springs* ☎ *406/741–2361 or 888/ 305–3106* ⊕ *www.symeshotsprings.com* 💰 *Baths $7* ☉ *Daily 8 AM–11 PM.*

Where to Stay & Eat

$–$$$$ ✕ **Ninepipes Lodge.** On the edge of the Ninepipe National Wildlife Refuge, the lodge has views of the snow-tipped Mission Mountains and the native-grass-edged wetlands full of birds. Dinners include tasty all-natural Angus beef steaks, seafood, and specials like beer-battered catfish or mushroom quesadillas. Breakfast is served on Saturday only. You can find inexpensive lodging here too ($50–$75) as well as an art gallery and a trading post next door. ⊠ *41000 US Highway 93, Charlo* ☎ *406/644–2588* ⚑ *Reservations essential* ▤ *AE, MC, V.*

¢–$$$$ ▦ **Cheff's Guest Ranch and Outfitters.** This 10,000-acre working cattle ranch at the base of the Mission Mountains lets you take part in ranching life in the summer and conducts pack trips from September through November. Hearty breakfasts start off days of trail rides, fishing for trout, bass, bullhead, and perch, and exploration on the nearby Ninepipe National Wildlife Refuge and Kicking Horse Reservoir in the valley below. Guests can join in duties such as milking cows, moving stock, and bucking bales of hay. A full range of options is available, from rooms with no services to cabins with all-inclusive packages. ⊠ *4274 Eagle Pass Trail, Charlo 59824* ☎ *406/644–2557* ₰ *406/644–2611* ⊕ *www.cheffguestranch.com* ➾ *7 rooms, 3 with bath; 2 cabins* ♨ *Dining room, some kitchens, some microwaves, pond, hot tub, fishing, mountain bikes, badminton, basketball, hiking, horseback riding, horseshoes, Ping-Pong, volleyball, library, piano, recreation room, shop, laundry facilities, meeting rooms, airport shuttle; no a/c, no room phones, no TV in some rooms, no smoking* ▤ *AE, MC, V* ☉ *Closed Dec.–May* ⏆ *FAP.*

☾ ¢–$$ ▦ **Twin Creek B&B.** The setting is first-rate at this contemporary B&B: two creeks meander through the property, located under the spectacular Mission Mountains, with views of Mission Valley farmland. Two tepees—you may stay in them for the ultimate Western night—and the resident St. Bernard dogs are popular with kids. Breakfast consists of homemade biscuits and huckleberry jam, ham, and eggs any way you like them. ⊠ *2295 Twin Creek Rd., Ronan 59864* ☎ *406/676–8800 or 877/524–8946* ₰ *406/676–2662* ⊕ *www.twincreeksbb.com* ➾ *7 rooms, 2 tepees* ♨ *Dining room, room service, in-room VCRs, in-room data ports, hot tub, spa, fishing, shop, babysitting, laundry facilities, business services, meeting rooms, free parking, some pets allowed; no smoking, no a/c* ▤ *AE, MC, V* ⏆ *BP.*

CAMPING ⛺ **Mission Meadows RV.** This grassy meadow near the highway is conveniently located near the bison range and fishing. ♨ *Flush toilets, full hookups, dump station, drinking water, guest laundry, showers, fire pits, picnic tables, food service, electricity, public telephone, general store* ➾ *20 full hookups, 70 partial hookups, 30 tent sites* ⊠ *205-102 Mud Creek La., 2 mi north of Ronan* ☎ *406/676–5182* ₰ *406/676–5182* ⌨ *$12 tent sites, $24 partial hookups, $29 full hookups* ▤ *D, MC.*

The Arts

☾ For more than a century, the four-day powwow during the **Arlee 4th of July Celebration** (⊠ Pow-Wow Rd., ½ mi east of U.S. 93, Arlee ☎ 406/745–0023 ⊕ www.visitmt.com) has drawn Native Americans from all over the West. Highlights are drumming, dancing, and singing contests; the parade; the traditional encampment; and arts, crafts, and food vendors. Gambling includes traditional stick games.

Shopping

The **Flathead Indian Museum and Trading Post** (✉ 1 Museum La., on U.S. 93, St. Ignatius ☎ 406/745–2951) has an extensive collection of authentic artifacts from local Native American tribes. On sale are arts, crafts, books, maps, and gifts.

Flathead Lake

⑩ *12 mi north of Ronan via U.S. 93.*

The 370-foot-deep Flathead Lake, with 180 mi of shoreline, is the largest natural freshwater lake in the western United States. It's a wonderful—and popular—place for sailing, fishing, and swimming. Wildhorse Island State Park, located in the lake, is home to bighorn sheep and other wildlife; the 2,165-acre island can be reached only by private boat. Cherry groves line the lake's shores, and toward the end of July farmers harvest them and sell cherries at roadside stands along the two highways that encircle the lake.

Polson, a quiet community of 4,000 on the southern edge of Flathead Lake, sits under the morning shadow of the jagged Mission Mountains. It's the largest town on the Flathead Indian Reservation. Picnic spots, lake access, and playgrounds are found at Boettcher, Sacajawea, and Riverside parks. Some other parks are for tribal members only; signs identify picnic areas that are closed to the public.

The Swan River empties into Flathead Lake at the small, idyllic resort community of **Bigfork.** The small town is filled with shops, galleries, restaurants, and a cultural center. Many summer events are so popular that you should make dinner and playhouse reservations a month in advance. This is a great spot to browse after you're finished with your outdoor activities. The rotating exhibits at **Bigfork Art and Cultural Center** (✉ 525 Electric Ave. ☎ 406/837–6927) display bronzes, paintings, and works in other mediums by Montana artists.

off the beaten path

MISSION MOUNTAINS WILDERNESS COMPLEX – From much of the Mission Valley and Flathead Indian Reservation you can see the Mission Mountains, on which there's a 73,877-acre wilderness area full of hiking, camping, and fishing opportunities. The area is probably best known for the 1,000-foot drops of Elizabeth and Mission falls. Glorious McDonald Peak looms at 9,280 feet; it's a favorite of grizzly bears, who gather on the snow fields to eat swarms of cutworm moths and ladybugs. Those who aren't tribal members must obtain a recreation permit to hike, fish, and camp here among the mountain lions, lynx, wolverines, black bears, and grizzlies. Recreational permits are available at local grocery and sporting-goods stores and most gas stations. Call the Flathead National Forest at the number below for camping permits and information on the recreation permits. ✉ *Mission Reservoir Rd., off U.S. 93* ☎ *406/758–5200* 🎫 *Recreational permit $25* ⊗ *Daily.*

Sports & the Outdoors

BOATING **Absolute Water Sport Rentals** (⊠ 303 U.S. 93, Polson ☎ 406/883–3900 or 800/358–8046) has everything from canoes and sea kayaks to deck boats and fishing boats. At **Dayton Yacht Harbor** (⊠ 299 C St., Dayton ☎ 406/849–5423 or 800/775–2990) you can rent a sailboat, go on an excursion, take sailing lessons, or moor your own sailboat near Wild Horse and Cromwell islands.

★ One of the most pleasant ways to see the lake is to take a **two-hour sail** (⊠ 150 Flathead Lake Lodge Rd., Bigfork ☎ 406/837–4391) on the historic *Questa* or the *Nor'Easter,* both 51-foot Q-class racing sloops built in the 1920s. They depart from Flathead Lake Lodge.

FISHING Take a charter trip on Flathead Lake with **A-Able Fishing Charters & Tours** (⊠ 63 Twin Acres Dr., Kalispell ☎ 406/257–5214 or 800/231–5214) to fish for lake trout and mackinaw. They take individuals and groups of up to 18 people. Fly-fish with **Two River Gear and Outfitter** (⊠ 603 Electric Ave., Bigfork ☎ 406/837–3474) on local streams, rivers, and lakes.

GOLF Wonderful views of mountains and Flathead Lake from **Eagle Bend** (⊠ 279 Eagle Bend Dr., Bigfork ☎ 406/837–7300 or 800/255–5641) are matched by the golfing on the 27-hole course. Each of the 27 holes of the **Polson Country Club** (⊠ 111 Bayview Dr. ☎ 406/883–8230 or 800/392–9795 ⊕ www.polsoncountryclub.com) has a view of the Mission and Swan mountain ranges and Flathead Lake.

HIKING **Jewel Basin Hiking Area** (⊠ 10 mi east of Bigfork via Hwy. 83 and Echo Lake Rd.) provides 35 mi of well-maintained trails among 27 trout-filled FodorsChoice alpine lakes. You'll find the nearest phone and hearty to-go trail lunches ★ at the Echo Lake Cafe at the junction of Hwy. 83 and Echo Lake Road. The **U.S. Forest Service** (⊠ 200 Ranger Station Rd. ☎ 406/837–7500) in Bigfork sells hiking maps.

KAYAKING World-class kayaking on the Swan River's Wild Mile draws boaters and spectators to the white water during spring and summer runoff. The annual **Bigfork Whitewater Festival** (⊠ 8155 Hwy. 35, Old Town Center, Bigfork ☎ 406/837–5888) celebrates the torrent every Memorial Day weekend with a water rodeo, races, and entertainment at local pubs and eateries.

MOUNTAIN Hundred of miles of unpaved roads are perfect for biking. Group tours, BIKING rentals and maps are available at **Mountain Mike's Rental Bikes** (⊠ 417 Bridge St., Bigfork ☎ 406/837–2453).

RAFTING Eight white-water miles of the lower Flathead River are covered by **Flathead Raft Co.** (⊠ 1503 U.S. 93 S, across from Super 1 Foods ☎ 406/883–5838 or 800/654–4359 ⊕ www.flatheadraftco.com). From June through September it provides wild rafting adventures, kayaking, and Native American interpretive trips between Kerr Dam and Buffalo Bridge. The outfitter will design family floats suitable for any age.

SKIING As you schuss runs of **Blacktail Mountain Ski Area** (⊠ Blacktail Mountain Rd., Lakeside ☎ 406/844–0999 ⊕ www.blacktailmountain.com), you'll glimpse Flathead Lake and surrounding peaks. This family-friendly mountain is known for inexpensive lift tickets; uncrowded, mostly intermediate slopes; a lovely log-accented lodge; and friendly staff.

Where to Stay & Eat

★ $$$–$$$$ ✕ **La Provence.** The garden dining here offers a flower-studded view down Bigfork's main street. Local artists' work decorates the whitewashed walls. The owner-chef specializes in French onion soup with Gruyère cheese served inside a large onion, and specials like venison tenderloin with figs and Bordeaux sauce. An international wine list and a traditional chocolate soufflé round out the Mediterranean meals. ⊠ *408 Bridge St., Bigfork* ☎ *406/837–2923* ⊟ *AE, MC, V* ☉ *Closed Sun.*

★ $$–$$$$ ✕ **Showthyme!** In Bigfork's former bank building, built in 1908, diners opt for street- or bay-side seating, or a table in the snug bank vault. Signature dishes include fresh ahi tuna with sweet soy ginger and wasabi over jasmine rice and locally raised organic beef. Save room for Benedictine chocolate truffle pie. ⊠ *548 Electric Ave., Bigfork* ☎ *406/ 837–0707* ⊟ *AE, DC, MC, V* ☉ *Closed Jan. No lunch.*

$$–$$$ ✕ **Swan River Café and Dinner House.** This relaxed yet elegant eatery serves such dishes as a succulent rack of lamb, pork tenderloin, pastas, fresh halibut in a sour cream-dill sauce, and fondues (which require advance reservation) inside or on the terrace overlooking Bigfork Bay. The Sunday brunch and dinner buffets are popular especially for the prime rib and Alaskan king salmon. ⊠ *360 Grand Ave., Bigfork* ☎ *406/837–2220* ⊟ *AE, D, MC, V.*

☉ $$$$ ▥ **Averill's Flathead Lake Lodge.** Since 1945 Averill's has been providing families a wholesome and active Western getaway. The beautiful green grounds are on the shore of the lake, where beach fires, canoeing, and sailing take place. The lodge, accommodations, and other buildings are all log-and-stone structures. Horseback rides set out both in the morning and evening, and you can learn to rope in the rodeo arena. Many activities such as rafting and guided fishing trips are available for an extra cost. It's BYOB at the bar. October through May, the lodge is open for corporate retreats only. ⊠ *150 Flathead Lake Lodge Rd., Flathead 59911* ☎ *406/837–4391* 🖷 *406/837–6977* ⊕ *www.averills.com* ⤶ *20 rooms, 20 cottages* ♨ *Dining room, 4 tennis courts, pool, lake, beach, boating, waterskiing, fishing, hiking, horseback riding, horseshoes, volleyball, children's programs (ages 3 and up), airport shuttle; no room TVs, no a/c, no smoking* ⊟ *AE, MC, V* ☉ *FAP.*

★ $$$–$$$$ ▥ **Mountain Lake Lodge.** This resort perched above crystalline Flathead Lake offers 30 well-appointed suites surrounding an outdoor pool on meticulously groomed grounds. From your room, enjoy sweeping views of the lake (best from the lakeside lodges) and surrounding mountains. The hotel is well situated for hiking, golfing, rafting, and lake cruising. The log-accented dining room is designed to let you watch the sunset while enjoying smoked pheasant and other delicacies. The dining room is open seasonally; the bar serves light dinners year-round. ⊠ *1950 Sylvan Dr. at Hwy. 35 mile marker 26.5, Bigfork 59911* ☎ *406/837–3800 or 877/823–4923* 🖷 *406/837–3861* ⊕ *www.mountainlakelodge.com* ⤶ *30 suites* ♨ *Restaurant, cable TV, pool, hot tub, bar, no-smoking rooms* ⊟ *AE, DC, MC, V.*

$$–$$$$ ⚏ **Marina Cay Resort and Conference Center.** In summer it's fun to arrive at this waterfront resort by boat; you can tie up next to the popular outdoor Tiki Bar. Most of the large, plainly decorated rooms here have views of Bigfork Bay. Luxury suites have private hot tubs, balconies, or patios. Nearby golf courses get lots of use from the guests. ⊠ *180 Vista La., Bigfork 59911* ☎ *406/837–5861 or 800/433–6516* 🖷 *406/837– 1118* ⊕ *www.marinacay.com* ⤳ *65 rooms* ⚏ *Restaurant, café, snack bar, some kitchens, cable TV, in-room data ports, pool, hot tub, dock, boating, jet skiing, marina, waterskiing, fishing, bicycles, bar, casino, shop, babysitting, laundry facilities, business services, convention center, no-smoking rooms* ⊟ *AE, D, MC, V.*

$–$$$ ⚏ **O'Duach'ain Country Inn Bed & Breakfast.** In a quiet lodgepole-pine forest outside of Bigfork, with horses grazing next door, this cozy and comfy B&B consists of a log home and guesthouse. The main house is light filled and has two stone fireplaces and a wraparound terrace; full breakfasts are served at a long dining room table. Each room is individually decorated in Old West style and the room in the main house has a step-up Queen Anne–style bed. The inn is a fun place for a wedding. ⊠ *675 Ferndale Dr., Bigfork 59911* ☎ *406/837–6851 or 800/837–7460* 🖷 *406/ 837–0778* ⊕ *www.montanainn.com* ⤳ *4 rooms, 1 suite* ⚏ *Dining room, hot tub, hiking; no room TVs, no a/c, no smoking* ⊟ *AE, MC, V* ⦿❘ *BP.*

CAMPING ⛺ **Flathead Lake state parks.** Five lakeside parks are scattered around Flathead, offering quiet camping, boat launches, and good views. Bigfork's Wayfarers, Lakeside's West Shore, and Polson's Big Arm, Finley Point, and Yellow Bay parks are all owned by Montana Fish, Wildlife and Parks. Reservations are a good idea in summer, as spots fill up fast with motor homes. Tent camps and canoe camps are reserved until early afternoon. ⚏ *Pit toilets, drinking water, fire grates, picnic tables, swimming (lake)* ⤳ *273 tent sites* ⊠ *490 N. Meridian Rd., Kalispell* ☎ *406/ 752–5501* 🖷 *406/257–0349* ⊕ *www.fwp.state.mt.us* ▣ *$15* ⊙ *May–Sept.*

☉ ⛺ **Polson/Flathead KOA.** Perched above Flathead Lake with incredible views of the Mission and Swan mountains, this grassy spot is convenient to the lake and town, and hosts can direct you to fossil and arrowhead hunting. Cabins have front porch swings. ⚏ *Flush toilets, full hookups, dump station, drinking water, guest laundry, showers, fire pits, picnic tables, electricity, public telephone, general store, play area, swimming (pool)* ⤳ *31 full hookups, 23 partial hookups, 21 tent sites; 12 cabins* ⊠ *200 Irving Flat Rd., Polson* ☎ *406/883–2130 or 800/562– 2130* 🖷 *406/883–0151* ⊕ *www.flatheadlakekoa.com* ▣ *$19–$28 tent sites, $27–$60 RV sites, $48–$160 cabins/cottages* ⊟ *AE, D, MC, V* ⊙ *Mid-Apr.–mid Oct.*

The Arts

Mid-May through early September, the repertory group **Bigfork Summer Playhouse** (⊠ 526 Electric Ave. ☎ 406/837–4886 ⊕ www. bigforksummerplayhouse.com) presents Broadway musicals and comedies every night except Sunday in the Bigfork Center for the Performing Arts. Phone orders for tickets are available from mid-May to the end of August, or by mail beginning in April. Children's workshops and theater are held in the same facility.

Enjoy summer theater with the **Port Polson Players** (⊠ Boetcher Park, U.S. 93 ☎ 406/883–9212). The high-quality amateur troupe puts on musicals, comedies, and dramas.

Summer Sundays at Bigfork's Everit L. Sliter Memorial Park hear live music—from orchestral to salsa—performed by local musicians and regionally known bands at the **River Bend Stage** (⊠ Bridge St. ☎ 406/837–4400).

Shopping

Bigfork's Electric Avenue is lined with galleries and eclectic gift shops and is recognized for unparalleled dining and sweets. Try the soft cookies and hot-out-of-the-oven cinnamon rolls baked daily and shipped nationwide from **Brookies Cookies** (⊠ 191 Mill St. ☎ 406/837–2447).

Filled to the brim with Montana history, regional travel, and other unique books, **Electric Avenue Books** (⊠ 490 Electric Ave. ☎ 406/837–6072) is a comfortable setting in which to browse. The shopkeeper offers tips on local events, restaurants, and out-of-the-way places.

Electric Avenue Gifts (⊠ 459 Electric Ave. ☎ 406/837–4994) carries folk-art gifts and souvenirs.

On Tuesday and Thursday in summer, see award-winning sculptor Eric Thorsen at work on clay sculptures and wood carvings in his studio, across the street from **Eric Thorsen Fine Art Gallery** (⊠ 547 Electric Ave. ☎ 406/837–4366).

You can pick up a tiny jar of huckleberry jam or honey at **Eva Gates Homemade Preserves** (⊠ 456 Electric Ave. ☎ 406/837–4356) or have one of the family-size jars of various berry flavors shipped back home.

The not-for-profit **Sandpiper Gallery** (⊠ 2 1st Ave., Polson ☎ 406/883–5956), located inside the Polson public library, shows the work of local and regional artists and presents an annual art show on the courthouse lawn the first Saturday in August.

en route When the last glacier receded from the area 10,000 years ago it left a 100-foot depth of fertile soil called glacier loam, perfect for agriculture. Two scenic routes—Hwy. 35 to Creston and Hwy. 82 to Kalispell—traverse this land, heading north from Bigfork, over the Flathead River (look for osprey nests atop poles), through fields of mint, seed potatoes, and hay, and past tree nurseries. **Gatiss Gardens** (⊠ 4790 Hwy. 35, at Broeder Loop Rd., Creston, 8 mi north of Bigfork ☎ 406/755–2418) has a gentle 1¼-mi trail past hundreds of perennials, bulbs, and shrubs.

Kalispell

⓫ *20 mi northwest of Bigfork via Hwy. 35.*

Main Street (U.S. 93) in busy downtown Kalispell is lined with galleries, jewelry stores, boutiques, and restaurants. This century-old city, the Flathead County seat, is a regional business and retail center for people from northwest Montana. An Andrew Carnegie library is now home to the Hockaday Museum of Art, and just a few blocks away, Kalispell's first school building has been turned into the Central School Museum. Pick up visitor information at the historic Great Northern Depot.

You can ring the old school bell at the **Central School Museum,** an 1894 Romanesque building. In the museum are galleries, activities, and displays concerning regional heritage and history. You'll also find a café, museum store, conference rooms, and reference library. ⊠ *124 2nd Ave. E* ☎ *406/756–8381* ⊕ *www.yourmuseum.org* ☑ *$5* ☉ *June–Aug., Mon.–Sat. 10–5; Sept.–May., Tues.–Sat. 10–5.*

A town highlight is the **Conrad Mansion National Historic Site Museum,** a 26-room Norman-style mansion that was the home of C. E. Conrad, the manager of a freighter on the Missouri River and the founder of Kalispell. Docents offer specialized tours for kids that focus on the clothing, activities, and food of the turn-of-the-20th-century era. Come Christmas, the mansion is lavishly decorated and filled with the wares of local artisans. ⊠ *4th St. between 6th and Woodland* ☎ *406/755–2166* ⊕ *www.conradmansion.com* ☑ *$8* ☉ *Guided tours mid-May–mid-Oct., Tues.–Sun., 10–4 on the hour; Christmas at the Mansion tours Thanksgiving–late Dec., Wed.–Sat., 11, 1 and 3.*

The **Hockaday Museum of Art,** housed in the renovated Carnegie library, presents contemporary art exhibits. The museum hosts the annual Hockaday Arts in the Park in late July at Depot Park, where vendors from around the Northwest sell fine art and crafts. ⊠ *302 2nd Ave. E, at 3rd St.* ☎ *406/755–5268* ⊕ *www.hockadayartmuseum.org* ☑ *$5* ☉ *June–Aug., Tues.–Fri. 10–6, Sat. 10–5, Sun. noon–4; Sept.–May, Tues.–Sat. 10–5.*

One of 20 city green spaces, **Woodland Park** has a popular swimming pool, a playground, ball fields, and a picnic area. Geese, ducks, peacocks, and black swans flutter to the pond, which in winter opens for ice-skating; there's a warming hut nearby. ⊠ *Conrad Dr. and Woodland Dr.* ☎ *406/758–7718 or 406/758–2800* ⊕ *www.kalispellchamber.com* ☑ *Free* ☉ *Daily dawn–dusk.*

Inside the historic **Great Northern Depot** is visitor information from the Kalispell Chamber of Commerce and the Flathead Convention and Visitors Bureau. Outside is the lovely Depot Park, where live music, arts shows, a gazebo, picnicking, and a playground attract both locals and travelers. ⊠ *15 Depot Park* ☎ *406/758–2800 or 800/543–3105* ⊕ *www. kalispellchamber.com* ☑ *Free* ☉ *Weekdays 8–5.*

off the beaten path

LONE PINE STATE PARK – At an elevation of 2,959 feet, you can view Kalispell, Flathead Lake, and the Whitefish Mountain Range from this 186-acre park. Features include a self-guided nature trail, a visitor center, nature interpretive programs, picnic areas, horse trails, and an archery range. ⊠ *4 mi southwest of Kalispell on Foyes Lake Rd., then 1 mi east on Lone Pine Rd.* ☎ *406/755–2706* ⊕ *www.fwp. state.mt.us* ☑ *$5 per vehicle* ☉ *Mid-Apr.–Oct., daily dawn–dusk.*

Sports & the Outdoors

GOLF   At **Big Mountain Golf Club** (⊠ 3230 U.S. 93 N ☏ 406/751–1950 or 800/ 255–5641) the challenging 18-hole links-style course has rolling fairways lined with native grasses and giant pine trees along the Stillwater River.

At one time, a private herd of bison grazed on what's now **Buffalo Hill Golf Club** (⊠ 116 N. Main ☏ 406/756–4530 or 888/342–1619 ⊕ www. golfbuffalohill.com) in the heart of Kalispell. This municipal 27-hole course, built in 1936, has tree-lined fairways along the Stillwater River.

HIKING   Every year from May through October, the **Montana Wilderness Association** (⊠ 43 Woodland Park Dr., No. 9 ☏ 406/755–6304 ⊕ www. wildmontana.org) offers free Wilderness Walks booklets describing dozens of trails in state. Join one of their free guided backcountry hikes, which vary from short wildflower walks to strenuous climbs.

SKYDIVING   Learn the fun of parachuting with **Skydive Lost Prairie** (⊠ Lost Prairie Rd.; 40 mi west of Kalispell on U.S. 2 to milepost 87, 4 mi north on Lost Prairie Rd. ☏ 406/858–2493 or 888/833–5867 ⊕ www. skydivelostprairie.com), where annually nearly 500 skydivers make about 7,000 jumps, some at the annual July Lost Prairie gathering, the largest gathering of skydivers in the northwestern U.S., with 400 to 500 jumpers.

TRAIL RIDING   Ride on an 800-acre ranch with **High Country Trails** (⊠ 2800 Foy's Lake Rd. ☏ 406/755–1283 or 406/755–4711), which also offers evening rides with an old-fashioned steak cookout.

Where to Stay & Eat

$$–$$$$ ✕ **Cafe Max.** The menu changes frequently in this cozy Main Street bistro. Appetizers, such as basil-lemon zest crepe with local goat cheese, are likely to have a French influence, whereas entrées have a Montana twist. Try the grilled buffalo fillet with huckleberry sauce or grilled Arctic char with poached prawns in basil and citrus butter. ⊠ *121 Main St.* ☏ *406/755–7687* ▤ *AE, MC, V* ⊗ *Closed Mon.*

$$–$$$$ ✕ **Painted Horse Grill.** Though the decor here is unusually bland, what's delivered to your table is likely to grab your attention. The calamari tempura is wonderfully tender, and cumin in the chiles rellenos gives the Southwestern appetizer an Indian twist. You can catch up on your vegetable intake here, as the salad greens are the freshest in the area and the cooked vegetables are nicely steamed. You can't go wrong with the creative entrées, including the roast curried duck. ⊠ *110 Main St.* ☏ *406/257–7035* ▤ *AE, MC, V* ⊗ *Closed Sun. No lunch Sat.*

$$–$$$ ✕ **Jordan's Barbecue.** Locals rave about the smoked ribs with Jordan's Juice—a potion that you can take home by the bottle. Try the stuffed baked potatoes, too. ⊠ *32 Village Loop, at the junction of Whitefish Stage Rd. and W. Evergreen* ☏ *406/755–9192* ▤ *AE, D, MC, V* ⊗ *Closed Sun.*

$$–$$$ ✕ **The Knead Cafe.** Come here for the best bread and soup in the valley. The café's baked goods, including croissants, fresh baguettes, and chocolate cakes, will entice you in, but it's worth your while to stay for a meal— try the curry shrimp or the New Orleans gumbo with shrimp and

chicken. The funky, mismatched dining tables and chairs are surrounded by local artwork. ✉ *25 2nd Ave. W* ☎ *406/755–7510* 🖃 *MC, V* ⊗ *No dinner Sun.*

$$–$$$$ 🏨 **Hampton Inn Kalispell.** This hotel 1 mi west of downtown features an indoor 24-hour guest pool and free extended buffet breakfast. The spacious rooms, Western decor, and river-rock fireplace in the lobby give the place a homey feel. ✉ *1140 U.S. 2 W, 59901* ☎ *406/755–7900 or 800/426–7866* 🖷 *406/755–5056* ⊕ *www.northwestinns.com* 📫 *120 rooms* ⚬ *Refrigerators, cable TV, in-room VCRs, indoor pool, no-smoking rooms* 🖃 *AE, D, DC, MC, V* �📶 *BP.*

$$$ 🏨 **WestCoast Kalispell Center Hotel.** Attached to the downtown Kalispell Center Mall, this no-surprises hotel has large, modern rooms and a solarium pool. The restaurant is well lighted by an atrium ceiling. ✉ *20 N. Main St., 59901* ☎ *406/751–5050 or 800/325–4000* 🖷 *406/751–5051* ⊕ *www.westcoasthotels.rdln.com* 📫 *132 rooms* ⚬ *Restaurant, cable TV, indoor pool, lounge, casino, business services, meeting rooms, free parking, no-smoking rooms* 🖃 *AE, D, DC, MC, V.*

$–$$ 🏨 **Cottonwood Hill Farm Inn.** In this renovated farmhouse, the three elegantly appointed guest rooms have views of the valley and surrounding peaks. Breakfasts, which can be taken outside on the deck, include panfried lake trout, fruits grown on the farm, and fresh baked goods with homemade jams and jellies; you can opt to take lunch and dinner here as well. The location is convenient to golf and water sports. ✉ *2928 Whitefish Stage Rd., 59901* ☎ *406/756–6404 or 800/458–0893* 🖷 *406/756–8507* ⊕ *www.cottonwoodhillfarm.com* 📫 *3 rooms* ⚬ *Dining room, room service, in-room VCRs, in-room data ports, bicycles, badminton, croquet, business services; no a/c, no kids under 12, no smoking* 🖃 *AE, MC, V* �📶 *BP.*

CAMPING ⛺ **Glacier Pines RV Park.** A bit of forest in the city, this spacious campground set among pines has paved roads and no maximum size limit or time limit. There are no tent sites, and it's open year-round. ⚬ *Flush toilets, full hookups, dump station, drinking water, guest laundry, showers, fire pits, picnic tables, electricity, public telephone, general store, play area, swimming (pool)* 📫 *75 full hookups* ✉ *1850 Hwy. 35 E, 1 mi east of Kalispell* ☎ *406/752–2760 or 800/533–4029* ⊕ *www.glacierpines.com* 💲 *$24* 🖃 *MC, V.*

Nightlife & the Arts

THE ARTS Live performances take place each Tuesday and Wednesday from 11:30 to 1:30 at **Depot Park** (✉ 1 Depot Park ☎ 406/758–7718). Performers vary from a one-man blues band to Montana mytho-poet entertainer Jack Gladstone.

★ For four days every October, the **Glacier Jazz Stampede** (✉ 1 Depot Park ☎ 406/755–6088 or 888/888–2308 ⊕ www.kalispellchamber.com/jazz) brings 15 toe-tapping jazz bands to four venues around downtown Kalispell and the surrounding valley.

Voices of the mountains blend at concerts by the **Glacier Orchestra and Chorale** (✉ 140 Main St. ☎ 406/257–3241), held in several venues around Kalispell and Whitefish.

NIGHTLIFE Cowboy boots and sneakers kick up the sawdust and peanut shells on the floor at **Moose's Saloon** (✉ 173 N. Main ☎ 406/755–2337), where tunes from the jukebox get the raucous crowd moving. You can order pizza to go with your beer.

Shopping

Browse through the large selection of Montana authors in **Books West** (✉ 101 Main St. ☎ 406/752–6900 or 800/471–2270), where you will find Western Americana, gifts, and U.S. Geological Survey maps.

Noice Studio and Gallery (✉ 127 Main St. ☎ 406/755–5321) features ongoing exhibits of paintings, sculpture, fiber arts, and photography by Montana artists such as Rudy Autio, Russell Chatham, and Marshall Noice, in a lovingly restored turn-of-the-20th-century building.

Sportsman Ski Haus (✉ U.S. 2 and U.S. 93 ☎ 406/755–6484 or 406/862–3111) is a good place to pick up skis, outdoor gear, clothing, and fishing tackle. It also has a store in Whitefish's Mountain Mall.

Whitefish

12 *15 mi north of Kalispell via U.S. 93.*

A hub for golfing, lake recreation, hiking, mountain biking, and skiing, Whitefish sits at the base of Big Mountain Ski and Summer Resort. Nine lifts serve 3,000 acres of powder skiing and provide outstanding winter and summer views (the mountain is closed mid-April–early June and late September–mid-November) into Glacier National Park and the Canadian Rockies. At Whitefish Lake, Native Americans once caught and dried whitefish. Euro-American settlers came a century ago to farm or join the timber or railroad industries; the sporty resort town now has 5,000 residents.

Skiers descend Big Mountain late fall through early spring, while summer attracts hikers to the Danny On Trail. The trail leads to the mountain summit, which can also be accessed via the Glacier Chaser chairlift. Numerous other activities, such as a kids' bike academy, art treks, art and music festivals, and nighttime stargazing events, keep the mountain busy throughout the warmer months. You can tackle mountain-bike trails, rent mountain scooters, try a 9-hole folf (Frisbee golf) course, and walk in the trees along an 800-foot path in the treetops, 60 feet above the forest floor. A nature center and a few gift shops and restaurants remain open mid-June–mid-September, daily 9–4:30.

If you want to check out a cross section of American life, drop by the Whitefish train station at 6 AM as a sleepy collection of farmers, cowboys, and skiers awaits the arrival of Amtrak's *Empire Builder,* en route from Seattle to Chicago. Inside the half-timber depot is the **Stumptown Historical Society's Museum.** The focus here is the Great Northern Railway, the nation's first unsubsidized transcontinental railway that passed through Whitefish. On display are lanterns, old posters, and crockery, as well as reminders of local history, such as the books of author Dorothy M. Johnson and photos of the Whitefish football team from 1922 through 1954, plus some real fun (look for the fur-covered trout). You can pick up a walking-tour map of Whitefish's historic district here. ✉ *500 Depot St.* ☎ *406/862–0067* 🖅 *Donations accepted* ☉ *June–Sept., weekdays 11–6, Sat. 11–3, Sun. 2–6; Oct.–May, weekdays 11–6, Sat. 11–3.*

Skiing & Snowboarding

The **Big Mountain Ski and Summer Resort** has been one of Montana's top ski areas since the 1930s, but it remains comfortably small. Eight miles from Whitefish, it's popular among train travelers from the Pacific Northwest and the upper Midwest. The snow season runs Thanksgiving through early April.

The mountain's most distinctive features are its widely spaced trees, which—when encased in snow—are known as snow ghosts. With 3,000 skiable acres, plus out-of-bounds areas for Sno-Cat skiing, the Big Mountain offers a lot of terrain to explore and many different lines to discover among those widely spaced trees. The pleasure of exploration and discovery—such as finding a fresh cache of powder many days after a snowstorm—is perhaps the main reason to ski the Big Mountain. Easy discovery comes with the help of free mountain tours by mountain ambassadors. They meet intermediate skiers near the bottom of the main quad chair, Glacier Chaser, at 10:30 AM and 1:30 PM daily.

In general, the pitch is in the intermediate to advanced-intermediate range; there's not a whole lot of super-steep or super-easy skiing. A sameness in pitch, however, doesn't mean a sameness in skiing. With trails falling away on all sides of the mountain, there is a tremendous variation in exposure and hence in snow texture; also take into consideration the number of trees to deal with and the views (the best being northeast toward Glacier National Park). Kids love the Super Pipe on the front side's Chair 3; they can spend the whole day on the north side, especially in the natural half pipe of George's Gorge, under Chair 7 (the Big Creek Express).

One of the Big Mountain's best features is its long high-speed quad, the Glacier Chaser, meaning that runs using most of the mountain's 2,300-foot vertical are interrupted by less than 10 minutes of lift-riding time. A negative is weather. Foggy days are not uncommon; at those times you're thankful that those snow ghosts are around as points of reference. 🖃 *Box 1400, 59937* ☎ *406/862–1900 or 800/858–4152* 🖷 *406/862–2922* ⊕ *www.skiwhitefish.com or www.big-mountain.com* ☉ *Thanksgiving–early Apr. and mid-June–mid-Sept., daily 9–4:30.*

FACILITIES 2,500-foot vertical drop; 3,000 skiable acres; 25% beginner, 50% intermediate, 25% advanced; 2 high-speed quad chairs, 1 quad chair, 4 triple chairs, 1 double chair, 3 surface lifts. Snow report ☎ 406/862–7669 or 800/847–4868.

LESSONS & PROGRAMS Group instruction in downhill is offered for $35 for a half day (plus a lift ticket); cross-country, telemark skiing, and snowboarding lessons are also available. Specialty clinics such as racing, mogul, and telemark techniques are provided, as well as children's programs. For information call the **Ski and Snowboard School** (☎ 406/862–2909).

LIFT TICKETS   A full-day ticket is $49; for night skiing (mid-December–March, Friday–Saturday 4:30–9), the charge is $14.

RENTALS   Full rental packages (skis, boots, and poles start at $20 per day. Snowboard rentals start at $28 per day.

BACKCOUNTRY SKIING & SNOWBOARDING   Because of an unusually liberal policy regarding skiing out-of-bounds, backcountry powder skiing and boarding are possible from the top of the Big Mountain. For the most part, the Big Mountain ski patrol does not prevent riders from crossing ski-area boundary ropes, although if you do so and get into trouble, you're responsible for paying rescue costs. Those who choose to travel out-of-bounds run a high risk of getting lost: It's easy to ski too far down the wrong drainage, creating the prospect of a tiring and excruciating bushwhack back to the base. For an introduction to the nearby backcountry, you might want to sign up with Big Mountain Ski and Snowboard School's **Sno-Cat-skiing** (☎ 406/862–2909) operation, which takes skiers on a four-hour off-piste adventure for the price of a lift ticket plus $100.

Although the backcountry avalanche danger varies with the winter snowpack, it's best to check the local avalanche forecast with **Glacier Country Avalanche Center** (☎ 406/257–8402) and to carry tranceivers, probe poles, shovels, and, most importantly, a knowledge of backcountry safety and first aid.

NORDIC SKIING   There are two machine-groomed track systems in the Whitefish area: both systems serve their purpose well enough, but don't expect inspiring views or a sense of wilderness seclusion. The **Big Mountain Nordic Center** (☎ 406/862–2946) has its own 10 km (6.2 mi) of groomed trails; the daily fee is $5. One advantage that **Glacier Nordic Touring Center** (✉ 1200 U.S. 93 W ☎ 406/881–4230 for snow report) on Whitefish Lake Golf Course has is that 2.8 km (1.6 mi) of its 12 km (7 mi) of groomed trail is for night skiing. A $5 per person donation is suggested. Rentals, lessons, and trail maps are available at the **Outback Ski Shack** (☎ 406/862–9498). Rentals and trail maps are available at **The Outpost Lodge on Big Mountain** (☎ 406/862–2946). Arrangements for cross-country lessons can be made through the **Ski and Snowboard School** (☎ 406/862–2909).

Sports & the Outdoors

BICYCLING   Of the 2,000 mi of county roads in the area, only 400 mi are paved, leaving dirt and gravel roads and innumerable trails open for discovery. You can rent bikes suitable to the terrain at **Glacier Cyclery** (✉ 326 E. 2nd St. ☎ 406/862–6446 ⊕ www.glaciercyclery.com). Monday-night group rides begin at the shop courtyard and lead to a variety of trails of varying degrees of difficulty. Bike maps, gear, and free air are available at this full-service shop.

CANOEING   You can paddle the Whitefish River Canoe Trail in your own boat or rent one from **Ski Mountain Sports** (✉ 242 Central Ave. ☎ 406/862–7541 ⊕ www.skimountainsports.com), which will outfit you for the trails, the hills, the mountain, and more. The river trail begins at Whitefish Lake and ends at a take-out spot at the Highway 40 bridge. Be sure to arrange a shuttle back to town if you don't want to return upstream.

DOGSLEDDING The dogs are raring to run at **Dog Sled Adventures** (✉ U.S. 93, 20 mi north of Whitefish, 2 mi north of Olney ☎ 406/881–2275 ⊕ www.dogsledadventuresmt.com). Your friendly musher will take care to gear the ride to the passengers, from kids to senior citizens; bundled up in a sled, you'll be whisked through Stillwater State Forest on a 1½-hour ride over a 12-mi trail. The dogs mush trails such as the Eskimo Rollercoaster, late November–mid-April. Reservations are necessary.

FISHING Toss a fly on one of the region's trout streams or lakes and you might snag a west slope cutthroat, rainbow trout, or grayling. By winter, you can dangle a line through a sawed hole in the ice of Whitefish Lake. The best place for fishing gear in Whitefish is **Lakestream Fly Fishing Shop** (✉ 334 Central Ave. ☎ 406/862–1298 ⊕ www.lakestream.com). Guided trips to secluded private lakes, equipment, and fly-fishing gear are sold at the shop. Advice is free. The **Tally Lake Ranger District** (☎ 406/863–5400) can recommend good fishing spots and sell you a fishing license.

GOLF The 27-hole **Whitefish Lake Golf Club** (✉ 1200 U.S. 93 W ☎ 406/862–4000 or 406/862–5960) had its modest beginning as an airstrip. You'll need reservations to play on the championship course.

SNOWMOBILING There are more than 200 groomed snowmobile trails in the Flathead region. Unless you are an experienced snowmobiler and expert at avalanche forecasting, you should take a guided trip. **Extreme Motorsports** (✉ 803 Spokane Ave. ☎ 406/862–8594 ⊕ www.wfmextrememotorsports.com) rents machines and clothing and leads guided tours.

Where to Stay & Eat

For lodging at the base of the Big Mountain Ski and Summer Resort, contact **central reservations** (☎ 800/858–4152), which handles everything from upscale Kandahar Lodge to dormitorylike Hibernation House, and various new-and-chic to older-yet-updated condominiums.

$$–$$$$ ✕ **Tupelo Grille.** In homage to Louisiana, native son and chef-owner Pat Carloss cooks up excellent dishes such as crawfish cakes with tarragon mustard, fried catfish, Acadian-style orange roughy, and his speciality, Tupelo filé gumbo with crawfish étouffée. Carloss rotates his well-chosen art collection in the dining room and further enlivens the atmosphere with piped-in New Orleans jazz, Dixieland, or zydeco music. ✉ *17 Central Ave.* ☎ *406/862–6136* ⓐ *Reservations essential* ▭ *AE, MC, V* ◷ *No lunch.*

$$–$$$$ ✕ **Wasabi Sushi Bar.** Not your typical Western ski-town eatery, Wasabi is an East-meets-West experience, serving Japanese cuisine in a relaxed, irreverent setting with pale green walls, a salmon-egg-orange ceiling, and rock and roll and reggae on the sound system. The fish may not be up to Tokyo standards, and servings are very small for the price, but it's more than passable for the northern Rockies, and there are other good options if you prefer your meal cooked, including tempura-fried soft-shell crab and chicken teriyaki with rice. ✉ *419 E. 2nd St.* ☎ *406/863–9283* ▭ *AE, MC, V* ◷ *Closed Mon. No lunch.*

$$–$$$$ ✕ **Whitefish Lake Restaurant.** In the historic clubhouse on the municipal golf course, dine on locals' favorites such as steak au poivre with

Madeira cream sauce, or fresh fish dishes such as halibut steak wrapped in herbs and phyllo dough, baked and served with garlic mashed potatoes. Hand-cut steaks, prime rib, and vegetarian pasta dishes are prepared with flair. You can also get a burger at the bar, but always save room for dessert: coffee-ice cream Mud Pie with Oreo cookie-crumb crust and fudge. ⊠ *1200 U.S. 93 N* ☎ *406/862–5285* ⌕ *Reservations essential* 🖃 *AE, D, MC, V* ⊗ *No lunch mid-Oct.–mid-Apr.*

$–$$$ ✕ **Pescado Blanco.** Mountain-Mexican fusion—fine Mexican cuisine with a Rocky Mountain flair—includes handmade tacos, burritos, enchiladas, fresh seafood, wild game, and a fresh salsa bar. In summer there's patio seating with mountain views. ⊠ *235 First St.* ☎ *406/862–3290* 🖃 *MC, V* ⊗ *Closed Sun.*

$–$$$ ✕ **Truby's.** Individual-size, wood-fired gourmet pizzas are the specialty here, but there are also options such as a Gorgonzola burger and hickory-smoked baby back ribs. On a warm evening, diners fill the patio garden area. The smoke-free bar has seven beers on tap, from the local Black Star brews to Guinness, and a good selection of wines. ⊠ *15 Central Ave.* ☎ *406/862–4979* 🖃 *AE, D, MC, V* ⊗ *No lunch Sun.*

¢–$ ✕ **Buffalo Cafe.** For the classic small-town café experience, this is the place.

FodorsChoice Locals and visitors happily blend in a casual, friendly atmosphere as they

★ dig into well-prepared breakfasts and lunches. (There's no dinner served.) You can start your day with pancakes ("bigger than bowling balls," the menu brags, but considerably lighter), biscuits and gravy, or any of a dozen egg dishes. At lunchtime, it's burgers, salads, grilled sandwiches, and Tex-Mex-style burritos and tacos; homemade milk shakes are worth the calories. This is comfort food at its best—familiar, filling, delicious, and served with a smile. ⊠ *516 Third St.* ☎ *406/862–2833* ⌕ *Reservations not accepted* 🖃 *AE, MC, V* ⊗ *No dinner.*

¢–$ ✕ **Montana Coffee Traders.** Coffees, fresh roasted locally, pastries, and homemade gelato are favorites with downtown shoppers. Unique hand-painted furniture, gifts, and bulk coffees and teas line the hangout's brick walls. Browse through the Saddest Pleasure Bookstore in the back of the café for local works, used books, and cards. ⊠ *110 Central Ave.* ☎ *406/862–7667* ⌕ *Reservations not accepted* 🖃 *AE, MC, V.*

¢–$ ✕ **Quickees Cantina.** You can count on great sandwiches by day, authentic Mexican by night. The fish tacos are Quckees' specialty. ⊠ *28 Lupfer* ☎ *406/862–9866* 🖃 *MC, V* ⊗ *Closed Sun.*

¢–$ ✕ **Tandoor.** The chef here adds Montana flavor to authentic contemporary Indian cuisine. On the menu are a variety of vegetarian, chicken, seafood, and local game dishes with hints of curry, coconut, and Bombay. ⊠ *235 Baker St.* ☎ *406/862–5490* 🖃 *No credit cards* ⊗ *No lunch.*

$$$–$$$$ ✕🏨 **Grouse Mountain Lodge.** Always a Whitefish favorite, the lodge is consistently booked solid in July and August. Public tennis courts and cross-country trails border the lodge, and there's a 36-hole golf course next door. Off-season you can book some bargain activity packages. The thoroughly modern lodge has a sunny lounge area with a lacquered slate floor, elk-horn chandeliers, soft-cushioned furniture, and a tall fireplace. The Grill at Grouse ($$–$$$$) focuses on steaks, ribs, and Pacific Northwest salmon baked on a cedar plank. Food is also served outside on the Deck and Patio ($–$$$), where there's shade and a large stone fire pit. Guest rooms are less refined but have standard modern furnishings and coffeemakers. Recently updated, with a wet bar and a microwave, the loft units are a good choice for families. During the holidays the lodge is decorated with twinkly flair. ⊠ *2 Fairway Dr., 59937* ☎ *406/862–3000, 877/862–1505, or 800/321–8822* 🖨 *406/863–2901* ⊕ *www.grousemountainlodge.com* ⇨ *133 rooms, 12 suites* ♨ *2 restaurants, cable TV, indoor pool, outdoor hot tubs, bicycles, cross-country skiing, downhill skiing, ski storage, bar, lounge, recreation room, babysitting, business services, meeting rooms, airport shuttle, car rental; no smoking* ⊟ *AE, D, DC, MC, V.*

$$$–$$$$ ✕▭ **Kandahar–The Lodge at Big Mountain.** Cafe Kandahar (no lunch, reservations recommended), the small, rustic dining room in this lovely mountain lodge, serves the finest meals on the mountain. In addition to dressed-up standards such as tournedos of beef and New York strip steak, you can choose from game dishes such as roast quail, elk rib chops, and duck with a spice-and-orange-vanilla bean jus, all prepared with a French provincial touch. In the rest of the lodge, the massive lobby fireplace and the Snug Bar are attractive public spaces, and the wood-accented guest rooms feature down comforters and cut-velvet duvets. You can catch a free two-minute shuttle to the slopes, then ski back to the lodge. ⊠ *3824 Big Mountain Rd.* ▭ *Box 278, 59937* ☎ *406/862–6247 (café), 800/862–6094, or 406/862–6098* 🖨 *406/862–6095* ⊕ *www.kandaharlodge.com* ⇨ *50 rooms* ♨ *Restaurant, some kitchens, cable TV, in-room data ports, hot tub, mountain bikes, hiking, cross-country skiing, downhill skiing, ski storage, sleigh rides, bar, shop, laundry facilities, meeting rooms, airport shuttle, free parking; no smoking, no a/c in some rooms* ⊟ *AE, D, MC, V* ⊙ *Closed mid-Apr.–June and Oct.–late Nov.* ▮⊙▮ *BP.*

$$$$ ▭ **Kintla Lodge.** This deluxe condo at the base of Big Mountain's beginner runs is reminiscent of the grand lodges of Glacier Park—in fact, it's named for one of the park's lakes. Wood accents, slate and carpeted floors, rustic decor, and ski-in, ski-out access make Kintla a top property on the mountain. Fireplaces, pine furniture, down comforters, and large windows all give the lodge a cozy feel. There's underground parking, and you'll be within walking distance of restaurants. ⊠ *3910 Big Mountain Rd., 59937* ☎ *406/862–2900 or 800/858–3830* 🖨 *406/862–1969* ⊕ *www.stayatbigmountain.com* ⇨ *20 rooms* ♨ *Kitchens, microwaves, refrigerators, cable TV, outdoor hot tub, sauna, mountain bikes, cross-country skiing, downhill skiing, ski storage, shop, laundry facilities, airport shuttle; no smoking* ⊟ *AE, D, MC, V.*

★ $$–$$$ ▭ **Garden Wall Inn B&B.** Most of what you see in this 1923 home is antique, from first-edition books about Glacier National Park and local history to bed linens with lace borders. All rooms are individually decorated and have down duvets. Special extras include a wake-up coffee tray delivered to your room and afternoon beverages and hors d'oeuvres in front of the fireplace. The three-course breakfast in the dining room is served on china from a Glacier National Park lodge. The innkeeper lives on the premises and shares cooking duties with the vivacious owner. The snow bus to the ski resort stops one block away. ⊠ *504 Spokane Ave., 59937* ☎ *406/862–3440 or 888/530–1700* ⊕*www.gardenwallinn.com* ⟳*3 rooms, 1 suite* ♻ *Dining room, bicycles, cross-country skiing, library, free parking; no room phones, no room TVs, no smoking, no a/c* ⊟ *AE, MC, V* ⍒ *BP.*

$$–$$$ 🔲 **Hidden Moose Lodge B&B.** At the foot of the road that climbs to Big Mountain, this two-story log lodge has a lively ski motif—a child's sled for a coffee table, an antique ski for handrail. Some of the rooms have their own Jacuzzis, and there's one outdoors as well. Rooms are individually decorated with rough-hewn pine furniture and ironwork, and each has its own entrance off a small deck. The living room's vaulted ceiling creates space for plenty of light and a 20-foot-high fireplace; the scene can be quite social, especially in summer. Breakfasts are a standout, and come evening, a glass of wine or bottle of locally brewed beer is on the house. The skier-owners may even share their favorite powder run on Big Mountain. ⊠ *1735 E. Lakeshore Dr., 1.9 mi from downtown, 59937* ☎*406/862–6516 or 877/733–6667* 🖷*406/862–6514* ⊕*www.hiddenmooselodge.com* ⟳*13 rooms* ♻ *Refrigerators, cable TV, in-room VCRs, hot tub, bicycles, meeting rooms; no smoking* ⊟ *AE, D, MC, V* ⍒ *BP.*

CAMPING   🛆 **Whitefish Lake State Park.** On Whitefish Lake in a shady grove of tall pines, this clean campground is very popular and fills early. It has a shallow bay for swimming, a boat launch, and views of the Whitefish Range. One downside is that trains rumble through at all hours. ♻ *Flush toilets, pit toilets, drinking water, fire grates, picnic tables, swimming (lake)* ⟳ *25 sites* ⊠ *State Park Rd., ½ mi from downtown on U.S. 93 N then 1 mi north on State Park Rd.* ☎ *406/862–3991 or 406/752–5501* 🖷 *406/257–0349* ⊕ *www.fwp.state.mt.us* ◨ *$15* ⊟ *AE, D, MC, V* ⊙ *May–early Oct.; primitive camping Oct.–Apr.*

Nightlife & the Arts

THE ARTS   The **O'Shaughnessy Cultural Arts Center** (⊠ 1 Central Ave. ☎ 406/862–5371) hosts a variety of year-round performances in an intimate theater setting.

Every June the founders-day celebration, **Stumptown Days** (⊠ Downtown Whitefish ☎ 406/862–3501 or 877/862–3548 ⊕ www.whitefishchamber. org) includes vintage window displays, historical walking tours, fiddlers, and the Stumptown Social.

The wild and the woolly show up in mid-January for the annual **Whitefish Winter Carnival** (🖅 Box 1120, 59937 ☎ 406/862–3501 or 877/862–3548 ⊕ www.whitefishchamber.org), where you may be chased by a yeti or kissed by a mountain man at the parade. There are activities on the Big Mountain, including a torchlight parade and the Spirit of Winter show by the Ski School. In town, events include snow-sculpting contests and skijoring races (skiers pulled by horse and riders).

Ride your favorite La-Z-Boy or just bring your camera to Big Mountain Ski and Summer Resort's **Annual Furniture Race** (⊠ 3910 Big Mountain Rd., 59937 ☎ 406/862–2900 ⊕ www.big-mountain.com) on the last day of skiing every April.

NIGHTLIFE Regional microbrews, herb-crusted pizza, and live funk and reggae most weekends draw a younger crowd to the smoke-free **Dire Wolf Pub** (✉ 845 Wisconsin Ave. ☎ 406/862–4500). A locals' hangout, **The Great Northern Bar and Grill** (✉ 27 Central Ave. ☎ 406/862–2816) may be stinky and smoky but it rocks with local bands and the occasional sort-of-big-name gig. The stage is surrounded by signs from Whitefish enterprises that are now defunct. Nonsmokers take refuge on the patio to enjoy a brew, a pile of nachos, and the cool summer evening. The microbrewery **Great Northern Brewing** (✉ 2 Central Ave. ☎ 406/863–1000) is open for free tastings of seven different beers, including the Black Star Wild Huckleberry. In winter it's open daily noon–8.

Shopping

From local history to best sellers, you'll find it at **Bookworks** (✉ 244 Spokane ☎ 406/862–4980), which has a fine selection of kids' books and handmade pottery.

☺ The largest toy shop in northwest Montana, **Imagination Station** (✉ 221 Central Ave. ☎ 406/862–5668) has fun, educational, and creative toys and gifts in all price ranges. It also has a downtown Kalispell location.

Sage and Cedar (✉ 214 Central Ave. ☎ 406/862–9411) sells lotions, potions, massage products, and perfumes.

Columbia Falls

🔞 *8 mi east of Whitefish via U.S. 93 and Hwy. 40.*

Many roadside attractions open during summer between the hard-working lumber town of Columbia Falls and Glacier National Park. Hands down, the most popular place on hot summer days is the **Big Sky Waterpark.** Besides the 10 waterslides and golf course, there are arcade games, bumper cars, a carousel, barbecue grills, a picnic area, and food service. ✉ *7211 U.S. 2 E, junction of U.S. 2 and Hwy. 206* ☎ *406/892–5025 or 406/892–2139* ⊕ *www.bigskywp.com* 🎟 *$20* ☺ *Memorial Day–Labor Day, daily 10–8.*

☺ Get lost in the maze at the **Amazing Ventures Fun Center**—a circuitous outdoor route made of plywood walls and ladders, with viewing areas where parents can watch their kids (and give directions when necessary). Other attractions include Bankshot Basketball, go-carts, 18 holes of miniature golf, thriller bumper boats in a pond, and a picnic area. ✉ *10265 U.S. 2 E, Coram* ☎ *406/387–5902* 🎟 *$6 per activity or $16.75 fun pass* ☺ *Memorial Day–mid-Sept., daily 9:30–8:30.*

☺ You've found the power center of Montana at the **House of Mystery–Montana Vortex,** a wacky roadside attraction where the laws of physics don't apply and other mystifying phenomena prevail. ✉ *7800 U.S. 2 E, Columbia Falls* ☎ *406/892–1210* 🎟 *$6* ☺ *Apr.–Oct., daily 9–7.*

Sports & the Outdoors

GOLF Flowers and tall pines line the greens of **Meadow Lake Golf Course** (✉ 100 St. Andrew's Dr. ☎ 406/892–8700 or 800/321–4653), where you'll find 18 holes, a pro shop, lodging, a restaurant, and a lounge.

LLAMA HIKES Lead your own llama with **Great Northern Llama Co.** (⊠ 600 Blackmer La. ☎ 406/755–9044 ⊕ www.gnranch.com) on a day trip, overnight trek, or fishing expedition.

Where to Stay & Eat

$$$–$$$$ ✕⌂ **Meadow Lake Golf Resort.** As the name indicates, the links are front and center here. The inn is just a few steps from the pro shop, and the veranda has views of the course, as well as the surrounding mountains and a pond. Condos and vacation homes, with private decks, barbecue grills, fireplaces, and simple, comfortable furnishings, line the fairways. The North Fork Grill ($$–$$$$) specializes in fresh salads, barbecue, and the chef's favorite, Buffalo Tip Stroganoff. You can dine outside in summer. ⊠ *100 St. Andrew's Dr., 59912* ☎ *406/892–8700 or 800/321–4653* ⊟ *406/892–0330* ⊕ *www.meadowlake.com* ⇨ *24 rooms, 100 condos, 20 vacation homes* ⚘ *Restaurant, some kitchens, some microwaves, some refrigerators, cable TV, in-room data ports, 18-hole golf course, putting green, pro shop, 2 pools (1 indoors), hot tub, massage, sauna, mountain bikes, billiards, Ping-Pong, cross-country skiing, bar, shop, laundry facilities, concierge, business services, meeting rooms, airport shuttle, no-smoking rooms* ⊟ *AE, D, DC, MC, V.*

CAMPING ⚞ **Columbia Falls RV Park.** The in-town location, with tall trees to shelter against the breeze, is convenient to the Big Sky Waterpark, shopping, the city pool, and the Flathead River. Pull-through spaces are adequate for large RVs, and the tent area is grassy, with electricity for some sites. ⚘ *Flush toilets, full hookups, picnic tables, electricity, public telephone, general store* ⇨ *40 full hookups, 10 tent sites* ⊠ *1000 3rd Ave. E, on U.S. 2* ☎ *406/892–1122 or 888/401–7268* ⊟ *406/892–2055* ⊕ *www. columbiafallsrvpark.com* ⚎ *$12–$16 tent sites, $28–$33 RV sites* ⊟ *D, MC, V* ☉ *May–Oct.*

Nightlife & the Arts

THE ARTS Enjoy plenty of holiday cheer and local color at the early December nighttime parade, **Night of Lights** (⊠ Nucleus Ave. ☎ 406/892–2072 ⊕ www. columbiafallschamber.com).

The outdoors echoes with the **Summer Concert Series** (⊠ Marantette Park on U.S. 2 E ☎ 406/892–2072) in the Don Lawrence Amphitheater Thursday from mid-June through late August. Types of music vary but are aimed to a broad audience; the Don Lawrence Big Band has a performance every year.

NIGHTLIFE Whether the owner's band is playing on the stage or cowboys are serenading a sparse crowd of locals during karaoke, the **Blue Moon Nite Club, Casino and Grill** (⊠ Hwy. 40 and U.S. 2, Columbia Falls ☎ 406/892–9925) is a hoot. The wooden dance floor gets a good scuffing on Western dance and country-swing nights. Two stuffed grizzly bears rear up near the entrance, and other species decorate the large saloon as well.

Shopping

Huckleberry Patch Restaurant & Gift Shop (⊠ 8868 U.S. 2 E, Hungry Horse ☎ 406/387–5670 or 800/527–7340 ⊕ www.huckleberrypatch. com) has been the huckleberry headquarters of the state for more than

50 years, selling the purple wild berry native to the region in all sorts of varieties, from jams to fudge-encased fruit.

en route Enter Glacier National Park through the back door by driving the **North Fork Road** (✉ From Nucleus Ave. drive north to the T, turn east and follow North Fork Rd. [Hwy. 486]). It's a rutted, bumpy, dusty gravel road that's teeming with wildlife along the North Fork of the Flathead River. The 40 mi to the Polebridge entrance station pass thick forests, some of which burned during fires of 2001 and 2003. You can opt out early and enter Glacier at the Camas Creek entrance gate and avoid rough roads.

SEELEY–SWAN VALLEY

Squeezed between two magnificent mountain ranges—the Missions on the west and the Swan Range on the east—the glacially formed Swan Valley is littered with lakes, sprinkled with homesteads, and frosted with snow for five months of the year. One road, Hwy. 83, winds along an 80-mi course that follows the Clearwater and Swan rivers, popular for boating and fishing—both winter ice fishing and summer trout fishing. Several trailheads lead into the Bob Marshall Wilderness from the Swan Valley. Modern amenities are as sparse as the population. Only about a thousand people reside here year-round, so you are much more likely to encounter a dozen deer than a dozen humans. With that in mind, it's imperative that you look out for deer and elk on the road, day and night. Summer visitors fill campgrounds and the few guest lodges. Besides snow-mobiling and cross-country skiing, winters bring snow, drippy weather, and low clouds. Do as the locals do: put up your hood, grab the gloves and boots, and head outdoors.

Seeley Lake

🄮 *120 mi south of Glacier National Park via U.S. 2, Hwy. 206, and Hwy 83.*

Bordered by campgrounds, hiking trails, and wildlife-viewing opportunities, this community of 2,400 centers on lovely Seeley Lake. Nearby is the Big Blackfoot River, a setting in *A River Runs Through It,* Norman McLean's reflection on family and fishing. Host to races and leisure outings, the Seeley Creek Nordic Ski Trails roll across hills and meadows. In winter 350 mi of snowmobile trails rip through the woods. The major industry, logging, which began in 1892, is evident on some hillsides.

Paddling on the 3½-mi **Clearwater Canoe Trail,** along an isolated portion of the Clearwater River, you may see moose and will likely see songbirds, great blue herons, and belted kingfishers. The Seeley Lake Ranger Station has free maps and directions to the put-in for the two-hour paddle. ✉ *3 mi north of Seeley on Hwy. 83* ☎ *406/677–2233* ⊕ *www.fs. fed.us/r1* ✑ *Free* ☉ *May–Oct.*

Ten days of events celebrate winter during the January **Seeley Lake Area Winterfest,** including a snow-sculpture contest, parade, kids' games, cross-country ski events, snowmobile fun runs, and more. ⊠ *Hwy. 83 S* ☎ *406/677–2880* ⊕ *www.seeleylakechamber.com* ⊙ *Mid- to late Jan., daily.*

Logging's colorful past is displayed in the big log barn at **Seeley Lake Museum and Visitors Center**, along with tools of the trade and visitor information. ⊠ *2920 Hwy. 83 S at mile marker 13.5* ☎ *406/677–2880* ⊕ *www.seeleylakechamber.com* ☎ *Free* ⊙ *Memorial Day–Labor Day, daily 9–5; Labor Day–Memorial Day, Mon. and Thurs.–Sat. 11–4, Sun. noon–4.*

off the beaten path

MORRELL FALLS NATIONAL RECREATION – A 2-mi hike leads to the lovely cascades of Morrell Falls. It is actually a series of falls, with the longest about a 100-foot drop. This is a moderately difficult family hike, perfect for a picnic (although it's wise to remember this is bear country). Maps and travel information are available at the Seeley Lake Ranger District office. ⊠ *From Hwy. 83, turn east on Morrell Creek Rd. and follow signs* ☎ *406/677–2233* ⊕ *www.fs.fed.us/r1* ☎ *Free* ⊙ *Daily.*

Sports & the Outdoors

★ You can romp in deep snows on the **Seeley Creek Nordic Ski Trails** at the edge of town. Trails are groomed for skate and classic skiing. Nearby are dogsled trails. The trail systems share a parking lot and covered picnic area where you can join a campfire to warm your toes. ⊠ *Forest Rd. 477; from Hwy. 83, turn east on Morrell Creek Rd., aka Cottonwood Lakes Rd., and drive 1 mi to trailhead* ☎ *406/677–2233* ⊕ *www.seeleylakechamber.com* ☎ *$4 donation requested* ⊙ *Dec.–Mar., daily.*

CROSS-COUNTRY
SKIING
You can ski a few kilometers on the **Double Arrow Resort** (⊠ Hwy. 83 at milepost 12, 2 mi south of Seeley Lake ☎ 406/677–2777 or 800/468–0777), where you may see moose in the willows.

Ski-touring equipment and maps from **Seeley Lake Recreational Rentals** (⊠ Hwy. 83 N ☎ 406/677–7368 ⊕ www.seeleyfunrentals.com) will take you to the winter trails. You can also rent snowmobiles, snowshoes, and summer toys like boats and bikes—reserve online.

DOGSLED RACING
Mushers and their dogs join the late-January **Seeley–Lincoln 100/200 Dog Sled Race** (⊠ Forest Rd. 477 ☎ 406/677–3016 ⊕ www.seeleylakechamber.com), which dashes through the snowy wooded trails from a dogsled trailhead at Seeley Creek. Spectators are welcome. To get there from Hwy. 83, turn east on Morrell Creek Road (aka Cottonwood Lakes Road) and drive 1 mi to the trailhead.

SNOWMOBILING
Rent snowmobiles from **Seeley Sport Rentals,** which also offers pontoon boats, canoes, and mountain bikes for summer adventures. (⊠ 3112 Hwy. 83 S ☎ 406/677–3680 ⊕ www.seeleysportrentals.com).

Where to Stay & Eat

$$–$$$$ ✕ **Lindey's Steak House.** Locals will send you here to watch the sun set over the lake while dining on the only thing on the menu: steak. Select cuts of prime rib, all 16-ounce portions, are served with potatoes, gar-

lic bread, and pickled watermelon rind served family style. ✉ *Hwy. 83, downtown Seeley Lake* ☎ *406/677–9229* ⊟ *AE, MC, V.*

$–$$$$ ✕**Cozy Corner Steak House.** From the outside it doesn't look like much, but this out-of-the-way charmer, a 1930s building with a log-cabin dining area, features some of the finest steaks around. Locals crowd into the remote restaurant south of town and east of Salmon Lake for the chicken-fried steak and the tempura prawns. ✉ *6070 Woodworth Rd. (Hwy. 67), 4 mi east of Hwy. 83* ☎ *406/677–5699* ⊟ *AE, D, MC, V.*

¢–$$ ✕**The Filling Station.** Friendly folks fill up on the simple food at this diner, which doubles as a bar and casino. Old standards are burgers with fries, porterhouse steaks, and huckleberry barbecue ribs served with baked beans and coleslaw. ✉ *Hwy. 83, downtown Seeley Lake* ☎ *406/677–2080* ⚐ *Reservations not accepted* ⊟ *AE, D, MC, V.*

$$–$$$$ ✕▥ **Double Arrow Resort.** The handsome, 60-year-old log main lodge combines European grace and Western trimmings on a 200-acre spread. The great room's stone fireplace is a guest gathering spot; nearby in the dining room ($$$–$$$$) the sophisticated menu features foie-gras salad, lobster and butternut squash ravioli, and rib-eye steak rubbed with cumin and charbroiled. Guest rooms and log cabins are simply furnished with a few antiques and fluffy comforters on brass beds. Early-20th-century log homes with antiques, knotty-pine interiors, and modern kitchens are popular with families. ✉ *Hwy. 83, milepost 12, 2 mi south of Seeley Lake, 59868* ⬚ *Box 747, Seeley Lake, 59868* ☎ *406/677–2777 or 800/468–0777* 🖷 *406/677–2922* ⊕ *www.doublearrowresort.com* ➳ *3 rooms, 12 cabins, 6 homes* ⚏ *Restaurant, some kitchens, cable TV, in-room data ports, driving range, 18-hole golf course, 2 tennis courts, pro shop, indoor pool, hot tub, massage, fishing, mountain bikes, horseback riding, cross-country skiing, sleigh rides, bar, piano, recreation room, shop, playground, laundry facilities, concierge, business services, convention center, meeting rooms, no-smoking rooms; no a/c* ⊟ *D, MC, V.*

CAMPING ⛰ **Big Larch.** Giant larch trees shade the large site, where fishing and boating are popular. There's a good beach for swimming, a horseshoes pit, handicapped-accessible picnicking, and marked nature trails. Shopping, laundry, and services are nearby. ⚑ *Flush toilets, dump station, drinking water, fire grates, picnic tables, ranger station, swimming (lake)* ➳ *50 sites* ✉ *Forest Rd. 2199; 1 mi north of Seeley Lake on Hwy. 83, and ½ mi west on Forest Rd. 2199* ☎ *406/677–2233* 🖷 *406/677–3902* ⊕ *www.fs.fed.us/r1* ⬙ *$10* ⊟ *AE, D, MC, V* ☉ *Mid-May–Sept.*

⛰ **Seeley Lake Forest Service Campground.** This busy campground among tall pines is on the lake, so mosquitoes can be pesky. Groceries, sports rentals, and restaurants are about 4 mi away. Reservations are recommended. ⚑ *Flush toilets, dump station, drinking water, fire grates, picnic tables, ranger station, swimming (lake)* ➳ *29 sites* ✉ *Boy Scout Rd.* ☎ *406/677–2233* 🖷 *406/677–3902* ⊕ *www.fs.fed.us/r1* ⬙ *$10* ⊟ *AE, D, MC, V* ☉ *Late May–Labor Day.*

Shopping

Find country fabrics in **Deer Country Quilts** (✉ Hwy. 83 ☎ 406/677–2730 ⊕ www.deercountryquilts.com), as well as thousands of bolts of flannels, batiks, and cotton in the store's lovely log lodge studio. Ask about receptions for quilters and the annual mid-July quilt show.

Beaver pelts, furs, blankets, and painted buffalo and elk hides hang from walls in the **Grizzly Claw Trading Company** (⊠ Hwy. 83 ☎ 406/677–0008 or 888/551–0008). Other one-of-a-kind items also are available, including pottery, jewelry, clothing, wood carvings, and furniture.

Holland Lake

⑮ *19 mi north of Seeley Lake via Hwy. 83.*

Outdoorsy types come to this 400-acre lake for fishing, boating, swimming, hiking, trail-riding, and camping in summer and ice fishing, cross-country skiing, snowshoeing, and snowmobiling in winter. To pursue any of the activities available in this remote setting, you must come equipped with your own canoe, motor launch, or snowmobile: your company will be kokanee salmon, rainbow trout, and bull trout, plus the handful of people who run Holland Lake Lodge. Maps for the numerous trails that depart from the lake area are available at the lodge or through the Forest Service office. Some routes climb the Swan Range into the Bob Marshall Wilderness.

The hike to **Holland Falls** is about 1½ mi from the lodge. The last bit is a steep climb, but it's well worth it for the view. *⊠ Holland Lake Rd.; from Hwy. 83, turn east on Forest Rd. 44 for 3 mi to Holland Lake Rd. ☎ 406/837–7500 ⊕ www.fs.fed.us/r1 ≊ Free ☉ Daily.*

Where to Stay & Eat

$–$$ ✕▦ **Holland Lake Lodge.** When the snow flies, this lodge is nearly buried, which makes for cozy fireside dining and relaxing. The log lodge sits on the lakeshore, where you can ski or snowshoe from the door. In summer, step off the cabin porch for a hike or a swim. Cabins are updated yet rustic. You can dine on trout in the restaurant ($$–$$$) while watching the wild fish jumping outside. *⊠ 1947 Holland Lake Rd., Swan Valley 59826 ☎ 406/754–2282 or 877/925–6343 ⊟ 406/754–2208 ⊕ www. hollandlakelodge.com ➾ 9 rooms, 6 cabins ⚫ Restaurant, snack bar, room service, lake, sauna, boating, fishing, mountain bikes, horseback riding, cross-country skiing, ski shop, lobby lounge, shop, business services, meeting rooms; no room phones, no room TVs, no smoking, no a/c ☰ AE, D, MC, V ⍟ FAP.*

CAMPING △ **Holland Lake Campground.** Large trees provide lots of shade for campers near the lake. The spot is popular with outfitters who pack horses into the nearby Bob Marshall Wilderness. Food service is available nearby at Holland Lake Lodge. *⚫ Pit toilets, dump station, drinking water, bear boxes, fire grates, picnic tables, swimming (lake) ➾ 40 sites ⊠ Holland Lake Rd. ☎ 406/837–7500 or 406/837–3577 ⊟ 406/ 837–7503 ⊕ www.fs.fed.us/r1 ≊ $12 ☰ AE, D, MC, V ☉ Mid-May–Sept.*

Bob Marshall Wilderness Area

 5 mi east of Hwy. 83 via Pyramid Pass Trail, Lion Creek Pass Trail, or Smith Creek Pass Trail.

The Bob Marshall, Scapegoat, and Great Bear wilderness areas take up 1.5 million rugged, roadless, remote acres within the Flathead National Forest. Preservation pioneer, forester, and cofounder of the Wilderness Society, Bob Marshall pushed Congress in 1964 to create the wilderness area that bears his name. Since then, little has altered the landscape, which runs 60 mi along the Continental Divide. More than 1,000 mi of trails enter the wilderness from near Seeley Lake at Pyramid Pass Trail and Holland Lake at Pyramid Pass, Condon's Lion Creek Pass, and Smith Creek Pass, where hikers are sure to meet outfitters and packhorses. An old airstrip at Shafer Meadows is used for float parties on the wild white-water Middle Fork of the Flathead.

Information on the Bob Marshall Wilderness is available through the **Flathead National Forest,** which has maps, listings of outfitters and access points, and safety information regarding travel in bear country. ⊠ *1935 3rd Ave. E, Kalispell 59901* ☎ *406/758–5200* ⊕ *www.fs.fed. us/r1* ✉ *Free* ☉ *Weekdays 8–4.*

A complete list of trails, elevations, and backcountry campsites can be found in the book *Hiking Montana's Bob Marshall Wilderness* by Erik Molvar, available at **Books West** (⊠ 101 Main, Kalispell 59901 ☎ 406/ 752–6900).

---

off the beaten path

SPOTTED BEAR – At the end of a long and often washboarded gravel road, Spotted Bear is a remote entrance into the Bob Marshall Wilderness. You'll find there a ranger station, outfitter's ranch, campground, swimming, and boating down the South Fork of the Flathead River to the Hungry Horse Dam. ⊠ *Forest Service Rd. 38; 55 mi from Hungry Horse on either E. or W. Hungry Horse Reservoir Rd.* ☎ *406/387–3800* ⊕ *www.fs.fed.us/r1* ✉ *Free* ☉ *Apr.–Oct.*

Sports & the Outdoors

FISHING Five-day pack and float trips with **Bob Marshall Wilderness Horse Pack and Float Expeditions** (⊠ 55 mi from Hungry Horse on either E. or W. Hungry Horse Reservoir Rd. toward Spotted Bear Ranger Station ☎ 406/755–7337 or 800/223–4333 ⊕ www.spottedbear.com) go deep into the backcountry for fly-fishing in the wilderness. This Orvis-endorsed expedition is limited to 12 people per trip.

Wilderness Lodge (⊠ West Side Hungry Horse Reservoir Rd., 55 mi east of Hungry Horse ☎ 406/387–4051) conducts three-day float and fishing trips in the wilderness area.

TRAIL RIDES Take a day ride or an overnight pack trip into the wilderness with **Diamond R Guest Ranch** (⊠ East Side Hungry Horse Reservoir Rd., 55 mi from Hungry Horse ☎ 406/756–1573 or 800/597–9465). Multiday pack trips with **Glacier Raft Company** (⊠ 11957 U.S. 2 E, West Glacier

CloseUp

OF DUDES & RANCHES

BY THE LATE 1800S, *stories of the jagged peaks and roaring rivers in the Rocky Mountains had caught the nation's imagination. Travelers headed west on the recently completed transcontinental railroads to see these wonders firsthand. They stayed where they could, which often meant rustic ranches. It worked out well—ranchers, starved for fresh faces and news from back home, were pleased to have the company. Soon ranches began hosting paying guests. These "dudes" stayed for*

weeks or months and participated in day-to-day operations. By 1940, there were more than 300 dude ranches in the United States and Canada. Today, you'd be hard pressed to find one of these places calling itself a dude ranch—"guest ranch" sounds better—and the typical stay is about a week. Activities include trail rides, barbecues, hoedowns, and sometimes opportunities to work the livestock. The week often culminates in a gymkhana, a series of competitive horseback events.

☎ 406/888–5454 or 800/235–6781) follow trails into the wilderness for campouts, fishing, and observing nature.

Where to Stay & Eat

$$$$ ▣ **Seven Lazy P Guest Ranch.** A snug haven in a rugged landscape, this
Fodor'sChoice 1,200-acre ranch is surrounded by pines and aspens deep in Teton
★ Canyon, an eastern gateway to the Bob Marshall Wilderness. The duplex cabins feel like a second home, with comfortable furniture, wood-paneled ceilings, rough-hewn wainscoting, and picture windows; enveloping sofas and chairs, a large stone fireplace, and more golden wood fill the main lodge. Three meals daily (included in the room rate) are served family style, and the food is memorable: a sausage-egg-and-cheese bake with homemade muffins for breakfast, grilled lemon-glazed salmon for dinner, and pies just out of the oven. They'll fortify you for a day of hiking, wildlife viewing, or guided horseback riding (also included in the room rate). In summer, multiday pack trips into the Bob Marshall give riders a glimpse of the Rockies as Lewis and Clark saw them. ⌂ *Box 178, Choteau 59422* ☎ *406/466–2044* ⊕ *www.sevenlazyp.com* ⇨ *3 rooms, 3 duplex cabins* ⌂ *Dining room, fans, refrigerators, billiards, hiking, horseback riding, piano, airport shuttle; no a/c, no room phones, no room TVs, no smoking* ▭ *No credit cards* ⊗ *Closed Nov.–Apr.* ⫶◎⫶ *FAP.*

★ **$$$$** ▣ **Spotted Bear Ranch.** Remote yet upscale, the two-bedroom log cabins here among the evergreens are cozy yet have generator power, flush toilets, showers, fireplaces, and views. The ranch, reachable by a rough road, specializes in fly-fishing expeditions. Dinners are served family style in the historic main lodge. ✉ *55 mi from Hungry Horse on either E. or W. Hungry Horse Reservoir Rd. toward Spotted Bear Ranger Station; winter address 115 Lake Blaine Dr., Kalispell 59901* ☎ *406/755–7337 or 800/223–4333* ▤ *406/755–7336* ⊕ *www.spottedbear.com* ⇨ *5 cabins* ⌂ *Dining room, snack bar, boating, fishing, horseback riding, shop, meeting rooms; no room phones, no room TVs, no smoking, no a/c* ▭ *AE, D, MC, V* ⊗ *Closed mid-Sept.–mid-June* ⫶◎⫶ *FAP.*

$ 🏠 **Wolf Willow Ranch.** There are two cabins—one fully equipped, the other rustic—on a family ranch outside of Bynum, 25 mi northwest of Choteau. Both sit just east of the foot of the mountains, with an inspirational view. The hiking and bird- and wildlife-waching for which the Rocky Mountain Front is known are right outside the door. One cabin is just like home, with a full kitchen and bath, living room with TV and VCR, and sleeping space (queen and twin beds) for four to six people, depending on how friendly they are. The other cabin has a loft and four bunk beds, a sofa, a propane stove and refrigerator, and an outhouse (in other words, no running water). ✉ Bynum, 59419 ☎ 406/469-2231 🛏 2 cabins 🚫 No credit cards.

CAMPING ⛺ **Spotted Bear Campground.** Alongside the South Fork of the Flathead River, this remote campground offers flat sites shaded by tall pines. Grizzly bears frequent the area, so a clean camp is imperative. Trailheads lead into wilderness areas. ⚓ *Pit toilets, dump station, drinking water, bear boxes, fire grates, picnic tables, ranger station, swimming (river)* 🛏 *13 sites* ✉ *Forest Service Rd. 38, 55 mi southeast of U.S. 2 at Hungry Horse* ☎ *406/756–5376* 📠 *406/758–5390* ⊕ *www.fs.fed.us/r1* 💳 *$10* 🚫 *AE, D, MC, V* ☻ *Late June–early Sept.*

MISSOULA

A fertile valley hemmed in by mountains cradles Missoula, the cultural center of northwest Montana. The largest metropolis around (population 57,000) is the home of the University of Montana. In the aptly nicknamed Garden City, maple trees line the residential streets and the Clark Fork River slices through the center of town; a 6-mi riverside trail passes the university en route to Hellgate Canyon. Missoula makes a good base for regional exploration by way of Interstate 90 east–west, U.S. 93 north–south, and numerous back roads.

In 1860 French trappers dubbed this trading settlement the Hell Gate when they discovered bones and bodies in the canyon following a bloody battle between Blackfeet and other Indians. Settlers did not arrive until more than 50 years after the Lewis and Clark expedition traveled through the area. Gold speculators, homesteaders, and the coming of the Northern Pacific Railroad in 1883 all helped establish the town.

Exploring Missoula

Missoula is home to the Adventure Cycling Association (formerly Bike Centennial), so it's no surprise that the city has more bicycles than people. Exploring by bicycle is popular and easy: downtown and the university district are relatively flat and have bike paths and bike traffic lanes; many storefronts are adorned with bike racks. Within the center of the city, walking is a good option, too, particularly given that parking is at a premium and that the university itself is a car-free zone. Dozens of walking and biking paths wend through town. The Missoula Valley and sights on the outskirts of town are best explored by car.

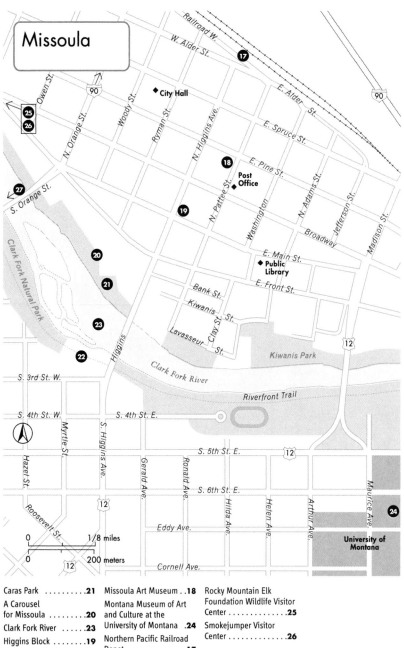

Missoula

What to See

㉑ Caras Park. Downtown's favorite green space, the park has a walking path along the Clark Fork River. A summer pavilion hosts live musical performances such as those at Downtown ToNight, a Thursday evening event that also features food and what the chamber of commerce likes to call a "beverage garden." ⊠ *Front and Ryman Sts.* ☎ *406/721–7275* ⊕ *www. ci.missoula.mt.us/parksrec* ⊠ *Free* ⊙ *Daily 6 AM–11 PM.*

㉒ A Carousel for Missoula. In downtown Caras Park, kids hop in the saddle of hand-carved steeds. The carousel's horses and chariots gallop on a lovingly restored 1918 frame, accompanied by tunes from the largest band organ in continuous use in the United States. The Dragon Hollow play area next to the carousel features a dragon, a castle, and many play structures. ⊠ *1 Caras Park* ☎ *406/549–8382* ⊕ *www.carrousel.com* ⊠ *Adults $1.50, kids 50¢ per ride; play area free* ⊙ *Memorial Day–Labor Day, daily 11–7; Labor Day–Memorial Day, daily 11–5:30.*

㉓ Clark Fork River. The heart of Missoula is defined by the Clark Fork River, which cuts through Hellgate Canyon between Mt. Sentinel and Mt. Jumbo, passes by the university, and slices through downtown. A 6-mi-long riverside trail and the connecting 2½-mi Kim Williams trail make for easy, pleasant walks, with picnic spots and benches along the way where you can watch the river. Take note: the powerful currents of the Clark Fork are dangerous—they've taken many lives over the years.

Council Grove State Park. History buffs appreciate this park's significance as the place where Isaac Stevens and the Pend d'Oreille and Flathead Kootenai Indians signed the Hell Gate Treaty in 1855 to establish the Flathead Indian Reservation. The park occupies 87 primitive acres; it has interpretive signs, a picnic area, fishing access, and a hiking trail. To get here, travel west from downtown on Interstate 90, exit at Reserve Street, then drive 2 mi south on Reserve and 10 mi west on Mullan Road. ⊠ *Off Mullan Rd.* ☎ *406/542–5500* ⊕ *www.fwp.state.mt. us* ⊠ *Free* ⊙ *Daily dawn–dusk.*

⑲ Higgins Block. This Queen Anne–style commercial structure, a granite, copper-domed corner building with red polychromed brick, occupies a block in the heart of downtown. On the National Register of Historic Places, it's now home to a deli, a bank, and several shops. ⊠ *202 N. Higgins Ave.* ⊕ *www.missouladowntown.com* ⊠ *Free* ⊙ *Tues. noon–8, Wed.–Sat. noon–6.*

㉗ Historical Museum at Fort Missoula. Fort Missoula, at the western edge of town, was established in 1877 at the height of the U.S. Army's conflict with the Nez Perce, led by Chief Joseph. The museum's indoor and outdoor exhibits, including 13 historic structures relocated from nearby sites, depict and explain the early development of Missoula County. The black 25th Infantry of bicycle soldiers arrived in 1888 to test bicycles for military use; near-life-size photos depict the soldiers during an expedition to Yellowstone National Park's Mammoth Terraces. Uniforms and artifacts are also on display. They ultimately rode one-speed bicycles from Missoula to St. Louis. Guided tours are available by appointment. ⊠ *Fort Missoula, Bldg. 322, accessed via South Ave.* ☎ *406/ 728–3476* ⊕ *www.fortmissoulamuseum.org* ⊠ *$3* ⊙ *Memorial*

Day–Labor Day, Mon.–Sat. 10–5, Sun. noon–5; Labor Day–Memorial Day, Tues.–Sun. noon–5.

★ ⑱ **Missoula Art Museum.** Each year, two dozen changing contemporary art exhibits join a permanent collection featuring works by E. S. Paxson, Walter Hook, and Rudy and Lela Autio and modern-day Indian artists. The 1903 Carnegie Library building, slated to reopen in summer 2006 after extensive remodeling to add handicap accessibility, will have expanded exhibit areas, and classrooms. ✉ *335 N. Pattee St., 1 block from the intersection with W. Broadway* ☎ *406/728–0447* ⊕ *www.artmissoula.org* 🖅 *Donations accepted* ☉ *Tues.–Sat. 10–3; call for occasional extended hours.*

⑳ **Montana Museum of Art and Culture at the University of Montana.** The university's art museum, divided into the Paxson Gallery and the Henry Meloy Gallery, hosts traveling exhibitions and has a permanent collection of more than 9,500 works, with an emphasis on contemporary art from the West. A highlight is the magnificent tapestry titled *Montana Horses* by Missoulian Rudy Autio. ✉ *Performing Arts and Radio/ Television Center, University of Montana* ☎ *406/243–2019* ⊕ *www. umt.edu/partv/famus* 🖅 *Free* ☉ *Tues.–Thurs. 11–3, Fri. and Sat. 4–8:30.*

⑰ **Northern Pacific Railroad Depot.** The construction of the Northern Pacific Railroad was instrumental in opening up the West to settlers, and the arrival of the line in Missoula is a key point in the city's history. The depot, opened in 1901, is an example of the Renaissance Revival architecture that dominates the north end of downtown. Today the depot houses private offices, but you can still look around inside, enjoy a picnic outside, and examine the "Crossings," a sculpture of giant red enamel Xs representing railroad trestles over mountain ravines. ✉ *N. Higgins Ave.* ☎ *406/ 543–4238* ⊕ *www.missouladowntown.com* 🖅 *Free* ☉ *Weekdays 9–5.*

⑳ **Old Milwaukee Railroad Depot.** A Missoula landmark along the river's south shore, this 1910 passenger depot, with Romanesque windows, a Spanish-style roof, two towers, and mission-style parapet walls, is on the National Register of Historic Places. It's now the site of the Boone and Crockett Club national headquarters, an organization founded in 1887 by Theodore Roosevelt to establish conservation of wild habitats. Open to the public are a gun collection, a library, and a display of a world-record-size taxidermied elk. ✉ *250 Station Dr., near the Higgins Ave. Bridge* ☎ *406/542–1888 or 888/840–4868* ⊕ *www.boone-crockett. org* 🖅 *Free* ☉ *Weekdays 8–5.*

 ⑳ **Rocky Mountain Elk Foundation Wildlife Visitor Center.** The visitor center features natural-history displays (including hands-on displays for kids), films, art, taxidermied animals, and a world-record-size pair of elk antlers. The foundation works to preserve wild lands for elk and other wildlife; since 1984, the nonprofit organization has saved more than 4 million acres from development. ✉ *2291 W. Broadway; look for the big bronze elk* ☎ *406/523–4545 or 800/225–5355* ⊕ *www.rmef.org* 🖅 *Donations accepted* ☉ *Memorial Day–Dec. 25, weekdays 8–6, weekends 9–6; Dec. 26–Memorial Day, weekdays 8–6, Sat. 9–6.*

★ ⑳ **Smokejumper Visitor Center.** A replica 1930s lookout tower, fire photos, videos, and murals explain wildland fire ecology and behavior, fire-fighting technique, and the nation's history of smoke jumping, which began here in 1942. Today, it's the largest smoke-jumper base in the nation. From Memorial Day through Labor Day, the center offers five tours daily given by firefighter guides who provide firsthand accounts of jumping into blazing forests. ⊠ *5765 Old Hwy. 10 W, 6 mi west of town, next to the airport* ☎ *406/329–4934* ⊕ *www.smokejumpers.com* ⊠ *Donations accepted* ☉ *Memorial Day–Labor Day, weekdays 8:30–5; Labor Day–Memorial Day weekdays 7:30–4; summer tours on the hr 10–11 and 2–4; by appointment rest of yr.*

Sports & the Outdoors

Bicycling

Nearly 30 trails thread through Missoula and can be found on the Missoulian's Hike, Bike, Run map, free online or by calling **Missoula Parks and Recreation** (☎ 406/721–7275 ⊕ www.missoulian.com/specials/hikebike/).

★ The folks at **Adventure Cycling** (⊠ 150 E. Pine St. ☎ 406/721–1776 or 800/755–2453 ⊕ www.adv-cycling.org) in downtown Missoula have good suggestions for nearby bike routes and an extensive selection of regional and national bike maps for sale. You can find bikes to rent or buy, cycling accessories, and cross-country ski gear at **Open Road Bicycles & Nordic Equipment** (⊠ 517 S. Orange St. ☎ 406/549–2453).

Fishing

Grizzly Hackle (⊠ 215 W. Front St. ☎ 406/721–8996) offers guided fly-fishing and outfitting for half-day to week-long float trips on the Bitterroot, Blackfoot, and Clark Fork rivers. Pick up supplies in the retail shop or sign up for a lesson.

Golf

Highlands Golf Club (⊠ 102 Ben Hogan Dr. ☎ 406/728–7360) has 9 holes and provides the best view of Missoula from the restaurant-bar Shadows Keep.

Larchmont Golf Course (⊠ 3200 Old Fort Rd. ☎ 406/721–4416), a relatively flat 18-hole municipal course, provides in-town golfing at reasonable rates ($22 for a round in midweek).

Rafting

Raft and kayak adventures with **Montana River Guides** (⊠ Sawmill Gulch Rd., 35 minutes west of Missoula on I–90, exit 70 at Cyr, cross the Cyr Bridge, turn left on Sawmill Gulch and look for the yellow rafts ☎ 406/273–4718 or 800/831–RAFT) splash down the Blackfoot and Bitterroot rivers and the rowdy Alberton Gorge of the Clark Fork River.

Skiing

Montana Snowbowl (⊠ Grant Creek Rd. ☎ 406/549–9696 or 406/549–9777 ⊕ www.montanasnowbowl.com) has slopes for advanced skiers who are hooked on steep, challenging runs, and powdery views of nearby Rattlesnake Wilderness. Telemarkers and geländesprung alpine ski jumpers add a colorful element to the scene. New skiers aren't neglected: groomed beginner and intermediate runs make up more than half the trails on the 950 acres here, 12 mi northwest of Missoula. Services include a restaurant, bar, and Geländesprung Lodge in the base area.

Where to Stay & Eat

★ **$$–$$$$** ✕ **The Bridge.** Snug inside an old dime-a-dance hall, this great find is known for its vegetarian dishes, Gorgonzola burger, and scallops and chanterelles over angel-hair pasta. You can sit at forest-green tables or an antique bar from Butte and wash everything down with one of 10 local microbrews. If you're in a hurry, call ahead and your order to go will be ready at the drive-through window just across the street. ⊠ *515 S. Higgins* ☎ *406/542–0638* ⊟ *AE, D, MC, V.*

★ **$$–$$$$** ✕ **Guy's Lolo Creek Steakhouse.** For a real taste of Montana, head for this steak house in a rustic log structure 8 mi south of Missoula, in Lolo. The dining room has a hunting-lodge atmosphere, replete with taxidermied wildlife on the walls. Although most diners opt for one of Guy's signature sirloins—cooked over a crackling open-pit barbecue and available in three sizes—there are other well-prepared meat, chicken, and seafood dishes from which to choose. ⊠ *6600 U.S. 12 W, Lolo* ☎ *406/273–2622* ⊟ *AE, D, MC, V* ☼ *Closed Mon. No lunch.*

$$–$$$ ✕ **Zimorino's Red Pies over Montana.** Some of the best pizza ever tossed under the Big Sky is served here. The pasta and bruschetta are top-notch, and you can wash it all down with a microbrew, wine, espresso, or Italian soda. Eat in, take out, or call for a delivery. ⊠ *424 N. Higgins Ave.* ☎ *406/721–7757* ⊟ *AE, D, MC, V.*

★ **$–$$$** ✕ **The Shack Cafe.** A longtime Missoula favorite for any meal, this elegant restaurant isn't in a shack but rather in a tastefully remodeled auto dealership. Swinging doors take you into the saloon, where there's an oak bar that arrived in Montana via steamship up the Missouri River a century ago. For dinner, try broiled lamb chops with rosemary butter or one of the specials. Breakfasts of elegant pastries and hearty omelets are popular with the locals. ⊠ *222 W. Main* ☎ *406/ 549–9903* ⊟ *AE, MC, V.*

¢–$$ ✕ **Tipus.** One of the few East Indian restaurants in the northern Rockies, vegetarian-only Tipus serves such delectables as traditional samosas, dals, chapatis, and fresh chutneys. Try the appetizer spicy yam fries with tamarind chili chutney. You can sit at the stainless-steel counter or a cozy table, or order takeout. ⊠ *115½ S. 4th W* ☎ *406/542–0622 or 877/ 705–9843* ⊟ *AE, D, MC, V.*

¢–$ ✕ **The Staggering Ox Downtown.** Reading the menu here is as much fun as eating the deli sandwiches, which are served on specialty breads shaped like a tin can. Evocative sandwich names include the Headbanger's Hoagie (with ham, salami, pepperoni, cream cheese, cheddar, Swiss, mozzarella, lettuce, and Italian dressing) and Chernobyl Melt Down (with turkey, salami, Swiss, sharp cheddar, cream cheese, veggies, and salsa). Like its sister restaurants in Helena and Spokane, this Staggering Ox is decorated with thrift-store artifacts hung from the ceiling and walls. ⊠ *123 E. Main* ☎ *406/327–9400* ⌆ *Reservations not accepted* ⊟ *AE, MC, V.*

¢–$ ✕ **Worden's Market & Deli.** Floorboards creak beneath you as you explore this old-fashioned market, which spills over with deli delicacies.

There's a huge selection of imported beer and groceries. With 150 cheeses to choose from, the sandwich possibilities are endless; have them pile on Black Forest ham and horseradish for a creation that will get you down the trail. There's limited seating both inside and outside, where Worden's espresso and fruit smoothie bar has a walk-up window. ⊠ *451 N. Higgins Ave.* ☎ *406/549–1223* ⌁ *Reservations not accepted* ⊟ *AE, D, MC, V.*

¢ ✕ **Bernice's Bakery.** Missoula's best bakery sells buttery croissants, muffins, scones, quiches, and other treats plus a tempting array of desserts, breads, and coffee from 6 AM to 10 PM. There's seating inside and outside, or you can eat alongside the nearby river. ⊠ *190 S. 3rd W* ☎ *406/728–1358* ⌁ *Reservations not accepted* ⊟ *D, MC, V.*

¢ ✕ **Taco Del Sol.** Locals, professors, and students hang out, study, and chow down on Mission-style burritos and fish tacos. Design your own and try a *horchata* (a sweet Mexican rice drink) or a Mexican soda. Beer and wine are also served. ⊠ *422 N. Higgins Ave.* ☎ *406/327–8929* ⊟ *No credit cards.*

$$–$$$$ ▥ **Hilton Garden Inn Missoula.** Brand-new in spring 2006, the hotel offers upscale rooms unlike any the town has seen before. Ample rooms are equipped with flat-screen TVs and workspace desks with ergonomic chairs. The Blue Canyon Kitchen and Tavern serves lunch and dinner, and the Grill serves breakfast. The Pavilion Pantry convenience mart has the sundries that you forgot, and all around are the views that you came for. ⊠ *3720 N. Reserve St., 59808* ☎ *406/532–5300 or 877/782–9444* 🖷 *406/532–5305* ⊕ *www.missoula.gardeninn.com* ➴ *146 rooms* ⌂ *2 restaurants, refrigerators, cable TV, in-room data ports, in-room broadband, indoor pool, gym, hot tub, laundry facilities, lounge, business services, meeting rooms, airport shuttle, no-smoking rooms* ⊟ *AE, DC, MC, V.*

$$–$$$$ ▥ **Wingate Inn.** Oversize guest rooms and a 24-hour self-service business center here are designed with the business traveler in mind, but two waterslides at the pool please kids as well. Rooms have cordless phones, lounge chairs, and large TVs; a few have Jacuzzis. The inn has a pleasant lobby that includes a breakfast area, and it's convenient to restaurants, historic sites, and the airport. ⊠ *5252 Airway Blvd., 59808* ☎ *406/541–8000 or 866/832–8000* 🖷 *406/541–8008* ⊕ *www.wingateinn.com* ➴ *100 rooms* ⌂ *Dining room, refrigerators, cable TV, in-room braodband, in-room data ports, indoor pool, gym, hot tub, laundry facilities, business services, meeting rooms, airport shuttle, no-smoking rooms* ⊟ *AE, D, DC, MC, V* ⊺⊙⊺ *BP.*

$$–$$$ ▥ **Holiday Inn Missoula–Parkside.** The Missoula member of the Holiday Inn chain is a large, comfortable hotel with a lush atrium in the center and modern rooms. The property's greatest asset is its location in Missoula's riverfront Bess Reed park, a stone's throw from the Clark Fork River and across the river from the university, a ¾-mi walk. Sunday brunch is served in the atrium. ⊠ *200 S. Pattee St., 59802* ☎ *406/721–8550 or 800/399–0408* 🖷 *406/728–3472* ⊕ *www.himissoula.com* ➴ *200 rooms* ⌂ *Restaurant, cable TV, indoor pool, gym, hot tub, bar, no-smoking rooms* ⊟ *AE, D, DC, MC, V* ⊺⊙⊺ *CP.*

☺ **$$** ▣ **C'mon Inn.** This hotel at the bottom of Grant Creek, near the Snowbowl ski area, has easy access to recreation and business in Missoula. The best family lodging in town, it features a spacious, tree-filled indoor courtyard with a pool, baby pool, five hot tubs, and a waterfall. The large guest rooms open onto the pool on the first floor and have balconies on the second. Some rooms have kitchens. ⊠ *2775 Expo Pkwy., off I–90, 59808* ☎ *406/543–4600 or 888/989–5569* 🖨 *406/543–4664* ⊕ *www.cmoninn.com* ⟨ *119 rooms* ⚱ *Indoor pool, gym, hot tubs, business services, no-smoking rooms* ⊟ *AE, DC, MC, V* ¡○¡ *CP.*

★ **$–$$** ▣ **Goldsmith's Bed and Breakfast.** Built in 1911 for the first president of the University of Montana, this lodging is on the bank of the Clark Fork River, at the end of a footbridge that leads to the campus. Within the prairie-style building, with big white eaves and a huge porch, are period furnishings, wool carpets, and fresh flowers. Each private room is unique; the honeymoon suite has a Japanese soaking tub and two suites have gas fireplaces. Public rooms include a library and TV sitting area. Breakfast offerings include French toast and crepes, served in the dining room or on the deck overlooking the Clark Fork River. ⊠ *809 E. Front St., 59801* ☎ *406/728–1585 or 866/666–9945* 🖨 *406/543–0045* ⊕ *www.goldsmithsinn.com* ⟨ *3 rooms, 4 suites* ⚱ *Library; no room TVs, no smoking* ⊟ *D, MC, V* ¡○¡ *BP.*

Camping

⚠ **Jellystone RV Park.** On the outskirts of town, this lively park is popular with families for the playground, miniature golf, swimming pools, and, a kid favorite, pictures with Yogi Bear. Camping cabins, which sleep four comfortably, have air-conditioning, refrigerators, and microwaves. ⚱ *Grills, flush toilets, full hookups, partial hookups, dump station, drinking water, guest laundry, showers, picnic tables, food service, electricity, public telephone, general store, swimming (pool)* ⟨ *110 full hookups, 10 tent sites; 3 cabins* ⊠ *I–90, Exit 96, ½ mi north* ☎ *406/543–9400 or 800/318–9644* 🖨 *406/543–9405* ⊕ *www.campjellystonemt.com* ⊠ *$26 tent sites, $29 partial hookups, $31 full hookups, $41 cabins* ⊟ *MC, V* ☺ *May–Oct.*

☺ ⚠ **Missoula KOA.** This lovely campsite in the Montana-born KOA chain is easy to reach from the interstate. It has two hot tubs, a game center, miniature golf, bike rentals, space for kids to play, and a petting zoo with miniature goats, peacocks, llamas, and more. ⚱ *Grills, flush toilets, full hookups, dump station, drinking water, guest laundry, showers, picnic tables, food service, electricity, public telephone, general store, swimming (pool)* ⟨ *146 full hookups, 31 tent sites; 19 cabins* ⊠ *3450 Tina Ave., I–90, Exit 101, 1½ mi south* ☎ *406/549–0881 or 800/562–5366* 🖨 *406/541–0884* ⊕ *www.missoulakoa.com* ⊠ *$23–$34 tent sites, $30 partial hookups, $46 full hookups, $42–$57 cabins* ⚱ *Reservations essential* ⊟ *AE, D, MC, V.*

Nightlife & the Arts

The wildest film stars in the world are up on the big screen at the week-long **International Wildlife Film Festival** (⊠ 718 S. Higgins Ave. ☎ 406/

728–9380 ⊕ www.wildlifefilms.org), which shows animal documentaries in early May at the Wilma and Roxy theaters in downtown Missoula. The festival includes seminars, panel discussions, a parade, and art displays. The organization also offers a summer film workshop and a September festival, "MontanaCINE: Cultures and Issues on Nature and Environment."

At the **Missoula Children's Theatre** (⊠ 200 N. Adams ☎ 406/728–1911 or 406/728–7529 ⊕ www.mctinc.org), year-round productions vary from Broadway musicals to community theater for and by children of all ages. From October to June, you can see local talent and guest artists (usually professionals) perform family favorites like *Fiddler on the Roof*. In summer, there's a theater camp where kids are the stars of the productions.

Performing on the stage at Missoula Children's Theatre, **Missoula Community Theatre** (☎ 406/728–7529) mounts productions such as *Paint Your Wagon* throughout the year.

The University of Montana's Department of Drama and Dance manages the **Montana Repertory Theater** (⊠ Montana Theatre, in the PARTV Building near the Adams Center ☎ 406/243–5288), a professional company that provides the region with a steady diet of popular Broadway shows.

Shopping

Take a break while touring downtown Missoula and have a cappuccino or a glass of fresh-squeezed orange juice at **Butterfly Herbs** (⊠ 232 N. Higgins Ave. ☎ 406/728–8780), or try the Butterfly Coffee Soda—a cold drink with multiple layers of sweetness. The shop also sells baked goods, candies, soaps, candles, china, and other odds and ends.

Works by Montana authors, a fine selection of regional books, and gift items are found at **Fact and Fiction** (⊠ 220 N. Higgins Ave. ☎ 406/721–2881). Readings, signings, and other literary events are scheduled year-round at this comfortable shop, where you're likely to rub elbows with an author browsing through the shelves.

At the outdoor **Missoula Farmers' Market** (⊠ N. Higgins Ave. on Circle Sq. between Railroad and Alder Sts. ☎ 406/543–4238 ⊕ www.missouladowntown.com) you can buy flowers, fresh fruits and vegetables, and unique handmade goods. It's held on Market Plaza, a two-block area downtown, every Saturday morning from mid-May to mid-October and Tuesday evenings from July through mid-September.

Whimsical artistry by Missoula natives is available at the **Monte Dolack Gallery** (⊠ 139 W. Front ☎ 406/549–3248 ⊕ www.montedolack.com), open Monday–Saturday for your laughing pleasure.

For locally made crafts, come to the **People's Market** (⊠ Pine St. between Higgins Ave. and Pattee St. ☎ 406/543–4238 ⊕ www.missouladowntown.com), open Saturday mornings from mid-May to mid-October.

BITTERROOT VALLEY

This history-filled valley south of Missoula was once home to Nez Perce who helped Lewis and Clark find their way through the mountains. The expedition's campsites, plus historic mansions and missions, are scattered in and around Stevensville, Hamilton, and Darby, towns founded by early settlers attracted by temperate weather and fertile soil. Flanked by the Bitterroot and Sapphire mountains, the valley is named for the state flower, the delicate pink rosette-shape bitterroot, which blooms in late spring; its roots were a staple of the Salish Indian diet. U.S. 93 threads through the heart of the verdant valley and along the Bitterroot River, an excellent fly-fishing spot. Back roads lead to wildlife refuges and numerous remote trailheads for biking and hiking. Beware of hazardous driving: now that the Bitterroot has been discovered, the two-lane roads fill with impatient drivers trying to pass slow-moving farm vehicles and RVs.

Stevensville

28 *25 mi south of Missoula via U.S. 93.*

Stevensville, population 1,550, sits on the site of the state's first non-Native American settlement, St. Mary's Mission, a restored treasure that dates back to 1841. Nearby Fort Owen is a partially restored 1850s trading post. The town itself is named for General Isaac Stevens, who was in charge of the Northwest Territory's military posts and Indian affairs. Today it's a mix of beautiful old homes and haphazard modern construction in a lush valley.

The **Lee Metcalf National Wildlife Refuge,** on the edge of town, is nearly as pristine as it was before development encroached upon the wilds in this part of the state. Within its 2,800 acres reside 235 species of birds, 41 species of mammals, and 17 species of reptiles and amphibians. Bald eagles, osprey, deer, and muskrats are frequently seen along the preserve's 2 mi of nature trails and in the wildlife-viewing area. Note that fishing is permitted on the river but not on the refuge ponds, and that both deer hunting with bows and waterfowl hunting are permitted during specific seasons. ✉ *115 W. 3rd St., 2 mi north of Stevensville* ☎ *406/777–5552* ⊕ *www.r6.fws.gov./leemetcalf/* ✉ *Free* ☉ *Daily dawn–dusk.*

★ **St. Mary's Mission,** established by Father Pierre DeSmet in 1841, was the first Catholic mission in the Northwest and the site of the first permanent non-Native American settlement in Montana. The site is run by a nonsectarian, nonprofit organization that encourages tour groups, school groups and individuals to explore the home of Father Anthony Ravalli, an Italian priest recruited to the mission by Father DeSmet in 1845. Ravalli was also Montana's first physician and pharmacist. On the site are a photogenic chapel, a priest's quarters, a pharmacy, Father Ravalli's log house, and the cabin of Chief Victor, a Salish Indian who refused to sign the Hell Gate Treaty and move his people onto the Flathead Reservation. A burial plot has headstones bearing the names of both Native Americans and white settlers. ✉ *4th St., from Main St., turn* *west at 4th and drive 3 blocks* ☏ *406/777–5734* ⊕ *www.saintmarysmission.org* ⊠ *$5* ⊙ *Mid-Apr.–mid-Oct., daily 10–5.*

Major John Owen established **Fort Owen** as a trading post 1850. The property also served as the headquarters of the Flathead Agency until 1860. It's worth a half-hour to visit the museum to see the restored barracks, artifacts, and some of the fort's original furnishings. ⊠ *Hwy. 269, ½ mi east of U.S. 93 at Stevensville* ☏ *406/542–5500* ⊕ *www.fwp.state.mt.us/parks* ⊠ *$4* ⊙ *Daily dawn–dusk.*

Historical items in the **Stevensville Museum** include the belongings of early settlers, particularly the missionaries who came to convert the Indians of the West. Other exhibits provide an overview of the area's original cultures (Salish, Nez Perce, and Lemhi Shoshone), background on Lewis and Clark's two visits, and a look at later residents, from orchard farmers to today's cybercommuters. ⊠ *517 Main St.* ☏ *406/777–3201* ⊠ *Donations accepted* ⊙ *Memorial Day–Labor Day, Thurs.–Sat. 11–4, Sun. 1–4.*

off the beaten path

TRAVELER'S REST STATE PARK – This park includes a Lewis and Clark camp on a floodplain overlooking Lolo Creek. The explorers stayed here from September 9 to 11, 1805, and again from June 30 to July 3, 1806. Archaeologists in 2002 found evidence of a latrine and a fire hearth, making this one of only a few locations with a physical record of the expedition's camp. Tepee rings suggest that Native Americans used the riverside location, too. Self-guided tours meander through cottonwoods and the historic campsite. Daily interpretive presentations and guided tours run during the summer, on the hour between 11 and 3. ⊠ *6550 Mormon Creek Rd., south of Lolo, ¼ mi west of U.S. 93, Lolo* ☏ *406/273–4253* ⊕ *www.travelersrest.org* ⊠ *$2* ⊙ *Memorial Day weekend–Labor Day, daily 8–8; Labor Day–Memorial Day weekend Mon.–Sat. 8–5.*

Sports & the Outdoors

FISHING **Anglers Afloat, Inc.** (⊠ 2742 Alpenglow Rd. ☏ 406/777–3421) leads trophy trout trips and gives fly-fishing and cooking lessons on the Bitterroot and Blackfoot rivers. During the mayfly, caddis, and salmon fly hatches, fish with **Backdoor Outfitters** (⊠ 227 Bell Crossing E ☏ 406/777–3861), along spring creeks, in private ponds, or on river float trips on the Bitterroot, Clark Fork, Blackfoot and Big Hole rivers.

Where to Stay & Eat

$–$$ ✕ **Frontier Cafe.** For a bit of town gossip and great burgers, stop in this classic small-town café, a dressed-down spot where the locals love to hang out. ⊠ *3954 U.S. 93 N* ☏ *406/777–4228* ⌖ *Reservations not accepted* ⊟ *AE, D, MC, V.*

¢–$$ ✕ **Food Fetish Cafe and Catering.** Dine to live music on Friday evening and at Sunday brunch in the historic Old Bank Building. The menu tends toward Western standards given a French accent, with a focus on Montana-made and -grown ingredients. Rotating exhibits of local art add color to the dining room. ⊠ *308 Main* ☏ *406/777–2133* ⌖ *Reservations not accepted* ⊟ *AE, MC, V* ⊙ *Closed Sun. and Mon.*

$ ⊞ **Big Creek Pines B&B.** All the spacious, airy rooms in this B&B along Big Creek have views of the Bitterroot and Sapphire mountains and come equipped with armoires and fluffy duvets. The innkeepers know the region; after your three-course breakfast of fruit smoothies, vegetable frittatas, or Danish pancakes, they can help with the day's itinerary. ⊠ *2986 U.S. 93 N, 59870* ☎ *406/642–6475 or 888/300–6475* 🖷 *406/ 642–6482* ⊕ *www.bigcreekpines.com* ⇌ *4 rooms* ⚭ *Dining room, some refrigerators, fishing, shop, meeting room, free parking; no room TVs, no smoking, no a/c* ⊟ *MC, V* ⦿ *BP.*

CAMPING ⚠ **Charles Waters Campground.** Located in the historical area of Stevensville, this is an access point to the Selway-Bitterroot Wilderness. Trails, fishing, picnic spots, and a bicycle campsite are sheltered among trees, affording glimpses of the surrounding mountains. A fire-ecology interpretive trail explores regrowth after recent forest fires. ⚭ *Pit toilets, drinking water, fire grates, picnic tables* ⇌ *22 sites* ⊠ *2 mi west of U.S. 93 on County Rd. 22, then 1 mi northwest on Forest Rd. 1316* ☎ *406/777–5461* 🖷 *406/777–7423* ⊕ *www.fs.fed.us/r1/bitterroot/* 🎫 *$10* ⊟ *AE, D, MC, V* ⊗ *Late May–early Sept.*

en route   A refreshing stop for wildlife viewing is the **Teller Wildlife Refuge** (⊠ Quast La., Corvallis ☎ 406/961–3507), a 1,200-acre private preserve dedicated to conservation, education, and research. Situated along 3 mi of the Bitterroot River, about 8 mi north of Hamilton, the refuge is home to otters, beavers, spotted frogs, and salamanders, as well as pileated woodpeckers, birds of prey, waterfowl, deer, and many native plants. An education center conducts numerous courses, including teachers' workshops, fly-fishing classes, and lectures. Conference groups of up to 26 may arrange to stay in the four homes on the refuge. To get here, take Route 269 to Quast Lane and follow the signs.

Hamilton

 36 mi south of Stevensville via U.S. 93.

Home to retirees, gentleman ranchers, and the Ravalli County Museum, Hamilton (pop. 5,000) is a gateway to the Selway-Bitterroot Wilderness. It was established by 19th-century industrialist Marcus Daly to house employees at his 22,000-acre Bitterroot Stock Farm. There he raised thoroughbred race horses, funding the venture with part of the fortune he made mining copper in Montana. His own home, the Daly Mansion, is open for tours.

★   Copper king Marcus Daly's 24,000 square-foot, 56-room **Daly Mansion**, with 24 bedrooms, 15 baths, and five Italian marble fireplaces, is the showplace of Hamilton. Daly's heirs opened the Georgian Revival–style house to the public, and today tours run on the hour. There's also a printed walking guide available to the extensive grounds. ⊠ *251 Eastside Hwy.* ☎ *406/363–6004* ⊕ *www.dalymansion.org* 🎫 *$7* ⊗ *Memorial Day weekend–Labor Day, daily 10–4; and for special events.*

Frequent festivities at the Daly Mansion include craft shows, Missoula Symphony performances, and even a Kentucky Derby Gala that celebrates Daly's dedication to racehorses. Call the **Chamber of Commerce** (☎ 406/363–2400) or the mansion to learn about events.

The **Ravalli County Museum,** in the former courthouse, contains exhibits on natural history, fly-fishing, Native Americans, Lewis and Clark, and other subjects related to the region. During the Sunday Series (most Sundays, 2 PM, $5), speakers share local history and lore. ⊠ *205 Bedford* ☎ *406/363–3338* ⊕ *www.cybernet1.com/rcmuseum* 🖙 *$3* ⊙ *Mon. and Thurs.–Sat. 10–4, Sun. 1–4.*

Hamilton is situated in the midst of the 1.6-million-acre **Selway-Bitterroot National Forest.** It includes the Bitterroot and Sapphire mountains and parts of the Selway-Bitterroot, Anaconda-Pintler, and Frank Church–River of No Return wildernesses; it's traversed by the Salmon and Selway rivers. More than 1,600 mi of trails wend through the forest, where visitors may encounter bears, elk, moose, deer, and bighorn sheep. There are also songbirds and birds of prey such as eagles and owls. The forest has three historically significant trails: the Continental Divide Scenic Trail, the Lewis and Clark Trail, and the Nez Perce Trail; some parts of the trails are open to hikers, other parts to bikes and vehicles. Wildfires of 2000 scorched parts of the forest; hikers should be alert to the danger of falling trees in the burnt-out areas. ⊠ *1801 North Ave.* ☎ *406/363–3131 or 406/777–5461* ⊕ *www.fs.fed.us/r1* 🖙 *Free* ⊙ *Daily.*

off the beaten path

SKALKAHO HIGHWAY – Three miles south of Hamilton, turn east onto Route 38, also known as the Skalkaho Highway, and you'll find yourself on a beautiful, seldom-traveled route leading into the Sapphire Mountains and on to the Georgetown Lake area near Anaconda. This fair-weather road is best traveled in summer, since 20 mi of it are gravel. Mountain bikers tour here, and there are plenty of hiking trails through the 23,000-acre Skalkaho Wildlife Preserve. Note that Forest Road 1352 into the preserve is closed October 15 to December 1, making that a fine time for nonmotorized travel. Only 10 mi of the Skalkaho Highway are plowed in winter, which means the area is excellent for cross-country skiing and snowshoeing.

Sports & the Outdoors

FISHING   There are two good options for fishing excursions in the area. You can float and fish with **Fly Fishing Adventures** (⊠ 112 Freezout La. ☎ 406/ 363–2398) on the Bitterroot River. Fishing trips with **Fly Fishing Always** (⊠ 1 Fisherman La. ☎ 406/363–0943) amble down the Bitterroot River looking for brown trout and west slope cutthroat. Scenic float trips are also available.

RODEO   See more than 300 of the country's top senior rodeo cowboys and cowgirls—even some 80-year-old team ropers—among the over-50-year-olds who rope and ride at the annual **Senior Pro Rodeo** (⊠ Ravalli County Fairgrounds ☎ 406/375–1400) in early July. There's a parade, food, cowboy poetry readings, arts-and-crafts booths, and live music.

TRAIL RIDES   Take a horse trip into the Selway-Bitterroot Wilderness with **Lightning Creek Outfitters** (⊠ 1424 Skalkaho Hwy. ☎ 406/363–0320), which also offers cowboy dinner rides and pack trips. Spend a full day or a summer week in the saddle with **Two Bear Outfitters** (⊠ 505 Camas Creek Loop ☎ 406/375–0070), which offers cookouts, too.

Where to Stay & Eat

¢–$$ ✕ **Spice of Life.** Wednesday night, when live music fills the air, is the time to visit this romantic spot in a historic building. Eclectic fare includes pasta, seafood, steak, Mexican, Thai, and Japanese specials. ⊠ *163 2nd Ave. S* ☎ *406/363–4433* ▭ *AE, MC, V* ☉ *No dinner Sun.–Tues.*

¢–$ ✕ **Bitter Root Brewing.** Meet the brewmaster, sample a Sawtooth Ale or "the Brewer's Whim," and enjoy the live music (Thursday and Saturday). This smoke-free brewpub offers free tastings daily and an eclectic menu from the grill, such as taquitos and flautas, bison burgers, and their specialty, hand-dipped fresh halibut-'n'-chips. ⊠ *101 Marcus St., one block east of town center* ☎ *406/363–7468* ▭ *AE, MC, V.*

¢–$ ✕ **A Place to Ponder Bakery and Cafe.** Excellent baked goods available in the small, smoke-free café include croissants, cookies, and cookie bars that go great with a cup of chai. Order a slice of pizza or a bowl of homemade soup, or get a packed lunch for the trail—particularly good is the chicken salad on outfitters bread, similar to croissant dough with cheese baked inside. There are a couple of seats, but business is primarily takeout. ⊠ *166 S. 2nd St.* ☎ *406/363–0080* ▭ *No credit cards* ☉ *No dinner. Closed Sun. and Mon.*

$–$$ ⌂ **Deer Crossing B&B.** The two deluxe rooms, two luxury suites, and two cabins are set on 25 acres of property surrounded by pastureland, pines, the Sapphire Mountains, and Como Peak. On this homestead, accommodations are outfitted with fireplaces, hot tubs, and Western furnishings. The hearty ranch breakfast consists of French bread custard, smoked ham, and a fruit platter, served on the deck in summers. Horses and pets are welcome. ⊠ *396 Hayes Creek Rd., 59840* ☎ *406/363–2232 or 800/763–2232* 🖷 *406/375–0771* ⊕ *www.deercrossingmontana.com* ⇥ *2 rooms, 2 suites, 2 cabins* ♿ *Dining room, fishing, hiking, horseback riding, babysitting, free parking, some pets allowed; no a/c, no room phones, no room TVs, no smoking* ▭ *AE, MC, V* ¶⊙¶ *BP.*

$ ⌂ **Best Western Hamilton Inn.** This clean and convenient hotel is typical of the chain's smaller properties. It's within walking distance of many of the town's sites and restaurants. A Continental breakfast and a newspaper are available in the lobby each morning. The "family room" suite features a fold-out bed alongside the two queens. ⊠ *409 S. 1st St., 59840* ☎ *406/363–2142 or 800/426–4586* 🖷 *406/363–2142* ⊕ *www.bestwestern.com* ⇥ *35 rooms, 1 suite* ♿ *Dining room, some microwaves, some refrigerators, cable TV, in-room data ports, hot tub, laundry facilities, business services, meeting rooms, no-smoking rooms* ▭ *AE, D, DC, MC, V* ¶⊙¶ *CP.*

CAMPING   ⚠ **Blodgett Canyon Campground.** From this undeveloped campsite along a canyon creek you have easy access to hiking and biking trails, fishing, and rock climbing. There's no garbage haul, so cleanliness depends on good camping etiquette. ♿ *Pit toilets, drinking water, fire grates, picnic tables, swimming (creek)* ⇥ *6 sites* ⊠ *Blodgett Canyon, 5 mi north-*

west of Hamilton ☎406/363–3131 ⊕*www.fs.fed.us/r1* ⊠*Free* ⚲*Reservations not accepted* ⊟ *No credit cards.*

The Arts
Two days in June are set aside as the **Annual Bitterroot Days** (⊠ Ravali County Museum, on Bedford St. between 2nd and 3rd Sts. ☎406/363–3338) to celebrate Montana's state flower and heritage. On display in the arts-and-crafts booths is an assortment of bitterroot art and memorabilia.

The annual **Bluegrass Festival** (⊠Hamilton Fairgrounds ☎406/381–0135 or 406/363–1250 ⊕ www.bluegrassfestival.org) draws musicians from around the West for three days in mid-July. The outdoor event also includes arts-and-crafts vendors, pickers' workshops, and food stands.

Summer comedies and spring Shakespeare are standard parts of the year-round schedule put on by the **Hamilton Players** (⊠100 Ricketts Rd. ☎406/375–9050) at the Hamilton Playhouse.

Shopping
You'll find all kinds of gifts and gear for the cabin in the **Bitterroot Trading Co.** (⊠206 W. Main ☎406/363–2782), including Western-style lodgepole-pine and hickory furniture, and regional jewelry.

Original Western art, including oils, watercolors, and prints, is available at the **Ponderosa Art Gallery** (⊠944 Springhill Rd. ☎406/375–1212 ⊕ www.ponderosaartgallery.com), which hosts special guest artists' shows.

Darby

30 *14 mi south of Hamilton via U.S. 93.*

This town of 900, site of the U.S. Department of Agriculture's first Forest Service ranger station, is a destination for wilderness adventurers. If you're driving through the Bitterroot Valley, take a break here and have a meal or do some shopping. Riders who come into town for a local brew often tie their horses along the sidewalks.

★ The one-room, lodgepole-pine-cabin **Alta Ranger Station** was constructed in 1899 by early forest rangers as the first ranger station in the country. Bicyclists often access forest roads from here. Rangers have maps and knowledge of the backcountry in surrounding mountains. ⊠ *6735 West Fork Rd.* ☎ *406/821–3269 or 406/821–3913* ⊕ *www.fs.fed.us/ r1* ⊠ *Free* ☉ *Daily dawn–dusk.*

One of the area's first hand-hewn-log homesteads, built in 1886, is now the **Darby Pioneer Memorial Museum**, a repository for pioneer artifacts, photographs, and memorabilia. ⊠ *334 Bunkhouse Rd. on U.S. 93* ☎ *406/821–4503* ⊕ *www.visitmt.com* ⊠ *Donations accepted* ☉ *June–Aug., weekdays 1–5.*

The **Painted Rocks State Park** reservoir is a great place to cool off. Boating, camping, and fishing are popular here with the locals. ⊠ *Hwy. 473, 23 mi southwest of U.S. 93* ☎ *406/542–5500* ⊕ *www.fwp.state.mt.us* ⊠ *Donations accepted.*

Sports & the Outdoors

BICYCLING   Seemingly endless miles of mountain-biking terrain open up in the Bitterroot National Forest, where several loop routes challenge riders along dirt roads. Within the 16 mountainous miles of the **Railroad–Daly Loop** you may see moose, deer, elk, or livestock. Remember that bicycles are forbidden in designated wilderness areas. For maps, directions, and other loop routes, stop in at the **Darby Ranger Station** (⊠ 721 Main ☎ 406/821–3913 ⊕ www.fs.fed.us/r1/bitterroot).

CROSS-COUNTRY
SKIING   Groomed trails for skate and classic skiing on the **Chief Joseph Cross-Country Ski Trails** (⊠ 1 mi east of U.S. 93 on Hwy. 43 ☎ 406/821–3201) cover more than 25 km (15 mi) over hills and through meadows.

DOWNHILL
SKIING   Ten feet of snow can accumulate at **Lost Trail Powder Mountain** (⊠ 7674 U.S. 93 S, Sula ☎ 406/821–3211 or 406/821–3742), which straddles the Montana–Idaho border. There are 45 runs, and lift tickets are inexpensive ($27).

FISHING   **Joe Biner's Rainbow Guide Service** (⊠ 5424 West Fork Rd. ☎ 406/821–4643 or 406/239–1192) will show you the ropes of trout fishing in the area. They also offer float trips.

LOGGING   The annual **Darby Logger Days** (⊠ at U.S. 93, just after Tin Cup Rd. ☎ 406/363–3582 ⊕ www.visitmt.com), held in mid-July in a field at the south end of town, celebrates forests and logging, which began in the region in the 1880s. Contests include log rolling, speed cutting, speed chopping, greased-pole climbing, and ax throwing.

TRAIL RIDES   See the Bitterroots on horseback with **Circle KBL Outfitters** (⊠ 171 Bunkhouse Rd. ☎ 406/821–0017 or 800/946–6778), who will take you on hour- or daylong trail rides and wilderness pack trips into the Bitterroot or Selway wildernesses.

Where to Stay & Eat

$–$$$ ✕ **The Rocky Knob.** This 1940s log lodge, a former brothel, is now a delightful eatery that specializes in hickory-smoked ribs and prime rib, with specials such as panfried trout topped with an herbed-crab–and–spinach sauce. Dine by one of the two fireplaces, or hang out in the lounge, where billiard games and fishing stories are popular. ⊠ *6065 U.S. 93 S, Conner, 13 mi south of Darby* ☎ *406/821–3520* ⊟ *MC, V.*

$$$$ ✕▣ **Triple Creek Ranch.** This ranch is definitely off the beaten path, but it's well worth the effort if you are seeking utter seclusion and indulgence. Luxurious log cabins tucked into ponderosa-pine forest offer the kind of privacy and pampering that attract celebrities to this year-round, adults-only resort. The humblest accommodations share a hot tub amid the trees, and the others (mostly one-bedroom suites) have roomy indoor Jacuzzis or hot tubs on decks overlooking the Bitterroot Range. Massive log beds, fireplaces, and his-and-her bathroom suites with steam showers redefine the term "cabin." The per-couple rate includes all drinks plus top-flight meals (dinner $$$$ for nonguests, excluding drinks) such as dry-aged New York steak and seared yellowfin tuna with fried oysters. Also included are on-ranch trail rides, fly-casting instruction, snowshoeing, and cross-country skiing. The staff has that rare blend of friendliness and discretion. ⊠ *5551 West Fork Rd., 59829* ☎ *406/*

821–4600 ⓐ 406/821–4666 or 800/654–2943 ⊕ www.triplecreekranch. com ⤴ 19 cabins ⚹ Restaurant, kitchenettes, minibars, cable TV, in-room VCRs, in-room data ports, putting green, tennis court, pool, hot tubs, massage, fishing, hiking, horseback riding, cross-country skiing, snowmobiling, bar, library, laundry service, business services, meeting room, airport shuttle; no smoking ⊟ AE, D, MC, V ⊠ FAP.

☾ **$$$$** ⊞ **Pepperbox Ranch.** Bring your cowboy hat for a relaxing stay on this working cattle ranch in the Bitterroot Mountains. From your log cabin (or teepee or covered wagon), you can step outside to fish, trail ride, photograph moose and elk, and hike, and kids can take archery and roping lessons. In the evening, cowboy entertainment, campfires, and wagon and buggy rides are offered. In winter, there's downhill and cross-country skiing. Meals, which are part of the all-inclusive package, are served family style in the main lodge and include fried chicken and ranch-raised beef; each ends with homemade pie. Private log cabins have spacious porches and handmade quilts. ⊠ *9959 West Fork Rd., 59829* ☎ *406/349–2920 or 800/994–2920* ⓐ *406/349–2039* ⊕ *www.pepperbox.com* ⤴ *4 cabins, 1 tepee, 1 wagon ⚹ Dining room, refrigerators, outdoor hot tub, mountain bikes, horseback riding, cross-country skiing, downhill skiing, shop, free parking, no-smoking rooms; no room phones, no room TVs, no a/c ⊟ MC, V ⊙ Closed Mar. and Apr. ⊠ FAP.*

$$–$$$ ⊞ **Tin Cup Lodge B&B.** On a clear day, you can see 80 mi of mountains and valley from this pleasant mountain-top log lodge in the foothills of the Bitterroot Range. Lodge rooms and cabins are appointed with Western flair, whimsical log furniture, and comforters; cabins have private hot tubs. ⊠ *582 Tin Cup Rd., 59829* ☎ *406/821–1620* ⓐ *406/821–0903* ⊕ *www.tincuplodge.com* ⤴ *4 rooms, 2 cabins ⚹ Dining room, room service, some microwaves, some refrigerators, cable TV, in-room VCRs, pond, hot tub, sauna, bicycles, billiards, recreation room, shop, laundry facilities, business services, meeting room, free parking; no phones in some rooms, no kids, no smoking, no a/c ⊟ AE, MC, V ⊠ BP.*

CAMPING ⛺ **Lake Como Lower Campground.** This popular reservoir-side site among the tall pines fills up fast during July and August. There's also an upper campground available when there's no vacancy here. Note that a $2-per-day vehicle pass is required to park at the trailheads, boat launch, and beach access. ⚹ *Pit toilets, drinking water, fire grates, picnic tables, swimming (lake)* ⤴ *12 sites* ⊠ *County Rd. 82, 4 mi north of Darby on U.S. 93, then 4.8 mi west on County Rd. 82* ☎ *406/821–3269 or 406/821–3913* ⊕ *www.fs.fed.us/r1* ⊞ *$14* ⊟ *AE, D, MC, V* ⊙ *Late May–early Sept.*

Shopping

Bitterroot Fly Company (⊠ 808½ N. Main ☎ 406/821–1624), an Orvis-endorsed fly shop, is a few minutes away from the convergence of the east and west forks of the Bitterroot River, a native Westlope cutthroat trout fishery. They sell rods, reels, clothing, and fishing supplies, and offer fly-tying clinics and guided float and wading trips on the Bitterroot, Bighole, Beaverhead, Madison, Clark Fork, Blackfoot, and Rock Creek rivers.

Lightfoot Cycles (✉ 179 Leavens Rd.; take West Fork Rd. 3 mi west from U.S. 93 ☎ 406/821–4750 or 866/821–4750 ⊕ www.lightfootcycles.com) makes unique handcrafted bicycles, tricycles, and quadracycles for touring, commuting, recreation, delivery, and industrial transport. Designers build cycles for special needs, including power-assisted cycles, that are sold around the globe.

Old West Gallery and Antiques (✉ 202 S. Main ☎ 406/821–4076) is a huge shop selling gifts, collectibles, Native American and Western art, and furniture. The kids are likely to be enamored of the Old West Candy Store inside, which features fudge and hand-dipped chocolates. You can have your family photo taken with Marilyn Monroe and John Wayne while you listen to a player piano and other music machines.

NORTHWEST MONTANA A TO Z

To research prices, get advice from other travelers, and book travel arrangements, visit www.fodors.com.

AIR TRAVEL

Northwest Montana has two principal airports: Missoula International, on U.S. 93 just west of Missoula, and Glacier Park International, 8 mi northeast of Kalispell and 11 mi southeast of Whitefish on U.S. 2. Both are serviced by major airlines; if you're coming from outside the Rockies area, the odds are that you'll have a connecting flight through a larger hub such as Denver, Salt Lake City, Minneapolis/St. Paul, Phoenix, or Calgary, Alberta.

🛪 Airlines & Contacts **Alaska/Horizon** ☎ 800/547-9308 ⊕ www.horizonair.com. **America West** ☎ 800/235-9292 ⊕ www.americawest.com. **Big Sky** ☎ 800/237-7788 or 406/247-3910 ⊕ www.bigskyair.com. **Delta** ☎ 800/221-1212 ⊕ www.delta-air.com. **Northwest** ☎ 800/225-2525 ⊕ www.nwa.com. **Skywest** ☎ 800/453-9417 ⊕ www. skywest.com. **SkyXpress** ☎ 866/354-8677 ⊕ www.skyxpress.ca. **United/United Express** ☎ 800/241-6522 ⊕ www.united.com.

🛪 Airport Information **Glacier Park International Airport** ✉ 4170 U.S. 2 E, Kalispell ☎ 406/257-5994 ⊕ www.glacierairport.com. **Missoula International Airport** ✉ 5225 U.S. 10, Missoula ☎ 406/728-4381 ⊕ www.msoairport.org.

BUS TRAVEL

Commercial buses that travel along U.S. 93 between Missoula and Whitefish depart daily and stop at several small towns en route.

🚌 Bus Information **Greyhound** ☎ 800/231-2222 ⊕ www.greyhound.com.

CAR RENTAL

Car rentals are available in East and West Glacier, Hamilton, Kalispell, Missoula, and Whitefish.

🚗 **Alamo/National Car Rental** ☎ 406/257-7144 or 800/227-7368 ⊕ www.nationalcar. com. **Avis** ☎ 406/257-2727 or 800/331-1212 ⊕ www.avis.com. **Budget** ☎ 406/755-7500 or 800/527-0700 ⊕ www.budget.com. **Dollar** ☎ 800/457-5335 ⊕ www. montanadollar.com. **Hertz** ☎ 406/758-2220 or 800/654-3131 ⊕ www.hertz.com. **Thrifty** ☎ 406/549-2277 or 800/344-1705 ⊕ www.thrifty.com.

CAR TRAVEL

Of Montana's 69,000 mi of public roads, there are certainly more gravel and dirt roads than paved. Many of the unpaved routes are in good shape, yet you'll need to slow down and, as on any Montana road, be on the lookout for wildlife, open-range livestock, farm equipment, unexpected hazards such as cattle crossing guards, and changing weather and road conditions. Snow can fall any month of the year. In more remote areas, carry an emergency kit with water, snacks, extra clothing, and flashlights. Gasoline is available along most paved roads. However, if you are traveling in more remote areas, be sure to gas up before leaving town. Note that cell phone coverage has increased in the state recently, yet in mountainous terrain, it's unlikely that you will have cell reception.

🚹 **Statewide Road Report** ☎ 511 or 800/226-7623 ⊕ www.mdt.mt.gov/travinfo/. **Montana Highway Patrol** ☎ 911, 406/388-3190, or 800/525-5555 ⊕ www.doj.state. mt.us/enforcement/highwaypatrol.asp.

EMERGENCIES

🚹 **Ambulance or Police** Emergencies ☎ 911.
🚹 **24-Hour Medical Care Kalispell Regional Medical Center** ⊠ 310 Sunnyview La., Kalispell ☎ 406/752-5111 ⊕ www.krmc.org. **Marcus Daly Memorial Hospital** ⊠ 1200 Westwood Dr., Hamilton ☎ 406/363-2211 ⊕ www.mdmh.org. **North Valley Hospital** ⊠ 6575 U.S. 93 S, Whitefish ☎ 406/863-3500 ⊕ www.nvhosp.org. **St. Joseph Hospital** ⊠ 6 13th Ave. E, Polson ☎ 406/883-5377 ⊕ www.saintjoes.org. **St. Patrick Hospital** ⊠ 500 W. Broadway, Missoula ☎ 406/543-7271 ⊕ www.saintpatrick.org.

LODGING

🚹 **Montana Bed & Breakfast Association** ☎ 800/453-8870 ⊕ www.mtbba.com. **Montana Dude Ranchers' Association** ⊠ 1627 W. Main, Suite 434, Bozeman, MT 59715 ☎ 406/284-9933 ⊕ www.montanadra.com. **Montana Innkeepers Association** ☎ 406/449-8408 ⊕ www.montanainnkeepers.com.

CAMPING Campgrounds across the region vary from no-services, remote state or federal campsites to upscale commercial operations. During July and August it's best to reserve a camp spot. Ask locally about bears and whether or not food must be stored inside a hard-side vehicle (not a tent). Avoid leaving pets alone at campgrounds because of wildlife confrontations, and because it's against the rules at most campgrounds.

🚹 **KOA, Kampgrounds of America** ☎ 406/248-7444 ⊕ www.koa.com. **Montana Fish, Wildlife and Parks** ☎ 406/444-2535 ⊕ www.fwp.state.mt.us/parks. **U.S. Forest Service** ☎ 406/329-3511 ⊕ www.fs.fed.us/r1.

MEDIA

NEWSPAPERS & MAGAZINES The only regional newspaper is the *Missoulian,* based in Missoula. Each community has a daily or weekly publication. The statewide magazine of recreation and travel, *Montana Magazine,* is published six times a year.

TELEVISION & RADIO National television affiliates are based in Missoula and Kalispell. Most lodging facilities offer cable or satellite TV. You can tune in to local radio stations from most places in northwest Montana. Public radio, KUMF, is based at the University of Montana in Missoula and broadcasts throughout the region. Near mountain passes and other road hazards you'll often see a sign identifying a radio station that broadcasts road information.

SPORTS & THE OUTDOORS

If you really want to get away from it all, plan a trip to the roadless 1.5 million acres of the Bob Marshall, Great Bear, and Scapegoat wilderness areas. Access is limited, although once you penetrate this huge wilderness tract, there are trails such as the 120-mi-long Chinese Wall, a reeflike stretch of cliffs in the Bob Marshall Wilderness. Remember that in bear country it's best to pursue outdoor activities in groups of four or more, make plenty of noise, and carry pepper spray.

BICYCLING Hill climbing, single track, dirt road, or easy cruising bike paths—northwest Montana is flush with cycling opportunities. Bicycle trail maps are available at local sports shops and U.S. Forest Service offices. Note that bicycles are not allowed in designated wilderness areas or on backcountry trails of national parks.

🏃 **Adventure Cycling Association** ☎ 406/721-1776 or 800/755-2453. **Glacier Cycling** ☎ 406/862-6440.

GUIDES & OUTFITTERS When heading into the backcountry, it's a good idea to hire a guide or outfitter who knows the local trails, weather patterns, and unique features. Outfitters offer rafting, hiking, horse-pack, and other trips into the remote mountains.

🏃 **Fishing Outfitters Association of Montana** 🗐 Box 67, Gallatin Gateway 59730 ☎ 406/763-5436 ⊕ www.foam-montana.org. **Montana Outfitters and Guides Association** 🗐 Box 1248, Helena 59624 ☎ 406/449-3578 ⊕ www.moga-montana.org.

HIKING Before lacing up your hiking boots, determine where you want to go, what you need to bring, and what you're likely to encounter on the trail. The book *Hiking Montana* by Bill Schneider has useful, basic hiking safety information and offers route details from several trailheads. U.S. Forest Service offices have local maps, trail guides, and safety information. If you're new to hiking, you may want to employ an outfitter that offers guided walks.

🏃 **Montana Fish, Wildlife and Parks** ☎ 406/444-2535 ⊕ http://fwp.state.mt.us/. **U.S. Forest Service regional office** ☎ 406/329-3511 ⊕ http://www.fs.fed.us/r1/.

SKIING Although there is a statewide ski areas' association, the best information for both downhill and cross-country skiing is available through the state tourism bureau. A free winter guide booklet is available as well as detailed information on the Web. For descriptions of many cross-country ski trails throughout the state, pick up a copy of the book *Winter Trails Montana*, by Jean Arthur, which details 40 trail systems in Montana's snowy regions. Novices to the slopes will be in good hands at the area's well-established ski schools.

🏃 **Travel Montana** ✉ 301 S. Park, Helena 59620 ☎ 406/841-2870 or 800/847-4868 ⊕ www.wintermt.com.

TOURS

Some out-of-state tour operators offer Montana trips. Local tour operators, including those listed below, provide a variety of options, including custom trips.

📧 Tour Operators **Adventure Cycling** ✉ 150 E. Pine, Missoula 59807 ☎ 406/721-1776 ⊕ www.adventurecycling.com. **Off the Beaten Path** ✉ 7 E. Beall St., Bozeman 59715 ☎ 800/445-2995 ⊕ www.offthebeatenpath.com. **Swan River Tours** ✆ Box 1010, Condon 59826 ☎ 877/696-1666 ⊕ www.swanrivertours.com.

TRAIN TRAVEL

Amtrak chugs across the Highline and the northwest part of the state, stopping in East Glacier, West Glacier, and Whitefish daily. Flathead Travel partners with Amtrak to offer package excursions to Glacier National Park and other northwest Montana destinations.

📧 Train Information **Amtrak** ☎ 800/872-7245 ⊕ www.amtrak.com. **Flathead Travel** ✉ 500 S. Main St., Kalispell 59901 ☎ 800/553-3400, 406/752-8700 🖷 406/752-8786 ⊕ www.flatheadtravel.com

VISITOR INFORMATION

📧 **Glacier Country** ✆ Box 1035, Bigfork 59911-1035 ☎ 406/837-6211 or 800/338-5072 ⊕ www.glacier.visitmt.com or www.glaciermt.com. **Travel Montana** ✉ 301 S. Park, Helena 59620 ☎ 406/841-2870 or 800/847-4868 ⊕ www.visitmt.com. **Bigfork Chamber of Commerce** ✉ 8155 Hwy. 35, Bigfork 59911 ☎ 406/837-5888 ⊕ www.bigfork.org. **Bitterroot Valley Chamber of Commerce** ✉ 105 E. Main St., Hamilton 59840 ☎ 406/363-2400 ⊕ www.bvchamber.com. **Missoula Chamber of Commerce** ✆ Box 7577, Missoula 59807 ☎ 406/543-6623 or 800/526-3465 ⊕ www.missoulachamber.com. **Whitefish Chamber of Commerce** ✉ 520 E. 2nd St., Whitefish 59937 ☎ 406/862-3501 or 877/862-3548 ⊕ www.whitefishchamber.org.

The Montana Plains

GREAT FALLS, BILLINGS, LITTLE BIGHORN,
THE BIG OPEN

WORD OF MOUTH

"[Eastern Montana] is high plains and arid, so the landscape through much of it is rather stark and rugged; washouts, dry creeks, etc. They don't call it Big Sky Country for nothing; at times it seems like you can see forever. (I actually like it because it is so different from what I am accustomed to and it reminds me of a Western movie, but some people can find it rather bleak.) The area around the Charles M. Russell National Wildlife Refuge and Fort Peck Lake is quite striking, and when you begin to come up on the mountains, it is truly awesome."

–Flyboy

By T. D. Griffith
& Dustin D.
Floyd

SPACE, LOTS OF SPACE, IS THE HALLMARK of eastern Montana's gently rolling plains. To escape stifling crowds and urban sprawl, you would do well in the wide-open plains of Big Sky Country. The state as a whole averages six people per square mile, but some of its prairies measure in reverse: one person per six square miles. Although largely devoid of the epic snow-covered peaks of the towering Rockies, the eastern two-thirds of Montana have an expansive beauty that seems to stretch endlessly beyond the horizon, beckoning you to bask in the isolated serenity of one of the least-populated places in the country—in a land of almost too much sky.

That's not to say that eastern Montana is flat and boring. In fact, the grassy plains are often broken up by geographical oddities such as badlands, glacial lakes, and ice caves. Occasional pine-covered foothills or snowcapped mountains even pop up, looking strangely out of place rising from the surrounding prairie. This topographical diversity makes the region a playground for lovers of the outdoors. Hiking, horseback riding, wrangling, boating, skiing, snowmobiling, caving, and some of the best fishing in the world are among the greatest attractions here. Beyond the blessings nature has bestowed upon the state are an ample number of historic sites, state parks, museums, and archaeological digs.

Paradoxically, the first- and third-largest cities in Montana are in the state's highly rural eastern region. The largest city in a 500-mi radius, Billings is a center for culture, shopping, entertainment, and medical care. Great Falls, straddling the Missouri River near a handful of thundering waterfalls, is one of Montana's greatest historical centers, with dozens of museums and interpretive centers that trace the state's varied cultural influences. Scattered in between these two cities are more than 100 small communities, some with no more than two dozen inhabitants. Although diminutive, sleepy, and dependent on the larger cities, each of these towns has its own distinct Western character, adding to the larger flavor of the region.

Exploring the Montana Plains

Most visitors to Montana neglect the eastern plains in their rush to get to the increasingly crowded forests and peaks farther west, but the grassy prairies that roll ever onward into the Dakotas and Canada should not be overlooked simply because they lack the majesty of a mountain range. Stop on the plains for their isolation, their serenity, and their sky. Unbroken by man-made objects (or even natural ones), the heavens don't just stretch upward—they stretch outward. At night the effect becomes even more intense, as millions of stars, undisguised by the lights of civilization, beam down from every direction onto an otherwise pitch-black landscape.

Major roads are few and far between in this part of the state. I–94 sweeps westward from North Dakota to Billings, where it joins I–90, which comes up from Wyoming's Bighorn Mountains and snakes west through the Rockies into Idaho. The only other Interstate is I–15, which threads north out of Idaho and onto the plains outside Helena before looping around Great Falls and heading to Canada. In the vast stretches of prairie out of reach of the interstates, the key thoroughfares are U.S. 2, also known as the Hi-Line, running east–west across the top of the state; U.S. 212, running southeast out of Billings into South Dakota; and U.S. 87, running north out of Billings.

About the Restaurants

Showy dress and jewelry matter little to most Montanans. A cowboy in dusty blue jeans, flannel shirt, and worn boots leaning against his rust-eaten Chevy could be a millionaire rancher and stockbroker, and the ponytailed woman behind the counter of the general store might be the town mayor. Because of this, no matter where you go to eat—whether the food is extravagant or simple, the prices expensive or dirt cheap—dress is casual. But despite the universal informality in dining, eastern Montana has a surprising number of upscale restaurants turning out sophisticated dishes. Good ethnic food, with the possible exception of Mexican and Native American cuisine, is scarce, however. Classic steak houses and local ma-and-pa eateries are ubiquitous.

About the Hotels

The strength of eastern Montana's hospitality doesn't lie in luxury resorts, bustling lodges, or crowded dude ranches, which are confined almost entirely to the western third of the state. The crown jewels of lodging on the plains are historic hotels and bed-and-breakfasts. Nearly every town with more than a few hundred residents has at least one of these properties, but no two are alike. From turreted Victorian mansions and rustic log ranch houses to Gothic manors and hulking sandstone inns with intricately carved facades, these lodgings have their own appeal and local flavor that set them apart from chain accommodations and commercial strip motels.

WHAT IT COSTS				
$$$$	**$$$**	**$$**	**$**	**¢**
RESTAURANTS over $22	$16–$22	$11–$16	$7–$11	under $7
HOTELS over $220	$160–$220	$110–$160	$70–$110	under $70

Restaurant prices are for a main course at dinner. Hotel prices are for two people in a standard double room in high season, excluding service charges and 4% tax.

Timing

Each season offers something different in Montana: summer brings warm, dry weather perfect for hiking, biking, and horseback riding; autumn yields throngs of wildlife for animal lovers and anglers; winter means plenty of snow for skiing, snowmobiling, and ice fishing. Although summer is the busiest season here—with good reason, since freezing temperatures can arrive as early as September and depart as late as May—many travelers are only passing through on their way farther west. The roads may be crowded, but the attractions, hotels, and restaurants are likely not. Winter can sometimes be just as busy as summer, as thousands of avid skiers rush through on their way to the slopes. Road conditions are generally poor in winter, especially when a heavy snowfall

Space, one of Montana's most abundant natural resources, can make traveling between major communities and attractions tedious. The drive from Great Falls to Billings, for instance, takes four hours. It's tempting to rush the drive in order to get from point A to point B, but that tactic can make you—and your traveling companions—batty with the vehicular version of cabin fever.

Break up long drives with side trips and random stops. Even if the trip could take only four or five hours, give yourself the entire day. Survey your route on a map before you set out and choose two or three possible stops along the way. Between Great Falls and Billings you might pause in the Big Snowy Mountains for a brisk hike. Break up the drive from Great Falls to Havre with lunch in Fort Benton, at the Union Grille in the Grand Union Hotel. Don't hesitate to stop in the random small town. You may not find much more than a gas station, but the locals will almost always offer friendly conversation and a few tall tales.

5

There is plenty to do in the two largest cities on the Montana plains. Lake Elmo State Park, ZooMontana, and Pictograph Cave State Monument are good stops in Billings, while the C. M. Russell Museum, Giant Springs State Park, and the Lewis and Clark National Historic Trail Interpretive Center are must-sees in Great Falls. Both cities make good base camps for further exploration: most of the region's attractions are day trips from these communities.

If you have the time, explore some of the state's smaller towns. These mini-municipalities have few obvious visitor attractions. You just have to do a little creative thinking in these remote villages. It may look a little primitive next to its big-city counterparts, don't hesitate to pay a visit to the local museum. Remember outdoor recreation opportunities, too: for example, Miles City may look a little dull at first glance, but it's the perfect base from which to float down the Yellowstone River to Pirogue Island State Park.

Indeed, the great outdoors are probably why you're in Montana to begin with. If you are unaccustomed to so much space, the state's endless plains and wide open skies may become wearisome after a while, but they can be every bit as beautiful as the mountain peaks that tower in the distance. Appreciate the empty countryside while you can. Once you're back home, you'll miss it.

---

closes down entire sections of highway. Spring is a hard season to define, as snowstorms can strike well into May. Autumn weather, although not completely predictable, is usually the most stable. Days are long and sunny, evenings are cool, and there are very few fellow travelers to contend with.

Numbers in the text correspond to numbers in the margin and on the Montana Plains, Billings, and Great Falls maps.

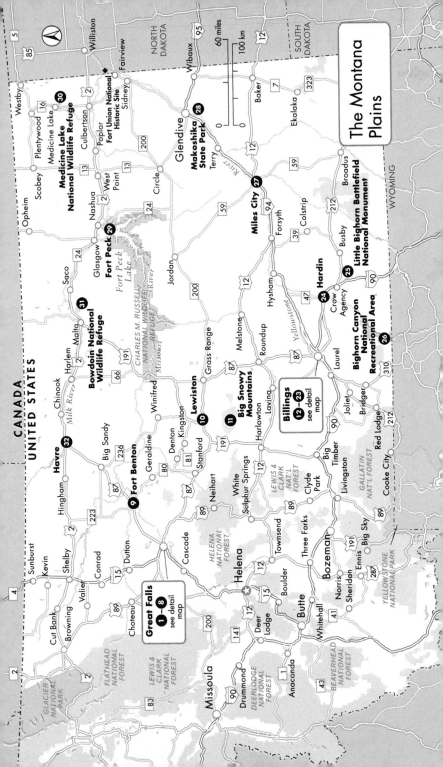

GREAT FALLS

One of Great Falls' greatest assets is its sense of history. Here, along the banks of the Missouri where the plains meet the Rockies, explorers Meriwether Lewis and William Clark encountered one of the more daunting obstacles of their expedition: the thundering waterfalls that gave the city its name. The interpretive center, guided boat trips, and paved trails that recall the passage of the two explorers in 1805 are impressive, but a slew of other museums and attractions celebrate other chapters in the city's history. From prehistoric buffalo jumps and famous Western artists to pioneering cowboys and the Missouri River fur trade, Great Falls has a storied past rich enough to make its people proud. And they are.

With 56,690 residents, Great Falls is no longer Montana's second-largest city, demoted in the 2000 census to third place, below the burgeoning mountain town of Missoula and its 363 extra residents. Great Falls is still the commercial and social hub for northern Montana and southern Alberta, with a bi-level mall, thriving downtown district, bustling civic center, and near-boundless opportunities for outdoor recreation.

Exploring Great Falls

This is a beautiful city for a sightseeing drive. Maple trees line the residential streets, the Missouri River slices through the center of town, and the Rockies sink their teeth into the distant horizon. Despite the curves of the river, most streets are straight and relatively easy to navigate, thanks largely to the flat terrain. However, with an Air Force base on the east side of town, a commercial airport on the west side, and only two bridges spanning the river in between, traffic can get heavy, especially in late afternoons and on weekends. Pedestrian paths are far less congested. A gorgeous 24-mi-long riverside trail, ideal for walking and cycling, passes the city's largest green space, Gibson Park, and one of the largest cold-water springs in the world.

a good tour

A good driving tour of Great Falls starts in the city's northeast corner along the southeastern banks of the Missouri. **Rainbow Falls ❶**, one of the half dozen or so waterfalls in the area, is below Rainbow Dam. Follow Giant Springs Road west along the river for several miles and you will come across several sights of interest: **Giant Springs State Park ❷**, where one of the largest freshwater springs in the world feeds a state fish hatchery before flowing into the tiny Roe River; the **Lewis and Clark National Historic Trail Interpretive Center ❸**, which focuses on the explorers' relations with Native Americans; and another set of waterfalls, **Black Eagle Falls ❹**. After visiting Black Eagle Falls, turn left onto 25th Avenue and follow it south until you reach 1st Avenue North. Turn right and drive west to the **Paris Gibson Square Museum of Art ❺**, at the center of the old town and housed in the city's first high school. Drive a couple of blocks farther west to 13th Street North, make a right, and drive to the **C. M. Russell Museum Complex ❻**, which holds the world's

most complete collection of art and personal effects of the famous cowboy artist. Drive west through the city's **historic district** to view hundreds of beautiful Victorian homes; the streets here are laid out in a perfect grid, so there's little chance of getting lost. Once you reach Park Drive North, follow it north to **Gibson Park** , the city's largest.

TIMING Depending on how much time you want to spend visiting the museums and wandering the historic district, this tour could keep you busy from sunrise to sunset. If you rush things, you might be able to finish in five or six hours. The parks and waterfalls take on their own special beauty when the snow falls, but biting winds might keep you from enjoying them for very long; the warmth of summer and the colors of autumn create perfect conditions for this tour.

The Main Attractions

Black Eagle Falls. On the north side of the historic part of town is 40-foot-high, 500-foot-wide Black Eagle Falls, one of the places where the Missouri River takes a sharp dive on its 500-foot descent through town. The adjoining golf courses and baseball diamond give the area plenty of green space and a seminatural feel, although it's hard not to notice the concrete dam looming above the falls. ⊠ *Intersection of U.S. 87 and 25th St. N.*

MONTANA'S GREATEST SON

CHARLES M. RUSSELL: The name is legendary in Montana. You'll see and hear it virtually everywhere you travel in this state, including at a massive national wildlife refuge that bears his name. But despite his near mythic status and the reverence his name evokes, people in these parts still prefer to call him simply "Charlie."

Born to a wealthy St. Louis family in 1864, Charlie could have enjoyed any of the luxuries high society had to offer. In fact, his parents spent most of his childhood trying to force refinement down his throat. When he didn't take to a private education in St. Louis, he was shipped off to military school in New Jersey. After the first semester he was sent home with instructions not to return. His parents noticed that Charlie always seemed to be drawing, so they sent him to art school. He was kicked out in a matter of days.

Charlie wanted nothing more than to go west and draw, so for his 16th birthday, his parents sent him with a family friend to a ranch in Montana, figuring that roughing it in the real world would cure him of his authority problems and fantasies. They were wrong. But it was far from easy for Charlie at first. He was terrible at his first job, herding sheep: He'd become so preoccupied with sketching that he wouldn't notice the animals wandering off. Eventually he was taken under the wing of mountain man Jake Hoover, and after a couple of years helping him trade with miners and ranchers, Charlie finally got himself a respectable cowboy job—wrangling cattle.

He spent the next 11 years working as a wrangler and painting or drawing nearly every day. During this time he befriended members of the Blood tribe, a branch of the Blackfeet Nation. For the rest of his life he would carry a deep respect for their culture and sympathy for their fate. "Those Indians have been living in heaven for a thousand years," he told a friend once, "and we took it away from 'em for forty dollars a month."

Eventually Charlie married. After a while, his wife, Nancy, persuaded him to work on his art full time, and in 1897 they moved to Great Falls, where Charlie built a studio. Within a few years he was showing work in New York galleries; not long after that he traveled to Europe. He hated going east, and in silent protest against the high-rises and factories he always wore his range clothes, including his trademark red sash.

Near the end of his life, health problems left Charlie tired and weak. The pain didn't bother him so much as the fact that he could no longer ride a horse. When he finally died in 1926, his hearse was pulled by horses—one of his last requests. Charlie's home was handed over to the city of Great Falls as a memorial. Local Native American tribes thought so much of him that they raised money to maintain the house and convert it into a museum.

Charlie's paintings and sculptures depict an era and a culture that were fading from the world during his lifetime. "The boosters say it's a better country than it ever was," he wrote to a friend in 1913 about the homesteading movement. "But it looks like hell to me. I liked it better when it belonged to God. It was sure his country when we knew it." Even his signature, which almost always included the symbol of a buffalo skull, commented on the end of the Western frontier. Some say his distinctive mark was a tribute to his Native American friends, whose free-roaming way of life died with the buffalo. But Charlie managed to save some of the spirit of the West he loved, in his more than 4,500 oil paintings, watercolors, sculptures, and illustrated letters.

❻ C. M. Russell Museum Complex. This 76,000-square-foot complex houses
Fodor'sChoice the largest collection of original art and personal objects of legendary
★ cowboy artist Charlie Russell (1864–1926). Russell's more than 4,000
works of art—sculptures, watercolors, oil paintings—primarily portray the vanishing era of the Old West. His studio and log home, built
at the turn of the 20th century, are adjacent to the main galleries. Also
here are collections of paintings by other 19th-century and modern
Western artists, interactive exhibits, and a research library. ⊠ *400 13th
St. N* ☎ *406/727-8787* ⊕ *www.cmrussell.org* ☜ *$8* ⊙ *May–Sept.,
Mon.–Sat. 9–6, Sun. noon–5; Oct.–Apr., Tues.–Sat. 10–5, Sun. 1–5.*

★ ❷ Giant Springs State Park. The freshwater springs here feed a state fish hatchery that covers 400 acres of parkland. According to residents, the waters that flow from the springs form the shortest river in the world, the
200-foot-long Roe River (Oregonians hold that their D River is shorter,
but most independent record-keepers side with Montana on the issue).
In addition to the hatchery, a visitor center, picnic grounds, a river
drive, hiking and biking trails, and a playground are all on-site. You can
also fish, attend educational programs, and take tours. ⊠ *4600 Giant
Springs Rd.* ☎ *406/454-5840* ⊕ *www.fwp.state.mt.us/parks/* ☜ *$5*
⊙ *Daily sunrise–sunset.*

❽ Gibson Park. This park, named for the insightful founder of Great Falls,
is the crown jewel of the city's 400-acre park system. The most popular features are the duck pond, the extensive flower gardens, and a small
café. There are also jogging paths, outdoor exercise equipment, basketball
courts, restrooms, a playground, a band shell, and prime picnicking spots.
⊠ *Park Dr. N and 1st Ave. N* ☎ *406/771-1265* ⊕ *www.ci.great-falls.
mt.us/people_offices/park_rec/* ☜ *Free* ⊙ *Daily dawn–dusk.*

Also Worth Seeing

❼ Historic district. There are more than 200 historic houses and small businesses here in the historic district, on the east bank of the Missouri River.
The structures reflect various architectural styles, including bungalow,
prairie, colonial, Queen Anne, Victorian, and Second Empire. You can
obtain a brochure for a one-hour self-guided walking tour of the area
from the **Great Falls Information Center** (⊠ *15 Upper River Rd.* ☎ *406/
771-0885 or 800/735-8535*). The area was laid out in a grid pattern
by city founder Paris Gibson, making it easy to navigate.

☝ ❸ Lewis and Clark National Historic Trail Interpretive Center. At this interpretive center next to the Missouri River you can trace the trail that
the Corps of Discovery traveled from 1804 to 1806 while in search of
an overland route to the Pacific Ocean. The center exhibits materials
used by the travelers and the Native Americans they met on their journey. Films, a self-guided tour, and costumed interpreters who conduct
daily demonstrations further illuminate the history. ⊠ *4201 Giant
Springs Rd.* ☎ *406/727-8733* ⊕ *www.fs.fed.us/r1/lewisclark/lcic.htm*
☜ *$5* ⊙ *Memorial Day–Sept., daily 9–6; Oct.–Memorial Day, Tues.–Sat.
9–5, Sun. noon–5.*

❺ Paris Gibson Square Museum of Art. Contemporary artwork of the northwest United States makes up the bulk of the collection here. In addition

to several exhibition halls and a photography collection, the museum has a bistro, a gallery, and a store. Near the center of town, the massive sandstone building that houses the museum was built as a high school in 1896 and converted into a museum in 1977. ⊠ *1400 1st Ave. N* ☎ *406/727–8255* ⊕ *www.the-square.org* ✉ *$5* ☉ *Memorial Day–Labor Day, Tues.–Fri. 10–5, weekends noon–5; Labor Day–Memorial Day, weekdays 10–5, Sat. noon–5.*

❶ **Rainbow Falls.** One of the waterfalls that gives the city its name, 50-foot-high Rainbow Falls is below Rainbow Dam, about 1½ mi east of Giant Springs State Park. The surrounding land is mostly owned by ranchers, although there are some trails cut into the hills near the falls. ⊠ *Giant Springs Rd.*

off the beaten path

SMITH RIVER – Flowing out of the Helena National Forest in the heart of Montana is the 60-mi Smith River. Like most other waterways in the state, it fluctuates with the seasons, ranging from a trickle in September to a raging torrent in June (thanks to the melting mountain snowpack). Although the river is popular for numerous activities, including camping on its banks, fishing, and swimming, the most prevalent activity on the Smith is floating. Floating is so popular, in fact, that Montana Fish, Wildlife & Parks limits the number of groups boating down the river to 700 per year. Despite the river's popularity, this is still Montana, and the sense of serene isolation that comes from the sight of towering mountains and open prairie will far outweigh any annoyance at seeing a few other boats during your journey. ⊠ *Between I–15 and U.S. 85* ☎ *406/454–5840* ⊕ *www.fwp.state.mt.us/parks/smith/* ✉ *Charges for use permits vary; call for details.*

ULM PISHKUN STATE PARK – For centuries Native Americans hunted bison by stampeding them off a cliff at this park named after the Blackfoot words for "deep blood kettle." This is one of the largest buffalo jumps in the United States. The mile-long cliff affords a spectacular view of the Rocky Mountains, the Missouri River, and the plains. An interpretive center focuses on the culture of the Plains Indians before white settlement. ⊠ *10 mi south of Great Falls on I–15 to the Ulm exit, then 3½ mi northwest* ☎ *406/866–2217* ⊕ *www.fwp.state.mt.us* ✉ *$2* ☉ *Memorial Day–Sept., daily 8–6; Oct.–Memorial Day, Wed.–Sat. 10–4, Sun. noon–4.*

Sports & the Outdoors

Unlike some of Montana's more westerly cities, Great Falls does not lie at the base of world-class ski runs or sheer cliffs for rock climbing. It is nevertheless popular with outdoor enthusiasts, largely because of its central location. Ski lodges and climbing trails are a short drive west, the pristine hunting grounds of the plains sit to the east, and stretching out north and south are Montana's famed blue-ribbon fishing streams. Not to be forgotten is the "Mighty Mo"—the Missouri River, a recreational playground that runs straight through the middle of the city.

The 24-mi **River's Edge Trail** (☎ 406/788–3313 ⊕ www.thetrail.org) follows the Missouri River through the city on both banks; four bridges connect the trail's two branches. The trail, which attracts bikers, joggers, and strollers, passes Gibson Park, the West Gate Mall, Giant Springs State Park, and several waterfalls and dams. More than 13 mi of the path, which is still under development, are paved; the remaining 11 mi are gravel.

Six blocks from the River's Edge Trail in downtown Great Falls is **Bighorn Wilderness Equipment** (⊠ 600 Central Ave. ☎ 406/453–2841), a sporting-goods superstore with everything from camping-stove fuel and freeze-dried food to ice-climbing equipment and kayaks. The store also rents bicycles and equipment.

Craig Madsen Montana River Outfitters (⊠ 923 10th Ave. N ☎ 406/761–1677 or 800/800–8218), facing the river on the north side of town, is known among locals for its guided trips along the river by canoe or horseback. You can also rent bicycles here for use on the River's Edge Trail.

Where to Stay & Eat

$$$–$$$$ ✕ **Eddie's Supper Club.** Campfire steak, lobster, prime rib, and shrimp are the entrées of choice at this casual Great Falls mainstay. The large booths and tables may hark back to the 1950s, but Eddie's serves some of the best burgers and steaks in town. There's live piano music on the weekends. ⊠ 3725 2nd Ave. N ☎ 406/453–1616 ▭ AE, D, MC, V.

$–$$$$ ✕ **Borrie's.** The dining is family style at this restaurant in Black Eagle, a small community that borders the northeast edge of Great Falls. Regulars favor the steaks, chicken, lobster, and burgers, although the huge portions of spaghetti, ravioli, and rigatoni are also popular. Historic photos of Great Falls line the walls, but the dim lighting makes all the furnishings look bland and dark. ⊠ 1800 Smelter Ave., Black Eagle ☎ 406/761–0300 ▭ AE, D, MC, V ☉ No lunch.

$–$$$$ ✕ **Jaker's.** The menu at this restaurant, part of a regional chain of steak houses, ranges from simple chicken sandwiches and pot roast to more elaborate dishes such as pan-seared oysters and fillet à la Jaker's, a steak topped with crab, asparagus, and béarnaise sauce. Dress is casual, although the cherrywood interior adds a feeling of sophistication. ⊠ 1500 10th Ave. S ☎ 406/727–1033 ▭ AE, D, DC, MC, V ☉ No lunch weekends.

★ **$–$$** 🏠 **Charlie Russell Manor.** A local attorney has restored and lavishly furnished this 1916 home in the historic district of Great Falls. Antiques fill the spacious rooms. The house also contains a sunroom, a study, a large dining room, and an English-style ballroom. Breakfasts are hearty, and there is on-site catering for special parties. ⊠ 825 4th Ave. N, 59401 ☎ 406/455–1400 or 877/207–6131 🖷 406/727–3771 ⊕ www. charlie-russell.com ⟲ 5 rooms ⚹ Dining room, in-room data ports, cable TV, meeting rooms; no smoking ▭ AE, MC, V ⑩ BP.

$ 🏠 **Best Western Heritage Inn.** Amenities such as outdoor tennis courts, a courtyard garden, balconies that overlook the indoor pool, and poolside rooms distinguish this modern chain hotel in a suburban area 3 mi from the airport. ⊠ 1700 Fox Farm Rd., 59404 ☎ 406/761–1900 or

800/548–8256 🖶 *406/761–0136* ⊕ *www.bestwestern.com* 🛏 *234 rooms* ⚓ *Restaurant, some microwaves, some refrigerators, cable TV with movies, tennis court, indoor pool, gym, hot tub, sauna, bar, casino, shop, laundry facilities, business services, meeting rooms, some pets allowed (fee), no-smoking rooms* ▤ *AE, D, DC, MC, V.*

$ **Collins Mansion Bed and Breakfast.** This gorgeous Victorian mansion,
Fodor'sChoice   built in 1891, looks like a circular building from the outside, thanks to
★   a massive wraparound porch. Oak chairs, wrought-iron beds, and miles of lace—on bedspreads, tables, and curtains—decorate the mansion. The spacious guest rooms all have baths, and the master suite has a fireplace. The B&B also has a gazebo, library, parlor, music room, and lounge with sattelite TV and VCR. Breakfast is served in your room, on the veranda, or in the dining room. ⊠ *1003 2nd Ave. NW, 59404* ☎ *406/452–6798 or 877/452–6798* 🖶 *406/452–6787* ⊕ *www.collinsmansion.com* 🛏 *5 rooms* ⚓ *Library; no room TVs, no smoking* ▤ *AE, MC, V* ⦿ *BP.*

$ **Townhouse Inn.** Frequent travelers to Great Falls return again and again to this modern hotel for its low prices and well-furnished, spacious rooms. Shades of beige, green, red, and blue decorate the motel-style rooms. An indoor courtyard has plants, a swimming pool, and a large hot tub. A small casino also offers distraction for road-weary guests. ⊠ *1411 10th Ave. S, 59405* ☎ *406/761–4600* 🖶 *406/761–7603* 🛏 *109 rooms* ⚓ *Restaurant, cable TV with movies, indoor pool, hot tub, sauna, casino, video game room, shop, meeting rooms, no-smoking rooms* ▤ *AE, D, DC, MC, V.*

¢   **Great Falls Inn.** Small but well appointed, this downtown hotel is accented by muted greens and reds, dark hardwood, and blazing white walls. Many of the guests of the inn stay here while using the services of the Great Falls Clinic and Benefis Healthcare Center next door. ⊠ *1400 28th St. S, 59405* ☎ *406/453–6000* 🖶 *406/453–6078* 🛏 *60 rooms* ⚓ *Some microwaves, some refrigerators, cable TV with movies, some pets allowed (fee), no-smoking rooms* ▤ *AE, D, MC, V* ⦿ *CP.*

Camping

⚠ **Fort Ponderosa Campground.** Horseshoes, miniature golf, and helpful hosts are some of the attractions of this friendly campground nestled against the Little Belt Mountains, 20 mi south of Great Falls. A small store here stocks propane and some basic provisions, and larger stores are in the nearby town of Belt, a short drive—or tube ride down the creek—away. If you don't bring your own shelter, you can stay in the A-frame chalet or the teepee. There's an extra $3 charge per night if you plan to use your RV's heater or air conditioner. ⚓ *Grills, laundry facilities, flush toilets, full hookups, partial hookups (electric), drinking water, showers, fire pits, picnic tables, food service, electricity, public telephone, general store, play area, swimming (creek)* 🛏 *25 full hookups, 25 partial hookups, 25 tent sites, 1 chalet, 1 teepee* ⊠ *568 Armington Rd.* ☎ *406/277–3232* 🖶 *406/277–3309* ⊕ *www.fortponderosa.com* 🗐 *$18 tent sites, $22 partial hookups, $25 full hookups, $45 chalet, $18 teepee* ▤ *MC, V* ⊙ *Apr.–Nov.*

⚠ **Great Falls KOA.** Regular evening entertainment at this campsite on the south edge of town includes bluegrass music, country humor, and a little cowboy poetry. The site is near three golf courses and has a large outdoor pool with a hot tub and sauna. ⚒ *Grills, swimming (pool), flush toilets, full hookups, partial hookups (electric and water), drinking water, showers, picnic tables, food service, electricity, public telephone, general store* ⤳ *80 full hookups, 60 partial hookups, 30 tent sites, 25 cabins* ⊠ *1500 51st St. S* ☎ *406/727–3191* ⊕ *www.koa.com* ⊡ *$33 tent sites, $40 partial hookups, $47 full hookups, $65 cabins* ⊟ *AE, D, MC, V.*

Shopping

★ Thanks to insightful city planners, Great Falls is blessed with a beautiful and extensive **downtown shopping district** full of the kind of old-fashioned stores that in other parts of the country are rapidly giving way to chain stores and shopping malls. Eat ice cream at a soda fountain, play with wooden cars at a toy store, and prepare for a trip down the Missouri at an outfitter's shop. Most of these businesses are in an area bounded by the Missouri River, 8th Street, 4th Avenue North, and 4th Avenue South.

★ A co-op run by a dozen local artists, **Gallery 16** (⊠ 608 Central Ave. ☎ 406/453–6103) has creations from more than 100 craftspeople whose works include paintings, jewelry, furniture, pottery, and sculpture. Gallery 16 also has a small gift shop at the Paris Gibson Square Museum of Art.

en route | Despite its name, the **Benton Lake National Wildlife Refuge** (⊠ 922 Bootlegger Trail ☎ 406/727–7400 ⊕ bentonlake.fws.gov/), about 20 mi north of Great Falls, isn't really a lake. Predominantly prairie and seasonal wetlands, the 19-square-mi marsh shelters hundreds of thousands of birds representing more than 240 species. The most common birds are ducks, geese, and swans. Come to watch, observe, and reflect; hunting is limited.

CENTRAL MONTANA

Although central Montana consists mostly of rolling plains carpeted with golden grasses, the general uniformity of the landscape is broken up by the occasional mountain range or swath of forest. There are other contrasts here as well, in this land where the pinnacles of the Rockies abut the ranches and farms of the prairie, and where old mining camps lie only a few miles from historic cow towns. Among the highlights of the region are its rivers: the Missouri, the Judith, and the Smith. They might not provide the kind of fishing found in Montana's famed Madison and Gallatin rivers, but they also aren't as crowded, and their rich history and stunning landscape make them the most popular Montana destinations you've probably never heard of. If you require regular doses of culture, you'll easily get bored in this land of seeming sameness, where you're considered a newcomer unless your grandparents are buried in the local cemetery.

Fort Benton

❾ *40 mi northeast of Great Falls via U.S. 87.*

The gateway to the wild and scenic Upper Missouri River, this town of 1,594 people has a rich and rugged past that's captured in a pair of excellent museums. Lewis and Clark first camped at this site less than an hour downriver from Great Falls, in 1805. As a quick and easy way to move people, the Missouri River was the lifeblood of 19th-century Fort Benton. The first steamboat arrived here in 1859, and the city once claimed distinction as the farthest inland port in the world. Throughout the 1860s gold taken from mines across the Montana was shipped downriver via Fort Benton; in 1866 alone, the town shipped 2½ tons of gold dust. The river still moves people today, not to seek their fortune in the goldfields but to paddle its placid waters amid the peaceful, serene, and beautiful countryside.

Montana's official agriculture museum, the **Museum of the Northern Great Plains** tells the story of three generations of farmers from 1908 until 1980. The 30,000 square feet of exhibition space hold a village of businesses from the homestead era, and a library. On display are the Hornaday-Smithsonian Bison, specimens taken from the Montana plains when it seemed likely that the species faced extinction. In 1886 the six buffalo were stuffed, then exhibited in the Smithsonian for more than 70 years. ⊠ *1205 20th St.* ☎ *406/622–5316* ⊕ *www.fortbenton.com/ museums/ag_museum.htm* 🎫 *$6* ⊙ *May–Sept., daily 10–5; off-season by appointment only.*

Fodor's Choice Covering the era from 1800 to 1900, the **Museum of the Upper Missouri**
★ highlights the importance of Fort Benton and the role it played as a trading post, military fort, and the head of steamboat navigation. Old Fort Benton is adjacent; considered the birthplace of Montana, with its 1846 blockhouse, this is the oldest standing structure in the state. ⊠ *Old Fort Park* ☎ *406/622–5316* ⊕ *www.fortbenton.com/museums/ muminfo.htm* 🎫 *$6* ⊙ *May–Sept., daily 10–5; off-season by appointment only.*

In 1805–06 Lewis and Clark explored the upper Missouri River and camped on its banks. Today the stretch designated the **Upper Missouri National Wild and Scenic River** runs 149 mi downriver from Fort Benton. Highlights include the scenic White Cliffs area, Citadel Rock, Hole in the Wall, Lewis and Clark Camp at Slaughter River, abandoned homesteads, and abundant wildlife. Commercial boat tours, shuttle service, and boat rentals—including rowboats, power boats, and canoes—are available in Fort Benton and Virgelle. ⊠ *Visitor Center, 1718 Front St.* ☎ *406/622–5185* ⊕ *www.mt.blm.gov/ldo/um/umnwsr.html* 🎫 *Free* ⊙ *Visitor center May–Oct., daily 8–5.*

Sports & the Outdoors

Although sparsely inhabited, this calm stretch of the Mighty Mo is becoming more and more popular with visitors. The benefit is no shortage of outfitters and guides offering their services at competitive prices.

★ The guided canoe trips offered by **Lewis and Clark Canoe Expeditions** (⊠ 812 14th St. ☎ 406/622–3698 or 888/595–9151 ⊕ www. lewisandclarkguide.com) last from one to seven days and can be customized to include horseback riding. You can also arrange for canoe rentals and a guide-only service, in which you provide transportation and food for your escort. The **Missouri River Canoe Company** (⊠ 7485 Virgelle Ferry Rd. N, Loma ☎ 406/378–3110 or 800/426–2926 ⊕ www.canoemontana. com/index.html), downriver from Fort Benton in the tiny town of Loma, provides canoe and kayak rentals by the day, outfitted excursions, and guided trips of one or four days. Also available are horseback-riding trips and lodging at Virgelle Merc, a restored homestead-era settlement with accommodations in cabins, B&B rooms, and even a sheepherder's wagon under the stars.

Where to Stay & Eat

$–$$$ ✕⊡ **Grand Union Hotel.** Perhaps the oldest hotel in Montana, the Grand Union was built on the bank of the Missouri in 1882 to serve steamboat and stage travelers. Filled with period pieces, the two-story building is as elegant as it ever was. Many of the spacious rooms have river views. With its dark-wood accents and Victorian-style lighting, the Union Grille Restaurant ($$$–$$$$) brings to mind the refinement cultivated by the Western frontier's elite. The menu might include seared sea scallops, charbroiled venison, and grilled buffalo tenderloin, and the wine list is populated by choices from California and Washington vineyards. Brunch is served on Sundays. ⊠ *1 Grand Union Sq., 59442* ☎ *406/ 622–1882 or 888/838–1882* 🖷 *406/622–5985* ⊕ *www.grandunionhotel. com* ⇩ *26 rooms* ⚬ *Restaurant, some in-room hot tubs, cable TV, bar, shop, business services, meeting rooms; no smoking* ⊟ *AE, D, MC, V* ⊙ *Restaurant closed Mon. in summer, Mon. and Tues. in winter. No lunch* ⎫◯⎧ *CP.*

$ ⊡ **The Riverbend Bed & Breakfast.** This log–and–wood-beam lodge nes-
Fodor'sChoice tles on a quiet stretch of the Missouri River 2 mi north of Fort Benton.
★ There are only two guest rooms, and only guests with advance reservations are given the B&B's precise location, so expect plenty of peace and solitude here. Because of its relatively remote location, outdoor activities are the primary pastime, and Riverbend's owners will gladly help you arrange day trips. Ask them about guided tours of nearby farms and historic sites, horseback riding excursions, and tee times at the local golf course. ⊠ *2 mi north of Fort Benton along the Missouri River, 59442* ☎ *406/622–5601* 🖷 *406/622–5601* ⊕ *www.riverbendbb. com* ⇩ *2 rooms* ⚬ *No room phones, no room TVs, no smoking, no a/c* ⊟ *No credit cards* ⊙ *Closed Oct.–Apr.* ⎫◯⎧ *BP.*

Shopping

There are thousands of bolts of quilting fabric at the **Quilting Hen** (⊠ 1156 Buck Bridge Rd., Carter ☎ 406/734–5297), about halfway between Great Falls and Fort Benton. The store specializes in unusual patterns and kits, including one based on the Lewis and Clark expedition.

Lewistown

① *90 mi southeast of Fort Benton via Hwys. 80 and 81.*

Begun as a small trading post in the shadow of the low-lying Moccasin Mountains, Lewistown has evolved into a pleasant town of 5,813 residents. Several locations are listed on the National Register of Historic Places, including the Silk Stocking and Central Business districts, Courthouse Square, Judith Place, and Stone Quarry. Self-guided-tour brochures are available at the the Lewistown Chamber of Commerce (⊠ 408 N. E. Main St. ☎ 406/535–5436 ⊕ www.lewistownchamber.com).

Nearly half the town—and several hundred visitors from across the country—turn out each year for the **Lewistown Chokecherry Festival.** Held the first Saturday after Labor Day, the annual harvest celebration includes contests, concerts, arts and crafts booths, a farmers' market, and a cook-off starring the wild-growing sour berry. ⊠ *Along Main St.* ☎ *406/ 535–5436* ⊕ *www.lewistownchamber.com/chokeche.htm.*

Pioneer relics, blacksmith and cowboy tools, guns, and Native American artifacts are displayed at the **Central Montana Museum.** ⊠ *408 N.E. Main St.* ☎ *406/535–5436* ☒ *Free* ⊙ *Daily 9–5.*

★ Discover the vistas that inspired Western artist Charles Russell on the **Charles Russell Chew-Choo,** a vintage 1950s-era train that travels through some of the most beautiful and remote landscapes in the state. The tour, which departs from Kingston, about 10 miles northwest of Lewiston, lasts 3½ hours and includes dinner. ⊠ *U.S. 191 north 2 mi, then Hanover Rd. west for 7½ mi* ☎ *406/538–8721, 800/860–9646* ⊕ *www. charlierussellchewchoo.com* ☒ *$90–$125, including dinner* ⊙ *June–Sept., Sat.; Also Dec. call for departure times.*

The regional **Lewistown Art Center** showcases artwork by local talent and hosts community art classes. ⊠ *801 W. Broadway St.* ☎ *406/538– 8278* ⊕ *www.lewistownartcenter.com* ☒ *Free* ⊙ *Tues.–Sat. 11:30–5:30.*

At the head of one of the purest cold-water springs in the world is the **Big Springs Trout Hatchery.** The state's largest cold-water production station nurtures several species of trout and kokanee salmon. The show pond, where you can view albino rainbow trout and fish weighing a monstrous 15 pounds, is a popular attraction, but the hatchery grounds are a sight in and of themselves. You can see the place where Big Spring Creek spurts from the earth, and the native wildlife—including white-tailed deer, beavers, wood ducks, and belted kingfishers—make frequent appearances. ⊠ *Hwy. 466, 5 mi south of Lewistown* ☎ *406/538–5588* ☒ *Free* ⊙ *Daily sunrise–sunset.*

off the beaten path

JUDITH RIVER – The tame, deserted Judith flows more than 60 mi from the Lewis and Clark National Forest through arid plains and sandy mesas before emptying into the Missouri. The scenery is stunning, but the variably low water levels and stifling hot summer sun are not conducive to float trips. This is, however, excellent fossil-hunting ground, and the **Judith River Dinosaur Institute,** based in Malta, sponsors frequent digs here. Most of the land surrounding the river is private, though, so check before you start wandering the banks looking for bones. As always, remember to leave fossils where you find them, and report anything significant to the Dinosaur Institute. ⊠ *North of Hwy. 200* ☎ *Dinosaur Institute 406/654–2323* ⊕ *www.montanadinosaurdigs.com.*

WAR HORSE NATIONAL WILDLIFE REFUGE – In 1958, this 3,192-acre area was established as a refuge and breeding ground for migratory birds and other wildlife. The refuge comprises three units: War Horse Lake, Wild Horse Lake, and Yellow Water Reservoir. The three units are geographically separate, but all are part of the larger Charles M. Russell National Wildlife Refuge, which encompasses more than 1 million acres along the Missouri River. Note that it's necessary to take gravel roads to reach fishing and wildlife areas. The Charles M. Russell Complex Headquarters is in Lewistown (505 Airport Rd.), with substations at Fort Peck, Jordan, and Roy. ⊠ *48 mi east of Lewistown on U.S. 87* ☎ *406/538–8706* ⊕ *refuges.fws. gov/* ⊡ *Free* ☉ *Daily; headquarters weekdays 8–4.*

Sports & the Outdoors

Lewistown has access to water—and plenty of it. From natural springs to alpine lakes to crystal-clear creeks fed by melting snow, there are all kinds of ways to get wet within a few short miles of town.

Ackley Lake State Park (⊠U.S. 87 to Hwy. 400, then 7 mi southwest ☎406/454–5840 ⊕ www.fwp.state.mt.us) has two boat ramps, great fishing, and a 23-site campground. It's to the north of the Little Belt Mountains, about 26 mi southwest of Lewistown. In a clearing outside Lewistown you can swim in the **Gigantic Warm Springs** (⊠ north on U.S. 191, then west on Hwy. 81 for 5 mi), a small spring-fed lake that keeps a constant temperature of 68°F. One of the most popular places in Frank Day City Park is the **Lewistown Municipal Swimming Pool** (⊠ S. 5th Ave. ☎406/538–4503), a 13,000-square-foot water park with two large slides.

Where to Stay & Eat

¢–$$ ✕ **The Mint Bar & Grill.** This quaint bar and grill serves an exceptional array of dishes, but you won't find them on the rather basic menu. You have a choice of seven to ten specials each night, ranging from simple sandwiches to salmon with lemon-tarragon beurre blanc to braised lamb shank over mashed potatoes. The separate bar, housed in the same restored 1914 brick building, has wainscotted walls and a hardwood floor. ⊠ *113 S. 4th Ave.* ☎ *406/538–9925* ▤ *D, MC, V* ⬿ *No smoking* ☉ *Closed Sun.*

¢–$ ▥ **Yogo Inn of Lewistown.** This inn takes its name from the Yogo sapphires mined nearby. Rooms are contemporary, spacious, and well furnished; some have four-poster beds. Many rooms face an indoor courtyard with a swimming pool and hot tub. Outside, the Centermark Courtyard take its name from surveyor documents buried here in 1912: they proclaimed the spot the geographical center of Montana. You can pick up the Charlie Russell Chew-Choo dinner train at the inn, and you can also arrange for Western buggy rides and ghost town tours. ⊠ *211 E. Main*

St., 59457 ☎ *406/535–8721 or 800/860–9646* 🖷 *406/538–8969*
⊕ *www.yogoinn.com* ⮠ *123 rooms* ⚐ *Restaurant, cable TV with movies, indoor pool, hot tub, bar, video game room, meeting rooms, some pets allowed (fee), no-smoking rooms* ▤ *AE, D, MC, V.*

Big Snowy Mountains

⑪ *40 mi south of Lewistown via Red Hill Rd.*

South of Montana's geographical center, an island of rocky peaks rises more than 3,000 feet from the sea of windswept prairie, beckoning scenery lovers and hard-core adventurers alike. A combination of evergreen forests and barren tundra, much of the Big Snowy Mountains area is undeveloped. More than 80% of its 106,776 acres are designated federal wilderness area—there are no homes, no commercial services, no industry, and very few roads. The result is almost total solitude for anyone who treks into the Big Snowies to explore their rocky pinnacles, icy caves, and tranquil forests. Few of the features of the Big Snowies are marked, but you can pick up a map of the area from any of the Lewis and Clark National Forest ranger stations scattered around central Montana, including the **Musselshell Ranger Station** (✉ 809 2nd St. NW, Harlowton ☎ 406/632–4391 ⊕ www.fs.fed.us/r1/lewisclark), 25 mi southwest of the mountains.

At 8,681 feet, **Greathouse Peak** (named for a Forest Service ranger who died in World War I) is the tallest mountain in the Big Snowies. Vehicles are permitted on some two-tracks that lead off Forest Service roads partially up the peak, but the simplest way up is to hike the 6 mi of unmarked trails that zigzag up the slope from Halfmoon Canyon. The main trail, which is only mildly strenuous, doesn't quite make it to the top; in order to reach the summit, you'll need to hike a few yards off the main path. You'll know you've reached the highest point when you see the two stone cairns. ✉ *Pack Trail* ☎ *406/566–2292* ☉ *Daily; automobile access June–Nov., other times by snowmobile only.*

The second-highest point in the Big Snowies is **Big Snowy,** also called Old Baldy. Just 41 feet shorter than Greathouse Peak, the 8,640-foot-high mountain makes an enjoyable climb. A two-track stretches almost to the summit, although fallen rocks block vehicle travel on the last stretch. The peak is a barren plateau with a small rocky outcropping marking the highest point. ✉ *Red Hill Rd.* ☎ *406/566–2292* ☉ *Daily; automobile access June–Nov., other times by snowmobile only.*

★ In the higher reaches of the mountains is pristine **Crystal Lake.** There's excellent hiking along interpretive and wildflower trails as well as camping, fossil hunting, and ice-cave exploration. The ice cave is a 6-mi hike from the 28-site campground; June is the best time to see the 30-foot ice pillars formed over the winter. There's a cabin for snowmobilers. No motorized boats are allowed on the lake. ✉ *Crystal Lake Rd.* ☎ *406/566–2292* ▦ *Free* ☉ *Daily; automobile access June–Nov., other times by snowmobile only.*

A 1909 limestone building in the town of Harlowton, 25 mi southwest of the mountains, houses the **Upper Musselshell Museum.** The collection primarily contains artifacts of the people who lived in, worked, and developed the land around the Upper Musselshell River. There are also fossils of dinosaurs and bison. ⊠ *11 S. Central St., Harlowton* ☎ *406/ 632–5519* ⊡ *$2* ☉ *Memorial Day–Labor Day, Tues.–Sat. 10–5.*

Sports & the Outdoors

In the evergreen forests and rocky slopes of the Big Snowies you can pursue numerous outdoor activities, including fishing, hiking, rock climbing, snowmobiling, and cross-country skiing. The utter isolation of the region enhances the experience but also means nearby outfitters are all but impossible to find. It's best to get supplied in the larger communities of Lewistown, Great Falls, or Billings before making the trek out to the mountains.

A small local outfitter, **Don's Store** (⊠ 120 2nd Ave. S, Lewistown ☎ 406/538–9408 or 800/879–8194 ⊕ www.montanaarchery.com) carries a wide selection of fishing gear and outdoor wear, plus some camera equipment. **High Plains Bike & Ski** (⊠ 222 W. Broadway St., Lewistown ☎ 406/538–2902) sells many brands of alpine and bicycling equipment and can rush-order cross-country-skiing equipment.

Where to Stay

¢–$ 🏨 **Corral Motel.** Family units, some with two bedrooms, and a nearby restaurant are the specialty of this hotel filled with modern furniture. Most rooms afford unobstructed views of the Musselshell River; the Castle, Crazy, and Big Snowy mountains are also clearly visible. ⊠ *U.S. 12 and U.S. 191, Box 721, Harlowton 59036* ☎ *406/632–4331 or 800/ 392–4723* 🖷 *406/632–4748* ⇝ *18 rooms, 6 2-bedroom units* ⌂ *Restaurant, some refrigerators, cable TV with movies, hot tub, bar, no-smoking rooms* ▭ *AE, D, MC, V.*

CAMPING 🏕 **Crystal Lake Campground.** Surrounded by thick stands of trees and tucked inside the lip of the crater that contains the waters of Crystal Lake, this primitive campground may be one of the most dramatic (and cold) places to pitch a tent in the state. There are year-round ice caves nearby, and heavy snows force the campground to close autumn through late spring. There's plenty of space separating the campsites. Call in advance to pay your fee. ⌂ *Grills, pit toilets, drinking water, picnic tables, swimming (lake)* ⇝ *23 sites* ⊠ *Crystal Lake Rd., 22 mi west of U.S. 87* ☎ *406/566–2292* 🖷 *406/566–2408* ⊕ *www.fs.fed.us/r1/ lewisclark* ⊡ *$8* ▭ *MC, V* ☉ *Mid-May–late Sept. (call to verify).*

en route Depending on how you entered and plan to leave the Big Snowy Mountains, any combination of U.S. 12, U.S. 191, U.S. 87, and I–90 will make a quick route to Billings. However, if you have the time, try getting off the main roads. The square of beautiful country between these four highways is the location of **Halfbreed Lake National Wildlife Refuge** (⊠ Molt-Rapelje Rd. ☎ 406/538–8706), part of the Charles M. Russell National Wildlife Refuge. The several thousand acres of Halfbreed encompass a lake, wetlands, creeks, and grassy plains. Wildlife includes grouse, elk, deer, and antelope. This is a favorite spot for birders, who say Halfbreed is one of the best places in the state to see migratory species.

BILLINGS

A bastion of civilization on an otherwise empty prairie, Billings is a classic Western city, full of the kind of history that shaped the frontier. The Minnesota and Montana Land and Improvement Company founded the town simply to serve as a shipping point along the Northwestern Railroad. In the spring of 1882 the settlement consisted of three buildings: a home, a hotel, and a general store, but before six months passed, 5,000 city lots had been sold and more than 200 homes and businesses had been erected. The city's immediate and consistent growth—spurred by the arrival of the railroad, its location on the Yellowstone River, and the entrepreneurial enthusiasm of cattle barons, merchants, and miners headed to the goldfields farther west—earned Billings the nickname "the Magic City."

The population of Billings has doubled every 30 years since its founding, and today the metropolitan area has more than 120,000 residents, making it not only the largest city in Montana, but also the largest city for 500 mi in any direction. Midway between Minneapolis and Seattle, and Denver and Calgary, Billings is one of the Northwest's premier trading centers. It's also an important regional center for medicine, education, culture, technology, and industry. Since the 1951 discovery of an oil field that stretches across Montana and the Dakotas into Canada, refining and energy production have played a key role in keeping the city vibrant and productive.

Exploring Billings

Over the years, city planners have done a fine job of laying out the constantly growing community of Billings. The primary residential districts are on the northern and western sides, the industrial parks are on the city's southern and eastern perimeters, and a lively downtown commercial district is sandwiched in between. There are plenty of major avenues to ease the flow of traffic between the sectors, and downtown streets are logically numbered, making navigation by car or foot relatively simple (note: some of the downtown streets are one-way). Remember that Billings, like most other Western cities, sprawls; expect to do far more driving than walking to reach your destination. Major residential and commerical development continues near Interstate 90 on the town's western edge, producing new freeway interchanges, strip malls, and chain hotels and motels. Keep in mind that I–90, which runs along the southern and eastern edges of Billings, is the primary route many locals use to commute to work, so do your best to avoid it in the early morning and early evening.

a good tour

Billings is surrounded by a distinct rock wall, aptly named the Rimrocks. Running along part of the wall is the **Rimrock Trail** ⑫, made up of several smaller trails, which has outstanding views and is a good place to start your tour of the city. After your hike, drive north on Main Street to **Lake Elmo State Park** ⑮, a popular recreational spot on the edge of town near Billings Heights. Head back down Main Street and then drive southwest on 6th Avenue North into the commercial district,

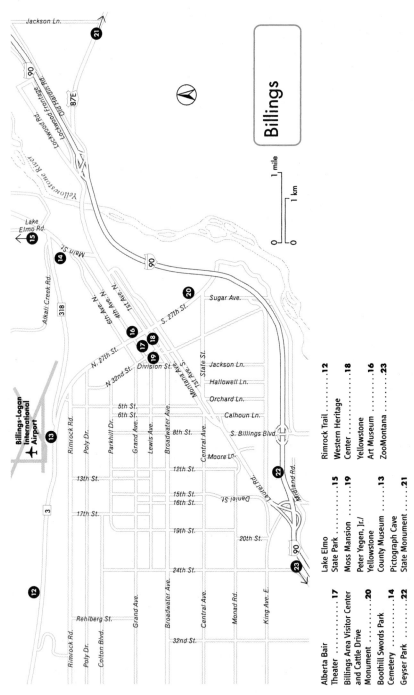

Billings

Billings-Logan
International
Airport

Jackson Ln.

Lockwood Frontage Rd.

Old Hardin Rd.

Yellowstone River

Lake
Elmo Rd.

Main St.

Alkali Creek Rd.

N. 27th St.

N. 32nd St.

Division St.

6th Ave. N.

4th Ave. N.

1st Ave. N.

S. 27th St.

Sugar Ave.

Jackson Ln.

Hallowell Ln.

Orchard Ln.

Calhoun Ln.

S. Billings Blvd.

Moore Ln.

Montana Ave. S.

State St.

Central Ave.

Laurel Rd.

Midland Rd.

Rimrock Rd.

Poly Dr.

Parkhill Dr.

Grand Ave.

Lewis Ave.

Broadwater Ave.

5th St.

6th St.

8th St.

12th St.

13th St.

15th St.

16th St.

17th St.

19th St.

20th St.

24th St.

Daniel St.

Rehlberg St.

32nd St.

Grand Ave.

Broadwater Ave.

Central Ave.

Monad Rd.

King Ave. E.

Poly Dr.

Colton Blvd.

1 mile

1 km

where several sights are grouped together. Make a left onto North 27th Street and drive to 4th Avenue North for the **Yellowstone Art Museum** ⑯, displaying Western and contemporary art. Park your car in the area and continue on foot one block south on North 27th Street to 3rd Avenue North; make a right and walk one block to North 28th Street to reach the **Alberta Bair Theater** ⑰. Walk south down North 28th Street to Montana Avenue, where you'll find the **Western Heritage Center** ⑱. To reach the turn-of-the-20th-century **Moss Mansion** ⑲ from the center, head north on North 28th Street for two blocks; make a left onto 2nd Avenue North and follow it west for several blocks to Division Street. Return to your car and drive south on 27th Street until you reach I–90; follow the interstate east for 2 mi to Exit 452. Turn right and follow Highway 87 south a few miles to the border of the Crow Indian Reservation, where you'll find the fascinating **Pictograph Cave State Monument** ㉑. For a bit of fun, head back into Billings and take I–90 west to **ZooMontana** ㉓, one of a handful of zoos in the region.

TIMING   You could easily spend one or even two days on this tour, depending on how much time you want to allocate to the sights and parks. In winter, this tour will take less time, as many of the outdoor sights close or are significantly less enjoyable.

The Main Attractions

⑰ **Alberta Bair Theater.** In the 1930s, 20th Century Fox built this Art Deco movie theater on land homesteaded by a successful sheep-ranching family. Saved from the wrecking ball by community groups in the 1980s, it is now a cultural center for the region. Aside from being home to the Billings Symphony Orchestra, the Alberta Bair hosts dance companies, theater troupes, and national music acts. The interior of the theater can only be seen during performances and on free group tours for 15 or more (reserve in advance). ⊠ *2801 3rd Ave. N* ☎ *406/256–6052 or 877/321–2074* ⊕ *www.albertabairtheater.org.*

☺ ⑮ **Lake Elmo State Park.** Surrounding a 64-acre reservoir in Billings Heights, this park is a popular spot for hiking, swimming, fishing, and nonmotorized boating. Although it's not far from downtown, the park is still wild enough to seem miles away from civilization. It's a popular venue for concerts and sporting events such as triathlons and the Montana Games. ⊠ *U.S. 87* ☎ *406/247–2940* ⊕ *www.fwp.state.mt.us* ⊠ *$5* ☉ *Daily sunrise–sunset.*

⑲ **Moss Mansion.** Dutch architect Henry Hardenbergh, who worked on the original Waldorf-Astoria and Plaza hotels in New York City, designed this house in 1903 for businessman P. B. Moss. The mansion still contains many of the elaborate original furnishings, ranging in style from Moorish to art nouveau. Guided tours are offered on the hour. ⊠ *914 Division St.* ☎ *406/256–5100* ⊕ *www.mossmansion.com* ⊠ *$7* ☉ *Sept.–May, daily 1–4; June–Aug., Mon.–Sat. 9–5, Sun. 1–4.*

㉑ **Pictograph Cave State Monument.** Once home to thousands of prehistoric hunters, this spot has yielded more than 30,000 artifacts related to early human history. A paved trail affords good views of the 2,200-year-old cave paintings depicting animal and human figures; if you bring binoc-

FodorśChoice
★

ulars, you'll be able to appreciate better the subtle detail of the artwork. Although there are three caves in the park, only one is open to the public. ⊠ *Coburn Rd. (U.S. 87)* ☎ *406/247–2940* ⊕ *www.pictographcave. org* ⊠ *$5 per vehicle* ☉ *May–Sept., daily 11–7.*

⑫ **Rimrock Trail.** Although its various routes may look straight and boring on a map, this trail system on the northern edge of Billings is actually a pleasant mix of paved urban paths and rugged dirt tracks, where elderly locals out for a Sunday stroll are just as content as extreme mountain bikers. Several individual trails make up the Rimrock system, which starts at Boothill Cemetery and winds past the airport up into the rocky formations that surround the city and give the trail its name. Expect fantastic views of the open plains and five distinct mountain ranges in some places, and the whir of jet engines and the sight of oil-refinery smokestacks in others. ⊠ *Airport Rd.* ☎ *406/245–4111.*

Ⓒ ⑱ **Western Heritage Center.** The permanent exhibits here include oral histories, artifacts, and kid-friendly interactive displays tracing the lives of Native Americans, ranchers, homesteaders, immigrants, and railroad workers who lived in the area between 1880 and 1940. Native American interpretive programs and tours to local cultural sites are available in summer. The impressive castlelike building that houses the center used to be the city's library and is just as interesting as the exhibits. ⊠ *2822 Montana Ave.* ☎ *406/256–6809* ⊕ *www.ywhc.org* ⊠ *Donations accepted* ☉ *Tues.–Sat. 10–5, Sun. 1–5.*

⑯ **Yellowstone Art Museum.** One of the premier art museums in a four-state region, Yellowstone displays Western and contemporary art from nationally and internationally known artists. Among the artists whose works are on permanent display are Charles M. Russell and Will James. The museum also occasionally borrows works by artists such as Monet and Rodin. ⊠ *401 North 27th St.* ☎ *406/256–6804* ⊕ *yellowstone. artmuseum.org* ⊠ *$7* ☉ *Tues.–Wed. and Fri.–Sat. 10–5, Thurs. 10–8, Sun. noon–5.*

Ⓒ ㉓ **ZooMontana.** Although it specializes in native northern-latitude temperate species, ZooMontana has plenty of exotic plants and animals, making it a favorite destination for locals and visitors alike. There's a small children's zoo with kid-friendly exhibits and displays. Because this is one of the only zoos in the region, it can be extremely busy in summer. ⊠ *2100 S. Shiloh Rd.* ☎ *406/652–8100* ⊕ *www.zoomontana. org* ⊠ *$6* ☉ *Daily 10–4.*

Also Worth Seeing

⑳ **Billings Area Visitor Center and Cattle Drive Monument.** A hero-size bronze sculpture of a cattle drover commemorates the Great Montana Centennial Cattle Drive of 1989 (which commemorated the drive of 1889) at this visitor center. You can take guided tours of the center, study the exhibits on the region, and gather all the information you'll need on area attractions. ⊠ *815 S. 27th St.* ☎ *406/252–4016 or 800/735–2635* ⊕ *billingscvb.visitmt.com* ⊠ *Free* ☉ *Weekdays 8–5.*

⑭ **Boothill Swords Park Cemetery.** Many of the city's early residents are buried at this cemetery atop the Rimrocks, north of historic Billings. Among

PAST & FUTURE ON THE PLAINS

IT'S NO WONDER that in the 1870s the Lakota Sioux, Northern Cheyenne, and Arapahoe hid out in southeastern Montana; 130 years later, this region may still be the last best place to hide in the lower 48. Most of the Montana plains didn't see white settlers until the 19th century was well along, and in some places nearly over. As a result, Montana's plains have an extremely brief documented history—perhaps that's why locals hang on dearly to remnants of the past. Even tiny settlements and cow towns have museums, which are essential community fixtures. Although often modest, such places are important for preserving the heritage of one of America's last frontiers. Among the finest are the C. M. Russell Museum Complex in Great Falls and Fort Benton's Museum of the Northern Great Plains.

It was in southeast Montana that Native Americans marked an epic and pivotal victory against the U.S. Army on the banks of the Little Bighorn. Here, a cavalry leader who may well have become president instead met defeat. The dramatic death of Lieutenant Colonel George Armstrong Custer redoubled the federal government's resolve to eradicate Native Americans; the policy of genocide endured until the massacre at Wounded Knee, in South Dakota, 14 years later.

Woven through the conflicts between whites and Native Americans is the ageless story of humanity's struggle with nature. This is rough and often unforgiving land, where too much rain and too much drought often defeated even the most dedicated settler. The government responded by building giant dams and laying asphalt ribbons. In large measure, they succeeded. Even where the horizon remains unbroken by power lines, residents have been brought into the mainstream by the Internet, satellite TV, and GPS navigation.

Boothill's residents are H. M. Muggins Taylor, the army scout who carried word of Custer's defeat through 180 mi of hostile territory to Fort Ellis; Western explorer Yellowstone Kelly; and several outlaws executed in the territorial days. ⊠ *Airport and Main Sts.* ☎ *406/657–8371.*

🖐 **22** **Geyser Park.** A favorite diversion for area visitors with children, Geyser Park has bumper boats, go-carts, a climbing wall, laser tag, and a miniature golf course with waterfalls and geyser pools. Each game operates on a ticket system. Concessions are rather pricey, so some families like to pack a cooler and eat in the picnic area. ⊠ *4910 Southgate Dr.* ☎ *406/254–2510* 💲 *$4–$5 per game* ⊕ *www.geyserpark.net* ☾ *Apr.–Oct., daily 11–11.*

13 **Peter Yegen Jr./Yellowstone County Museum.** Although there isn't enough evidence to prove it, some documents suggest that this log cabin was built in 1877 as a trading post on the Yellowstone River by frontiersman Paul McCormick before it was moved to downtown Billings in 1893. In Billings it served as a gentlemen's club for many years, frequented by the likes of Teddy Roosevelt and Buffalo Bill Cody, before it was moved again, in 1949, to its present location at the entrance to Billings Logan International Airport. The structure today serves as a small museum that interprets Montana's frontier history. Check out the chuck wagon, barbed-wire collection, and the creepy-looking tools from the city's first dentist office. A veranda here affords unparalleled views of the Bighorn, Pryor, and Beartooth mountains more than 100 mi to the south. ⊠ *1950 Terminal Circle* ☎ *406/256–6811* ⊕ *www.pyycm.org* 🖃 *Free* ☉ *Feb.–Dec., weekdays 10:30–5, Sat. 10:30–3.*

Sports & the Outdoors

The Rimrocks are easily the dominant feature of Billings. These 400-foot rock walls provide a scenic backdrop for numerous recreational pursuits. One of the most popular is mountain biking; suitable terrain for beginners, experienced thrill seekers, and everyone in between can be found within a short driving distance.

Golf

Perhaps surprisingly, Billings has more than half a dozen golf courses. Ranging from quick 9-hole executives in the middle of town to grand 18-hole country-club courses set against the Rimrocks, the golfing venues around the city are diverse in design and often have exceptional views of the surrounding country.

Circle Inn Golf Links (⊠ 1029 Main St. ☎ 406/248–4202), on top of the Rimrocks in Billings Heights, is a 9-hole public course that doesn't discriminate: men and women tee off from the same spot. A creek runs along three of the holes, and there's a bunker on one hole. Just below the Rimrocks near the airport is the 18-hole **Exchange City Golf Course** (⊠ 19th St. W ☎ 406/652–2553), a casual course with a winding creek and plenty of hills on the front nine. A public 18-hole course near Lake Elmo State Park in Billings Heights, the **Lake Hills Golf Club** (⊠ 1930 Clubhouse Way ☎ 406/252–8950) is in a wooded area frequented by grouse, antelope, and pheasant. Its two lakes and 444-yard final hole are its most famous features. The **Peter Yegen Jr. Golf Club** (⊠ 3400 Grand Ave. ☎ 406/656–8099), an 18-hole public course, is set against the walls of the Rimrocks. Although not very wooded, the course has plenty of water hazards and bunkers.

Mountain Biking

The **Bike Shop** (⊠ 1934 Grand Ave. ☎ 406/652–1202), owned by a local family since the 1970s, sells, rents, and services mountain bikes. **DVS Bikes** (⊠ 520 Wicks La., Suite 12 ☎ 406/256–3900) specializes in BMX and freestyle bikes but also sells mountain bikes and equipment. **Scheels All Sports** (⊠ Rimrock Mall, 1233 W. 24th St. ☎ 406/656–9220 ⊠ 300 S. 24th St. W ☎ 406/656–9220) sells mountain and street bikes, in addition to other sporting goods. Head to the **Spoke Shop** (⊠ 1910 Broadwater Ave. ☎ 406/656–8342) for street bikes, mountain bikes, and equipment.

Where to Stay & Eat

$$–$$$$ ✕ **George Henry's.** With its stained glass and tearoom-style table settings, this restaurant in an 1882 Victorian house is elegant yet surprisingly laid-back. It's popular with businesspeople, who come here for lunch and dinner meetings. Favorites include steak Oscar (steak with béarnaise sauce, crab, and asparagus), roasted crispy duck, quiche, and seafood pasta. ⊠ *404 N. 30th St.* ☎ *406/245–4570* ☒ *AE, D, DC, MC, V* ☉ *Closed Sun.*

$$–$$$$
Fodor's Choice
★
✕ **Juliano's.** Hawaiian-born chef Carl Kurokawa has won so many culinary awards, they'd probably fill a closet. But Carl isn't about trophies and plaques—he's about food. His menu changes monthly; past entrées have included roasted ostrich, grilled elk, spicy watermelon salad, chicken with leeks and roasted tomato, and sea bass. Inspired by Pacific and European flavors, yet distinctly American, Carl's cooking is some of the best in the state. The building, with its tin ceiling, is almost as impressive, having once been a stable for the turn-of-the-20th-century sandstone mansion next door. Lunch is fast and inexpensive. Reservations are a good idea. ⊠ *2912 7th Ave. N* ☎ *406/248–6400* ☒ *AE, D, MC, V* ☉ *Closed Sun. No dinner Mon. or Tues.*

$$–$$$$
✕ **The Granary.** A restored flour mill houses this restaurant, which ages its own beef. Seafood is also on the menu, and the salad bar is superb. Like the outdoor seating options at most Billings restaurants, the veranda here is very popular in the summer. ⊠ *1500 Poly Dr.* ☎ *406/259–3488* ☒ *AE, D, DC, MC, V* ☉ *Closed Sun.*

★ **$$–$$$$**
✕ **The Rex.** Built in 1910 by Buffalo Bill Cody's chef, this restaurant was saved from the wrecking ball and restored in 1975. Today it's one of the best steak houses in the city. The dining room and bar are big and airy, enhanced by wooden beams that impart an almost Southwestern look, but the outdoor patio is perhaps the most popular place to dine on such dishes as roasted buffalo, prime rib, Italian beef sandwiches, jerk steak with mango chutney, and Vietnamese noodle salad. The kitchen stays open until 11 PM, making the restaurant especially popular with the after-theater crowd. ⊠ *2401 Montana Ave.* ☎ *406/245–7477* ☒ *AE, D, DC, MC, V.*

$–$$$
✕ **Enzo Bistro.** People come to this attractive chalet-style building for European specialties such as the Mediterranean meat loaf with basil, cumin, and kalamata olives, and kids' favorites such as pizzas and pastas. ⊠ *1502 Rehberg La., at Grand Ave.* ☎ *406/651–0999* ☒ *AE, DC, MC, V* ☉ *No lunch.*

¢–$$$
✕ **Bruno's.** On the residential west side of town, this family-style Italian restaurant sits in the shadow of the Rimrocks. The building's exterior is unremarkable, but traditional Italian music and artfully displayed antique pasta machines, old olive-oil cans from Italy, and utensils the owners have picked up over their decades in the restaurant business create a warm dining environment. Locals come here for the homemade pasta; the veal, made-from-scratch meatballs, and specialty pizzas are also delicious. There's a full bar, plus a modest selection of Italian wines and beers. Olive oils and pastas are for sale at the building's entrance. ⊠ *2658 Grand Ave.* ☎ *406/652–4416* ☒ *D, MC, V* ☉ *Closed Sun. No lunch.*

$–$$
✕ **Thai Orchid.** When chef Lex Manraksa moved from Thailand to Billings, he brought with him authentic Thai cooking and spices Montana had never seen before. His downtown eatery is now a community fixture and gets especially popular with the business crowd around lunchtime. Manraksa is especially happy to talk with Thai-food connoisseurs and then serve them some superspicy traditional dishes; for the uninitiated he has plenty of milder dishes reminiscent of Chinese fa-

vorites. Expect plenty of beef, chicken, and pork, but also look for entrées highlighting shrimp, oyster, and duck. ⊠ *2926 2nd Ave. N* ☎ *406/ 256–2206* ⊟ *MC, V* ☉ *Closed Sun.*

¢–$$ ✕ **Pug Mahon's.** Good Irish stews, pasties, and traditional fish-and-chips are the highlights of this authentic Irish pub, which serves dozens of imported beers and whiskies. The Sunday brunch is wildly popular. Be sure to try one of the 22 varieties of omelet. ⊠ *3011 1st Ave. N* ☎ *406/259– 4190* ⊟ *MC, V* ☉ *No dinner Sun.*

¢–$ ✕ **The Beanery Bar and Grill.** Located downtown in Billings's 19th-century train depot, the Beanery has a large outdoor patio that's a great spot for people-watching in summer. The bar inside is contemporary, but the old-fashioned signs and period light fixtures hark back to the building's railroad past. The menu has fewer than a dozen items, and the food here is simple. Especially noteworthy are the wraps (such as fajita or Caesar wraps), which are praised by downtown business folk out for a quick lunch, and the legendary barbecue-pork sandwich. ⊠ *2314 Montana Ave.* ☎ *406/896–9200* ⊟ *AE, MC, V* ☉ *Closed Sun.*

¢ ✕ **Poet Street Market.** The distinctive sandwiches include roast beef with blue cheese, turkey with cranberry-apple compote on pumpkin bread, and artichoke hearts with white cheddar cheese on olive bread. The soups, salads, and pizzas are equally creative. It's difficult to leave without ordering dessert: catching sight of fresh concoctions such as chocolate Bavarian torte, bourbon spice cake, or sour cream pear tart is enough to make you hungry again. ⊠ *905 Poly Dr.* ☎ *406/245–9501* ⊟ *AE, MC, V* ☉ *Closed Sun.*

$$–$$$ 🏨 **Sheraton Billings.** The downtown location of this high-rise is convenient, and the contemporary rooms are spacious. Some rooms overlook the mountain ranges outside the city. The hotel encloses a pleasant and large central courtyard; the pool area is big and luxurious. ⊠ *27 N. 27th St., 59101* ☎ *406/252–7400 or 800/588–7666* 🖷 *406/252–2401* ⊕ *www.sheraton.com* ⇆ *282 rooms* ⚇ *Restaurant, some refrigerators, cable TV with movies, in-room data ports, indoor pool, gym, hot tub, video game room, shop, business services, meeting rooms, some pets allowed (fee), no-smoking floor* ⊟ *AE, D, DC, MC, V.*

$–$$ 🏨 **Best Western Billings.** A round-the-clock restaurant next door and proximity to I–90 make this chain hotel a good stop for last-minute or late arrivals. It's also very close to a water park, making it a favorite among guests with children. ⊠ *5610 S. Frontage Rd., 59101* ☎ *406/248– 9800 or 800/528–1234* 🖷 *406/248–2500* ⊕ *www.bestwestern.com* ⇆ *80 rooms* ⚇ *Some in-room hot tubs, cable TV with movies, indoor pool, hot tubs, laundry facilities, business services, meeting rooms, some pets allowed (fee), no-smoking rooms* ⊟ *AE, D, DC, MC, V* ⦿ *CP.*

$–$$ 🏨 **Historic Northern Hotel.** A 1940 fire destroyed the original 1905 building and the hotel was rebuilt, but it still provides a sense of the city's past. Rooms follow an American West theme, with woven rugs and bedspreads and a gaming table. Guest-room views—of the Pryor Mountains, rolling plains, or Rimrocks—are glorious. The massive fireplace is the focus of the comfortable lobby—a common gathering place for guests and locals. The Golden Belle serves Continental cuisine in surroundings that are fancier than usual for Montana. ⊠ *19 Broadway, at 28th St., 59101* ☎ *406/245–5121 or 800/542–5121* 🖷 *406/259–9862*

⊕ *www.historicnorthernhotel.net* ⤵ *160 rooms* ⚐ *Restaurant, gym, bar, shop, laundry facilities, meeting rooms, cable TV, no-smoking rooms* ⊟ *AE, D, DC, MC, V* ⍾ *CP.*

$–$$ ⊡ **Josephine Bed and Breakfast.** Within walking distance of downtown is this lovely historic home with five theme rooms—such as the Garden Room, with its floral fabrics. You're welcome to relax in the guest parlor, with a piano and a TV with VCR, or in the library. Breakfast is served at your convenience; afterward, you can work off your meal with a free guest pass to the local YMCA. ⊠ *514 N. 29th St., 59101* ☎ *406/248–5898 or 800/552–5898* ⊕ *www.thejosephine.com* ⤵ *5 rooms* ⚐ *Some in-room hot tubs, cable TV, some in-room data ports; no smoking* ⊟ *AE, D, MC, V* ⍾ *BP.*

¢–$$ ⊡ **C'mon Inn.** Five hot tubs and an indoor pool attract families to this lodging near the major roads and the interstate. Even in winter, there's a garden inside the woodsy, tropical courtyard. There are wood-burning fireplaces in the lobby. ⊠ *2020 Overland Ave., 59102* ☎ *406/655–1100 or 800/655–1170* ⊟ *406/652–7672* ⊕ *www.cmoninn.com* ⤵ *80 rooms, 8 suites* ⚐ *Some in-room hot tubs, microwaves, refrigerators, indoor pool, gym, hot tubs, cable TV, video game room, Internet, meeting rooms; no smoking* ⊟ *AE, D, DC, MC, V* ⍾ *CP.*

$ ⊡ **Quality Inn Homestead.** A delightful outdoor sundeck and an indoor swim center are the main attractions here. The rooms are contemporary in design and average in size; the two-room suites are a favorite among families. The on-site car rentals are a bonus for business travelers. A complimentary full breakfast is made to order. ⊠ *2036 Overland Ave., 59102* ☎ *406/652–1320* ⊟ *406/652–1320* ⊕ *www.qualityinn.com* ⤵ *120 rooms, 60 suites* ⚐ *Restaurant, some microwaves, some refrigerators, cable TV with movies, indoor pool, hot tub, sauna, laundry facilities, business services, no-smoking rooms* ⊟ *AE, D, DC, MC, V* ⍾ *BP.*

¢–$ ⊡ **Dude Rancher Lodge.** As you might expect from the lodge's name, a Western theme pervades this downtown institution, right down to the lantern-style light fixtures, wood paneling, and custom-made carpet "branded" with the symbols of several area ranches. Breakfast, which costs extra, is full and hearty. ⊠ *415 N. 29th St., 59101* ☎ *406/259–5561 or 800/221–3302* ⊟ *406/259–0095* ⊕ *www.duderancherlodge.com* ⤵ *57 rooms* ⚐ *Restaurant, some microwaves, some refrigerators, cable TV with movies, some pets allowed (fee), no-smoking rooms* ⊟ *AE, D, DC, MC, V.*

¢ ⊡ **The Carlin Hotel.** Opened in 1910 for railroad passengers, the Carlin fell into disrepair, as did much of Billings's downtown district, with the demise of rail travel. It was luxuriously restored in 2002, however, and now has suites fully furnished for extended stays (there's a minimum one-week stay). The suites, decorated almost entirely in black, white, and bright primary colors, are distinctly modern. The bathrooms are tiled, and the kitchens have dishwashers and hardwood floors. There's a restaurant and martini bar on the first floor. ⊠ *2501 Montana Ave., 59101* ☎ *406/245–7515* ⊕ *www.carlinhotel.com* ⤵ *8 suites* ⚐ *Restaurant, microwaves, refrigerators, cable TV with movies, bar, in-room data ports; no smoking* ⊟ *AE, D, MC, V.*

¢ **Riverstone Billings Inn.** Bright white walls stand out against curtains and upholstery in dark red and green tones. Because of the inn's location along Billings's medical corridor and its squeaky-clean image, many people who come to town for a hospital visit stay here. ✉ *880 N. 29th St., 59101* ☎ *406/252–6800 or 800/231–7782* 🖷 *406/252–6800* 🌐 *www.billingsinn.com* *59 rooms, 3 suites* *Some microwaves, some refrigerators, cable TV, laundry facilities; no smoking* 💳 *AE, D, DC, MC, V* 🍽 *CP.*

Nightlife & the Arts

Nightlife

★ The **Carlin Martini Bar and Nightclub** (✉ Carlin Hotel, 2501 Montana Ave. ☎ 406/245–2503) offers live entertainment most nights, ranging from rock and blues bands to comedians and DJs. **Casey's Golden Pheasant** (✉ 222 N. Broadway ☎ 406/256–5200) combines the Old West and the 1950s: the 1870s bar is solid mahogany, but the mural on the ceiling depicts 1950s rock stars, and neon signs hang from the walls. Bands play almost every night of the week; the music varies but usually falls somewhere in the rock, blues, R&B, reggae, and jazz categories. A young crowd gathers at **Eleven: 11** (✉ 2526 Montana Ave. ☎ 406/238–0011) to play pinball, air hockey, and pool. The music is almost exclusively punk rock, and modern art by regional artists decorates the walls. No alcohol is served here.

The Arts

The **Alberta Bair Theater** (✉ 2801 3rd Ave. N ☎ 406/256–6052 or 877/321–2074 🌐 www.albertabairtheater.org) presents music, theater, dance, and other cultural events. It's the home theater for the Billings Symphony Orchestra.

Something of a community art center, the **Bill McIntosh Gallery** (✉ 2507 Montana Ave. ☎ 406/252–2010) displays the work of local and regional artists in all mediums. The gallery also offers art classes and sells a significant selection of art supplies. From paintings and etchings to sculpture and vintage rifles, the **Meadowlark Gallery** (✉ 118 N. 29th St. ☎ 406/294–8575 or 800/727–3949) showcases all kinds of Western artwork. The owners are experts on painter-etcher Hans Kleiber, and they love to talk with interested customers. The works of modern artists living in the region are shown at the downtown **Toucan Gallery** (✉ 2505 Montana Ave. ☎ 406/252–0122). The artwork varies from traditional paintings and sculptures to painted quilts, object collages, and dolls.

Shopping

Al's Bootery and Repair Shop (✉ 1820 1st Ave. N ☎ 406/245–4827) corrals your toes into fancy cowboy boots ranging from $50 to $1,800. Billing itself as "a deli for the mind," **Barjon's Books** (✉ 2718 3rd Ave. N ☎ 406/252–4398 or 800/788–4318) sells incense, Celtic statuary, Native American medicine wheels, books on Buddhism, and more. The store regularly hosts readings and talks by guests who include New Age authors and Buddhist monks. A large downtown warehouse built in 1928 has been converted into the charming **Depot Antique Mall** (✉ 2223 Montana Ave. ☎ 406/245–5955 or 877/245–5955), which sells a varied collection that includes furniture, china, branding irons, and more. Unlike many other antiques shops, this one welcomes children. **Rand's Custom Hats** (✉ 2205 1st Ave. N ☎ 406/248–7688 or 800/346–9815 ⊕ www.randhats.com) creates cowboy hats for working cowboys and movie stars and will custom-fit a felt fur hat. Prices range from $300 to $2,000. Rand's also sells leather carrying cases.

| en route | Although the route will take you slightly out of the way, take I–94 on your way to Hardin and stop at **Pompey's Pillar National Historic Landmark** (✉ I–94, 25 mi east of Billings ☎ 406/875–2233), the only physical evidence of the Lewis and Clark expedition. When William Clark saw this small sandstone mesa rising out of the prairie along the Yellowstone River on July 25, 1806, he climbed to the top to survey the area and then marked it with his signature and the date. His graffiti, along with other engravings by early-19th-century fur traders and homesteaders, is still visible. The interpretive center is open only in summer, but you can climb to the top of the mesa and view the signature year-round. The landmark was heavily publicized in 2002 when it was named one of America's 11 most endangered landmarks by the National Trust for Historic Preservation. Despite the national attention and concern, four massive grain elevators and a loading terminal for trucks and railcars were built less than a mile from the site. The view from the top is still well worth the 10-minute hike, despite the industrial intrusion. To get to Hardin, continue east on I–94 for a few miles and then head south on Highway 47. |

SOUTHEAST MONTANA

As with most of eastern Montana, the word that comes to mind in the state's far southeastern reaches is "big." Characterized by badlands, shallow canyons, grassy hills, and, above all, treeless plains, the land here survives on annual rainfall that just barely exceeds that of a desert. Aside from the livestock, this land belongs to ranchers and Native Americans—specifically the Crow and Northern Cheyenne, who both have reservations here. Few settlements in the region have more than 1,000 people. When you find them, residents are friendly and almost always willing to show you around town—which typically consists of their home and the general store they run next door.

Hardin

24 *50 mi east of Billings via I–90.*

Although its roots are firmly planted in cattle ranching, Hardin makes a significant portion of its living as a visitor gateway to the Little Bighorn Battlefield National Monument just a few miles to the south. It's also a popular base for exploring the several state parks and national recreation areas nearby. With 3,334 residents, Hardin is among the largest communities in southeast Montana, making it a convenient stop for people traveling to the western part of the state from South Dakota.

The **Arapooish State Fishing Access Site,** a mile north of Hardin, is a favorite spot among locals, who pack the family up, set up in a shaded picnic area, cast a line into the Bighorn River, and have a cookout. It's also a prime bird-watching venue. ⊠ *Hwy. 47* ☎ *406/237–2940* ⊕ *www. fwp.state.mt.us* ☜ *Free* ☉ *Apr.–Oct., daily sunrise–sunset.*

Focusing on Native American and early homestead settlement, the 24-acre **Bighorn County Historical Museum and Visitor Information Center** complex comprises 20 historic buildings that have been relocated to the site, including a one-room schoolhouse, a barn, a smithy, teepees, and a log cabin. The center also serves as an official Montana State Visitor Center. ⊠ *I–90, Exit 497* ☎ *406/665–1671* ⊕ *www.museumonthebighorn. org* ☜ *Free* ☉ *June–Aug., daily 8–8; Sept.–May, daily 8–5.*

★ During the third week in August, a stretch of land along the Bighorn River becomes the "teepee capital of the world" when the **Crow Fair and Rodeo,** official fair of the Crow tribe, begins north of the town of Crow Agency. The festival focuses on traditional dances and activities, with the powwow a central part of the gathering. Sports tournaments are nearly as important, and the events, ranging from archery and horse racing to basketball and softball, inspire a healthy rivalry among the various reservation communities. ⊠ *Bighorn River north of Crow Agency, 14 mi south of Hardin on I–90* ☎ *406/638–3793* ☜ *Free.*

Where to Stay & Eat

¢ ✕ **Purple Cow.** This family eatery with a friendly staff is a favorite among

Fodor'sChoice travelers, largely because heading eastward it's one of the last restau-

★ rants until Belle Fourche, South Dakota, more than 200 mi away. The shakes and malts here are fantastic, as are the burgers and steaks. Chicken and simple salads are also on the menu. Portions are generous, so you might want to consider splitting some items, such as the delectable BLT. ⊠ *I–90, Exit 495* ☎ *406/665–3601* ☰ *MC, V.*

¢–$$ 🏨 **American Inn.** The massive waterslide that towers above the outdoor pool is the most noticeable feature of this lodging off I–90. Tans, browns, and dark reds decorate the guest rooms, a bracing chance from the decor from the sterile beiges and pastels of most chain hotels. ⊠ *1324 N. Crawford Ave., 59034* ☎ *406/665–1870* ☒ *406/665–1492* ⬎ *43 rooms* ⌂ *Restaurant, some in-room hot tubs, some refrigerators, cable TV, pool, hot tub, bar, laundry facilities, meeting rooms, some pets allowed (fee), no-smoking rooms* ☰ *AE, D, MC, V.*

★ ¢ 🏨 **Hotel Becker Bed and Breakfast.** Built in 1908 for railroad passengers, this three-story brick hotel with yellow awnings is on the National Register of Historic Places. Depression-era items, such as handmade quilts, decorate the rooms. Owner Mary Slattery, a Hardin native, is more than happy to direct you to local points of interest—or, at the very least, to the Chamber of Commerce across the street in the old train depot. You can use the phone and TV in the living room, since the guest rooms don't have these amenities. ⊠ *200 N. Center St., 59034* ☎ *406/665–2707* ⬎ *7 rooms, 5 with bath* ⌂ *Meeting room; no room phones, no room TVs, no smoking* ☰ *No credit cards* ☉ *Closed Oct.–May* ❙❀❙ *CP.*

CAMPING ⛺ **Grandview Campground.** Cable TV, a copy machine, nightly ice-cream socials, movie rentals, and regular book swaps are some of the extras at this full-service campground. On the edge of town, in the narrow corridor between downtown Hardin and I–90, it lies next door to the Hardin Community Activity Center, giving you access to an Olympic-size indoor pool and fitness facilities. The owner is a font of knowledge on Hardin and takes great pride in the community. The Grandview is open year-round, but only a few electric sites are available in winter. *⌂ Swimming (indoor pool), guest laundry, flush toilets, full hookups, dump station, drinking water, showers, picnic tables, electricity, public telephone, play area ↪ 50 full hookups, 30 tent sites ⊠ 1002 N. Mitchell ☎ 406/665–2489 or 800/622–9890 ⊕ www.grandviewcamp. com ☒ $17 tent sites, $25 full hookups ☐ MC, V.*

Little Bighorn Battlefield National Monument

㉕ *17 mi south of Hardin via I–90.*

When the smoke cleared on June 25, 1876, neither Lieutenant Colonel George Armstrong Custer (1839–76) nor his 200 or so blue-shirted troopers were alive to tell the story of their battle against several thousand Northern Plains warriors led by Sitting Bull (circa 1831–90) and Crazy Horse (1842–77). It was a Pyrrhic victory for the tribes; the loss pushed the U.S. government to redouble its efforts to clear them off the plains. Now the Little Bighorn Battlefield, on the Crow Indian Reservation, memorializes the warriors who took part in the conflict, with monuments and an interpretive center. The site, windswept prairie along the Little Bighorn River, remains largely undeveloped. Note that there are rattlesnakes around the area, and also beware of touching the flesh-piercing yucca plants. Talks by park rangers contain surprises for even the most avid history buff. *⊠ Battlefield Rd. ☎ 406/638–3204 ⊕ www. nps.gov/libi ☒ $10 per vehicle ☉ Memorial Day–July, daily 8–9; Aug.–Labor Day, daily 8–8; Sept.–Oct., daily 8–6; Nov.–Mar., daily 8–4:30; Apr.–late May, daily 8–6.*

The interpretive exhibits at the **Little Bighorn Battlefield Visitor Center** explain the events that led to and resulted from the battle, as well as the deeper issues regarding the historical conflict between white and Native American culture. You also can sign up for guided tours here, and perhaps listen to one of the special interpretive talks. *⊠ Battlefield Rd. ☎ 406/638–3204 ☉ Memorial Day–July, daily 8–9; Aug.–Labor Day, daily 8–8; Sept.–Oct., daily 8–6; Nov.–Mar., daily 8–4:30; Apr.–late May, daily 8–6.*

The old stone superintendent's house is now the **White Swan Memorial Library,** which has one of the most extensive collections of research material on the Battle of the Little Bighorn. You can view the material by appointment only; contact the visitor center for more information.

Among those interred at **Custer National Cemetery,** near the visitor center, are Custer's second-in-command, Marcus Reno; some of Custer's Native American scouts; and soldiers originally buried at frontier military posts that were abandoned as the West became settled. There are many soldiers from more modern wars buried here as well, from World

Wars I and II to Korea and Vietnam. Note that you can visit the cemetery without paying the park entrance fee.

For more than 120 years the only memorial to those killed in the battle was the towering obelisk of the **7th Cavalry Monument.** The hike to the monument, at the top of Last Stand Hill, isn't difficult, but it can seem long on a scorching summer day. Although the hill isn't particularly high, it affords a good overall view of the battlefield site.

★ Until the **Indian Memorial** was unveiled in 2003, the battlefield's only monument paid tribute to the immediate losers. Although they are meant to honor Native Americans who died on both sides (Custer had a few Crow and Arikara scouts), the three bronze riders of the memorial represent the united forces of the Lakota Sioux, Northern Cheyenne, and Arapahoe, who defeated the government troops. The wooden posts off to the side form a "spirit gate" welcoming the dead riders. The text, images, and pictographs are accounts of the battle from the perspective of the three united tribes.

Scattered around the battlefield are short white **markers** indicating the places where soldiers died. Although the markers may look like graves, the actual bodies are interred elsewhere, including that of Custer, whose remains rest at the military academy at West Point. One marker belongs to Custer's younger brother, Thomas, the most decorated soldier of the Civil War. Only three markers represent Native American warriors, in part because no one knows exactly where they fell: the Native American survivors buried their dead immediately after the battle in traditional fashion.

After Custer's defeat, two of his officers held their ground against the Native American forces at **Reno-Benteen Battlefield.** The seven companies lost only 53 men during the two-day siege; more soldiers might have shared Custer's fate had not the advance of several thousand fresh troops caused the Native Americans to break camp and flee the region. The site is a 5-mi drive southeast along Battlefield Road.

> **off the beaten path**

CHIEF TWO MOON MONUMENT – Lakota leaders Crazy Horse and Sitting Bull are the most famous Native Americans associated with the Battle of the Little Bighorn, but Cheyenne chief Two Moon was just as well respected among his people. The owner of the general store (and one of the only residents) in the nearby town of Busby became acquainted with the young and friendly chief and built a monument to him in the 1930s. A likeness of the chief, who served as the model for the head side of the buffalo nickel, adorns the memorial. ⊠ *U.S. 212, 25 mi east of Crow Agency, Busby.*

ROSEBUD BATTLEFIELD STATE PARK – Eight days before Custer's defeat, 1,500 Lakota Sioux and Northern Cheyenne warriors met 1,000 troops under the command of General George Sherman along Rosebud Creek, 35 mi southeast of what would soon become the Little Bighorn Battlefield. For six hours the armies fought up and down a 10-square-mi patch of land. When the dust had settled, neither side could claim victory. The very lack of a victor was enough proof for some that the Native Americans had become a dangerous fighting force. A Third Cavalry officer present at the battle later wrote that the Lakota "were the best cavalry soldiers on earth." A local rancher saved 3,000 acres of the battlefield from coal developers, and the area is now a state park. The land remains much the way it did in 1876, so enjoy the peaceful emptiness—and watch out for rattlesnakes. ⊠ *25 mi east of Crow Agency on U.S. 212, 20 mi south on Hwy. 314, 3 mi west on county rd.* ☎ *406/234–0900* ⊕ *www.fwp.state.mt.us/parks/* ☜ *Free* ☉ *Daily, 24 hrs.*

Where to Eat

¢–$ ✕ **Custer Battlefield Trading Post and Cafe.** With its stock of T-shirts, inexpensive jewelry, and dreamcatchers, the trading post is touristy, but the small attached restaurant is quite good—as evidenced by the locals who regularly congregate here. Steak is the dish of choice, and there are no fewer than three ways to get it on a sandwich. The several variations of Indian taco made by the Crow cooks are especially popular. If tacos aren't your style, try a buffalo burger. ⊠ *I-90 at U.S. 212* ☎ *406/638–2270* ⊕ *www.laststand.com* ▤ *D, MC, V.*

| en route | North of Bighorn Canyon is the tiny settlement where Father Prando, a Jesuit missionary, founded the **St. Xavier Mission** (⊠ Mission Ave. ☎ 406/784–4500) in 1887. This was the first mission to the Crow tribe and, as such, offered the people their first primary school. Although the town is barely inhabited, the church and school are still in use and may be visited. Now called Pretty Eagle School, after a Crow chief, the school provides a free primary and secondary education for 120 students from homes as far as 45 mi away. |

Bighorn Canyon National Recreation Area

❷❻ *40 mi southwest of Little Bighorn Battlefield National Monument via I-90 and Hwy. 313.*

Centered around a 60-mi-long lake, this park stretches between the Pryor and Bighorn mountains, well into Wyoming. Not only a favorite destination for boaters and anglers, it is a fine place to visit just for the breathtaking views from the hills and cliffs above the lake. Really just a wide spot on the Bighorn River, the lake fills much of Bighorn Canyon, whose steep walls, carved by geological upheaval and the force of wind and water, are too rugged for casual access. People who traveled and lived nearby spent little or no time on the river until the Yellowtail Dam was built to create a lake and generate hydroelectric power. Shortly after the Army Corps of Engineers completed the dam in the 1960s, Congress declared the lake and surrounding land a national recreation area. Most people visit the park by boat, which is the only way within the park to get directly from the northern unit, in Montana, to the southern unit, much of which is in Wyoming. Most of the major sights are accessible by boat, but you can also reach them by driving north from Wyoming on Highway 37. If you're visiting from Wyoming, Lovell makes a good base for exploring the area. ☎ *307/548–2251 or 406/666–2412* ⊕ *www. nps.gov/bica/* ☜ *$5 per vehicle* ☉ *Daily, 24 hrs.*

The **Yellowtail Dam Visitor Center** in the northern unit is the starting point for guided tours of the dam. Exhibits within the center focus on the life of Crow Chief Robert Yellowtail, the Crow people, the history of the Bighorn River, the dam's construction, and the wildlife in the area. Note that on the dam tour you must ascend three short flights of stairs. ⊠ *Hwy. 313, Fort Smith* ☎ *406/666–3218* ⊕ *www.nps.gov/bica/* 🖃 *Included in $5 admission to recreation area* ☉ *Memorial Day–Labor Day, daily 9–5.*

The old **Hillsboro Dude Ranch** complex is probably the best known and easiest to reach of the four ranch ruins within the recreation area. There are old log cabins, cellars, chicken coops, and other buildings that belonged to Grosvener W. Barry, one of the area's more colorful characters in the early 20th century. Barry attempted three gold-mining ventures, all of which failed, before opening a dude ranch here. Later on he attempted to turn the ranch into a town, built a post office, and had himself proclaimed postmaster in 1915. He died five years later. The town never really took off, however, and was completely abandoned during World War II. ⊠ *Hwy. 37* ⊕ *www.nps.gov/bica/* 🖃 *Included in $5 admission to recreation area.*

When Spanish explorers introduced horses to the Americas, some of the animals inevitably escaped and roamed wild across the land. Their descendants populated the two continents ahead of the settlers who would come centuries later. You can see some of the last members of these breeds in the **Pryor Mountain Wild Horse Range**, the first such nationally designated refuge. Some 200 horses, generally broken into small family groupings, roam these arid slopes with bighorn sheep, elk, deer, and mountain lions. Coat variations such as grulla, blue roan, dun, and sabino indicate Spanish lineage, as do markings such as dorsal stripes, zebra stripes on the legs, and a stripe on the withers. The best way to view the herds is simply to drive along Highway 37 and look out your window. From the northern unit you'll have to reach the refuge by boat, or you can head to the town of Pryor (on the Crow Reservation in Montana) in a four-wheel-drive vehicle and take a gravel road through the range; the road eventually hooks back up with Highway 37 across the border in Wyoming. A road system circles the refuge, but, again, a four-wheel-drive vehicle is necessary. ⊠ *Hwy. 37* ☎ *406/896–5000* 🖃 *Included in $5 admission to recreation area.*

Fodor'sChoice
★

★ **Devil's Canyon Overlook,** a few miles north of the Wyoming border, affords breathtaking views of the point where narrow Devil's Canyon joins sheer-walled Bighorn Canyon. The overlook itself is on a cliff 1,000 feet above the lake. Look for fossils in the colorful rock layers of the canyon walls. ⊠ *Hwy. 37* ⊕ *www.nps.gov/bica/* 🖃 *Included in $5 admission to recreation area.*

The **Crooked Creek Ranger Station**, past the south entrance of the park in Wyoming, houses exhibits about the four historic ranches within the recreation area. A small shop sells books related to the local history and geology. ⊠ *Hwy. 37, WY* ☎ *307/548–7326* ⊕ *www.nps.gov/bica/* 🖃 *Included in $5 admission to recreation area* ☉ *Daily; hrs vary by season.*

The main visitor center for the park, the **Bighorn Canyon Visitor Center** has geological and historical exhibits on the area, as well as a film about the canyon. Two shorter movies, one on the Pryor Mountain wild horses and the other about Medicine Wheel National Historic Landmark (east of Lovell), are shown on request. A small store sells books and other regional items. The center is in the town of Lovell, Wyoming, about 11 mi southwest of the recreation area's south entrance. ⊠ *U.S. 310 at U.S. 14A, Lovell WY* ☎ *307/548–2251* ⊕ *www.nps.gov/bica/* ⌑ *Free* ☉ *Memorial Day–Labor Day, daily 8–6; Labor Day–Memorial Day, daily 8–5.*

off the beaten path

CHIEF PLENTY COUPS STATE PARK – Although many Plains Indian tribes, notably the Cheyenne and Lakota Sioux, opposed the intrusion of whites into their lands, the Crow did not. Hoping that U.S. troops would keep the rival Cheyenne and Lakota off their lands, the Crow allied themselves with the U.S. government. Ultimately, the army protected Crow territory from the other tribes—but only so it could be settled by whites. Despite the betrayal, the last traditional chief of the Crow, Plenty Coups, strongly encouraged his people to adopt modern ways and cooperate with the U.S. government. At his request, his home and general store in the town of Pryor were preserved as a state park after his death. Note the blending of modern and traditional ways, such as the room of honor in the rear of his log home, meant to parallel the place of honor along the back wall of a teepee. The guides here are especially interested in helping children understand the site. ⊠ *1 mi west of Pryor on county rd., Pryor* ☎ *406/252–1289* ⊕ *www.fwp.state.mt.us/parks/* ⌑ *$2* ☉ *May–Sept., daily 8–8.*

Sports & the Outdoors

The Lewis and Clark expedition and, later, fur traders avoided the Bighorn River at all costs, for the narrow channel, high canyon walls, and sharp rocks were treacherous. With the construction of the Yellowtail Dam in the 1960s, however, the water levels in the canyon rose above most rocky obstacles and created new access points along the shore of the now tamed river. It wasn't long before boaters answered the call of the new lake, which varies from wide basins to narrow passages through the canyon walls. The fishing here—for largemouth bass, rainbow and brown trout, walleye, yellow perch, and more—is excellent, both above and below the dam, although many come simply to rest on the water and enjoy the calm winds and pleasant views. An extended drought that lowered water levels shut down the lake's marinas and boat launches in 2001. The marinas reopened in 2003, but fishing and boating will likely be affected for several more years.

Because canyon walls create sharp turns and bottlenecks in the lake, there are some boating speed limits.

Boats can be docked or rented in the northern unit of the park at **Ok-A-Beh Marina** (⊠ off Hwy. 313, on the north end of the lake ☎ 406/665–2216). The facilities here aren't luxurious, but you'll find a basic eatery, a few groceries, tackle, a swimming area, and reasonable rates. One of the most popular boat launches in the southern unit is **Barry's Landing** (⊠ Hwy. 37 ☎ 406/666–2412). There isn't much here—not even electricity—but the scenic campground, shaded picnic area, and central location are big draws. Many boats in the southern unit are based at

CloseUp

WALKING ALONE

THE TOTAL ISOLATION possible in this great and empty land is a rare thing. Eastern Montana is one of the few places left in the world where you can feel truly alone.

As any local will tell you, a stroll through a wildlife refuge or a drive along a quiet county road is an excellent way to take some time for yourself. You don't need to pull out your yoga mat to absorb the solitude; just try to make time—even if it's only a few minutes—to take a walk by yourself. No kids, no spouse, not even the family dog—just you, the rocks, the grass, and the incredible sky that stretches endlessly into the distance.

Towering canyon walls make Bighorn Canyon National Recreation Area a good place to withdraw from civilization, so long as you're far enough away from the lake and its motorboats. Another distinctive place to experience Montana's silence is among the eerie rock formations of the badlands in Makoshika State Park.

Near Havre, the Bear Paw Mountains are among the most ancient in the world. The Big Snowy Mountains have miles of peaceful old-growth forest in which to wander, and the Charles M. Russell National Wildlife Refuge is so sprawling that it's easy to lose yourself—no kidding, so be sure to take a map with you wherever you go.

Horseshoe Bend Marina (✉ Hwy. 37, WY ☎ 307/548–7230), which has boat rentals, a beach, a small general store, a modest restaurant, and the largest campground in the park. A nearby buildup of silt from the Shoshone and Bighorn rivers has made boat launching here a tricky business, and the facilities may one day move farther up the lakeshore.

Camping

⚠ **Black Canyon Campground.** This campground, about 5 mi south of the Ok-A-Beh Marina up the small Black Canyon Creek, is accessible only by boat, and only during high water. Hiking in is impossible, both because of the terrain and because the private property that surrounds it is within Crow Nation boundaries. It's very primitive, but the isolation is unmatched. ⚲ *Pit toilets, bear boxes, fire pits, picnic tables, swimming (lake)* ⤴ *17 sites* ✉ *Black Canyon Creek* ☎ *406/666–3218* ⊕ *www.nps.gov/bica/* ✉ *$5 included in admission to recreation area* ⚲ *Reservations not accepted.*

⚠ **Horseshoe Bend Campground.** The proximity to the marina in the southern unit makes this, the largest campground in the park, especially popular, although never very busy. It's open all year for tent and RV camping, but most services are unavailable in winter. ⚲ *Flush toilets, dump station, drinking water, fire pits, picnic tables, food service, electricity,* *public telephone, general store, swimming (lake)* ⤳ *54 sites* ✉ *Hwy. 37, WY* ☎ *307/548–7230* ⊕ *www.nps.gov/bica/* ⌷ *$5 included in admission to recreation area* ⌂ *Reservations not accepted.*

⚠ **Medicine Creek Campground.** The best way to get to this campground in the southern unit is by boat, although it's possible to hike in. Just north of Barry's Landing, the isolated site offers a good central location without the summer bustle of some other camping spots. ⚲ *Grills, pit toilets, picnic tables, swimming (lake)* ⤳ *6 sites* ✉ *Medicine Creek* ☎ *307/548–2251* ⊕ *www.nps.gov/bica/* ⌷ *$5 included in admission to recreation area* ⌂ *Reservations not accepted.*

Miles City

27 *160 mi northeast of Bighorn Canyon National Recreation Area via Hwy. 313 and I–94.*

History buffs enjoy the ranch town of Miles City (population 8,487), at the confluence of the cottonwood-lined Tongue and Yellowstone rivers. The federal Fort Laramie Treaty of 1868 stated that this land would be "Indian country as long as the grass is green and the sky is blue." The government reneged on its promise only six years later, when gold was found in the Black Hills of South Dakota to the southeast. White settlers streamed into the area, setting in motion events that led to the Battle of the Little Bighorn. After the battle the army built a new post less than 2 mi from where Miles City would be founded. In time the ranchers took over, and in 1884, the last of the great herds of bison was slaughtered near here to make room for cattle. Ranching has been a way of life ever since.

★ The third weekend in May, Miles City holds its famed **Bucking Horse Sale,** a three-day event with a rodeo and a giant block party. Rodeo-stock contractors come from all over the country to buy the spirited horses sold here. ✉ *Fairground Rd. at Main St.* ☎ *406/234–2890 or 877/632–2890* ⊕ *www.buckinghorsesale.com* ⌷ *$8.*

★ Although the holding tanks of an old water-treatment plant don't seem like the best location for fine art, the **Custer County Art Museum,** in the town's 1910 wastewater facility overlooking the Yellowstone River, is actually very attractive. The permanent exhibit reflects the town's Western heritage; the traveling shows are a bit more varied. ✉ *Water Plant Rd.* ☎ *406/234–0635* ⊕ *www.ccac.milescity.org* ⌷ *Free* ⊙ *Oct.–May., daily 1–5, June–Sept., daily 9–5.*

The **Range Riders Museum,** built on the site of the 1877 Fort Keogh, is jammed to the rafters with saddles, chaps, spurs, guns, and other frontier artifacts. Some of the nine museum buildings of this complex were once part of the fort, which was abandoned in the 1920s after being used as a remount station during World War I. ✉ *Old Hwy. 10, across the Tongue River Bridge on west end of Main St., Exit 135 off I–94* ☎ *406/ 232–4483 or 406/232–6146* ⊕ *www.mcchamber.com/communit/ rrmuseum.htm* ⌷ *$5* ⊙ *Apr.–Oct., daily 8–6.*

Pirogue Island State Park, a 269-acre chunk of land in the middle of the Yellowstone River, is completely undeveloped; the only way to access the park is by floating down the river or fording with a vehicle in times of low water. The cottonwood trees are an excellent habitat for waterfowl, raptors, and deer, and the geology of the island makes it prime agate-hunting ground. ⊠ *1 mi north of Miles City on Hwy. 59, 2 mi east on Kinsey Rd., then 2 mi south on county rd.* ☎ *406/234–0900* ⊕ *fwp.mt.gov/lands/site_283962.aspx* ⊠ *Free* ☉ *Daily 5 AM–10 PM.*

Where to Stay & Eat

¢–$$ ✕ **Mama Stella's Pizza.** You can always opt for pepperoni and a traditional red marinara sauce for your pizza, but you may want to try one of Mama Stella's imaginative creations, such as pizza topped with white Alfredo sauce. Unusual toppings include broccoli, sauerkraut, and asparagus. There are also several sandwiches, including the signature "paco," a thick tortilla stuffed with spicy taco goodies. Mama delivers and stays open until midnight on weekends—no small accomplishment in a town with fewer than 9,000 residents. It's in the Trail's Inn Bar and Comedy Club. ⊠ *607 Main St.* ☎ *406/234–2922* ▭ *V.*

¢–$ ⊞ **Best Western War Bonnet Inn.** The two-room family suites and free admission to a nearby fitness facility make this chain hotel stand out. It's on the edge of town near I–94. ⊠ *1015 S. Haynes Ave., 59301* ☎ *406/234–4560* ⊟ *406/234–0363* ⊕ *www.bestwestern.com* ⤸ *54 rooms, 3 suites* ⚬ *Cable TV with movies, indoor pool, hot tub, laundry facilities, business services, no-smoking rooms* ▭ *AE, D, DC, MC, V* ⊠⚬ *CP.*

Nightlife & the Arts

NIGHTLIFE   The downtown **Trail's Inn Bar and Comedy Club** (⊠ 607 Main St. ☎ 406/234–2922) draws regional and national comedy acts. Satisfy your munchies at the on-site Mama Stella's Pizza restaurant.

THE ARTS   The **Wool House Gallery** (⊠ 419 N. 7th St. ☎ 406/232–0769), located in a 1909 railroad building, showcases the work of Alice Walden, a talented local who does most of her work in painted steel. Her innovative pieces range from historical Western characters and animals to ornate birdbaths and benches. She also displays a few oil paintings.

Shopping

★   The craftspeople at **Miles City Saddlery** (⊠ 808 Main St. ☎ 406/232–2512 ⊕ www.milescitysaddlery.com), in business since 1909, custom-design saddles of legendary quality. They also craft saddlebags, holsters, and other leather goods. Even if you're not buying, this is worth a stop.

THE BIG OPEN

In the Big Open, you can revel in wild grasslands, stark badlands, unhindered skylines, and spectacular sunsets, far from the rumble of jetliners, the roar of traffic, and the ringing of cell phones. A great triangle bounded by the Yellowstone River to the south, the Missouri River to the north, and U.S. 87 to the west, the region comprises nearly 10% of the state of Montana. Its residents, however, represent less than 1% of the state's total population, and the number is shrinking. This is a region with barely 1,000 people between the two largest towns (Jordan, with 364 residents, and Circle, with 644), where the livestock outnumbers the people 100 to one. One winter the tumbleweeds clogged a highway so badly that the state had to send out snowplows to clear the way. A visit here means forsaking resorts, fancy restaurants, and shopping centers.

Makoshika State Park

★ ❷ *84 mi northeast of Miles City via I–94 and N. Merrill Ave.*

Named after the Lakota word for "bad land," Makoshika State Park encompasses more than 11,000 acres of Montana's badlands, distinct rock formations also found in Wyoming and the Dakotas. The bare rock walls and mesas of the park create an eerie moonscape that is only occasionally broken by a crooked pine or juniper tree warped by the hard rock and lack of water. Practically a desert, the badlands are excellent fossil grounds, and the remains of tyrannosaurs and triceratops have been found here. Because it's south of the Yellowstone River, near the ranching town of Glendive (population 4,729), Makoshika is technically outside the boundaries of the Big Open. However, many people equate the barren rocks and empty sky of the park with the Big Open's dry and unpeopled plains, and Makoshika is usually considered part of the region. ⊠ *Makoshika State Park Rd.* ☎ *406/377–6256* ⊕ *www.fwp. state.mt.us/parks/* ☐ *$5 per vehicle* ☉ *Daily, 24 hrs.*

At the entrance of the park is the small **Visitor Information Center,** with information on the history and geology of the park. A few fossils are on display, including a triceratops skull. ☎ *406/377–6256* ☉ *Daily 9–5.*

Interpretive signs explain the geology of the rock layers visible on the ½-mi loop of the **Cap Rock Nature Trail,** which begins on Cains Coulee Road, a few miles from the park entrance. The trail affords excellent views of a natural rock bridge. Beginning at the campground, the 1½-mi **Diane Gabriel Trail** loops through both badlands and prairie terrain. At the halfway point a duck-billed-dinosaur fossil is embedded in a cliff. The ½-mi **Kinney Coulee Trail** starts about 4 mi south of the park entrance and leads 300 feet down a canyon. The terrain here is a bit more forested than elsewhere in the park, but the rock formations are the real stars.

Where to Stay

$ 🏨 **Charley Montana Bed & Breakfast.** Built by ranching mogul Charles Krug in 1907, this solid brick home looks like a fortress compared with its stick-built Victorian contemporaries. Indeed, with more than 25 rooms and 8,000 square feet, this place sometimes seems more like a castle than a B&B. The interior is decidedly soft, however, and much of the Krug family's period furniture is still in use. The local owners are eager to help you plan your itinerary. ⊠ *103 N. Douglas, Glendive 59330* ☎ *888/395–3207* ⊕ *charley-montana.com* ➥ *5 rooms* ♨ *Dining room, library; no room phones, no room TVs, no smoking* ☐ *AE, D, MC, V* ⏐◯⏐ *BP.*

CAMPING ⛺ **Makoshika State Park Campground.** This small campground doesn't offer much in the way of amenities, but the views of the surrounding sheer cliffs and stone bluffs are incredible. There's a Frisbee-golf course nearby. Some facilities are at the nearby visitor center. ♨ *Grills, flush* *toilets, drinking water, fire pits, picnic tables, electricity, public telephone, ranger station* ⤴ *22 sites* ⊠ *Makoshika State Park Rd.* ☎ *406/377– 6256* ⊕ *www.fwp.state.mt.us/parks/* ⊡ *$12* ▭ *No credit cards.*

en route The drive from Makoshika State Park to Fort Peck will take you along the Hi-Line, otherwise known as U.S. 2, for a few miles through the **Fort Peck Indian Reservation** (⊠ U.S. 2 ☎ 406/768– 5155). Like most of Montana, much of the land here is empty; at nearly 2 million acres, the reservation is home to only 6,800 tribal members. However, the reservation does have a bustling industrial center, a community college, and an interesting tribal cultural center and museum in Poplar. The diversity of the reservation is somewhat unusual: three bands of the Nakota Sioux and two bands of the Assiniboine live here. Two of the most important towns are Poplar and Wolf Point, both on U.S. 2.

Fort Peck

❷❾ *147 mi northwest of Makoshika State Park via Hwy. 200S, Hwy. 13, U.S. 2 and Hwy. 117.*

Fort Peck itself is nearly a ghost town today, with 240 residents; at night, the lights of ranch houses here are few and far between. It owes its existence to Fort Peck Dam, built on the Missouri River during the Great Depression. In those years, the West was in poor condition, and desperate families in Montana struggled against drought and unemployment. President Franklin Roosevelt's answer was one of the largest New Deal projects, the Fort Peck Dam, a source of water and jobs. Constructing the 250-foot-high, 4-mi-long dam required seven years and scores of workers, many of whom settled in the government-built town, aptly named Fort Peck. Some built their own settlements nearby, with names like New Deal, Square Deal, and Wheeler. But when the dam was finished and work dried up by 1940, so did the settlements.

When the mayor of the nearby town of Glasgow learned of the government's plans to build what would become the largest dam on the Missouri, he was aghast. "Hell," he said, "a dam like that might cost a million dollars." In fact, it cost $156 million. Part of the money was used to build the **Fort Peck Visitor Center and Museum**, in the lobby of Power Plant No. 1, northeast of town. Interpretive displays recount the history and significance of the dam's construction, along with the larger history of the area. There are also some dinosaur fossils on display, including a triceratops skull. Guided tours of the dam and its power plants depart from here. ⊠ *Lower Yellowstone Rd.* ☎ 406/526–3431 or 406/526– 3421 ⊕ *www.nwo.usace.army.mil* ⊡ *Free* ☉ *Memorial Day–Labor Day, daily 9–5.*

At the peak of dam construction, nearly 11,000 workers lived in Fort Peck; together with their families, they made up a thriving population center of 50,000. To help keep the populace entertained, the Army Corps of Engineers built a movie house in 1934. It was supposed to be a temporary structure, but it instead it eventually became the **Fort Peck**

Summer Theater. The chalet-style building is a venue for live entertainment weekend nights in summer. ✉ *110 5th St.* ☎ *406/228–9219* 💲 *$12* ☽ *June–Aug., Fri.–Sun. 7–midnight.*

Sports & the Outdoors

Stretching 134 mi across the border between the Big Open and the Hi-Line (U.S. 2), Fort Peck Lake is a prime outdoor-adventure destination. Fishing is especially popular here. Walleye are likely the lake's most well-known fish, but other species include northern pike, trout, perch, and salmon. Outfitters are hard to come by, so be sure to get most of your supplies before coming here. The lake is the venue for the annual **Governor's Cup Walleye Tournament** (☎ 406/228–2222) in July.

The **Fort Peck Dredge Cuts** (✉ Hwy. 117 ☎ 406/228–3700), also known as the Fort Peck Trout Pond, is a state fishing access site on the north shore of the lake. It has a boat launch. The **Rock Creek Marina** (✉ 652 South Rock Creek Rd. ☎ 406/485–2560) has marina facilities, a boat launch, and a modern campground.

Where to Stay

¢–$ 🏨 **Fort Peck Hotel.** Just about every piece of furniture in this barnlike wooden building dates from the hotel's construction during the Great Depression. Inside, the hardwood floors, thick beams, sturdy rafters, and Western style transport you back to the 1930s. The computer in the lounge and cable TV in the rooms, however, will bring you back into the 21st century. Accommodations are small and modest. Most bathrooms have showers, but some have massive claw-foot bathtubs. The adjoining rustic dining room serves three square meals a day for an additional charge. The hotel is popular with hunters. ✉ *175 S. Missouri St., 59223* ☎ *406/526–3266 or 800/560–4931* 🖷 *406/526–3472* 🛏 *37 rooms* 🍴 *Dining room, cable TV, Internet, business services, meeting rooms; no room phones, no room TVs, no smoking* ⊟ *AE, D, MC, V.*

CAMPING ⛺ **Downstream Campground.** This large and wooded campground is one of a few developed camping facilities on Fort Peck lake, which is managed by the Army Corps of Engineers. 🚻 *Grills, flush toilets, pit toilets, partial hookups (electric), dump station, drinking water, showers, picnic tables, electricity, public telephone, play area, swimming (lake)* 🛏 *71 partial hookups, 3 tent sites* ✉ *Hwy. 24 N* ☎ *406/526–3224* 🖷 *406/526–3593* 💲 *$10 tent sites, $12 partial hookups* ⊟ *AE, D, MC, V.*

Charles M. Russell National Wildlife Refuge

1 mi south of Fort Peck via Missouri Ave.

Bordering the shores of Fort Peck Lake—and encompassing the town of Fort Peck itself—is the massive Charles M. Russell National Wildlife Refuge, a 1.1-million-acre preserve teeming with more than 200 species of birds, including bald eagles and game birds; 45 different mammals, including elk, antelope, prairie dogs, and deer; and a variety of fish and reptiles. But this is also a refuge for history: each year scientists from around the country march into the preserve, and each year they find something new, whether it's dinosaur bones, buffalo jumps, teepee rings, or an old homesteader's shack. Charlie Russell, whose evocative paintings depicted a West about to be overrun by railroads, highways, and smokestacks, would surely be proud of the conservation being accomplished in his name—although he might not mind if there were a few more watering holes on the outskirts of this great tract of remote and undeveloped land. The refuge is open for hiking, horseback riding, fishing, boating, and other activities. Several access roads run through the area; most of these are unpaved, aside from U.S. 191, which runs north–south through the western edge of the refuge. ☎ *406/538–8706* ⊕ *cmr.fws.gov* ✉ *Free* ☉ *Daily, 24 hrs.*

There are three staffed **field stations** (✉ U.S. 91, Hwy. 200, and Hwy. 24 ☎ 406/538–8706 ⊕ cmr.fws.gov) in the refuge: the **Sand Creek Wildlife Station**, the **Jordan Wildlife Station**, and the **Fort Peck Wildlife Station**. Although they have no public facilities, they are conveniently scattered around the park, and the rangers will help you with directions or problems.

★ Hundreds of elk congregate in evening in the fall at the **Slippery Ann Wildlife Viewing Area** (✉ U.S. 191). During the autumn mating season, the bulls violently lock horns while herds of cows come to watch. Be sure to bring binoculars and zoom lenses for your camera, because you must keep your distance from these massive animals.

A refuge within a refuge, the **UL Bend National Wildlife Refuge** consists of more than 20,000 acres of wilderness entirely within the boundaries of the Charles M. Russell National Wildlife Refuge. Its primary mission at the moment is to rescue one of the nation's most endangered animals: the black-footed ferret. The ferrets depend on the high concentration of prairie dog towns for food. There are also plenty of grouse and burrowing owls, who use abandoned prairie dog tunnels for homes. ✉ *UL Bend National Wildlife Refuge Rd.* ☎ *406/538–8706* ⊕ *cmr.fws.gov* ✉ *Free* ☉ *Daily, 24 hrs.*

THE HI-LINE

The Hi-Line is named for U.S. 2, which connects Houlton, Maine, with Everett, Washington. The most northerly road traveling east–west across the United States, the highway plows a path almost straight through northern Montana until it reaches the Rockies. Remote prairies, northern wetlands, and scattered forests make this area both a haven for wildlife and for the few people who live here. U.S. 2 is the region's lifeline, connecting otherwise isolated communities with the rest of the country. From the descendants of wheat farmers and cattle ranchers to a half-dozen Native American tribes and two dozen German-speaking Hutterite colonies, the people of the Hi-Line are a hardy bunch, enduring the bone-chilling winters and poor economy for a quiet bit of land and a caring community. This is a place where you know your neighbors—all of them—and visitors often make the weekly paper. There may not be a Starbucks on every corner, or even a movie theater within 100 mi, but Hi-Line residents wouldn't have it any other way.

Medicine Lake National Wildlife Refuge Complex

③⓪ *230 mi northeast of Charles M. Russell National Wildlife Refuge via Larb Creek Rd. and U.S. 2.*

Established in 1935, this refuge sandwiched between U.S. 2 and the Canadian border encompasses more than 30,000 acres of wetlands that provide ideal habitat for waterfowl and migrating birds. Dozens of mammal species, including bear and bobcats, and a variety of butterflies and moths make their home here. There are few facilities available, but that's the point. ✉ *223 North Shore Rd.* ☎ *406/789–2305* ⊕ *medicinelake.fws. gov* ✑ *Free* ⊙ *Daily sunrise–sunset.*

Winding through the central unit of the refuge is the **Auto Tour Route,** an excellent way to get a peek at the animals that call this pristine park home. Most of the route is open only during daylight hours.

The **Observation Tower,** adjacent to the refuge headquarters, provides a good overview of the lakes in the refuge and the surrounding terrain. From above the trees and tall reeds, you can see the distinct lakes and ponds, as well as the sand hills around the borders. Birders often congregate in the **Grouse Observation Blind,** 2¼ mi east of the refuge headquarters, to take a good look at the resident bird species. The covered area is also good for watching other wildlife.

> off the beaten path

FORT UNION TRADING POST NATIONAL HISTORIC SITE – Just across the border in North Dakota, near the confluence of the Missouri and Yellowstone rivers, is one of the most famous fur-trading posts on the upper plains. Founded in 1828 by John Jacob Astor's American Fur Company, Fort Union bustled with activity well into the 1860s, despite its remote location and an outbreak of smallpox that wiped out up to 90% of some neighboring Native American tribes. By the conclusion of the Civil War, however, the fort had outlived its usefulness, and in 1867 it was dismantled, its pieces used to construct nearby Fort Buford. But the site was not forgotten, and in 1941 the grounds of the old post were established as a state park; in 1966 this became a national historic site. The fort has been reconstructed, and you can wander through any number of interpretive exhibits relating to the fur trade and Native American life in the mid-19th century. ✉ *15550 Rte. 1804, Williston, ND* ☎ *701/ 572–9083* ⊕ *www.nps.gov/fous/* ✑ *Free* ⊙ *Sept.–May, daily 9–5:30; June–Aug., daily 8–8.*

Bowdoin National Wildlife Refuge

③① *200 mi west of Medicine Lake National Wildlife Refuge via U.S. 2.*

An oxbow of the Missouri River before the last ice age, Bowdoin National Wildlife Refuge is a massive series of lakes and wetlands a few miles east of Malta. Before the government started to administer the refuge, water levels would drastically vary by season, making it a poor breeding ground for birds—but an excellent breeding ground for disease. Since the construction of several dikes and water channels in the 1930s, however, the water levels of the lakes have remained fairly constant, and the 15,000-acre preserve now shelters numerous birds and mammals. Aside from typical prairie animals and field songbirds, there are sizeable populations of pelicans, gulls, and herons. Several protected species also live here, including the piping plover, black-footed ferret, bald eagle, and peregrine falcon. ☎ *406/654–2863* ⊕ *bowdoin.fws.gov* ⊠ *Free* ☉ *Daily during daylight hrs.*

As the main road through the refuge, the **Bowdoin Refuge Autotour Route** affords excellent views of the terrain and wildlife. Old U.S. 2 is another main route, but it doesn't compare to the slower and far more scenic experience of the Autotour.

The **Bowdoin Wildlife Refuge Headquarters,** at the main entrance to Bowdoin, provides information on refuge conditions, species lists, and instructions for a drivable tour route. ⊠ *Bowdoin Refuge Autotour Rte.* ☎ *406/654–2863* ⊕ *bowdoin.fws.gov* ⊠ *Free* ☉ *Weekdays 8–5.*

Birders and wildlife photographers come to the **Pearce Waterfowl Production Area Bird Blind,** on the northeast edge of the refuge, for great views.

<table>
<tr><td>

off the
beaten
path

</td><td>

PHILLIPS COUNTY HISTORICAL MUSEUM – This museum in the town of Malta, a ranching community of about 2,000 people, is an official repository for fossils found in the Judith River basin. The highlight of the dinosaur display is a reconstructed albertosaur skeleton, which towers above the rest of the collection. You can also see some significant homesteading artifacts, including exhibits related to outlaws who spent time here: Butch Cassidy, the Sundance Kid, Kid Curry, the Tall Texan, and other members of the Wild Bunch gang. ⊠ *431 U.S. 2, Malta* ☎ *406/654–1037* ⊕ *www. montanadinosaurdigs.com/museum.htm* ⊠ *Free* ☉ *May–Sept., Mon.–Sat. 10–5, Sun. 12:30–5; Oct.–Apr., by appointment only.*

</td></tr>
</table>

Where to Stay

¢ 🏨 **Maltana Hotel.** Easy to find, this downtown hotel is within walking distance of Malta's Amtrak station and a few blocks from the junction of U.S. 2 and 191. The rooms are modest but modern, with data ports and coffeemakers—unusual finds in a small, isolated town. ⊠ *138 1st Ave. E, Malta 59538* ☎ *406/654–2610* 🖷 *406/654–1663* ⚐ *19 rooms* ♨ *Cable TV, in-room data ports, airport shuttle, no-smoking rooms* ▭ *AE, D, MC, V.*

Havre

32 *103 mi west of Bowdoin National Wildlife Refuge via U.S. 2.*

Mainly a place to stay when visiting Fort Assinniboine, the town of Havre (population 9,621) is the trading center for a wide area of extreme north-central Montana and southern Alberta and Saskatchewan. It lies between the Milk River and Bear Paw Mountains, and in a preserve south of town you can fish, picnic, or just enjoy the view.

Displays at the **H. Earl Clack Memorial Museum** include murals, artifacts, dioramas, and military and mining exhibits that explore the lives of Plains

Indians and Havre's early settlers and ranchers. Many of the artifacts come from nearby Fort Assinniboine and the Wahkpa Chu'gn Archaeological Site, a major buffalo jump; you can arrange for tours of these sites through the museum. ⊠ *306 3rd Ave.* ☎ *406/265–4000* ⬚ *$3* ☉ *Labor Day–Memorial Day, Tues.–Sat. 1–5; Memorial Day–Labor Day, Tues.–Sat. 10–5.*

★ Once the largest military fort west of the Mississippi and known as the "West Point of the West," **Fort Assinniboine** was established in 1879 in the aftermath of the Battle of the Little Bighorn. At its peak, the fort had more than 100 brick and stone buildings and nearly 500 men. The soldiers stationed here brought along their families, who lived on the post; the small ranching community of Havre, 6 mi away, was still in the process of becoming a full-fledged town. As a result, the Victorian-era fort became a cultural center as well as a military one, hosting plays and dances along with parades and training exercises. This was one of the more culturally diverse posts of its day, with Native American, black, and white soldiers. Its mission was to keep indigenous tribes in check, though there was some speculation that the post's northern location reflected the ambitions of some U.S. senators to acquire Canada. The fort is now a museum, and many of the imposing buildings still stand, although they appear eerily deserted. In fact, a few are storage or administrative facilities for the Northern Research Agricultural Center. Others are open to public tours, which begin at the H. Earl Clack Memorial Museum. ⊠ *306 3rd Ave.* ☎ *406/265–4383* ⬚ *$3* ☉ *May–Sept., hrs vary so call ahead.*

★ The **Havre Beneath the Streets** tour takes you to a bordello, an opium den, a bakery, and other stops in an underground business center dating from the early days of the frontier—the equivalent of an underground mall. ⊠ *120 3rd Ave.* ☎ *406/265–8888* ⬚ *$10* ☉ *Sept.–May, Mon.–Sat. 10–4; June–Aug., daily 9–5.*

Set in the ancient Bear Paw Mountains, about 10 mi south of town, is the 10,000-acre **Beaver Creek Park,** the largest county park in the country. It's a favorite spot for locals, who come here to fish in the two lakes, camp, picnic, and enjoy the scenery. ⊠ *Hwy. 234* ☎ *406/395–4565* ⬚ *$5 per vehicle* ☉ *Daily, 24 hrs.*

Where to Stay & Eat

¢–$$ ✕ **Lunch Box.** There are daily soup and sandwich specials at this family-style deli; two soups are made fresh daily. The menu lists a lot of healthful choices, with 70 sandwiches, as well as salads, nachos, baked potatoes, lattes, and espresso. ⊠ *213 3rd Ave.* ☎ *406/265–6588* ▭ *MC, V* ☉ *Closed Sun.*

$ ▦ **Best Western Great Northern Inn.** A clock tower, colorful flags, and off-white stones and bricks decorate the proud exterior of this spacious hotel. Contemporary furnishings fill the rooms, and an annex separates the business suites from the rest of the hotel. ⊠ *1345 1st St., 59501* ☎ *406/ 265–4200 or 888/530–4100* 🖷 *406/265–3656* ⊕ *www.bestwestern. com* ⇆ *63 rooms, 12 suites* ⌂ *Restaurant, some in-room hot tubs, cable TV with movies, indoor pool, hot tub, bar, laundry facilities, business* *services, airport shuttle, some pets allowed (fee), no-smoking rooms* ⊟*AE, D, DC, MC, V* |◎| *CP.*

The Arts
Focusing on the pencil drawings of a local artist, the **Old Library Gallery** (⊠ 439 4th Ave. ☎ 406/265–8165) also displays paintings and pottery; most have a connection with local history and culture.

THE MONTANA PLAINS A TO Z

To research prices, get advice from other travelers, and book travel arrangements, visit www.fodors.com.

AIR TRAVEL
Within eastern Montana, commercial flights—generally via Salt Lake City, Seattle, Denver, or Phoenix—are available only to Billings and Great Falls; small commuter and charter flights serve other towns. Because the region is so isolated, flights here from anywhere in the country can be pricey—often more expensive than coast-to-coast flights.

🛂 Airlines & Contacts **Big Sky** ☎ 800/237-7788 ⊕ www.bigskyair.com. **Delta** ☎ 800/221-1212 ⊕ www.delta.com. **Horizon** ☎ 800/252-7522 ⊕ horizonair.alaskaair.com. **Northwest** ☎ 800/225-2525 ⊕ www.nwa.com. **United** ☎ 800/864-8331 ⊕ www.ual.com.

AIRPORTS
Both Billings Logan and Great Falls are international airports, but only because they have occasional service to and from Canada. Because Billings and Great Falls have direct service to only a few cities in the western part of the country, some residents of the region drive as far as Bismarck, North Dakota; Rapid City, South Dakota; or Gillette, Wyoming, to catch departing flights.

🛂 Airport Information **Billings Logan International Airport** ⊠ 1901 Terminal Circle, Billings ☎ 406/238-3420 ⊕ www.flybillings.com. **Great Falls International Airport** ⊠ Airport Dr., Great Falls ☎ 406/727-3404 ⊕ www.gtfairport.com.

BUS TRAVEL
Several bus companies connect most communities of 1,000 residents or more; smaller towns may not have service. Expect high ticket prices; depending on where you're going, taking the bus can be almost as expensive as flying, and because of the great expanse of Montana, it can take infinitely longer.

🛂 Bus Information **Greyhound Bus Lines** ☎ 406/245-5116 or 800/231-2222 ⊕ www.greyhound.com. **Karst Stages** ☎ 406/556-3500 ⊕ www.karststage.com. **Powder River Transportation** ☎ 307/674-6188. **Rimrock Stages** ☎ 406/245-7696 or 800/255-7655 ⊕ www.rimrocktrailways.com. **Silver Eagle Shuttle Inc.** ☎ 406/256-9793 ⊕ www.montanacustomtours.com.

CAR RENTAL
Rental cars are easily acquired in Billings and Great Falls; the airports are your best bet.

🛂 Avis ☎ 800/831-2847 ⊕ www.avis.com. **Budget** ☎ 800/527-0700 ⊕ www.budget.com. **Hertz** ☎ 800/654-3131 ⊕ www.hertz.com. **National** ☎ 800/227-7368 ⊕ www.nationalcar.com.

CAR TRAVEL

It is virtually impossible to travel around the Montana plains without a car. One of the best things about driving here is the lack of traffic. Aside from a little bustle in Great Falls or Billings on weekdays in the late afternoon, gridlock and traffic jams are unheard-of here. The largest driving hazards be slow-moving farming or ranching equipment, wranglers on horseback, herds of grazing livestock that refuse to move off the highway, and deer bounding over ditches in the evening. Driving gets a little hairy in winter, but not because of the amount of snow that falls, which is generally very little. Whiteouts, when winds tearing across the plains whip up the tiniest bit of snow into ground blizzards, are the most common hazard. Large drifts and slick roads become more problematic at higher elevations.

For information on road conditions, contact the Montana Department of Transportation.

🔢 **Montana Department of Transportation** ☎ 800/226–7623 or 511 ⊕ www.mdt.mt. gov/travinfo. **Montana Highway Patrol** ☎ 406/444–3780 ⊕ www.doj.state.mt.us/ department/.

EMERGENCIES

🔢 Ambulance or Police **Emergencies** ☎ 911 or 800/525–5555.
🔢 24-Hour Medical Care **Benefis Healthcare** ✉ 1101 26th St. S, Great Falls ☎ 406/ 455–5000 ⊕ www.benefis.org. **Deaconess Billings Clinic** ✉ 2800 10th Ave. N, Billings ☎ 406/657–4000 ⊕ www.billingsclinic.com. **St. Vincent Healthcare** ✉ 1233 N. 30th St., Billings ☎ 406/657–7000 ⊕ www.stvincenthealthcare.org.

LODGING

The Montana Innkeepers Association's simple Web site accesses a large database of lodgings throughout most of the state. However, many of the smaller inns and motels in Montana's eastern reaches do not belong to the association.

🔢 **Montana Innkeepers Association** ☎ 406/449–8408 ⊕ www.montanainnkeepers.com.

CAMPING Camping in Montana is incredibly easy: many federal and state-owned lands allow camping for little or no charge, and you can often set up shop wherever you like, so long as you don't light a fire. In the more developed towns and cities there is almost always a campground or two with some more modern conveniences, such as hot showers and flush toilets.

Contact Montana Fish, Wildlife & Parks for information on camping in state parks and the U.S. Forest Service for information on camping at national parks in the area.

🔢 **Montana Fish, Wildlife & Parks** ☎ 406/444–2535 ⊕ www.fwp.state.mt.us/parks.
U.S. Forest Service ☎ 406/329–3511 ⊕ www.fs.fed.us/r1.

MEDIA

NEWSPAPERS & MAGAZINES The *Billings Gazette* is by far the most widely read newspaper in Montana; it even has a strong following among people in Wyoming and the Dakotas. Its only competitor in the immediate vicinity is the *Great Falls Tribune*. Where the *Gazette* tends to focus on the southern Montana plains and environs, the *Tribune* finds its niche farther north.

TELEVISION &
RADIO
Radio and TV signals are few and far between in this incredibly vast region. You might not even find a station by pushing the "seek" button on your car radio. Many people subscribe to cable television simply so they can get two or three local stations. The major broadcasters are CBS/KTVQ Channel 2 and NBC/KULR Channel 8 in Billings, and ABC/KFBB Channel 5, CBS/KRTV Channel 3, and NBC/KTGF Channel 16 in Great Falls.

SPORTS & THE OUTDOORS

BOATING
Although the plains are dry, dams have tamed a few of the major rivers that run through the region, creating ideal venues for water sports. Motorized boating, including jet skiing, is usually not restricted, even in the massive Charles M. Russell National Wildlife Refuge. Marinas rent out boats on Fort Peck Lake, Bighorn Lake, and a few of the other reservoirs scattered around the plains. Extended droughts can sometimes put the marinas out of business—at least temporarily—or force them to move to another location. If you're interested in boat rentals on a specific lake or river, call Travel Montana for information on a marina that serves that location.

🚩 **Travel Montana** ⊠ 301 S. Park Ave., Helena 59620 ☎ 406/841-2870 or 800/847-4868 ⊕ www.visitmt.com.

FISHING
Although the eastern two-thirds of Montana are decidedly drier than the western regions, small mountain-fed creeks and reservoirs on a few major rivers are plentiful. Unlike the blue-ribbon streams of the higher elevations, the babbling brooks of the lowlands seldom attract crowds.

🚩 **Montana Fish, Wildlife & Parks** ⊠ 1420 E. 6th Ave., Helena 59620 ☎ 406/444-2535 ⊕ www.fwp.state.mt.us.

TRAIN TRAVEL

Amtrak serves the isolated communities of the Hi-Line. The tracks run nearly parallel to U.S. 2 the entire length of the state. Trains stop in the towns of Glasgow, Malta, Havre, Wolf Point, and Cut Bank, among others.

🚩 **Train Information Amtrak** ☎ 800/872-7245 ⊕ www.amtrak.com.

VISITOR INFORMATION

🚩 **Tourist Information Billings Convention and Visitors Bureau** ⊠ 815 S. 27th St., Billings 59107 ☎ 406/252-4016 or 800/735-2635 ⊕ www.billingscvb.visitmt.com. **Great Falls Convention and Visitors Bureau** ⊠ 710 1st Ave. N, Great Falls 59401 ☎ 406/761-4434 ⊕ greatfallscvb.visitmt.com. **Travel Montana** ⊠ 301 S. Park Ave., Helena 59620 ☎ 406/841-2870 or 800/847-4868 ⊕ www.visitmt.com.

Cody, Sheridan & Northern Wyoming

6

By T. D. Griffith & Dustin D. Floyd

PINE-CARPETED HILLSIDES AND SNOWY MOUNTAIN SUMMITS give way to windswept prairies and clean-flowing rivers where the Great Plains meet the mighty Rocky Mountains. Northern Wyoming's epic landscape is replete with symbols of the American frontier: the ranch, the rodeo, and the cowboy.

It may be that no state in the union exalts cowboy life as Wyoming does. The concept of the dude-ranch vacation—where urban folk learn to rope, ride, and rodeo with weathered ranchers and professional cattle drivers—started in northern Wyoming, at Eaton's Guest Ranch just outside Sheridan. Numerous other guest ranches are strewn across the grassy plains here, from the acres of dusty plains east of Cody to the alpine meadows of the Big Horn Mountains. Most Big Horn-area dude ranches run pack trips into these high, rugged peaks, sometimes for days at a time. Even if you prefer a warm bed to sleeping under the stars, don't be deterred, and certainly don't leave the state without getting on a horse at least once: try a shorter trail ride or a pack trip that ends at a furnished cabin.

The outdoors are northern Wyoming's primary draw. Take the time to appreciate the wide-open spaces before you: take a hike, go fishing, ride a bike, or get out into the snow. Much of this territory is just as empty as it was when the first white people arrived here more than a century ago. Even though Europeans settled in Wyoming as early as 1812, the state's population is the smallest in the nation, at only 493,782 permanent residents. But the few that have dwelt in this place have been history makers. This part of Wyoming has a rich and storied past that encompasses icons such as gunslingers, gamblers, miners, mule skinners, and warriors. Some of the most famous (and infamous) figures of the Old West passed through here, including Buffalo Bill Cody, Wild Bill Hickok, Calamity Jane, and Butch Cassidy and the Sundance Kid, the latter of whom took his name from one of the region's towns.

Exploring Northern Wyoming

Northern Wyoming is a point of convergence. Here mountains meet prairies, forests meet ranches, and country towns meet Western cities. Most settlements have no more than a few hundred people; only three surpass 10,000 residents. Casper, on the banks of the North Platte River in the center of Wyoming, is on or near five of the major pioneer trails of the mid-19th century, including the Oregon and Mormon trails. Gillette, in the Powder River basin near Devils Tower National Monument, and Sheridan, on the edge of the Big Horn Mountains 100 mi to the northwest, are both in Wyoming's energy country, although ranching (both dude and cattle) are mainstays of the communities. Cody, with only 8,973 residents, is the largest community between the Big Horn Mountains and Yellowstone National Park, a convenient stop for visitors on their way to the natural treasures further west.

About the Restaurants

Although not every community here has the eclectic mix of dining options common in more urban areas, there are plenty of small restaurants

6

Many people travel through northern Wyoming on their way to visit the wonders of Yellowstone National Park to the west. This is one of the most logical ways to see the area, but beware: the empty spaces between towns and the wide-open road might tempt you to speed through the region too quickly. Give yourself enough time to allow for occasional stops, and don't hesitate to overnight in one of the area's small towns. You won't just be breaking up the car ride, you'll get to visit some of the American West's hidden gems. Planning ahead is imperative—hotels, gas stations, and restaurants can be few and far between.

If you're headed into Wyoming from the east along I-90, be sure to stop at Sundance and Devils Tower National Monument. The towns of Gillette, Buffalo, and Sheridan are also worth your time, and are ideal places to spend the night. You have your choice of guest ranches and mountain lodges here, and you can take the opportunity to explore both the Wyoming plains and the foothills of the Big Horns. Take either U.S. 14 or U.S. 16 through the mountains and stretch your legs in the Cloud Peak Wilderness Area, a prime spot for outdoor recreation, whether it's a 15-minute hike or a daylong ski trip. West of the Big Horns, the two highways meet up near Basin; from here, U.S. 14 is a straight shot to Cody and U.S. 310 is a scenic route through the arid plains near Lovell and Deaver.

An alternative for those interested in pioneer trails and stagecoach routes is to head south from Buffalo via I-25 to the eastern Wyoming towns of Casper, Douglas, and Lusk. They lie in flatter landscape and offer less in the way of visitor services, but this is where you'll find the National Historic Trails Interpretive Center, Fort Fetterman State Historical Site, and similar attractions. From here, head back north on U.S. 20 to Thermopolis and either travel northeast into the Big Horns on U.S. 16 or northwest toward Cody and Yellowstone National Park on Hwy. 120.

---

and local cafés with inimitable appeal. The larger communities often have several ethnic eateries from which to choose, serving everything from traditional Mexican and Native American specialties to old-world Italian and modern Korean dishes. The real strength of the region's dining, however, lies with the basics. In almost any small-town watering hole, you can order up some of the freshest and best-tasting beef and buffalo in the world. Whether it's prime rib and mashed potatoes with sunflower bread, or charred rib eye with corn on the cob, the area's best meals are simple yet filled with a flavor found only in the West.

About the Hotels

Just as diverse as the area's landscape, which fades from small Western cities into vast lengths of open prairie and forested mountains, are its accommodations. In the population centers, lodgings range from new chain hotels with wireless Internet access to elegant and historic stone inns decorated with buffalo skins and Victorian furniture. Move beyond

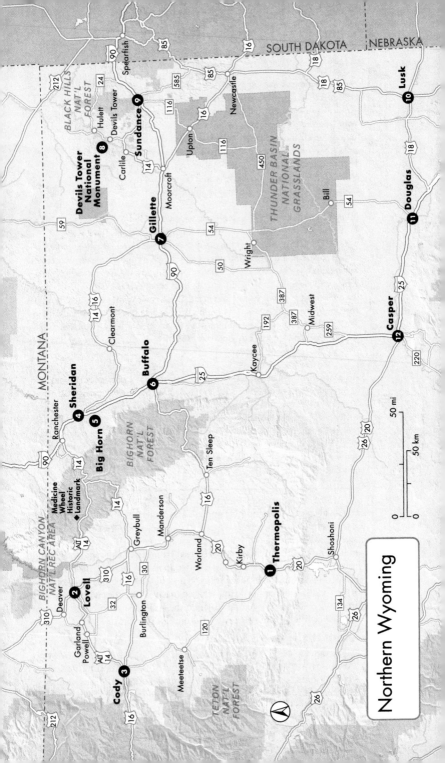

Northern Wyoming

these cities, however, and everything changes. Campgrounds abound in the open countryside. On the prairie, expect sprawling guest ranches alongside cold mountain-fed creeks. In the higher elevations, look for charming bed-and-breakfasts on mountain slopes with broad alpine vistas. But whatever the type of accommodation, all kinds of amenities are available, from the ordinary to the unconventional, including saunas, hot tubs, horseback riding, fly-fishing lessons, and square dancing. Perhaps the greatest benefit of all, however, is the isolation. In what some might call a welcome change in this era of information overload, many rural lodgings don't have in-room televisions or telephones, and some areas don't have cell phone service.

WHAT IT COSTS					
	$$$$	**$$$**	**$$**	**$**	**¢**
RESTAURANTS	over $22	$17–$22	$12–$16	$7–$11	under $7
HOTELS	over $220	$161–$220	$111–$160	$70–$110	under $70

Restaurant prices are for a main course at dinner, excluding sales tax of 4%–7%. Hotel prices are for two people in a standard double room in high season, excluding service charges and 5%–10% tax.

Timing

People come to experience northern Wyoming in all four seasons—sometimes all in the same week. The weather here is notoriously difficult to predict, as warm Chinook winds can shoot January temperatures into the 70s and freak storms can drop snow in July. On the whole, however, Mother Nature behaves herself and gives the area pleasantly warm summers and refreshingly snowy winters. Most travelers flock to the region between June and August, availing themselves of the higher temperatures optimal for outdoor activities. Many more come to ski or snowmobile the pristine powder of the Big Horn Mountains in the winter.

Temperatures in both seasons can be extreme, however. Thermometers often register a week of triple digits in August in the lower elevations. Snow begins to blanket the mountain slopes in late September and begins to recede only in late May. Spring, especially in the mountains, is sometimes nothing more than a week or two of rain between the last winter snowfall and the warm sunshine of summer. Autumn, on the other hand, is full of pleasantly warm days, cooler nights, and vivid colors. Additionally, the only crowds to fight are small pockets of hunters, anglers, and local leaf peepers.

THE BIG HORN BASIN

Rich in Native American history, Old West flavor, and natural wonders, this broad basin is flanked by the Absaroka and Owl mountains to the west and the Big Horns to the east. The Bighorn River flows north along the eastern edge of the basin and up into Montana. Here, straddling the two states, is Bighorn Canyon National Recreation Area; most of the recreation area lies in Montana, but the southern portion is easily accessible in Wyoming via Highway 37.

Numbers in the text correspond to numbers in the margin and on the Northern Wyoming map.

Thermopolis

❶ *133 mi east of Dubois via U.S. 26/287 to Shoshoni, then north on U.S. 20.*

Native Americans, particularly the Shoshone, considered Thermopolis' hot mineral springs and surrounding land neutral territory. In 1896 they ceded the ground to the U.S. government as a "gift of the waters," stipulating that the springs should remain available for the free use of all people. You can take the waters gratis at the state bathhouse, but private pools charge a fee.

The land that is now **Hot Springs State Park** was sacred to Native Americans because of its healing waters. You can partake of these waters by soaking indoors or outside at the free hot mineral pools at the Wyoming State Bath House. **Star Plunge** is a commercial facility within the park with indoor and outdoor hot mineral pools, soak tubs, and a waterslide. You can hike or bike on the trails within the park, and you may even spot a bison herd. ⊠ *U.S. 20* ☎ *307/364–2176 or 307/864–3765* ⊕ *wyoparks.state.wy.us/hsslide.htm* ✉ *Park and state bathhouse free, Star Plunge $9* ☉ *Park daily 24 hrs; state bathhouse Mon.–Sat. 8–5:30, Sun. noon–5:30; Star Plunge daily 9–9.*

Ⓒ Among the dinosaur remains displayed at the **Wyoming Dinosaur Center** is a replica of "Stan," the second-largest and most complete Tyrannosaurus rex in the world, measuring 40 feet long and weighing in at nearly six tons. Kids can try their hand at paleontology by digging in the dinosaur quarry; regular digs are scheduled for children ages 8–13 and 13–17. ⊠ *110 Carter Ranch Rd.* ☎ *307/864–2997* ⊕ *www.wyodino.org* ✉ *$6, dig tours (summer only) $6* ☉ *Mid-May–mid-Sept., daily 8–8; mid-Sept.–mid-May, daily 10–4. Dig tours daily 10–4, weather permitting (generally May–Sept.).*

Sports & the Outdoors

GOLF **Legion Town & Country Club** (⊠ 141 Airport Rd. ☎ 307/864–5294) has a 9-hole course with views of Hot Springs State Park and the Wind River canyon.

RAFTING **Wind River Canyon Whitewater** (⊠ 210 Hwy. 20 S ☎ 307/864–9343 or 888/246–9343) leads white-water floats down the Wind River. Trips range from a couple of hours to full-day trips that include lunch. Scenic floats and fishing trips are also available.

Where to Stay & Eat

$–$$ ✕▦ **Holiday Inn of the Waters.** The rooms are standard at this hotel within
FodorsChoice Hot Springs State Park, but the extra amenities—including a hot min-
★ eral swimming pool, a large hot mineral soaking pool, and a health club—
and the hotel's proximity to the commercial mineral swimming pools

set it apart. There's also a nearby jogging trail, and winter lodging-meal-activity packages are available. A collection of game animals from around the world decorates the Safari Dining Room ($$–$$$$), which serves bison raised on the nearby Red Canyon Ranch, prime rib, and steaks. ✉ *Hot Springs State Park, 115 E. Park St., 82443* ☎ *307/864–3131* 🖷 *307/864–3131* ⊕ *www.thermopolis-hi.com* ⤳ *80 rooms* ⬤ *Restaurant, room service, in-room data ports, pool, health club, outdoor hot tub, spa, hiking, bar, laundry service, some pets allowed, nosmoking rooms* ▭ *AE, D, DC, MC, V.*

Lovell

❷ *46 mi east of Cody via Alternate U.S. 14.*

This small community makes a convenient, if bare-bones, base for exploring the Bighorn Canyon National Recreation Area, which overlaps the Wyoming–Montana border. On the Wyoming side, Bighorn Lake is popular with boaters and anglers; most of the main attractions, including the majority of the Pryor Mountain Wild Horse Range, lie on the Montana side. (For further information, *see* Chapter 5.)

The main visitor center for Bighorn Canyon National Recreation Area, the **Bighorn Canyon Visitor Center** has geological and historical exhibits on the area, as well as a film about the canyon. ✉ *U.S. 310 at Alternate U.S. 14* ☎ *307/548–2251* ⊕ *www.nps.gov/bica/* 🎫 *Free* ⊗ *Memorial Day–Labor Day, daily 8–6; Labor Day–Memorial Day, daily 8–5.*

More than 155 species of birds, including white pelicans, bald eagles, and great blue herons, inhabit the 19,424-acre **Yellowtail Wildlife Habitat Management Area,** as do numerous other animal species, including red fox, mule deer, and cottontail rabbits. ✉ *Hwy. 37, 33 mi east of Lovell* ☎ *307/527–7125* 🎫 *Free* ⊗ *Daily.*

off the beaten path

MEDICINE WHEEL NATIONAL HISTORIC LANDMARK – A ring of rocks 80 feet in diameter, this ancient site is the best preserved of nearly 150 Native American stone wheels found in Wyoming, South Dakota, Montana, Alberta, and Saskatchewan. Evidence such as the 28 spokes (one for each day of the lunar cycle) leading from the edge of the wheel to a central cairn has persuaded some that the wheel was an ancient spiritual observatory much like England's Stonehenge may have been. To protect the area, access to the wheel is restricted to foot travel; it's a 1½-mi hike to the site from the parking lot (people with disabilities may drive to the site). Up in the Big Horn Mountains, at an elevation of 9,642 feet, the site affords views of the entire Big Horn Basin. At this elevation, you'll want to bring a coat or sweatshirt. ✉ *30 mi east of Lovell on Alternate U.S. 14* ☎ *307/548–6541* ⊕ *wyoshpo.state.wy.us/medwheel.htm* 🎫 *Free* ⊗ *Daily 24 hrs.*

Where to Stay & Eat

¢–$ ✕ **Lange's Kitchen.** This homey diner-style grill is a local institution, partly because it's the only restaurant in town. Workers at the nearby

FORGING THE FRONTIER

NORTHERN WYOMING is one of the least-populated areas in the United States. Although white people ventured through starting in the early 19th century—John Colter, a member of the Lewis and Clark expedition, visited in 1807—it wasn't until the 1850s and 1860s that significant numbers of permanent settlers arrived. Fur trappers and mountain men trickled in during the early 1800s, but for many years the land remained largely in the hands of the Lakota Sioux, the Arapahoe and the Crow.

No Rush

Unlike the bordering states of Montana, South Dakota, and Colorado, Wyoming never experienced a population boom from a gold or silver rush. The 1848 discovery of gold in California brought the first wave of northern Wyoming settlers when it sparked a massive migration of people eager to seek their fortune in the West.

Most used well-established pioneer trails that, in many cases, intersected almost in the center of Wyoming, near the present-day city of Casper. Like Sheridan and many other settlements in this area, Casper was founded as a military fort to protect travelers from Native American tribes.

The Indian Wars

As elsewhere, the indigenous people of northern Wyoming were angered by the U.S. government's blatant trespassing. Tensions flared into the Indian Wars of the late 19th century, and in this region Fort Phil Kearny saw the Fetterman Battle of 1866 and the Wagon Box Fight of 1867. The Lakota, Arapahoe, and Crow maintained firm control of the area until after the 1870s, when the Army finally subdued them and forced them onto reservations.

Cattle Country

American cattle ranchers took over the land and began establishing railroads and shipping points, such as Gillette and Buffalo, to transport their stock back east. Buffalo erupted in the Johnson County War of 1892, a conflict between big cattle barons and local ranchers that was immortalized in The Virginian, Owen Wister's 1902 novel.

Ranching continues to make a major economic contribution, and the dude ranch (a concept credited to Eaton's Guest Ranch, which opened outside Sheridan around the turn of the 20th century) has blended the traditional cowboy way of life with tourism.

An Energy-Powered Economy

In the late 20th century energy resource development emerged as northern Wyoming's largest economic force, thanks to vast deposits of coal and natural gas. Evidence of this is the Wyodak power plant that dominates Gillette: just outside town, a conveyor belt that runs underneath the interstate transports fuel from a coal mine on the north side of I–90 to a coal-fired generator on the south side. The future of northern Wyoming, the most recently settled area of one of the nation's youngest states, seems assured as its rich energy resources become increasingly valuable.

sugar refinery and bentonite plants come here for the kind of down-home cooking that sticks to your insides: biscuits and gravy, homemade oatmeal, hamburgers, shrimp baskets, tacos, halibut strips, and liver and onions. If you're not in the mood for a full meal, you can enjoy brewed coffee and tea in the coffee shop out front. Lange's is open from 6 AM to 2 PM, so you won't be able to get late lunch or dinner here. ⊠ *483 Shoshone Ave.* ☎ *307/548–9370* ☰ *MC, V* ⊘ *No dinner.*

¢ ▦ **Cattleman Motel.** Lodgepole-pine furniture fills the clean, simple Western-style rooms at this basic one-story motel. It's near the center of town. ⊠ *470 Montana Ave., 82431* ☎ *307/548–2296 or 888/548–2269* 🖶 *307/548–2483* ➥ *13 rooms* ♢ *Cable TV, hot tub, some pets allowed, no-smoking rooms* ☰ *AE, D, MC, V* ⸤◯⸥ *CP.*

CODY

❸ *84 mi northwest of Thermopolis via Hwy. 120; 52 mi east of Yellowstone via U.S. 14/16/20.*

Cody, founded in 1896 and named for Pony Express rider, army scout, and entertainer William F. "Buffalo Bill" Cody, is the eastern gateway community for Yellowstone National Park. The North Fork Highway—as the route leading east to Yellowstone is locally known—follows the North Fork of the Shoshone River past barren rock formations strewn with tumbleweeds, then enters lush forests and green meadows as the elevation increases roughly 3,000 feet in 70 mi. Cody is within easy reach of Shoshone National Forest, the Absaroka Range, the Washakie Wilderness, and the Buffalo Bill Reservoir.

But Cody is much more than a base for exploring the surrounding area. Several excellent museums make up the outstanding Buffalo Bill Historical Center, and the Western lifestyle is alive and well on dude ranches and in both trendy and classic shops. Part of the fun in Cody is sauntering down Main Street, stopping by the Irma Hotel (built by Buffalo Bill and named for his daughter) for some refreshment, and attending the nightly rodeo.

Pick up a brochure ($1 donation) with a self-guided walking tour of the town's historic sites at the Chamber of Commerce on Sheridan Avenue.

The **Wyoming Vietnam Veterans Memorial** is a small-scale version of the Vietnam Veterans Memorial wall in Washington, D.C. The Cody memorial recognizes the Wyoming residents who died during the conflict. ⊠ *U.S. 14/16/20, east of Cody.*

The **Cody Mural,** at the Church of Jesus Christ of Latter-day Saints, is an artistic interpretation of Mormon settlement in the West. Edward Grigware painted the scene on the domed ceiling in the 1950s. ⊠ *1010 Angler Ave.* ☎ *307/587–3290 or 307/587–9258* ⸤➘⸥ *Free* ⊘ *June–mid-Sept., Mon.–Sat. 8–8, Sun. 3–8.*

On the west side of Cody is one of the finest museum complexes in the
Fodor$Choice West: the **Buffalo Bill Historical Center,** which houses five museums in one.
★ The **Buffalo Bill Cody Museum** is dedicated to the incredible life of William F. "Buffalo Bill" Cody. Shortly after Cody's death, some of his

friends took mementos of the famous scout and Wild West showman and opened the Buffalo Bill Museum in a small log building. The museum has since been moved to the historical center and includes huge posters from the original Wild West shows, as well as personal effects such as clothing, guns, saddles, and furniture. The **Cody Firearms Museum** traces the history of firearms through thousands of models on display, from European blunderbusses to Gatling guns and modern firearms. Included are examples of Winchester and Browning arms, as well as a model of an arms-manufacturing plant. Through exhibits, outdoor activities, tours, and seminars, the **Draper Museum of Natural History** explores the Yellowstone ecosystem. There are children's discovery areas in addition to life-size animal mounts. Recordings play the sounds of wolves, grizzly bears, birds, and other animals that make their home in the Yellowstone area. At the **Plains Indian Museum,** interactive exhibits and life-size dioramas explore the history and culture of the Lakota, Blackfeet, Cheyenne, Shoshone, and Nez Perce tribes. Among the exhibits are rare medicine pipes, clothing, and an earth-house interpretive area. The **Whitney Gallery of Western Art** is devoted to the West's greatest artists. On display are works by such masters as Frederic Remington, Charles M. Russell, Albert Bierstadt, George Catlin, and Thomas Moran, plus contemporary artists such as Harry Jackson, James Bama, and Peter Fillerup. ⊠ *720 Sheridan Ave.* ☎ *307/587–4771* ⊕ *www.bbhc.org* ⊒ *$15 (2 days)* ☉ *Apr., daily 10–5; May, daily 8–8; June–mid-Sept., daily 7 AM–8 PM; mid-Sept.–Oct., daily 8–5; Nov.–Mar., daily 10–3.*

☁ **Cody Nite Rodeo,** more dusty and intimate than big rodeos such as Cheyenne Frontier Days, offers children's events, such as goat roping, in addition to the regular adult events. Contact the Cody Chamber of Commerce for more information. ⊠ *West Cody Strip* ☎ *800/207–0744* ⊕ *www.codyniterodeo.com* ⊒ *$10–$12; seat prices vary with location* ☉ *June–Aug., daily at 8:30 PM.*

Summer evenings, the **Cody Gunslingers Shootout** takes place on the porch at the Irma Hotel. ⊠ *1192 Sheridan Ave.* ☎ *307/587–4221* ⊒ *Free* ☉ *June–late Sept., daily at 6 PM.*

If you give the folks at **Cody Trolley Tours** an hour of your time, they'll take you on a journey through 100 years of Cody history. The tour takes in historic sites, scenery, geology, and wildlife attractions. A combination ticket also grants you admission to the Buffalo Bill Historical Center. ⊠ *Ticket booth in front of Irma Hotel, 1192 Sheridan Ave.* ☎ *307/527–7243* ⊕ *www.codytrolleytours.com* ⊒ *Tour ticket $13, combination ticket with Buffalo Bill Historical Center $22* ☉ *Early June–Sept., Mon.–Sat. at 9, 11, 1, 3, and 6:30; Sun. at 9, 11, 1, and 3.*

Dioramas at **Tecumseh's Wyoming Territory Old West Miniature Village and Museum** depict early-Wyoming and Native American history and Western events. The gift shop sells deerskin clothing handmade on the premises. ⊠ *142 W. Yellowstone Hwy.* ☎ *307/587–5362* ⊒ *Free* ☉ *June–Aug., daily 8–8; May and Sept., daily 10–6; rest of yr by appointment.*

On Cody's western outskirts, off the West Yellowstone Highway, is **Old Trail Town,** a collection of historic buildings from Wyoming's frontier days. Also here are a cemetery for famous local mountain men and Native American and pioneer artifacts. The buildings aren't fancy and the displays are rustic, so you really get a feel for an Old West town. Sometimes in summer Bobby Bridger, great-grandnephew of mountain man Jim Bridger, performs his "Ballad of the West" ($12) in the barn here. The three-night program describes the settlement of the West and includes stories of mountain men, Buffalo Bill Cody, and the Lakota. ⊠ *1831 Demaris Dr.* ☎ *307/587–5302* ✑ *$6* ☉ *May–Sept., daily 8–8.*

Fishing and boating on the Buffalo Bill Reservoir are popular activities at **Buffalo Bill State Park,** west of Cody. A visitor center here focuses on the history of the reservoir, which was completed in 1910. ⊠ *47 Lakeside Rd., west of Cody on U.S. 14/16/20* ☎ *307/587–6076* ⊕ *wyoparks. state.wy.us/BBslide.htm* ✑ *Park $4, camping $4* ☉ *Park daily 24 hrs, visitor center May–Sept., daily 8–8.*

The **Shoshone National Forest** was the country's first national forest, established in 1891. You can hike, fish, mountain bike, and ride horses in warmer weather, and snowmobile and cross-country ski in winter. There are picnic areas and campgrounds. ⊠ *U.S. 14/16/20, west of Cody* ☎ *307/527–6241* ⊕ *www.fs.fed.us/r2/shoshone/* ✑ *Free* ☉ *Daily 24 hrs.*

off the beaten path

CHIEF JOSEPH SCENIC BYWAY – In 1877, a few members of the Nez Perce tribe killed some white settlers in Idaho as retribution for earlier killings by whites. Fearing that the U.S. Army would punish the guilty and innocent alike, hundreds of Nez Perce fled on a five-month journey toward Canada that came to be known as the Nez Perce Trail. Along the way they passed through what is now Yellowstone National Park, across the Sunlight Basin area north of Cody, and along the Clarks Fork of the Shoshone River before turning north into Montana. To see the rugged mountain area they traveled through, follow Highway 120 north 17 mi to Highway 296, the Chief Joseph Scenic Byway. The byway eventually leads to Cooke City and Red Lodge, Montana. Along the way you'll see open meadows, pine forests, and a sweeping vista of the region from the top of Dead Indian Pass.

Sports & the Outdoors

Canoeing, Kayaking & Rafting

To get out on the Shoshone River, charter a guided trip. In Cody it's not possible to rent equipment for unguided trips.

Family river trips on the Shoshone River are offered by **River Runners** (⊠ 1491 Sheridan Ave. ☎ 307/527–7238). **Wyoming River Trips** (⊠ Buffalo Bill Village, 1701 Sheridan Ave. ☎ 307/587–6661 or 800/586–6661) arranges Shoshone River trips.

Fishing

The fish are big at the private **Monster Lake** (☎ 800/840–5137), filled with rainbow, brook, and brown trout weighing up to 10 pounds. For a fee you can fish all or part of the day at this lake on the east side of town; accommodations are available as well.

You can buy fishing tackle, get information on fishing in the area, or take a guided half- or full-day trip with **Tim Wade's North Fork Anglers** (✉ 1107 Sheridan Ave. ☎ 307/527–7274). Walk-ins are welcome.

Golf

Olive Glenn Golf and Country Club (✉ 802 Meadow La. ☎ 307/587–5551 or 307/587–5308) is a highly rated 18-hole course open to the public; a Jacuzzi, pool, and two tennis courts are also here.

Horseback Riding

Ride for one to four hours or all day with **Cedar Mountain Trail Rides** (✉ U.S. 14/16/20, 1 mi west of rodeo grounds ☎ 307/527–4966). You can ride horses into Shoshone National Forest with **Goff Creek Lodge** (✉ 995 E. Yellowstone Hwy. ☎ 307/587–3753); lunch rides are also available.

Skiing

In the Wood River valley near Meeteetse, 32 mi south of Cody, **Wood River Ski Touring Park** (✉ 1010 Park Ave. ☎ 307/868–2603) has 32 km (20 mi) of cross-country trails.

Where to Stay & Eat

$–$$$ ✕ **Maxwell's.** A turn-of-the-20th-century Victorian structure with huge windows and a porch houses this upscale contemporary restaurant that serves free-range beef entrées, homemade soups, pastas, and sandwiches. The baby-back pork ribs are always a good bet, and the Mediterranean pizza with Greek olives, feta cheese, and fresh tomatoes is also a good, very filling choice. In summer there's outdoor dining on the deck. ✉ 937 *Sheridan Ave.* ☎ 307/527–7749 ▭ *AE, D, MC, V.*

$–$$$ ✕ **Proud Cut Saloon.** At this popular downtown eatery and watering hole, owner Del Nose serves what locals call "kick-ass cowboy cuisine": steaks, prime rib, shrimp, fish, and chicken. Western paintings, vintage photographs of Cody country, and large game mounts decorate the place. ✉ *1227 Sheridan Ave.* ☎ 307/527–6905 ▭ *D, MC, V.*

¢–$ ✕ **La Comida.** Making no claim to authentic Mexican cooking, this restaurant nevertheless receives praise for its "Cody-Mex" cuisine. You may order enchiladas, burritos, tacos, and chiles rellenos, but they won't be as spicy as similar foods would be in the Southwest. Mexican wall hangings contribute to the festive atmosphere. ✉ *1385 Sheridan Ave.* ☎ 307/587–9556 ▭ *AE, D, DC, MC, V.*

★ **$$–$$$$** ▥ **Cody Guest Houses.** You have several house-rental options here, from a Victorian guest house with lace curtains and antique furnishings to a four-bedroom lodge with a fireplace. The 10 different guest houses have one to four bedrooms, and all of them have been lovingly restored and elegantly decorated. These houses are meant to make you feel truly at home, so you'll find refrigerators, full kitchens, outdoor barbecue grills, and children's play areas at most of them. ✉ *1525 Beck*

Ave., 82414 ☎ *307/587–6000 or 800/587–6560* 🖷 *307/587–8048*
⊕ *www.codyguesthouses.com* ⬐ *10 houses* ⚭ *Kitchens, laundry facilities; no TV in some rooms, no a/c in some rooms, no smoking* ▤ *AE, D, MC, V.*

$$$ ⊡ **Rimrock Dude Ranch.** Dating to 1956, this is one of the oldest guest ranches on the North Fork of the Shoshone River. Rimrock offers both summer and winter accommodations and activities, from horseback riding in the surrounding mountain country to snowmobile trips in Yellowstone National Park. Lodging is in one- and two-bedroom cabins. There's a one-week minimum stay. ✉ *2728 North Fork Rte., 82414* ☎ *307/587–3970 or 800/208–7468* 🖷 *307/527–5014* ⊕ *www. rimrockranch.com* ⬐ *9 cabins* ⚭ *Dining room, refrigerators, pool, hot tub, fishing, horseback riding, snowmobiling, airport shuttle; no smoking, no room TVs, no a/c* ▤ *MC, V* †⦶† *FAP.*

Ↄ $$–$$$ ⊡ **UXU Ranch.** One of the cabins at the UXU guest ranch is a historic late-19th-century stage stop moved to the site and decorated with Molesworth-style furnishings made by New West of Cody; other cabins here date to the 1960s or 1920s. The ranch, along the North Fork of the Shoshone River, offers outstanding horseback riding, pack trips into the nearby mountains, and the opportunity to really get away from it all. There's a minimum one-week stay. ✉ *1710 North Fork Hwy., Wapiti 82450* ☎ *307/587–2143 or 800/373–9027* 🖷 *307/587–8307* ⊕ *www. uxuranch.com* ⬐ *11 cabins* ⚭ *Dining room, hot tub, fishing, hiking, horseback riding, bar, children's programs (ages 6 and up), playground, no-smoking rooms; no a/c, no room phones* ▤ *MC, V* †⦶† *FAP.*

$$ ⊡ **Best Western Sunset Motor Inn.** This inn sits on a large grassy property with shade trees and has an enclosed play area for children. Numerous amenities, clean rooms, and a quiet and relaxed atmosphere make this a favorite with families. It's a block from the Buffalo Bill Historical Center. ✉ *1601 8th St., 82414* ☎ *307/587–4265 or 800/624–2727* ⊕ *www.bestwestern.com* ⬐ *116 rooms, 4 suites* ⚭ *Restaurant, cable TV, indoor-outdoor pool, gym, hot tub, playground, laundry facilities, some pets allowed; no smoking* ▤ *AE, D, DC, MC, V.*

$–$$ ⊡ **Buffalo Bill Village.** This downtown development comprises three lodgings, which share many facilities. The Buffalo Bill Village Resort consists of log cabins with modern interiors, and the Holiday Inn Convention Center and the Comfort Inn are typical chain hotels. The downtown shopping district begins one block to the west, and there's also a grocery store a block away. ✉ *1701 Sheridan Ave., 82414* ☎ *307/587–5544 or 800/527–5544* ⊕ *www.blairhotels.com* ⬐ *Buffalo Bill Village Resort 83 cabins; Comfort Inn 75 rooms; Holiday Inn 189 rooms* ⚭ *Restaurant, pool, gym, bar, meeting room, airport shuttle, no-smoking rooms* ▤ *AE, D, DC, MC, V.*

$–$$ ⊡ **Lockhart Inn.** The former home of Cody author Caroline Lockhart, this inn has rooms named after her characters and books. Western antiques decorate the rooms, many of which have claw-foot tubs. It's on the main western strip of Cody, which is convenient to area attractions. ✉ *109 W. Yellowstone Ave., 82414* ☎ *307/587–6074 or 800/377–7255* ⬐ *7 rooms* ⚭ *Dining room, cable TV; no smoking* ▤ *D, MC, V* †⦶† *BP.*

$ ▦ **Irma Hotel.** This hotel named for Buffalo Bill's daughter retains some frontier charm, with brass beds and period furniture in many rooms, a large restaurant, and an elaborate cherrywood bar. If you want true history, be sure to stay in one of the 15 rooms of the original 1902 hotel and not in the annex, which has standard hotel-style contemporary rooms. In summer, locals stage a gunfight on the porch Tuesday–Saturday at 6 PM. ⊠ *1192 Sheridan Ave., 82414* ☎ *307/587–4221 or 800/745–4762* ⊟ *307/587–1775* ⊕ *www.irmahotel.com* ⬐ *40 rooms* ⚏ *Restaurant, bar, no-smoking rooms* ⊟ *AE, D, DC, MC, V.*

$ ▦ **Yellowstone Valley Inn.** Located 16 mi west of Cody and 32 mi east of Yellowstone National Park's east entrance, this sprawling and peaceful property offers basic accommodations in a mountain setting. Rooms are in the motel or duplex cabins, and campsites are available. ⊠ *3324 Northfolk Hwy., 82414* ☎ *307/587–3961 or 877/587–3961* ⊟ *307/587–4656* ⊕ *www.yellowstonevalleyinn.com* ⬐ *15 motel rooms, 20 cabin rooms* ⚏ *Restaurant, picnic area, cable TV, bar, laundry facilities, meeting rooms, some pets allowed; no room phones, no smoking* ⊟ *AE, D, MC, V.*

Camping

There are 32 campgrounds within **Shoshone National Forest** (☎ 307/527–6241 ⊕ www.fs.fed.us/r2/shoshone); some have only limited services, and others have hookups and campground hosts.

⚠ **Cody KOA.** This campground on the southeast side of town serves free pancake breakfasts. There's also a free shuttle to the Cody Nite Rodeo, and you can arrange to take a horseback ride. ⚏ *Grills, flush toilets, full hookups, partial hookups (electric and water), drinking water, guest laundry, showers, picnic tables, general store, swimming (pool)* ⬐ *78 tent sites, 68 full-hookups, 54 partial hookups, 21 cabins, 1 cottage* ⊠ *5561 U.S. 20 (Greybull Hwy.)* ☎ *800/562–8507* ⊟ *307/587–2369* ⊕ *www.codykoa.com* ✉ *$26 tent sites, $31 partial hookups, $42 full hookups, $45–$51 cabins $126 cottage* ⊟ *AE, D, DC, MC, V* ⊙ *May–Oct.*

⚠ **Dead Indian Campground.** You can fish in the stream at this tent campground adjacent to the Chief Joseph Scenic Byway (Highway 296). There are hiking and horseback-riding trails, plus nearby corrals for horses. ⚏ *Pit toilets, drinking water, bear boxes, fire grates, picnic tables, swimming (creek)* ⬐ *12 sites* ⊠ *17 mi north of Cody on Hwy. 120, then 25 mi northwest on Hwy. 296* ☎ *307/527–6241* ⊕ *www.fs.fed.us/r2/shoshone* ✉ *$5* ⊟ *No credit cards* ⊙ *May–Oct.*

⚠ **Deer Creek Campground.** At the head of the South Fork of the Shoshone River, this small, tree-shaded campground for tents provides hiking access to the Absaroka Range and the Washakie Wilderness. ⚏ *Pit toilets, drinking water, fire pits, picnic tables* ⬐ *7 sites* ⊠ *47 mi west of Cody on South Fork Hwy. (Hwy. 291)* ☎ *307/527–6241* ⊕ *www.fs.fed.us/r2/shoshone* ✉ *Free* ⊙ *May–Oct.*

⚠ **Ponderosa Campground.** Within walking distance (three blocks) of the Buffalo Bill Historical Center, this is a large facility with separate areas for tents and RVs. You can even stay in a tepee or pitch your own tent or tepee in a primitive camping area (without any nearby facilities) known as the OK Corral in the canyon above the Shoshone River. ⚭ *Grills, flush toilets, full hookups, dump station, drinking water, guest laundry, showers, picnic tables, public telephone, general store, play area* 🚏 *137 full hookups, 50 tent sites; 8 tepees* ✉ *1815 8th St.* ☎ *307/587–9203* 🖙 *$21 tent sites and tepees, $38 full hookups* ▭ *No credit cards* ☾ *May–Oct.*

Nightlife & the Arts

Nightlife

A trip to Cody isn't complete without a chance to scoot your boots to live music, usually provided by the local band West, at **Cassie's Supper Club and Dance Hall** (✉ 214 Yellowstone Ave. ☎ 307/527–5500). The tunes are a mix of classic country, the band's Western originals, and today's hits.

The Arts

Impromptu jam sessions, nightly concerts, and a symposium of educational and entertaining events related to cowboy music are all part of the **Cowboy Songs and Range Ballads** (☎ 307/587–4771 ⊕ www.bbhc. org). In addition to classic range ballads there's original music by performers from across the West. Events are held over the course of a few days in late March or early April at the Buffalo Bill Historical Center and other venues.

The two-day **Plains Indian Powwow** (✉ 720 Sheridan Ave. ☎ 307/587–4771 ⊕ www.bbhc.org), in late June, brings together hoop dancers, traditional dancers, and jingle dancers from various tribes. The performances take place at the Buffalo Bill Historical Center.

Sculptures and paintings by such artists as James Bama, Chris Navarro, and Frank McCarthy are displayed at **Big Horn Galleries** (✉ 1167 Sheridan Ave. ☎ 307/527–7587). **Simpson Gallagher Gallery** (✉ 1161 Sheridan Ave. ☎ 307/587–4022) showcases and sells contemporary representational art by Harry Jackson, Margery Torrey, and Geoff Parker.

Shopping

The **Cody Rodeo Company** (✉ 1273 Sheridan Ave. ☎ 307/587–5913) sells cowboy hats, plus housewares with a cowboy or rodeo motif. Head to ★ the **Custom Cowboy Shop** (✉ 1286 Sheridan Ave. ☎ 307/527–7300) to stock up on top-quality cowboy gear and clothing, ranging from hats and vests for men to women's shirts and jackets; there's even gear for your horse here. Also available are CDs by top Western recording artists such as Ian Tyson, Don Edwards, and Michael Martin Murphey.

Flight West (✉ 1155 Sheridan Ave. ☎ 307/527–7800) sells designer Western women's wear, leather goods for men and women, books, gifts, and jewelry. Women shop at the **Plush Pony** (✉ 1350 Sheridan Ave. ☎ 307/587–4677) for "uptown Western clothes" ranging from leather belts to stylish skirts, jackets, and dresses. The **Wyoming Buffalo Company** (✉ 1270 Sheridan Ave. ☎ 307/587–8708 or 800/453–0636) sells buffalo-meat products, such as sausage and jerky, in addition to specialty foods such as huckleberry honey. Chock-full of souvenirs and trinkets, the **Yellowstone Gift Shop** (⌧ 1237 Sheridan Ave. ☎ 307/587–4611 or 800/788–9429) also has a huge selection of turquoise jewelry.

POWDER RIVER BASIN & THE BLACK HILLS

The rolling grassland of the Powder River Basin, in the far northeastern corner of Wyoming, is the ancestral homeland of the Lakota Sioux. On its western edge, the Big Horn Mountains are both a popular winter recreational area and a beautiful backdrop for the communities of Sheridan, Big Horn, and Buffalo. As you drive east, the mountains give way to coal mines (particularly around Gillette), oil fields, and family ranches, many of which were established in the 19th century by Basque sheepherders. Now one of the least-populated parts of America, the basin encompasses the vast Thunder Basin National Grasslands.

The Black Hills border the Powder River Basin to the east, where a couple of hundred thousand acres of Black Hills National Forest spill out of South Dakota into Wyoming. Thickly wooded with pine, spruce, and fir trees, the rocky slopes stand in stark contrast to the prairie below. Some of the most famous characters of the American West roamed across this soil, including Wild Bill Hickok, Calamity Jane, and the Sundance Kid, who took his name from a local town.

Sheridan

❹ *147 mi north of Casper via I–25 and I–90.*

Proximity to the Big Horn Mountains and Bighorn National Forest makes Sheridan a good base for hiking, mountain biking, skiing, snowmobiling, and fly-fishing, while the small city's European-flavored cowboy heritage makes it an interesting stop for history buffs. Soon after trappers built a simple cabin along Little Goose Creek in 1873, the spot became a regional railroad center. Cattle barons, many of them English and Scottish noblemen, established ranches that remain the mainstay of the economy. Sheridan still has ties to Britain's aristocracy; in fact, Queen Elizabeth II herself has paid the town a visit. Recently, coal mines and oil wells to the east have brought much-needed jobs and tax income to this community of 15,804 residents.

Built in 1923 as a vaudeville theater called the Lotus, the **Wyo Theater** was closed and nearly demolished in the early 1980s. A strong show of support from the community saved the building, and now the refurbished art deco structure hosts everything from orchestras and ballets to lectures and Broadway revivals, especially in the summer. ⌧ *42 N. Main St.* ☎ *307/672–9084* ⊕ *www.wyotheater.com.*

Local cowboy legend Don King owns **King's Saddlery and Ropes.** A saddle maker since the 1940s, King now lets his sons run the business. Besides selling high-quality equipment to area ranchers and professional rodeo performers, King's has crafted gear for many celebrities, including Queen Elizabeth II. Behind the store is a museum full of King's own collection, including saddles from the pre–Civil

DROPPING A LINE

CASTING into a clear stream or placid blue lake is a popular pastime all over Wyoming, with good reason: the waters of the entire state teem with trout, pike, whitefish, catfish, and bass of all kinds. Most fishing enthusiasts stick to the land near Yellowstone, leaving the blue-ribbon streams of northern Wyoming relatively underutilized. The Bighorn River, Powder River, Crazy Woman Creek, Keyhole Reservoir, and Buffalo Bill Reservoir are all excellent angling venues.

Fly-fishing is especially big here, and there's no shortage of outfitters to equip you, both in the towns and in the wilderness. Anyone with a pole—be it an experienced fly-fisher or novice worm dangler—is respected out here. All the same, if you're a beginner, you'd do well to hire a guide. Tackle-shop staff can direct you to some good fishing spots, but you're more likely to find the choicest locations if you have an experienced local at your side.

War era and medieval Japan. ⊠ *184 N. Main St.* ☎ *307/672–2702* ◻ *Free* ☉ *Mon.–Sat. 8–5.*

A Flemish Revival mansion built in 1913 for John B. Kendrick, cattleman and one of Wyoming's first governors and senators, is now the **Trail End State Historic Site.** The furnishings and exhibits in the home are designed to depict early-20th-century ranching on the Plains. Highlights include elegant hand-carved woodwork and a third-floor ballroom. ⊠ *400 Clarendon Ave.* ☎ *307/674–4589* ⊕ *www.trailend.org* ◻ *$2* ☉ *Mar.–May and Sept.–mid-Dec., daily 1–4; June–Aug., daily 9–6.*

Fodor'sChoice
★ Evidence of the area's old-world ties can be found at the **Sheridan Inn,** just a few miles from downtown near the old railroad depot. Modeled after a hunting lodge in Scotland, the 1893 building sports 69 gables in a show of architectural splendor not often seen around these parts. On the National Register of Historic Places, the inn once lured the likes of Herbert Hoover, Will Rogers, and Ernest Hemingway, and Buffalo Bill auditioned performers here for his Wild West Show. The original Buffalo Bill Bar, an oak-and-mahogany monstrosity on the main floor, is said to have been a gift sent from England by Queen Victoria. Lunch and dinner are served all year, although patrons are no longer permitted to bring their horses inside. ⊠ *856 Broadway* ☎ *307/674–5440* ⊕ *www.sheridaninn.com* ◻ *Free, self-guided tour $2, guided tour $5* ☉ *Hrs vary by season; call for current schedule.*

Sports & the Outdoors

Like every other community on the edge of the Bighorn National Forest, Sheridan abounds with opportunities for outdoor recreation. A love of sports seems to be a common thread among people here, whether they're visitors or locals, winter enthusiasts or sun seekers, thrill hunters or quiet naturalists. Because of Sheridan's proximity to U.S. 14, a mountain highway near hundreds of miles of snowmobile trails and alpine streams, the town is especially popular among sledders in the winter and fly-fishers in the summer and autumn.

FLY-FISHING More of a custom adventure company than an outfitter, **Angling Destinations** (⊠ 151 Powder Horn Rd. ☎ 800/211–8530) arranges multiday fishing trips to some of the most remote locations of Wyoming, Montana, and Idaho, as well as international destinations. For the less experienced angler, **Big Horn Mountain Sports** (⊠ 334 N. Main St. ☎ 307/672–6866) provides fly-fishing lessons and guided trips and rents and sells complete fly-fishing gear (including flies, rods, reels, waders, and hats). The full-service **Fly Shop of the Big Horns** (⊠ 227 N. Main St. ☎ 800/253–5866) offers sales, rentals, guided trips, and a fly-fishing school, a 2½-day class covering everything from casting to landing and releasing. **World Flyfishing Journeys** (⊠ 1349 Fort Rd. ☎ 307/673–1732) leads guided fishing trips in the Big Horns and Powder River country.

SKIING & **Bear Lodge** (⊠ Off U.S. 14A, Burgess Junction ☎ 307/752–2444), an
SNOWMOBILING hour northwest of Sheridan, rents Polaris snowmobiles by the half day or full day. Guided tours are available; reserve ahead. There's also a small service shop and parts store here.

Where to Stay & Eat

$–$$$$ ✕ **Oliver's Bar and Grill.** Soft yellows and greens decorate this modern restaurant with an open kitchen and paintings from local artists on the walls. The menu lists fairly typical salads, burgers, and chicken dishes year-round, but it also frequently includes seasonal items such as Copper River salmon from Alaska, which is available here for only three weeks in early summer. You can watch your meal being prepared if you sit at the kitchen bar. ⊠ 55 N. Main St. ☎ 307/672–2838 ▭ MC, V.

¢–$$ ✕ **Silver Spur.** This hole-in-the-wall is sometimes mistaken for an abandoned building, but it's actually a popular breakfast spot serving bacon, hash browns, omelets, and other fried favorites. For lunch there are burgers and Philly cheesesteak sandwiches. Contractors often meet here to conduct business over breakfast and lunch. ⊠ 832 N. Main St. ☎ 307/673–7330 ▭ No credit cards ☉ No dinner.

$ ✕▨ **Sheridan Holiday Inn.** The soaring atrium of this five-story lodging, which is five minutes from downtown by car, has a waterfall and is filled with overstuffed chairs and couches. The rooms are typical of chain hotels, but most have some Western-style touches, and some look out on the Big Horn Mountains. Two restaurants ($$), the Greenery and Scooter's Bar and Grill, serve burgers, steak, chicken, and pasta. Sunday brunch is an elegant and extensive buffet. ⊠ 1809 Sugarland Dr., 82801 ☎ 307/672–8931 or 877/672–4011 ▤ 307/672–6388 ⊕ www.holidayinnrockies.com ⇌ 212 rooms, 7 suites ⌂ 2 restaurants, cable TV with movies and video games, putting green, indoor pool, gym, hair salon, hot tub, sauna, racquetball, bar, video game room, business services, convention center, meeting rooms, airport shuttle, some pets allowed (fee), no-smoking rooms ▭ AE, D, DC, MC, V.

$$$–$$$$ ▨ **The Ranch at Ucross.** If you're looking to get in touch with yourself—or your traveling companion—the banks of Piney Creek may well be the place. In the foothills of the Big Horns, this tranquil Old West–style ranch is as relaxed as it gets. The four bedrooms in the restored 1912

house, as well as modern rooms and cabins around the property, are given a warm Western feel by gnarled wood lamps, quilt-covered beds, and comfy throws for cool nights. Most accommodations open onto spacious decks where you can read, watch the sun set, or just gaze at the Canadian geese, grazing horses, and towering cottonwoods. Do some mountain-stream fishing or take a pack trip to mountain lakes. Managers Scott and Becky Christensen, the consummate hosts, handle family reunions and retreats with unusual aplomb. ⊠ *2673 U.S. Hwy. 14, Clearmont 82835* ☎ *307/737–2281* 🖷 *307/737–2211* ⊕ *www. blairhotels.com* 🖙 *25 rooms, 6 cabins* ⚷ *Dining room, pool, fishing, hiking, horseback riding, meeting rooms, tennis courts, basketball, lounge, in-room data ports, some pets allowed; no room TVs, no smoking* ⊟ *AE, D, MC, V* ⭤ *FAP.*

$$$ 🏨 **Eaton's Guest Ranch.** This is the place credited with creating the dude ranch, back in the late 19th century, and it's still going strong as a working cattle ranch. Its location, west of Sheridan on the edge of the Bighorn National Forest, makes it ideal for horseback riding, fishing, cookouts, and pack trips. The ranch can accommodate 125 guests, and reservations for the summer should be made by March. The facilities are a collection of one-, two-, and three-bedroom cabins and the main lodge. There's a one-week minimum stay mid-June through August and a three-day minimum stay the rest of the season. ⊠ *270 Eaton's Ranch Rd., Wolf 82844* ☎ *307/655–9285 or 800/210–1049* 🖷 *307/655–9269* ⊕ *www.eatonsranch.com* 🖙 *51 cabins* ⚷ *Dining room, pool, fishing, hiking, horseback riding, meeting rooms; no a/c, no room TVs, no smoking* ⊟ *D, MC, V* ⊗ *Closed Oct.–May* ⭤ *FAP.*

$ 🏨 **Best Western Sheridan Center Motor Inn.** The rooms at this lodging popular with tour groups are typical of chain motels, but some have lodgepole-pine furniture and blue and green tones. The motel consists of four buildings connected by a sky bridge over Main Street. ⊠ *612 N. Main St., 82801* ☎ *307/674–7421* 🖷 *307/672–3018* ⊕ *www. bestwestern.com* 🖙 *138 rooms* ⚷ *2 restaurants, cable TV, indoor pool, sauna, spa, bar, video game room, meeting rooms, no-smoking rooms* ⊟ *AE, D, DC, MC, V.*

$ 🏨 **Mill Inn.** A former flour mill near a bridge has been converted into this motel on the east side of town. The building has six stories, but the top four floors are business offices. Furniture from a dude ranch fills much of the motel, giving it a definite Western style. ⊠ *2161 Coffeen Ave., 82801* ☎ *307/672–6401 or 888/357–6455* 🖷 *307/672–6401* ⊕ *www.sheridanmillinn.com* 🖙 *45 rooms* ⚷ *Gym, cable TV, no-smoking rooms* ⊟ *AE, D, MC, V* ⭤ *CP.*

CAMPING ⛺ **Big Horn Mountain KOA Campground.** On the banks of Big Goose Creek minutes away from downtown Sheridan is this KOA, a well-developed campground with a basketball court, horseshoe pits, and a miniature-golf course. ⚷ *Flush toilets, full hookups, drinking water, showers, picnic tables, food service, electricity, public telephone, play area, swimming (pool)* 🖙 *40 full hookups, 12 tent sites; 6 cabins* ⊠ *63 Decker Rd.* ☎ *307/ 674–8766* ⊕ *www.koakampgrounds.com* 🕮 *$22 tent sites, $35 full hookups, $32–$79 cabins* ⚷ *Reservations essential* ⊟ *AE, D, MC, V.*

⚠️ **Foothills Motel and Campground.** In the tiny town of Dayton, 20 mi west of Sheridan, this campground nestles in a cottonwood grove on the Tongue River, at the base of the Big Horns. In addition to tent and RV sites, there are cabins here. They are clean and well equipped with cable TV and showers, except for one: an aged and rustic log cabin heated by a woodstove. ⚠️ *Flush toilets, full hookups, partial hookups (electric and water), drinking water, guest laundry, showers, picnic tables, electricity, public telephone, play area, swimming (river)* 🛶 *12 full hookups, 10 partial hookups, 30 tent sites; 10 cabins* ✉️ *101 N. Main St., Dayton* ☎️ *307/655–2547* 🌐 *www.foothillscampground.com* 💲*$15 tent sites, $19 partial hookups, $21 full hookups, $30–$45 cabins* 🚫 *No credit cards.*

The Arts
A stronghold of frontier culture, the **Bozeman Trail Gallery** (✉️ 190 N. Main St. ☎️ 307/672–3928) has a varied collection of artifacts and art from the American West, ranging from vintage Colt revolvers and leather saddles to Cheyenne Sioux moccasins and Navajo rugs. The gallery also maintains a collection of significant Western paintings from artists such as Carl Rungius and Ernest Martin Hennings.

Shopping
The suburban malls that have drained so many downtowns are absent in Sheridan; instead, Main Street is lined with mostly homegrown—and sometimes quirky—shops.

In a break from typical gift stores stocked with rubber tomahawks, the **Best Out West Mall** (✉️ 109 N. Main St. ☎️ 307/674–5003) is a two-story bazaar of Western paraphernalia, with booths hawking everything from spurs to rare books. Some items are new, but most are antiques. For an excellent selection of both local and general-interest books, try the **Book Shop** (✉️ 117 N. Main St. ☎️ 307/672–6505). On occasion, local authors will spend several hours here signing their books. The **Crazy Woman Trading Company** (✉️ 120 N. Main St. ☎️ 307/672–3939) sells unique gifts and antiques, including deluxe coffees and T-shirts sporting a black bear doing yoga. Murphy McDougal, the store's CEO (and the owners' golden retriever), is usually sleeping near the front door.

Big Horn

🔵 *10 mi south of Sheridan via Hwy. 335.*

Now a gateway to Bighorn National Forest, this tree-lined town with mountain views was originally a rest stop for emigrants heading west. An outpost on the Bozeman Trail, which crossed Bozeman Pass, Big Horn City in the mid-19th century was a lawless frontier town of saloons and roadhouses. After pioneers brought their families to the area in the late 1870s, the rowdy community quieted down. It never officially incorporated, so although it has a post office, fire department, and school, there is no bona fide city government.

A hand-hewn-log blacksmith shop, built in 1879 to serve pioneers on their way to the goldfields of Montana, houses the **Bozeman Trail Mu-**

seum, the town's historical repository and interpretive center. The jewel of its collection is the Cloud Peak Boulder, a stone with names and dates apparently carved by military scouts just two days before the Battle of the Little Bighorn, which was fought less than 100 mi to the north in 1876. The staff is very friendly to children, and there are some old pipe organs that kids are encouraged to play. ⊠ *335 Johnson St.* ☎ *307/672–5705 or 307/674–1600* ☜ *Free* ◷ *Memorial Day–Labor Day, weekends 11–6.*

If you're not staying at a ranch and you want to get a look at one of the West's finest, visit the **Bradford Brinton Memorial,** south of Big Horn on the old Quarter Circle A Ranch. The Brinton family didn't exactly rough it in this 20-room clapboard home, complete with libraries, fine furniture, and silver and china services. A reception gallery displays changing exhibits from the Brinton art collection, which includes such Western artists as Charles M. Russell and Frederic Remington. ⊠ *239 Brinton Rd.* ☎ *307/672–3173* ⊕ *www.bradfordbrintonmemorial.com/* ☜ *$4* ◷ *Mid-May–Labor Day, daily 9:30–5.*

Big Horn is an access point to the 1.1-million-acre **Bighorn National Forest,** which has lush grasslands, alpine meadows, rugged mountaintops, canyons, and deserts. There are numerous hiking trails and camping spots for use in the summer, and it's a popular snowmobiling area in the winter. ⊠ *Ranger station, 1969 S. Sheridan Ave.* ☎ *307/672–0751* ⊕ *www.fs.fed.us/r2/bighorn.*

Sports & the Outdoors

Perhaps the most unexpected sport to be found in the outdoor playground of the Bighorn National Forest is polo. The game has been played at the **Big Horn Equestrian Center** (⊠ Near state bird farm, on Hwy. 28, west of Big Horn ☎ 800/453–3650) ever since upper-class English and Scottish families settled the area in the 1890s. You can watch people at play for free on Sundays in the summer. The 65 acres here are also used for other events, including youth soccer and bronc riding.

Where to Stay & Eat

$–$$$ ✕ **Bozeman Trail Inn.** A wood-slat building with a false front and tin roof, this is the oldest operating bar in Wyoming, established in 1882. The inn's only sign is painted on a mock covered wagon that's perched above the door. The kitchen serves standard burgers and sandwiches for lunch, steak and seafood for dinner, and prime rib on the weekends. ⊠ *1506 Warren St.* ☎ *307/672–9288* ▭ *MC, V* ◷ *Closed Sun. and Mon.*

$–$$ 🏠 **Spahn's Big Horn Mountain Bed and Breakfast.** Ron and Bobbie Spahn have guest rooms and cabins at their soaring log home in the Big Horn Mountains. The rooms have tongue-and-groove woodwork and peeled-log beams; ruffled curtains and peeled-log beds complete the look. It's more than a traditional B&B: you can participate in horseback riding, cookouts, and guided tours that include a wildlife-viewing trip. Family-style dinners, including fresh grilled steaks, are served by arrangement. ⊠ *Hwy. 335, 7 mi south of Big Horn, Box 579, 82833* ☎ *307/674–8150* 🖷 *307/674–8150* ⊕ *www.bighorn-wyoming.com* ➪ *3* *rooms, 2 cabins* ♿ *Some kitchens, library, piano; no a/c, no room phones, no room TVs, no smoking* ⊟ *No credit cards* ⍑⚪⍑ *BP.*

¢–$ 🏨 **Wagon Box Resort.** On the edge of the tiny town of Story, 14 mi south of Big Horn, the Wagon Box lies at the base of the Big Horn Mountains. The rooms and cabins are furnished modestly in Western style; the cabins have fireplaces and porches with swings. This is a great spot for outdoor recreation—from hiking and fishing to horseback riding and barbecuing—and your hosts are happy to help you plan whatever activity suits your fancy. There are even horse corrals at the campground next door, so planning a quick ride or a major expedition into neighboring Bighorn National Forest is a breeze. ⊠ *109 N. Piney Rd., Story 82842* ☎ *307/683-2444* 🖷 *307/683-2443* ⊕ *www.wagonbox.com* ⍩ *15 rooms, 6 cabins* ♿ *Restaurant, some kitchens, some kitchenettes, hot tub, sauna, fishing, hiking, horseback riding, bar, some pets allowed, no-smoking room; no a/c, no room phones, no room TVs* ⊟ *AE, D, MC, V.*

Buffalo

❻ *25 mi south of Big Horn via I–90, U.S. 87, and Hwy. 335.*

Buffalo is a trove of history and a hospitable little town in the foothills below Big Horn Pass. Here cattle barons who wanted free grazing and homesteaders who wanted to build fences fought it out in the Johnson County War of 1892. Nearby are the sites of several skirmishes between the U.S. military and Native Americans along the Bozeman Trail.

The **Jim Gatchell Memorial Museum** is the kind of small-town museum that's worth stopping for if you're interested in the history of the region, including the Johnson County War. It contains Native American, military, outlaw, and ranching artifacts collected by a local druggist who was a close friend of area Native Americans. ⊠ *100 Fort St.* ☎ *307/684-9331* ⊕ *www.jimgatchell.com* ⍑ *$4* ⊙ *Mid-Apr.–Dec., Mon.–Sat. 9–8, Sun. noon–5.*

★ Signs bearing a buffalo symbol mark the **Clear Creek Trail** (☎ 307/684–5544 or 800/227–5122), which consists of about 11 mi of trails following Clear Creek through Buffalo and past historic areas. The trail has both paved and unpaved sections that you can traverse on foot or by bicycle. Along it you see the Occidental Hotel (made famous by Owen Wister's novel *The Virginian*), a brewery and mill site, and the site of Fort McKinney, now the Veterans' Home of Wyoming. You can also use the trail for wildlife viewing, photography, and access to fishing.

★ The frontier army occupied the military installation at **Fort Phil Kearny State Historic Site** for only a couple of years in the mid-1860s. Considered a hardship post by officers and enlisted men alike, the fort protected travelers headed to Montana's goldfields and later distracted Native Americans from the construction of the transcontinental railroad to the south. Eventually the constant attacks by the Plains Indians paid off, and the fort was abandoned in 1868 as part of the Fort Laramie Treaty. No original buildings remain at the site—they were likely burned by the Cheyenne as soon as the soldiers left—but fort buildings are marked and the visitor center has good details. The stockade around the fort was re-created after archaeological digs in 1999. ⊠ *12 mi north of Buffalo on I–90* ☎ *307/684–7629 or 307/777–7014* ⊕ *www.philkearny.vcn.com* 🎫 *$2* ⊗ *Mid-May–Sept., daily 8–6.*

The **Fetterman Massacre Monument** (⊠ 12 mi north of Buffalo, off I–90; obtain directions at Fort Phil Kearny) is a rock monolith dedicated to the memory of Lieutenant William J. Fetterman and his 80 men, who died in a December 21, 1866, battle against Lakota warriors led by Red Cloud.

Sports & the Outdoors

The forested canyons and pristine alpine meadows of the Big Horn Mountains teem with animal and plant life, making this an excellent area for hiking and pack trips by horseback. The quality and concentration of locals willing to outfit adventurers are high in Buffalo, making it a suitable base camp from which to launch an expedition.

The folks at **South Fork Mountain Outfitters** (⊠ 16 mi west of Buffalo on U.S. 16 ☎ 307/267–2609 or 307/684–1225) can customize about any sort of adventure you'd like to undertake in the Big Horns, whether it's hiking, fishing, horseback riding, snowmobiling, or cross-country skiing. The company can arrange for all of your food and supplies and provide a guide, or render drop-camp services for more experienced thrill seekers.

FLY-FISHING The **Sports Lure** (⊠ 66 S. Main St. ☎ 800/684–7682) stocks rods, reels, flies, books, and outdoor wear. You can also arrange for lessons and guided fishing trips.

HORSEBACK Located on a 24,000-acre working ranch, the **Powder River Experience** RIDING & PACK (⊠ U.S. 14, Clearmont ☎ 307/758–4381 or 888/736–2402) gives you TRIPS the chance to ride on the open range or to pack into the backcountry for an overnight stay at a log cabin. You're also encouraged to watch or personally experience as many ranch activities as you wish, whether it's branding, cattle driving, or calving.

Trails West Outfitters (⊠ 259 Sunset Ave. ☎ 307/684–5233 or 888/283–9793 ⊕ www.trailswestoutfitters.com) arranges multiday pack trips in the Bighorn and Shoshone national forests. The company also operates shorter wilderness excursions and drop camps for more independent adventurers.

Where to Stay & Eat

$$–$$$$ ✕ **The Virginian Restaurant.** Named for the 1902 Owen Wister novel that made Buffalo famous, this is the dining room of the beautifully restored Occidental Hotel. Dishes like buffalo rib eye, chateaubriand, shrimp scampi, swordfish, chicken marsala, and filet mignon with béarnaise sauce are served amid antique mirrors, Western art, and Victorian lamps; many items are original to the building. Period light fixtures hang from the original brass-colored tin ceiling, and wainscoting accents the maroon-colored walls. ⊠ *10 N. Main St.* ☎ *307/684–0451* ▤ *AE, D, MC, V.*

$$–$$$$ ✕ **Winchester Steak House.** You can tie up your car in front of the hitch racks before this Western-style eatery in a false-front building. The Winchester has steak and more steak, plus a large rock fireplace and small bar. Locals rave about the place. ⊠ *117 Hwy. 16 E* ☎ *307/684–8636* ▭ *MC, V.*

★ **$–$$** ✕ **Colonel Bozeman's Restaurant and Tavern.** This eatery, which is literally on the Bozeman Trail, serves decent food amid Western memorabilia. Local favorites include buffalo steak and prime rib. You can dine outdoors on the deck. ⊠ *655 E. Hart St.* ☎ *307/684–5555* ▭ *AE, D, MC, V.*

¢–$$ ✕ **Deerfield Boutique and Espresso Bar.** For a change from steak and potatoes, try this café in a renovated historic theater with high ceilings and old wallpaper. The place serves a wide selection of tortilla wraps and specialty sandwiches such as lemon-ginger chicken pita, and turkey and Swiss on focaccia. In summer there are chilled soups, such as tomato wine, cream of cantaloupe, and spinach cucumber. The Polynesian and mandarin orange salads are equally refreshing. Deerfield is next to Clear Creek, on a quiet side street in downtown Buffalo. ⊠ *7 N. Main St.* ☎ *307/684–7776* ▭ *MC, V.*

¢–$ ✕ **Tom's Main Street Diner.** This tiny, clean place dishes up huge burgers and sandwiches in short order. A few mounted buck trophies line the walls above the tables, and you may notice a book or two lying on the counter about Gerry Spence, one of America's more famous lawyers and the NBC legal consultant during the O. J. Simpson trial. If Tom is cooking, see if you can spot the family resemblance—Tom and Gerry are brothers. ⊠ *41 N. Main St.* ☎ *307/684–7444* ▭ *AE, D, MC, V.*

★ ☺ **$$$$** ▦ **Paradise Guest Ranch.** Not only is this dude ranch—with a stunning location at the base of some of the tallest mountains in the range—one of the oldest (circa 1905), but it's also very progressive, as evidenced by its adults-only month (September) and a women-only week. The rest of the summer there are extensive children's programs, with everything from overnight pack trips to rodeo training. Adult programs involve sing-alongs, fancy barbecues, and square dances. The wranglers are very careful about matching riders to appropriate horses; multiday trips for veterans lead into Bighorn National Forest and the Cloud Peak Wilderness Area. Cabins are simple; some have fireplaces. There's a one-week minimum stay. ⊠ *Hunter Creek Rd., off U.S. 16, Box 790, 82834* ☎ *307/684–7876* 🖷 *307/684–9054* ⊕ *www.paradiseranch.com* ⬎ *18 cabins* ⚃ *Dining room, kitchenettes, pool, pond, hot tub, massage, fishing, basketball, hiking, horseback riding, horseshoes, bar, library, piano, recreation room, shops, children's programs (ages 6–18), playground, laundry facilities, meeting rooms, airport shuttle, travel services; no a/c, no room phones, no room TVs* ▭ *No credit cards* ☽ *Closed Oct.–Apr.* ⎇⊙⎇ *FAP.*

$$–$$$ ▦ **Occidental Hotel.** Founded in 1879 to serve emigrants on the Bozeman Trail, the Occidental was immortalized in the 1902 Owen Wister novel, *The Virginian*, about the Johnson County War. From 1918 to 1976 it was owned by a single family, who kept all of the hotel's original furnishings and architectural accents intact. A lavish 2003 restoration spruced up the Victorian-style rooms and the tin-ceilinged lobby and restaurant. Most spectacular of the rooms are the spacious Clear Creek Suite, with its six-post cherrywood bed, adjoining sitting room, and spacious bathroom, and the elegant Teddy Roosevelt Suite, furnished with a high-backed walnut bed, an antique hardwood desk, and a claw-foot tub. In the saloon downstairs, the 25-foot bar, stained-glass accents, and tin ceiling are better than new—except for 23 bullet holes. ⊠ *10 North Main St., 82834* ☎ *307/684–0451* ⊕ *www.occidentalwyoming.com* ⤳ *7 rooms* ⫶ *Cable TV, some pets allowed, Internet room; no smoking* ⊟ *AE, D, MC, V* ¶⊙∣ *CP.*

$ ⌂ **Comfort Inn.** Several blocks from downtown, this motel is close to Clear Creek Trail, the city's bike and walking path. Rooms have generic motel furnishings, including desks and coffeemakers. ⊠ *65 U.S. 16 E, 82834* ☎ *307/684–9564 or 800/228–5150* ⊕ *www.comfortinn.com* ⤳ *41 rooms* ⫶ *Cable TV with movies, hot tub, some pets allowed (fee), no-smoking rooms* ⊟ *AE, D, DC, MC, V* ¶⊙∣ *CP.*

¢ ⌂ **Blue Gables Motel.** Old West collectibles and quilts add warmth to this highway-side motel's homey log cabins clustered in a U-shape. A few tent sites and a two-bedroom house are also available nearby. ⊠ *662 N. Main St., 82834* ☎ *307/684–2574 or 800/684–2574* ⊕ *www. bluegables.com* ⤳ *17 rooms* ⫶ *Microwaves, pool; no smoking* ⊟ *D, MC, V.*

CAMPING ⚠ **Deer Park Campground.** Although one section of this campground is quiet and relaxed, reserved for campers over 55, the main campsites are busy. In addition to a heated pool and a hot tub, Deer Park offers guided fishing excursions during the day (for a fee) and free ice-cream socials at night. Rates vary dramatically, depending on the number of site occupants. ⫶ *Flush toilets, full hookups, partial hookups (electric and water), drinking water, showers, picnic tables, electricity, public telephone, swimming (pool)* ⤳ *33 full hookups, 33 partial hookups, 34 tent sites* ⊠ *146 U.S. 16* ☎ *307/684–5722 or 800/222–9960* ⊕ *www. deerparkrv.com* ⊴ *$17–$29 tent sites, $23–$35 partial hookups, $27–$41 full hookups* ⚠ *Reservations essential* ⊟ *MC, V* ⊙ *May–Sept.*

Nightlife

Regulation pool tables and live country music and dancing every Friday and Saturday night (no cover charge) make the **White Buffalo Saloon** (⊠ 106 U.S. 16 ☎ 307/684–0101) a local favorite. The gift shop sells T-shirts, shot glasses, and other kitsch emblazoned with the White Buffalo logo.

Shopping

Cast-iron chandeliers with a Western flair are the signature products of
★ **Frontier Iron Works** (⊠ 659 Trabing Rd. ☎ 307/684–5154 or 800/687–6952). They also craft distinctive furniture ranging from bar stools and patio sets to wall sconces and fireplace screens.

Gillette

❼ *70 mi east of Buffalo on I–90.*

With 19,646 residents, Gillete is the metropolis of the Powder River Basin. Thanks to the region's huge coal mines, it's one of Wyoming's wealthiest cities, and as a result it has an excellent community infrastructure that includes the Cam-Plex, a multiuse events center that hosts everything from crafts bazaars and indoor rodeos to concerts and fine-arts exhibits. Gillette is also a gateway town for Devils Tower National Monument, the volcanic plug that is one of the nation's most distinctive geological features and a hot spot for rock climbers.

Gillette has worked hard to make itself presentable, but you don't have to look very hard to find a shovel bigger than a house at one of its giant strip mines. Once a major livestock center, from which ranchers shipped cattle and sheep to Eastern markets, the city now mines millions of tons of coal each year and ships it out to coal-fired power plants. In fact, if Gillette (and surrounding Campbell County) were its own nation, it would be the world's sixth-greatest producer of coal. Currently the county turns out nearly a third of all American-mined coal. Gillette, however, is a big fish in a small pond, one of only two incorporated towns in the county (the other is Wright, population 1,347).

Anything from a rodeo or crafts show to a concert or melodrama could be going on at the **Cam-Plex,** Gillette's multiuse facility. There's something scheduled almost every day; call or check the Web site for details. ⊠ *1635 Reata Dr.* ☎ *307/682–0552, 307/682–8802 for tickets* ⊕ *www. cam-plex.com* ⊠ *$8–$13* ☽ *Call for schedule.*

You can fish, boat, swim, and camp at **Keyhole State Park.** Bird-watching is a favorite activity here, as up to 225 species can be seen on the grounds. ⊠ *353 McKean Rd.* ☎ *307/756–3596, 307/756–9529 marina information* ⊕ *wyoparks.state.wy.us/keslide.htm* ⊠ *$2 resident vehicle, $4 nonresident vehicle; camping $6 resident vehicle, $12 nonresident vehicle.*

Local artifacts, including bits, brands, and rifles, make up the collection at the Campbell County–run **Rockpile Museum.** The museum's name comes from its location next to a natural rock-pile formation that served as a landmark for pioneers. ⊠ *900 W. 2nd St.* ☎ *307/682–5723* ⊕ *wyshs.org/mus-rockpile.htm* ⊠ *Free* ☽ *June–Aug., Mon.–Sat. 9–8, Sun. 12–6; Sept.–May, Mon.–Sat. 9–5.*

At the **Eagle Butte Coal Mine,** 17 mi south of Gillette, shovels and haul trucks dwarf anything you're likely to see in a science-fiction movie. There's a surprising amount of wildlife, from falcons to deer to bobcats, dwelling in and around the huge pits. You can register for the summer tours of the mine at the Gillette Visitors Center. ⊠ *Gillette Visitors Center, Flying J Travel Plaza, 1810 S. Douglas Hwy.* ☎ *307/686–0040 or 800/544–6136* ⊠ *Free* ☽ *Tours June–Aug., daily 9 AM–11 AM.*

off the beaten path

THUNDER BASIN NATIONAL GRASSLANDS – An 890-square-mi wilderness preserve that stretches from the edge of the Black Hills almost to the center of Wyoming, Thunder Basin truly is the outback of America. Except for a handful of tiny towns, deserted highways, and coal mines, it is entirely undeveloped. Farmers from the east settled this area at the end of the 19th century, hoping to raise crops in the semiarid soil. Experienced only with the more humid conditions east of the Rockies, the farmers failed, and the region deteriorated into a dust bowl. Most of the land has reverted to its natural state, creating millions of acres of grasslands filled with wildlife. Among the many species are one of the largest herds of pronghorn in the world (numbering approximately 26,000), prairie dogs, and burrowing owls that live in abandoned prairie dog holes. U.S. 116 and U.S. 450 provide the best access; a few interior dirt roads are navigable only in dry weather. The grasslands, though, are most impressive away from the highways. Take a hike to get a real sense of the vast emptiness of this land. ⊠ *U.S. 450* ☎ *307/745–2300* ⊕ *www.fs.fed.us/r2/mbr/* ☞ *Free* ⊙ *Daily, 24 hrs.*

Sports & the Outdoors

Although the town isn't on the slope of a mountain range or on the edge of a forest, there are plenty of sporting opportunities in Gillette—thanks largely to its own residents. The community as a whole is especially fitness conscious, and as a result, the town has many recreational facilities—including a multisport recreation center and two health clubs—that cities of a similar size lack. There are also more than 37 mi of developed walking trails within the city limits, including paths on the north end of town, off West Warlow Drive, in McManamen Park, a prime bird-watching spot.

An indoor track, gymnasium, five racquetball/handball courts, squash court, free-weight room, golf driving range, junior Olympic pool with a waterslide, locker rooms, and steam rooms are all part of the **Campbell County Recreation Center and Pool** (⊠ 1000 Douglas Hwy. ☎ 307/682–7406 ⊕ www.ccprd.com). It costs $3 to use the recreation center and pool. Also here are the Campbell County Ice Arena, the Bell Nob golf course, and the Cam-Plex picnic area.

ICE-SKATING   The **Campbell County Ice Arena** (⊠ 121 S. 4J Rd. ☎ 307/687–1555), attached to the Campbell County Recreation Center and Pool, is open year-round for ice-skating. The arena accommodates public skating sessions, skating lessons, local hockey teams, and even figure skating.

Where to Stay & Eat

$$–$$$$ ✕ **The Chophouse.** In the middle of a ranching town in the middle of ranching country, it's no surprise that more than half of this restaurant's menu is devoted to beef. Chef Ray Marini, who helped open the first American restaurant in the Soviet Union, uses only certified Angus, and only cuts that have been aged to his standards. The remainder of the menu is split between pasta and dishes made with fresh fish flown in at Marini's request. Of course, the beef dishes—including the massive 22-ounce bone-in rib eye—remain house favorites. The two dining rooms are on the ground floor of a renovated century-old hotel: one is cheerfully decorated in a Western motif, the other is accented with dark-wood trim and artwork by Frank Sinatra, one of the owner's favorite celebrities. ⊠ *113 S. Gillette Ave.* ☎ *307/682–6805* ▤ *AE, MC, V.*

¢–$$ ✕ **Hong Kong.** Lunches here are served fast and cheap (between $5 and $6) and include more than 30 different dishes, such as Mongolian beef and cashew chicken. They're popular with the business crowd, so you might want to avoid the noon lunch rush. ✉ *1612 W. 2nd St.* ☎ *307/682–5829* ▱ *AE, D, MC, V.*

$ 🏨 **Best Western Tower West Lodge.** Shades of beige and teal decorate the large, comfortable rooms of this hotel on the west side of town. Among the public spaces are an outdoor courtyard and a lobby with leather couches and chairs grouped around the fireplace. ✉ *109 N. U.S. 14/16, 82716* ☎ *307/686–2210* ▤ *307/682–5105* ⊕ *www.bestwestern.com* ⇒ *189 rooms* ⟡ *Restaurant, indoor pool, gym, hot tub, bar, no-smoking rooms* ▱ *AE, D, DC, MC, V.*

$ 🏨 **Clarion Western Plaza.** Travelers with a yen for exercise appreciate the gym and a pool of lap-swimming proportions at this motel with everything under one roof. Rooms are decorated in soft teal and mauve. The on-site Sierra Café serves steak and seafood. ✉ *2009 S. Douglas Hwy., 82718* ☎ *307/686–3000 or 800/686–3068* ▤ *307/686–4018* ⊕ *www.westernplaza.com* ⇒ *146 rooms, 13 suites* ⟡ *Restaurant, cable TV, indoor pool, gym, hot tub, sauna, video game room, Internet room, business services, meeting rooms, no-smoking rooms* ▱ *AE, D, DC, MC, V.*

$ 🏨 **Quality Inn.** This motel right off I–90 has large rooms but no frills, except for a free Continental breakfast. There's one other perk: antelope often graze nearby. ✉ *1004 E. U.S. 14/16, 82716* ☎ *307/682–2616 or 800/621–2182* ▤ *307/687–7002* ⊕ *www.qualityinn.com* ⇒ *80 rooms* ⟡ *Cable TV, no-smoking rooms* ▱ *AE, D, DC, MC, V* ⑩ *CP.*

Nightlife & the Arts

NIGHTLIFE   Pop and country performers make occasional appearances at Gillette's **Cam-Plex** (✉ 1635 Reata Dr. ☎ 307/682–0552, 307/682–8802 for tickets ⊕ www.cam-plex.com).

THE ARTS   Founded in 1986, the **Powder River Symphony** (✉ 1635 Reata Dr. ☎ 307/660–0919) continues to perform on a regular basis at the Cam-Plex Heritage Center, a 960-seat auditorium within Cam-Plex. The orchestra is composed of area musicians of all ages, and they play everything from Beethoven to Andrew Lloyd Webber.

Shopping

The people of Campbell County take their gardening seriously, as any observer can tell by walking into the **Sunrise Greenhouse** (✉ 7568 A U.S. 59, Wright, 38 mi south of Gillette ☎ 307/464–0889) in the springtime. A community institution, this greenhouse not only keeps local and exotic plants in stock but also carries an extensive selection of flowers for special occasions.

Devils Tower National Monument

★ ❽ *65 mi northeast of Gillette via I–90 and U.S. 14.*

As you drive east from Gillette, the highways begin to rise into the forested slopes of the Black Hills. A detour north will take you to Devils Tower, a rocky, grooved butte that juts upward 1,280 feet above the plain of the Belle Fourche River. Native American legend has it that the tower was corrugated by the claws of a bear trying to reach some children on top, and some tribes still revere the site, which they call Bear Lodge. Geologists attribute the butte's strange existence to ancient volcanic activity. Rock climbers say it's one of the best crack-climbing areas on the continent. The tower was a tourist magnet long before a spaceship landed here in the movie *Close Encounters of the Third Kind*. Teddy Roosevelt made it the nation's first national monument in 1906, and it has attracted a steadily increasing throng of visitors ever since—up to nearly half a million people a year.

When you visit Devils Tower, take some time to stop at the **visitor center,** a few miles beyond the park entrance. Exhibits here explain the geology, history, and cultural significance of the monument, and a bookstore carries a wide selection of materials relating to the park. Park rangers can provide updated information on hiking and climbing conditions. ⊠ *Hwy. 110* ☎ *307/467–5283* ⊕ *www.nps.gov/deto/* ⌂ *Cars $10; motorcycles, bicycles, and pedestrians $5* ☉ *Butte daily 24 hrs; visitor center Apr. and May, daily 8:30–4:30; June–Aug., daily 8–8; Sept. and Oct., daily 9–5.*

At the **Prairie Dog Town** between Devils Tower and the Belle Fourche River, you can observe the rodents in their natural habitat. Prairie dogs were once plentiful on the Great Plains, but ranching and development have taken their toll; today, the only sizeable populations of the animal are found on protected federal lands. ⊠ *Hwy. 110* ☎ *307/467–5283* ⊕ *www.nps.gov/deto/* ⌂ *Free* ☉ *Daily 24 hrs.*

Sports & the Outdoors

HIKING Aside from affording excellent views of Devils Tower and the surrounding countryside, the hiking trails here are a good way to view some of the geology and wildlife of the Black Hills region. The terrain that surrounds the butte is relatively flat, so the popular **Tower Trail,** a paved 1⅓-mi path that circles the monument, is far from strenuous. It's the most popular trail in the park, though, so if you're looking for more isolation, try the 1½-mi **Joyner Ridge Trail** or the 3-mi **Red Beds Trail.** They're a bit more demanding, but the views from the top of Joyner Ridge and the banks of the Belle Fourche River are more than adequate rewards. Both the Tower and Red Beds trails start at the visitor center; Joyner Ridge Trail begins about a mile's drive north from there.

ROCK CLIMBING Climbing is the premier sporting activity at Devils Tower. Acclaimed as one of the best crack-climbing areas in North America, the monument has attracted both beginners and experts for more than a century. There are few restrictions when it comes to ascending the granite cone. Although climbing is technically allowed all year, there is generally a voluntary moratorium in June to allow for peaceful religious rites performed by local Native American tribes. Additionally, the west face of the formation is closed intermittently in the summer to protect the prairie falcons that nest there.

Before ascending Devils Tower you should sign in at the **visitor center** (⌂ Hwy. 110 ☎ 307/467–5283) and discuss conditions with park officials. You can obtain a list of park-licensed guides here; courses are offered at all skill levels and sometimes include excursions into the Rockies or South Dakota. Some tour operators continue to guide climbs during the voluntary ban in June.

Camping

⌂ **Belle Fourche Campground.** Tucked away in a bend of the Belle Fourche River, this campground is small and spartan, but it is the only place in the park where camping is allowed. ⌂ *Flush toilets, drinking water, picnic tables ⌂ 30 sites ⌂ Hwy. 110 ☎ 307/467–5283 ⌂ 307/467–5350* ⊕ *www.nps.gov/deto/camp.htm ⌂ $12 ⌂ Reservations not accepted* ⊟ *No credit cards ⊙ Apr.–Oct.*

⌂ **Devils Tower KOA.** Less than a mile from Devils Tower, this campground literally lies in the shadow of the famous stone monolith. The view of the sheer granite walls above red river bluffs is one of the property's greatest assets. Another is the bordering Belle Fourche River, which nurtures several stalwart cottonwood and ash trees that provide at least some areas with shade. Weather permitting, the campground stages a nightly outdoor showing of *Close Encounters of the Third Kind.* ⌂ *Grills, flush toilets, full hookups, partial hookups (electric and water), drinking water, guest laundry, showers, picnic tables, general store, swimming (pool), play area, public telephone ⌂ 56 full hookups, 30 tent sites, 11 cabins ⌂ Hwy. 110 ☎ 307/467–5395 ⊕ www. devilstowerkoa.com ⌂ $24 tent sites, $33 partial hookups, $58 cabins ⊟ AE, D, DC, MC, V ⊙ May–Sept.*

Shopping

At **Devils Tower Trading Post** (⌂ 57 Hwy. 110 ☎ 307/467–5295), at the entrance to Devils Tower National Monument, you can purchase informative books, Western art, buffalo hides, clothing, knickknacks, and souvenirs. A giant Harley-Davidson flag (supposedly the world's largest) flies over the store, so it's no wonder that bikers overrun the place during the massive Sturgis Motorcycle Rally the first week of August. The old-fashioned ice-cream parlor, which also serves a mean sarsaparilla, is a real treat in the heat of summer.

Sundance

❾ *31 mi southeast of Devils Tower National Monument via U.S. 14.*

A combination of traditional reverence and an infamous outlaw's date with destiny put Sundance on Wyoming's map, and continues to draw visitors today. Native American tribes such as the Crow, Cheyenne, and Lakota consider Sundance Mountain and the Bear Lodge Mountains to be sacred. Before whites arrived in the 1870s the Indians congregated nearby each June for their Sun Dance, an important ceremonial gathering. The event gave its name to this small town, which in turn gave its name to the outlaw Harry Longabaugh, the Sundance Kid, who spent time in the local jail for stealing a horse. Ranch country and the western Black Hills surround the town.

★ Thousands of buffalo bones are piled atop each other at the **Vore Buffalo Jump,** where Native Americans forced buffalos to plunge to their deaths in the era when hunting was done with spears rather than fast horses and guns. ⊠ *Frontage Rd.* ☎ *307/283–1000* ⊕ *www. sundancewyoming.com/vore.htm* ☒ *Free* ☉ *Daily.*

Projects by local young people are displayed at the **Crook County Fair and Rodeo** during the first week in August, from cooking and clothing to livestock projects. There also are live music shows, basketball tournaments, a Dutch oven cook-off, pig wrestling, and a rodeo with sheepdog trials and team roping events. ⊠ *Fairgrounds Loop Rd.* ☎ *307/ 283–2644* ⊕ *www.wyomingfairs.org* ☒ *Free.*

Where to Stay & Eat

¢–$$ ✕ **Aro Restaurant and Lounge.** This large family diner in downtown Sundance has a cowboys-and-Indians theme and an extensive, well-priced menu. Standards include burgers, prime rib, Southwestern smothered burritos, Reuben sandwiches, and a huge Devils Tower brownie sundae dessert. ⊠ *203 Cleveland St.* ☎ *307/283–2000* ▤ *D, MC, V.*

¢–$$ ✕ **Country Cottage.** This one-stop shop in the center of town sells flowers, gifts, and simple meals, including submarine sandwiches. There's a modest seating area with some booths and small tables. ⊠ *423 Cleveland St.* ☎ *307/283–2450* ▤ *MC, V.*

¢–$$ ✕ **Log Cabin Cafe.** Locals crowd this small log-cabin restaurant full of country crafts for burgers, steaks, and seafood. Because the place is always packed, service can be slow, but the staff is always friendly. ⊠ *1620 E. Cleveland St.* ☎ *307/283–3393* ▤ *MC, V.*

¢–$$ 🛏 **Bear Lodge Motel.** A cozy lobby, a stone fireplace, and wildlife mounts on the walls distinguish this downtown motel. Hardwood furniture and patterned bedspreads add a slightly Western touch to the spacious, simple bedrooms. DVDs and players are available for use at no charge. ⊠ *218 Cleveland St., 82729* ☎ *307/283–1611* 🖷 *307/283–2537* ⊕ *www.bearlodgemotel.com* ⇨ *33 rooms* ♨ *Cable TV with movies, hot tub; no-smoking rooms* ▤ *AE, D, DC, MC, V.*

$ 🛏 **Sundance Mountain Inn.** Clean but basic rooms, friendly service, and a comfortable poolside area make this one-story ranch-style motor inn a nice place to stay. It's convenient to I–90 and across the street from area restaurants. ⊠ *26 Hwy. 585, 82729* ☎ *307/283–3737 or 888/347–2794* 🖷 *307/283–3738* ⊕ *www.sundancemountaininn.com* ⇨ *42 rooms* ♨ *Cable TV, indoor pool, hot tub, laundry facilities, some pets allowed (fee), Wi-Fi, no-smoking rooms* ▤ *AE, D, DC, MC, V* ⋈ *CP.*

¢–$ 🛏 **Best Western Inn at Sundance.** Dark-green carpeting and plum-color drapes decorate the spacious rooms of this hotel. With its inlaid cedar accents and comfortable deck chairs, the room housing the indoor pool is surprisingly stylish for a chain hotel. ⊠ *2719 Cleveland St., 82729* ☎ *307/283–2800 or 800/238–0965* 🖷 *307/283–2727* ⊕ *www. bestwestern.com* ⇨ *44 rooms* ♨ *Cable TV with movies, indoor pool, hot tub, shop, laundry facilities, in-room data ports, meeting rooms, some pets allowed (fee), no-smoking rooms* ▤ *AE, D, DC, MC, V* ⋈ *CP.*

THE NORTH PLATTE RIVER VALLEY

Sweeping down from the Colorado Rockies into the very center of Wyoming, the North Platte River was a key waterway for emigrants because its valley was one of the few places where wagons could safely cross the mountains. A deep pioneer legacy survives here, where several trails converged along the Platte and Sweetwater rivers and snaked through South Pass. Some of the travelers put down roots, and the North Platte River valley remains one of Wyoming's important agricultural areas.

Much of this area is cattle country, for one simple reason: it's flat and dry. On some of the westernmost ranges of short grassland before the Rockies thrust up from the plains, the land is relatively treeless. The human presence consists largely of fences, livestock, a few small cow towns, and the bustling Western city of Casper. Today a hefty share of central Wyoming's wealth derives from its deposits of oil, uranium, and bentonite.

Lusk

🔟 *140 mi northeast of Cheyenne via I–25 and U.S. 18.*

Proudly rural, the 1,500 townspeople of Lusk often poke gentle fun at themselves, emblazoning T-shirts with phrases such as "End of the world, 12 miles. Lusk, 15 miles." You'll see what they mean if you visit this seat of Niobrara County, whose population density averages 524 acres of prairie per person. If you find yourself traveling the main route between the Black Hills and the Colorado Rockies, a stop in this tiny burg is worth the time for a quick lesson in frontier—particularly stage-coach—history. You can also find gasoline and food, rare commodities on the open plain.

Lusk owes its existence to rancher Frank S. Lusk, who cut a deal with the Wyoming Central Railroad in 1886. The railroad originally planned to build its route through central Wyoming along the Cheyenne–Deadwood Stage Line, which ran between the territorial capital and the Black Hills gold-rush town. Officials selected Silver Cliff, where Ellis Johnson ran a store, saloon, and hotel, as the area's station. When Johnson tried to raise the price for his land, the railroad changed its plans and bought from Lusk. The rail line bypassed Silver Cliff for the station named Lusk.

The stagecoach line that passed through Lusk played a role in the development of the Black Hills, but Lusk became a different sort of pioneering town in the 1990s. Town leaders installed fiber-optic cable lines and obtained computers for schools, public facilities, and homes, placing Lusk on the frontier of technology when other small Wyoming towns had barely even heard of the Internet. The media spotlight shone briefly on the town that led the state of Wyoming into the 21st century.

Artifacts from early settlement days and the period when the Cheyenne–Deadwood Stage Line was in full swing are some of the displays at the **Stagecoach Museum.** You also can get information about the Texas Cattle Trail. ⊠ *322 S. Main St.* ☎ *307/334–3444 or 800/ 223–5875* ≊ *$2* ☉ *May–Aug., weekdays 10–6; Sept. and Oct., weekdays 10–4.*

You can still see the remains of one of the Cheyenne–Deadwood Stage Line stops at the **Historic Hat Creek Stage Station.** Also here are an old schoolhouse and post office out in the tallgrass plains. You can wander among the buildings whenever you like, but to see the insides you must call for a tour. ⊠ *15 mi north of Lusk on U.S. 85, then 2 mi east on gravel Rd.* ☎ *307/334–2950, 307/334–2134 for private tour* ≊ *Free* ☉ *Daily.*

Where to Stay & Eat

$–$$$ ✕ **El Jarros.** At the center of town, this festive restaurant is filled with Ted DeGrazia prints, strung with lights, and decked in bright, warm colors. Try the fajitas, barbecue ribs, or spicy shrimp stir-fry, and complement your meal with an icy margarita. Note that the restaurant closes between 2 and 5. ⊠ *625 S. Main St.* ☎ *307/334–5004* ▤ *MC, V.*

¢–$ ✕ **Pizza Place.** A casual atmosphere and good food come together at this downtown eatery. Pizza, calzones, and sub sandwiches made with homemade bread are on the menu, and there's also a salad bar. ⊠ *218 S. Main St.* ☎ *307/334–3000* ▤ *No credit cards.*

$ ▥ **Covered Wagon.** With a covered wagon on the front portico, an indoor pool, and an outdoor playground, this U-shape hotel is an inviting place for families with kids. ⊠ *730 S. Main St., 82225* ☎ *307/334– 2836 or 800/341–8000* ⎙ *307/334–2977* ⇆ *51 rooms* ♨ *Indoor pool, hot tub, sauna, cable TV, playground, laundry facilities, meeting rooms, no-smoking rooms* ▤ *AE, DC, MC, V* ⎢◯⎢ *CP.*

¢–$ ▥ **Best Western Pioneer Court.** Although the exterior of this motel near downtown and the Stagecoach Museum is unremarkable, the lobby is attractive, with a ceramic-tile floor, hardwood trim, and wrought-iron tables and lamps. There are some extra-large rooms that can accommodate up to eight people. ⊠ *731 Main St., 82225* ☎ *307/334– 2640* ⎙ *307/334–2640* ⊕ *www.bestwestern.com* ⇆ *30 rooms* ♨ *Restaurant, cable TV, pool, bar, no-smoking rooms* ▤ *AE, D, DC, MC, V.*

¢ ▥ **Rawhide Motel.** The standard-size rooms are rustic but warm, and service is friendly at this affordable, locally owned motel in downtown Lusk. It's within walking distance of area restaurants. ⊠ *805 S. Main St., 82225* ☎ *307/334–2440 or 888/679–2558* ⎙ *307/334–2440* ⇆ *19 rooms* ♨ *Cable TV, some pets allowed, no-smoking rooms* ▤ *AE, D, MC, V.*

en route Off U.S. 18 on the drive from Lusk to Douglas is **Glendo State Park,** which surrounds Glendo Reservoir, a human-made lake on the North Platte River. Rich in history, the park encompasses parts of the Oregon, Utah, and California trails (although many stretches of the old trails are now under water) and several prehistoric and historic Native American camps. In addition to a marina there are several hundred campsites at various places on the lakeshore. ⊠ *State Rd. 319* ☏ *307/735–4433* ⊕ *wyoparks.state.wy.us/glslide.htm* 🖃 *$4 per vehicle* ⊙ *Daily.*

A few miles east of Glendo State Park lies a vast stone quarry initially mistaken for the work of early Spanish explorers. Archaeologists later determined the site, known as the **Spanish Diggings,** to be the work of various indigenous tribes on and off for the past several thousand years. Tools and arrowheads carved from the stone quarried here, including quartzite, jasper, and agate, have been found as far away as the Ohio River valley. To see the diggings you'll have to drive through Glendo State Park.

Douglas

🄫 *55 mi west of Lusk via U.S. 18 and I–25.*

Douglas is best known for two things: the Wyoming State Fair, which has been held here annually since 1905, and the jackalope. A local taxidermist assembled the first example of the mythical cross between a jackrabbit and an antelope for display in a local hotel. There's an eight-foot-tall concrete jackalope statue in Jackalope Square in downtown Douglas, and many businesses sell jackalope figures and merchandise.

Surveyors plotted the town of Douglas (named for Stephen A. Douglas, the presidential candidate who lost to Abe Lincoln) in 1886, in preparation for the construction of the Fremont, Elkhorn, and Missouri Valley Railroad. The railroad, which owned the town site, prohibited settlement before the rails arrived. Eager to take up residence, a few enterprising souls built shelters on Antelope Creek, outside the official boundaries. When the railroad arrived on August 22, they put their structures on wheels and moved them into town.

The weeklong **Wyoming State Fair and Rodeo,** held in early August each year at the Wyoming State Fairgrounds, includes a carnival, livestock judging, commercial exhibits, and a Professional Rodeo Cowboys Association rodeo. ⊠ *400 W. Center St.* ☏ *307/358–2398* ⊕ *www. wystatefair.com* 🖃 *$4* ⊙ *Early Aug.; call for exact dates.*

At the **Wyoming Pioneer Memorial Museum,** the emphasis is on the Wyoming pioneer settlers and overland immigrants, but this small state-operated museum on the state fairgrounds also has displays on Native Americans and the frontier military. ⊠ *400 W. Center St.* ☏ *307/358–9288* ⊕ *wyoparks.state.wy.us/PMslide.htm* 🖃 *Free* ⊙ *June–Aug., weekdays 8–5, Sat. 1–5; Sept.–May, by appointment.*

Overland immigrants sometimes visited **Ayres Natural Bridge** (⊠ *Off I–25* ☏ *307/358–2950*), a rock outcrop that spans LaPrele Creek. It's now a small but popular picnic area and campsite where you can wade in the creek or simply enjoy the quiet.

Built in 1867 to protect travelers headed west, the army post here is preserved today as the **Fort Fetterman State Historic Site.** Although the fort was never very large and had difficulty keeping its soldiers from deserting, its location on the fringes of the Great Sioux Indian Reservation made it an important outpost of civilization on the Western frontier. After white settlers overran the Black Hills and the government did away with the reservation, soldiers from here helped end armed Plains Indian resistance—and thus put an end to the fort's usefulness. Two buildings, the ordnance warehouse and officers' quarters, survived decades of abandonment and today house interpretive exhibits and artifacts related to the area's history and the fort's role in settling the West. The remains of other fort buildings can still be seen, as can the ruins of Fetterman City, which died out when Douglas was founded several miles to the south. ⊠ *Hwy. 93* ☏ *307/358–2864 or 307/777–7629* ⊕ *wyoparks.state.wy.us/FFslide.htm* ✉ *$1 residents, $2 nonresidents* ☉ *Memorial Day–Labor Day, daily 9–5.*

The **Medicine Bow National Forest, Douglas District** (⊠ Douglas Ranger District, 2250 E. Richards St. ☏ 307/358–4690 ⊕ www.fs.fed.us/r2/mbr/), southwest of Douglas in the Laramie Peak area, includes four campgrounds ($5 for camping; campground closed in winter) and areas where you can fish and hike.

Where to Stay & Eat

$$–$$$ ✕ **Plains Trading Post.** Antique furnishings and portions of old bank buildings set the scene at this restaurant, where the menu is diverse but basic—chicken, burgers, steaks—and the portions are large. It's open 24 hours a day, a rarity even in the larger cities. ⊠ *841 S. 6th St.* ☏ *307/358–4484* ▤ *MC, V.*

$–$$ ✕ **The Koop.** Serving breakfast and lunch, this place is known for its burgers and fries. The fries are unusual, since each curly fry is made from a whole potato. ⊠ *108 N. 3rd St.* ☏ *307/358–3509* ▤ *MC, V* ☉ *No dinner.*

$ ✕▦ **Best Western Douglas Inn.** With its cathedral ceiling and fireplace, the atrium lobby is an impressive entranceway into this chain hotel. The location is convenient, next to I–25 on the north side of town and close to the Wyoming State Fairgrounds. The restaurant's menu ($$–$$$$) of mostly American dishes includes exotic choices such as ostrich and buffalo steak. ⊠ *1450 Riverbend Dr., 82633* ☏ *307/358–9790* ▤ *307/358–6251* ⊕ *www.bestwestern.com* ⇄ *117 rooms* ⚬ *Restaurant, cable TV with movies, pool, gym, hot tub, sauna, video game room, laundry facilities, meeting rooms, some pets allowed (fee), no-smoking rooms* ▤ *AE, D, DC, MC, V.*

¢–$$ ▦ **Morton Mansion.** The huge, covered wraparound porch of this inn on a quiet, residential street is perfect for relaxing. The mansion was built in 1903 in the Queen Anne style. Antiques and floral patterns decorate the guest rooms, and the attic suite has two bedrooms, a private living room, and a full kitchen. ⊠ *425 E. Center St., 82633* ☏ *307/358–2129* ▤ *307/358–6590* ⊕ *www.mortonmansion.com* ⇄ *3 rooms, 1 suite* ⚬ *Dining room, cable TV; no kids under 10, no smoking* ▤ *AE, D, MC, V* ◉ *CP.*

CAMPING ⛺ **Esterbrook Campground.** Nestled among pine trees near Laramie Peak, 30 mi south of Douglas, Esterbrook is only a few miles from Black

Mountain Lookout, one of the few staffed fire lookouts remaining in the country. During fire season (generally mid-June through September) be sure to ask the ranger-in-residence before exploring his or her home. ♿ *Pit toilets, drinking water, fire grates, picnic tables, ranger station* ⬅ *12 sites* ✉ *Forest Rd. 633* ☎ *307/358–4690 or 307/358–1604* ⊕ *www.fs.fed.us/r2/mbr/recreation/camping/douglas/esterbrook.shtml* ⌨ *$5* ♿ *Reservations essential* ▭ *No credit cards* ☉ *Mid-May–mid-Oct.*

Casper

⓬ *50 mi west of Douglas via I–25.*

Several excellent museums in Casper illuminate central Wyoming's pioneer and natural history. The state's second-largest city, it's also one of the oldest. Some of the first white people to venture across Wyoming spent the winter here in 1811, on their way east from Fort Astoria in Oregon. Although they didn't stay, they helped to forge several pioneer trails that crossed the North Platte River near present-day Casper. A permanent settlement eventually arose, and was named for Lieutenant Caspar Collins; the spelling error occurred early on, and it stuck. The town has grown largely as a result of oil and gas exploration, and sheep and cattle ranchers run their stock on lands all around the city.

Five major immigrant trails passed near or through Casper in the period between 1843 and 1870. The best known are the Oregon Trail and the Mormon Trail, both of which crossed the North Platte River in the vicinity of today's Casper. The **National Historic Trails Interpretive Center** examines the early history of the trails and the military's role in central Wyoming. Projected onto a series of screens 11 feet high and 55 feet wide, a film shows Wyoming trail sites and scenes of wagon travelers. You can climb into a wagon to see what it was like to cross the river, or learn about Mormon pioneers who traveled west with handcarts in 1856. ✉ *1501 N. Poplar* ☎ *307/265–8030* ⊕ *www.wy.blm.gov/nhtic* ⌨ *$6* ☉ *Apr.–Oct., daily 8–7; Nov.–Mar., Tues.–Sat. 9–4:30.*

FodorsChoice ★

The **Fort Caspar Historic Site** re-creates the post at Platte Bridge, which became Fort Caspar after the July 1865 battle that claimed the lives of several soldiers, including Lieutenant Caspar Collins. A post depicts life at a frontier station in the 1860s, and sometimes soldier reenactors go about their tasks. Museum exhibits show the migration trails. ✉ *4001 Fort Caspar Rd.* ☎ *307/235–8462* ⊕ *www.fortcasparwyoming.com* ⌨ *May–Sept. $2, Oct.–Apr. $1* ☉ *Museum June–Aug., Mon.–Sat. 8–7, Sun. noon–7; May and Sept., Mon.–Sat. 8–5, Sun. noon–5; Oct.–Apr., weekdays 8–5, Sun. 1–4. Fort buildings June–Aug., Mon.–Sat. 8:30–6:30, Sun. 12:30–6:30; May and Sept., Mon.–Sat. 8:30–4:30, Sun. 12:30–4:30.*

The **Casper Planetarium** has multimedia programs on astronomy. There are also interactive exhibits in the lobby and a gift shop. Public programs, which last an hour, are scheduled regularly in the summer. ✉ *904 N. Poplar St.* ☎ *307/577–0310* ⊕ *ncsdweb.ncsd.k12.wy.us/planetarium/*

$2.50 ⊙ *Lobby exhibits weekdays 8–5. Public programs June–Aug., Mon.–Sat. 7 PM–8 PM; Sept.–May, Sat. 7 PM–8 PM; call to confirm.*

The **Werner Wildlife Museum,** near the Casper College campus, has displays of birds and animals from Wyoming and around the world. ⊠ *405 E. 15th St.* ☎ *307/268–2676* ⊕ *www.caspercollege.edu/lifescience/ werner* ⊡ *Free* ⊙ *Mid-May–Labor Day, daily 10–5; Labor Day–mid-May, weekdays 2–5.*

Casper College's **Tate Earth Science Center and Geological Museum** displays fossils, rocks, jade, and the fossilized remains of a brontosaurus, plus other dinosaur bones. ⊠ *125 College Dr.* ☎ *307/268–3068* ⊕ *www. caspercollege.edu/tate/webpage.asp* ⊡ *Free* ⊙ *Weekdays 9–5, Sat. 10–4.*

★ A showcase for regional artists and mostly modern artwork, the **Nicolaysen Art Museum and Discovery Center** also exhibits works by national artists. The building's early-20th-century redbrick exterior and contemporary interior are an odd combination, but this makes the museum all the more interesting. There are hands-on activities, classes, children's programs, a research library, and a Discovery Center. ⊠ *400 E. Collins Dr.* ☎ *307/235–5247* ⊕ *www.thenic.org* ⊡ *Donations accepted* ⊙ *Memorial Day–Labor Day, Tues.–Fri. 10–7, Sat. 10–5, Sun. noon–4; Labor Day–Memorial Day, Tues.–Sat. 10–5, Sun. noon–4.*

off the beaten path

INDEPENDENCE ROCK STATE HISTORIC SITE – This turtle-shape granite outcrop became an important site on the Oregon, California, and Mormon trails. Tradition dictated that travelers had to arrive at the rock by July 4 in order to reach the West Coast before winter set in. Many of these pioneers carved their names in the rock, and some are still legible more than a century later. The rock face looks steep but is relatively easy to climb without any special equipment. Midway between Casper and Rawlins, the site includes a rest stop with bathrooms and picnic tables. ⊠ *Hwy. 220, 54 mi southwest of Casper* ☎ *307/777–6323* ⊕ *wyoparks.state. wy.us/IRslide.htm.*

DEVIL'S GATE – Local Shoshone and Arapaho tribes believed this deep cleft in the mountains through which the Sweetwater River flows was cut by a giant tusked beast in a fit of anger. Although Devil's Gate is only 30 feet wide at the base, the sheer walls of the ⅓-mi-long canyon rise more than 300 feet high. There are interpretive panels along the highway, and you can still see the ruts carved by the wagons that followed the pioneer trails nearby. Devil's Gate is less than 6 mi south of another pioneer-trail landmark, Independence Rock. ⊠ *Hwy. 220, 59 mi southwest of Casper.*

HANDCART RANCH – The Martin's Cove Visitor Center, run by the Church of Jesus Christ of Latter-day Saints, has exhibits on the Sun family and their ranch, which operated here from 1872 until the church bought the Sun Ranch in 1997. The Oregon, California, and

Mormon trails cross the ranch, which is particularly important to the Mormons because two groups of pioneers traveling with handcarts to Salt Lake City became stranded in the area by snowstorms in 1856. They had left the area along the Missouri River near Omaha, Nebraska, too late in the year to cross the mountains before winter set in. A 3½-mi trail leads to Martin's Cove, where the handcart pioneers found shelter from the cold. You can push one of 100 handcarts up the trail to get a feel for this mode of transportation. The carts are loaned for free on a first-come, first-served basis; none are loaned after 3:30 and none on Sunday. ⊠ *Hwy. 220, 60 mi southwest of Casper* ☎ *307/328–2953* ⊕ *www.handcart.com* ✉ *Free* ⊗ *Daily 8–7.*

Sports & the Outdoors

With thousands of acres of empty grassland and towering mountains only miles away, the landscape around Casper is full of possibilities for enjoying the outdoors. Casper Mountain rises up 8,000 feet no more than 20 minutes from downtown, providing prime skiing and hiking trails.

Edness Kimball Wilkins State Park (⊠ I–25, 6 mi east of Casper ☎ 307/577–5150) is a day-use area with picnicking, swimming, fishing, and a 3-mi walking path.

HIKING Much of Casper Mountain is taken up by private land, but there are some public trails, including mountain-bike routes and the Braille Trail, a simple hike with plaques (in braille) that describe the views and ecology of the mountain. The trails can get a little crowded in the summer. Contact the **Casper Convention and Visitors Bureau** (⊠ 330 S. Center St. ☎ 307/234–5362 or 800/852–1889 ⊕ www.casperwyoming.org) for more information.

The **Platte River Parkway** hiking trail runs adjacent to the North Platte River in downtown Casper. Access points are at Amoco Park at 1st and Poplar streets, or at Crosswinds Park, on North Poplar Street near the Casper Events Center.

SKIING Perched on Casper Mountain a few miles outside of town is **Hogadon Ski Area** (⊠ Casper Mountain Rd. ☎ 307/235–8499), with a vertical drop of 600 feet. Less than a quarter of the runs are rated for beginners; the rest are evenly divided between intermediate and expert trails. Also here are a separate snowboard terrain park and a modest lodge. **Mountain Sports** (⊠ 543 S. Center ☎ 307/266–1136) provides more than just ski and snowboard sales. It also runs Wyomaps, which sells personal Global Positioning System products and provides custom mapping services.

Where to Stay & Eat

$$$–$$$$ ✕ **Armor's.** A quiet dining room with cozy booths and tables makes this a popular place for a special dinner. In addition to standards such as steaks and prime rib, the menu lists blackened and Cajun entrées. ⊠ 3422 S. Energy La. ☎ 307/235–3000 ▭ AE, D, DC, MC, V.

$$–$$$$ ✕ **Poor Boys Steakhouse.** Reminiscent of a frontier mining camp or Western town, this steak house has blue-and-white-check tablecloths and chair backs, quick service, and large portions of steak, seafood, and chicken. Salad comes in a bucket and is served with fresh, hot bread. Try the Moonshine Mama—grilled chicken breast smothered in mushrooms and Monterey Jack and cheddar cheeses—or enjoy a tantalizingly tender filet mignon with shrimp. For dessert try the Dutch apple pie or Ashley's Avalanche—a huge plate of ice cream, a white-chocolate brownie, cherry-pie filling, chocolate sauce, and whipped cream. ⊠ *739 N. Center St.* ☎ *307/237–8325* ⊟ *AE, D, DC, MC, V.*

$–$$$ ✕ **El Jarro.** Usually crowded and always noisy, this place serves hearty portions of Mexican cuisine. The beef fajitas are a favorite, second only to the fine margaritas, which come in glasses the size of bowls. The place is decorated with bright colors, which only seem to encourage the generally rowdy bunch at the bar. ⊠ *500 W. F St.* ☎ *307/577–0538* ⊟ *AE, MC, V.*

$–$$$ ✕ **Sanfords Grub and Pub.** This lively spot decorated with 20th-century memorabilia may be a brewery, but children are welcome here in the heart of downtown. The extensive menu includes pastas, pizzas, and calzones. If you're a vegetarian, this is your best bet in Casper for its variety of meatless dishes. ⊠ *241 S. Center St.* ☎ *307/234–4555* ⊟ *AE, D, DC, MC, V.*

$ 🏨 **Hampton Inn.** The rooms in this clean and very quiet lodging have coffeemakers, large cable TVs, dark floral spreads, and an easy chair with an ottoman. The small restaurant, Cafe José's, serves authentic Mexican food, including enchiladas, flautas, and chimichangas. ⊠ *400 W. F St., 82601* ☎ *307/235–6668* 🖨 *307/235–2027* ⊕ *www.hamptoninn. com* ➦ *121 rooms* ♿ *Restaurant, cable TV with movies, pool, sauna, meeting rooms; no smoking* ⊟ *AE, D, DC, MC, V* ⦿ *CP.*

$ 🏨 **Parkway Plaza.** With a large convention center, the Parkway is one of Casper's busiest motels. The rooms are quiet and large, with double vanities, one inside the bathroom and one outside. Furnishings are contemporary in the rooms but Western in the public areas. The pool has wading and diving sections. Attached to the hotel is Old Town, a small amusement park with an arcade, miniature-golf course, and a NASCAR-sanctioned go-kart track. ⊠ *123 W. Center St., 82601* ☎ *307/235–1777 or 800/270–7829* 🖨 *307/235–8068* ⊕ *www.parkwayplaza.net* ➦ *285 rooms* ♿ *Restaurant, coffee shop, cable TV with movies, indoor-outdoor pool, gym, hair salon, hot tub, sauna, bar, video game room, playground, laundry facilities, business services, convention center, no-smoking rooms* ⊟ *AE, D, MC, V.*

¢ 🏨 **Best Western Ramkota Hotel.** This full-service location, off I–25, has everything under one roof, from dining options to business services. Muted blues, greens, and mauves decorate the large, contemporary rooms, some of which have whirlpool tubs. ⊠ *800 N. Poplar St., 82601* ☎ *307/266–6000* 🖨 *307/473–1010* ⊕ *www.bestwestern.com* ➦ *229 rooms* ♿ *Restaurant, café, some in-room hot tubs, cable TV with movies, in-room data ports, indoor pool, hot tub, bar, business services, convention center, no-smoking rooms* ⊟ *AE, D, DC, MC, V.*

The Arts

Both the Casper Symphony Orchestra and the Casper College Theater Department perform at the 465-seat **Gertrude Krampert Theater** (✉ Casper College, 125 College Dr. ☎ 307/268–2500). **Stage III Community Theater** (✉ 4080 S. Poplar St. ☎ 307/234–0946) presents plays and other dramatic performances at various times.

Shopping

The largest shopping center in a 175-mi radius, the **Eastridge Mall** (✉ 601 S.E. Wyoming Blvd. ☎ 307/265–9392), anchored by such standbys as Sears, JCPenney, Target, and Bon Marché, is popular and important to locals. There are also a few local stores here, including JAAG Racing, the largest NASCAR store in the state, and Corral West Ranchwear, which occasionally hosts roping competitions in the central court.

CODY, SHERIDAN & NORTHERN WYOMING A TO Z

To research prices, get advice from other travelers, and book travel arrangements, visit www.fodors.com.

AIR TRAVEL

CARRIERS   For the most part, airlines connect the region only to Denver, Minneapolis, or Salt Lake City, although some carriers occasionally have seasonal routes to smaller cities such as Billings.

Delta Air Lines serves Casper and Cody from Salt Lake City. Northwest Airlines connects Casper and Minneapolis. United Airlines flies from Denver into Casper, Gillette, Sheridan, and Cody.

🖪 Airlines & Contacts **Delta Air Lines** ☎ 800/221-1212 ⊕ www.delta.com. **Northwest Airlines** ☎ 800/225-2525 ⊕ www.nwa.com. **United Airlines** ☎ 800/241-6522 ⊕ www.ual.com.

AIRPORTS

The region's major airports are Casper's Natrona County International Airport, Gillette's Campbell County Airport and Cody's Yellowstone Regional Airport. Sheridan County Airport has one or two flights daily to and from Denver, plus charter service.

The Campbell County Airport is 6 mi north of Gillette and 106 mi east of Sheridan. Natrona County International Airport is 12 mi west of Casper. Yellowstone Regional Airport is on the edge of Cody, about a mile from downtown.

🖪 Airport Information **Campbell County Airport** ✉ 2000 Airport Rd., Gillette ☎ 307/686-1042 ⊕ ccg.co.campbell.wy.us/airport/. **Natrona County International Airport** ✉ 8500 Airport Pkwy., Casper ☎ 307/472-6688 ⊕ www.casperwyoming.org/airport/. **Sheridan County Airport** ✉ 908 W. Brundage La. ☎ 307/674-4222. **Yellowstone Regional Airport** ✉ 3001 Duggleby Dr., Cody ☎ 307/587-5096 ⊕ www.flyyra.com.

BUS TRAVEL

National bus service from Greyhound Lines is only available through Powder River Transportation, a regional carrier that connects the area to the larger hub cities of Cheyenne and Rapid City, South Dakota. Casper, Gillette, Sheridan, Cody, and nearly every smaller town in northern and central Wyoming are well served by Powder River Transportation.

Greyhound Lines ☎ 307/634-7744 or 800/231-2222 ⊕ www.greyhound.com. **Powder River Transportation** ☎ 307/682-0960.

CAR RENTAL

The three major airports in the region are the best places to find car rentals. Make rental reservations early; between business travelers and tourists, which both peak in summer, rental agencies are often booked.

Avis ☎ 800/831-2847 ⊕ www.avis.com. **Budget** ☎ 800/527-0700 ⊕ www.budget.com. **Dollar** ☎ 800/527-0700 ⊕ www.dollar.com. **Hertz** ☎ 800/654-3131 ⊕ www.hertz.com. **National** ☎ 800/227-7368 ⊕ www.nationalcar.com.

CAR TRAVEL

Unless you're traveling with a package tour, a car is essential here. I–90 cuts directly through northeastern Wyoming, hitting the towns of Sheridan, Buffalo, Gillette, and Sundance. I–25 runs south from Buffalo through the Big Horns to Casper, Douglas, Cheyenne, and eventually Denver. There are no interstate highways west of the Big Horns, so U.S. 14–one of two routes that cross the mountain range–is the main road in this part of the state, connecting Cody with I–90.

Because the territory in this part of the world is so sparsely populated, it's almost impossible to find gas and repair shops at your convenience. There are few towns along the major routes here, including the interstates, so it's wise to plan your trip in advance. Although most of the country has gone to 24-hour credit-card gas pumps, these pieces of technology haven't hit the smaller towns in Wyoming, and it's rare to find a gas station open past the early evening unless you're in Gillette, Sheridan, Casper, or Cody. If you're driving in a particularly remote region, it's wise to take along extra water. Although the communities here employ great fleets of snowplows in the winter, it can sometimes take them time to clear the upper elevations. Some passes in the Big Horns close entirely. Keep in mind, too, that residents are used to driving in a little snow and ice, so the plows will come out only if accumulations are substantial.

Contact the Wyoming State Highway Patrol for information on road conditions.

Wyoming State Highway Patrol ☎ 888/996-7623 ⊕ whp.state.wy.us.

EMERGENCIES

Ambulance or Police Emergencies ☎ 911.

24-Hour Medical Care Campbell County Memorial Hospital ✉ 501 S. Burma St., Gillette ☎ 307/682-8811 ⊕ www.ccmh.net. **Sheridan County Memorial Hospital** ✉ 1401 W. 5th St., Sheridan ☎ 307/672-1000 ⊕ www.sheridanhospital.org. **West Park Hospital** ✉ 707 Sheridan Ave., Cody ☎ 800/654-6447 ⊕ www.westparkhospital.org. **Wyoming Medical Center** ✉ 1233 E. 2nd St., Casper ☎ 307/577-7201 ⊕ www.wmcnet.org.

LODGING

CAMPING The opportunities to camp in this region are almost limitless. There are countless campgrounds in the Big Horns, and a few on the prairies below. Most of the public land within the national forests and parks is open for camping, provided that you don't light any fires. Keep in mind when selecting your campsite that the majestic peaks of the Big Horns are home to black bears and mountain lions.

MEDIA

NEWSPAPERS Most small communities have their own newspapers that print at least once a week with local reports and weather forecasts, but the papers of the bigger communities tend to serve as the printed-news mainstays of the whole area. The *Casper Star-Tribune* is the largest and most comprehensive newspaper, although the *Gillette News-Record* and the *Sheridan Press* are also detailed and available every day. Some of the larger newsstands carry all three, plus papers from nearby cities like Cheyenne and Rapid City, South Dakota. Because most of the people here are staunchly conservative, most of the papers are as well.

TELEVISION & If you're not near Casper, Gillette, or Sheridan, chances are you won't
RADIO pick up many stations, either on the television or radio. Many rural communities have cable just to get the regional affiliates. In fact, the only major stations that broadcast from this area are in Casper: FOX/ KFNB Channel 20, CBS/KGWC Channel 14, UPN/KWYF Channel 26, NBC/KCWY Channel 13, and ABC/KTWO Channel 2. Other stations come from nearby Cheyenne, Billings, Montana, and Rapid City, South Dakota.

The radio waves, both AM and FM, are dominated largely by country- or Christian-music stations. In central Wyoming, KWYY 95.5 FM and KTWO 1030 AM play country, and KCSP 90.3 FM plays contemporary Christian music. In the Big Horn Basin, you'll probably be able to pick up KZMQ 100.3/101.1 FM, a country station, and KCGL 104.1 FM, which plays classic rock. For news, talk, and sports, tune to KODI 1400 AM.

SPORTS & THE OUTDOORS

FISHING Besides the local chambers of commerce, the Wyoming Game and Fish department is your best bet for updated information on the numerous fishing opportunities in this region. The countless local outfitters, guides, and community organizations can also provide information.
🖪 **Wyoming Game and Fish** ✉ 5400 Bishop Blvd., Cheyenne 82006 ☎ 307/777-4600 ⊕ gf.state.wy.us/.

SKIING & The Big Horns receive a substantial amount of snow each year, turning
SNOWMOBILING the mountains into a winter playground. Even the flatter land that lies below is conducive to scenic sledding and cross-country skiing, and there are miles of groomed trails for that purpose. Because there is no one agency that keeps track of conditions in the area, your best sources of information on winter sports are individual outfitters and businesses, or the local chambers of commerce.

VISITOR INFORMATION

There are plenty of publications, ranging from small booklets to thick magazines, geared to visitors to the area, especially for those headed to the Black Hills. Many of these publications can be found at hotels and restaurants, usually for free (although you should expect 50%–75% of these magazines to be dedicated to advertisements).

Wyoming Tourist Information Buffalo Chamber of Commerce ✉ 55 N. Main St., Buffalo 82834 ☎ 307/684-5544 or 800/227-5122 ⊕ www.buffalowyo.com. **Campbell County Chamber of Commerce** ✉ 314 S. Gillette Ave., Gillette 82716 ☎ 307/682-3673 ⊕ www.gillettechamber.com. **Casper Chamber of Commerce** ✉ 500 N. Center St., Casper 82601 ☎ 307/234-5311 or 800/852-1889 ⊕ www.casperwyoming.org. **Casper Convention and Visitors Bureau** ✉ 330 S. Center St., Casper 82602 ☎ 307/234-5362 or 800/852-1889 ⊕ www.casperwyoming.org. **Cody Country Chamber of Commerce** ✉ 836 Sheridan Ave., Cody 82414 ☎ 307/587-2777 ⊕ www.codychamber.org. **Gillette Convention and Visitor's Bureau** ✉ 1810 S. Douglas Hwy., Gillette 82718 ☎ 307/686-0040 or 800/544-6136 ⊕ www.visitgillette.net. **Park County Travel Council** ✉ 836 Sheridan Ave., Cody 82414 ☎ 307/587-2297 ⊕ www.yellowstonecountry.org. **Sheridan Chamber of Commerce** ✉ Box 707, Sheridan 82801 ☎ 307/672-2485 ⊕ www.sheridanwyomingchamber.org.

The South Dakota Black Hills

7

WITH DEADWOOD, MOUNT RUSHMORE & THE CRAZY HORSE MEMORIAL

WORD OF MOUTH

"We really wanted to see Deadwood and weren't disappointed. There were reenactors on the streets. In the early evening there was the reenactment of the shooting of Wild Bill and the subsequent trial of Jack McCall. We really enjoyed the trial."

—mlm59

"We were pleasantly surprised by Mount Rushmore. We'd expected it to be tacky and touristy, but the visitors center is very nice."

—lynnss1

"I would start the day in the Badlands at sunrise—makes all the difference in the colors you'll see."

—Souette

By T. D. Griffith & Dustin D. Floyd

"AN EMERALD ISLE IN A SEA OF PRAIRIE," as they are sometimes called, the Black Hills rise up from the western South Dakota plains just over the Wyoming state line and about 150 mi east of the Big Horn range of the Rocky Mountains. They aren't as high—Harney Peak, their tallest summit, measures 7,242 feet—and they cover a territory only 50 mi wide and 120 mi long, but these ponderosa-covered mountains have a majesty all their own. Alpine meadows, thick forests, and creek-carved canyons: the landscape of the Black Hills and badlands region more closely resembles Big Horn and Yellowstone country than it does South Dakota's typical flat farmland.

The Black Hills are anchored by Rapid City; with 60,876 residents, it's the largest city for 350 mi in any direction. Perhaps better known, however, are the region's 19th-century frontier towns, including Spearfish, Lead, and Deadwood. The Black Hills also can claim one of the highest concentrations of public parks, monuments, and memorials in the world. Among the more famous are Badlands National Park, Jewel Cave National Monument, and Mount Rushmore National Memorial, whose giant stone carvings of four U.S. presidents have retained their stern grandeur for more than 60 years.

As in neighboring Wyoming and Montana, outdoor recreation reigns supreme in the Black Hills. Whatever your pleasure—hiking, mountain biking, rock climbing, horseback riding, fishing, boating, skiing, snowmobiling, cross-country skiing—you can do it here, before a backdrop of stunning countryside.

Exploring the South Dakota Black Hills

Numbers in the text correspond to numbers in the margin and on the South Dakota Black Hills and Badlands National Park maps.

The 2 million acres of the Black Hills are about evenly split between private property and the Black Hills National Forest. Fortunately for visitors, the national forest is one of the most developed in the United States. Roads are generally numerous and well maintained, and navigation is easy. Towns with services are plentiful (compared with the Wyoming plains to the west), so you needn't worry about how much gas you've got in your tank or where you'll find a place to stay at night. Rapid City, the largest community in the region, is the most popular base for exploration of the Black Hills. The northern towns of Deadwood and Spearfish, however, have almost as many services with less traffic and fewer tourists.

About the Restaurants

Like neighboring Wyoming, the Black Hills are not known for culinary diversity, and no matter where you go in this part of the world, beef is king. Nevertheless, thanks to a growing population and increasing numbers of visitors, the area is beginning to see more dining options. Rapid City and Spearfish have an abundance of national chain restaurants, and both communities have local eateries that specialize in Continental, contemporary, Native American, and traditional American cooking. Although dining in Deadwood's casinos usually involves an all-you-can-eat buffet, the tiny town also claims some of the best-ranked restaurants in South Dakota. Don't be afraid to try wild game dishes: buffalo, pheasant, and elk are relatively common ingredients in the Black Hills.

About the Hotels

New chain hotels with modern amenities are plentiful in the Black Hills, but when booking accommodations consider a stay at one of the area's historic properties. From grand brick downtown hotels to intimate Queen Anne homes converted to bed-and-breakfasts, historic lodgings are easy to locate. Many have been carefully restored to their late-19th-century grandeur, down to antique Victorian furnishings and authentic Western art. Other distinctive lodging choices include the region's mountain lodges and forest retreats. Usually built along creeks or near major trails, these isolated accommodations often attract outdoor enthusiasts.

	WHAT IT COSTS				
	$$$$	$$$	$$	$	¢
RESTAURANTS	over $22	$16–$22	$11–$16	$7–$11	under $7
HOTELS	over $220	$160–$220	$110–$160	$70–$110	under $70

Restaurant prices are for a main course at dinner, excluding sales tax of 4%–7%. Hotel prices are for two people in a standard double room in high season, excluding service charges and 5%–10% tax.

Timing

Weather forecasters hate the Black Hills. Snow can fall in the upper elevations every month of the year, while temperatures in January sometimes register above 60°F. However, anomalies like these rarely last more than a day or two. For the most part, expect the thermometer to range between 80°F and 100°F in summer, and know that winter temperatures can plunge below 10°F. Most visitors come in the warmer months from June to September, an optimal time for outdoor activities. Thanks to an average annual snowfall of 150 inches, more winter-sports enthusiasts are beginning to discover the area's skiing and snowmobiling opportunities. Nevertheless, the colder months are the least crowded in the Black Hills.

The shoulder seasons are nearly as unpopular as the winter months. This makes sense in spring, generally a snowy and rainy time of the year. Autumn, on the other hand, is the perfect time to visit the Black Hills. The days are pleasantly warm, the nights are cool, and if you arrive before mid-October you'll be treated to an incredible display of fall colors. Your only competition for space will be small groups of sportsmen and the occasional photographer out capturing images of colorful leaves.

DEADWOOD

❶ *42 mi northwest of Rapid City via I–90 and U.S. 14A.*

Fodor'sChoice Its brick-paved streets plied by old-time trolleys, illuminated by period
★ lighting, and lined with original Victorian architecture, Deadwood today owes much of its historical character to casinos. In 1989, South Dakota

Every small town in the Black Hills has something to offer—a fact that you may find surprising. In fact, this region has the highest concentration of parks, monuments, and memorials in the United States, qualifying the Black Hills and badlands as more than just a stopover on the way to and from the huge national parks of western Montana and Wyoming. If you have the time, your must-see list should go beyond Rapid City, Mount Rushmore, and Deadwood. Sure, you can see the highlights of southwesternmost South Dakota in 24 or 48 hours, but if you spend five days or more here you will be amply rewarded.

You might consider a top-down approach, first exploring the Northern Hills around Deadwood. The historic sites, scenery, and casinos will keep you busy, but don't be afraid to explore the hidden treasures of the outlying towns: The new Tri-State Museum in Belle Fourche, the High Plains Western Heritage Center in Spearfish, and the Homestake Visitor Center in Lead are all worth seeing. Afterward, you can move into the central Black Hills, spending some time in Rapid City to shop, check out the Journey Museum, and sample the local cuisine. Rapid City makes a good base for a day trip to nearby Mount Rushmore and Hill City, a tiny town with a vibrant art-gallery district and its own winery. When you've covered the central region, shift down to the southern hills and visit Wind Cave National Park, Crazy Horse Memorial, Jewel Cave National Monument, and the historic towns of Custer and Hot Springs—where naturally warm water still bubbles up from the earth. You can approach Badlands National Park to the east as a separate region if you have the time, or you might simply make it a day trip.

Spending a day in each subregion will allow you to explore most of the key attractions in the Black Hills. If you have time to spare, you will probably want to add the central and northern Black Hills, which are relatively densely populated and naturally offer more to see and do than the southern hills and badlands.

---

voters approved limited-stakes gaming for the town, on the condition that a portion of revenues be devoted to historic preservation. Since then, more than $170 million has been dedicated to restoring and preserving this once infamous gold-mining boomtown, which has earned recognition as a National Historic Landmark. Small gaming halls, good restaurants, and hotels occupy virtually every storefront on Main Street, just as they did back in Deadwood's late-19th-century heyday. You can walk in the footsteps of legendary lawman Wild Bill Hickok, cigar-smoking Poker Alice Tubbs, and the fabled Calamity Jane, who swore she could outdrink, outspit, and outswear any man—and usually did.

Several of the storefronts on **Main Street** belong to souvenir shops that typically peddle rubber tomahawks and plastic pistols to tourists. Some of the more upscale stores carry high-quality Western wear, Black Hills–gold jewelry, and fine art. Ice-cream parlors are never hard to find in summer.

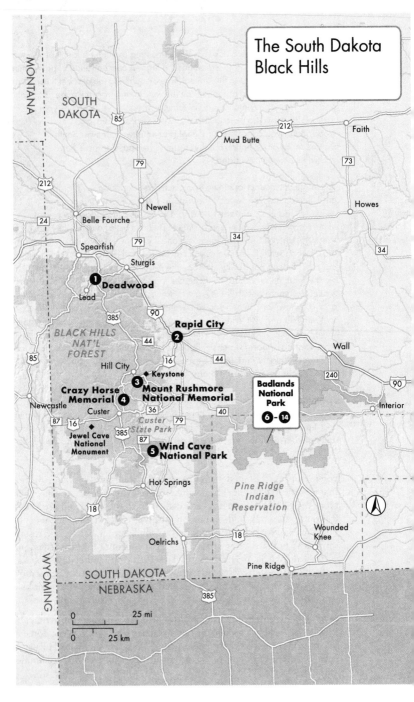

The South Dakota Black Hills

MONTANA

SOUTH DAKOTA

85

212   Faith

Mud Butte

79   73

24

212

Newell   Howes

Belle Fourche

79   34

Spearfish

Sturgis   34

1 Deadwood

Lead

385   90

Rapid City

2

BLACK HILLS
NAT'L
FOREST   44

Wall

85   16

44   240

Hill City

◆ Keystone

**3 Mount Rushmore
National Memorial**

90

**Crazy Horse
Memorial 4**

Badlands
National
Park   Interior

Newcastle   Custer

6 - 14

87 16   36   40

79

Jewel Cave
National
Monument   385

87   **Wind Cave
5 National Park**

Hot Springs   Pine Ridge
Indian
Reservation

18

Wounded
Knee

Oelrichs   18

WYOMING

SOUTH DAKOTA   Pine Ridge

NEBRASKA   385

0 ____ 25 mi

0 ____ 25 km

Exploring Deadwood

Because most of Deadwood was laid out before the advent of automobiles, the city today is entirely walkable. Strung in a roughly straight line along the bottom of a gulch, the main points of interest are difficult to miss. The best strategy is to park in one of the lots on Main or Sherman street and begin your pedestrian adventure from there.

TIMING   Deadwood's historical sites and museums require at least a full day, and a hiking or skiing excursion would take another entire day. If you plan to enjoy the saloons, card tables, and slot machines, add more time to your itinerary. Deadwood is especially popular in summer, which can make traffic and parking tricky; if you can, aim for a visit in early autumn, when the weather is still good and crowds have thinned.

The Main Attractions

A tour of the restored **Adams House Museum** includes an explanation of the tragedies and triumphs of two of the community's founding families (the Franklins and the Adamses) who lived here. The 1892 Queen Anne–style mansion was closed in the mid-1930s and sat empty for more than 50 years, preserving the original furniture and decor that you see today. ⊠ *22 Van Buren St.* ☎ *605/578–3724* ⊕ *www.adamsmuseumandhouse.org* ✉ *$5* ☉ *Memorial Day–Labor Day, Mon.–Sat. 9–6, Sun. noon–4; Labor Day–Memorial Day, Mon.–Sat. 10–3.*

☪ The **Adams Museum,** between the massive stone-block post office and the old railroad depot, houses three floors of displays that include the first locomotive used in the area, photographs of the town's early days, and a reproduction of the largest gold nugget (7¾ troy ounces) ever discovered in the Black Hills (the original is in the museum vault). ⊠ *54 Sherman St.* ☎ *605/578–1714* ⊕ *www.adamsmuseumandhouse.org* ✉ *Donations accepted* ☉ *Memorial Day–Labor Day, Mon.–Sat. 9–7, Sun. noon–5; Labor Day–Memorial Day, Mon.–Sat. 10–4.*

Mount Moriah Cemetery, also known as Boot Hill, is the final resting place of Wild Bill Hickok, Calamity Jane, and other notable Deadwood residents. The aging landmark was revitalized by extensive restoration work in 2003, including the addition of a visitor center that houses a leather Bible, stained-glass window, and pulpit chairs from the first and second Methodist churches of Deadwood that were destroyed in 1885 and 2003, respectively. From the top of the cemetery you'll have the best panoramic view of the town. ⊠ *Top of Lincoln St.* ☎ *605/722–0837* ✉ *$1* ☉ *Memorial Day–Labor Day, daily 7 AM–8 PM; Labor Day–end of Sept., daily 9–5.*

A heroic-scale bronze sculpture of three Native Americans on horseback driving 14 bison off a cliff is the centerpiece of **Tatanka: Story of the Bison,** on a ridge above Deadwood. The attraction, owned by *Dances with Wolves* star Kevin Costner, also includes an interpretive center with a re-enactment of a Lakota Sioux encampment and Lakota guides who explain Plains Indian life circa 1840. ⊠ *U.S. 85* ☎ *605/584–5678* ⊕ *www.storyofthebison.com* ✉ *$7.50* ☉ *Mid-May–Sept., daily 9–5.*

Also Worth Seeing

You can pan for gold and join guides on a journey into the **Broken Boot Gold Mine,** a remnant of Deadwood's early days. You may not find any gold, but if nothing else, you'll leave with a souvenir stock certificate. ⊠ *U.S. 14A* ☎ *605/578–9997* ✆ *Tour $5, gold panning $5* ⊙ *May–Aug., daily 8–5:30; Sept., daily 9–4:30.*

Before it closed in 2001, the Homestake Gold Mine was the deepest and the longest continually operating gold mine in the western hemisphere. The mine's history is preserved at the **Homestake Visitor Center,** where you can embark on a guided surface tour (in summer only) of the mine's remains and view the massive Open Cut, a giant man-made bowl nearly a mile long and 900 feet deep. Tours of the underground passages (which plunge more than 8,000 feet below the surface) are no longer offered, but the visitor center has several displays of historic mining equipment. ⊠ *160 W. Main St., Lead* ☎ *605/584–3110 or 888/701–0164* ✆ *$6* ⊙ *May–Aug., daily 8–6; Sept.–Apr., Mon.–Sat. 8:30–5.*

off the
beaten
path

HIGH PLAINS WESTERN HERITAGE CENTER – Founded to honor the pioneers and Indians of a region now covered by five states—the Dakotas, Wyoming, Montana, and Nebraska—the center features artifacts such as an original Deadwood-Spearfish stagecoach and life-size dioramas of an American cattle drive. Outdoor exhibits include a sod home, a log cabin, a one-room schoolhouse, herds of bison and longhorn steers, antique farm equipment and, in summer, an entire antique farm. Often on the calendar are cowboy poetry, live music, festivals, reenactments, talks on area ghost towns, and the Campfire Series of historical talks. ⊠ *825 Heritage Dr., Spearfish* ☎ *605/642–9378* ⊕ *www.westernheritagecenter.com* ✆ *$4* ⊙ *Daily 9–5.*

TRI-STATE MUSEUM – Artifacts of regional ranchers and pioneer families are showcased in this museum's interpretive exhibits. You can see historical photos and items from the everyday life of 19th-century homesteaders, such as dolls, clothing, and dinnerware. The museum occupies a spacious building near the bank of the Belle Fourche River. ⊠ *415 5th Ave., Belle Fourche* ☎ *605/723–1200* ⊕ *www.tristatemuseum.com* ✆ *Free* ⊙ *Mon.–Fri., 10–4, Sat. 10–2, Sun. 12–2.*

Sports & the Outdoors

Deadwood makes a good base for a winter sports vacation in the Black Hills, particularly if you like snowmobiling and cross-country skiing. The surrounding Northern Hills are especially popular, both for their stunning scenery and heavy snows. The rocky peaks and deep canyons are the most dramatic here, and the snowfall is the heaviest. In some years the area around Deadwood sees as much as 180 inches of the white stuff, although the yearly average hovers around 150 inches. However, the climate here is more variable than in the Rockies, so snow won't blanket the region all winter. Often a spell of 50°F, 60°F, or even 70°F weather will hit the region for a week or so after a big snowfall, quickly melting the fresh powder. Before you make firm plans, be sure to check weather reports.

The first week of August each year, the community of **Sturgis** becomes South Dakota's largest city when more than half a million motorcylists invade for the **Sturgis Motorcycle Rally** (✉ 13 mi east of Deadwood on U.S. 14 ☎ 605/720–0800 ⊕ www.sturgismotorcyclerally.com). Begun in 1940 by a handful of bike owners, the event has grown into one of the largest gatherings of Harley-Davidson owners in the world. Motorcycle shows, concerts, motorcycle tours, and national racing events are just some of the activities that fill this 10-day festival. Most hotels within a 100-mi radius are totally booked for the festival up to a year in advance.

Fishing

Custom Caster (✉ 21207 Thunder La., Lead, 8 mi southwest of Deadwood ☎ 605/584–2217) is a one-man operation that specializes in hand-tied flies and custom-made rods. Owner Dale Peters also sells name-brand rods and reels.

Hiking & Bicycling

The railroad didn't reach Deadwood until 1891, in part because of the narrow canyons and sharp grades of the northern Black Hills. Although the old tracks have since outlived their usefulness for trains, they still help people get around thanks to a rails-to-trails program.

Beginning in Deadwood and running the length of the Black Hills from north to south, the **Mickelson Trail** (⊕ www.ridethetrail.com) incorporates more than 100 converted railroad bridges and four tunnels in its 117-mi-long course. Although the grade seldom exceeds 4%, parts of the trail are strenuous. A $2 day pass lets you hike or bike on the trail ($10 for an annual pass); passes are available at self-service stations along the trail, some state park offices, and through the South Dakota Game, Fish, and Parks Web site (⊕ www.state.sd.us/gfp/). A portion of the trail is open for snowmobiling in winter.

Deadwood Bicycles (✉ 180 Sherman St. ☎ 605/578–1345), in a restored engine house at the beginning of the Mickelson Trail, provides bike sales, service, and rentals, including bikes for men, women, and children, plus tandems. There's also a modest selection of rock-climbing equipment.

Skiing

Heavy snowfalls and lovely views make the Black Hills prime cross-country skiing territory. Many trails are open to snowmobilers as well as skiers, so most skiers stick to the quieter trails closed to motorized traffic. Many of these trails run along the rim or at the bottom of narrow canyons and gulches, affording outstanding views of some spectacular country. Depending on the freeze-thaw cycle, you may catch a glimpse of frozen waterfalls, particularly in Spearfish Canyon.

Although the Black Hills don't have the massive peaks that give Colorado, Wyoming, and Montana some of the best downhill skiing in the world, a couple of rocky slopes in the Northern Hills are both steep enough and snowy enough to support modest ski resorts, with runs of respectable intermediate level.

The groomed **Big Hill Trails** (✉ 7 mi south of Spearfish on Tinton Rd., 15 mi west of Deadwood ☎ 605/673–9200) travel all around Spearfish Canyon. The trees here are gorgeous, ranging from the ubiquitous ponderosa and Black Hills spruce to quaking aspen and paperbark birch. The towering canyon walls, abundant wildlife, and stark contrast between the evergreens and the bare trees make this a particularly outstanding trail.

The runs at **Deer Mountain Ski Area** (✉ 3 mi south of Lead on U.S. 85 ☎ 605/717–0422 ⊕ www.skideermountain.com) aren't as challenging as those on nearby Terry Peak, but this slope has a massive beginner's area and the only night skiing in the Black Hills. There are also about 10 mi of groomed cross-country trails. Rentals, regular classes, and inexpensive personal lessons are available, and there's a modest lodge. Perched on the sides of a 7,076-foot mountain, **Terry Peak Ski Area** (✉ 2 mi south of Lead on U.S. 85 ☎ 605/584–2165 or 800/456–0524 ⊕ www.terrypeak.com) claims the second-highest mountain summit in the Black Hills. The runs here are challenging for novice and intermediate skiers and should at least keep the experts entertained. The view from the top is spectacular; on a clear day you can see into Wyoming, Montana, and North Dakota.

Skiers and snowboarders will find a good selection of equipment for sale or rent at **Terry Peak Ski and Sport** (✉ 2 mi south of Lead on U.S. 85 ☎ 605/584–3644 or 866/250–1606 ⊕ www.buymyskis.com), just outside the entrance to Terry Peak Ski Area. Skis, boards, boots and outdoor wear are all available here, typically at prices lower than those charged on the slopes.

Snowmobiling

Trade and travel magazines consistently rank the Black Hills among the top snowmobiling destinations in the country for two simple reasons: dramatic scenery and an abundance of snow. You'll find both throughout the area, but especially in the Northern Hills.

Trailshead Lodge (✉ 21 mi southwest of Deadwood on U.S. 85 ☎ 605/584–3464 ⊕ www.trailsheadlodge.com), near the Wyoming border, has a small restaurant, a bar, gas, a repair shop, and dozens of brand-new snowmobiles for rent by the day. In summer (or during warm spells in winter when the snow melts) the lodge caters to bicyclists, horseback riders, hunters, and hikers.

Where to Stay & Eat

★ **$$$–$$$$** ✕ **Jakes.** This restaurant owned by actor Kevin Costner is among South Dakota's best dining experiences. Cherrywood pillars inlaid with etched-glass lights, white-brick fireplaces, and a pianist add to the elegance of the atrium dining room. Among the menu's eclectic offerings are buffalo roulade, Cajun seafood tortellini, filet mignon, and fresh fish. ✉ 677 Main St. ☎ 605/578–1555 ⚑ Reservations essential 🖃 AE, D, DC, MC, V.

★ **$$–$$$$** ✕ **Deadwood Thymes Bistro.** Located across from the historic courthouse and post office buildings, away from the Main Street casinos, this has a quieter, more intimate feel than the other restaurants in town. That's just fine for owner and executive chef Mike Chaput, who's worked hard to create a European-style café. The food here is easily among the best in town. The menu changes frequently, but expect dishes like brioche French toast, salmon quiche, Parisian grilled ham and Swiss, Thai burrito with peanut sauce, and lamb chops marinated in white wine and mustard and served with parsley-gin sauce. The wine list features imports, and desserts are incredible. You might find raspberry cheesecake, chocolate angel food cake with a whiskey-bourbon sauce, or tiramisu. ⊠ *87 Sherman St.* ☎ *605/578–7566* ▤ *MC, V.*

★ **$–$$$** ✕ **Deadwood Social Club.** On the second floor of historic Saloon No. 10, this warm restaurant surrounds you with wood and old-time photographs of Deadwood's past. The decor is clearly Western, but the food is northern Italian, a juxtaposition that keeps locals and visitors coming back time and again. The menu stretches from wild-mushroom pasta-and-seafood nest with basil cream to chicken piccata and melt-in-your-mouth rib eyes. The ever-growing wine list had nearly 200 selections at last count. Reservations are a good idea. ⊠ *657 Main St.* ☎ *605/578–1533* ▤ *AE, MC, V.*

¢–$ ✕ **Moonshine Gulch Saloon.** Although 25 mi south of Deadwood in the middle of a very empty section of the forest, the ghost town of Rochford is worth visiting. Once the site of a prosperous gold camp, the town now has about 15 residents and even fewer buildings. The saloon (between the Rochford Mall, the self-proclaimed "Small of America," and one-room Rochford University) stays quite busy in the summer despite its remote location. After you order your sarsaparilla soda and hamburger, look up and admire the collection of baseball caps and currency on the ceiling. ⊠ *Rochford Rd., Rochford* ☎ *605/584–2743* ▤ *MC, V.*

$–$$ ✕🏠 **Bullock Hotel.** Built by Deadwood's first sheriff, Seth Bullock, in 1895, this pink granite hotel has been meticulously restored. Victorian reproduction furniture adorns the cozy lobby and bar, and the rooms are also decorated in a Victorian style. The suites have hot tubs. You can order a steak or hamburger at the casual and relaxed downstairs restaurant ($–$$$), complete with a period fireplace. ⊠ *633 Main St., 57732* ☎ *605/578–1745 or 800/336–1876* 🖷 *605/578–1382* ⊕ *www. historicbullock.com* ⮑ *29 rooms, 7 suites* ♻ *Restaurant, room service, some in-room hot tubs, cable TV with movies, bar, casino, business services, meeting rooms, no-smoking rooms* ▤ *AE, D, MC, V.*

$ ✕🏠 **Deadwood Gulch Resort.** Perched on the banks of Whitewood Creek where it bubbles steadily down into Deadwood, this family-style resort has a deck with a view of the hills. Although the resort is about a mile from downtown, trolleys run frequently to other hotels, casinos, and attractions closer to the main drag. The resort also has a casino of its own. The Creekside Restaurant ($–$$$) is decorated like an old saloon and serves hearty breakfasts and some of the best burgers in town. The giant salads here are also favorites, largely because of the side of sunflower bread and the homemade apricot dressing. ⊠ *U.S. 85, 57732* ☎ *605/578–1294 or 800/695–1876* 🖷 *605/578–2505* ⊕ *www. deadwoodgulch.com* ⮑ *98 rooms* ♻ *Restaurant, cable TV with movies,* *in-room data ports, pool, hot tub, snowmobiling, bar, casino, meeting rooms, no-smoking rooms* 🖃 *AE, D, DC, MC, V* 🍴 *BP.*

$ 🏨 **Franklin Hotel.** Built in 1903, the imposing Franklin Hotel has housed many famous guests in its time, including John Wayne, Teddy Roosevelt, and Kevin Costner. It still has its original banisters, ceilings, and fireplace. The guest rooms are Victorian style, with reproduction furniture, lace on hardwood tables, and flowery bedspreads. A bar on the second floor spills out onto the veranda above the white-columned hotel entrance, affording a great view down Main Street. The fabled Franklin reopened in spring 2006 following a major face-lift. ⊠ *700 Main St., 57732* 📞 *605/578–2241 or 800/688–1876* 📠 *605/578–3452* ⊕ *www. historicfranklinhotel.com* ↳ *81 rooms* △ *Room service, cable TV with movies, bar, casino, business services, meeting rooms, no-smoking rooms* 🖃 *AE, D, DC, MC, V.*

$$–$$$ 🏨 **Holiday Inn Express.** Although the exterior of this four-story building was built to resemble the much older brick facades of Deadwood's Main Street, the guest rooms are equipped with standard chain-hotel furnishings. Three suites have fireplaces and whirlpool tubs. ⊠ *22 Lee St., 57732* 📞 *605/578–3330 or 888/777–4465* 📠 *605/578–3335* ⊕ *www.ichotelsgroup.com* ↳ *78 rooms, 22 suites* △ *Cable TV with movies and video games, in-room data ports, indoor pool, gym, hot tub, casino, laundry facilities, meeting rooms, no-smoking rooms* 🖃 *AE, D, DC, MC, V* 🍴 *CP.*

$$–$$$ 🏨 **Mineral Palace.** As at the other hotels built in town since gaming was reintroduced in 1989, the architecture of Mineral Palace blends in with the historic buildings of Deadwood. The rooms have modern furnishings, but floral bedspreads, burgundy carpeting, and hardwood trim give them a slightly Victorian look. One deluxe suite has a hot tub and fireplace. ⊠ *601 Main St., 57732* 📞 *605/578–2036 or 800/847–2522* 📠 *605/578–2037* ⊕ *www.mineralpalace.com* ↳ *57 rooms, 6 suites* △ *Restaurant, room service, some in-room hot tubs, cable TV with movies and video games, in-room data ports, bar, laundry facilities, business services, meeting rooms; no smoking* 🖃 *AE, D, MC, V.*

$$–$$$ 🏨 **Spearfish Canyon Lodge.** Located about midway between Spearfish and Deadwood, near the bottom of Spearfish Canyon, this lodge-style hotel commands some of the best views in the Black Hills. Limestone cliffs rise nearly 1,000 feet in all directions. The rush of Spearfish Falls is only a ¼-mi hike away, while the gentle flow of Roughlock Falls is a mi-long hike through pine, oak, and aspen from the lodge's front door. The rooms are furnished in natural woods, and fabrics are dark maroon and green. It's especially popular for weddings. ⊠ *10619 Roughlock Falls Rd., Lead 57754* 📞 *877/975–6343 or 605/584–3435* 📠 *605/584–3990* ⊕ *www.spfcanyon. com* ↳ *54 rooms* △ *Restaurant, room service, some in-room hot tubs, cable TV with movies, in-room data ports, bar, laundry facilities, business services, meeting rooms; no smoking* 🖃 *AE, D, MC, V.*

Nightlife

There are more than 80 gaming establishments in Deadwood, most of them small and personal. They generally serve other functions as well—as restaurants, saloons, gift shops—and have only a few blackjack and poker tables and slot machines. That means you can easily amuse yourself once you've dropped your last quarter.

Live rock bands play in the bars on weekends, actors portray Wild West characters outside the hotels during the day, and comedians do their schtick from time to time in the restaurants.

Expect a family crowd in the day and a rowdier bunch at night at the **Bodega and Big Al's Buffalo Steakhouse Stockade** (⊠ 658 Main St. ☎ 605/578–1300). Most evenings you can listen to live country or rock music; the entertainment moves outdoors in summer, when bands play in the stockade section. The Bodega has a rough past; from the 1890s up until 1980, the upper floors were used as a brothel. The rooms now sit empty, although the secret buzzers and discreet back doors were only removed in the 1990s. It doesn't offer live music, but the casino **Midnight Star** (⊠ 677 Main St. ☎ 605/578–1555) is owned by actor Kevin Costner and decorated throughout with props and costumes from his movies. The bar on the first floor is named for and modeled after the bar in the film *Silverado,* in which Costner starred. Wood accents, stained glass, and plush carpeting give the structure an elegant Victorian look.

★ Billing itself as a "museum with a bar," the **Old Style Saloon No. 10** (⊠ 657 Main St. ☎ 605/578–3346) is littered with thousands of artifacts, from vintage photos and antique lighting to a stuffed two-headed calf and the chair in which Wild Bill Hickok was supposedly shot. A reenactment of his murder takes place four times daily in the summer. At night, come for some of the region's best bands, lively blackjack tables, and quiet bartenders who cater to noisy customers. The **Silverado** (⊠ 709 Main St. ☎ 605/578–1366 or 800/584–7005), sprawling over half a city block at the top of Main Street, is among Deadwood's largest gaming establishments. Although the wood paneling and brass accents around the bars recall Deadwood's Wild West past, the red carpets, velvet ropes, and bow tie-clad staff give the place modern polish. The prime rib-and-crab buffet on Friday and Saturday nights attracts regulars from more than 100 mi away.

en route   The easiest way to get from Deadwood to Rapid City and the central Black Hills is east through Boulder Canyon on U.S. 14A, which joins I–90 in Sturgis. However, it's worth looping north and taking the long way around on **Spearfish Canyon Scenic Byway,** a 20-mi route past 1,000-foot limestone cliffs and some of the most breathtaking scenery in the region. Cascading waterfalls quench the thirst of quaking aspen, gnarled oaks, sweet-smelling spruce, and the ubiquitous ponderosa pine, which grow right off the edges of rocky precipices. The canyon is home to deer, mountain goats, porcupines, and bobcats. Near its middle is the old sawmill town of Savoy, a jumping-off point for scenic hikes to Spearfish Falls and Roughlock Falls. The canyon opens onto the small city of Spearfish and its several restaurants, hotels, and Black Hills State University.

BLACK HILLS BOOMS & BUSTS

LIKE MANY MOUNTAIN RANGES in the American West, the Black Hills were settled only after a glint of gold winked at a prospector. That prospector didn't show up in southwestern South Dakota until 1874, largely because the small Black Hills mountain range lay at the center of the Great Sioux Indian Reservation.

Established by the 1868 Treaty of Fort Laramie, the reservation was intended to be the home of the Lakota Sioux for time immemorial. An illegal expedition by George Armstrong Custer and his Seventh Cavalry, however, turned up gold near present-day Custer State Park that fateful day in 1874. White men quickly wrested the sacred land known to the Lakota as the Paha Sapa (literally "Hills Black") from their hands, and white settlers and gold-seekers soon overran the last unexplored region of the United States.

Deadwood, Past & Present

A bigger gold strike in 1876 sent thousands of people northward, where brand-new Deadwood suddenly became the largest settlement in the state. Legends like Wild Bill Hickok, Calamity Jane, and Seth Bullock lived and died here. Gold, gambling, and prostitution fueled Deadwood's economy for years, until each profit source was depleted or shut down. When legalized gaming returned to the Black Hills in 1989, the huge revenues transformed Deadwood into one of the largest ongoing historic preservation projects in the United States. The city's brick-paved Main Street, complete with period lights and stone Victorian facades, appears much as it did back in the 1890s.

Making Mount Rushmore

As mining faded, tourism supplanted it as the dominant industry in the Black Hills. With the backing of state leaders, sculptor Gutzon Borglum began carving the four presidential heads of Mount Rushmore in 1927. Eighty percent of the sculpture was "carved" with dynamite in 14 years of dusty work. All told, the memorial cost about $1 million to carve (compared with $56 million to improve visitor facilities at the turn of the 21st century).

Almost as soon as it was completed in 1941, Mount Rushmore became the second-biggest visitor draw—after Yellowstone National Park—in four states; in 2005 it attracted 2.8 million visitors. They boosted businesses at privately operated attractions nearby, such as the Depression-era Reptile Gardens and the Wall Drug Store, famed for its free ice water. The establishment of other national and state parks, including Jewel Cave National Monument, Badlands National Park, and Custer State Park, further fueled the development of the tourism industry.

Digging Deep

Nevertheless, mining and timber remained important parts of the local economy. Opened in 1876 in Deadwood's sister city, Lead, the Homestake Gold Mine became the longest-operating gold mine in North America. When the mine finally closed in 2001, its main shaft was more than 8,000 feet deep, making it the deepest in the world. Its new owner, the State of South Dakota, is developing a temporary scientific laboratory in the underground passages, where sensitive experiments will be shielded from cosmic rays. The goal is to persuade the National Science Foundation to build a permanent, federally funded facility that will spur high-tech industry in the area.

MOUNT RUSHMORE & THE BLACK HILLS

The central Black Hills, one of the most developed and best-traveled parts of the region, is anchored by Rapid City. The largest population center in a 350-mi radius, it's the cultural, educational, medical, and economic hub of a vast region. Most of the numerous shops, hotels, and restaurants in the city cater specifically to tourists, including a steady flow of international visitors; some signage displays information in multiple languages and the metric system. A four-lane highway, U.S. 16, links the city to Mount Rushmore National Memorial, the massive mountain tribute to four American presidents.

Rapid City

➋ *42 mi southeast of Deadwood via U.S. 14A and I–90.*

A good base from which to explore the Black Hills, South Dakota's second-largest city (population 60,876) is a cross between a progressive 21st-century city and a Western town. Locals refer to Rapid City as "West River," meaning west of the Missouri. Cowboy boots are common here, and business leaders often travel by pickup truck or four-wheel-drive vehicle. At the same time, the city supports a convention center and a modern, acoustically advanced performance hall.

★ The **Journey Museum** combines the collections of the **Sioux Indian Museum,** the **Minnilusa Pioneer Museum,** the **Museum of Geology,** the **State Archaeological Research Center,** and a private collection of Native American artifacts into a sweeping pageant of the history and evolution of the Black Hills. A favorite among visitors is the tepee in the Sioux Indian Museum; you have to crouch down and peer inside to watch a holographic Lakota woman talk about the history and legends of her people. ✉ *222 New York St.* ☎ *605/394–6923* ⊕ *www.journeymuseum. org* 🎫 *$7* ☉ *Memorial Day–Labor Day, daily 9–5; Labor Day–Memorial Day, Mon.–Sat. 10–5, Sun. 1–5.*

The **South Dakota Air & Space Museum** has a model of a Stealth bomber that's 60% actual size. Also here are General Dwight D. Eisenhower's Mitchell B-25 bomber and more than two dozen other planes, as well as a once-operational missile silo. The museum is open year-round, but tours are not available in winter. ✉ *2890 Davis Dr.* ☎ *605/385–5188* 🎫 *Free, tour $5* ☉ *Mid-May–mid-Sept., daily 8:30–6; mid-Sept.–mid-May, daily 8:30–4:30.*

Although they were released in the early 1990s, the films *Dances with Wolves* and *Thunderheart* continue to generate interest and business in the Black Hills. The **Ft. Hays Dances with Wolves Movie Set** displays photos and shows a video taken during the making of the film. A chuck-wagon dinner show ($15) is offered Memorial Day through Labor Day. ✉ *Ft. Hays Dr. and U.S. 16* ☎ *605/394–9653* ⊕ *www.rushmoretours.com/ forthays.html* 🎫 *Free* ☉ *Mid-May–mid-Sept., daily 7:30 AM–8 PM.*

☾ On the west side of Rapid City is **Storybook Island,** a park on the banks of Rapid Creek that lets children romp through scenes from fairy tales and nursery rhymes. A children's theater troupe, sponsored by the Black Hills Community Theater, performs regular shows on a modest outdoor stage here and hosts workshops and acting programs. ⊠ *1301 Sheridan Lake Rd.* ☎ *605/342–6357* ⊕ *www.storybookisland.org* ✉ *Donations accepted* ☉ *May–Sept., daily 9–7.*

★ ☾ **Reptile Gardens,** on the bottom of a valley between Rapid City and Mount Rushmore, is western South Dakota's answer to a zoo. In addition to the world's largest private reptile collection, the site also has a raptor rehabilitation center. Birds that cannot be rereleased into the wild are used in educational shows, as are many reptile species. No visit here is complete without watching some alligator wrestling or letting the kids ride the giant tortoises. ⊠ *8955 S. U.S. 16* ☎ *605/342–5873* ⊕ *www.reptilegardens.com* ✉ *$12.50* ☉ *Apr.–Oct., daily 8–7.*

☾ At the drive-through wildlife park **Bear Country U.S.A.,** you encounter black bears, wolves, and other North American wildlife. There's also a walk-through wildlife center with bear cubs, wolf pups, and other offspring. ⊠ *13820 S. U.S. 16* ☎ *605/343–2290* ⊕ *www.bearcountryusa.com* ✉ *$12* ☉ *May–Oct., daily 8–6.*

Sports & the Outdoors

The Black Hills are filled with tiny mountain creeks, especially on the wetter western and northern slopes, that are ideal for fly-fishing. Rapid Creek, which flows down from the Central Hills into Pactola Reservoir and finally into Rapid City, is a favorite fishing venue for the city's anglers, both because of its regularly stocked population of trout and for its easy accessibility (don't be surprised to see someone standing in the creek casting a line as you drive through the center of town on Highway 44). Also popular are nearby Spearfish, Whitewood, Spring, and French creeks, all within an hour's drive of Rapid City.

Although they'll take you on a guided fly-fishing trip any time of the year, the folks at **Dakota Angler and Outfitter** (⊠ *513 7th St.* ☎ *605/341–2450*) recommend fishing between April and October. The guides lead individuals and groups on half- and full-day excursions, and they cater to all skill levels.

Where to Stay & Eat

$$–$$$$ ✕ **Firehouse Brewing Company.** Brass fixtures and firefighting equipment ornament the state's first brewpub, in a 1915 firehouse. The five house-brewed beers are the highlight here, and the menu includes such hearty pub dishes as pastas, salads, and gumbo. Thursday nights buffalo prime rib is the specialty. Kids' menus are available. ⊠ *610 Main St.* ☎ *605/348–1915* ⚲ *Reservations not accepted* ▭ *AE, D, DC, MC, V* ☉ *No lunch Sun.*

$$$ ✕ **Fireside Inn Restaurant & Lounge.** One of the two dining rooms here has tables arranged around a slate fireplace; you can also dine on an outdoor deck, weather permitting. The menu offers more than 50 entrées, including prime rib, seafood, and Italian dishes. ⊠ *Hwy. 44, 6½ mi west of town* ☎ *605/342–3900* ▭ *AE, D, DC, MC, V.*

$–$$$ ✕ **Botticelli Ristorante Italiano.** With a wide selection of delectable veal and chicken dishes as well as creamy pastas, this Italian eatery provides a welcome respite from the traditional Midwestern meat and potatoes. The artwork and traditional Italian music in the background give the place a European air. ☒ *523 Main St.* ☎ *605/348–0089* ▤ *AE, MC, V.*

$–$$$ ✕ **Minerva's.** A pub and pool room complement this spacious restaurant next to hotels and the city's largest shopping mall. Specialties include linguine Minerva (chicken breast served on linguine with pesto, vegetables, pine nuts, and a cream sauce), rotisserie chicken, and a scrumptious rib eye with grilled onions and new potatoes. ☒ *2111 N. LaCrosse St.* ☎ *605/394–9505* ▤ *AE, D, DC, MC, V.*

$$$ ✕ **Flying T Chuckwagon.** Ranch-style meals of barbecued beef, grilled chicken, potatoes, and baked beans are served on tin plates in this converted barn. Dinner, served between 5 and 6:30, is followed by a Western show with music and cowboy comedy. The prix fixe includes dinner and the show. In summer it's a good idea to buy tickets in advance. ☒ *U.S. 16, 6 mi south of town* ☎ *605/342–1905 or 888/256–1905* ⊕ *www. flyingt.com* ▤ *MC, V* ☉ *Closed mid-Sept.–mid-May. No lunch.*

$ ✕ **Golden Phoenix.** Great food, low prices, convenient parking, and re-

Fodor'sChoice laxed, friendly, and quick service make this one of South Dakota's best

★ Chinese restaurants. The chef-owner, who often socializes with the locals who frequent his establishment, spices up traditional dishes from all over China with cooking elements from his native Taiwan. Try the Mongolian beef, sesame chicken, or Hunan shrimp. Local businesspeople crowd in for the daily lunch specials. ☒ *2421 W. Main St.* ☎ *605/348– 4195* ▤ *AE, D, DC, MC, V.*

★ $–$$ ✕🏨 **Alex Johnson Hotel and Landmark Restaurant.** Native American motifs and artwork predominate at this landmark hotel dedicated to the Lakota peoples. The hotel opened in 1928, and rooms have reproductions of their original furniture. A torch chandelier in the lobby is made of Lakota war lances. The Landmark Restaurant ($$$$) is popular for its lunch buffet and for such dinner specialties as prime rib, beef Wellington, freshwater fish, and wild game. ☒ *523 6th St., 57701* ☎ *605/342–1210 or 800/ 888–2539* ⊕ *www.alexjohnson.com* ➥ *143 rooms, 2 suites* ⚏ *Restaurant, room service, cable TV with movies, bar, shop, business services, meeting rooms, no-smoking rooms* ▤ *AE, D, DC, MC, V.*

$$–$$$$ 🏨 **Radisson Hotel Rapid City/Mount Rushmore.** Murals of the surrounding landscape and a large Mount Rushmore mosaic in the marble floor distinguish the lobby of this nine-floor hotel in the heart of downtown Rapid City. Decorated in gold and beige, the rooms here are unremarkable, with one exception: most feature Sleep Number beds, whose comfort level can be adjusted by users. The popular accommodation stands between the interstate and U.S. 16, the highway that leads into the southern Black Hills and Mount Rushmore. ☒ *445 Mt. Rushmore Rd., 57701* ☎ *605/348–8300* 🖷 *605/348–3833* ⊕ *www.radisson.com/ rapidcitysd* ➥ *176 rooms, 5 suites* ⚏ *Cable TV with movies, indoor pool, gym, hair salon, shop, business services, meeting rooms, Wi-Fi, no-smoking rooms* ▤ *AE, D, DC, MC, V.*

★ $$–$$$ 🏨 **Audrie's Bed & Breakfast.** Victorian antiques and the hint of romance greet you at this out-of-the-way B&B, set in a thick woods 7 mi west of Rapid City. Suites, cottages, and creek-side cabins sleeping two come with old-world furnishings, fireplaces, private baths, hot tubs, and big-screen TVs. Bicycles and fishing poles can be obtained free from the office. ⊠ *23029 Thunderhead Falls Rd., 57702* ☏ *605/342–7788* ⊕ *www. audriesbb.com* ⇨ *2 suites, 7 cottages and cabins* ⚹ *Some in-room hot tubs, cable TV with movies, fishing, bicycles, shop; no kids, no smoking* ▤ *No credit cards* |◯| *BP.*

$–$$ ▣ **Holiday Inn Rushmore Plaza.** This eight-story hotel has a central lobby with an atrium, glass elevators, and a 60-foot waterfall. Rooms are generally spacious, decorated in warm tones of red, gold, and oak. Located in the parking lot of the Rushmore Plaza Civic Center, it often fills up for major events at the facility, such as the Black Hills Stock Show and Rodeo or the Sturgis Motorcycle Rally. Be sure to book ahead. ⊠ *505 N. 5th St., 57701* ☏ *605/348–4000* ☖ *605/348–9777* ⊕ *www. holidayinnrapidcity.com* ⇨ *205 rooms, 1 suite* ⚹ *Restaurant, room service, cable TV with movies, indoor pool, gym, hot tub, sauna, bar, business services, meeting rooms; no smoking* ▤ *AE, D, DC, MC, V* |◯| *CP.*

CAMPING ⚠ **Whispering Pines Campground and Lodging.** Block party–style cookouts are followed by movies every night here as long as the weather is good. Located 16 mi west of Rapid City in Black Hills National Forest, the campground lies exactly midway between Deadwood (22 mi to the north) and Mount Rushmore (22 mi to the south). In addition to RV and tent sites, cabins are available at a reasonable price. ⚹ *Flush toilets, full hookups, partial hookups (electric and water), dump station, drinking water, guest laundry, showers, fire pits, picnic tables, food service, electricity, public telephone, general store, play area, swimming (lake)* ⇨ *26 full hookups, 2 partial hookups, 45 tent sites; 5 cabins* ⊠ *22700 Silver City Rd.* ☏ *605/341–3667* ☖ *605/341–3667* ✉ *$15 tent sites, $20 partial hookups, $22 full hookups, $33–$40 cabins* ⚹ *Reservations essential* ▤ *D, MC, V* ☉ *May–Sept.*

The Arts

At the **Dahl Fine Arts Center** (⊠ 713 7th St. ☏ 605/394–4101), across from the downtown Rapid City Public Library, exhibits by local artists rotate regularly, but there is one permanent piece: a 180-foot oil-on-canvas mural depicting United States economic history from the colonization by the Europeans to the 1970s. The Black Hills Community Theater performs in the modest theater here on a regular basis.

The technically and architecturally advanced **Rushmore Plaza Civic Center Fine Arts Theater** (⊠ 444 Mt. Rushmore Rd. N. ☏ 800/468–6463) hosts about a half-dozen touring Broadway shows in winter. It's also the venue for the Vucurevich Speaker Series, a program that has attracted prominent names such as the humorist Dave Barry, the late astronomer Carl Sagan, and former Secretary of State Colin Powell.

Shopping

One of the world's top collections of Plains Indian artwork and crafts makes **Prairie Edge Trading Company and Galleries** (⊠ 6th and Main Sts. ☏ 605/342–3086 or 800/541–2388) seem more like a museum than a store and gallery. With a collection ranging from books and CDs to artifact reproductions and artwork representing the Lakota, Crow, Cheyenne, Shoshone, Arapaho, and Assiniboin tribes of the Great Plains, Prairie Edge is one of the crown jewels of downtown Rapid City.

Mount Rushmore National Memorial

❸ *24 mi southwest of Rapid City via U.S. 16 and U.S. 16A.*

Fodor'sChoice
★

At Mount Rushmore, one of the nation's most famous sights, 60-foot-high likenesses of Presidents George Washington, Thomas Jefferson, Abraham Lincoln, and Theodore Roosevelt grace a massive granite cliff, which, at an elevation of 5,725 feet, towers over the surrounding countryside and faces the sun most of the day. The memorial is equally spectacular at night in June through mid-September, when a special lighting ceremony dramatically illuminates the carving.

Sculptor Gutzon Borglum began carving Mount Rushmore in 1927 and, with the help of some 400 assistants, almost finished it in 1941. In consultation with U.S. Senator Peter Norbeck and State Historian Doane Robinson, Borglum chose the four presidents to signify the birth, growth, preservation, and development of the nation. In six and a half years of carving over a 14-year period, the sculptor and his crew drilled and dynamited a masterpiece, the largest work of art on earth. Borglum died in March, 1941, leaving his son, Lincoln, to complete the work only a few months later.

Follow the Presidential Trail through the forest to gain excellent views of the colossal sculpture, or stroll the Avenue of Flags for a different perspective. Also on-site are an impressive museum, indoor theaters where films are shown, an outdoor amphitheater for live performances, and concession facilities. The nightly ranger program and lighting of the memorial is reportedly the most popular program in all of the national parks system.

The **Mount Rushmore Information Center,** between the park entrance and the Avenue of Flags, has a small exhibit with photographs of the presidents' faces as they were being carved. There's also an information desk here, staffed by rangers who can answer questions about the memorial or the surrounding Black Hills. A nearly identical building across from the information center houses restrooms, telephones, and soda machines. ⊠ *Beginning of Ave. of Flags* ☎ *605/574–2523* ⊕ *www.nps. gov/moru* ⊡ *Free; parking $8* ☉ *May–Sept., daily 8 AM–10 PM; Oct.–Apr., daily 8–5.*

The **Avenue of Flags,** which runs from the entrance of the memorial to the museum and amphitheater at the base of the mountain, represents each state, commonwealth, district, and territory of the United States. Waving from granite posts on both sides of the walkway, the flags are in alphabetical order and have engravings at their base listing the date of admittance to the Union.

Underneath the viewing platform and at the top of the amphitheater is the **Lincoln Borglum Museum,** a giant granite-and-glass structure with permanent exhibits on the carving of the mountain, its history, and its significance. Also here are a bookstore, a theater that shows an orientation film, and an area for temporary exhibits. ⊠ *End of Ave. of Flags* ☎ *605/574–3165* ⊡ *Free* ☉ *Apr. and May, daily 8–7; June–Sept., daily 8 AM–10 PM; Oct.–Mar., daily 8–5.*

Running around the Lincoln Borglum Museum toward the Mount Rushmore carving is the **Presidential Trail** (⊠ near Lincoln Borglum Museum), an easy hike along a boardwalk and down some stairs to the very base of the mountain. Although the trail is thickly forested, you'll have more than ample opportunity to look straight up the noses of the four giant heads.

Built in 1939 as Gutzon Borglum's on-site workshop, the **Sculptor's Studio** displays tools used by the mountain carvers, a $\frac{1}{12}$ scale model of the memorial, and a model depicting the unfinished Hall of Records. Borglum intended the Hall of Records to be a storehouse for documents that would explain the mountain carving to any future archaeologists. He died before he could complete the chamber, however. An incomplete version of the hall, behind the heads at the top of the mountain, was sealed in 1998. ⊠ *¼ mi from Lincoln Borglum Museum* ⊡ *Free* ☉ *May–Sept., daily 9–6.*

Founded in the 1880s by prospectors searching the central Black Hills for gold deposits, the small town of **Keystone** (⊠ U.S. 16A ☎ 605/666–4896 or 800/456–3345) now serves the millions of visitors who pass through here each year on their way to Mount Rushmore, 2 mi away. The touristy town has some 700 hotel rooms—more than twice the number of permanent residents. Its 19th-century buildings house dozens of gift shops, restaurants, and attractions that range from wax museums and miniature golf courses to alpine slides and helicopter rides.

Where to Stay & Eat

$$–$$$$ ✕ **Creekside Dining.** Dine on very good American cuisine at this casual Keystone restaurant with a patio view of Mount Rushmore. Chef Bear's finest dishes are the hearty platters of prime rib, buffalo, lamb, chicken, and fish. The desserts, which include bread pudding, crème brûlée, and peach cobbler, are also excellent. A kids' menu is available. ⊠ *610 U.S. 16A, Keystone* ☎ *605/666–4904* ⊟ *MC, V* ☉ *Closed Nov.–May.*

★ ¢–$ ✕ **Buffalo Dining Room.** The only restaurant within the bounds of the memorial affords commanding views of Mount Rushmore and the surrounding ponderosa pine forest, and exceptional food at a reasonable price. The menu includes New England pot roast, buffalo stew, and homemade rhubarb pie. You can choose to end your meal with a "monumental bowl of ice cream." ⊠ *Beginning of Ave. of Flags* ☎ *605/574–2515* ⊟ *AE, D, MC, V* ☉ *No dinner mid-Oct.–early Mar.*

$–$$$ ⬚ **Roosevelt Inn.** This midsize inn less than 1 mi from the east entrance of Mount Rushmore is one of the closest hotels to the "faces" (although you cannot see them from the inn itself). Standard motel-style furnishings fill the rooms, some of which have balconies. Mountain-view rooms are especially inviting in autumn. ⊠ *206 Old Cemetery Rd., Keystone 57751* ☎ *605/666–4599 or 800/257–8923* ⊟ *605/666–4535* ⊕ *www.rosyinn.com* ⬚ *21 rooms* ⬚ *Restaurant, cable TV, indoor pool, hot tub; no smoking* ⊟ *AE, MC, V* ⦿ *CP.*

$$ ⬚ **Buffalo Rock Lodge B&B.** A large, native-rock fireplace surrounded by hefty logs adds to the rustic quality of this lodge decorated with Western artifacts. There's an extensive view of Mount Rushmore from an oversize deck surrounded by a plush pine forest filled with wildflowers. ✉ *Playhouse Rd., Box 641, Keystone 57751* ☎ *605/666–4781 or 888/564–5634* ⊕ *buffalorock.net* ➭ *3 rooms* ♨ *In-room hot tubs, fishing, hiking, some pets allowed; no smoking, no room TVs* ▭ *DC, MC, V* ⓧ *CP.*

$–$$ ⚏ **Best Western Four Presidents.** In the shadow of Mount Rushmore in downtown Keystone, the hotel lies within walking distance of the town's major attractions, including several restaurants. Short pack tours into the hills by horseback can be arranged next door. ✉ *U.S. 16A, Keystone 57751* ☎ *605/666–4472* ⊞ *605/666–4574* ⊕ *www.bestwestern.com* ➭ *45 rooms, 5 suites* ♨ *Room service, some in-room hot tubs, microwaves, cable TV with movies, indoor pool, gym, laundry facilities, business services; no smoking* ▭ *AE, D, DC, MC, V* ⊙ *All but 3 rooms closed Nov.–Apr.* ⓧ *CP.*

Shopping

The **Mount Rushmore Bookstore** (✉ Lincoln Borglum Museum, end of Ave. of Flags ☎ 800/699–3142) carries a selection of books, CDs, and videos on the memorial, its history, and the entire Black Hills region. There are also some titles on geology and Native American history. The **Mount Rushmore Gift Shop** (✉ Beginning of Ave. of Flags ☎ 605/574–2515), across from the Buffalo Dining Room, hawks any number of souvenirs, from shot glasses and magnets to T-shirts and baseball caps. You can also buy Black Hills–gold jewelry and Native American art.

en route   The fastest way to get from Mount Rushmore to Crazy Horse Memorial and the southern Black Hills is along Highway 244 west and U.S. 16/U.S. 385 south. This route, like all of the drives in the Black Hills, is full of beautiful mountain views, but the **Peter Norbeck National Scenic Byway** is an even more stunning, though much longer, route. Take U.S. 16A south into Custer State Park, where buffalo, bighorn sheep, elk, antelope, and burros roam free, then drive north on Highway 87 through the Needles, towering granite spires that rise above the forest. A short drive off the highway reaches 7,242-foot Harney Peak, the highest point in North America east of the Rockies. Highway 87 finally brings you to U.S. 16/U.S. 385, where you head south to the Crazy Horse Memorial. Because the scenic byway is a challenging drive (with one-lane tunnels and switchbacks) and because you'll likely want to stop a few times to admire the scenery, plan on spending two to three hours on this drive. Note that stretches of U.S. 16A and Highway 87 may close in winter.

Crazy Horse Memorial

❹   *15 mi southwest of Mount Rushmore National Memorial via Hwy. 244*
FodorśChoice *and U.S. 16.*
★

Designed to be the world's largest sculpture (641 feet long by 563 feet high), the tribute to Crazy Horse, the legendary Lakota leader who defeated General Custer at Little Bighorn, is a work in progress. So far the warrior's head has been carved out of the mountain, and the head of his horse is starting to emerge; when work is underway you can expect to witness frequent blasting. Self-taught sculptor Korczak Ziolkowski conceived this memorial to Native American heritage in 1948, and after his death in 1982 his family took on the project. The completion date is unknown, since activity is limited by weather and funding. Near the work site stands a very good orientation center, the Indian Museum of North America, Korczak's studio/home and workshop, indoor and outdoor sculpture galleries, and a restaurant. ☎ *605/673–4681* ⊕ *www.crazyhorse.org* ✉ *$10 per adult or $24 per carload for more than 2 adults* ⊙ *May–Sept., daily 8 AM–9 PM; Oct.–Apr., daily 8–4:30.*

When Ziolkowski agreed to carve Crazy Horse, he determined that he wouldn't stop with the mountain. He wanted an educational institution to sit at the base of the mountain, complete with a center showcasing examples of Native American culture and heritage. The construction in 1972 of the **Indian Museum of North America,** built from wood and stone blasted from the mountain, was the initial step in that direction. The permanent collection of paintings, clothing, photographs, and artifacts represents many of the continent's tribes. There is also a space for temporary exhibits that often showcases works by modern Native American artists. ⊠ *Ave. of the Chiefs* ☎ *605/673–4681* ✉ *Free* ⊙ *May–Sept., daily 8 AM–9 PM; Oct.–Apr., daily 8–4:30.*

off the beaten path

CUSTER STATE PARK – Down the road less traveled, in 71,000-acre Custer State Park, scenic backcountry is watered by crisp, clear trout streams. Elk, antelope, deer, mountain goat, bighorn sheep, mountain lion, wild turkey, prairie dog, and the second-largest (behind the one in Yellowstone National Park) publicly owned herd of bison in the world walk the pristine land. Some of the most scenic drives in the country roll past finger-like granite spires and panoramic views. Each year at the Buffalo Roundup and Arts Festival, thousands of spectators watch the park's 1,450 bison thunder through the hills at the start of a Western-themed art and food expo. ⊠ *U.S. 16A, 4 mi east of Custer* ☎ *605/255–4515* ⊕ *www.custerstatepark.info* ✉ *$2.50–$23* ⊙ *Year-round.*

JEWEL CAVE NATIONAL MONUMENT – The strange beauty of the crystal-lined caverns of Jewel Cave prompted the federal government to make it a national monument in 1908. So huge is the cave—it's the second-longest cave in the world, behind Kentucky's Mammoth Cave—that only an estimated 5% of its length has been mapped. Wander the dark passageways, and you will be rewarded with the sight of tiny crystal Christmas trees, hydromagnesite balloons that would pop if you touched them, and delicate calcite deposits dubbed "cave popcorn." Year-round, you can take ranger-led tours, from a simple half-hour walk to a lantern-light or wild caving tour. Above ground, the cave entrance and ponderosa forest provide superb habitat for several species of bats. ⊠ *U.S. 16, 15 mi west of Custer* ☎ *605/673–2288* ⊕ *www.nps.gov/jeca* ✉ *$4–$27* ⊙ *Sept.–Apr., daily 8–4:30; May–Aug., daily 8–7.*

Where to Stay & Eat

$–$$ ✕ Laughing Water Restaurant. This airy pine restaurant with windows facing the mountain sculpture is noted for its fry bread and buffalo burgers. There's a soup-and-salad bar, but you'd do well to stick to the Native American offerings; try the Indian taco or "buffaloski" (a Polish-style sausage made with Dakota buffalo). A kids' menu is available. ⊠ *Ave. of the Chiefs* ☎ *605/673–4681* ☰ *AE, D, MC, V* ☉ *Closed Nov.–Apr.*

$–$$$$ ✕🏨 State Game Lodge and Resort. Once the summer White House for Presidents Coolidge and Eisenhower, this stately stone-and-wood lodge in Custer State Park has well-appointed rooms and isolated pine-shaded cabins, many right on the banks of a creek. The cabins are simple and spartan, the motel rooms are comfortable, and the lodge rooms are almost stately, with elegant hardwood furniture and massive stone fireplaces. The menu at the excellent, upscale Pheasant Dining Room ($$–$$$$) is varied; the place is known for pheasant and buffalo specialties. In addition to a salad bar and lunch buffet, there's a kids' menu. ⊠ *16 mi east of Custer on U.S. 16A* 🏠 *HCR 83, Box 74, Custer 57730* ☎ *605/255–4541 or 800/658–3530* 🖷 *605/255–4706* ⊕ *www.custerresorts.com* ⮑ *7 lodge rooms, 40 motel rooms, 33 cabins* ⌂ *Restaurant, picnic area, some kitchenettes, bar, some pets allowed; no a/c in some rooms, no phones in some rooms, no room TVs, no smoking* ☰ *AE, D, MC, V* ☉ *Closed Oct.–Mother's Day.*

★ $–$$$ ✕🏨 Sylvan Lake Resort. This spacious stone-and-wood lodge in Custer State Park affords fantastic views of pristine Sylvan Lake and Harney Peak beyond. The rooms in the lodge are large and modern, and there are rustic cabins, some with fireplaces, scattered along the cliff and in the forest. The Lakota Dining Room ($–$$$) has an exceptional view of the lake, and its lovely veranda constructed of native stone is the perfect place to sip tea and watch the sunrise. On the menu are buffalo selections, including steaks, and rainbow trout. You can canoe, fish, and swim in the lake, and there are numerous hiking trails here. ⊠ *16 mi east of Custer on U.S. 16A* 🏠 *HC 83, Box 74, Custer 57730* ☎ *605/574–2561 or 800/658–3530* 🖷 *605/574–4943* ⊕ *www.custerresorts.com* ⮑ *35 rooms, 31 cabins* ⌂ *Restaurant, lake, boating, fishing, shops, meeting room; no smoking* ☰ *AE, D, MC, V* ☉ *Closed Oct.–Mother's Day.*

$–$$ 🏨 Strutton Inn B&B. Set on 4 acres near the town of Custer and a few miles from Crazy Horse, this luxurious three-story Victorian home has a 140-foot veranda with a gazebo on each corner looking out over a lovely garden and the Black Hills beyond. Most of the guest rooms of the well-furnished retreat are decorated with pastels, frills, and floral patterns. The rooms have king-size beds but no TVs; there is, however, a 46-inch big-screen TV in the common room. Antique-doll and crystal collections fill the house. ⊠ *U.S. 16* 🏠 *R.R. 1, Box 55 S, Custer 57730* ☎ *605/673–2395 or 800/226–2611* 🖷 *605/673–2395* ⊕ *www.struttoninn.com* ⮑ *9 rooms* ⌂ *In-room hot tubs, outdoor hot tub; no room phones, no room TVs, no smoking* ☰ *MC, V* ⍾ *BP.*

Shopping

With handmade items representing the Lakota, Navajo, Huichol, Acoma, and other tribes, **Korczak's Heritage** (⊠ Ave. of the Chiefs ☎ 605/673–

4681) is more than a simple gift shop. In addition to hand-crafted items such as jewelry and dream catchers, Korczak's carries sculpture and prints by Native American artists. The store also sells food and clothing, and gift items hewn from stones blasted from the mountain.

Wind Cave National Park

❺ *28 mi southeast of Crazy Horse via U.S. 16 and Hwy. 87.*

At Wind Cave National Park, which has more than 117 mi of mapped underground passageways and more than 44 square mi of aboveground wilderness preserve, you can go spelunking, discover curious speleothems (cave formations), and hike or watch wildlife all in one day. The cave holds a world of wonders: perfect examples of mineral boxwork (thin spikes of calcite that create a honeycomb pattern), gypsum beard that sways in the heat of a lamp, and delicate helicite balloons that would burst at the touch of a finger. Amazingly, 95% of Wind Cave, already ranked the fifth-longest cave in the world, has yet to be navigated. Outside, bison, elk, deer, and pronghorn roam prairies, granite-walled canyons, and ponderosa pine forests near the cave. Theodore Roosevelt made Wind Cave the country's seventh national park, and the first dedicated to preserving a cave, on January 3, 1903.

Besides being the primary place to get general park information, the **Wind Cave Visitor Center,** on top of the cave, has three exhibit rooms with displays on cave exploration, cave history, cave formations, the Civilian Conservation Corps, park wildlife, and resource management. ⊠ *Off U.S. 385, 3 mi north of the park's southern border* ☎ *605/745–4600* ⊕ *www.nps.gov/wica* ⊠ *Free* ☉ *Mid-Apr.–mid-Sept., daily 8–5; mid-Oct.–early Apr., daily 8–4:30.*

★ You can choose among five different ranger-led **cave tours** (⊠ Wind Cave Visitor Center, off U.S. 385 ☎ 605/745–4600) of Wind Cave if you visit from June through August; the rest of the year, only one or two tours are available. All tours depart from the visitor center, and on each you pass incredibly beautiful cave formations, including extremely well-developed boxwork. The least-crowded times to visit in summer are mornings and weekends. The cave is 53°F year-round, so bring a sweater, and be sure to wear comfortable, closed-toe shoes. Tour schedules, program times, and meeting points are subject to change, so call ahead.

The **Candlelight Cave Tour,** available twice daily from early June through Labor Day, takes you into a section of the cave that has no paved walks or lighting. Everyone on the tour carries a lantern similar to those used in expeditions in the 1890s. The $9 tour lasts two hours and covers 1 mi of the cave; reservations are essential. Children under 8 are not admitted.

On the **Fairgrounds Cave Tour,** available five times daily from early June through Labor Day, you visit some of the largest rooms in the cave, including the Fairgrounds room, which holds examples of nearly every type of calcite formation found in the cave. There are some 450 steps, leading up and down, on this 1½-hour tour; the cost is $9.

You don't need to go far to see boxwork, popcorn, and flowstone formations. Just take the relatively easy, one-hour **Garden of Eden Cave Tour,** which covers only about ¼ mi and 150 stairs. It's available seven times daily early June through Labor Day, and three times daily October through early June; the cost is $7.

The popular, 1¼-hour **Natural Entrance Cave Tour** takes you ½ mi into the cave, over 300 stairs (most heading down), and out an elevator exit. Along the way are the natural opening where the cave's discoverers first entered, and some significant boxwork deposits along the middle level. The tour costs $9 and leaves nine times daily from early June through Labor Day, and seven times daily for the rest of September.

For a serious caving experience, sign up for the challenging, extraordinary, four-hour **Wild Caving Tour.** After some basic training in spelunking, you crawl and climb through fissures and corridors, most lined with gypsum needles, frostwork, and boxwork. You'll also see artifacts left by early explorers. Expect to get dirty. Wear shoes with good traction, long pants, and a long-sleeve shirt. The park provides knee pads, gloves, and hard hats with headlamps. You must be at least 16 to take this tour; 16- and 17-year-olds must show signed consent from a parent or guardian. Tours cost $23 and are available at 1 PM daily early June through mid-August, and at 1 PM weekends mid-August through Labor Day. Reservations are essential.

★ One of the best birding areas in the park is **Wind Cave Canyon** (⌧ About ½ mi east of visitor center). As you hike down the trail, the steep-sided canyon widens to a panoramic view east across the prairies.

You can take in panoramic views of the park and surrounding hills from **Rankin Ridge Lookout Tower,** which at 5,013 feet is the highest point in the park. To get here you must hike the 1-mi Rankin Ridge loop, which starts 6 mi north of the visitor center on Highway 87.

Like many small communities in the Black Hills, **Hill City** (⌧U.S. 16 ☎605/574–2368 or 800/888–1798) has boomed and gone bust along with the mining and timber industries. Unlike many of those small towns, however, Hill City has successfully reinvented itself as a vibrant arts community. Today this town of 780 residents can claim no fewer than seven art galleries in addition to a natural history museum, a winery, a brewery, a vintage steam locomotive line, and dozens of small craft stores, restaurants and hotels. Its 19th-century Main Street is always bustling with visitors and locals; even in the sleepy winter months Hill City stays busy with a Victorian Christmas celebration and a dogsled race.

off the
beaten
path

MAMMOTH SITE – During the construction of a housing development in the 1970s, earthmoving equipment uncovered this prehistoric sinkhole where giant mammoths came to drink, got trapped, and died more than 26,000 years ago. More than 50 of the fossilized woolly beasts have been unearthed since digging began, and many can still be seen in situ. A structure was built on top of the sinkhole, allowing year-round access to the site for visitors and paleontologists. You can watch the excavation in progress and take guided tours of this unique discovery. ⊠ *U.S. 18, Hot Springs, 15 mi south of Wind Cave National Park* ☎ *605/745–6017 or 800/325–6991* ⊕ *www. mammothsite.com* ⊠ *$7* ☉ *Daily; hrs vary, call ahead.*

Sports & the Outdoors

HIKING There are more than 30 mi of hiking trails within the boundaries of Wind Cave National Park. Hiking into the wild, untouched backcountry is perfectly safe, provided you have a map (available from the visitor center) and a good sense of direction. Remember that wild animals, including coyotes and bison, are roaming the same territory that you are. Although bison may appear to be nothing more than big hairy cows, they are very wild. They can easily weigh a ton and if threatened can outrun a horse. Bison are especially unpredictable during the rut, or mating season, in late July and August. Admire their majestic power and typically peaceful nature from a distance.

If you want to get away from the crowds, head for the **Boland Ridge Trail.** It's a strenuous hike of more than 2½ mi up to Boland Ridge, but the panorama from the top is well worth it—sunset from this remote point is absolutely spectacular. The trailhead is off Forest Service Road 6, 1 mi north of the junction with Forest Service Road 5.

Constructed to celebrate South Dakota's 100th birthday, the **Centennial Trail** bisects the Black Hills from north to south, covering 111 mi of territory. Designed for bikers, hikers, and horses, this trail is rugged but accommodating (note, however, that bicycling on the trail is not allowed within park boundaries). Pick up the trail off Highway 87, 2 mi north of the visitor center.

The difficult, roughly 8½-mi, **Highland Creek Trail** is the longest and most diverse trail within the park, traversing mixed-grass prairies, ponderosa pine forests, and the riparian habitats of Highland Creek, Beaver Creek, and Wind Cave Canyon. The southern trailhead stems from Wind Cave Canyon trail 1 mi east of U.S. 385. The northern trailhead is on Forest Service Road 5.

From the Centennial trailhead on Highway 87, the just over 2-mi **Lookout Point Trail** follows the prairie, traverses Lookout Point, and ends at Beaver Creek. Cross over to the Centennial Trail to make a loop of nearly 5 mi.

SPELUNKING **Edge Sports** (⊠ 922 Main St., Rapid City ☎ 605/716–9912), offers a good selection of equipment for the seasoned outdoor enthusiast. Cavers will find a solid inventory of clothing and gear, but hikers, skateboarders and rock climbers won't be disappointed. **The Edge** store on the way to the ski slopes in the northern Black Hills (⊠ 32 Baltimore St., Lead ☎ 605/722–7547), maintains a good stock of winter sports equipment for sale and rent during the snowy months.

Where to Stay & Eat

¢–$ ✕ **Alpine Inn.** With its rustic wood construction, pastoral paintings, lacy tablecloths, and beer steins, the Alpine Inn brings a version of old-world charm to the Old West. The lunchtime menu changes daily but always has selections of healthful sandwiches and salads—and no fried food. Filet mignon is the only item on the dinner menu, but it's one of the best steaks around. Weather permitting, lunch is served on the veranda overlooking Main Street. Hard liquor is not served. ⊠ *225 Main St., Hill City* ☎ *605/574–2749* ⌲ *Reservations not accepted* ▭ *No credit cards* ☉ *Closed Sun.*

$–$$ ▣ **Best Western Hot Springs.** Near U.S. 385, and three blocks from downtown Hot Springs, this hotel offers easy access to the Mueller Civic Center. Family suites are available, and some rooms overlook a little river. ⊠ *737 S. 6th St., Hot Springs 57747* ☎ *605/745–7378 or 800/228–5150* ⎙ *605/745–3240* ⊕ *www.bestwestern.com* ⇄ *51 rooms* ⌂ *Some in-room hot tubs, microwaves, cable TV with movies, indoor pool, exercise equipment, hot tub, laundry facilities, business services, some pets allowed (fee), no-smoking rooms* ▭ *AE, D, MC, V* ⑩ *CP.*

CAMPING ⛺ **Elk Mountain Campground.** If you prefer a relatively developed campsite and relative proximity to civilization, Elk Mountain is an excellent choice. You can experience the peaceful pine forests and wild creatures of the park without straying too far from the safety of the beaten path. There are only tent sites, and Sites 24 and 69 are reserved for campers with disabilities. ⌂ *Flush toilets, running water (non-potable), fire grates, public telephone* ⇄ *75 sites* ⊠ *½ mi north of the visitor center* ☎ *605/745–4600* ⊡ *$5–$10* ▭ *No credit cards* ☉ *Apr.–late Oct.*

Shopping

The **Prairie Berry Winery** (⊠ 23837 U.S. 385, Hill City ☎ 605/574–3898) nestles in some pines off the main highway between Hill City and Keystone. Owned and operated by the Vojta family, who have been making wine in South Dakota since the mid-1870s, the spacious facility has a tasting room and outdoor patio. The grape wines are good by Midwestern standards, while the varieties made from fruit such as currants, chokecherries, and plums offer something a little different. Especially enjoyable are the wines made from a South Dakota specialty—honey. The **Wind Cave Gift Shop** (⊠ U.S. 385 ☎ 605/745–4600) at the visitor center carries a modest selection of books, videos, slides, and maps about the Black Hills, Wind Cave, and geology.

> **en route** Built on the "wall" of the South Dakota badlands, the town of **Wall** (⊠ I–90, Exit 110 ☎ 605/279–2665 or 888/852–9255) was founded in 1907 as a railroad station for the Chicago and Northwestern Railroad. The town (population 818) borders Buffalo Gap National Grasslands and is only a few miles north of the Pinnacles entrance to Badlands National Park. It is a popular base for exploring the two wildernesses.

Wall Drug Store (⊠ 510 Main St. ☎ 605/279–2175), a South Dakota original, made its mark during the Great Depression, when the owners decided to hand out free ice water to road-weary motorists en route to the Black Hills. Today its four art-gallery dining rooms serve burgers and steaks, and its Western Mall has 14 shops. The place also has a life-size mechanical Cowboy Band and Chuckwagon Quartet. In the early morning, the restaurant fills with area ranchers who stop to talk weather and politics, grab a doughnut, and down a cup of black coffee before heading out to the range. Copies of their brands line some of the walls. Wall Drug Store opens daily at 6:30 AM and closes at 7 PM.

BADLANDS NATIONAL PARK

★ *140 mi northeast of Wind Cave via Hwy. 87, U.S. 16, and I–90.*

So stark and forbidding are the chiseled spires, ragged ridgelines, and deep ravines of South Dakota's badlands that Lieutenant Colonel George Custer once described them as "hell with the fires burned out." Although a bit more accessible than the depths of the underworld, the landscape is easily the strangest in the Great Plains. Ruthlessly ravaged over the ages by wind and rain, the 380 square mi of wild terrain continue to erode and evolve, sometimes visibly changing shape in a few days. Despite harsh conditions, a community of prairie creatures, from bison and bald eagles to rattlesnakes and pronghorn, thrives on the untamed territory. Fossil evidence—there are more Oligocene fossil deposits in the badlands than anywhere else in the world—shows that mammals have roamed the area for more than 35 million years. Within the ancient rock formations paleontologists have traced the evolution of such mammals as horses, cats, sheep, rhinoceroses, and pigs, and have identified various birds and reptiles. The park, established as a national monument in 1939, was designated a national park in 1978. ☎ 605/433–5361 ⊕ *www.nps.gov/badl* ⬚ *Cars $10; motorcycles, bicycles, and pedestrians $5* ☉ *Daily, 24 hrs.*

Exploring Badlands National Park

The park is divided into three units: the North Unit, which includes the Badlands Wilderness Area, and the southern Stronghold and Palmer units, which are within the Pine Ridge Indian Reservation. The National Park Service and the Oglala Sioux Tribe manage the southern units together. The North Unit is far more user-friendly and attracts the majority of visitors. Much of the southern two units is accessible only on foot or horseback, or by a high-clearance four-wheel-drive or ATV.

The most popular way to see the park is to spend a half-day driving Hwy. 240, otherwise known as Badlands Loop Road, which conveniently runs parallel to I–90. For a closer look, consider a trip into the southern units (this will likely require a second day) and a stop at the White River Visitor Center, where you should register with park officials if you plan to take any significant hikes.

a good tour

Arriving in the park via the Northeast Entrance (off I–90 at Exit 131), drive south on Badlands Loop Road (Hwy. 240) until you reach the **Ben Reifel Visitor Center** ⑥. Pick up some brochures and maps, and if the entrance booth was closed, pay your park entrance fee here. Try one of the marked hikes nearby: the **Cliff Shelf Nature Trail** is less than ½ mi northeast of the visitor center and makes for a quick walk. Several others, including the **Door Trail**, are within easy driving distance.

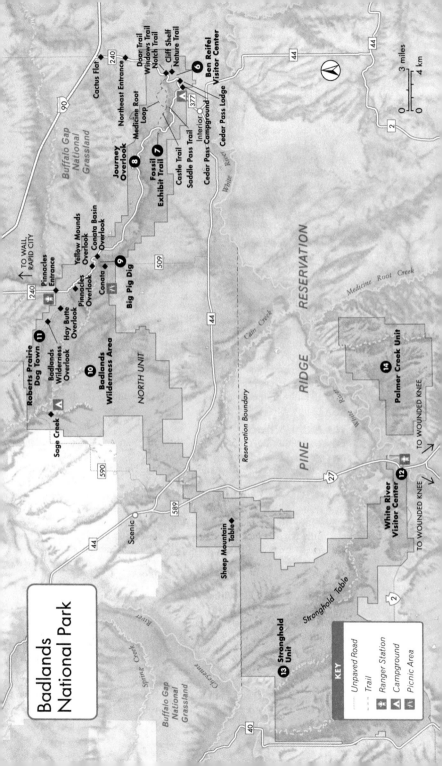

Badlands National Park

KEY

- ---- Unpaved Road
- ····· Trail
- 🏠 Ranger Station
- ▲ Campground
- ⛱ Picnic Area

TO WALL, RAPID CITY →

Buffalo Gap National Grassland

Cactus Flat

Northeast Entrance

Door Trail
Windows Trail
Notch Trail
Cliff Shelf Nature Trail
Ben Reifel Visitor Center

6

Medicine Root Loop

Journey Overlook

8

Fossil Exhibit Trail **7**

Castle Trail
Saddle Pass Trail

Interior
Cedar Pass Campground
Cedar Pass Lodge

White River

Pinnacles Entrance

Yellow Mounds Overlook
Conata Basin Overlook

Pinnacles Overlook
Conata

Big Pig Dig **9**

Hay Butte Overlook

Roberts Prairie Dog Town **11**

Badlands Wilderness Overlook

Badlands Wilderness Area **10**

NORTH UNIT

Sage Creek

Scenic

RESERVATION

Medicine Root Creek

Cain Creek

Reservation Boundary

PINE RIDGE

Palmer Creek Unit **14**

White River

TO WOUNDED KNEE

White River Visitor Center **12**

TO WOUNDED KNEE

Sheep Mountain Table

Stronghold Table

Stronghold Unit **13**

Buffalo Gap National Grassland

Spring Creek

Cheyenne River

3 miles
4 km
0
0

N

From the visitor center, drive northwest on Badlands Loop Road for about 5 mi to the **Fossil Exhibit Trail** ❼. After a short walk around the loop, continue northwest to the **Journey Overlook** ❽ for a view over the rugged land. Farther up the road, near the Conata Picnic Area, you'll find the **Big Pig Dig** ❾, a fossil site still being excavated by paleontologists. Badlands Loop Road next takes you past the massive **Badlands Wilderness Area** ❿, which covers 100 square mi to the west. Provided the road is dry, take a side trip 5 mi down Sage Creek Rim Road to **Roberts Prairie Dog Town** ⓫, inhabited by a huge colony of the chattering critters. Double back to the main road to drive north to the town of Wall and I–90 or to return to the visitor center, next door to Cedar Pass Lodge.

If you're feeling adventurous, take a second day to explore the two southern units of the park. Start at the **White River Visitor Center** ⓬ for a talk with park rangers about your hiking options. You can head directly into the **Stronghold Unit** ⓭, or make a 2-mi trek across private land (you must obtain permission; park rangers can point you in the right direction) to the **Palmer Creek Unit** ⓮. Neither unit has any services or marked trails, so bring maps and plenty of water.

TIMING It's possible to complete a trip around Badlands Loop Road in less than five hours, but give yourself an entire day to soak up the spirit of the land. A visit to either of the southern units can easily become a multiday wilderness pack trip. For the most comfortable weather throughout the park, avoid late July, early August, and November through March: the strong rays of the sun turn the bare-rock badlands into an oven in high summer, while cold, snow-laden winds drive through mercilessly in winter.

The Main Attractions

❿ Covering about 25% of the park, the 100-square-mi **Badlands Wilderness Area** (✉ 25 mi northwest of Ben Reifel Visitor Center on Hwy. 240) is part of the largest prairie wilderness in the United States. About two-thirds of the Sage Creek region is mixed-grass prairie, making it an ideal grazing ground for bison, pronghorn, and many of the park's other native animals. The Grassy Tables Overlook 2 mi northwest on Sage Creek Rim Road and the Pinnacles Overlook 1 mi south of the Pinnacles Entrance on Hwy. 240 are the best places to get an overview of the wilderness area. Feel free to park beside the road and hike your own route into the untamed, unmarked prairie, but remember that any water in this region is unfit for drinking—be sure to pack your own.

❻ Although the **Ben Reifel Visitor Center** is at the extreme eastern edge of the park, in the developed Cedar Pass area, it's a good idea to stop here first to pick up park brochures and maps. A lodge, campground, amphitheater, and six trails are less than 2 mi away. ✉ *Badlands Loop Rd. (Hwy. 240), Interior* ☎ *605/433–5361* 💲 *Free* 🕑 *June 4–Aug. 19, daily 7 AM–8 PM; Aug. 20–Sept. 9, daily 8–6; Sept. 10–June 3, daily 9–4.*

In a depression by the Conata Basin picnic area, paleontologists dig for
❾ fossils and field questions from curious visitors at the **Big Pig Dig** (✉ 17

mi northwest of Ben Reifel Visitor Center on Hwy. 240). This site was named for a large fossil originally thought to be the remains of a pre-historic pig, although it actually turned out to be a small, hornless rhinoceros. The dig is open and staffed June through August; contact the Ben Reifel Visitor Center for hours.

★ ☾ ❼ Fossils of early mammals are displayed under glass along the ¼-mi **Fossil Exhibit Trail** (⊠ 5 mi northwest of Ben Reifel Visitor Center on Hwy. 240), which is wheelchair-accessible and great for kids.

❽ From **Journey Overlook** (⊠ 7 mi northwest of Ben Reifel Visitor Center on Hwy. 240) you can see Bigfoot Pass, where Sioux chief Big Foot and his band traveled through the badlands on their way to that fateful battle at Wounded Knee, on December 29, 1890, when U.S. troops killed more than 200 Sioux men, women, and children.

⓫ Once a homestead, **Roberts Prairie Dog Town** (⊠ 5 mi west of Badlands Loop Rd. on Sage Creek Rim Rd.) is now owned by the largest colony of black-tailed prairie dogs in the country.

Also Worth Seeing

The ½-mi loop of **Cliff Shelf Nature Trail** (⊠ 1 mi east of Ben Reifel Visitor Center) winds through a wooded prairie oasis in the middle of dry, rocky ridges and climbs 200 feet to a peak above the White River valley for an incomparable view. Look for chipmunks, squirrels, and red-wing blackbirds in the wet wood, and eagles, hawks, and vultures at hilltop.

The ¾-mi round-trip **Door Trail** (⊠ 2 mi east of Ben Reifel Visitor Center) leads through a natural opening, or door, in a badlands rock wall. The eerie sandstone formations and passageways beckon, but it's recommended that you stay on the trail. The first 100 yards of the trail are on a boardwalk.

If you're feeling especially adventurous, you may want to hike into the ⓮ **Palmer Creek Unit** (⊠ 2 mi east of White River Visitor Center). This is the most isolated section of the park—no recognized roads pass through its borders. You must obtain permission from private landowners to pass through their property; contact the White River Visitor Center for more information. If you plan on exploring here, count on spending two days—one day in and one day out.

⓭ With few paved roads and no campgrounds, the **Stronghold Unit** (⊠ north and west of White River Visitor Center), in the southwestern section of the park, is difficult to access without a four-wheel-drive or high-clearance vehicle. However, if you're willing to trek, the unit's isolation provides a rare opportunity to explore badlands rock formations and prairies completely undisturbed. From 1942 to 1968 the U.S. Air Force and South Dakota National Guard used much of the Stronghold Unit as a gunnery range. Hundreds of fossils were destroyed by bomber pilots, who frequently targeted the large fossil remains of an elephant-size titanothere (an extinct relative of the rhinoceros), which gleamed bright white from the air. Beware of such remnants as old automobiles turned targets, unexploded bombs, shells, rockets, and other hazardous materials. If you see unexploded ordnance while hiking in the Stronghold

Unit, be sure to note the location so you can report it to a ranger later. Steer clear of it and find another route.

Within the Stronghold Unit, the 3-mi-long **Stronghold Table** (⊠ 7 mi west of White River Visitor Center) can be reached only by crossing a narrow land bridge just wide enough to let a wagon pass. It was here in 1890, just before the Massacre at Wounded Knee, that some 600 Sioux gathered to perform one of the last known Ghost Dances, a ritual in which the Sioux wore white shirts that they believed would protect them from bullets. Permission from private landowners is required to gain access to the table. Contact the White River Visitor Center for more information.

⑫ Any visit to the Stronghold or Palmer unit should be preceded by a stop at the **White River Visitor Center** for maps and information about road and trail conditions. You can also see fossils and Lakota artifacts and learn about Sioux culture past and present. In the early and late summer, be sure to call the Ben Reifel Visitor Center first to check operating hours, as the White River Visitor Center is open only for a short time. ⊠ *25 mi south of Hwy. 44 via Hwy. 27* ☎ 605/455–2878 ☉ *June–Aug., daily 10–4.*

Sports & the Outdoors

Bicycling

Bicycles are permitted only on designated roads, which may be paved or unpaved. They are prohibited on closed roads, trails, and the backcountry. Flat-resistant tires are recommended.

In the Stronghold Unit on the Pine Ridge Indian Reservation, the 7-mi **Sheep Mountain Table Road** (⊠ 14 mi north of White River Visitor Center on Hwy. 27) is ideal for mountain biking. At the top of this high, flat mesa you can take in great views of the area. This is a dirt road and should be biked only when dry. The terrain is level for the first 3 mi; then it climbs the table and levels out again.

Bird & Wildlife Viewing

If you're interested in the park's diverse wildlife, bring along a pair of binoculars. Especially around sunset, get set to watch the badlands come to life. Jackrabbits, bats, prairie dogs, gophers, porcupines, foxes, coyotes, skunks, bobcats, horned lizards, prairie rattlers, deer, pronghorn, bighorn sheep, and bison all call the badlands home. Although very rare, weasels, mountain lions, and the endangered black-footed ferret can also be spotted roaming the park. Additionally, more than 215 bird species have been recorded in the area, including herons, pelicans, cormorants, egrets, swans, geese, hawks, golden and bald eagles, falcons, vultures, cranes, doves, and cuckoos.

Scheels All Sport (⊠ 2200 N. Maple Ave., Rapid City ☎ 605/342–9033), in Rapid City's Rushmore Mall, is one of the few places in the area to carry a wide selection of all-weather hiking clothes and binoculars suitable for wildlife viewing.

Hiking

The isolation and otherworldliness of the badlands are best appreciated on a hike. Take time to examine the dusty rock beneath your feet, and be on the lookout for fossils and animals. Remember to bring at least a liter of water per person.

If the marked trails and overlooks off Badlands Loop Road aren't challenging enough, you might consider a trek into the **Badlands Wilderness Area** (⊠ 25 mi northwest of Ben Reifel Visitor Center on Hwy. 240), a 100-square-mi parcel of grassy steppes and rocky canyons east of the highway and south of Sage Creek Rim Road, near the Pinnacles entrance. There are no services here and very few visitors, even in summer. Before you venture out, it's a good idea to check in with park staff at one of the visitor centers.

The easy **Castle Trail** (⊠ 5 mi north of Ben Reifel Visitor Center) stretches for 5½ mi one way from the Fossil Exhibit trailhead on Badlands Loop Road to the parking area for the Door and Window trails. If you choose to follow the Medicine Root Loop, which detours off the Castle Trail, you'll add ½ mi to the trek.

One of the park's more interesting hikes, the 1½-mi round-trip **Notch Trail** (⊠ 2 mi north of Ben Reifel Visitor Center) takes you over moderately difficult terrain and up a ladder. Winds at the notch can be fierce, but it's worth lingering for the view of the White River valley and the Pine Ridge Indian Reservation.

The **Saddle Pass Trail** (⊠ 2 mi west of Ben Reifel Visitor Center), which connects with Castle Trail and Medicine Root Loop, is a steep ¼-mi climb up and down the side of "The Wall," an impressive rock formation.

The 200-yard round-trip **Window Trail** (⊠ 2 mi north of Ben Reifel Visitor Center) ends at a natural hole, or window, in a rock wall. Looking though, you'll see more of the distinctive badlands pinnacles and spires.

Horseback Riding

The park has one of the largest and most beautiful territories in the state in which to ride a horse. Riding is allowed in most of the park except for some marked trails, roads, and developed areas. The mixed-grass prairie of the Badlands Wilderness Area is especially popular with riders.

Gunsel Horse Adventures (☎ 605/343–7608 ⊕ www.gunselhorseadventures. com) arranges pack trips into the badlands and Buffalo Gap National Grasslands. The four-day trips are based in one central campsite and are all-inclusive; you bring your own sleeping bag and personal effects.

Where to Stay & Eat

¢–$ ✕🏨 **Cedar Pass Lodge.** Each small white cabin at this lodging within the park has two twin beds and views of the badlands peaks. A gallery at the lodge displays the work of local artists, and the gift shop is well stocked with local crafts, including turquoise and beadwork. There are also hiking trails on the premises. Enjoy a hearty meal of steak, trout, or Indian tacos and fry bread in the restaurant ($–$$), with its dark, knotty-pine walls under an exposed-beam ceiling. ⊠ *1 Cedar St. (Hwy. 240), Interior 57750* ☎ *605/433–5460* 🖷 *605/433–5560* ⊕ *www.cedarpasslodge. com* ⇆ *24 cabins* ⚹ *Restaurant, picnic area, hiking, some pets allowed; no room phones, no room TVs, no smoking* ▱ *AE, DC, MC, V* ⊗ *Closed Oct.–Apr.*

¢–$ 🏠 **Badlands Ranch and Resort.** This 2,000-acre ranch lies outside the national park, and the ranch house and cabins have spectacular views of the badlands. The grounds—complete with gazebo, duck ponds, picnic areas, and a bonfire site—are ideal for summer family vacations and reunions. The ranch house has a Jacuzzi tub set in wooden a deck. ⊠ *Hwy. 44* ⌁ *HCR 53, Box 3, Interior 57750* ☎ *605/433–5599* 🖷 *605/433–5598* ⊕ *www. badlandsranchandresort.com* ⇆ *4 rooms, 7 cabins* ⚹ *Picnic area, kitchenettes, cable TV with movies, pond, hot tub* ▱ *AE, D, MC, V.*

CAMPING There are no designated campgrounds in the Stronghold and Palmer units, but you may pitch a tent anywhere that's at least ½ mi from a road or trail. Be careful of the remains of military gunning. Despite these historical reminders of civilization, camping in the Stronghold or Palmer unit lets you experience the sheer isolation of the badlands. Note that fires are not allowed anywhere within the park.

○ ⚠ **Badlands KOA.** The green, shady sites spread over the 31 acres of this campground southeast of Interior are pleasant and cool after a day among the dry rocks of the national park. White River and a small creek border the property on two sides. ⚹ *Flush toilets, full hookups, partial hookups (electric and water), dump station, drinking water, showers, fire grates, picnic tables, public telephone, general store, play area, swimming (pool)* ⇆ *44 full hookups, 38 partial hookups, 62 tent sites* ⊠ *4 mi south of Interior on Hwy. 44* ☎ *605/433–5337* ⊕ *www.koa. com* ⊠ *$25 tent sites, $26 partial hookups, $32 full hookups* ▱ *MC, V* ⊗ *May–early Oct.*

⚠ **Cedar Pass Campground.** Although it has only tent sites, this is the most developed campground within the park, and it's near the Ben Reifel Visitor Center, Cedar Pass Lodge, and a half-dozen hiking trails. You can buy $1 or $2 bags of ice at the lodge. ⚹ *Flush toilets, pit toilets, dump station, drinking water, public telephone, ranger station* ⇆ *96 sites* ⊠ *Hwy. 377, ¼ mi south of Badlands Loop Rd.* ☎ *605/ 433–5361* ⊕ *www.cedarpasslodge.com* ⊠ *$10* ⚹ *Reservations not accepted* ▱ *No credit cards.*

⚠ **Sage Creek Primitive Campground.** The word to remember here is "primitive." If you want to get away from it all, this lovely, isolated spot surrounded by nothing but fields and crickets is the right camp for you. There are no designated campsites, and the only facilities are pit toilets and horse hitches. ⚹ *Pit toilets* ⊠ *25 mi west of Badlands Loop Rd. on Sage Creek Rim Rd.* ☎ *No phone* ⊠ *Free.*

Shopping

The **Cedar Pass Gift Store** (⊠ 1 Cedar St. ☎ 605/433–5460) at the Cedar Pass Lodge carries a small selection of handmade gifts and Native American crafts.

SOUTH DAKOTA BLACK HILLS A TO Z

To research prices, get advice from other travelers, and book travel arrangements, visit www.fodors.com.

AIR TRAVEL

CARRIERS Delta Air provides a connection to the Black Hills from Salt Lake City, Northwest Airlines offers service from Minneapolis, United Airlines flies from Denver, and Allegiant Air has a twice-a-week run from Las Vegas. Seasonal routes sometimes open up other cities: A summer route on United has started to provide service to Chicago; occasional connections to regional cities like Billings and Sioux Falls also are offered.

🛂 **Airlines & Contacts Allegiant Air** ☎ 800/432-3810 ⊕ www.allegiantair.com. **Delta Air** ☎ 800/221-1212 ⊕ www.delta.com. **Northwest Airlines** ☎ 800/225-2525 ⊕ www.nwa.com. **United Airlines** ☎ 800/241-6522 ⊕ www.ual.com.

AIRPORTS

Although there are several landing strips and municipal airports in the Black Hills, the only airport with commercial service is in Rapid City. Rapid City Regional Airport is 11 mi east of town on Hwy. 44.

🛂 **Airport Information Rapid City Regional Airport** ✉ 4550 Terminal Rd., Rapid City ☎ 605/393-9924 ⊕ www.rapairport.org.

BUS TRAVEL

Greyhound Lines provides national service out of Rapid City. Jefferson Lines serves Wall and Rapid City, with connections to most Midwestern and Southern cities. Powder River Transportation connects Rapid City with the smaller towns in eastern and northern Wyoming. Gray Line of the Black Hills provides charter service and tours within the Black Hills region.

🛂 **Gray Line of the Black Hills** ☎ 605/342-4461 ⊕ www.blackhillsgrayline.com. **Greyhound Lines** ☎ 307/634-7744 or 800/231-2222 ⊕ www.greyhound.com. **Jefferson Lines** ☎ 888/864-2832 ⊕ www.jeffersonlines.com. **Powder River Transportation** ☎ 307/682-0960.

CAR RENTAL

Rapid City Regional Airport is the best place to find car rentals. Make rental reservations early; Rapid City is visited by many business travelers and rental agencies are often booked.

🛂 **Avis** ☎ 800/831-2847 ⊕ www.avis.com. **Budget** ☎ 800/527-0700 ⊕ www.budget.com. **Casey's Auto Rental Service** ✉ 1318 5th St., Rapid City ☎ 605/343-2277 ⊕ www.caseyscorner.com. **Dollar** ☎ 800/527-0700 ⊕ www.dollar.com. **Hertz** ☎ 800/654-3131 ⊕ www.hertz.com. **National** ☎ 800/227-7368 ⊕ www.nationalcar.com.

CAR TRAVEL

Unless you come the the Black Hills on an escorted package tour, a car is essential. I–90 cuts directly through South Dakota from west to east, connecting the northern towns of Spearfish, Sturgis, and Deadwood (which lies about 8 mi off the interstate) with Rapid City. From there the interstate turns straight east, passing Wall and Badlands National Park on its way to Sioux Falls.

Minor highways of importance include U.S. 385, which connects the interior of the Black Hills from south to north, and U.S. 16, which winds south of Rapid City toward Mount Rushmore and Crazy Horse Memorial. Hwy. 44 is an alternate route between the Black Hills and the badlands. Within the Black Hills, seven highway tunnels have limited clearance; they are marked on state maps and in the state's tourism booklet.

Snowplows work hard to keep the roads clear in winter, but you may have trouble getting around immediately after a major snowstorm, especially in upper elevations. Unlike in the Rockies, where even higher elevations make some major roads impassable in winter, the only Black Hills roads that close permanently in the snowy months are minor dirt or gravel Forest Service roads.

Contact the South Dakota State Highway Patrol for information on road conditions.
🚹 **South Dakota State Highway Patrol** ☎ 511 ⊕ hp.state.sd.us.

EMERGENCIES
🚹 Ambulance or Police **Emergencies** ☎ 911.
🚹 **24-Hour Medical Care** **Rapid City Regional Hospital** ✉ 353 Fairmont Blvd., Rapid City ☎ 605/719-1000 ⊕ www.rcrh.org. **Spearfish Regional Hospital** ✉ 1440 N. Main St., Spearfish ☎ 605/644-4000 ⊕ www.rcrh.org.

LODGING

CAMPING   Camping is one of this region's strengths. There are countless campgrounds in the Black Hills and in the badlands below. Most of the public land within the national forests and parks is open for camping, provided that you don't light any fires. Keep in mind when selecting your campsite that while the Black Hills don't have any native bears, there is a significant population of mountain lions.

LODGING RESERVATIONS   Black Hills Central Reservations, also known as CenRes, handles reservations for hotels, campgrounds, lodges, ranches, and B&Bs in the Black Hills.
🚹 **Black Hills Central Reservations** ☎ 800/529-0105 ⊕ www.blackhillsvacations.com.

MEDIA

NEWSPAPERS   Most towns have their own newspapers that print local reports and weather forecasts at least once a week. The *Rapid City Journal* is the main newspaper for the Black Hills.

TELEVISION & RADIO   Although many TV stations broadcast in the Black Hills, the deep canyons and tall hills often prevent reception. Many residents subscribe to cable simply so they can tune in to local stations. ABC/KOTA Channel 3, based in Rapid City, broadcasts across western South Dakota, western Nebraska, and much of northern Wyoming. Also available in Rapid City, the Black Hills, and parts of eastern Wyoming are CBS/KCLO Channel 15, FOX/KEVN Channel 7, NBC/KNBN Channel 21, PAX/KPAX Channel 24, WB/KWBH Channel 27, and PBS/KBHE Channel 9.

Most radio stations in the Black HIlls have a country-music format, although classic rock is popular as well. KIQK 104.1 FM, KOUT 98.7 FM, and KIMM 1150 AM play country; rock stations are KDDX 101.1 FM and KSQY 95.1 FM; and KRCS 93.1 FM presents the Top 40.

SPORTS & THE OUTDOORS

FISHING Besides the local chambers of commerce, the South Dakota Game, Fish, and Parks Department is your best bet for updated information on regional fishing locations and their conditions. Local outfitters, guides, and community organizations can also provide information.

🖪 **South Dakota Game, Fish, and Parks** ✉ 523 E. Capitol Ave., Pierre 57501 ☎ 605/773-3485 ⊕ www.state.sd.us/gfp/.

SKIING & Because there is no one agency that keeps track of conditions in the area, SNOWMOBILING your best sources of information on winter sports are local chambers of commerce, ski lodges and outfitters.

TOURS

Gray Line of the Black Hills offers bus tours of the region, including trips to Mount Rushmore and Black Hills National Forest.

🖪 **Gray Line of the Black Hills** ☎ 605/342-4461 ⊕ www.blackhillsgrayline.com.

VISITOR INFORMATION

Numerous publications, ranging from small booklets to thick magazines, provide information—and lots of advertising—to visitors headed to the Black Hills. You can pick up many of these at hotels and restaurants, usually for free.

🖪 **South Dakota Tourist Information Black Hills, Badlands and Lakes Association** ✉ 1851 Discovery Circle, Rapid City 57701 ☎ 605/355-3600 ⊕ www.blackhillsbadlands.com. **Deadwood Area Chamber of Commerce & Visitor Bureau** ✉ 735 Main St., Deadwood 57732 ☎ 605/578-1876 or 800/999-1876 ⊕ www.deadwood.org. **Rapid City Chamber of Commerce and Convention & Visitors Bureau** ✉ Civic Center, 444 N. Mt. Rushmore Rd. Box 747, Rapid City 57709 ☎ 605/343-1744 or 800/487-3223 ⊕ www.rapidcitycvb.com. **USDA Forest Service Buffalo Gap National Grasslands Visitor Center** ✉ 708 Main St. ⌂ Box 425, Wall 57790 ☎ 605/279-2125.

Cheyenne, Laramie & Southern Wyoming

8

WORD OF MOUTH

"The Snowy Range mountains are fantastic! I like them better than Rocky Mountain National Park, and they are not heavily visited. Last time I was there, a 'heavily used trail' had 300 people on it per season; moderate was only 30."
—travellyn

"Flaming Gorge is definitely worth seeing. The view is really spectacular, especially around sunset, when the rocks are very red (hence the 'Flaming') because of the light conditions."
—John

"Fossil Butte is the home of many interesting fish fossils. The extraordinary clarity with which the fossils are preserved is remarkable."
—brookwood

By Candy
Moulton

A JOURNEY ACROSS SOUTHERN WYOMING takes you through a wonderfully diverse landscape, from the wheat fields of the southeast to the mountains of the Snowy Range to the stark and sometimes hauntingly beautiful Red Desert, where wild horses still roam freely. Cheyenne, the largest city in Wyoming and the state capital, is the cornerstone community at the eastern edge of the state and host to the annual Cheyenne Frontier Days rodeo. Evanston, a town settled by railroad workers in 1869, anchors the western edge of the state. In between are the cities of Laramie, Rock Springs, and Green River, all of which owe their origin to the construction of the Union Pacific Railroad.

Several smaller communities with unique museums, access to diverse recreational opportunities, and one-of-a-kind personality lure travelers away from I-80, the main route through the region. Medicine Bow has a rich cowboy heritage portrayed in Owen Wister's 1902 Western novel, *The Virginian*. Saratoga has a resort flavor and some of the best dining and lodging of any small town in the state. Encampment and Baggs are little, slow-paced, historically rich towns. In these and other towns across the region you can travel back in time by attending re-creations of mountain man rendezvous, cowboy gatherings, and other historical events.

Once covered by an ocean and now rich in fossils, southwest Wyoming's Red Desert, or Little Colorado Desert, draws people in search of solitude (there's plenty of it), pioneer trails (more miles of 19th-century overland emigrant trails than anywhere else in the country), and recreation ranging from wildlife watching to fishing and boating on Flaming Gorge Reservoir, south of the town of Green River. The region is rich in history as well: here, John Wesley Powell began his 1869 and 1871 expeditions down the Green River, and Jim Bridger and Louis Vasquez constructed the trading post of Fort Bridger, now a state historic site. And all across the region, evidence remains of the Union Pacific Railroad, which spawned growth here in the 1860s as workers laid the iron rails spanning the continent.

Exploring Southern Wyoming

Once you explore this region, it becomes apparent why Wyoming has earned the nickname the "Cowboy State." The plains remain a prime grazing spot for wild horses, cattle, and sheep. As you drive west, the plains give way to the snowcapped mountains of the appropriately named Snowy Range. After a few more hours driving west you'll reach the Red Desert, with unique rock formations and herds of wild horses and pronghorn.

I-80 is the major artery through this region, running from Cheyenne at the southeast corner of the state west to Evanston in the southwest corner of the state.

About the Restaurants

Almost anywhere you dine in southern Wyoming, beef plays a prominent role on the menu; prime rib and steak are often specialties. Standard fare at many small-town restaurants includes burgers and sandwiches, and several eateries serve outstanding Mexican dishes. The pickings can be a bit slim for vegetarians, although most menus have at least one vegetable pasta dish or meatless entrée. Jeans and a T-shirt are acceptable attire for most places (even if the folks at the next table happen to be dressed up). Cowboy hats are always welcome.

About the Hotels

Because I–80 traverses this region, there are countless chain motels, but many other interesting accommodations are available. Southern Wyoming has a large number of independent lodging properties ranging from bed-and-breakfasts to lodges to historic hotels. Dude ranches are a unique lodging experience that let you sample a taste of wrangling life, and you can even stay in a remote mountain cabin in the heart of the national forest.

WHAT IT COSTS					
	$$$$	**$$$**	**$$**	**$**	**¢**
RESTAURANTS	over $22	$17–$22	$12–$16	$7–$11	under $7
HOTELS	over $220	$161–$220	$111–$160	$70–$110	under $70

Restaurant prices are for a main course at dinner, excluding sales tax of 4%–7%. Hotel prices are for two people in a standard double room in high season, excluding service charges and 5%–10% tax.

Timing

The best time to visit southern Wyoming is in summer or fall, when most lodging properties and attractions are open (some smaller museums, sights, and inns close between Labor Day and Memorial Day). Summer is the season for most local community celebrations, including the region's longest-running and biggest event, Cheyenne Frontier Days, held the last full week in July.

Some areas, particularly around Laramie, Centennial, Saratoga, and Encampment, are great for winter sports, including cross-country skiing, snowmobiling, and ice fishing. Bear in mind that in parts of southern Wyoming it can—and often does—snow every month of the year, so even if you're visiting in July, bring some warm clothes, such as a heavy jacket and sweater.

CHEYENNE

Cheyenne is Wyoming's largest city, but at just over 50,000 people it is not a place where you'll have to fight traffic or wait in lines—except, perhaps, during the last nine days in July, when the annual Cheyenne Frontier Days makes the city positively boom. Throughout the year it offers a decent variety of shopping, plus attractions ranging from art galleries to museums to parks.

Born in 1867 as the Union Pacific Railroad inched its way across the plains, Cheyenne began as a rowdy camp for railroad gangs, cowboys, prospectors heading for the Black Hills, and soldiers. It more than lived up to its nickname: "Hell on Wheels." But unlike some renegade railroad tent cities, which disappeared as the railroad tracks pushed far-

All across southern Wyoming you can immerse yourself in cowboy and Old West heritage. Some of your driving can take you along pioneer emigrant trails; you can hike or ride horses on other segments. A good place to start your explorations is at one of the two major frontier-era forts, Fort Laramie (northeast of Cheyenne) and Fort Bridger (in the southwest), that served emigrants heading to Oregon, California, and Utah. From Fort Laramie, drive to Cheyenne, where you can see one of America's most complete horse-drawn wagon collections. Continue west to learn about territorial and frontier justice at the historic prisons in Laramie and Rawlins. For a rare treat, spend some time visiting the region's small museums, which preserve evocative relics of the past. Start with the Grand Encampment Museum, Medicine Bow Museum, Little Snake River Valley Museum (in Baggs), and Carbon County Museum (in Rawlins), then head west to tour the Sweetwater County Historical Center in Green River and Ulrich's Fossil Museum west of Kemmerer.

If you like to spend time in the outdoors, by all means take the scenic routes. From Cheyenne, follow Highway 210, which provides access to Curt Gowdy State Park. Traveling west of Laramie, head into the Snowy Range and Sierra Madre Mountains by taking Highway 130, which links to Saratoga by way of Centennial, or take Highway 230 to Encampment and then travel over Battle Highway (Hwy. 70) to Baggs. The mountain country of the Snowy Range and Sierra Madres provides plenty of opportunity for hiking, horseback riding, mountain biking, fishing, and camping. There are hundreds of thousands of acres to explore on trails ranging from wheelchair accessible paths to incredibly difficult tracks for experienced backcountry travelers only. The action continues in winter, when snowmobilers ride free-style across open country (rather than on trails), cross-country skiers glide through white landscapes, and snowshoers explore hushed forests. The lakes that attract anglers during summer are equally busy in winter, when ice fishing rules. In the southwestern part of the region, water sports in Flaming Gorge National Recreation Area and hiking at Evanston's Bear River State Park are among your options.

For a firsthand Western experience, stay at one of the guest ranches near Cheyenne, Laramie, or Saratoga, where you can take part in cowboy activities and ride horses. Wild horses range freely in Southwest Wyoming's Red Desert, even though the area is being heavily developed for energy production. You can spot the magnificent creatures west of Baggs and north and south of Rock Springs.

ther west, Cheyenne established itself as a permanent city, becoming the territorial capital in 1868. Its wild beginnings gave way in the late 19th century to respectability with the coming of the enormously wealthy cattle barons, many of them English. They sipped brandy at the Cheyenne Club and hired hard cases such as Tom Horn (1860–1903) to take care of their competitors—which in many cases meant killing rustlers—on the open range.

Southern Wyoming

Cheyenne became the state capital in 1890, at a time when the rule of the cattle barons was beginning to weaken after harsh winter storms in the late 1880s and financial downturns in the national economy. But Cheyenne's link to ranching didn't fade, and the community launched its first Cheyenne Frontier Days in 1897, an event that continues to this day. During the late July celebration—the world's largest outdoor rodeo extravaganza—the town is up to its neck in bucking broncs and bulls and joyful bluster. There are parades, pageantry, and parties that require the endurance of a cattle hand on a weeklong drive.

Exploring Cheyenne

Numbers in the text correspond to numbers in the margin and on the Cheyenne, Southern Wyoming, and Laramie maps.

I–25 runs north–south through the city; I–80 runs east–west. Central Avenue and Warren Avenue are quick north–south routes; the former goes north one way and the latter runs south one way. Several major roads can get you across town fairly easily, including 16th Street (U.S. 30), which gives you easy access to downtown. Most places of interest are in the downtown area. Most shopping is also downtown or along Dell Range Boulevard on the north side of town. Note that there are a few one-way streets in the downtown area.

a good tour

Park your car at the **Old West Museum ❶**, within Frontier Park; this museum houses displays on the history of the region, plus the largest collection of horse-drawn vehicles anywhere in Wyoming. After you tour the museum, cross the street for a stroll through the **Cheyenne Botanic Gardens ❷**.

Head south on Carey Avenue; make a left on 24th Street to reach the **Wyoming State Capitol ❸**. Park along the street or turn right onto Central Avenue to look for parking. Take a self-guided tour of the capitol building, and note the statue out front of Esther Hobart Morris, who helped make Wyoming the first state to grant women the right to vote. Cross Central Avenue to the **Wyoming State Museum ❹**, housing artifacts from across the state.

TIMING   You could visit all of the sights within the city in a day. Several sights close on Sunday.

The Main Attractions

❷ **Cheyenne Botanic Gardens.** A vegetable garden, roses and other flowers, cacti, and both perennial and annual plants bloom within the greenhouse conservatory and on the grounds here. ⊠ *710 S. Lions Park Dr.* ☎ *307/637–6458* ⊕ *www.botanic.org/* 🖃 *Donations accepted* ☉ *Conservatory weekdays 8–4:30, weekends 11–3:30; grounds stay open into the evening.*

❻ **Curt Gowdy State Park.** You can fish, boat, hike, and picnic at this park named for Wyoming's most famous sportscaster, who got his start at local radio stations in the 1940s. The park, which is 20 mi west of the city, is particularly pleasant in summer and spring, when the wildflowers are in bloom. ⊠ *1351 Hyndslodge Rd., off Hwy. 210 (Happy Jack Rd.)* ☎ *307/632–7946* ⊕ *http://wyoparks.state.wy.us/CGslide.htm*

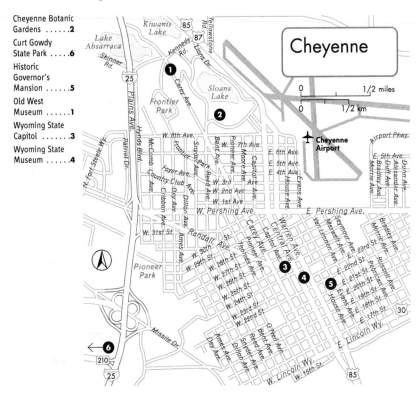

🚘 *$2 resident vehicles, $4 nonresident vehicles* ⊙ *Daily 24 hrs; entrance fee station, 7 AM–11 PM.*

① **Old West Museum.** This museum within Frontier Park houses some
FodorśChoice   30,000 artifacts—including 125 carriages, the largest collection of horse-
★   drawn vehicles in the state—relating to rodeos, ranching, and Cheyenne
Frontier Days. Guided tours are geared toward children. During Frontier Days the museum hosts the Governor's Invitational Western Art Show
and Sale, which exhibits works by top Western wildlife and landscape
artists from across the country. ⊠ *4610 N. Carey Ave.* ☎ *307/778–7290
or 800/266–2696* ⊕ *www.oldwestmuseum.org* 🚘 *$5* ⊙ *Sept.–May,
weekdays 9–5, Sat. 11–4; June–Aug., weekdays 8:30–5, weekends 9–5;
extended hrs during Frontier Days, in late July.*

④ **Wyoming State Museum.** Several permanent exhibits are dedicated to
exploring the heritage, culture, and landscape of Wyoming, covering
everything from natural resources to wildlife to historical events.
There's a hands-on exhibit geared to children, and the museum hosts
several additional temporary exhibits each year. ⊠ *Barrett Building,
2301 Central Ave.* ☎ *307/777–7022* ⊕ *wyomuseum.state.wy.us*
🚘 *Free* ⊙ *May–Oct., Tues.–Sat. 9–4:30; Nov.–Apr., Tues.–Fri. 9–4:30,
Sat. 10–2.*

Also Worth Seeing

5 **Historic Governor's Mansion.** Between 1905 and 1976 (when the state built a new residence for the governor), 19 Wyoming first families made their home in this Colonial Revival building. Period furnishings and ornate chandeliers remain in nearly every room. ⊠ *300 E. 21st St.* ☎ *307/777–7878* ⊕ *wyoparks.state.wy.us/HGMslide.htm* 🖼 *Free* ☉ *Tues.–Sat. 9–5.*

3 **Wyoming State Capitol.** Construction on this Corinthian-style building, now on the National Register of Historic Places, was authorized by the Ninth Territorial Legislative Assembly in 1886. The dome, covered in 24-karat gold leaf and visible from all roads leading into the city, is 50 feet in diameter at the base and 146 feet high. Standing in front is a statue of Esther Hobart Morris, a proponent of women's suffrage. One of Wyoming's nicknames is the "Equality State" because of its early advocacy of women's rights. Thanks to Wyoming's informal ways, it's not unusual to find the governor wandering the halls of the capitol. You can take a self-guided tour of state offices and the Senate and House chambers. ⊠ *Capitol Ave.* ☎ *307/777–7220* ⊕ *www.state.wy.us* 🖼 *Free* ☉ *Sept.–Apr., weekdays 8–5; May–Aug., weekdays 8–5, Sat. 9–5.*

Sports & the Outdoors

Golf

The **Airport Course** (⊠ 4801 Central Ave. ☎ 307/637–6418) has 18 holes. There's a 9-hole course at **Little America Hotel and Resort** (⊠ 2800 W. Lincolnway ☎ 307/775–8400). Play 18 holes of golf at **Prairie View** (⊠ 3601 Windmill Rd. ☎ 307/637–6420).

Where to Stay & Eat

★ **$$–$$$$** ✕ **Little Bear Steakhouse.** Locals rave about this classic American steak house decorated with a Western theme. The seafood selections are diverse and well prepared. Try the New York strip steak or the rib eye; salmon is fixed in several ways. ⊠ *1700 Little Bear Rd.* ☎ *307/634–3684* ▭ *AE, D, DC, MC, V.*

$–$$$ ✕ **The Albany.** Historic photographs of early Cheyenne set the tone for this downtown icon, a place that seems as old as the city itself (the structure was built circa 1900). It's a bit dark, and the booths are a bit shabby, but the American food is solid. Now if only you could get the walls to tell their stories. No doubt they've heard it all, as many of the movers and shakers in Cheyenne's past (and a few in its present) have eaten here. The menu lists hot and cold sandwiches, salads, and burgers, plus prime rib, steak, pork, lamb, and seafood. ⊠ *1506 Capitol Ave.* ☎ *307/638–3507* ▭ *AE, D, DC, MC, V.*

$–$$$ ✕ **Texas Roadhouse.** Close to the Dell Range Boulevard shopping district, this steak house also serves chicken, pork, and pasta. Favorite menu items include the portobello-mushroom chicken sandwich and barbecue ribs. The Western atmosphere includes buckets of peanuts; when you eat the peanuts, throw the shells on the hardwood floor just like cowboys did in the 1800s. You can wet your whistle at the bar. ⊠ *1931 Bluegrass Circle* ☎ *307/638–1234* ▭ *AE, D, MC, V.*

CloseUp

CHEYENNE FRONTIER DAYS

ONE OF THE PREMIER EVENTS in the Cowboy State is Cheyenne Frontier Days, held the last full week of July every year since 1897. The event started as a rodeo for ranch-riding cowboys who liked to show off their skills; now it consumes all of Cheyenne for nine days, when 250,000 to 300,000 people come into town.

Parades, carnivals, concerts, and more fill the streets and exhibition grounds, but rodeo remains the heart of Frontier Days, drawing the best cowboys and cowgirls each year. There is no rodeo quite like this one, known by the trademarked nickname "Daddy of 'Em All."

By the Numbers
Cheyenne Frontier Days includes: nine afternoon rodeos; nine nighttime concerts; eight days of Indian dancing (Saturday–Saturday); four parades (Saturday, Tuesday, Thursday and Saturday); three pancake breakfasts (Monday, Wednesday and Friday); one U.S. Air Force air show (Wednesday); and one art show (all month).

The Rodeos
Dozens of the top Professional Rodeo Cowboys Association contenders come to Cheyenne to face off in bull riding, calf roping, saddle bronc or bareback bronc riding, and steer wrestling. Women compete in barrel racing; trick riders and wisecracking rodeo clowns break up the action. In one of the most exciting events, three-man teams catch a wild horse and saddle it, then one team member rides the horse around a track in a bronc-busting rendition of the Kentucky Derby. Frontier Days wraps up with the final rodeo, in which the top contestants from a week's worth of rodeos compete head-to-head.

Extracurriculars
Each night, concerts showcase top country entertainers such as Kenny Chesney, Toby Keith, and Tim McGraw (be sure to buy tickets in advance). Members of the Northern Arapaho and Eastern Shoshone tribes from the Wind River Reservation perform the Indian dances at a temporary Native American village where they also drum, sing, and share their culture. The parades show off a huge collection of horse-drawn vehicles, and the free pancake breakfasts feed as many as 12,000 people in two hours. Crowds descend on the midway for carnival rides and games.

Boots & Books
Of course, there's plenty of shopping: at the Western wear and gear trade show you can buy everything from boots and belts to home furnishings and Western art. And you can pick up regional titles at book signings by members of the Western Writers of America.

Plan Ahead
Cheyenne Frontier Days entertains both kids and adults, in large numbers. It not only takes over Cheyenne but fills lodgings in nearby Laramie, Wheatland, Torrington, and even cities in northern Colorado. If you plan to attend, make your reservations early—some hotels book a year out.

For further information and to book rodeo and concert tickets, contact **Cheyenne Frontier Days** (✉ Box 2477, Cheyenne 82003 ☎ 307/778-7222 locally, 800/543-2339 in WY, 800/227-6336 elsewhere ⊕ www.cfdrodeo.com). The Web site is a useful resource: you can buy tickets online, see a schedule of activities, and order a brochure, all well in advance of the event itself.

\$–\$\$ ✕ **Snake River Grill & Pub.** This downtown spot in the historic Union Pacific Railroad Depot has its own brewery. The bar looks out on the trains that still pass through Cheyenne. Eat sandwiches, stone-oven pizzas, pasta, fresh fish, or steak in the bar or the adjacent restaurant. ☒ *115 W. 15th St., Suite 1* ☎ *307/634–7625* ▤ *AE, D, MC, V.*

¢–\$ ✕ **Los Amigos.** Mexican sombreros, serapes, and artwork on the walls complement the south-of-the-border food at this local favorite south of downtown. Deep-fried tacos and green chili are popular items, and the portions are big. ☒ *620 Central Ave.* ☎ *307/638–8591* ▤ *MC, V* ☉ *Closed Sun.*

\$\$ ✕▥ **Best Western Hitching Post Inn.** State legislators frequent this hotel, known to locals as "The Hitch." With its dark-wood walls, the hotel has an elegance not found elsewhere in Cheyenne. It books country-and-western performers in the lounge. The Cheyenne Cattle Company restaurant (\$\$–\$\$\$\$) serves steak and other dishes in a quiet, relaxed dining room. Next door at the Ikon Center are miniature golf, laser tag, and ice-skating. ☒ *1700 W. Lincolnway, 82001* ☎ *307/638–3301* 🖷 *307/778–7194* ⊕ *www.hitchingpostinn.com* ⤵ *166 rooms* ⌂ *Restaurant, coffee shop, room service, refrigerators, in-room data ports, cable TV, indoor-outdoor pool, gym, lobby lounge, dance club, shop, laundry service, business services, convention center, airport shuttle, no-smoking rooms* ▤ *AE, D, DC, MC, V.*

\$–\$\$ ✕▥ **Little America Hotel and Resort.** An executive golf course is the highlight of this resort at the intersection of I–80 and I–25. Most guest rooms are spread among several buildings clustered around the swimming pool, and some are attached to the common public areas via a glassed-in breezeway. The 24-hour coffee shop (¢–\$\$\$) serves sandwiches, chicken, steak, and seafood (try the hot turkey sandwich); sit at linen-covered tables or in large booths in the dining room (\$–\$\$\$\$), which has piano music. On the menu there you will find seafood, steak, and prime rib. ☒ *2800 W. Lincolnway, 82001* ☎ *307/775–8400 or 800/235–6396* 🖷 *307/775–8425* ⊕ *www.littleamerica.com* ⤵ *188 rooms* ⌂ *Restaurant, coffee shop, room service, some minibars, refrigerators, in-room data ports, cable TV, 9-hole golf course, pool, gym, bar, lounge, nightclub, shops, laundry service, business services, convention center, airport shuttle, no-smoking rooms* ▤ *AE, D, DC, MC, V.*

\$\$ ▥ **Nagle Warren Mansion.** This delightful Victorian mansion B&B, built
FodorsChoice in 1888, has gorgeous woodwork, ornate staircases, and period furniture and wallpaper. Antiques furnish the lavish rooms, which are named for figures associated with the mansion's history; some rooms have gas fireplaces. Close to downtown, the B&B is near restaurants and within walking distance of shops. ☒ *222 E. 17th St., 82001* ☎ *307/637–3333 or 800/811–2610* 🖷 *307/638–6879* ⊕ *www.naglewarrenmansion.com* ⤵ *12 rooms* ⌂ *Dining room, in-room data ports, gym, hot tub, library, piano, meeting rooms, no-smoking rooms, cable TV; no a/c* ▤ *AE, MC, V* ◉ *BP.*

¢–\$ ▥ **Rainsford Inn.** Elegant surroundings and a B&B atmosphere welcome you on historic "Cattleman's Row" in the heart of downtown Cheyenne. The Cattle Baron Corner suite has dark-wood furniture and ornaments ranging from ropes to boots. It overlooks 17th Street, where Cheyenne's cattle barons lived in the late 1800s. One room is suitable for people with disabilities and includes a roll-in shower. The third-floor Grandma's Attic is a very private retreat. All rooms have whirlpool tubs, one has a gas fireplace, and a full breakfast is included. ⊠ *219 E. 18th St., 82001* ☎ *307/638–2337* ⊟ *307/634–4506* ⊕ *www.rainsfordinnbedandbreakfast. com* ⤴ *6 rooms* ♿ *Dining room, library, no-smoking rooms* ⊟ *AE, MC, V* ⦿ *BP.*

Camping

⚠ **Curt Gowdy State Park.** In rolling country with pine forest and a profusion of wildflowers during spring and summer, Curt Gowdy is a good camping spot about 20 mi west of the city. The park has picnic sites and areas for swimming, boating, and fishing. The campsites can be used for tents or trailers. ♿ *Flush toilets, pit toilets, dump station, drinking water, fire pits, picnic tables, public telephone, play area, swimming (lake)* ⤴ *150 sites* ⊠ *1351 Hyndslodge Rd., off Hwy. 210* ☎ *307/632–7946 or 877/996–7275* ⊕ *wyoparks.state.wy.us/cgslide.htm* ⊡ *$6 for Wyoming residents, $12 for nonresidents* ⊟ *No credit cards.*

⚠ **Terry Bison Ranch.** In addition to being a full-service campground and RV park with a restaurant and occasional entertainment, this is a working bison ranch, with nearly 2,000 head on the property. ♿ *Flush toilets, full hookups, drinking water, guest laundry* ⤴ *88 full hookups, 100 tent sites; 7 cabins, 17 bunkhouse rooms* ⊠ *I–25 Service Rd. near the Colorado state line* ☎ *307/634–4171* ⊟ *307/634–9746* ⊕ *www. terrybisonranch.com* ⊡ *$15 tent sites, $25 full hookups, $38 bunkhouse rooms, $79 cabins* ⊟ *D, DC, MC, V.*

⚠ **Wyoming Campground and Mobile Home Park.** Two of the attractions at this campground are a swimming pool and Internet service. It's on the south side of Cheyenne. ♿ *Flush toilets, full hookups, partial hookups (electric), dump station, drinking water, guest laundry, showers, picnic tables, electricity, public telephone, play area, swimming (pool)* ⤴ *50 full hookups, 20 partial hookups, 50 tent sites* ⊠ *I–80, Exit 377* ☎ *307/547–2244* ⊡ *$14–$27 tent sites, $17–$31 partial hookups, $19–$34 full hookups* ⊟ *AE, D, DC, MC, V* ⦿ *May–Oct.*

Nightlife & The Arts

For an evening of live rock and roll (country and western during Cheyenne Frontier Days) that you can enjoy on a large dance floor, try the **Cheyenne Club** (⊠ 1617 Capitol Ave. ☎ 307/635–7777). The dance floor and rock and roll beckon at **The Outlaw** (⊠ 3839 E. Lincolnway ☎ 307/635–7552). You'll find live country and western plus rock and roll Tuesday through Saturday, dancing, and drinks at **Rockin' Cowboy Club** (⊠ 312 S. Greeley Hwy. ☎ 307/637–3800).

A wide variety of cultural events, including concerts, theater productions, dance recitals and performances by the Cheyenne Symphony Orchestra take place at **Cheyenne Civic Center** (⊠ 510 W. 20th St. ☎ 877/691–2787 ⊕ www.cheyenneciviccenter.org). Original oil paintings, sculpture and other art is sold at **Manitou Gallery** (⊠ 1715 Carey Ave. ☎ 307/635–0019).

Shopping

Cheyenne's **Frontier Mall** (⊠ 1400 Dell Range Blvd. ☎ 307/638–2290) houses 75 specialty shops and four major department stores. It's as typical an American mall as you'll find. For the best women's Western-style clothing in the city, ranging from belts, pants, shirts, and skirts to leather jackets, visit **Just Dandy** (⊠ 212 W. 17th St. ☎ 307/635–2565). **Wrangler** (⊠ 16th and Capitol Sts. ☎ 307/634–3048) stocks a full line of traditional Western clothing, ranging from Wrangler and Rocky Mountain jeans to Panhandle Slim shirts, Resistol hats, and Laredo boots. There are sizes and styles for the entire family. Handcrafted furniture, artwork, and Western home items are available at **Wyoming Home** (⊠ 509 W. Lincolnway ☎ 307/638–2222).

A Side Trip to Fort Laramie National Historic Site

❼ *105 mi north of Cheyenne via Hwys. 25 and 26.*

Fodor'sChoice
★

Fort Laramie is one of the most important historic sites in Wyoming, in part because its original buildings are extremely well preserved, but also because it played a role in several significant periods in Western history. Near the confluence of the Laramie and North Platte rivers, the fort began as a trading post in 1834, and it was an important provisioning point for travelers on the Oregon Trail in 1843, the Mormon Trail in 1847, and the California Trail in 1849, when it also became a military site. In 1851 the first treaty between the U.S. government and the Northern Plains Indians was negotiated near the fort, and in 1868 a second Fort Laramie Treaty led to the end of the First Sioux War, also known as Red Cloud's War. Costumed interpreters reenact scenes of military life and talk about the fur trade, overland migration, and relations between settlers and Native Americans. ⊠ *Goshen County Rd. 270, 3 mi west of town of Fort Laramie* ☎ *307/837–2221* ⊕ *www.nps.gov/ fola* 🎫 *$2* ☉ *Site daily 8–dusk; visitor center daily 8–5.*

en route

Although I–80 connects Cheyenne and Laramie more quickly, the drive between the two cities on **Happy Jack Road** (Highway 210) is very scenic, particularly in spring and early summer, when wildflowers are in full bloom. The road winds over the high plains, past Curt Gowdy State Park, and provides access to the Vedauwoo Recreation Area before linking back to I–80, 7 mi east of Laramie at the **Lincoln Monument.** At this state rest area you can obtain information about the region and view a larger-than-life sculpture of the 16th president.

The **Vedauwoo Recreation Area,** in the Medicine Bow–Routt National Forest, is a particularly unusual area and a great place for a picnic. Springing out of high plains and open meadows are glacial remnants in the form of huge granite boulders piled skyward with reckless abandon. These one-of-a-kind rock formations, dreamscapes of gray stone, are great for hiking, climbing, and photography. There's also camping here. ⊠ *31 mi west of Cheyenne off I–80 or Hwy. 210* ☎ *307/745–2300* ⊕ *www.fs.fed.us/r2/mbr* 🎫 *Free, camping $10* ☉ *Daily 24 hrs.*

LARAMIE

The historic downtown of Laramie, nestled in a valley between the Medicine Bow Mountains and the Laramie Range, has several quaint buildings, some of which date back to 1868, the year after the railroad arrived and the city was established. For a time it was a tough "end-of-the-rail" town. Vigilantes took care of lawbreakers, hanging them from convenient telegraph poles. Then, in 1872, the city constructed the Wyoming Territorial Prison on the bank of the Little Laramie River. One of its most famous inmates was Butch Cassidy. The prison has since closed, and things have calmed down in this city of approximately 30,000. It's now the center of open-plains ranching country and the site of the University of Wyoming, the only university in the state.

You can get brochures from the Laramie Chamber of Commerce, on South 3rd Street, for a self-guided tour of the late-19th-century Victorian architecture. Also available are the "Architectural Walking Tour" brochure, which focuses on the historic residences in the downtown area, and the "Laramie Antique Trail" guide, with locations of antiques shops in and around downtown.

Exploring Laramie

I–80 skirts the south and then west sides of town; U.S. 287 (3rd Street within the city) bisects Laramie from north to south. Grand Avenue, which borders the University of Wyoming, is the primary east–west route through Laramie.

a good tour

Begin your tour of Laramie at **Wyoming Territorial Prison State Historic Site ❽**, location of the restored Wyoming Territorial Prison and several other historic displays. When you're ready to leave the park, turn left out of the parking lot and follow Clark Street east to 6th Street; turn right and drive a few blocks south to Ivinson Avenue. The **Laramie Plains Museum ❾** stands on the corner of 6th and Ivinson. Get back in your car and travel east on Ivinson to 15th Street, turn left on 15th to Willett Drive, and turn right (east) on Willett to reach a large building that looks like an upside-down funnel. This is the **American Heritage Center ⓭**, with collections on American and Western history.

TIMING Plan on spending most of a day on this tour. Note that several museums close on Sunday and/or Monday and that the Wyoming Territorial Park is open only in summer.

The Main Attractions

⓭ **American Heritage Center.** The center houses more than 10,000 photographs, rare books, collections of papers, and memorabilia related to such subjects as American and Western history, the petroleum industry, conservation movements, transportation, and the performing arts. Permanent and temporary art displays also fill the museum space. ✉ *2111 Willet Dr.* ☎ *307/766–4114* ⊕ *www.uwyo.edu/ahc* ✉ *Free* ☉ *Sept.–May, weekdays 8–5, Sat. 11–5; June–Aug., weekdays 7:30–4:30.*

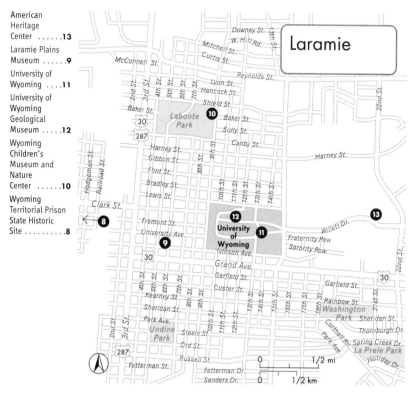

9 **Laramie Plains Museum.** Edward Ivinson, a businessman and philanthropist and one of Laramie's first settlers, built the mansion that houses this museum in 1892; it's now on the National Register of Historic Places. Inside is a growing collection of historical artifacts from the Laramie plains area. ⊠ *603 Ivinson Ave.* ☎ *307/742–4448* ⊕ *www. laramiemuseum.org* 🖃 *$5* ⊗ *Mid-June–mid-Aug., Tues.–Sat. 9–5, Sun. 1–4; mid-Aug.–mid-June, Tues.–Sat. 1–4.*

12 **University of Wyoming Geological Museum.** This is one of the University of Wyoming's most notable museums, in a building with a dinosaur statue out front. Inside, a skeleton of an apatosaurus is 15 feet high and 75 feet long; it's believed the animal would have weighed 30 tons. Other exhibits explore the dinosaur family tree, meteorites, fossils, and earthquakes. ⊠ *Northwest corner of University of Wyoming campus* ☎ *307/ 766–2646 or 307/766–4218* ⊕ *www.uwyo.edu/geomuseum* 🖃 *Free* ⊗ *Weekdays 8–5, weekends 10–3.*

☝ **10** **Wyoming Children's Museum and Nature Center.** Here children are encouraged to explore, make noise, experiment, play, imagine, discover, and invent. The hands-on exhibits emphasize wildlife, nature, and some local history. Live animals include Hissy, a great horned owl. The museum is on the edge of Labonte Park, which has playground equipment and plenty of grassy space in which children can burn off some energy. ✉ *968 N. 9th St.* ☎ *307/745–6332* ⊕ *www.wyshs.org/mus-wychildrens. htm* ✍ *$3* ☉ *Memorial Day–Labor Day, Tues.–Thurs. 9–4, Fri. 1–5, Sat. 10–3; Labor Day–Memorial Day, Tues.–Thurs. 9–4, Sat. 10–3.*

❽ Wyoming Territorial Prison State Historic Site. Perhaps because of the bedlam of the early days, Laramie became the site of the Wyoming Territorial Prison in 1872. Until 1903, it was the region's federal and state penal facility, locking down Butch Cassidy and other infamous frontier outlaws. Today the restored prison is a state historic site that brings to life the legends of frontier law and justice. The Warden's house and a broom factory are being restored and may open in 2006. In addition to the prison, the park contains a 19th-century railroad display and a replica frontier town, where there are occasional living-history programs. The Horse Barn Dinner Theater has periodic programs as well. ✉ *975 Snowy Range Rd.* ☎ *307/745–6161 or 800/845–2287* ⊕ *www. wyoprisonpark.org* ✍ *$5* ☉ *Park, mid-Apr.–Oct., daily 9–6; frontier town, June–Aug., weekends 9–6.*

Also Worth Seeing

⓫ University of Wyoming. In addition to having several museums and attractions, the university hosts year-round events—from concerts to football games. You can join a tour or just pick up information on the university at the **UW Visitor Center** (✉ 14th St. and Grand Ave. ☎ 307/ 766–4075). The **Anthropology Museum** (☎ 307/766–5136) houses numerous Native American exhibits. Among the artwork displayed in the **Art Museum** (☎ 307/766–6622) are paintings, sculpture, photography, and folk art from America, Europe, Africa, and Asia. Kids especially enjoy looking at the butterflies, mosquitoes, and other crawling and flying critters at the **Insect Museum** (☎ 307/766–2298). You can learn about the stars and watch laser shows at the university's **planetarium** (☎ 307/ 766–6514). The **Rocky Mountain Herbarium** (☎ 307/766–2236) focuses on Rocky Mountain plants but also includes other examples of flora from the Northern Hemisphere. Call individual museums for opening times and fees (most of them are free). ✉ *13th St. and Ivinson Ave.* ⊕ *www.uwyo.edu.*

Sports & the Outdoors

Bicycling

Mountain-biking trails are scattered throughout the Medicine Bow–Routt National Forest and the Happy Jack recreation area, east of Laramie. For information, trail maps, and rentals, see Mike or Doug Lowham at the **Pedal House** (✉ 207 S. 1st St. ☎ 307/742–5533).

Cross-Country Skiing

The Medicine Bow–Routt National Forest and the Happy Jack recreation area have numerous cross-country trails. For information and rentals, contact **Cross Country Connection** (✉ 117 Grand Ave. ☎ 307/721–2851).

Golf

Enjoy the links at the 18-hole **Jacoby Park Golf Course** (✉ Off N. 30th St. ☎ 307/745–3111).

Where to Stay & Eat

$$$–$$$$ ✕ **Cavalryman Supper Club.** It's the food, not the look of the place, that attracts people to this restaurant on the plains, 1 mi south of Laramie on U.S. 287. Menu highlights include prime rib, steak, and lobster. Every dinner includes deep-fried mushrooms, soup and salad, and dessert. There is a lounge area with dining on the upper and lower floors. ⊠ *4425 S. 3rd St.* ☎ *307/745–4578* 🖃 *AE, DC, MC, V* ⊘ *No lunch.*

$–$$$ ✕ **The Overland Fine Eatery.** Patio dining and a superb wine list enhance
Fodor'sChoice the food—pasta, chicken, quiche, beef, and seafood—at this restaurant
★ in the historic district, right on the railroad tracks. Sunday brunch might include such unique entrées as yellowfin tuna and eggs, a buffalo-chili omelet, or avocados Benedict. ⊠ *100 Ivinson Ave.* ☎ *307/721–2800* 🖃 *AE, D, MC, V.*

$$–$$$ 🛏 **Laramie Comfort Inn.** On busy Grand Avenue, this Comfort Inn is close to restaurants and fast-food chains, as well as War Memorial Stadium at the University of Wyoming. One of the three suites has a whirlpool. ⊠ *3420 Grand Ave., 82070* ☎ *307/721–8856 or 800/228–5150* 🖷 *307/721–5166* ⊕ *www.comfortinn.com* ➪ *55 rooms, 3 suites, 1 efficiency apartment* ⟁ *Indoor pool, gym, hot tub, cable TV, no-smoking rooms* 🖃 *AE, D, DC, MC, V* ⊺⊙⊺ *CP.*

¢–$ 🛏 **Howard Johnson Inn.** At this white-brick motel, the lobby and halls are rustic Western knotty pine, and the rooms are basic, with contemporary furnishings. The property includes a convenience store, a 24-hour restaurant, and a liquor store. It's on the western edge of town, at the Snowy Range Road exit off I–80. ⊠ *1555 Jackson St., Exit 311 off I–80, Box 580, 82070* ☎ *307/742–8371* 🖷 *307/742–0884* ➪ *112 rooms* ⟁ *Restaurant, indoor pool, hot tub, cable TV, no-smoking rooms, bar* 🖃 *AE, D, DC, MC, V.*

Camping

⛺ **Laramie KOA.** This campground on the west side of town has lots of grassy space and some trees. Bicycles are provided for free, and for an extra fee you can have satellite TV and telephone service for your RV. Modem service is also available at no extra charge. There are one- and two- bedroom cabins. ⟁ *Flush toilets, full hookups, drinking water, picnic tables, general store, play area* ➪ *116 full hookups, 30 tent sites; 8 cabins* ⊠ *1271 W. Baker St., I–80 at Curtis St. exit* ☎ *307/742–6553* 🖷 *307/742–5039* ⊕ *www.koa.com* ⊠ *$10–$16 tent sites, $27 full hookups, $35–$45 cabins* 🖃 *D, DC, MC, V.*

Nightlife & the Arts

Nightlife

On weekends you can kick up your heels to live country and western music at the **Buckhorn** (⊠ 114 Ivinson Ave. ☎ 307/742–3554), or listen to a DJ upstairs at the Parlour Bar any night. Take a spin around the dance floor at the **Cowboy Saloon** (⊠ 108 S. 2nd St. ☎ 307/721–3165) on weekends. On Thursdays September through May the place hops with college kids who aren't old enough to be in the bar at other times; no alcohol is served then, but there is usually live music, dance contests, and other events. A young set often congregates at the **Drawbridge Tavern** (⊠ 1622 Grand Ave. ☎ 307/745–3490), which hosts rock bands. College students gather and shoot pool at **Mingles** (⊠ 3206 Grand Ave. ☎ 307/721–2005).

The Arts
Dinner theater is performed at the **Horse Barn Dinner Theater** (⊠ 975 Snowy Range Rd. ☎ 307/745–6161 or 800/845–2287).

The **University of Wyoming's Fine Arts Program** (⊠ East end of Fraternity and Sorority Row ☎ 307/766–5249) regularly holds concerts by classical and popular performers. The **University of Wyoming Fine Arts Center** (⊠ East end of Fraternity and Sorority Row ☎ 307/766–3327) periodically hosts productions by the University of Wyoming Department of Theater and Dance.

Shopping

Laramie's most interesting shopping is found in a shopping district called **Landmark Square** along Ivinson Avenue and Grand Avenue. Stores here sell artwork, clothing, and handcrafted items.

Books
Chickering Bookstore (⊠ 203 S. 2nd St. ☎ 307/742–8609) showcases regional authors, self-help books, and a good selection of children's titles. **The Grand Newsstand** (⊠ 214 Grand Ave. ☎ 307/742–5127) has the best selection of Western and regional titles in the city. **The Second Story** (⊠ 105 Ivinson Ave. ☎ 307/745–4423), in an old, antiques-laden upstairs suite of offices, stocks only "personally recommended books," some of them signed by visiting authors.

Crafts & Gifts
★ **Curiosity Shoppe** (⊠ 206 S. 2nd St. ☎ 307/745–4760) sells antiques, pottery, and hand-embroidered and -crocheted items. **A Touch of Country** (⊠ 312 S. 2nd St. ☎ 307/721–2171) has folk art, pottery, baskets, country pine furniture, and a year-round Christmas Shoppe.

Specialty Foods
Laramie's **Whole Earth Granary** (⊠ 111 Ivinson Ave. ☎ 307/745–4268) sells organic whole grains and flours, 50 varieties of coffee, herbal extracts, essential oils, and fresh seafood flown in weekly, including live Maine lobster.

IN & AROUND THE SNOWY RANGE

Mountain lakes and streams, aspens and pines, camping areas, and trails for hiking, cross-country skiing, and snowmobiling draw outdoor enthusiasts to the Snowy Range, which encompasses portions of both the Laramie and Brush Creek districts of Medicine Bow–Routt National Forest. The Snowy Range Pass, a stretch of Highway 130 running west from Centennial toward Saratoga, climbs as high as 10,847 feet; driving through the pass, which is open only in summer, takes you past stunning views of the surrounding peaks, including 12,013-foot Medicine Bow Peak. The high elevation means snow caps the mountain peaks in the range year-round.

Medicine Bow

⑭ *60 mi northwest of Laramie via U.S. 30.*

When novelist Owen Wister (1860–1938) first visited Medicine Bow—the town he would immortalize in his 1902 classic Western tale *The Virginian*—he noted that the community looked "as if strewn there by the wind." Today the town still looks somewhat windblown, although the small business district is anchored by the Virginian Hotel, built in the early 1900s and named in honor of the book. This is a community of 320 struggling for survival, with an economy based on the vagaries of agriculture and mining. Although the town sits at the intersection of U.S. 30 (Lincoln Highway) and Wyoming Route 487, you'll seldom encounter much traffic here, except during the fall hunting season (the area is particularly noted for its antelope hunting) and when there are football or basketball games at the University of Wyoming. On those days, expect a crowd on the road and fans talking of sports at the Virginian Hotel.

You can learn about the history of this small town at the **Medicine Bow Museum,** housed in an old railroad depot built in 1913. Owen Wister's summer cabin was relocated to the premises and stands next door. ⊠ *405 Lincoln Pl.* ☎ *307/379–2225, 307/379–2581 tour appointments* ⊕ *www.medicinebow.org/museum.htm* ⊠ *Free* ⊙ *Memorial Day–Sept., weekdays 10–5 and by appointment.*

Where to Stay & Eat

¢–$ ✕⊞ **Virginian Hotel.** Inspired by the Owen Wister novel *The Virginian,* **Fodor'sChoice** this sandstone hotel was built in 1909 and has been operating nearly ★ continuously ever since. Claw-foot tubs, tulip-shape lights, and high beds with comforters fill the Victorian-style rooms. The rooms in the main hotel don't have TVs, phones, or radios (most don't even have electrical outlets), but the atmosphere more than makes up for the lack of amenities. In the main hotel, only the suites have private bathrooms; rooms in the Bunkhouse Motel annex have TVs and bathrooms. The dining room ($–$$), with antique oak furniture and 19th-century photographs, serves American fare such as steak and chicken. Saturday nights usually bring dancing to a live band. ⊠ *404 Lincoln Hwy., Box 127, 82329* ☎ *307/379–2377* ⌖ *26 rooms, 4 suites in hotel; 12 rooms in Bunkhouse Motel* ⚬ *Restaurant, bar, no-smoking rooms; no phones in some rooms, no TV in some rooms, no a/c* ⊟ *MC, V.*

Centennial

⑮ *30 mi west of Laramie via Hwy. 130; 90 mi south of Medicine Bow via U.S. 30 and Hwy. 130.*

Snuggled up against the mountains of the Snowy Range, Centennial lies at the head of the glacial Centennial Valley. As the community closest to the Snowy Range, the town makes a good base from which to take part in numerous recreational activities, including hiking, cross-country skiing, snowmobiling, and downhill skiing. This small town has a few hardy year-round residents, and many more people who summer in the area.

The former Centennial Railroad Depot now houses the **Nici Self Museum,** at the eastern edge of town. The museum displays ranching, farming, and mining equipment, plus artifacts typical of what you'd find in a pioneer home; there's also an outdoor-equipment exhibit. ⊠ *2740 Hwy. 130* ☎ *307/742–7158 or 307/634–4955* ⊕ *wyshs.org/mus-nici.htm* 🖼 *Donations accepted* ☉ *Mid-June–Labor Day, Fri.–Mon. 1–4.*

You can hike, picnic, fish, ski, snowmobile, or take photographs in the 400,000 acres of **Medicine Bow–Routt National Forest, Laramie District** (⊠ Laramie office: 2468 Jackson St., Laramie 82070 ☎ 307/745–2300, 877/444–6777 for camping ⊕ www.fs.fed.us/r2/mbr/), and that is the short list. The Laramie District has 19 developed campgrounds; dispersed camping is also allowed. Lodgings such as cabins, forest guard stations, and even a fire lookout tower high in the Snowy Range are available for rent in summer.

Sports & the Outdoors

CROSS-COUNTRY SKIING
The same trails that serve hikers in summer cater to cross-country skiers in winter in the Lower Snowy Range trail system. You can access several trails on Highway 130 west of Centennial in the Medicine Bow–Routt National Forest, including the Corner Mountain Trail (3 mi west of Centennial), Little Laramie Trail (5 mi west of Centennial), and the Green Rock Trail (9 mi west of Centennial). There is also a cross-country-skiing trail system at Snowy Range Ski and Recreation Area. Many of the trails are interconnected, so you can combine short trails for a longer ski trip.

HIKING
Dozens of miles of hiking trails slice through the Medicine Bow–Routt National Forest west of town. Major trailheads are on Highway 130, including trailheads for the 7-mi Corner Mountain Trail (3 mi west of Centennial), 7-mi Little Laramie Trail (5 mi west of Centennial), and 9-mi Medicine Bow Peak Trail (9 mi west of Centennial). The easy 1-mi Centennial Trail takes off from the Centennial Visitor Center at the forest boundary. More difficult is the 4½-mi Barber Lake Trail, which starts at Barber Lake and incorporates ski trails and old forest roads. Most hikers follow this trail downhill one way and instead of doubling back use two vehicles to shuttle between Barber Lake and the Corner Mountain trailhead (the Barber Lake Trail hooks up with part of the Corner Mountain trail).

Trail maps and information are available at the **Centennial Visitor's Center** (⊠ Hwy. 130, 1 mi west of Centennial ☎ 307/742–6023).

SKIING & SNOWBOARDING
Downhill skiing and snowboarding are available 7 mi west of Centennial at the **Snowy Range Ski and Recreation Area** (⊠ 5414 Mountain Mist Ct. ☎ 307/745–5750 or 800/462–7669 ⊕ www.snowyrange.com). There are slopes for beginners and experienced skiers, plus some cross-country-skiing trails.

Where to Stay & Eat

$$–$$$ ✕⊡ **Vee Bar Guest Ranch.** Along the Centennial Valley's Little Laramie River, 21 mi west of Laramie and 9 mi east of Centennial, this family-operated guest ranch builds its summer activity program around horse-back riding. Lodging is in 9 individual cabins and 4 lodge suites. You can buy an all-inclusive week or stay as a nightly B&B guest; October through April only the B&B plan is offered. B&B guests, and those not staying at the ranch, may eat in the dining room ($$–$$$) by reservation only. ⊠ *2091 Hwy. 130, Laramie 82070* ☎ *307/745–7036, 800/ 483–3227* 🖷 *307/745–7433* ⊕ *www.vee-bar.com* ⏎ *9 cabins, 4 lodge rooms* ⚭ *Dining room, refrigerators, Wi-Fi, exercise equipment, hot tub, fishing, hiking, horseback riding, cross-country skiing, babysitting, play-ground, laundry facilities; no a/c, no room TVs, no smoking* ⊟ *AE, D, MC, V* ⌖ *FAP.*

$ ✕⊡ **Old Corral Hotel & Steak House.** A crowd of Western carved-wood characters greets you on the front lawn of this log restaurant and hotel. Walking into the steak house ($$–$$$$), with its woodstove and ranch decorations, is like stepping into the Old West. Hand-hewn pine beds and dressers decorate the hotel rooms, and you have access to a deck with picnic tables and a hot tub, a pool room, and a TV room with videos. The lower level of the on-site gift shop sells T-shirts and Christmas decorations; upstairs there are antique replicas, including Native American pipes and outlaw paraphernalia. In winter you can rent snowmobiles. ⊠ *2750 Hwy. 130, 82055* ☎ *307/745–5918* 🖷 *307/742–6846* ⊕ *www. oldcorral.com* ⏎ *35 rooms* ⚭ *Restaurant, picnic area, cable TV with movies, some in-room VCRs, in-room data ports, outdoor hot tub, shop, laundry service, no-smoking rooms, some pets allowed; no a/c* ⊟ *D, MC, V* ⊗ *Closed mid-Oct.–mid-Dec. and mid-Apr.–mid-May.*

$–$$$ ⊡ **Rainbow Valley Resort.** Just outside town in a forest of pine and aspen, these cabins afford views of the Centennial Valley. The cabins, which have rustic pine furniture, sleep 3 to 10 people and have full kitchens and out-door gas grills; there's a two-night minimum stay. A common area has a basketball court and a horseshoe-pitching area. ⊠ *68 Rainbow Valley Rd., Box 303, 82055* ☎ *307/745–0368* ⊕ *www.rainbowvalleyresort. com* ⏎ *6 cabins* ⚭ *Kitchens, basketball, hiking, horseshoes; no room phones, no smoking, no room TVs, no a/c* ⊟ *MC, V.*

CAMPING In addition to the campgrounds listed here, there are several others in both the Laramie and Brush Creek districts of the **Medicine Bow–Routt National Forest** (☎ 877/444–6777, 307/745–2300 Laramie District, 307/ 326–5258 Brush Creek District ⊕ www.fs.fed.us/r2/mbr/).

⚠ **Brooklyn Lake.** On the east side of Snowy Range Pass, at an elevation of 10,200 feet, this small campground sits beside Brooklyn Lake and is surrounded by pine forest. You can fish in the lake and use non-motorized boats. All campsites have views of the lake. ⚭ *Pit toilets, fire pits, picnic tables* ⏎ *19 sites* ⊠ *Hwy. 130, 7 mi west of Centennial on Hwy. 130, then 2 mi east on Brooklyn Lake Rd./Forest Rd. 317* ☎ *307/ 745–2300* ⊕ *www.fs.fed.us/r2/mbr/* 🖾 *$10* 🕭 *Reservations not ac-cepted* ⊟ *No credit cards* ⊗ *July–Sept.*

⚠ **Nash Fork.** Pine trees surround this simple campground at an elevation of 10,200 feet. Each site can accommodate an RV or a tent, but

CloseUp

RELIVING HISTORY

THE RICH HISTORY of southern Wyoming lives on in its museums, forts, and towns, where sometimes you can not only observe but also relive a bit of that history. Arapaho, Ute, Shoshone and other Native American tribes lived and hunted in this area before it developed as a travel corridor for westbound emigrants in the mid-19th century. The first towns came with construction of the Union Pacific Railroad; white settlement grew as ranchers began raising cattle and miners started mining coal and other minerals.

Hell on Wheels
The Union Pacific Railroad pushed across southern Wyoming in 1868–69. It spawned "hell-on-wheels" cities where there was little law, but many hard-working men and early entrepreneurs who set up hotels and saloons, eating establishments and laundry services.

Most of the settlements were temporary, with businesses housed in tents; they folded up and followed the railroad tracks as they pushed west. Some of the tent towns, though, developed into permanent cities: Cheyenne, Laramie, Rawlins, Green River, and Evanston. Their old rail depots now serve as restaurants, museums, and visitor's centers.

King Coal
Coal mining started with the construction of the Union Pacific. In 1868 Wyoming's first coal mines appeared east of Rawlins, in the small town of Carbon. Now the southwestern corner of the state, from Rawlins to Evanston, is experiencing a new minerals boom, feeding the fuel-hungry nation on the remains of the prehistoric animals that once thrived here. Mining exhibits figure prominently at the museums in Hanna, Encampment and Green River; Evanston's museum features displays on the area's Chinese mining heritage.

Cowboy Culture
Texas cattlemen pushed the first herds into Wyoming in the 1870s. Soon the cattle spread to ranges all across the southern part of the territory, and homesteaders and small ranchers were supplanted by big operations.

The region's cowboy culture was popularized throughout the United States by the 1902 publication of Owen Wister's classic Western novel, The Virginian, partly set in Medicine Bow. With no television, radios, or phones in most rooms, a stay in the town's Virginian Hotel, built in 1909, transports you back into southern Wyoming's past. It's the perfect place to settle into an armchair with a copy of Wister's novel.

Taking the Waters
Where Native Americans and, later, white travelers and settlers soaked away aches and pains in the hot mineral springs at Saratoga, you can combine history with relaxation and take a dip in the Hobo Pool Hot Springs.

Experience a different kind of living history at Fort Laramie National Historic Site and Fort Bridger State Historic Site, where costumed interpreters portray the lives of 19th-century people who came through this land: mountain men and women, Pony Express riders, and pioneers on their way to Oregon, California, and Utah.

there are no hookups. ♿ *Pit toilets, drinking water, fire grates, fire pits, picnic tables* ✇ *27 sites* ✉ *Hwy. 130, 8 mi west of Centennial* ☎ *307/ 745–2300* ⊕ *www.fs.fed.us/r2/mbr/* ▣ *$10* ⌂ *Reservations not accepted* ▭ *No credit cards* ☉ *July–Oct.*

⚠ **Ryan Park.** During World War II this was the site of a camp for German prisoners, and you can still see some of the building foundations. The campground on the east side of Snowy Range Pass lies at an elevation of 8,000 feet. It has access to stream fishing as well as to hiking on forest trails and two-track roads. Just west of the small community of Ryan Park, it is 20 mi southeast of Saratoga. ♿ *Pit toilets, fire pits, picnic tables, drinking water* ✇ *19 sites* ✉ *Hwy. 130, 20 mi southeast of Saratoga* ☎ *307/326–5258* ⊕ *www.fs.fed.us/r2/mbr/ or www. reserveusa.com* ▣ *$10* ▭ *No credit cards* ☉ *May–Sept.*

Shopping

Leather purses, children's and regional-history books, clothing, ice cream, and baked goods are sold at the **Country Junction** (✉ 2742 Hwy. 130 ☎ 307/745–3318), on the eastern edge of Centennial and within walking distance of the Nici Self Museum. Antiques, wood furniture, ★ and a 5¢ cup of coffee are available at **J&N Mercantile** (✉ 2772 Hwy. 130 ☎ 307/745–0001), along with Wyoming products such as goat's-milk lotion, "cowboy bubble bath" (a bag of beans), and jewelry.

en route Highway 130 between Centennial and Saratoga is known as the **Snowy Range Scenic Byway.** This paved road, which is in excellent condition, crosses through the Medicine Bow–Routt National Forest, providing views of 12,013-foot Medicine Bow Peak and access to hiking trails, 10 campgrounds (6 right near the road), picnic areas, and 100 alpine lakes and streams. Gravel roads lead off the route into the national forest. Maps are available from the **Centennial Visitor's Center** (✉ Hwy. 130, 1 mi west of Centennial ☎ 307/742–6023).

At the top of the 10,847-foot Snowy Range Pass, about 10 mi west of Centennial, take a short walk to the Libby Flats Observation Site for views of the Snowy Range and, on clear days, Rocky Mountain National Park to the southwest in Colorado. Lake Marie, a jewel of a mountain lake at an elevation of approximately 10,000 feet, is also here. On the Saratoga side of the mountain, the road passes through pine forest and descends to the North Platte River valley, with cattle ranches on both sides of the highway. Note that there is ongoing construction near the junction of Highways 130 and 230, 8 mi south of Saratoga. Also, the byway is impassable in winter and therefore is closed between approximately mid-October and Memorial Day.

Saratoga

⑯ *49 mi west of Centennial via Hwy. 130, Memorial Day–early Oct.; rest of yr, 140 mi west of Centennial via Hwy. 130 east to Laramie, Hwy. 230 west to Encampment, and Hwy. 130 north or east to Laramie, I–80 west to Hwy. 130 and then south.*

Tucked away in a valley formed by the Snowy Range and Sierra Madre mountains, Saratoga is a rarely visited treasure. Fine shopping and dining happily combine with elegant lodging facilities and a landscape that's ideal for outdoor activities. This is a good spot for river floating and blue-ribbon fishing: the North Platte River bisects the region, and there are several lakes and streams nearby in the Medicine Bow–Routt National Forest. You can also cross-country ski and snowmobile in the area. The town first went by the name Warm Springs, but in an attempt to add an air of sophistication to the place, townsfolk changed the name to Saratoga in 1884 (after Saratoga Springs, New York).

★ Hot mineral waters flow freely through the **Hobo Pool Hot Springs,** and the adjacent swimming pool is heated by the springs. People have been coming here to soak for generations, including Native Americans, who considered the area neutral territory. Hardy folk can do as the Native Americans did and first soak in the hot water, then jump into the adjacent icy waters of the North Platte River. ☒ *201 S. River St.* ☎ *307/ 326–5417* 💲 *Free* ⊙ *Hot springs year-round, daily 24 hrs; pool Memorial Day–Labor Day, daily 9–8 (sometimes closed for lessons).*

The former Union Pacific Railroad depot houses the **Saratoga Historical and Cultural Association Museum,** with displays of local artifacts related to the history and geology of the area. Outdoor exhibits include a sheep wagon and a smithy. A nearby gazebo is used for occasional musical and historical programs in summer. ☒ *104 Constitution Ave.* ☎ *307/ 326–5511* ⊕ *www.saratoga-museum.org* 💲 *Donations accepted* ⊙ *Memorial Day–Labor Day, Tues.–Sat. 1–4.*

Sports & the Outdoors

CANOEING & RAFTING ★
Stoney Creek Outfitters (☒ 216 E. Walnut St. ☎ 307/326–8750 ⊕ www. grmo.com) offers guided canoe and raft expeditions on the North Platte River, plus canoe and drift-boat rentals.

CROSS-COUNTRY SKIING & SNOWMOBILING
Extensive trail networks in the Medicine Bow–Routt National Forest are good for novice and experienced cross-country skiers and snowmobilers. For trail conditions, contact the **Hayden/Brush Creek Ranger District** (☎ 307/326–5258 or 307/327–5481 ⊕ www.fs.fed.us/r2/mbr) of the Medicine Bow–Routt National Forest.

Snowmobile rentals, including full- and half-day guided treks into the Snowy Range or Sierra Madres, are available from **Platte Valley Outfitters** (☒ 1st St. and Bridge Ave. ☎ 307/326–5750).

FISHING
Brook trout are prevalent in the lakes and streams of Medicine Bow–Routt National Forest, and you can also find rainbow, golden, cutthroat, and brown trout, as well as splake. You can also drop a fly in the North Platte River. **Stoney Creek Outfitters** (☒ 216 E. Walnut St. ☎ 307/326–8750 ⊕ www.grmo.com) rents tackle and runs fishing trips on the Upper North Platte.

Where to Stay & Eat

$–$$ ✕ **Lazy River Cantina.** Mexican music and sombreros greet you at this downtown restaurant, which also includes a bar and lounge where locals and visitors take their shot at darts. The entrées include tacos, enchiladas, burritos, and chimichangas, served in one of two small rooms. You can sit in a booth and watch folks and traffic on busy Bridge Avenue. ⊠ *110 E. Bridge Ave.* ☎ *307/326–8472* ▭ *MC, V* ☻ *Closed Tues.*

★ **$–$$** ✕▥ **Saratoga Inn Resort.** With leather couches in the common areas, pole-frame beds, and Western art, this inn is as nice as any place in Wyoming. Some rooms are in the main lodge, which has a double fireplace lounge that opens both to the central sitting room and the back porch; other rooms are in separate buildings surrounding a large expanse of lawn and a hot-mineral-water swimming pool. There are five outdoor hot tubs filled with mineral water, three of them covered with teepees, a 9-hole public golf course, and tennis courts. The inn coordinates year-round activities—including fishing and horseback riding—with Brush Creek Guest Ranch. The Silver Saddle Restaurant ($$–$$$) serves steak, pasta, and seafood in a quiet, cozy setting with a fireplace to warm you in fall or winter. ⊠ *601 E. Pic-Pike Rd., Box 869, 82331* ☎ *307/326–5261* 🖷 *307/326–5109* ⊕ *www.saratogainn.com* ⇋ *50 rooms* ♻ *Restaurant, room service, cable TV, driving range, 9-hole golf course, putting green, 2 tennis courts, pro shop, pool, outdoor hot tub, fishing, horseback riding, bar, lobby lounge, shop, business services, meeting rooms, no-smoking rooms* ▭ *AE, DC, MC, V.*

¢–$$ ✕▥ **Wolf Hotel.** This downtown 1893 hotel on the National Register of
Fodor'sChoice Historic Places is well maintained by its proud owners. Although some
★ of the guest rooms are small, all of them have simple Victorian charm (note that the rooms are on the second and third floors, and there is no elevator; there also is no way to control the heat in individual rooms). The fine restaurant ($–$$$$), bar, and lounge also have Victorian furnishings, including dark-green wallpaper, antique oak tables, crystal chandeliers, and lacy drapes. Prime rib and steaks are the specialties, and seafood and lamb are also on the menu. Dinner reservations are strongly recommended. ⊠ *101 E. Bridge Ave., 82331* ☎ *307/326–5525* ⊕ *www. wolfhotel.com* ⇋ *5 rooms, 4 suites* ♻ *Restaurant, bar, lounge, no-smoking rooms; no TV in some rooms, no a/c* ▭ *AE, DC, MC, V.*

$$$ ▥ **Brush Creek Guest Ranch.** On this 6,000-acre working cattle ranch you get a chance to ride horses, work cattle, or just relax. Take advantage of the Orvis-endorsed fishing program, go rafting on North Platte River, or have a dip in the hot pool; in winter go cross-country skiing, snowshoeing, or snowmobiling (bring your own machine or rent one from the ranch). At night, retire to your small country cabin or to your room on the second floor of the main lodge. Ranch manager Kinta Blumenthal grew up on the ranch and can talk history or cattle. ⊠ *Brush Creek Rd. off Hwy. 130, 20 mi southeast of Saratoga and Encampment, 82331* ☎ *307/327–5241* ⊕ *www.brushcreekranch.com* ⇋ *13 rooms* ♻ *Dining room, picnic area, fishing, mountain bikes, hiking, horseback riding, cross-country skiing, snowmobiling, bar, snowshoeing, library, children's programs (ages 8–12); no smoking, no room phones, no room TVs* ▭ *MC, V* ⦿ *FAP.*

Nightlife & the Arts

NIGHTLIFE Local bands often play country-and-western music on weekend nights at the **Rustic Bar** (⊠ *124 E. Bridge Ave.* ☎ *307/326–5965*).

THE ARTS   A juried art show, music, and other activities are part of the **Platte Valley Festival of the Arts,** held each year during the weekend closest to the Fourth of July. Obtain information from the **Saratoga-Platte Valley Chamber of Commerce** (⊠ 115 W. Bridge Ave., Box 1095, 82331 ☎ 307/326–8855).

Shopping

Oil paintings, sculpture, and photographs are among the fine-art pieces showcased at **Blackhawk Gallery** (⊠ 100 N. 1st St. ☎ 307/326–5063). For gift items, women's clothing, and household goods ranging from spackle wear to china, stop by **The Cottage** (⊠ 102 E. Bridge Ave. ☎ 307/326–8504). The **Hat Creek Saddlery** (⊠ 107 W. Bridge Ave. ☎ 307/326–5755) sells handcrafted leather goods, boots, and hats. Locally-designed women's clothing, including dresses, pantsuits, and even fur coats, is available at **Laura M** (⊠ 114 E. Bridge Ave. ☎ 307/326–8187). If you want pampering, try the services at **Red Sage Spa & Artistry Salon** (⊠ 106 E. Bridge Ave. ☎ 307/326–8066). They offer reflexology, Reiki, warm stone massage, and salt glows, and sell candles and scented oils.

Encampment

🕡 *18 mi south of Saratoga via Hwys. 130 and 230.*

This is the gateway community to the Continental Divide National Scenic Trail, accessed at Battle Pass, 15 mi west on Highway 70. When completed, this trail will run from Canada all the way south to Mexico along the Continental Divide. Encampment is also a good place to launch trips into four nearby wilderness areas in the Hayden District of Medicine Bow–Routt National Forest—Platte River, Savage Run, Encampment River, and Huston Park—where you can go hiking, fishing, mountain biking, snowmobiling, and cross-country skiing.

Encampment got its start in 1838, when trappers held a rendezvous on a stream flowing from the Sierra Madre range. They called the site Camp le Grande, and the name stuck. When copper miners struck it rich in 1897, the community that sprang up became Grand Encampment. But the copper boom went bust by 1910, and Grand Encampment dropped the "Grand," even though the town survived as an agricultural and logging center. Most logging operations have since gone the way of mining here, leaving agriculture as the mainstay of the area. Recreation is a quickly emerging industry, but there's still a lot of quiet mountain country to explore, and it's not yet crowded in this town of 400 residents.

The modern interpretive center at the **Grand Encampment Museum** holds exhibits on the history of the Grand Encampment copper district and logging and mining. A pioneer town of original buildings includes the Lake Creek stage station, the Big Creek tie hack cabin, the Peryam homestead, the Slash Ridge fire tower, a blacksmith shop, a transportation barn, and a two-story outhouse. Among the other relics are three original towers from a 16-mi-long aerial tramway built in 1903 to transport copper ore from mines in the Sierra Madres. You can take guided tours, and there's also a research area. A living-history day, with music, costumes, and events, takes place the third weekend in July. ⊠ *807 Bar-*

nett Ave. ☎ *307/327–5308* ⊕ *www.grandencampmentmuseum.org* 🖃 *Donations accepted* ◔ *Memorial Day weekend 10–5; June–Labor Day, Mon.–Sat. 10–5, Sun. 1–5; Sept., weekends 1–5.*

☕ The ranching and cowboy lifestyle is the focus of the three-day **Grand Encampment Cowboy Gathering** (⊠ 807 Barnett Ave. ☎ 307/326–8855), held in mid-July. Cowboy musicians and poets perform during afternoon and evening concerts, and there's a stick-horse rodeo for children. Events take place at the Grand Encampment Museum and other venues around town.

The **Medicine Bow–Routt National Forest, Hayden District** covers 586,000 acres, including the Continental Divide National Scenic Trail and the Encampment River, Huston Park, Savage Run, and Platte River wilderness areas. The local **Forest Service office** (⊠ 204 W. 9th St. ☎ 307/327–5481 ⊕ www.fs.fed.us/r2/mbr) can provide information on hiking, fishing, camping, cross-country skiing, and snowmobiling trails.

Sports & the Outdoors

CROSS-COUNTRY SKIING & SNOWMOBILING A network of cross-country trails in Medicine Bow–Routt National Forest, the **Bottle Creek Ski Trails** (⊠ Hwy. 70, 6 mi southwest of Encampment ☎ 307/327–5720) include several backcountry trails suitable only for expert skiers. There are also easier routes for skiers of all levels. Some trails double as snowmobile trails. All of them are free. For more information in town, go to the Trading Post.

For ski rentals and sales as well as trail information contact Mark Rauterkus at the **Trading Post** (⊠ Junction of Hwys. 70 and 230 ☎ 307/327–5720 ⊕ www.wyomingcarboncounty.com/html/trading.html).

HIKING There are extensive trails in the Sierra Madre range west of Encampment, ranging from developed paths around Bottle Creek to wilderness trails through Huston Park and along the Encampment River. For hiking information, contact the Forest Service office of the **Medicine Bow–Routt National Forest, Hayden District** (⊠ 204 W. 9th St. ☎ 307/327–5481).

HORSEBACK RIDING Rick Stevens of **Horseback Adventures** (☎ 307/326–5569 or 307/326–5751) can lead a trail ride geared to your riding level. You can choose among rides in the Snowy Range, Sierra Madres, or desert country throughout Carbon County.

Where to Stay & Eat

$–$$$ ✕ **Bear Trap Cafe.** People come for the large portions of hearty but basic food at this log building with the look and feel of a Western hunting lodge. The menu is strong on burgers, steaks, fish, and chicken. ⊠ *120 E. Riverside Ave., Riverside, 2 mi northeast of Encampment* ☎ *307/327–5277* ⊟ *MC, V* ◔ *Closed Mon.*

¢–$ ✕ **Pine Lodge Restaurant.** Regular offerings here include burgers and sandwiches; on some evenings there is Mexican food or prime rib. The bar is in a separate room. ⊠ *518 McCaffrey St.* ☎ *307/327–5203* ⊟ *MC, V.*

¢–$$ 🛏 **Cottonwood Cabins.** In the quiet little town of Riverside, just across the street from the town park, these cabins have wood furniture, country quilts, outdoor grills, picnic tables, and full kitchens. ⊠ *411 1st St.,*

Riverside 82325 ☎ *307/327–5151* 🖷 *307/327–5151* ⤳ *3 cabins* ⚷ *Picnic area, BBQs, kitchens, cable TV; no a/c, no room phones, no smoking* ▱ *D, MC, V.*

$ ⊡ **Spirit West River Lodge.** Beside the Encampment River, this massive log
Fodor'sChoice structure has walls of lichen-covered rocks and large windows over-
★ looking the water and surrounding scenery. Stained glass and Western
artwork—most of it by owner R. G. Finney, who is known for his wildlife
bronzes and paintings—fill the lodge. His wife, Lynn, who serves the full
breakfast, is a Senior Olympic gold medalist in cycling and a native of
the area. She can direct you to the best cycling routes and cross-country-skiing trails. The lodge has a mile of private-access fishing on the Encampment River, and each room has a private entrance off a deck
overlooking the river. The three-bedroom guesthouse ($$–$$$$) has a
full kitchen and private access, as well as river frontage. ⊠ *¼ mi east of
Riverside on Hwy. 230, Box 605, 82325* ☎ *307/326–5753* 🖷 *307/327–
5753* ⤳ *4 rooms, 1 cabin* ⚷ *Pond, exercise equipment, fishing, bicy-
cles, bar, piano; no room TVs, no a/c, no smoking* ▱ *MC, V* ⦿ *BP.*

CAMPING △ **Hog Park.** In the Sierra Madres west of Encampment, this large camp-
★ ground sits beside a high mountain lake at 8,400 feet; some of the camp-
sites have views of the water. You can use motorized boats and other
watercraft on the lake. Hiking, horseback riding, and mountain-biking
roads and trails abound, and there is a boat dock here as well. ⚷ *Pit toi-
lets, fire pits, picnic tables, drinking water* ⤳ *50 sites* ⊠ *20 mi south-
west of Encampment; 5 mi west on Hwy. 70 then 15 mi southwest on
Forest Rd. 550* ☎ *307/326–5258* ⊕ *www.fs.fed.us/r2/mbr/* 🖾 *$10*
⤹ *Reservations not accepted* ▱ *No credit cards* ⦿ *Mid-June–Sept.*

△ **Lazy Acres Campground.** The Encampment River runs past this small
campground with plenty of big cottonwood trees for shade. There are
pull-through RV sites, tent sites, one small cabin (you provide bedding,
stove, and cooking utensils), and four no-frills motel rooms. There's also
an on-site fly-fishing shop. ⚷ *Flush toilets, full hookups, guest laundry,
showers* ⤳ *17 full hookups, 14 partial hookups, 2 tent sites; 1 camp-
ing cabin, 4 motel rooms* ⊠ *Hwy. 230, Riverside* ☎ *307/327–5968*
⊕ *www.wyomingcarboncounty.com/lazy.htm* 🖾 *$16 tent sites, $18–22
partial and full hookups, $27 cabin, $34–$45 motel rooms* ▱ *MC, V*
⦿ *Mid-May–Nov.*

△ **Six Mile Gap.** There are only nine sites at this campground on a hill-
side above the North Platte River. Some are pull-through camper sites
and others are walk-in tent sites. Trails follow the river, which you can
cross during low water to reach the Platte River Wilderness Area. ⚷ *Pit
toilets, fire pits, picnic tables, drinking water* ⤳ *19 sites* ⊠ *Hwy. 230,
26 mi east of Encampment, then 2 mi east on Forest Rd. 492* ☎ *307/
326–5258* ⊕ *www.fs.fed.us/r2/mbr/* 🖾 *$10* ⤹ *Reservations not ac-
cepted* ▱ *No credit cards* ⦿ *July–Sept.*

Shopping
Aunt Martha's This 'n That (⊠ 705 Freeman St. ☎ 307/327–5090) car-
ries antiques and baskets, pottery, and other gift items. Roxana John-
son sells hand-knitted and hand-sewn clothing for all ages at **Ewe to You**
(⊠ 705 Freeman St. ☎ 307/327–5558).

en route

As you make your way west to Baggs over the **Battle Highway** (Highway 70), you'll cross the Continental Divide and the Rocky Mountains. This route takes you through the mining country that was developed during the 1897–1908 copper-mining boom in the Sierra Madres; interpretive signs along the way point out historic sites. In 1879, Thomas Edison was fishing near Battle Pass with a bamboo rod when he began to ponder the idea of a filament, which led to his invention of the incandescent lightbulb. Note that this section of the highway closes to car travel in winter, though it stays open for snowmobiles.

Baggs

18 *60 mi west of Encampment via Hwy. 70.*

Settled by cattle and sheep ranchers, the Little Snake River valley—and its largest community, Baggs—is still ranch country. Two emigrant trails passed nearby: the south branch of the Cherokee Trail (circa 1849–1850) crosses near the community, and the Overland Trail (1862–1865) lies farther to the north. Notorious outlaw Butch Cassidy frequented the area, often hiding out here after pulling off a train or bank robbery. To the west of Baggs, large herds of wild horses range freely on public lands. The town is on the southern edge of what is now a major oil, gas, and coalbed methane field, so large numbers of equipment trucks, big water trucks, and field workers ply the roads. Motels and restaurants stay busy.

Ranch paraphernalia, handmade quilts, a doll collection, and the original 1870s-era cabin of mountain man James Baker are exhibited at the **Little Snake River Valley Museum.** ⊠ *No. 2 N. Savery Rd.* ☎ *307/383-7262* ⊕ *lsrvmuseum.homestead.com/homepage.html* 🎫 *Donations accepted* ☉ *Memorial Day–late Oct., daily 11–5.*

Where to Stay & Eat

¢–$ ✕ **Wagon Wheel Cafe.** Generous portions of steak, chicken, and seafood are dished up at low prices at this small café. Hamburgers are served on homemade buns. The café can also provide a sack lunch that is bound to assuage any appetite. ⊠ *20 N. Penland St.* ☎ *307/383-7515* ▤ *MC, V.*

¢ ✕🏨 **Drifter's Inn.** Drifter's has no-frills motel rooms adjacent to a restaurant ($–$$$) and lounge. Menu items range from burgers and steaks to chicken and fish. Friday nights there's prime rib, and Saturday nights are reserved for steak and shrimp. ⊠ *210 Penland St., 82321* ☎ *307/383-2015* 🖷 *307/383-6282* 🛏 *51 rooms* 🖒 *Restaurant, cable TV, bar, some pets allowed, no-smoking rooms; no a/c* ▤ *AE, D, MC, V.*

Rawlins

19 *70 mi northeast of Baggs via Hwy. 789 and I–80.*

The northern gateway to the Medicine Bow–Routt National Forest, Rawlins stands at the junction of U.S. 287 and I–80. Started as one of the Union Pacific's hell-on-wheels towns, this was an important transportation center as early as 1868, when miners heading for the goldfields at South Pass to the north rode the rails to Rawlins or points nearby,

CloseUp
WYOMING'S COWBOY SYMBOL

ASK ANY OLD-TIMER in Cheyenne, Laramie, Lander, or Pinedale who the cowboy is on the Wyoming license plate's bucking-horse symbol, and you'll probably get four different answers. Artist Allen True, who designed the symbol, once said he had no particular rider in mind, but that hasn't stopped Wyoming residents from attributing the rider to regional favorites. Several well-known cowboys are often mentioned, including Stub Farlow of Lander and Guy Holt of Cheyenne (who later ranched near Pinedale).

True was not the first person to create this bucking-horse design, however. The symbol evolved over a number of years, beginning with a 1903 photograph by Professor B. C. Buffum of cowboy Guy Holt riding Steamboat, one of five horses recognized as the most difficult bucking horses of all time. In 1921, the University of Wyoming used that photograph as a model for the bucking-horse-and-cowboy logo on its sports uniforms.

But by that time there was already another Wyoming bucking-horse symbol. During World War I, George Ostrom, a member of the Wyoming National Guard serving in Germany, had a bucking-horse-and-rider design painted on a brass drum. His 148th Field Artillery unit soon adopted the logo for its vehicles as well, and it became known as the Bucking Bronco Regiment from Wyoming. And which horse was the symbol modeled after? In the case of the Wyoming National Guard logo, the horse was Ostrom's own mount, Red Wing.

Using Allen True's design, the state of Wyoming first put the bucking bronco on its license plate in 1936, and the well-known, trademarked symbol has been there ever since.

then went overland to the gold diggings. The town became a large sheep-raising center at the turn of the 20th century. Kingpins in the sheep industry, such as George Ferris and Robert Deal, also backed the development of the Grand Encampment Copper Mining District in the Sierra Madres after miner Ed Haggarty discovered copper there in 1897.

Declines in sheep raising, long Rawlins's mainstay industry, have hurt the community economically, as have downturns in regional mineral production. But the city of 10,000 is still home to many railroad workers and employees of the Wyoming State Penitentiary outside of town. In summer there are weekly free concerts in the park.

About 70 mi north of Rawlins via U.S. 287 and Highway 220 are several sights of interest that are grouped together: Independence Rock State Historic Site, Devil's Gate, and Handcart Ranch (⇨ *see* Casper *in* Chapter 6).

At the **Carbon County Museum** you can see a gruesome pair of shoes made from the skin of Big Nose George Parrott. Parrott was an outlaw who was lynched in 1881 after he attempted to escape from the county jail, where he was being held awaiting execution for his role in the murder of two law-enforcement officers, the first officers to die in the line of duty in Wyoming. After his death, Parrott's body was used for "medical study," and he was ultimately skinned (which is how they made the shoes). Other more traditional articles, including one of the six original Wyoming state flags, illuminate the area's settlement. ⊠ *901 W. Walnut St.* ☎ *307/328–2740* ☒ *Free* ⊙ *June–Sept., Tues.–Sat. 10–noon and 1–5; Oct.–May, Tues.–Sat. 1–5; tours by appointment.*

You can fish, boat, and water-ski on the Seminoe Reservoir, the primary attraction within **Seminoe State Park.** This is also a popular spot for camping and picnicking. It's on a Bureau of Land Management backcountry byway, Carbon County Road 351, which links Sinclair with Alcova. ☎ *307/320–3013* ⊕ *wyoparks.state.wy.us* ☒ *$2 resident vehicle, $4 nonresident vehicle; $6 camping* ⊙ *Daily 24 hrs.*

Cold steel and concrete, the Death House, and the Yard are all part of the tour of the **Wyoming Frontier Prison,** which served as the state's penitentiary from 1901 until 1981. There are occasional midnight tours and a Halloween tour. ⊠ *500 W. Walnut St.* ☎ *307/324–4422* ⊕ *www. wyomingfrontierprison.com* ☒ *$4.25* ⊙ *Memorial Day–Labor Day, daily 8:30–5:30; Apr.–Memorial Day and Labor Day–Oct., call for limited hrs; rest of yr by appointment.*

Where to Stay & Eat

$–$$$ ✕ **Cappy's.** The chicken-fried steak, T-bone steak, and enchiladas are all equally good at this family-owned restaurant on the west side of the city. ⊠ *2351 W. Spruce St.* ☎ *307/324–4847* ☰ *AE, D, MC, V.*

★ $–$$ ✕ **Rose's Lariat.** Some of the best authentic Mexican food in Wyoming is served in this tiny eatery. Try the enchiladas or tamales. If you can't handle it hot and spicy, order a sandwich, a hamburger, or one of the Italian dishes on the menu. ⊠ *410 E. Cedar St.* ☎ *307/324–5261* ☰ *No credit cards* ⊙ *Closed Sun. and Mon.*

$–$$ ✕ **Sanfords Grub & Pub.** This downtown restaurant looks like an antiques store packed with road signs, memorabilia from the 1960s and later, and other vintage decorations. The huge menu includes beef, chicken, pasta, sandwiches, and salads. ⊠ *401 Cedar St.* ☎ *307/324–2921* ☰ *AE, D, DC, MC, V.*

$–$$ ✕ **Su Casa.** The only place in Wyoming to rival the Mexican menu at Rose's Lariat is 6 mi east of Rawlins in Sinclair. The menu includes shrimp, beef, and chicken fajitas, green chili, enchiladas, and Navajo tacos. Try the chiles rellenos (fried cheese-stuffed peppers) or shredded beef enchiladas. Takeout is available. ⊠ *705 E. Lincoln Ave., Sinclair* ☎ *307/ 328–1745* ☰ *No credit cards* ⊙ *Closed Mon.*

$ ✕🖼 **Best Western Cottontree Inn.** This is Rawlins's finest motel, with spacious guest rooms decorated in greens and mauves. The inviting public areas with easy chairs are great for relaxing. There are regular water aerobics classes at the indoor pool. The Hungry Miner ($–$$$) restaurant serves melt-in-your-mouth corn bread and homemade soups. ⊠ *23rd and W. Spruce Sts., Box 387, 82301* ☎ *307/324–2737* ☒ *307/324–5011* ⊕ *www.cottontree.net* ⇆ *122 rooms* ⅋ *Restaurant, cable TV, in-room data ports, Wi-FI, indoor pool, hot tub, sauna, bar, laundry service, busi-*

ness services, meeting rooms, free parking, some pets allowed, no-smoking rooms ⊟ *AE, D, DC, MC, V.*

$ ✕🖽 **Quality Inn.** Formerly the Lodge at Rawlins, this motel on the east side of town near the 287 bypass has just about everything you could ask for under one roof, from a game room to business services to a barber shop. It's convenient to shops and a grocery store; a free pass gives you full gym access at the Rawlins Recreation Center. Fat Boys Bar & Grill ($–$$$) serves sandwiches, steak, meat loaf, pot roast, and shepherd's pie. ⊠ *1801 E. Cedar St., 82301* ☎ *307/324–2783 or 877/729–5467* 🖨 *307/328–1011* ⊕ *www.thelodgeatrawlins.com* 🛏 *132 rooms* ⟁ *Restaurant, cable TV, microwaves, refrigerators, in-room data ports, Wi-Fi, pool, bar, recreation room, laundry service, business services, meeting rooms, free parking, some pets allowed (fee), no-smoking rooms* ⊟ *AE, D, DC, MC, V.*

CAMPING ⚠ **RV World Campground.** There are pull-through RV sites and tent sites at this campground on the west side of Rawlins. ⟁ *Grills, flush toilets, full hookups, dump station, drinking water, guest laundry, showers, picnic tables, swimming (pool)* 🛏 *90 full hookups, 11 tent sites* ⊠ *3101 Wagon Circle Rd.* 🖾 *307/328–1091* 🖂 *$8 tent sites, $22 full hookups* ⊟ *MC, V* ⊙ *Mid-Apr.–Sept.*

⚠ **Western Hills Campground.** There are pull-through RV sites, grassy tent sites, and an 18-hole miniature golf course at this year-round campground on the west side of Rawlins. Barbecue, play horseshoes, or browse the gift shop. You have access to immediate phone hookup, a TV area, and a public computer. ⟁ *Flush toilets, full hookups, drinking water, guest laundry, showers, picnic tables, fire pits, play area* 🛏 *115 full hookups, 80 tent sites* ⊠ *2500 Wagon Circle Rd.* 🖾 *307/324–2592* 🖂 *$16 tent sites, $25–$27 full hookups* ⊟ *MC, V.*

Shopping

Western and wildlife art, antiques, and clothing are among the items available at **Cedar Chest Galleries** (⊠ 416 W. Cedar St. ☎ 307/324–7737).

en route | If you're heading west from Rawlins to Rock Springs on I–80, you'll be following the path of the Cherokee Trail, the Overland Trail, and the Union Pacific Railroad into the **Great Divide Basin and Red Desert**, a landscape of flat sands and sandstone outcrops and bluffs. The best time to appreciate the beauty of this desert country, which spreads for thousands of acres west of Rawlins, is early morning (traveling west) and late afternoon (traveling east), when the sun creates wonderful shadows and makes the land glow. If you're headed east in the morning or west in the afternoon, you'll be driving with the sun in your eyes, so this may be a good time to take a break from driving.

SOUTHWEST WYOMING

Known as the Red Desert or the Little Colorado Desert, this is a unique area of Wyoming, with a combination of badlands, desert, and mountains. Although it may appear to be desolate, there's a wealth of wildlife in this region, including the largest free-ranging herd of pronghorn in the world (numbering around 50,000) and one of the largest herds of wild horses (numbering in the hundreds) in the United States. Southwest Wyoming is known for its mineral resources and for the dinosaur fossils that have been found here. Its southwesternmost corner has close ties to Utah. Not only are many communities predominantly Mormon, but with Salt Lake City about an hour away, Evanston residents also shop and attend cultural events there.

Rock Springs

⑳ *106 mi west of Rawlins via I–80.*

Thousands of acres of public land attract people to this area to see wild horses, hike, and explore 19th-century emigrant trails. Coal mining has always defined the community of Rock Springs, established when the Union Pacific Railroad pushed through the area in the late 1860s. The mines drew laborers from a variety of nationalities, making this a real melting pot of cultures. Sprawled at the base of White Mountain, Rock Springs, population 24,000, is the site of Western Wyoming Community College, a facility known for its paleontological resources.

The Red Desert to the north and east is home to hundreds of wild horses; you can often catch a glimpse of them from area highways.

Dinosaurs, placed throughout the building, are among the prehistoric animal and plant specimens on display at the **Western Wyoming Community College Natural History Museum.** Species range in age from 67 million to 180 million years old. Don't miss the fossilized fish and the baby alligator. The museum also has rotating exhibits. ⊠ *2500 College Dr.* ☎ *307/382–1600* ☜ *Free* ☉ *Daily 8–7.*

Where to Stay & Eat

¢–$$$ ✕ **Bitter Creek Brewery.** Choose one of 18 different burgers and wash it down with a Bob (a local brew that has won awards at brew fests in Denver and Laramie) or a Coal Porter (a beer named in honor of the coal-mining heritage of this community). Wraps, soups, steaks, and chicken are also on the menu. The brewery, in a long, narrow room with a concrete floor and blond-oak furniture, has an upbeat, contemporary atmosphere. ⊠ *604 Broadway* ☎ *307/362–4782* ☰ *AE, D, MC, V.*

¢–$ ✕ **Boschetto's European Market.** Rock Springs's population has been a melting pot of nationalities since its earliest settlement as a coal-mining town. With its wide selection of cheeses, sausages, spaghetti, and other foods, Boschetto's, a European-style market and deli, caters to the variety of folks living here. The dining room sparkles with a tile floor, black-and-white chairs, and small white-linen-covered tables. Takeout is available. ⊠ *6717 Broadway* ☎ *307/382–2350* ☰ *AE, D, DC, MC, V.*

¢–$ ✕ **Grubs Drive-In.** Burgers and fries are the specialty at this tiny diner, and the same family has been dishing them up since the 1950s. There's not a lot of room in here: you sit at a horseshoe-shape counter elbow-to-elbow with the other diners. ⊠ *415 Paulson St.* ☎ *307/362–6634* ☰ *MC, V.*

$–$$ ☒ **Holiday Inn.** A fireplace in the lobby sets the mood at this west-side motel, which in 2004 beefed up its inventory with 57 new executive rooms—some with jetted tubs and all with Wi-Fi. An indoor pool has its own space in a separate room to the left side of the lobby. Light-color furniture fills the guest rooms; chairs and ottomans within the rooms are nice for relaxing. Note that the ground-floor rooms have exterior entrances. There is air-conditioning in public spaces only. ☒ *1675 Sunset Dr., 82902* ☎ *307/382–9200* ☒ *307/632–1064* ⊕ *www.holiday-inn. com* ↷ *170 rooms, 1 suite* ↺ *Restaurant, refrigerators, cable TV, Wi-Fi, indoor pool, gym, hot tub, bar, business services, convention center, meeting rooms, airport shuttle, no-smoking rooms, some pets allowed (fee)* ☰ *AE, D, DC, MC, V.*

$ ☒ **Ramada Limited.** Cherrywood furniture—including a desk, end tables, and an easy chair—decorates the rooms here. A free Continental breakfast is served by the fireplace in the breakfast room. Near the White Mountain Mall, the hotel is on the west side of town; take Exit 102 off I–80. ☒ *2717 Dewar Dr., 82902* ☎ *307/362–1770, 888/307–7890 reservations only* ☒ *307/362–2830* ⊕ *www.ramada.com* ↷ *129 rooms, 2 suites* ↺ *In-room data ports, cable TV, no-smoking rooms, pool, gym, laundry service, some pets allowed* ☰ *AE, D, DC, MC, V* ◎ *CP.*

CAMPING   ⚠ **Rock Springs KOA.** Tent sites, camping cabins, and plenty of RV space make up this campground on the west side of the city. There's plenty to keep you busy here, including basketball, horseshoes, tetherball, and a video game room. ↺ *Grills, flush toilets, full hookups, dump station, drinking water, guest laundry, showers, picnic tables, swimming (pool), play area* ↷ *100 full hookups, 20 tent sites* ☒ *86 Foothill Blvd.* ☎ *307/ 362–3063 or 800/562–8699* ⊕ *www.koa.com* ☒ *$19 tent sites, $19–$27 full hookups, $40 camping cabins* ☰ *D, MC, V* ◷ *Apr.–mid-Oct.*

The Arts

Programs ranging from art shows to concerts are presented throughout the year by the **Community Fine Arts Center** (☒ 400 C St. ☎ 307/ 362–6212). Every June the center hosts International Day in recognition of the 56 nationalities of people who settled and live in Rock Springs. The center's Halseth Gallery houses a permanent collection of more than 400 mostly American paintings, prints, drawings, and photographs, including artwork by Norman Rockwell, Grandma Moses, and Rufino Tamayo.

en route   Wild horses, antelope, desert elk, coyotes, hawks, and sage grouse are among the wild animals you might see on the **Pilot Butte Wild Horse Scenic Loop Tour** (☎ 307/362–3771), which also takes you past such prominent features as Pilot Butte, the Killpecker Sand Dunes, and segments of the Overland Trail. Along the route there are pullouts with interpretive panels.

This loop links Rock Springs and Green River; it takes two to three hours to drive the 50-mi route, half of which is on gravel roads, between the two towns. From Rock Springs, travel north for 14 mi on Highway 191. Turn left onto Sweetwater County Road 4-14 and follow the route for 2½ mi before turning left onto

Sweetwater County Road 4-53, which will take you to Green River, 33½ mi away.

Green River

㉑ *12 mi west of Rock Springs via I–80.*

A town of more than 13,000, Green River attracts those who want to explore the waterways of the Green River drainage in the nearby Flaming Gorge National Recreation Area. Of all the towns along the Union Pacific Railroad, this is the only one that predated the arrival of the rails in the late 1860s. It began as a Pony Express and stage station on the Overland Trail. In 1869 and again in 1871, explorer John Wesley Powell (1834–1902) launched expeditions down the Green and Colorado rivers from nearby sites.

A golf tournament, bull-riding competition, parade, arts festival in the park, and concerts are all part of **Flaming Gorge Days** (☎ 307/875–5711 ⊕ www.flaminggorgedays.com), a four-day celebration held each June in Green River. Tickets can be purchased for individual events; it costs $6 to $8 to attend the bull-riding competition, and concert tickets start at $25.

off the beaten path

SEEDSKADEE NATIONAL WILDLIFE REFUGE – Prairie and peregrine falcons, Canada geese, and various species of hawks and owls inhabit this 25,000-acre refuge. Trumpeter swans also occasionally use the area. Within or near the refuge there are homestead and ranch sites, Oregon Trail crossings, and ferries that cross the Green River, as well as the spot where Jim Bridger and Henry Fraeb built a trading post in 1839. Visitor information and restrooms are available 24 hours. ✉ *37 mi north of Green River on Hwy. 372* ☎ *307/875–2187* ⊕ *www.r6.fws.gov/refuges/seedskad* ⌑ *Free.*

Sports & the Outdoors

A stroll on the paved path by the Green River takes you along the route that John Wesley Powell followed on his expedition down the waterway in 1869. Along the way you can visit Expedition Island, the Green Belt Nature Area, and the Scotts Bottom Nature Area. Access **Expedition Island** off 2nd Street, southwest of the railroad yard in Green River; wild birds, squirrels, and rabbits inhabit the grassy, tree-shaded island. Downstream from Expedition Island on the south bank of the river is the **Green Belt Nature Area,** with interpretive signs, nature paths, and numerous birds, including waterfowl. Farther south is **Scotts Bottom Nature Area,** where you'll find more interpretive signs related to the wildlife that lives in this riparian habitat.

Where to Stay & Eat

$–$$$ ✕ **Denali Grill and Bakery.** A Mount Denali theme pervades this down-home restaurant with artificial pine trees galore, twig curtain rods, pictures of moose and bears, and iron caribou silhouettes on the walls. The owners pride themselves on their homemade breads, soups, and sandwiches. Local favorites are the baby-back barbecue ribs and the chicken-fried steak.

Bread pudding, pecan torte, and lemon crunch pie are some of the home-made desserts, or end your meal with "moose balls," a confectionery delight. ☒ *375 Uinta Dr.* ☏ *307/875–4654* ▭ *AE, D, MC, V.*

★ ¢–$$$ ✗ **Don Pedro's Family Restaurant.** Heaping plates of sizzling fajitas, enchiladas, burritos, and other traditional Mexican fare are served in a two-room restaurant where serapes, Mexican sombreros, and cactus provide decoration. ☒ *520 Wilkes, Suite 10* ☏ *307/875–7324* ▭ *AE, D, MC, V.*

$–$$ ✗ **Penny's Diner.** The name pretty much says it all—a 1950s-style 24-hour diner with a bright shiny look, reminiscent of a railcar, and flashing neon lights. Try a burger, fries, and a milk shake. The diner is part of the Oak Tree Inn. ☒ *1172 W. Flaming Gorge Way* ☏ *307/875–3500* ▭ *AE, D, DC, MC, V.*

$–$$$ ▥ **Little America.** This one-stop facility stands alone in the Red Desert, and it can be a real haven if the weather becomes inclement. The hotel, founded in 1934, is the original of the small chain. The rooms are large and comfortable, with mauve and green comforters and lots of floral pillows; a small number of them have only showers, and no bathtubs, in the bathrooms. A full-service fuel station and a convenience store are also on the premises. ☒ *I–80, 20 mi west of Green River, Box 1, Little America 82929* ☏ *307/875–2400 or 800/634–2401* 🖷 *307/872–2666* ⊕ *www.littleamerica.com* ⇗ *140 rooms* ⅙ *Restaurant, some refrigerators, some in-room data ports, pool, gym, bar, playground, laundry facilities, business services, no-smoking rooms* ▭ *AE, D, DC, MC, V.*

¢–$ ▥ **Oak Tree Inn.** This two-story inn in four buildings on the west side of town is 20 mi from Flaming Gorge and has views of unique rock outcroppings above the city. Contemporary furnishings fill the rooms, which are decorated in shades of mauve and green. ☒ *1170 W. Flaming Gorge Way, 82935* ☏ *307/875–3500* 🖷 *307/875–4889* ⇗ *192 rooms* ⅙ *Restaurant, some refrigerators, cable TV, exercise equipment, hot tub, laundry facilities, some pets allowed (fee); no smoking* ▭ *AE, D, DC, MC, V.*

Flaming Gorge National Recreation Area

㉒ *20 mi south of Green River via Hwy. 530 or Hwy. 191.*

The Flaming Gorge Reservoir of the Flaming Gorge National Recreation Area is formed by Green River water held back by Flaming Gorge Dam. Here you can boat and fish, as well as watch for wildlife. The area is as rich in history as it is spectacularly beautiful. Mountain men such as Jim Bridger and outlaws such as Butch Cassidy found haven here, and in 1869, on his first exploration down the Green River, John Wesley Powell named many local landmarks: Flaming Gorge, Horseshoe Canyon, Red Canyon, and the Gates of Lodore. The recreation area straddles the border between Wyoming and Utah; most of the park's visitor services are in Utah. There are marinas, lodging, food, campgrounds, places to rent horses and snowmobiles, and trails for mountain bikes. The Ashley National Forest administers the area. ☏ *801/784–3445, 800/277–7571 for information on reservoir elevations and river flows, 877/444–6677 TDD, 877/833–6777 for campground reservations* ⊕ *www.fs.fed.us* ▨ *Free* ⊙ *Daily 24 hrs.*

Sports & the Outdoors

BOATING **Buckboard Marina** (⊠ Hwy. 530, 25 mi south of Green River ☎ 307/ 875–6927) provides full marina services, including boat rentals, a marina store, and an RV park.

FISHING Bob and Marsha Tynsky of **Sweetwater Fishing Adventures** (⊠ 1125 Florida , Green River ☎ 307/875–9609) lead guided fishing trips within Flaming Gorge.

Camping

⚠ **Buckboard Crossing.** The campsites at this campground on the west side of Flaming Gorge can be used for tents or RVs, though only a few sites have electrical hookups for RVs. There's a boat dock here. ♿ *Flush toilets, dump station, drinking water, showers, fire pits, picnic tables, general store* ⤳ *53 sites* ⊠ *23 mi southwest of Green River on Hwy. 530, then 2 mi east on Forest Rd. 009* ☎ *435/784–3445 for information, 307/875–6927, 877/444–6777 for reservations* ⊕ *www.reserveusa. com* 💲 *$17* ⊟ *AE, D, MC, V* ☉ *Mid-May–mid-Sept.*

⚠ **Firehole Canyon.** Located in the Flaming Gorge National Recreation Area, this campground has great canyon views. You can pitch a tent or park an RV on the campsites here, but there are no hookups for RVs. There's a beach area nearby, plus a boat ramp. ♿ *Flush toilets, drinking water, showers, fire pits, picnic tables* ⤳ *40 sites* ⊠ *13 mi south of Green River on Hwy. 191, then 10 mi west on Forest Rd. 106* ☎ *435/ 784–3445 for information, 877/444–6777 for reservations* ⊕ *www. reserveusa.com* 💲 *$13–$26* ⊟ *AE, D, MC, V* ☉ *Mid-May–early Sept.*

Fort Bridger State Historic Site

★ ☺ ㉓ *51 mi west of Green River via I–80.*

Started in 1843 as a trading post by mountain man Jim Bridger and his partner Louis Vasquez, Fort Bridger was under the control of Mormons by 1853 after they either purchased the fort or forced the original owners to leave—historians aren't sure which. As the U.S. Army approached during a conflict known as the Mormon War of 1857, the Mormons deserted the area and burned the original Bridger post. Fort Bridger then served as a frontier military post until it was abandoned in 1890. Many of the military-era buildings remain, and the Bridger post has been rebuilt and is staffed by a mountain man and woman. You can attend interpretive programs and living-history demonstrations during the summer, and the museum has new exhibits about the fort's history. The largest mountain-man rendezvous in the intermountain West occurs annually at Fort Bridger over Labor Day weekend, attracting hundreds of buckskinners and Native Americans plus thousands of visitors. ⊠ *Exit 34 off I–80* ☎ *307/782–3842* ⊕ *wyoparks.state.wy.us/FBslide.htm* 💲 *$2–$4* ☉ *Grounds year-round, daily 8–sunset. Museum Apr. and Oct., weekends 9–4:30; May–Sept., daily 9–5:30.*

Camping

⚠ **Fort Bridger RV Camp.** There's plenty of grass for tents, and room for RVs as well at this campground near Fort Bridger. ♿ *Grills, flush toilets, full hookups, drinking water, guest laundry, showers, picnic tables*

39 full hookups, 20 tent sites ⊠ *64 Groshon Rd.* ☎ *307/782–3150*
$15 tent sites, $19 full hookups ⊟ *No credit cards* ⊙ *Apr.–mid-Oct.*

Shopping

★ The fort's re-created **Bridger/Vazquez Trading Post** sells goods typical of
the 1840s, when the post was first established, including trade beads,
clothing, and leather items. It's open May–September, daily 9–5.

Kemmerer

㉔ *34 mi north of Fort Bridger via Hwy. 412, 35 mi north of Evanston via
Hwy. 189.*

This small city serves as a gateway to Fossil Butte National Monument.
Probably the most important person in Kemmerer's history was James
Cash Penney, who in 1902 started the Golden Rule chain of stores here.
He later used the name J. C. Penney Company, which by 1929 had 1,395
outlets. Penney revolutionized merchandising in western Wyoming.
Before the opening of Penney's stores, the coal-mining industry dominated the region, and miners were used to working for the company
and purchasing their supplies at the company store—which often
charged whatever it wanted, managing to keep employees in debt. But
when Penney opened his Golden Rule, he set one price for each item
and stuck to it. Later he developed a catalog, selling to people unable
to get to town easily.

A unique concentration of creatures is embedded in the natural limestone outcrop at **Fossil Butte National Monument,** indicating clearly that
this area was an inland sea more than 50 million years ago. Many of
the fossils—which include fish, insects, and plants—are remarkably
clear and detailed. Pronghorn, coyotes, prairie dogs, and other mammals find shelter within the 8,198-acre park, along with numerous
birds, such as eagles and falcons. You can hike the fossil trails and unwind at the picnic area. A visitor center here houses an information desk
and exhibits of fossils found in the area, including a 13-foot crocodile.
⊠ *15 mi west of Kemmerer via U.S. 30* ☎ *307/877–4457* ⊕ *www.nps.
gov/fobu* ⊠ *Free* ⊙ *Park daily 24 hrs. Visitor center June–Aug., daily
8–7; Sept.–May, daily 8–4:30.*

The **Fossil Country Frontier Museum,** housed in a former church, has fossils and displays related to early settlement in the area. ⊠ *400 Pine Ave.*
☎ *307/877–6551* ⊠ *Free* ⊙ *June–Aug., Mon.–Sat. 9–5; Sept.–May,
Mon.–Sat. 10–4.*

At **Ulrich's Fossil Gallery** you can view fossils from around the world and
even buy some specimens, particularly fish fossils. Ulrich's also runs fossil-digging excursions at private quarries; call for more information. ⊠ *U.S.
30* ☎ *307/877–6466* ⊠ *Gallery free, fossil-digging excursions $65*
⊙ *Daily 8–6; fossil digs June–Sept., daily at 9.*

Where to Stay & Eat

$ ✕ **Busy Bee.** This local favorite on the main street of town serves hearty
homemade fare such as chicken-fried steak, chicken dinners, hamburgers, and omelets. The theme is cows: cow pictures and ceramic heifers

dot the walls and counters. ✉ *919 Pine St.* ☎ *307/877–6820* 🚫 *No credit cards.*

¢ 🏨 **Energy Inn.** Southwestern colors decorate the basic rooms, and you have access to a fax machine and a microwave in the lobby. A few miles south of Kemmerer in Diamondville, the motel caters to energy industry workers; ten ground-floor kitchenette units are for extended stays. ✉ *3 Hwy. 30, Diamondville 83101* ☎ *307/877–6901* ⊕ *www. energyinn.net* 🔌 *31 rooms, 10 kitchenette units* ♨ *Some kitchenettes, refrigerators, cable TV, in-room data ports, Wi-Fi, no-smoking rooms* 🚫 *AE, D, DC, MC, V.*

Shopping

To understand Kemmerer's roots, stop at the **J C Penney store** (✉ *722 JC Penney Dr.* ☎ *307/877–3164*), which is where James Cash Penney began his merchandising career. This small retail establishment, known as the "mother store," sells clothing.

Evanston

㉕ *48 mi south of Kemmerer via U.S. 189; 86 mi west of Green River on I–80; 80 mi east of Salt Lake City, Utah, on I–80.*

Like other raucous towns established as the Union Pacific laid its tracks across Wyoming, Evanston started as a tent city. Many of the rail workers were Chinese. Today Evanston celebrates that railroad and Chinese history at Depot Square, with the UP Railroad Depot and a model of a Chinese joss house. The town makes a decent base for visiting Fort Bridger State Historic Site and Fossil Butte National Monument.

Wildlife, from ducks and Canada geese to herds of bison and elk, is abundant in **Bear River State Park,** and you can hike and ski on the park's trails, which have picnic shelters. You also can fish here. The park connects to Evanston's Bear Pathway, a paved trail that for much of its length is fully accessible to people with disabilities. ✉ *601 Bear River Dr.* ☎ *307/789–6547* ⊕ *http://wyoparks.state.wy.us/BRslide.htm* 🎫 *Free* ⊙ *Daily 24 hrs.*

The **Uinta County Historical Museum** houses displays on Chinese culture and local history, including historic photographs of the area, ranching and railroad paraphernalia, and Native American artifacts. ✉ *36 10th St.* ☎ *307/783–0370* 🎫 *Free* ⊙ *Memorial Day–Labor Day, weekdays 9–5, weekends 10–4; Labor Day–Memorial Day, weekdays 9–5.*

Sports & the Outdoors

The **Bear River Outdoor Recreation Alliance** (🏠 Box 2600, Evanston 82930 ☎ 307/789–1770) has a series of trails used for mountain biking and hiking in summer and as Nordic ski trails in winter. These trails can be found in and around Evanston and Uinta County. There's also a system of yurts for overnight stays. The trails are a cooperative project of the Alliance, the U.S. Forest Service, Evanston Parks and Recreation Department, and the Wyoming and Utah state parks divisions. You can obtain information from Evanston's **Visitors Information Center/**

Depot Square (✉ 920 Front St., Evanston 82930 ☎ 307/789–1472) or by writing Bear River Outdoor Recreation Alliance.

Where to Stay & Eat

$–$$$ ✕ **Legal Tender.** Within the Best Western Dunmar Inn, this restaurant has the most "upscale" atmosphere in the community, but it's not pretentious. It's quiet with lots of faux greenery and a floral carpet. The varied menu includes steak, seafood, chicken, and pasta, and there's a full salad bar. ✉ *1601 Harrison Dr.* ☎ *307/789–3770* ▭ *AE, D, DC, MC, V.*

$–$$ ✕ **Don Pedro's Family Mexican Restaurant.** This small, family-owned restaurant serves authentic Mexican food. Sombreros, serapes, and Mexican music create the appropriate mood in which to dine on sizzling fajitas or the special *molcajete,* a stew of beef and chicken. ✉ *909 Front St.* ☎ *307/789–2944* ▭ *AE, D, DC, MC, V.*

$ ✕ **Hunan Garden.** Evanston's Chinese culture comes through in this restaurant with green walls and Chinese lamps that serves Hunan, Szechuan, and Mandarin dishes. Among the house specialties on the extensive menu are walnut prawns, double-face noodles (chicken, prawns, and beef sautéed with vegetables), and black-pepper beef or lamb. You can also order set dinners for two or more that include hot-and-sour soup, cheese puffs, barbecue-pork egg rolls, sweet-and-sour prawns, Hunan chicken, and Mongolian beef. ✉ *933 Front St.* ☎ *307/789–3908* ▭ *MC, V.*

¢–$$ ▥ **Pine Gables Inn B&B.** Built in 1883 in Victorian style, this house, the only B&B in town, is on the National Register of Historic Places. The rooms have murals, hand-painted by the house owner; antique furnishings; and nooks and crannies that are a fun part of the architecture. There is a large Jacuzzi in the suite. Some of the rooms have fireplaces and claw-foot tubs. ✉ *1049 Center St., 82930* ☎ *307/789–2069 or 800/ 789–2069* ⊕ *www.cruising-america.com/pinegables* ⤵ *3 rooms, 1 suite* ⌂ *Library; no room TVs, no a/c, no smoking* ▭ *AE, MC, V* ¶◎¶ *BP.*

$ ▥ **Best Western Dunmar Inn.** The rooms are spread over a large area that's a bit mazelike (you have to drive or walk a ways to your room from the main lobby and restaurant), but they are large and well appointed, with a desk and easy chairs. In the "business plus" rooms, you have free phone calls and the option of a Continental or full breakfast. The public spaces are casual and inviting, and there is live music in the bar most weekend nights. ✉ *1601 Harrison Dr., Box 0768, 82931* ☎ *307/789–3770 or 800/654–6509* ⊟ *307/789–3758* ⊕ *www.bestwestern.com* ⤵ *165 rooms* ⌂ *Restaurant, cable TV, in-room data ports, pool, gym, hot tub, bar, convention center, business services, no-smoking rooms* ▭ *AE, D, MC, V.*

¢ ▥ **High Country Inn.** Dark-green carpeting, neutral-tone walls, and mauve-and-green accents decorate the rooms at this inn overlooking a golf course. The lobby has lots of oak trim and an aquarium. You can have a microwave and refrigerator in your room on request, or even participate in off-track betting. ✉ *1936 Harrison Dr., 82930* ☎ *307/789– 2810* ⊟ *307/789–5506* ⊕ *www.highcountryinn.net* ⤵ *113 rooms, 2 suites* ⌂ *Restaurant, cable TV, pool, exercise equipment, bar, laundry service, business services; no smoking* ▭ *AE, D, DC, MC, V.*

SOUTHERN WYOMING A TO Z

To research prices, get advice from other travelers, and book travel arrangements, visit www.fodors.com.

AIR TRAVEL

CARRIERS Great Lakes Airlines/United Express connects Cheyenne, Laramie, and Rock Springs to Denver, Colorado.

🛪 Airlines & Contacts **Great Lakes Aviation/United Express** ☎ 307/432-7000 in Cheyenne, 307/742-5296 in Laramie, 800/554-5111 ⊕ www.greatlakesav.com/.

AIRPORTS

Cheyenne, Laramie, and Rock Springs' Sweetwater County Airport are the major airports in the area, with service to and from Denver only; there is no commercial service to other communities in the region. Many visitors to southeastern Wyoming prefer to fly into Denver International Airport and drive the 90 mi north to Cheyenne.

If you only need to get to and from the airport or bus station and the capitol area from Cheyenne Airport, you can make do with cabs. Try Checker Cab or Yellow Cab.

🛪 Airport Information **Cheyenne Airport** ⊠ 200 E. 8th Ave., Cheyenne ☎ 307/634-7071 ⊕ www.cheyenneairport.com. **Laramie Airport** ⊠ 3 mi west of Laramie off Hwy. 130 ☎ 307/742-4165 ⊕ www.laramieairport.com. **Sweetwater County Airport** ⊠ 382 Hwy. 370, Rock Springs ☎ 307/352-6880 ⊕ www.rockspringsairport.com.

🛪 Taxis **Checker Cab** ☎ 307/635-5555. **Yellow Cab** ☎ 307/638-3333.

BUS TRAVEL

Greyhound Lines connects Cheyenne, Evanston, Laramie, Rawlins, and Rock Springs to such hubs as Denver and Salt Lake City.

🛪 Bus Information **Greyhound Lines** ☎ 800/231-2222 ⊕ www.greyhound.com ⊠ 1503 Capitol Ave., Cheyenne ☎ 307/634-7744 ⊠ 1936 W. Lincoln Hwy., Evanston ☎ 307/789-2810 ⊠ 4700 Bluebird La., Laramie ☎ 307/742-9663 ⊠ 2217 E. Cedar St., Rawlins ☎ 307/324-4196 ⊠ 1695 Sunset Dr., Suite 114, Rock Springs ☎ 307/362-2931.

CAR RENTAL

Rental agencies can be found at airports and at other locations in the larger cities.

🛪 Local Agencies **Avis** ⊠ Cheyenne Airport ☎ 307/632-9371 ⊠ Sweetwater County Airport, Rock Springs ☎ 307/362-5599. **Dollar** ⊠ 300 E. 8th Ave., Cheyenne ☎ 307/632-2422. **Enterprise** ⊠ 800 W. Lincolnway, Cheyenne ☎ 307/632-1907 ⊠ Sweetwater County Airport ☎ 307/362-0416. **Hertz** ⊠ Cheyenne Airport ☎ 307/634-2131 ⊠ Laramie Airport ☎ 307/745-0500 ⊠ Sweetwater County Airport, Rock Springs ☎ 307/382-3262.

CAR TRAVEL

A car is essential to explore southern Wyoming. I–80 is the major route through the region, bisecting it from east to west. In places it runs parallel to U.S. 30. Other major access roads include U.S. 287, connecting Laramie and Medicine Bow; Highway 130, serving Centennial and Saratoga; Highway 230, running through Encampment; and Highway 70, connecting Encampment and Baggs.

Although distances between towns can be extensive, gasoline and other automobile services are available in each community and at various points roughly 20 to 40 mi apart along I–80. When traveling here in winter, be prepared for whiteouts and road closings (sometimes for hours, occasionally for more than a day). Always carry a blanket and warm clothing when driving in winter, along with a safety kit that includes snack food and water. Cell-phone service is getting better but is still sporadic in areas where mountains might interfere with cell towers.

Note that the Snowy Range Pass section of Highway 130, between Centennial and Saratoga, and the Battle Highway section of Highway 70, west of Encampment, close during cold weather, generally from mid-October until Memorial Day.

Contact the Wyoming Department of Transportation for information on road conditions.

Wyoming Department of Transportation ☎ 307/777-4484, 307/772-0824 from outside Wyoming for road conditions, 888/996-7623 from within Wyoming for road conditions ⊕ www.wyoroad.info/. **Wyoming Highway Patrol** ☎ 307/777-4301, 800/442-9090 for emergencies, #4357 (#HELP) from a cell phone for emergencies ⊕ whp.state. wy.us/index.htm.

EMERGENCIES

Ambulance or Police Emergencies ☎ 911.

24-Hour Medical Care Evanston Regional Hospital ⊠ 190 Arrowhead Dr., Evanston ☎ 307/789-3636 or 800/244-3537 ⊕ www.evanstonregionalhospital.com. **Ivinson Memorial Hospital** ⊠ 255 N. 30th St., Laramie ☎ 307/742-2141 ⊕ www.ivinsonhospital. org. **Memorial Hospital of Carbon County** ⊠ 2221 Elm St., Rawlins ☎ 307/324-2221 ⊕ www.imhcc.com. **Memorial Hospital of Sweetwater County** ⊠ 1200 College Dr., Rock Springs ☎ 307/362-3711. **United Medical Center East** ⊠ 2600 E. 18th St., Cheyenne ☎ 307/634-2273 ⊕ www.umcwy.org. **United Medical Center West** ⊠ 214 E. 23rd St., Cheyenne ☎ 307/634-2273 ⊕ www.umcwy.org.

LODGING

CAMPING Just about every community in the region has private campgrounds and RV parks. The Wyoming Campground Association can provide information on these campgrounds.

You can also camp on public lands managed by the U.S. Forest Service and local Bureaus of Land Management; these camping opportunities range from dispersed camping with no facilities to campgrounds with water, fire pits, and picnic tables. Some of the best camping spots are in the Medicine Bow–Routt National Forest near the communities of Centennial, Saratoga, Encampment, and Baggs. Camping near lakes and reservoirs is possible west of Cheyenne at Curt Gowdy State Park and south of Green River at Flaming Gorge National Recreation Area.

Curt Gowdy State Park ☎ 307/632-7946 ⊕ wyoparks.state.wy.us/cgslide.htm. **Flaming Gorge National Recreation Area** ☎ 801/784-3445, 877/833-6777 for campground reservations ⊕ www.fs.fed.us/r4/ashley/recreation/flaming_gorge. **Kemmerer District Bureau of Land Management** ☎ 307/828-4500 ⊕ www.wy.blm.gov/kfo/info. htm. **Medicine Bow-Routt National Forest** ☎ 307/745-8971 ⊕ www.fs.fed.us/r2/ mbr. **Rawlins District Bureau of Land Management** ☎ 307/328-4200 ⊕ www.wy.blm. gov/rfo/. **Rock Springs District Bureau of Land Management** ☎ 307/352-0256

⊕ www.wy.blm.gov/rsfo/. **U.S. Forest Service** ☎ 303/275-5350 ⊕ www.fs.fed.us/r2.
Wyoming Campground Association ☎ 307/684-5722 ⊕ www.campwyoming.org/.

DUDE RANCHES If you want to experience a bit of the wrangling life, consider a stay at
a dude ranch. Professional cattle drivers and ranchers will teach you to
rope, ride, and rodeo. The Wyoming Dude Ranchers Association can
help you find a ranch to suit your interests and needs.
🖪 **Wyoming Dude Ranchers Association** ☎ 307/455-2084 ⊕ www.wyomingdra.com.

MEDIA

NEWSPAPERS & Major newspapers in the region include the *Wyoming State Tribune-*
MAGAZINES *Eagle,* published in Cheyenne; the *Laramie Daily Boomerang;* the *Rawlins Daily Times;* the *Rock Springs Rocket Miner;* the *Green River Star;*
and Evanston's *Uinta County Herald.* The *Casper Star-Tribune* covers
the entire state and includes a weekly events section each Thursday.

TELEVISION & Cheyenne has ABC/ KKTU Channel 8 and CBS/KGWN Channel 5. NBC/
RADIO KUSA Channel 9, broadcast out of Denver, reaches much of southern
Wyoming. Rock Springs and Evanston pick up Salt Lake City TV sta-
tions, including ABC/KTVX Channel 4, CBS/KTUV Channel 2, and NBC/
KSL Channel 5.

You can listen to country music in and around Cheyenne on the following
radio stations: KFBC 1240 AM, KHAT 96.7 FM, KGYN 95.1 FM, and
KOLZ 100.7 FM. Cheyenne's KLEN 106.3 FM and KIGN 101.9 FM
play rock and roll; KGAB 650 AM has talk radio. Evanston's KEVA
1240 AM and KOTB 106.1 FM play country. In Green River listen to
KFRZ 92.1 FM for country music. Among the stations broadcast out
of Laramie are KOWB 1290 AM and KCGY 95.1 FM, both of which
play country music. Kemmerer is served by KMER 950 AM, which plays
oldies. Rock Springs has oldies on KRKK 1360 AM, country on KQSW
96.5 FM, and rock and roll on KSIT 104.5 FM.

SPORTS & THE OUTDOORS

SKIING & Numerous trail systems in the Medicine Bow–Routt National Forest,
SNOWMOBILING Snowy Range, and Sierra Madres are popular with cross-country skiers
and snowmobilers. Centennial, Encampment, Laramie, and Saratoga make
particularly good bases for cross-country skiing, and you can access some
downhill-skiing terrain from Centennial as well.

TOURS

The Cheyenne Trolley takes a $6, two-hour tour of the historic down-
town area and Frances E. Warren Air Force Base, including 20–25 minutes at the Old West Museum. The trolley runs from mid-May to
mid-September, Monday–Saturday at 10 and 1:30, Sunday at 11:30. Tickets are sold at the Cheyenne Area Convention and Visitors Bureau on
weekdays and at the Wrangler shop on weekends. For a self-guided walking tour of the downtown and capitol area in Cheyenne, contact the
Cheyenne Area Convention and Visitors Bureau.

Large herds of wild horses range freely on public lands west of Baggs,
and you can see the animals by taking a four-wheel-drive tour with Wild

Horse Country Tours. Tours start at $200 for two people. Having grown up here, guides John and Esther Clark are very knowledgeable about the area.

Rick Stevens of Horseback Adventures in Saratoga will take you out for a day, or on an overnight pack trip into the mountain and desert country of south-central Wyoming.

🚩 Tour Operators **Cheyenne Trolley Ticket Sales** ⊠ Cheyenne Area Convention and Visitors Bureau, One Depot Square, 121 W. 15th St., Suite 202 ☎ 307/778–3133 ⊕ www. cheyenne.org ⊠ Wrangler shop, 16th and Capitol Sts. ☎ 307/634–3048. **Horseback Adventures** ℗ P.O. Box 1681, Saratoga 82331 ☎ 307/326–5569. **Wild Horse Country Tours** ℗ Box 11, Baggs 82391 ☎ 307/383–6865

VISITOR INFORMATION

🚩 Tourist Information **Albany County Tourism Board (Laramie)** ⊠ 210 E. Custer St., Laramie 82070 ☎ 307/745–7339 or 800/445–5303 ⊕ www.laramie-tourism.org. **Carbon County Visitor's Council)** ℗ Box 856, Saratoga 82331 ☎ 800/228–3547 ⊕ www. wyomingcarboncounty.com. **Cheyenne Area Convention and Visitors Bureau** ⊠ One Depot Square, 121 W 15th St., Suite 212, Cheyenne 82001 ☎ 307/778–3133 or 800/426– 5009 ⊕ www.cheyenne.org. **Evanston Chamber of Commerce** ⊠ 36 10th St., Evanston 82931 ☎ 307/783–0370 ⊕ www.etownchamber.com. **Green River Chamber of Commerce** ⊠ 541 E. Flaming Gorge Way, Green River 82935 ☎ 307/875–5711 or 800/354– 6743 ⊕ www.grchamber.com. **Kemmerer Chamber of Commerce** ⊠ 800 Pine Ave., Kemmerer 83101 ☎ 307/877–9761 ⊕ www.kemmererchamber.com/. **Laramie Chamber of Commerce** ⊠ 800 S. 3rd St., Laramie 82070 ☎ 307/745–7339 or 866/876–1012 ⊕ www.laramie.org. **Medicine Bow–Routt National Forest** ⊠ 2468 Jackson St., Laramie 82070 ☎ 307/745–8971 ⊕ www.fs.fed.us/r2/mbr. **Rawlins-Carbon County Chamber of Commerce** ⊠ 519 W. Cedar St., Rawlins 82301 ☎ 307/324–4111 or 800/ 228–3547 ⊕ www.rawlinscarboncountychamber.com. **Rock Springs Chamber of Commerce** ⊠ 1897 Dewar Dr., Rock Springs 82902 ☎ 307/362–3771 or 800/463–8637 ⊕ www.tourwyoming.com. **Saratoga-Platte Valley Chamber of Commerce** ⊠ 106 N. First St. ℗ Box 1095, Saratoga 82331 ☎ 307/326–8855 ⊕ www.saratogachamber.info. **Sweetwater County Joint Travel & Tourism Board** ⊠ 79 Winston Dr., Rock Springs 82902 ☎ 307/354–6457 ⊕ www.tourwyoming.com. **Visitors Information Center/ Depot Square** ⊠ 920 Front St., Evanston 82930 ☎ 307/789–1472.

INDEX

PHOTO CREDITS

Cover Photo (Jackson Lake and the Grand Tetons, Wyoming): *David Jensen.* F14, *Eric Horan/age fotostock.* F15, *Michael Javorka/viestiphoto.com.*

NOTES

NOTES

NOTES

NOTES

NOTES

ABOUT OUR WRITERS

Jean Arthur writes for travel and adventure publications from her Montana home. Her nonfiction books include *Timberline and a Century of Skiing on Mount Hood,Hellroaring: Fifty Years on the Big Mountain,* and *Winter Trails Montana.* She is a regular contributor to *Ski Trax, Horizon Air,* and *Montana* magazines and numerous newspapers, including as the *Christian Science Monitor.* When not writing, she travels Montana's front-country and backcountry by boot, bicycle, or ski.

Deadwood resident **Dustin Floyd** is a fifth-generation South Dakotan who studied at Oxford University before graduating from Coe College in Cedar Rapids, Iowa. In addition to his duties as executive editor of *Deadwood Magazine,* Dustin is a media-relations specialist for TDG Communications, responsible for developing partnerships and coordinating for organizations such as the United Kingdom's Sky One television network, London's News of the World, and the Travel Channel. A member of the Western Writers of America and an avid traveler, he regularly writes history and travel features for national publications.

Candy Moulton has spent years traveling through Wyoming—her native state—researching her nonfiction books: *Roadside History of Wyoming; Legacy of the Tetons: Homesteading in Jackson Hole; The Grand Encampment: Settling the High Country; Wagon Wheels: A Contemporary Journey on the Oregon Trail; Writer's Guide to Everyday Life in the Wild West from 1840 to 1900; Writer's Guide to Everyday Life: Native Americans in the 1800s;* and *Steamboat: Legendary Bucking Horse.* She has also written *Roadside History of Nebraska* and *Salt Lake City Uncovered.* She is the editor of *Roundup,* the official publication of Western Writers of America, and is a regular contributor to Fodor's. Candy makes her home near Encampment, Wyoming.

Award-winning journalist and photographer **Tom Griffith** attended the University of London and graduated from the University of Wisconsin before pursuing a career in the newspaper business that took him to Montana and Arizona. He is former director of communications for the Mount Rushmore Preservation Fund and author of three books about the memorial—*America's Shrine of Democracy, The Four Faces of Freedom,* and *A Sculptor's Son*—as well as dozens of history- and travel-related magazine articles. When he's not reading or writing, Tom enjoys mountain biking and hiking in the Black Hills and teaching his two children the intricacies of trout fishing.